Attributing Knowledge

Attributing Knowledge

What It Means to Know Something

JODY AZZOUNI

OXFORD
UNIVERSITY PRESS

Oxford University Press is a department of the University of Oxford. It furthers the University's objective of excellence in research, scholarship, and education by publishing worldwide. Oxford is a registered trade mark of Oxford University Press in the UK and certain other countries.

Published in the United States of America by Oxford University Press
198 Madison Avenue, New York, NY 10016, United States of America.

First issued as an Oxford University Press paperback, 2025

Library of Congress Cataloging-in-Publication Data
Names: Azzouni, Jody, author.
Title: Attributing knowledge : what it means to know something / Jody Azzouni.
Description: New York, NY, United States of America : Oxford University Press, 2020. |
Includes bibliographical references and index.
Identifiers: LCCN 2020007416 | ISBN 9780197508817 (hardback) | ISBN 9780197803042 (paperback) |
ISBN 9780197508824 (updf) | ISBN 9780197508831 (epub) | ISBN 9780197508848 (online)
Subjects: LCSH: Knowledge, Theory of.
Classification: LCC BD161 .A99 2020 | DDC 121—dc23
LC record available at https://lccn.loc.gov/2020007416

Paperback printed by Marquis Book Printing, Canada

For Arnie

In 2012, Geoffrey Hinton changed the way machines see the world.

Cade Metz (2017a)

Contents

Acknowledgments

This book grew out of a larger book project in epistemology that I started in the fall of 2015. Despite repeated, substantial, and lengthy interruptions, I had enough material for a class in advanced epistemology by the spring of 2017. My thanks to Cody Abramson, Megan Entwistle, Raul Ibarra Herrera, Jiali Liu, Kiku Mizuno, James Withers, Qiong Wu, and Douglas Yetman. The material they saw, however, largely isn't in this book—a later version of (most of) that material will appear in a subsequent book, *Challenging Knowledge*.

"Penultimate" versions of chapters 1 through 5 of *this* book, in turn, were largely written during the late fall of 2016, in the summer and fall of 2017, and finally in the first two months of 2018; and so, by the spring of 2018, I had enough material to give a second class on advanced epistemology without repeating what I'd done the first time. My thanks for their comments and commentary to Alex Sarappo, Daniel Schwartz, and Asa Lukas Zabarsky; they helped turn what I thought were final versions of material into earlier chapters of a still unfinished book. (This is something I find myself saying *a lot*. I'm grateful for the teaching advantages that the good students at Tufts University give me year after year.) Florence Bacus, Noelle Ballesteros, Monika Greco, Shao-An Hsu, Patrick McKee, Tianyi Zhao, and Yingsa Zhang—members of my Spring, 2020 class on Advanced Epistemology—deserve thanks for their reactions to the full manuscript then available (essentially: the book before copyediting). They were great!—extremely focused and helpful (as a number of additions to the book I added during the copyediting phrase indicate). I also thank Eric Dean for substantial detailed comments and suggestions on the entire February 2019 version of the book, many of which were taken up when I finalized the manuscript; I must similarly thank Corey Dethier for substantial detailed comments and suggestions on the same version of the manuscript (also many of which I used). I thank Ram Neta for numerous helpful suggestions that I applied throughout that (version of the) manuscript. His comments were sent anonymously; I subsequently credited him when I learned who that particular anonymous reader of the manuscript was. All the references to "Ram Neta" in this book that aren't dated are to that set of comments—ones I received on June 24, 2019, from Oxford University Press, and that I used while working up the for-copyediting version of the manuscript in September and October 2019. Thanks to Jeff McConnell for his comments (and corrections) to the introduction and to Brian Epstein for sensibly urging that I segregate the linguistic content of the introduction from the rest of the introductory material.

I also want to thank Otávio Bueno and Markus Gabriel for inviting me to the conference "Metaphysics, Science, and Skepticism I," at the University of Bonn on June 29, 2017; there I presented a talk on knowledge attributions to animals and artifacts that's (now) part of chapter 1. Otávio Bueno continued to comment on (and oppose) my views on this repeatedly during our stay in Bonn and then in Munich (thanks, Otávio, and thanks to the audience, who mostly agreed with one another that my paper was really a talk on how much nonphilosophers like metaphors—contrary to how I'd advertised it). My thanks to Megan Entwistle for finding many of the useful quotations from the animal literature that appear in chapter 1—and for putting some nice blue decorative stripes on my PowerPoint slides for the June 29 talk. Thanks are also due to the gracious audience at Colby College on April 11, 2019 (and to Dan Cohen for making the occasion possible), and to the organizers of the joint 2019 Suffolk County Community College spring philosophy conference and the Long Island Philosophical Society conference (and specifically to Lowell Kleiman and Matthew Konig) for inviting me to be the keynote speaker on April 13, 2019. On both occasions I presented material from the general introduction and chapter 1. I also did so for my October 18, 2019, talk at the University of Rochester; my thanks to the audience there.

My thanks, finally, to the philosophy department at Tufts and to Tufts University as well for granting me an unpaid leave during the academic year 2018–2019. The temporary unemployment I subsequently enjoyed enabled me to finish this book (chapters 6–11 and the appendix) and much of my next book. I also have to thank Sound Bites, Le Pain Quotidien (especially Anastasia, Jhanil, Karla, Laura, and Nancy), and the Amtrak quiet car, places where I wrote (and rewrote) most of this book.

I'd like to also thank Wendy Keebler, for wonderful copyediting, Peter Ohlin—as always—and everyone else at *Oxford University Press* who helped make this book possible.

So many people have been helpful that it's with sorrow that I must announce that despite their interventions and my own best efforts, I know (many?) falsehoods remain, and maybe one or two contradictions as well—all horribly my own fault. (I have—as Quine once put it about himself—erred indelibly in print. Worse, I know this happens *each time* I publish something.)

I described myself as turning explicitly to a book in epistemology in the fall of 2015. But of course, epistemological topics are naturally thought about (at least by me) for a whole lifetime. Although I didn't predict this book or some of its claims, significant groundwork was done in writing my earlier books and even before, during childhood ruminations. Many years ago (in 1991 or 1992), I was on an elevator at Clark Street with my friend and former student

Aaron Lipeles. How we got onto this topic I don't remember, but I audibly said (the elevator was quiet except for the two of us) that I wonder *all the time* whether we always know what we know, and whether we know what we know we know—or even whether this makes any sense. Someone behind us chortled sardonically. I paused for just a moment and then said to Aaron (who was momentarily puzzled, and then laughed), "But then I quit philosophy, got a job on Wall Street, and made millions and millions of dollars. So now I'm much, much happier."

Speaking of millions (and maybe billions), I mustn't forget to thank one individual who also deserves a compliment—although, in this case, only a backhanded one. After all, I could never have anticipated (not in millions of years, and maybe not in billions) that while I was writing a book on epistemology, a president of the United States would have such *deliberately* poor cognitive practices and habits that he'd be an implicit (and sometimes explicit) foil for so much of what I would claim in the book. So it goes. And thanks for that, Mr. President.

Attributing Knowledge

Introduction

Part 1

i Epistemology: What It Is

We attribute a great deal of knowledge to ourselves and to others.[1] We do this on our own (silently, sometimes), as well as in conversation, by claiming that we and others "know" all sorts of things. We do this explicitly with the word "know(s)" and other words closely aligned with it—"recognize(s)," "realize(s)," "learn(s)," "acknowledge(s)," etc.—and with sensorily colored verbs like "see(s)," "hear(s)," and "feel(s)." We do it tacitly by speaking in ways or in contexts that reveal presuppositions that we or others have knowledge. All of us—philosophers and nonphilosophers alike—are pretty aware that we indispensably rely on the knowledge we take ourselves and others to possess.

This is a ubiquitous and perennial fact of ordinary life. As children we quickly realize that we don't know what others, especially adults, seem to know; we go to school to "learn."[2] And as adults in professional life, or, for that matter, in any area of life we can imagine ever being in, we face "learning curves" where we must acquire new knowledge to function competently. This is as true in lofty professions dedicated to discovering surprising new facts (and elaborating far-reaching theories) about our universe, such as cosmology and genetics, as it is in those professions in which knowledge is largely applied—in medicine, as well as in the humanities. Knowledge is indispensable *everywhere*: in carpentry, during garbage collecting, while plumbing—not to mention the knowledge that's needed by CEOs, CIOs, accountants, small business owners, journalists, politicians, and even chronic liars. *All of us* have to know many things. Those of us who live alone on islands, in caves, or on mountaintops (if there *are* any of us like that any

[1] Pinillos (2012, 193) cites a study by Oxford Dictionaries that shows that "'knows' is the 59th most commonly used word of the English language, edging out words like 'take,' 'person' and 'good.'" (He gives the citation *Oxford English Corpus*, www.oxforddictionaries.com/page/oecfactslanguage/the-oec-facts-about-the-language and writes that he retrieved it on 02/06/2011.) Wierzbicka (1996) powerfully argues that "know(s)" belongs to a family of words—"think(s)," "see(s)," and "hear(s)" are others—that look to be lexical universals.

[2] Anyone interacting with children sees how early "know" is acquired and correctly deployed by them: "Where's your purple dinosaur?" "I don't know." "Know(s)" is among the most typically used "mental state" words by young children. Shatz, Wellman, and Silber (1983).

Attributing Knowledge. Jody Azzouni, Oxford University Press (2020). © Oxford University Press.
DOI: 10.1093/oso/9780197508817.001.0001.

longer) need lots of knowledge, just as those of us do who live in groups. Many of us—professionally—study other humans or animals; many of us design or otherwise implement sophisticated artifacts like the numerous bots, robots, and other forms of artificial intelligence now populating our world. It's routine for those of us who do this or who otherwise implement the existence of these artifacts (who sell them, for example, or represent companies that make them), or who just interact with them, to attribute knowledge to these mechanisms. (Alexa, we say, knows *a lot*.) We routinely, that is, attribute knowledge to humans, to animals, and to—this isn't a bad word to use—machinery.

We also attribute knowledge to ourselves *collectively*. "We now know the genetic basis of most colon cancers," we may read on a blog. The typical writers of such sentiments (and pretty much all their readers) haven't the training in genetics, or even in basic biology, to say much more beyond vague generalities about what this knowledge that we all "have" comes to—although Wikipedia may know more about this. Nevertheless, we routinely attribute knowledge this way to ourselves because we belong to vaguely delineated groups of people who all talk with and read one another. "We" know things that, in fact, only some or very few of us—as individuals—understand much about.

We not only (apparently) have a great deal of knowledge; we also constantly challenge the knowledge we seem to have and that we attribute to one another, both individually and collectively. "That's not true" and "you don't know that" are things we sometimes say—perhaps often—when objecting to something someone else has just tacitly or explicitly claimed to know. While doing this, we often evaluate one another's evidence for the things we take ourselves (and others) to know. Some people (the rest of us think) are "conspiracy nuts"—that is, people who willingly believe all sorts of bizarre things on recognizably bad evidence, or without any evidence at all. We are often, both in highly sophisticated ways and in ordinary ways, testing and relying on evidence for what we take ourselves to know. The statistical tools that social psychologists routinely use to design their experiments are sometimes misused; the evidence is faulty, and the experimenters, consequently, don't know what they thought they knew.[3] Those of us who have witnessed crimes, and have to testify about what we've seen, similarly sometimes misremember or mischaracterize what we saw. We instead recall the sloppy ways we *described* what happened to friends (or to ourselves) right after the event instead of remembering what actually happened. Our evidence is faulty—or our use of that evidence is, anyway.

Perhaps, though, the evidence we have doesn't show what we think it shows; perhaps that evidence is insufficient to rule out other possibilities we should take

[3] These concerns have made it into the popular literature. See, for example, Dominus (2017).

seriously. Perhaps, more dramatically, when *all* our evidence is examined carefully, it will become clear that we haven't any good evidence at all, or evidence sufficient for showing anything we think we know; perhaps we don't know much or any of the things we take ourselves to know. This is a fear everyone—nearly enough—has had at one time or another; it's a recurring theme in movies and television (e.g., *The Truman Show*, the *Matrix* series): perhaps *nothing* is as it appears. Perhaps nothing that we think is true *is* true.

This is the basic tension central to our ubiquitous practices of attributing and challenging knowledge: on the one hand, we and everyone around us seem to have enormous amounts of knowledge. We seem to, anyhow, given how much knowledge we *attribute* to ourselves and others—to people, animals, drones, GPS systems, and autonomous vehicles. Our ignorance is great, we'll admit—in sober moments anyway—but nevertheless we know *a lot*. On the other hand, when we examine how we routinely challenge our own and others' knowledge claims, or when we challenge our apparent knowledge systematically—something that some philosophers warn us only philosophers seem to want to do—it looks like we actually don't know *anything*.

This is *epistemology*. This subject, as the etymology of the word indicates, is perhaps the most ancient of philosophical subjects—its concerns date to or before the recorded origins of intellectual life among the ancient Greeks. Perhaps the subject matter of epistemology, rather than a topic to be studied systematically is instead a motley of glittering *puzzles*. It can certainly be taught that way, one damn puzzle after another: everything from evil demons and mad scientists (who fool their victims about—well—everything they *can*) to trilemmas about justification (infinite, circular, or arbitrary stopping points) to straightforward-seeming arguments that result in bizarre-sounding claims, like if you know something you should be dogmatic about it (because, after all, anything challenging what you *know* just *has to be* misleading). Or perhaps—like many areas of contemporary philosophy, actually—it's a battlefield of wounded and dying definitions surrounded by murderous counterexamples. We can study these wars of words and concepts for years (so it seems): definitions of knowledge, then counterexamples, then evasively modified definitions, then fiercer, less evadable counterexamples, then . . .

Epistemology, as a result, is populated with numerous positions, each convincing only to its few proponents—and commonly not even to all of *them* (some philosophers modestly saying: I *think* this is right . . .). This and the weird self-reflectiveness that's typical of the subject are puzzling all by themselves: how can a topic area constituted, nearly enough, only of severely designed *arguments* succeed so little in persuading other professionals in the field? How can this be in a post-twentieth-century setting, where, if we've learned anything new from the brilliant burst of twentieth-century results in *logic*, we've certainly (and finally) learned what logic *is*, and consequently, we've supposedly learned what a *good argument* is?

Half of the foregoing (mess) is the topic of this book. For, as I've intimated, epistemology divides sharply into the study of two aspects of our relationship to knowledge and the word "know(s)." There are, first, the attributions of knowledge—to ourselves and to others. And second, there are the challenges to purported knowledge—again, to ours and to that of others as well. There are puzzles, ancient and modern, about both aspects of our knowledge practices. But (and maybe this is surprising) for the most part, the puzzles (and therefore the issues that need investigation) fall fairly neatly into the division I've drawn between attributing knowledge and challenging it. I'll briefly indicate why.

There is, to begin with, the question of what the words that we use mean, words like "know(s)," "justif(y/ies)," "remember(s)," and so on. Do these words have stable invariant definitions? Are they instead contextually shifty, or are they just vague? Correspondingly, do these words—"know(s)," in particular—refer to the mental states of agents and/or to relations that these agents have to the world, or (instead) do they refer to nothing special in particular? And "justification" needs clarification too: how are justifications structured: can they be circular or infinite, or must there be "stopping points"? These are among the questions that arise when we ask what we're attributing to agents when we attribute knowledge to them.

When focusing on how knowledge is challenged, of course, the foregoing is relevant. But other questions arise too. *How*, exactly, is knowledge challenged? How are those challenges met? Can they be met? In the course of analyzing these latter questions, not only does the topic of (Cartesian) scepticism arise, but so do more detailed issues about the nature of the possibilities that are crucially deployed to challenge knowledge. Are these possibilities *logical* possibilities or some other species of modality? And questions also arise about the debates between purported knowers and their challengers. Is there (always) a burden of proof on purported knowers to justify what they claim to know, or is the burden instead on the challenger to provide a *genuine* challenge? This book, as I said, takes up the attribution of knowledge and largely leaves for future work the intricacies of how knowledge is challenged and, more generally, the puzzles of Cartesian scepticism.

ii The Importance of Words

With respect to the specifics of knowledge attribution, it must be admitted at the outset that epistemology is (or is like) a special science—it faces, anyway, all the drawbacks and challenges that special sciences face. Specifically, to understand what we do when we attribute knowledge, we need to already understand what have become classified as topics in linguistics and philosophy of language.[4] We need to understand the properties of the words we use, "know(s)" in particular—but not just that word, of course; "recognize(s)," "justif(y/ies)," "believe(s)," and many others are also relevant.

In some subject areas, knowing about words isn't that important. To make progress in zoology, we must acquire a nomenclature, but we don't really need to learn *its* peculiarities—we just need to study the animals themselves that the nomenclature labels. This isn't always true. In chemistry, instead, we must acquire a nomenclature that we also have to learn to manipulate (e.g., and this is a simple example, we need to learn how to "balance equations"). Mathematics and physics offer many other (quite sophisticated) examples of the same thing—including diagrams with, nearly enough, syntactic properties the sheer manipulation of which belongs to the mathematical/scientific discovery process. The ordinary language that surrounds knowledge—"infer(s)," "see(s)," etc.—is, remarkably, similarly complex; although our childhood acquisition of this system of words enables us to use it *effortlessly*, its intricate structure is hard to theorize about. Rather surprisingly, it eludes simple characterizations the way that the specialized nomenclatures of mathematics and the hard sciences elude simple characterizations—and unlike the straightforward terminology of zoology.

It's tempting, nevertheless, to think: "knowledge" is one thing, knowledge quite another. Let's study knowledge and leave "knowledge" for linguists. This won't work, not any better than its cousin view works in metaphysics, the one about "exist(s)" and what exists. Subtleties about knowledge are hidden in how we use the ordinary words "know(s)," "see(s)," "infer(s)," "recognize(s)," and others. These *words* are hardly the whole story, of course—but they're a crucial part of it.

Some of the main lessons of this book result from a close examination of the primary insight of the post-Gettier literature: "know(s)" and other related words haven't definitions. Of course (this is philosophy!), not everyone thinks this *is* an insight—there are treasure hunters still searching for definitions in the good old-fashioned way. Furthermore, some philosophers, while extolling this post-Gettier lesson, simultaneously offer characterizations of knowledge that, if successful, would be actual definitions of the word.

[4] It's thus no surprise that DeRose (2017, vii) describes the first volume of his papers (2009) in epistemology "more as philosophy of language." Similarly unsurprising is that scepticism isn't taken up in that first volume but delayed to DeRose's second volume of papers. Despite these resemblances, *this* book is primarily a book on *epistemology*—as I'll indicate later in this introduction.

Consider Williamson (2000, chapter 1). He describes the failures of the post-Gettier literature as resulting from the undefinability of "know(s)," and he characterizes undefinability as a common property of many of our ordinary words (he cites Fodor (1998)); in the same chapter, however, he *also* characterizes knowing "as the most general factive mental state." This is a characterization (a *definition*) that—in his view—picks out the extension of "know(s)" uniquely! Lewis (1996) also gives a definition of "know(s)," namely "S knows P if S can eliminate every possibility in which not P." (Lewis sees this condition as necessary and not merely sufficient because he treats it as threatening us with scepticism, which it wouldn't do if it weren't necessary.) Lewis contextualizes the definition, but it remains a definition nevertheless.

What both these philosophers give up, however, is a definition designed along the lines the post-Gettier literature strived for: an additional ingredient, X, to be added to the "traditional" tripartite set of necessary conditions—truth, belief, and justification—resulting in a set of conditions necessary *and* sufficient for knowledge.

It turns out that the bearing of linguistic matters on epistemology is intricate enough that I dedicate part 2 of this introduction to describing linguistic preliminaries that the reader needs in order to fully appreciate the evidence for the substantial epistemology that follows in later chapters.

iii Some of the Distinctive Epistemic Claims I Attempt to Establish in This Book

Epistemology exhibits its *special scienceness* in ways other than the relevance of linguistics to it. Epistemologists need to understand—at least broadly speaking—what we demand *of* someone or something in order for us to attribute knowledge to her, him, them, or *it*. Since knowledge is attributed to agents (ourselves and others) on the basis of facts about those agents—in particular, facts about the resources (sensory and otherwise) of those agents—we also need to understand, at least in a general way, how those agents acquire knowledge, what it is about their senses, about how they communicate with one another, and so on, that enables knowledge acquisition and transmission.

This is a point about epistemology that Quine (1969) seems to have first announced publicly—at least in a way that drew attention from philosophers. Naturalized epistemology is a research area, so he claimed, that relies on background sciences. He specified only psychology, but other sciences are relevant too. Regardless of Quine's dramatic claims (subsequently widely debated by philosophers in his wake), it's simply true that to understand the role of evidence in knowledge attributions, we must consider aspects of the sciences—both in respect of being subject areas *of* knowledge and as areas in which the means of knowledge are studied: various branches of linguistics, psychology, social psychology, and sociology are relevant to the latter concerns. It's here, incidentally, that the role and nature of reliability arise.

Because epistemology is a special science—more accurately, because it's the study of a certain distinctive cognitive phenomenon—there is the empirical possibility that the subject area of epistemology is a hot mess (as Williams (1996) suggests) in the sense that there is nothing illuminatingly general to say about it. On the contrary (I hope to show in this book): Epistemology is the study of a major deep-seated part of our cognitive anatomy. And, as with any study of our cognitive anatomy, it's not always clear what the "moving parts," the "cognitive levers," or suchlike are. (Metaphorically: what the muscles are, the bones . . .) This is especially the case in epistemology. For almost all of this book (chapters 1–8), it may appear that one jigsaw-puzzle piece after another is being picked up and analyzed without much of an attempt at assembling anything: this bit of usage is being analyzed (Moorean paradoxes), then that bit (assertion norms), then this (metacognition), then that (justification). As a result, the reader may (on occasion) wonder: Yes, but where is this all *going*? It's only in the last three chapters that everything's assembled into a systematic epistemic *landscape*; only then does a quite unified, cohesive, and (I think) compelling picture of knowledge attribution emerge in which a small number of central moving pieces are shown to be the machinery of our epistemic practices.

Three of the prime movers are the factivity of "know(s)," the vagueness of the word, and its compatibility with the fallibility of knowing agents.[5] These (as illustrated in the last three chapters of the book) are the key to unlocking epistemology. As important, however, are a number of items that are shown *not* to be prime movers, items that many philosophers have thought (for many years) to be central to the operations of knowledge.

Here is a rough description of several *negative* epistemic claims that I attempt to establish that illustrate the last sentence. That is, the concept of knowledge is minimal in the principles it obeys, and correspondingly broad in the range of possible epistemic agents it allows. Among other things, if an agent S know(s) *p*, then it *doesn't* necessarily follow (although it *can* be true) that:

> S believes *p*,
> S rationally believes *p*,
> S is certain of *p*,

[5] What I call "social role" epistemologists try to show instead that their specified one or another social role for knowing attributions, *to indicate acceptable testifiers, to reassure*, etc., are such linchpins. No—as I argue in section 11.5.

S is sure/confident of *p*,
S is conscious of *p*,
S is conscious (at all),
S can justify *p* (in the sense that S is aware of, or grasps, or can grasp, or can articulate, reasons that justify *p*),
S knows that S knows that *p*,
S understands *p*.

That is, an agent can know *p*, although she doesn't believe *p*, she wouldn't be rational to believe *p*, she could be wrong about *p* (in an appropriate sense of this), she needn't be confident or sure of *p*, she needn't be conscious of *p* (or conscious at all, or capable of consciousness), nor need she be able to justify *p*. Finally, she needn't have any iterated knowledge attitudes toward what she knows.

These results free "know(s)" from many entailments that, implicitly and explicitly, philosophers have attached to the word. Some may fear that this leaves us with little to say about "know(s)" that's positive. Not so (as the size of this book sadly indicates): "know(s)" I also show—using the standard jargon—is invariant, intellectualist (pure), but vague. The usage data that philosophers have used to show that "know(s)" is contextual in one or other ways, or sensitive to the agent's pragmatic needs, is either specious or can be explained by the word's vagueness alone.

Furthermore, that knowledge attributions allow agents to be fallible has important implications. Because all knowing agents are fallible (but in different ways), no easily stated closure condition on knowledge is true. Nor are parity conditions true—under identical circumstances, two agents (both, say, holding lottery tickets for the same lottery drawing and knowing the same facts about that lottery) will differ in that one agent can know that he'll lose while another won't know this (and *only* because she'll *win*).

Some hedged versions or other of conditions on "know(s)" that philosophers have wanted remain. Williamson (2000), for example, regards "know(s)" as the most general factive mental state. Subsidiary claims of his that accompany this definition of the knowledge state are true, e.g., that if φ is a factive mental state, then, if an agent φs that *p*, the agent knows that *p*; for example, if an agent S sees that *p*, then S knows that *p*. A hedged version of an agent knowing *p* implying that agent is confident or certain of *p* holds; this is so only when lacking that confidence damages an agent's methods of knowing *p*. As I intimated, there are also agent-relative hard-to-state hedged closure conditions that hold of "know(s)."

Apart from these various hedged conditions, "know(s)" is governed by two necessary conditions. The easily stated one, as I mentioned, is factivity: If S know(s) *p*, then *p*. The second can only be stated vaguely: If S know(s) *p*, then S has come to know *p* by a process that, to some extent, is reliable. The vagueness is ineliminable: "know(s)" is vague because the (tacit) standards for knowledge are vague. This, as I'll show, can't be strengthened into a sufficient condition. For the same reason, a reliable process that's sufficient for knowledge for an agent in some circumstances won't be sufficient for knowledge for another agent in other circumstances—where, for example, the circumstances and agents differ only insofar as one agent will win a lottery and the other won't.

Given all this, exactly how cognitively minimal can agents be and yet still be knowers? Pretty minimal: Knowers range from (i) sophisticated humans who (regularly) engage in iterated cognition, and have knowledge, about their own knowledge states—such humans focus not just on what they know but on how they know it; further, such humans regularly recognize subtle implications of what they know, and know these things as well—to (ii) unsophisticated humans who rarely, if ever, engage in iterated cognition, and who, when they evaluate questions about how they know what they know, often get it wrong—as well as knowing little or next to nothing about what follows from that knowledge—to (iii) nonhuman animals who, despite knowing things, and indeed, often knowing a lot, nevertheless know little or nothing about what they know, and little or nothing about what their knowledge implies, to (iv) insects, drones, and driverless cars, which despite all that they know, aren't (and shouldn't be) regarded as conscious, and (unless designed otherwise) know almost nothing (or nothing at all) about what they know.

iv Brief Synopses of the Chapters in This Book

Before giving synopses, I'll note that the jigsaw-pieces look of the earlier chapters, 1–8, is due to the fact that I'm mostly establishing the negative theses I've listed in iii. Only in the last three chapters are my positive theses established and explored.

In chapter 1, I start—naturally—with some empirical usage data. We routinely attribute knowledge to many kinds of agents—not just self-conscious thoughtful humans but various animals, insects, and mechanisms. The application of many epistemic words, "know(s)," "see(s)," "realize(s)," etc., aren't metaphors or special-case extensions of these words. The lesson of the chapter: There seem to be quite limited "mental-state" requirements on the epistemic agents that "know(s)" attributions can be applied to. We readily attribute knowledge to cameras, GPS systems, insects, drones, autonomous vehicles, not to mention humans and other animals—both sophisticated and unsophisticated. In particular, as I mentioned earlier, "believe(s)" attributions, as well as attributions of consciousness (meant in the sense of the possession of an "inner life"), uncouple from knowledge attributions. Beings don't have to be conscious of what they know, or be conscious *at all*; they don't have to believe p to know p.

In chapters 2 and 3, I turn to undercutting still-popular epistemic contextualisms (as well as impurity positions like "subject-sensitive invariantism"). These positions are undercut, nearly enough, by a close examination of the usage data the positions are supposedly supported by. My objections can be summarized neatly: these views fail to account for *all* the usage data that's available—in particular, they don't account for how we explicitly respond to purported cases of "shifting knowledge standards" when we *compare cases* to one another. For then we resist that our knowledge standards—whatever they are—can contextually shift; this contrasts with how we experience *genuine* context shiftiness in standard cases of such, e.g., "tall." I establish, thus, that our ordinary concept of knowledge is pure (intellectualist) and not contextual.

In chapter 4, I turn to another recently popular topic in epistemology: assertion norms. I say: There no assertion norms. My basis for this claim is an analysis of Moorean remarks and criticisms of knowledge claims that shows instead that held-in-common background assumptions are what are behind our judgments that Moorean remarks are weird, or that criticisms of knowledge claims are legitimate. What undercuts norm views, and this is a matter of re-examining the usage data about remarks and criticisms, is that Moorean remarks are often perfectly acceptable, and criticisms of knowledge claims are often illegitimate. I thus undercut *the* usage data that assertion-norm views need for support.

In chapter 5, I turn to iterated "know(s)" claims. A close examination of usage is again required to unearth the many ways in which we confound iterated and ground-floor cognitive attributions and self-attributions, including "know(s)" ones. The KK and K¬K theses are wrong (that if we know *p*, then we know that we know *p*, and if we don't know *p*, then we know that we don't know *p*); but more important are the details of when *specific* iterated cognition attributions are legitimate. Included in this chapter are important subtleties in the ways in which we attribute the possession of concepts to epistemic agents. This matters to the discussion of some of the empirical literature surveyed in chapter 6, where I look at both illustrative thought experiments and real-world animal studies to see how and when we can attribute ground-floor and higher-order cognitions to agents.

Inferential "justification" is analyzed in chapter 7. In the course of giving a definition for "justif(y/ies)"—that is, while characterizing justifications—I discuss Agrippa's trilemma, in particular, the infinitist leg of the trilemma that only recent philosophers have argued is viable. I conclude that it isn't viable. Important to showing this is a close evaluation of recent work by Atkinson and Peijnenburg (2017) and some of the surrounding literature.

Chapter 8 focuses on "representational justification." The primary polemical target is a group of philosophers whom I (perhaps unfairly) lump together: Aikin,

BonJour, Brandom, and Williams, among others. These philosophers subscribe to one or another version of Sellars's argument against "the Given": that nothing nonpropositional can function as a justifier. While giving a definition for "justif(y/ies)," I undercut several arguments found in the literature for this widely believed claim. A satisfying result is that our ordinary practice of pointing to things in the world, like chairs, to justify claims, such as "that's a chair," is fully sustained.[6]

Chapter 9 explores the vagueness of "know(s)," and how that handles the usage phenomena that (heretofore) it's looked like only some sort of contextualist view can handle. Crucial to this project is getting clear about what vagueness is; Williamson's (1994) well-known characterization of vagueness is rejected; so is his argument against KK.

In chapter 10, I turn explicitly to fallibilism. I show how numerous factors in our ordinary usage practices conspire to make it appear that ordinary attributions of knowledge to agents require them to be infallible. In particular, I explain why "I know *p*, but possibly not *p*" seems unacceptable, and I show against Fantl and McGrath (2009) why fallibilism is compatible with intellectualism. Solutions to the lottery paradox and Kripke's dogmatism paradox are ventured. Knowledge closure, as well as closure principles for rational belief, is denied (but none of these denials will help us against scepticism).

Chapter 11, finally, steps back and uses the foregoing results to give an overview of the meaning of "know(s)" and its indispensable role/function. In the conclusion, I (rashly?) make some promises about future work.

In the appendix, I solve the surprise exam paradox. My primary aim in doing so is to dislodge the apparent significance the paradox has seemed (to some philosophers—Harman, Kripke, Williamson, and Wright among them) to have for epistemology. Although certain epistemic facts discussed earlier in the book are relevant to the solution of the paradox (e.g., that we sometimes aren't iteratively cognizing even though we're talking as if we are), most aren't. In particular, the failure of KK (relatedly, that epistemic agents needn't grasp iterations of their ground-floor knowledge) isn't pertinent to a solution. And, because of the meaning of "know(s)," misleading-evidence-undercutting-knowledge solutions don't work either.

[6] There's a cast of mind I can easily put myself into where it strikes me as outrageous that this popular view about justification was *ever* taken seriously by *anyone*: that only something propositional can play the role of a justifier. (Davidson [1986, 310] writes, for example, "what distinguishes a coherence theory is simply the claim that nothing can count as a reason for holding a belief except another belief." Leave aside the nomenclatural point that this *doesn't* distinguish a coherence theory; Davidson means to claim, in any case, that it's true that only beliefs can justify beliefs.) But, as I've just parenthetically indicated, sober philosophers did (and do) have this position for reasons that deserve respectful attention, so I suppress this cast of mind in what follows.

Part 2

Consider this part of the introduction a compendium of linguistic and methodological points that are presupposed in the rest of the book. Sometimes I'll be explicit about this. I rely heavily, for example, on the material from introduction sections v and vii in the first chapter—the points made in these sections directly prevent treating the usages I discuss in chapter 1 as metaphors or nonliteral expressions. Other material, from introduction sections viii, ix, and x, is used throughout the book, but is especially needed to appreciate the description I give of "know(s)" in chapter 11. Lastly, introduction section xi defends my general approach, one used throughout the book, against attacks on it that, generally, attempt to undermine the distinctively linguistic approach to usage data that I take here.

The reader, therefore, can read the material that follows in a preliminary way to grasp the overall assumptions and the structure of the arguments, returning to it (if needed) when specific claims are relied on later in the book.

v Insights from Lexical Semantics: Ambiguity and Polysemy

The important point issuing from contemporary lexical semantics and the fledgling theory of concepts[7]—anticipated by Wittgenstein (1963)[8]—isn't that definitions for most of our words (important *and* unimportant) don't exist. That's true, of course, but the crucial result is that the behavior of our definitionless words is more subtle and constrained than most philosophers *still* realize—especially epistemologists. I'll first illustrate the important behavior of ordinary words that I need for the studies in this book with a philosophically non-contentious word, "climb(s)."[9]

[7] "Fledgling" not because it's young by scientific standards but because it hasn't "matured," as Kuhn would have put it. There are several current competing paradigms. I'm most drawn to prototype theory because it's empirically well verified and because it fits best with those theories of the lexicon that I also think are empirically well verified; I discuss this momentarily. For some of the early experimental work prototype theory is based on, see Rosch and Mervis (1975) and Rosch (1978).

[8] Well, maybe not. Although the denial of necessary and sufficient conditions for most natural-language words is genuinely insightful, Wittgenstein's influential remarks about "family resemblances"—and the accompanying analogy of words with games—are dangerously misleading. Words and their uses aren't like games *at all*, because games really are open-ended. Words, however (because of the natural-language constraints governing them), are limited both in the variety of them possible across (natural) public languages and in their evolution within those languages. Although the details of these constraints still aren't fully clarified, we know enough today to know that this is true. See, for some particulars about this, the forthcoming discussion on the contemporary philosopher's tendency to see ambiguity or metaphor in places it doesn't exist.

[9] I've drawn this material—and the material to follow on "see(s)"—from Jackendoff (1990, 35–36) and Jackendoff (1983, especially 118–121, 144–145, and 150–151). Jackendoff (1990, 290 n. 9) credits Fillmore (1982) with first giving the forthcoming characterization of "climb(s)." Jackendoff (1990,

Consider the following sentences:

1. Bill climbed (up) the mountain.
2. Bill climbed down the mountain.
3. The snake climbed (up) the tree.
4. ?*The snake climbed down the tree.

Jackendoff describes "climbing" as involving two independent conceptual conditions: (i) an individual is traveling upward; (ii) the individual is moving with characteristic effortful grasping motions.[10] The interesting point is that these conditions are independent insofar that if only one or the other is violated (as in, respectively, 2 and 3), the resulting usage is still acceptable, although if *both* are violated, the result is unacceptable, as in 4. So we have two *linked* conditions on the meaning of "climb(s)," neither of which is necessary but either of which is sufficient.[11] Although either alone suffices for correct usage, they're nevertheless linked by their effects on typicality intuitions, by how they allow certain usages and not others (as I indicate momentarily), and by their inducing a default assumption about what's being described (as I indicated in note 11).[12]

This *doesn't* show that the word "climb" as used in these cases is ambiguous, nor does it show that one condition is central and the other is in some sense nonliteral or "metaphorical," or one that applies only in special cases. As Jackendoff (1990, 35) writes, "Rather, [1], which satisfies both conditions at once, is more "stereotypical" climbing. Actions that satisfy only one of the conditions, such as [2 & 3] are somewhat more marginal but still perfectly legitimate instances of climbing." Thus, a plane can climb to 2,000 feet (just as the temperature can climb

290 n. 10) credits Miller and Johnson-Laird (1976) with the forthcoming characterization of "see(s)." My thanks to Ray Jackendoff for a (brief) conversation on this topic on February 12, 2018.

[10] He describes "clambering" as "a convenient term" for these typical effortful grasping motions. I'm not sure it fits (do *squirrels* clamber?), but I'll go along for the sake of the illustration because I haven't anything better that can be said *quickly*. Wierzbicka (1996, 165–166) criticizes this characterization of "climb(s)" because trains "climb" mountains only if they move slowly enough. This looks right, and some clause about speed (appropriate to the kind of thing that's climbing and/or to what it's climbing on, if anything) needs to be incorporated into these conditions.

[11] Jackendoff (1983, 1990) calls a set of conditions operating on a lexical item in this way a "preference rule system." An important fact about how preference rules operate is that, without further information, the default assumption is that *both* conditions are operative. This explains why "The monkey climbed the tree" is assumed to be a description of the monkey going *up*—unless specified otherwise. The information that nullifies the default, presumably, doesn't need to be syntactically explicit; otherwise we'd expect climbing planes to be clambering planes.

[12] Are these conditions disjunctively necessary? I suspect they may be de facto disjunctively necessary in the case of "climb"—that is, there are only two linked conditions for "climb," but this isn't required by the meaning of the word. (My thanks to Ram Neta for pressing me to be more explicit about this.) I should add that I'll refine Jackendoff's apparatus slightly—introducing the notion of *sufficiency regions* for words—before applying it to "know(s)" in section 11.3.

to 120 degrees Fahrenheit), but we never describe planes or the temperature as "climbing down." Planes aren't "stereotypical" climbers—but that doesn't make the application of "climb" to planes nonliteral or metaphorical. It would be a mistake (but one that philosophers typically make with the words *they* care about) to treat "climbing" planes and temperatures as metaphors, and in this way attempt to impound as a necessary *and* sufficient condition on climbing the clambering (up trees) that bears and squirrels, say, engage in, but not planes, the temperature, or social climbers.

Now consider a philosophically significant word, "see":

5. Bill saw Harry.
6. Bill saw things that weren't there.
7. Bill saw the sign, but he didn't notice it at the time.
8. *Bill saw things that weren't there, but he didn't notice them at the time.

Jackendoff (1990, 36) writes, "The two preference conditions for *x sees y* are roughly that [i] x's gaze makes contact with y, and [ii] x has a visual experience of y."[13] As with "climbing," 5 is a stereotypical use which satisfies both conditions; still acceptable, however, are uses satisfying only one or the other of these conditions (such as 6 and 7); unacceptable are uses that violate both, as 8 does.[14]

Let's return to "climb(s)" as an illustration, in order to see the kinds of empirical arguments that can be used to show when words should be taken to be operating ambiguously, when metaphorically, and when neither. Why *isn't* "climb(s)," when applied to planes and temperatures, a metaphorical extension of its proper use with respect to bears, squirrels, and the like? An important piece of evidence against this is that we haven't the *freedom* that we would have in our use of the word if it were perceived as a mere metaphorical extension. We *can't* say, "The temperature is finally climbing down," although if the application of "climb(s)" to temperature were a metaphorical extension of a use of "climb(s)" that allows both "climbing" up and down, it's hard to see why it would be restricted in this way. The same is true for "social climbing," which might sound like a better

[13] Jackendoff's examples (instead of my 6 and 8) are "Bill saw a vision of dancing devils" and "Bill saw a vision of dancing devils, but he didn't notice it at the time." I dislike his examples because I want to substitute "had" for "saw" in them; and some others to whom I've shown Jackendoff's examples react similarly. (The same seems true of "hallucination"—we *have* hallucinations; it's awkward, although not impossible, to say, "I saw hallucinations.") No matter, there are plenty of examples with "see(s)" where no substitution of "had" works, e.g., "He often sees angels, demons, and devils," "We all saw the holes in the cheese," "Sarah is seeing dancing devils again, so we're taking her back to the doctor," and so on.

[14] No one should expect much philosophical or scientific depth from conditions like these. They're intended to exhaust our linguistic competence—semantically speaking—but nothing further. They won't even resolve straightforward questions like "when I gaze at someone's eyes, am I gazing at their corneas?" (I'm grateful to Ram Neta for urging me to be explicit about this.)

candidate for a metaphorical extension of "climb(s)." Here too, socially climbing *down* is ruled out.

Suppose this is right: why isn't "climb(s)" instead ambiguous, with two related meanings? There are several connected considerations against this. As Jackendoff mentions, speaker-hearers have a tripartite set of responses to the uses of words: *typical, atypical* (which in turn is open to grading), and *wrong*. "Wrong," incidentally, will instead be a judgment of "metaphorical" if, for example, the usage appears in a poem, e.g., "the snake slowly climbed its way down from heaven . . ."[15] Thus the typicality intuitions used to support prototype theories of concepts are nicely explained by Jackendoff's model of the lexicon. Specifically, his model explains why we don't have the kind of ambiguity intuitions with "climb(s)" that we have with genuinely ambiguous words, like "bank" (Jackendoff (1990, 35)).

Another important piece of evidence that can be applied to test for ambiguity is the conjunction-reduction test.[16] Utilize one instance of the same word to cover the two cases and see if the resulting expression reads bizarrely. For example, these are fine: "Bill and the snake climbed up the same tree at the same moment" or "When he stepped through the door, Bill saw dancing side by side both Harry, who was real, and a devil, who wasn't." On the other hand, we can't replace "The colors are light and the feathers are light," with #"The colors and feathers are light."[17] This test is evidence that neither "climbed" nor "saw" is ambiguous, as they're used here, although "light" is. Notice further that although "see(s)" isn't ambiguous, as far as Jackendoff's two independent preference rules (i) and (ii) mentioned right after (5)–(8) are concerned, the English word *is* ambiguous because an instance of it can be governed by those meaning conditions or can instead convey "understanding," e.g., as in "I see what you meant." #"I see the stove and what you meant" fails the conjunction-reduction test.

More evidence: A symptom of a word's ambiguity is that it fails a substitution test which (when the test can be relied on) shows that the word's different meanings are operating in different syntactic frames.[18] So, for example, "in the house" can be replaced with "inside the house," but "in the milk" can't be replaced

[15] This said, I'm slightly less comfortable with Jackendoff's verdict on snakes than I am about temperatures, planes, and social climbers. And some others I've queried on this share my misgivings: many of us have no problem with snakes climbing up and down trees being an acceptable usage. Others, like Jeff McConnell (email, June 25, 2018), don't like snakes climbing *at all*. (He thinks, I guess, that they can only *slither*.) On the other hand, I balk at *snails* climbing down. That's just not a *thing*. (Joke.) I discuss idiolectical phenomena, and the importance of taking account of them, later in this introduction.

[16] For discussion of this, and other tests for ambiguity, see Zwicky and Sadock (1975). For a nice overview of the topic, see Sennet (2016).

[17] I'll generally use # to indicate a bizarreness reaction, typically a semantic one. Sometimes, if I'm following closely the discussion of an author who uses * for this, I'll do the same.

[18] See Wierzbicka (1996) for numerous applications of this point about syntax in order to determine across languages when one word (with one meaning) is present and when, instead, ambiguity is operative. I should add that Wierzbicka's (1996) project *is* to provide definitions for lexical items

with "inside the milk" (Wierzbicka [1996, 95]). This test shows "in" is ambiguous. A conjunction-reduction test yields the same result. Consider "the sugar is in the jar on the cupboard or it's in the Kool-Aid." But #"the sugar is in the jar on the cupboard or the Kool-Aid."[19]

Generally, both tests must be applied with care, and a single application of either alone isn't conclusive. #"Bill and the temperature climbed up and down all day" sounds bad—so "climb(s)" flunks this application of the conjunction-reduction test. Also bad is the substitution of "inside" for "in" in "in the garden." Nevertheless, "in" as used in "in the house" and "in the garden" seems to mean the same. This latter usage passes the conjunction-reduction test: "Harry is either in the garden or the house."[20]

A word can flunk a substitution test not because it's ambiguous but because the word substituted for it is governed by special conditions (e.g., "inside"); a word can flunk a specific instance of the conjunction-reduction test despite not being ambiguous if a constraint on one of its sufficient conditions is encoded syntactically in the sentence the conjunction-reduction test is employing, as with "climbed up and down all day."[21]

So, whether a word is ambiguous or not is (perhaps unsurprisingly) a subtle empirical matter. Typicality intuitions matter (as well as folk intuitions that a word is being used metaphorically or just incorrectly); so does the *pattern* of substitution failures and successes, as well as the *pattern* of successes and failures of the conjunction-reduction test.[22] (And, of course, there are other tests I haven't talked about—e.g., contradiction and entailment tests.) This said, there may still seem to be something stipulative here: why *can't* we nevertheless insist that

in terms of semantic primitives (ones that occur in every language). I won't pause to evaluate the prospects of this ambitious goal; I only want to observe that her definitions *aren't* meant to provide necessary and sufficient conditions because exceptions are allowed. Strictly speaking, therefore, her project is irrelevant to the hallowed traditional one where definitions *are* supposed to provide necessary and sufficient conditions *without* exceptions.

[19] "The sugar is in the jar on the cupboard or the refrigerator" is OK. See Sennet (2016, section 3.1), however, for misgivings about "in." Although this doesn't fault the application of the test, you *can* say (about a frozen block of milk) that "there is a mouse inside the milk" (Janet Chumley, email, June 25, 2018). See note 20 for a diagnosis of this.

[20] The complications here arise, most likely, because gardens are conceptualized as having two-dimensional boundaries and houses as having three-dimensional boundaries. That's what makes replacing "in" with "inside" awkward. My thanks to Eric Dean (personal communication, May 25, 2019) for this.

[21] This is related to the default property of preference-rule systems mentioned earlier.

[22] Consider "run(s)" to describe what animals do, as opposed to what refrigerators do. Is it, when so used, ambiguous, or is it like "climb(s)"? I think the evidence indicates ambiguity. For example, I can run in place, but a refrigerator—or motor—can't (except facetiously). I can also go running, although a refrigerator can't. #"The refrigerator and I stopped running at the same time." Etcetera. For a wealth of interesting examples on "run(s)," see Alston (1971). His discussion is still good—although limited in the tests for ambiguity that he considers.

"climb(s)" or "see(s)" has *two* meanings, each of which is structured as Jackendoff describes them: with two sufficient conceptual conditions neither of which is necessary? Why must we say that it's a single meaning that's structured this way?

Theorists *could* go this way[23] (and perhaps they have with respect to the notion of "polysemy"—see the discussion three paragraphs later). If, however, purportedly distinct usages of words pass a pattern of substitution and conjunction-reduction tests, this indicates that *we* conceptualize them (to that extent) together, and that's an indication that speaker-hearers don't understand these usages to come apart in meaning the way our imagined theorists insist upon. In part this conceptual unity turns on exactly how the various sufficient (but not necessary) conditions are related. For example, the things we "see," according to both sufficient conditions that Jackendoff distinguishes, play similar if not identical roles in our lives: we use our eyes to see both in the same way; we take what we "see" to be true (all things being equal) and as open to questions of existence; furthermore, we have the same responses to what we "see" (again, all things being equal), and so on.

Closely related to this point is that how speaker-hearers individuate concepts comes apart from how theorists, plying this imagined line, would individuate them. This too is a serious drawback (when comparing the virtues of theories), especially if there are theories available (of concepts *and* of the lexicon) that accommodate speaker-hearers better. Lastly, the primary motivation apparently behind this maneuver is to preserve the hallowed tradition of concepts having exceptionless necessary and sufficient conditions, and correspondingly, words with exceptionless necessary and sufficient conditions. The right view about this is revealed by the powerful conceptual structures embodied in mathematics and in the sciences: terms (and the corresponding concepts) with exceptionless necessary and sufficient conditions are largely *invented*. They aren't particularly prevalent in natural languages—apart from jargon and kinship vocabularies (see Fodor et al. (1980)).

The lexical data—that determines the presence of ambiguity (or its absence)—isn't an arbitrary matter that philosophers *cum* theorists can tweak at their pleasure to fit abstract theoretical virtues, such as elegance or simplicity. These are properties of words that are instead indicated by usage *independently* of philosophical views on the matter.[24]

Once upon a time (during the dark ages of semantics, back when it was practiced by the likes of Ayer ((1940)), attribution of ambiguity to words was empirically unprincipled. Philosophers relied on their *direct* (and varying) intuitions

[23] Theorists could also insist that space has a Euclidean structure, despite the current tight relationship between non-Euclidean geometry in general relativity and the evidence for that particular package of mathematics and physics. Underdetermination of a theory by data is a fact of life (as any philosopher of science will point out)—especially if stubborn theorists are willing to pay for the extra cost of ad hoc complexity.

[24] Contrast this lesson in philosophical method with the aprioristic methodology Hazlett (2010, 503) demands; he writes, "Following Grice, I take the positing of polysemy to be a vice, ceteris

about the ambiguity of particular words, and not on the intricate interplay of usage factors—that I've described—that are now used to recognize the presence of ambiguity. Empirically unprincipled distinctions are tempting vices for some philosophers because their "intuitions" can be used to dictate an answer, *this* or *that*, independently of the empirical facts, and in a way that supports philosophical proclivities. I've suggested in the foregoing that the situation has changed with respect to ambiguity: we (now) have ways of systematically bringing to bear *different* aspects of usage all of which go beyond sheer speaker-hearer "intuitions" about whether they "hear" one or more meanings—devices, for example, like the conjunction-reduction test, ellipsis, and anaphora.

Polysemy (currently) is a different matter.[25] Theorists have distinguished the meanings of words even in cases where tests for ambiguity *fail*. Consider the word "bank."[26] That this word is ambiguous between a side-of-a-river reading and a financial-institution reading is shown by the conjunction-reduction test:

9. The bank was slippery after the rain.
10. The bank dropped the mortgage rate.
11. #The bank was slippery after the rain and dropped the mortgage rate.

Consider, however, the following:

12. The bank was bailed out by the government, which damaged its standing.
13. The bank's refurbishments improved the queuing problem, which was popular with the customers.
14. The bank was bailed out by the government, which damaged its standing, but its refurbishments improved the queuing problem, which was popular with the customers.

Here, Collins argues, "bank" carries distinct but not unrelated meanings, one denoting an institution (that can be bailed out) and the other a building or group of them that can be refurbished and involve queuing.[27]

paribus, for a linguistic theory." Later, he presses a popular (but false) cliché about scientific methodology: "The method here resembles that used in science—rival theories will be described, compared, and a winner chosen on the basis of simplicity, elegance, and explanatory success." (By "polysemy," I take Hazlett to mean "ambiguity," and not what I subsequently call "polysemy." If Hazlett were speaking specifically of "polysemy," he'd be making a better case—alas—as I will indicate.)

[25] This very terminology, "polysemy," now standard, is misleading. Some philosophers use "polysemy" to mean "ambiguous in several ways," or they otherwise slur over what's emerged as an important linguistic distinction between ambiguity and polysemy.

[26] I draw the discussion of this example from Collins (2017, 678–679).

[27] Collins (2017, 678–679) writes: "In standard terminology, we say that *bank* is *ambiguous* with respect to denoting a financial institution or a side of a river, whereas it is *polysemous* with respect

The empirical problem the notion of polysemy faces (in contrast to ambiguity) is that, without the corresponding linguistic tools available for ambiguity, there is an opening for methodological pronouncements and sheer philosophical debate to dictate whether polysemy is present or not. Collins (2017, 679), as I quoted with "bank," and as he also claims with "book"—when he notes that one can both memorize and burn books—presses the ontological distinction between the items he takes to be polysemously referred to. But it's open to some metaphysicians to claim, against him, that—after all—there are (according to these metaphysicians) "queer entities" out there, ones that can be memorized *and* burned or bailed out *and* refurbished. In noting the metaphysical option here for denying polysemy, I'm not claiming Collins is wrong; I'm pointing out that the discussion has unpleasantly skittered out of empirical linguistics and into metaphysics.[28]

Some philosophers, reveling in the empirically anchorless latitude that polysemy offers, are resurrecting Ayer's old tendency to see ambiguity everywhere—but now in the guise of polysemy. And the only tool they offer for determining the presence of polysemy is the direct impression of multiple readings. It's better to recognize that polysemy is (currently) in the kind of theoretical flux that ambiguity was back in Ayer's time, and to be *very* careful about relying on it in philosophical argument.[29]

What about "see" and "climb"? Are *they* polysemous? Against this are the points already raised, how Jackendoff's preference conditions are linked *linguistically*. I mean by this not merely that the distinct "meanings" survive the tests for ambiguity (which is true for all polysemy) but in addition—as I mentioned—how they're connected to psychological results about *typicality*. In this respect,

to denoting a financial institution or a building serving the institution. The crucial feature to bear in mind with the polysemous case here is that although the two senses are clearly intimate, they are ontologically quite distinct. A bank as an institution, say, could close down all of its branches and remain the same bank. More generally, we reckon there not to be the one entity out there in the world that can receive bailouts and be carpeted, say. Moreover, no such queer entity appears to be licensed by, or be otherwise explanatorily relevant for, our bare linguistic competence with the expressions."

[28] Collins seems to suggest otherwise with the sentence, quoted here in note 27, "Moreover, no such queer entity appears to be licensed by, or be otherwise explanatorily relevant for, our bare linguistic competence with the expressions." He may mean by this that the positing of such an entity is linguistically idle apart from providing a single referent for what would otherwise be a polysemous word. I'm not sure that succeeds as an objection against determined anti-polysemists. One might—here's another strategy—hope to show that even the most metaphysically rich view is outstripped by polysemy phenomena. I doubt it; metaphysical inventiveness is notorious.

[29] On the other hand, one can, like Hofweber (2016), see "semantic underspecification" *everywhere*, and thus polysemy as extremely widespread. Hofweber's only empirical test for the presence of polysemy, as mentioned, is the "hearing" of multiple readings. The result (in my view) is a muddying-together of quite distinct linguistic phenomena—not just a tendency to blend ambiguity with polysemy (as with the word "get," which Hofweber describes as polysemous even though it fails the conjunction-reduction test) but, worse, a tendency to read Gricean implicatures as instead exhibitions of polysemy. See Azzouni (forthcoming b) on this.

"see" and "climb" are like "bird," which is *not* seen as polysemous as between, say, "robin" and "penguin," as opposed to "bank," "London," or "book," which *are* seen as polysemous, as Collins (and others) argue.[30]

vi Insights from Lexical Semantics: Retraction and the Factivity of "Know(s)"

Warnings about attributions of polysemy in place, I turn now to illustrating how lexical semantics bears on epistemology a bit further by looking at another aspect of "know(s)" that (I think) is clearly dictated by usage. A view almost universal among philosophers (and linguists, when they focus on the issue) is the factivity of "know(s)"—that if an agent knows *p*, then *p*. There are philosophers, however, who oppose this, and Hazlett is among them.[31] He offers examples like the following (my numbering) (Hazlett (2010, 501); the original sources are in his notes 13–16):

15. Everyone knew that stress caused ulcers, before two Australian doctors in the early 80s proved that ulcers are actually caused by bacterial infection.
16. He figures anything big enough to sink the ship they're going to see in time to turn. But the ship's too big, with too small a rudder . . . it can't corner worth shit. Everything he knows is wrong.
17. In school we learned that World War I was a war to "make the world safe for democracy," when it was really a war to make the world safe for the Western imperial powers.[32]
18. I had trouble breathing, sharp pains in my side, several broken ribs and a partially collapsed lung, and I was in the middle of nowhere without any real rescue assets—it was then that I realized I was going to die out there.

Hazlett employs a strategy used by *many* philosophers—he focuses *only* on the acceptability of these individual cases *without* paying attention to retraction

[30] Because the polysemy of "London," "book," and the like aren't very visible to speaker-hearers (in part because usage doesn't seem to be sensitive to polysemy), I suspect the cases being labeled as polysemy aren't actually linguistic matters at all but aspects of how we conceptualize objects—real and not real—that we talk about. This is a speculation, however, that I must pursue elsewhere.

[31] Sosa (2000, 8), too, notes that: "The term 'know' and its cognates are sometimes so used as to make it true that the medieval just 'knew' that the earth was flat (a view confirmed by the OED). In some ordinary contexts if someone is very sure that *p*, that makes it true to say that they 'know' that *p*." This isn't the right characterization of these *usages*; rather, they will be retracted under push-back ("Medievals *knew* the earth was flat? Because then it *was*? Um, you're kidding, right?"); dictionaries and compendiums of usage, generally, don't take account of retraction. (They should!) In any case, Sosa's attempt to use this purported usage as a reason to derail the significance of language to epistemology fails.

[32] "Learn" is different from "realize" and "know," which are both uniformly factive; you can "learn" things that are false—this is in the sense of "cognitively acquiring" them.

phenomena: when speakers systematically withdraw claims (or fail to withdraw claims) under pressure.[33] In 15, 16, and 18, and in all other cases of factive words, like "know(s)," "realize(s)," and the like, that I know of, speaker-hearers usually withdraw the knowledge claim under even light pressure.[34]

Especially with a word as complex in its usage as "know(s)," which has intricate semantic/pragmatic relationships with "evidence," as well as with a battery of other verbs—"see(s)," "infer(s)," "believe(s)," "regret(s)," and so on—it's especially important to consider *all* aspects of usage; this includes retraction phenomena. As I'll indicate in chapter 2, the major problem with treating "know(s)" as contextual is that it does *not* retract the way that acknowledged contextual words do.[35]

[33] I discuss this further in chapter 2, with respect to the supposed usage evidence for contextualism. MacFarlane (2005) is especially good on retraction. Turri (2011) is good on criticisms of Hazlett (2010).

[34] Hazlett (2010, 503), it should be noted, rhetorically helps his claim along with remarks like: "most people do not find the claim that nothing false can be known to be obvious." I have no idea what this can mean. People universally do *not* continue to claim they knew (even worse, know) what they have now discovered to be false. ("Yes, 2 + 2 = 5 isn't true, but—luckily—I still know it.") What I think *is* true is that "knowledge," a *mass term*, allows the inclusion of falsehoods. In this respect, if falsehoods are, from the point of view of knowledge, impurities, it's like other mass terms, although this has no impact on the factivity of the verb "know(s)"; see the discussion of "knowledge" in section 2.2.

[35] I'll only describe in this note another systematic failure to take account of ordinary usage because I'm unable to classify the nature of the failure within the taxonomy I'm (implicitly) using in this introduction. Schaffer's case for his "contrastivism" begins with the claim that, according to the contrastivist, Moore doesn't simply either know that he has hands or that he doesn't (as dogmatists and sceptics respectively argue). Instead, Schaffer (2005, 235) claims that "Moore knows that he has hands rather than stumps; but . . . Moore does not know that he has hands rather than vat-images of hands." Schaffer isn't primarily making an *epistemic claim* that know(s)-that remarks always occur in response to questions (e.g., "Do I have hands rather than stumps?" "Do I have hands rather than vat-images of hands?"). His contrastivism position relies on a claim about *usage*—we can't say that S knows *p*, we can only say that S knows *p* rather than *q*. As a claim about usage (and therefore, as a suitable constraint on the *semantics* of knowledge attributions), this is plainly false. A great deal of what we know (and take ourselves to know) aren't answers to questions or matters that have been "researched" or the like, although, of course, knowledge claims can be framed (often artificially) in this way. S knows that *p can* be of the form S knows that *p* rather than *q*—after all, a proposition of any form can be substituted for *p*—including syntactically more restricted forms like "*p* rather than *q*." Schaffer (2005) treats (by fiat) all knowledge ascriptions as if they all belong to a syntactically restricted subset of knowledge ascriptions. A related suggestion (equally valuable, that is) would be to insist, perhaps on the grounds that indicative claims *p* are always made in relation to background conditions of one sort or another, that indicative sentences are all (semantically) of the form, If *q*, then *p*, and thus should be semantically analyzed as conditionals. One could then attempt to analyze *all* indicatives by exploring various (traditional) semantic approaches to conditionals (and testing them against intuitions we have for these restricted indicatives. The project undertaken in Schaffer and Szabó (2014) offers a semantic analogy only for knowledge attributions of the restricted form, S knows *p* rather than *q*, in terms of A-quantification over a contextually variable domain of situations. For all the technical bravado the paper exhibits, little is gained by narrowing the syntactic properties of the sentences substitutable for *p* in "know(s) that *p*" to the point that the results found don't bear on the word as it freely operates in natural languages.

DeRose (2009, 153) tries to minimize the importance of retraction evidence by instead employing something he tendentiously calls "The methodology of the straightforward," which

> takes very seriously the simple positive and negative claims speakers make utilizing the piece of language being studied, and puts a very high priority on making those natural and straightforward uses come out true, at least when that use is not based on some false belief the speaker has about some underlying matter of fact. Relatively little emphasis is then put on somewhat more complex matters, like what metalinguistic claims speakers will make and how they tend to judge how the content of one claim compares with another (e.g. whether one claim contradicts another).

Leave aside the dubious hint that retraction *must be* understood to be a matter of metalinguistic judgment—as opposed to a ground-floor "oops!" reaction.[36] Dual process theories have become prominent in the psychological literature, the key idea being that judgments can be either fast and relatively automatic processes or slow and deliberate ones. Exactly what's involved in these different forms of judgment is contested, but a lot of evidence supports the psychological reality of the distinction (see Evans and Frankish (2009) for a review as of 2009). Thompson, Prowse Turner, and Pennycook (2011) is typical in its design. The point, for us, is that syllogistic reasoning tasks, in these researchers' studies, are *not* operationalized via intuitive first-pass responses but instead as closer to settled careful analytic responses. As I said, this is typical; it's the immediate responses that are treated as involving heuristics and, potentially, the biases that heuristics are prone to. In particular, experimental design takes the emergence of fallacious inference during "fast thinking" as evidence of heuristics and not as evidence that "imply" or "infer" actually designates (to the participants) reasoning processes *defined* by the contours of such heuristics. Were researchers using DeRose's "methodology of the straightforward," however, the "fast thinking" applications would be definitive of the usage of these notions and not the thoughtful "slow" thinking.

With a word like "know(s)," one with the complex relationships to other words (and concepts) that I've alluded to—relationships that humans are tacitly and often explicitly aware of—it's hard to motivate DeRose's methodology. Worse still, as Nagel (2010, 306) points out, after discussing important (and well-established) psychological biases, such as epistemic egocentrism and the availability heuristic, "the possibility that such biases are interfering with our intuitive

[36] For an extensive discussion of the quite vexing issue of when verbal behavior betrays metacognitive vs. a ground-floor response, see chapters 5 and 6.

responses . . . should perhaps make us more cautious about using such responses as a point of departure for our theories of knowledge." Nagel is speaking of "intuitive responses" to a specific case she has given, but her point easily generalizes.[37] The recognition throughout the psychological literature that immediate responses are (all things considered) most likely to involve shortcut heuristics (with accompanying artifacts of failure), as well as intrusions of bias, cuts against DeRose's suggested methodology. It becomes a case of special pleading: let's use a specific methodology for *knowledge* by treating it (by fiat) as a unique psychological case.[38]

vii Insights from Lexical Semantics: Literality and Metaphoricality

I turn now to other properties of the words I'm concerned with, "know(s)," "see(s)," "infer(s)," etc. A theme I explore in this book is that, in addition to the lexical evidence available for my view, the characterizations of the words (and concepts of) "know(s)," "see(s)," and the like that I offer are in any case ones that capture their functionally linked interactions, especially as they're exemplified in speech acts. These roles are splintered apart (or unnaturally constrained) by earlier philosophical attempts to treat certain usages of these words as instead metaphors or symptoms of polysemy.

An important example of this that I've mentioned already is the almost universal tendency of philosophers to think that ontologically noncommitting uses of "seeing" hallucinations, visions, and the like are second-class; they're derivative, or special cases, or metaphors. Even Austin (1962)—despite his unusual language sensitivities—is completely mistaken about "see(s)," "perceive(s)," and the like, although the view of Ayer's that he opposes—that "see(s)" and "perceive(s)" have many distinct meanings—is equally implausible.[39]

[37] Also see the discussion on DeRose's "methodology of the straightforward" by Gao, Gerken, and Ryan (2017, 83).

[38] Ram Neta suggests that DeRose's methodology of the straightforward can be defended if it's presumed that the words studied—"know(s)," in particular—are individuated by the use of shortcut heuristics. The latter result, however, must be established *empirically*, and not imposed upon the data by a methodological presumption the way DeRose tries to.

[39] Wierzbicka (1996, 134), in passing, writes: "an oasis that I can see in the distance may be simply a mirage (and so may not be there at all, in the place where I see it), and an apparition which someone can see in a place may not be really there." And then she cites Bishop Berkeley on seeing a silver speck in the sky not implying *there is* a silver speck in the sky (which indicates that Berkeley's English was the same on this point as ours is). See Azzouni (2010, chapter 2) for a discussion of the philosophical significance of the ontologically noncommitting uses of these verbs. I should also add that the intrusion of "virtual reality" into our ordinary life is bringing with it many more examples of non-ontologically committing uses of "see(s)," "hear(s)," and so on, that philosophers will find increasingly hard to sideline. (See Rothman (2018) for recent examples in popular writing.) It's crucial, as I indicated in Azzouni (2010, chapter 2), and I'm stressing again here, that these uses can involve a

Why have philosophers misunderstood these words for so long—even ones who (like Austin) reject necessity/sufficiency definitions on words? In part, but only in part, it's a leftover of the tendency to nevertheless see word meanings as *acting as if* they have necessary and sufficient conditions. By failing to appreciate that the meanings of many words are constituted of multiple sufficient (but not necessary) conditions like "climb(s)" and "see(s)" are, we're forced to an artificial dichotomy. Making one set of conceptual conditions necessary and sufficient either requires the other conceptual conditions to be metaphorical, or if not—if the other conceptual conditions are also necessary and sufficient—the result must be ambiguity. A second reason is that philosophers mistake intuitions of atypicality effects as instead intuitions of metaphor or nonliterality.[40] Consider Yablo (1998, 256) on the word "calm":

> Is "calm" literal in connection with people and metaphorical as applied to bodies of water, or the other way around—or literal in connection with these and metaphorical when applied to historical eras?

Why must we *choose*? Why is it obvious that *some* of these usages *must be* metaphorical? Regardless of the origins of these various sufficient conceptual conditions on the same word "calm"—after all, one or another of these usages might *originally* have been due to a metaphorical extension of an ancestor of our contemporary "calm"—that shouldn't stop us from recognizing that ordinary usage currently treats *all* the applications of "calm" that Yablo mentions as acceptable. Only the assumption that the perceived meaning of a single word can't have multiple conceptual conditions none of which is necessary but each of which is sufficient prevents us from recognizing that Yablo's choices are artificially restricted.[41]

simultaneous perception of something real and not real. Notice also that both conditions on "see(s)" restrict usage in a way that a metaphorical extension of the word from one usage to the other wouldn't be perceived as doing. Finally, special-case arguments that uses of "see(s)" in VR are specialized, are undercut by both usages appearing identically in a wide class of syntactic constructions like the following: "Only when I put on my glasses could I see the intricate pattern" and "Only when I put on my VR goggles could I see the dancing hobbits."

40 Philosophers, however, are often opportunistic vis-à-vis the lexical data: no philosopher claims that penguins—despite similar intuitions of atypicality—are only "metaphorically" birds.

41 Well, what *about* "calm"? There is a tendency to think that meanings can be individuated on the sheer grounds that the entities the words are applied to are quite different: e.g., emotional beings, bodies of water, and historical eras. But this isn't true—in particular, a certain pattern of non-erratic *behavior*, as in this case, may be the only necessary condition of the correct application of the word. Again, what's needed is an examination of the pattern of usages the word appears in, e.g., said by someone who lives near a beach, "I'm always calm when the ocean is too." Jackendoff (1990, section 1.6.2) gives illustrations of how lexical items are routinely generalized across ontological categories. What about "rise"? (Otávio Bueno has asked me this, personal communication, October 26, 2018.) Consider the following two sentences: "The levitator and the temperature in the room he was

That conditions on the meanings of words can be independently sufficient the way they are in the cases of "climb(s)," "see(s)," and "calm," in addition, impels a different view of the presence of metaphor in ordinary language from that of Yablo and Quine before him, and indeed, still presumed by many philosophers. Metaphors and nonliterality are (almost) everywhere in natural language, these philosophers tell us; literal usage, on the other hand, is rare. This impression, as I said, is common but misguided. Philosophers want to sideline most of the usages they identify as nonliteral because of theoretical assumptions that such usages (if literal) would contradict. Typical is the following sentiment, expressed by Williams (2001, 32): "It may be that externalist attributions of knowledge, say to children and animals, are less than literal"—although atypical is his care in immediately noting that this "is not immediately obvious." Philosophers, however, often imperially dictate literality and nonliterality on the basis of their theoretical needs, ignoring—meanwhile—pushback from usage. This ignoring of linguistic evidence, despite an ineradicable impression of ad hocness, looks more respectable when accompanied by a characterization of metaphor (and pretense) as "almost everywhere" in language. The view on metaphor and nonliteral usage that issues from contemporary lexical semantics is this, however: metaphor and pretense appear in language largely when and how the folk experience them as appearing—pretty rarely because they're creative, idiosyncratic (and cognitively difficult) language acts. People *knowingly* wrench usage, either in poetry, in advertising, or with explicit forms of pretense. Metaphor isn't going on invisibly among us *all the time*. If right, these linguistic facts prevent philosophers from using metaphor as an unprincipled tool to sideline the systematic usages that children acquire when they learn words.

Epistemology, dangerously but unavoidably, relies on facts of usage. If we (routinely) attribute knowledge to animals, to timid students who sincerely doubt or deny the knowledge they nevertheless exhibit, and to mathematicians who offer confused proofs for theorems they know, it's simply not acceptable to deny these are legitimate uses of the word "know(s)." Epistemological theorizing has to yield to usage, not the other way around.[42] Because of an implicit bias

levitating in rose at the same time. And this was the clue that Houdini used to figure out the levitator's trick!" "Rise" isn't being used metaphorically; it isn't ambiguous. (And, I would argue, it isn't polysemous either.) But what about a locution like, "each morning I rise together with the Sun"? Isn't to speak of the Sun rising a metaphor? And yet this passes the conjunction reduction test. (I owe this question to Florence Bacus, Monika Greco, Shao-An Hsu, Patrick McKee, Jeff McConnell, Tianyi Zhao, and Yingsa Zhang.) No, it's not a metaphor: the Sun, indeed, looks just like it's rising—it's a natural application of the word. It's wrong, however, and most of us know that (but use it anyway). Persistence in the use of a word wrongly, however—no matter how convenient—doesn't make it metaphor. (And it's passing the conjunction reduction test proves this.)

[42] Whatever the value of "rational equilibrium" is supposed to be, it's not meant to deny *data*.

philosophers have toward centralizing certain cases as indicating the meanings of words (and the accompanying marginalization of other ones), in almost every chapter of this book I've had to remind philosophers of cases that have been previously overlooked or sidelined in order to show that (various) generalizations about knowledge that have been elevated to truisms must instead be denied. Not only have cases, like timid students, been largely ignored, but many others haven't been noticed at all, like the previously mentioned mathematicians who give bad proofs for results they've discovered (and nevertheless *know*)—I discuss these in chapter 8—or the spokespeople in chapter 4 who can coherently utter Moorean remarks that deny their own knowledge of, or beliefs in, what they're nevertheless asserting.

viii Insights from Lexical Semantics: Semantic Entailments

Just because a natural-language expression doesn't have a definition in the vernacular doesn't mean we can't create one after we've empirically studied the word's extension for a while. Ancient words—"gold," "copper," "water," and some others—are success stories. Leaving aside issues of purity, these words acquired definitions because of the development of the science of molecules—so I'm talking about the late nineteenth/early twentieth century. These definitions, that is, leave intact—nearly enough—the extensions of the original pretheoretical words; they emerge by embedding the original words (and what they referred to) into a new theoretical context (with new coined vocabulary!) and by designing definitions on the basis of other words that are only now (semantically) connected to the now-defined words. I think something similar can happen with *certain* epistemic words, "justify" among them.

Yet still further fallout from the inertial tendency to see the meanings of words in terms of necessary and sufficient conditions (even among philosophers who have officially rejected the possibility of definitions for our ordinary words) is to see presumed entailments among words (on the basis of their supposed meanings) when in fact such entailments are often restricted to those words only when they're used according to certain sufficient conceptual conditions but not other equally legitimate ones. The most important example of this involves the traditional tripartite definition of knowledge: a knowing agent must believe what she knows. This is false; there are usages where we attribute knowledge to agents even when they sincerely deny they believe what we take them to know. We, generally, allow that mechanisms know things even though we will, while using a certain conceptual condition on "believe(s)," deny they believe anything. The sufficient conceptual condition on "believe(s)" in play in this case requires consciousness. But that's not always the case with "believe(s)": it also has a contrastive role with "know(s)," where consciousness *isn't* required. We will say, for example, that an autonomous car believes that a shadow on the road in front of it is a pothole (because it doesn't know that what's ahead isn't a shadow), even though we will simultaneously deny that the car is conscious. The word "see(s)" is similarly complex: machines see things even though they're not conscious (see section 1.3 on all this).[43]

Another rather different kind of example (that nevertheless bears on epistemology) is this. The verb "infer(s)" has both factive and nonfactive conceptual sufficient conditions, even though "know(s)" "acknowledge(s)," and "regret(s)" don't. We can't draw the conclusion from A inferring *p* from *q* that A therefore knows *q* unless the factive conceptual sufficient condition on "infer(s)" is in play.[44]

I say more about these important lexical facts, and how they bear on epistemology, in later chapters, especially in chapter 11. Meanwhile, I should single out two other important results about the purported semantic entailments of "know(s)" that I show in this book. This is that, first, knowledge doesn't imply metaknowledge, and cognition doesn't imply metacognition. Second, an agent's knowledge (whatever it amounts to) has no systematic constraints on it of the form: If S knows *p*, then S *must know q, r*, . . ., etc. Common (explicit and implicit) views in epistemology require denials of both these facts; such views require

[43] I suspect that "see(s)" hasn't a third conceptual sufficient condition beyond the two Jackendoff attributes to it. Rather, condition [i] on x's seeing y, "x's gaze makes contact with y," doesn't require a visual *experience*. These conditions have to be refined a bit in formulation—in particular, "gaze" won't do—but I forgo attempting this for reasons I give in section 11.3.

[44] "Infer(s)" can be used nonfactively? Certainly. "John inferred from Sam's ambiguous gestures that Sam was going to shoot him, but John was wrong" is OK; "John knew on the basis of Sam's ambiguous gestures that Sam was going to shoot him, but John was wrong," is *not* OK. The word "remember(s)" is complicated. Williamson (2000, 37–38) distinguishes between "remember(s)" and "remember(s) that," and bundles this distinction together with "perceive(s)" and "perceive(s) that," arguing that the verbs accompanied with "that" are factive, although without "that" they needn't be. (I discuss Williamson's views on this in more detail in section 1.4.) The data for "remember(s)" and "remember(s) that" is more involved than Williamson or other philosophers have realized. Moore (1959, 210–211) criticizes Russell for claiming that (199) "in dreams we often remember things that never happened" because (although Moore doesn't use this jargon) he thinks the word operates factively: I remember *p* entails *p*. Some of us, however, find the following unproblematic: "I *clearly* remember putting my keys in this drawer although obviously I didn't." Equally unproblematic, it seems to me (and others), is: "I clearly remember that I put my keys in this drawer although obviously I didn't." *But* some of us, on the other hand, *do* find both of these problematic, and want to substitute something like, "I *seem to* remember putting my keys in this drawer although obviously I don't remember this since it didn't happen," or "I seem to remember that I put my keys in this drawer although obviously I didn't." I've found—over the many years I've queried people in classes, in bars, at one or two funerals, about these examples and variants of them—that Americans divide pretty evenly on this. That "remember(s)" and "remember(s) that" idiolectically shift between speakers this way—apart from, as far as I can tell, the standard factors of gender, age, and geography (among others)—although "know(s)" doesn't, I think, betrays something important about the different roles and functions of these words. The functions and roles of words affect their potential for "idiolectical drift."

instead that knowing agents must be idealized reasoners of one or another sort. Knowing beings must be capable of reflecting on their sources of knowledge, their means of justification, their own mental states (and the content of those mental states, concepts and suchlike), their knowledge must be closed under rules of inference (e.g., modus ponens), and so on.

It's true that metaknowledge not being implied by knowledge is widely acknowledged these days (especially since Williamson (2000)), but the rest of what I say about this isn't widely acknowledged (or, pretty much, acknowledged at all)—in particular, the important fact that the knowledge of any agent can be *fragmentary* is unrecognized. Correspondingly unrecognized is that knowers can be quite cognitively limited both in what they know and in what they're *capable* of knowing. That knowledge can be fragmentary, interestingly, is hinted at by the very syntax of the verb "know": apparently involved is only a relationship between an agent and a specific item of knowledge, independently of other specific items of knowledge, e.g., S knows *p*. This syntax is compatible, of course, with rich descriptive (or normative) truth conditions underwriting this relationship; my point, however, is that the syntax also compatible with the knowledge relationship between S and *p* involving *no* other items of knowledge—and (so I try to show in this book) this syntactic hint is borne out.

The shocking bit (perhaps) isn't that this is true. Almost everyone plying views in this ballpark realizes that humans (in practice) fail to meet various epistemic ideals. What's shocking, perhaps, is that such ideals aren't constraints on how we *use* epistemic words, or on what they mean—this is true of "know(s)" in particular. That is (and in particular), knowing about *p* doesn't require knowing anything about knowing about *p*; knowing that *p* doesn't require other metacognitive resources either: it doesn't require the agent to grasp the concept of justification, or the implications of what it means to justify one's knowledge claims or (for that matter) to have any notion of justification at all. More generally, it doesn't require agents to grasp or understand that they have concepts that apply to the world around them. Knowing that *p* doesn't require agents to grasp semantic notions like truth and falsehood. It may be (it probably is) that knowing agents must have or be able to *deploy* concepts *of some sort* (see section 6.3)—but that's not a reflexive ability: no self-knowledge of *any sort* is required for *that*. Finally, there is no requirement—normative or otherwise—that knowing agents be rational. Knowledge is compatible with gross irrationality.[45]

[45] Other epistemic words, "see," for example, are similarly assumed by philosophers to have rich requirements for their application to agents. The point of the quotation from Metz that this book opens with is that Hinton is being credited for changing the way machines see the world; he isn't being credited for changing the way we use the word "see," so that it can *now* be applied to machines.

The denials of these Kantian (and indeed Cartesian—for Descartes seems to be an important node point for all of these views)[46] metacognitive and knowledge-systemic presumptions are (partially achieved) insights of the reliabilist tradition in epistemology. But pressing these insights further to old and new puzzles in epistemology solves them in fresh ways unanticipated by reliabilists. Moore's paradox (so called), the justification trilemma, the KK thesis, the lottery paradox, Kripke's dogmatism paradox, and others are resolved in linked illuminating ways once we see, in particular, the implications of separating cognition from metacognition.

ix The Lexical Analysis of Words Versus the Functional Analysis of Them

Some philosophers have attempted to characterize epistemology in terms of the *function* of epistemic words. Craig (1990, 11) writes, for example, that "briefly and roughly, the concept of knowledge is used to flag approved sources of information."[47] Craig, in the course of his book, very ingeniously shows how this characterization of the role of "know(s)" explains properties of the word, for example, why in most cases of attributions to knowing agents, we expect them to believe what they know. A significant aspect of his approach is that it handles apparent counterexamples to his thesis by accommodating them: if a word has a certain role—e.g., flagging approved sources of information—that's nevertheless compatible with it being applied (at times) to agents who can't function as approved sources because they're maliciously insincere, etc. It also explains why, although we have the impression that knowers believe what they know, we can correctly attribute knowledge to someone who doesn't believe what they know.

In general, characterizing a word or phrase in terms of its (purported) functional role can be quite illuminating, but it can never be a complete analysis for a straightforward reason: a functional analysis of a word, if successful, reveals genuine "design features" of that word—how we use it, in particular, in speech acts. But the design features of a word are always based on the syntactic/semantic properties of that word that make its design features possible—that make it possible for us to use the word as we do. For example (and focusing here only on

[46] I've come to realize, however, that these views significantly precede Descartes. See Pasnau (2017). I suppose that's the fate of every "original" figure; the more history we learn the more subtle the question becomes of how that person stands out from her peers and earlier influential figures. I'll continue to describe these views as "Cartesian" in pretty much the same way that, in philosophy of mathematics, "Platonic" is used (by me and others) to describe non-nominalistic views—regardless of how far these non-nominalistic views are from Plato's original views.

[47] My thanks to Ram Neta for urging me to discuss how my approach differs from Craig's.

syntax), we can use the word "know" to flag an approved source of information because it's a verb that relates an agent *to* an item of information. If it were an intransitive verb or a preposition, it couldn't do this—or as successfully. Consider a screwdriver. We can functionally characterize a screwdriver as a tool that enables us to place screws in various materials. The rigidity of the shaft of the screwdriver, the shape of its handle, etc., are essential to our being able to use it this way.

Importantly, only characterizing the design features of a word leaves out a description of the properties of the word which explain *how* the word exhibits design features or fails to exhibit them. This isn't just true of words—as I've just indicated—it's true of anything to which design features can be attributed. In an important sense, if we want to understand anything which we can characterize in terms of design features, a pen, for example, we must include, and perhaps describe first, the properties that make those design features possible.

In biology, we—professionals and amateurs—often describe various biological entities, cells, organs, skill sets of animals, etc., functionally: the heart is "designed" to pump blood; blood, in turn, is a transport system for, among other things, oxygen. These functional characterizations aren't meant to indicate the presence of a designer; they shouldn't be so understood, anyway. Nor do they indicate a certain causal/evolutionary history: e.g., that the contemporary "heart" resulted from an evolutionary process of selection. None of this need be true. Instead, descriptions of functionality characterize a certain causal role abstractly—stepping away from the details of exactly what a heart is (in various animals), what it's made of, in a word, *how* it manages the function so described. Again, these details matter, especially when we need to refine a description of a function to include conditions on when something described as having that function or role fails to follow through, or the ways in which other things having the same function or role differ from it.

An example: Hemoglobin is a molecule (with such-and-such properties) that enables oxygen transport in humans; hemocyanin is instead the active oxygen carrier in the octopus. The ocellated icefish, however, has no (and needs no) active oxygen carrier, because there is so much oxygen in the very cold water it lives in. These different mechanisms matter because they affect exactly how (and when) the oxygen-carrying function of blood can work and when it can misfunction—hemocyanin doesn't transport oxygen well in very cold water, so the octopus needs other biological mechanisms to compensate.

What corresponds to biological machinery in the case of speech acts and the functions/roles of certain phrases is the stuff of language itself: syntax and semantics. Broadly speaking, therefore, I focus on the language machinery of "know(s)," and the words it's related to, and read off from that (along with other background considerations) its functional role. My distinctive epistemic claims arise from this. My approach thus differs significantly from Craig's insofar as although I too want to eventually extract descriptions of the roles/functions of "know(s)," and, more broadly, knowledge attributions, I'm primarily (and first) concerned with the "machinery" that enables those functions. Craig, instead, goes directly for that role itself and reads his claims about epistemology directly from it. (I'll explore further the differences between my approach and Craig's—as well as those of other social-role epistemologists, Lawlor (2013) and Reynolds (2017), later in section 11.5.)

One interesting way Craig's and my approaches can yield very different results is because (on my view) there are invariably misfittings between the design roles of words or phrases and the syntactic/semantic machinery that enables those design roles. These misfittings can take more than one form. For example, there can be various failures, ways in which a design role is (sometimes) not executed successfully. And there can be other ways that a word can be used, because of its syntactic/semantic properties that aren't in accord with its design roles. Any adequate understanding of a word, thus, requires recognizing both its design role and its syntactic/semantic machinery, and an understanding of the specific ways that these interact. In general, how these interact will be particular to the specific words and phrases being studied.[48]

x An example: "True"

I want to illustrate these points—especially about how design function can be in tension with syntactic/semantic machinery—with the word "true."[49] This case is illuminating, in part, because "true" is less complex in various respects than "know." The lesson is the same one, however: a number of philosophical puzzles directly arise because of a clash that occurs between the design role of words—how we use them—and the syntactic/semantic properties of those words that enable these words, to the extent that they can, to be used in the execution of their design roles.

[48] Some philosophers will surely want to argue that words and sentences only have what I've described as design features as their properties because, ultimately, there are only speech acts; my distinction presupposes a specious division between the uses of words and sentences and the words and sentences themselves—but there are no such things as words and sentences, at least not in the sense of things whose properties can be independently assessed apart from how we use them in speech acts. (See, e.g., Alston (2000, 50).) As I argue in Azzouni (2013b), our experience of language induces precisely this "specious" division, and it's supported further by our *use* of language being infiltrated by our conscious awareness of pragmatic factors that play into, among other things, what we experience as implicated, although our grasp of syntax (and semantics) largely isn't so infiltrated. There is much more to say about this, but I must defer this to my previous (and future) work.

[49] In doing so, I'm relying heavily on earlier work of mine; see, specifically, Azzouni (2006) and Azzouni (2018)—but I'm characterizing the landscape differently.

A claim originally due to Quine (1970) is that "true" is needed for what has subsequently come to be called "blind truth ascription." "True" appears idle in usages like "'John is running' is true" or even "It's true that John is running," since one can—more directly—just say that John is running without detouring through a claim that a sentence that says this is true. But this is false of statements like "Everything that follows from Peano arithmetic is true," or "Einstein's theory of general relativity is true" (if one can't state general relativity).

We can, thus, hypothesize that the role/function of "true" is to enable the assertion of blind truth ascriptions.[50] Along those lines, philosophers have claimed, additionally, that "true" *is* a device of blind truth ascription or that it *is* a device of generalization. Others, hypothesizing that, in a certain respect, statements of the form *"John is running" is true if and only if John is running* are central to our understanding of the word "true," and noting that the right-hand side doesn't have quotation marks, have called "true" a device of disquotation, or a device of semantic descent and ascent. The thought here is that the blind-truth-ascription role of the truth predicate is to enable a shift from talking *about* a set of sentences "All the consequences of Peano arithmetic" to a kind of *assent* to those sentences. However: These are acceptable descriptions—if they're acceptable—only as hypotheses about the functional role of the word "true."

What *is* the word "true"?[51] "True" is, syntactically and semantically, an *ordinary* adjective, like "blue," "flat," and so on. The sense in which these other adjectives are "devices" of generalization is only (semantically) that they apply, in principle, to more than one thing. They're not devices of generalization, for example, in the sense that quantifiers ("most," "all," "a number of") are. No more than any other word or sentence are they devices for assertions—of any sort. This is how we *use* sentences, to make assertions, but we also use sentences in other ways, and sometimes we don't use sentences at all—they're just present. It's important to keep separate questions of how we use something—and derivatively, what its design features are—from what it is, what its properties are (apart from

[50] In claiming this, as I've already warned, we shouldn't be saying that the word was originally introduced into the language to fulfill this purpose; no diachronic claims about language are being made. Rather, the point is only that the only nonredundant use of the predicate "true" by speaker-hearers is this one. By "nonredundant," I don't mean that some other piece of language—invented or present—can't do the same thing; rather, what's meant is that any other piece of language that can play this role will do the same thing in the sense that a truth predicate can be extracted from it, e.g., by a definition.

[51] Here I'm shifting from the question of its functional role to the question, as we might put it, of what it actually is (what kind of thing is being used to fulfill the functional role that "true" is hypothesized to have in English?). Compare: we've shifted from describing the functional role of a pen (to make detectable traces on a medium) to the question, but what *is* a pen?—and now (unlike with the word "true") there are *lots* of answers because there are many kinds of pens. There are many different kinds of mechanisms and materials that can be used to make something a pen—that can be used to make something that can satisfy the role we want pens for.

those design features) that enable those design features. "True" in this latter respect is the same as, as ordinary as, any other adjective.

The philosophically central role of "true," in conjunction with certain historical developments, has made discussion of the word's properties contentious (in contrast to its fellow adjectives). For example, what sorts of things does it characterize? Sentences? Propositions? I largely won't explore this concern here. Another issue concerns its definability. Assume, for expository purposes, that the word is an adjective that applies to sentences. Can the kinds of sentences it's applied to be characterized in some way apart from the fact that they're all true? If so, it seems this would yield a definition for the word "true" itself. For example, suppose all the sentences that are true are ones that can be characterized as bearing a certain kind of relationship to the world—call this a correspondence relation C. Then we can define "true" this way: s *is true* iff_{def} s *is C*. The project of attempting to define "true" this way has a long historical pedigree: characterizations of "true," for example, as correspondence, coherence, etc., are part of this tradition. Call this a property definition of "true."

But another sort of definition seems possible that's different in flavor from property definitions, and this other approach is possible because "true," unlike most other adjectives, applies to sentences which can explicitly appear *in* a definition of it, although this isn't true—for example—of a definition of a word that holds of a kind of fish (we can't put the kind of fish *in* the definition the way we can with sentences). Suppose (falsely) that there were only three sentences in the universe that the word "true" applied to, S_1, S_2, and S_3.[52] Then we could define "true" easily enough like so: s is true iff $s = S_1$ or $s = S_2$ or $s = S_3$. That's to say, we could give a "list." The difference between these two kinds of definitions is clear, I think. In the first, we utilize a property, other than "true," that holds of all and only the true sentences. In the second, we list the sentences themselves. Whether one definition is more valuable than the other turns solely on what property is used in the property definition. If we think the property is informative in some way that a list isn't, we prefer the first definition. For example, if we feel we don't understand "what truth is," we may like a definition in terms of correspondence or coherence. Otherwise, a list definition is fine.

But what if we don't know which sentences are true? Can we manage a list definition anyway? Yes. Again, imagine that there are only three sentences, S_1, S_2, or S_3, in the language. We can give the following alternative definition: s is true iff ($s = S_1$ & S_1) or ($s = S_2$ & S_2) or ($s = S_3$ & S_3). We thus now list every sentence, and append a condition under which that sentence will be true (the condition for any

[52] Suppose, for example, the language in question only had three primitive sentences, and no connectives, not even negation, perhaps just "The sky is blue," "Grass is green," and "Snow is white."

sentence S_i to be true is simply S_i). Tarski's (1983) famous definition is, apart from important and innovative technical complexities, a definition of this last form.[53]

The considerations about definitions don't directly bear on the function/role issue of the word "true." These definitions only indicate what sentences, in fact, are true. To figure out the word's role is to see why (and when) we want to assent to the truth of certain sentences. This is where the point about blind truth ascriptions arises: that we often want to assent to sentences but we can't assert them (say them, write them down) is part of the story of why we want to use the truth predicate this way.

The reason this is only part of the story is that a necessary supplementation is why there is nothing else in the language that can do the same job. It's right here where a *puzzle knot* arises in discussions of "true." In natural languages, English specifically, we can describe sentences of any other language as true. In particular, the following is grammatical: "Chaque champignon est vénéneux" is true. This raises two complications with the second sort of definition. The first is that the list becomes infinite. We can ask, and the answer isn't trivial, whether definitions based on infinite lists exist in English. Let's agree that they do exist (via ellipses, for example), and let's consider the harder second problem. This is that, although the quotation name, "Chaque champignon est vénéneux," is a name—in *English*—of a French sentence, the French sentence that it's a name of *isn't* an *English* sentence. This creates a problem with list definitions (and, thus, with Tarskian approaches to defining truth) although not with the first sort of definition of truth. List definitions require us to *use* the sentences listed; but we can't use, in any definition *in* English, a sentence of another language. We can name such sentences in English, but we can't use the sentences themselves.[54]

At this point, the project of defining the natural-language word "true," as it's used in natural languages (as an adjective that can be applied to sentences of *any* language), takes on the flavor of questions of definition generally. Many, if not most, words of natural languages don't have definitions, as I earlier noted. Sometimes a word can acquire a definition (necessary and sufficient conditions) via supplementation of natural language: this is what happened to "gold."

[53] Things get complicated if the set of sentences of a language is infinite: We can't write the list down, or so it seems. I turn to discussing a generalization of this problem shortly.

[54] In Azzouni (2004), I called this "the transcendence of the vernacular 'true.'" "True," as it occurs in English, and (I believe) in other languages, can be applied to sentences of any other language. Also see Azzouni (2006, chapter 2). Right here, of course, philosophers are tempted to posit "propositions" that sentences of natural languages "express," and claim that although French sentences aren't themselves in English, every sentence of French expresses a proposition that an English sentence also expresses. Then list definitions using propositions become possible. There is a large debate over whether what's expressible in any natural language is expressible in any other natural language. I think the answer is no—if only because words without definitions in the vernacular, e.g., "proton," don't occur in every natural language. (Of course, philosophers can trivialize the question by treating any natural language as capable of absorbing the resources of any other natural language.)

Sometimes it can't. If a characterization (apart from truth) of all and only the true sentences can be sustained, then a definition of the first sort can be managed; if natural languages can be augmented with specialized devices of some sort, perhaps a definition of the second sort can be managed. To define "true," therefore, there must be another property that all and only true sentences have that enables a property definition, or we need some sort of language tool that enables us to refer to the sentences of any language in a way that simultaneously enables us to *assent* to them even though we can't *assert* them because they aren't part of English.[55]

It could easily be both that no other property of sentences is coextensive with "true" and that no such device can be introduced into natural languages. If so, the word "true" is primitive, in the sense that necessary and sufficient conditions for a sentence being true—statable in English—are impossible.[56]

So, here are some results about the natural-language expression "true" that are gleaned from this discussion: (i) The function/role that the word satisfies is one that allows speakers to assent to a sentence or a set of sentences that, for whatever reason (ignorance, number of sentences), they can't assert—e.g., state aloud, or write down, etc. They need, that is, a language device that indicates (or describes) a sentence or set of sentences and then marks them—somehow—*as* asserted by the speaker. (ii) The word that's available for this purpose in English (and in every natural language) is an ordinary adjective applied to sentences. That "true" is an adjective explains why there are uses of it that go beyond its application to

[55] I invented a formal device (see Azzouni (2001; 2006)), the anaphorically unrestricted quantifier that quantifies into nominal positions (as ordinary, e.g., first-order, quantifiers do) and simultaneously into sentential positions (as prosentential quantifiers do). Such a quantifier allows, for example, $(x)(\text{True}x \leftrightarrow x)$. This says, in distorted English: "For each thing, *x*, it is true if and only if it," where "it" here is functioning as a pronoun in both a nominal and a sentential position. Such a device allows quantification over sentences regardless of what language they're located in, and so it can be used to define a truth predicate that holds of sentences of other languages in addition to the one it occurs in. As the weirdness of the distorted English indicates, nothing like this occurs in English, and (I hypothesize) in any natural language. Although natural languages are open to vocabulary augmentation, and shifts in syntax, and although anaphorically unrestricted quantifiers are formally well behaved (i.e., they're axiomatizable and the axioms are complete with respect to a straightforward model theory), the constraints on how natural-language syntax can change—although not well understood—are nevertheless severe. The anaphorically unrestricted quantifier, I believe, because it exhibits simultaneous anaphora in both nominal and sentential positions cannot occur in natural languages.

[56] The claim that the truth role is exhausted by its blind-ascription role—that there is no other nonrhetorical use (often called "substantial," e.g., explanatory) we put it to—is a nontrivial claim needing argument. Also, that no other property definition for "true" is possible is also a nontrivial claim needing argument. (See Azzouni (2018) for a full discussion of this.) I should also add that list definitions are completely compatible with property definitions—when these are both available. However, I think property definitions all fail because, roughly, sentences are true for all sorts of reasons—some because of the correspondence of their terms to the world that the sentence describes accurately, some by stipulation, some by what's, broadly speaking, coherence, and many by combinations of these. "True," thus, is what can be called a metaphysically neutral notion. Again, see Azzouni (2018) for discussion of this.

sentences, such as "true friend." How the word, that is, is extended metaphorically (or literally) is explained by what piece of syntax it is—its being an adjective and not, say, a quantifier. (iii) Other sorts of language items we can dream up that could also be used to fulfill this function/role are ones that, for one reason or another, cannot belong to English and other natural languages.[57] (iv) It's an empirical question whether a word is susceptible to a natural-language definition, now or any time in the future. This turns on the semantic/syntactic properties of the word, and aspects of the world—sometimes, but not always, what the word refers to. In the case of "true," I hypothesize that because this word is used by speaker-hearers with respect to sentences that aren't English, it can't be defined in English.

The foregoing analysis of "true" shows, I hope, how subtle the interplay between the role/function of a word and its syntactic/semantic properties can be. One shouldn't, for example, simply try to read off the meaning of a word from its role/function—not even as a hypothesis.[58]

xi Xphilosophy and the Threat of Idiolectical Scepticism

A striking fact about the lexical results I've cited in the foregoing is the kind of evidence linguists support them with.[59] In particular, what *doesn't appear* as evidence for these results are the sociological questionnaire surveys that have, in the twenty-first century, become so popular within a recently emerged philosophical subdiscipline: "experimental philosophy" (hereafter, "xphilosophy"). In lexical semantics (and in linguistics, generally), by contrast, within-language results are verified by (professional and non-professional) readers checking *their own usage*; across-language results are similarly verified by native speakers of those languages. These evidential methods, I should add, are empirically respectable;

[57] Why, for example, couldn't "true" have been a sentence operator rather than an adjective? This may just prove to be a contingent fact about natural languages, but I think it's not; I think the desirability of locutions like "true short sentences" motivates "true" as an adjective. Thus, I hypothesize that, although "It's true that John is running" looks like a use of "true" as a sentence operator, it's not genuinely so.

[58] Lawlor (2013, 42), for example, expresses cautiousness about reading the meaning of "know" from a characterization of what she takes to be the word's speech-act assurance role. Nevertheless, she thinks that the role does "provide some hints about what the meaning might be—something like 'has conclusive reason for believing what is in fact the case.'" In the course of this book, I'll argue that both this strategy and the resulting characterization of the meaning of "know" are mistakes. Speech acts, and the rules (if any) governing such speech acts, should be guides to the meaning of the words that are used in those acts *only insofar as* claims are made during those speech acts that are recognized (by speaker-hearers) to be true or false. (I thank Ram Neta for drawing my attention to Lawlor's book.)

[59] What follows is cribbed, in part, from Azzouni (forthcoming d).

the explanation is that although each speaker-hearer speaks an idiolect, among same-language speaker-hearers those idiolects are extremely close.

What's the evidence for this extreme closeness? Stalnaker (1974; 1978; 2002) describes the pragmatic presuppositions—tacit and explicit—shared by conversants as their *common ground*.[60] Included in this common ground (so say I) is that the conversants share the same language. (I'm leaving aside cases where native speakers of different languages struggle to communicate in one or another language that one or both of them recognizably speak poorly in.) And, thus, an important part of this common ground is massive agreement on word usage. We do not converse—we cannot converse—with those who don't "speak our language." Call this *the common-language presupposition*.

Three points about this fundamental presupposition of conversation—*massive agreement* on word usage: First, it's compatible with an internalist (Chomskian) view of language; no ontological assumption of an external public language is needed (see Azzouni (2013b)). More specifically, perfect overlap of the idiolects of speaker-hearers, who "speak the same language," isn't needed; speaker-hearers recognize they may not agree on the meanings of certain words or about whether a phrase is grammatical or makes sense. Nevertheless, the feeling that we're conversing with someone who speaks our language breaks down with too much disagreement on words.[61]

Thus, second, this massive agreement is compatible with highly salient differences. Speaker-hearers often say to one another, "I don't use that word that way." These differences are often (but not invariably) due to demographic (and other) factors that experimental philosophers, and those studying slurs, have focused on.[62] Regardless, even where common ground is distorted by political/sociological vectors (or verbal incompetence), massive agreement remains a default.

[60] Stalnaker's common-ground notion is inspired by an undeveloped allusion to it in Grice's William James lectures (Stalnaker [2002, 701 n. 1]). As Stalnaker develops the notion, it's enmeshed in intractable complexities due to the infinitely iterated propositional attitudes of the participating individuals; this is because he explicates it in terms of the Lewis/Schiffer notion of common knowledge or mutual belief (Lewis (1969), Schiffer (1972)). I reject this reductive project of characterizing common knowledge or mutual belief in terms of the individual propositional attitudes of the individuals sharing that knowledge or belief; I instead treat the notions of common knowledge and mutual belief as primitives governed by sets of conditions, e.g., "*p* is *mutually believed* by a set of individuals R iff for all *x* in R, *x* believes *p*," and the like. I leave the details of this and its defense for another time.

[61] How much disagreement makes conversants uncomfortable? I suspect 10 percent easily does it. This is a testable question, although I don't know of studies.

[62] Slurs, it seems to me, explicitly violate common-ground assumptions: a necessary condition on something being an "insult" is that its application *isn't* common ground between the insulted and the insulting. Expertise, I should add, potentially endangers common-ground assumptions as well, but since normal speaker-hearers defer to the usage practices of purported experts, this minimizes if not eliminates the danger. I describe expertise phenomena in the next paragraph.

Third, the common-language presupposition is compatible with enormous ignorance—on the part of most speaker-hearers—about the applications of their words. This too is recognized: speaker-hearers understand that to know a word (to "understand the meaning of a word") doesn't require always being able to pick out what the word refers to. We recognize that people vary in how well they recognize things, and that there are "experts" others defer to. But a rank hobbyist (or a child) may be much better than I am at picking out gold, antiques, or authentic coins; and people recognizably need instruments or specialized knowledge to realize a home is infested with carpenter ants or that lead is in their drinking water. Specialized knowledge is unevenly distributed and isn't restricted to "experts."

Here is the most important point. *The common-language presupposition* supports standard evidential practices in lexical semantics—and in linguistics, more broadly. In particular, this common-language presupposition is undisturbed by ordinary conversation, both as it occurs among same-language speakers and during other activities (such as reading scientific results) which are sophisticated versions of ordinary conversation; it's, notably, undisturbed when English-speaking readers *read* Chomsky, Jackendoff, and other linguists. I'll next bring the common-language presupposition to bear on currently vexed questions of philosophical methodology; but I need some background first.

Many philosophers claim there is a special method to philosophy, "the method of cases." This is a supposed method of presenting real or imagined cases to a philosophical audience to elicit "intuitions." Malmgren (2011), Pust (2000), Neta (2012), and Ichikawa and Jarvis (2009) are only a few of the many (recent) philosophers who think this—or something like it—is *the* method (or the *primary* method) of philosophy. Other philosophers, who accept that the "method of cases" is a distinguishable *method* that philosophers employ, argue that empirical studies are required—social-psychological ones (primarily questionnaire studies)—to determine the trustworthiness of these intuitions. Included in the characterization of "trustworthiness" that's to be empirically verified are (among other things) to what extent these intuitions are shared, e.g., whether they vary concomitantly—and inappropriately—with various demographic factors (for example, race, socioeconomic class, age) and whether the judgments elicited vary according to other (truth-unworthy) factors, such as time of day, temporal relationship to the presentation of other questions (and scenarios), lunch, the conditions of the furniture in the room the person making the judgments is in, and so on.

Of course, what "intuitions" are, what they are of, and whether philosophers use them at all are all hotly debated. Deutsch (2015) and Cappelen (2012) have recently denied that philosophers use "intuitions"; more specifically, they deny that there is any such "method of cases."[63] Although I agree with

[63] Among those who believe there is a distinctive philosophical method of cases, and criticize it from various perspectives—empirical and otherwise—are Baz (2012) and many of the authors

Deutsch and Cappelen about there being no distinctively philosophical "method of cases," and with them that "intuition" is vague philosophical jargon that doesn't pick out anything significant, my reasons for having these views differ from theirs.

I claim, contrary to Deutsch and Cappelen (and others), that philosophical thought experiments, first and foremost, reveal aspects of usage. They are designed, that is, to show that aspects of usage refute (or support) a targeted language generalization. I claim, further, that only along with additional assumptions (which are often tacitly buried in a philosopher's presentation of a thought experiment) do they establish anything more substantial—for example, philosophical claims in epistemology, metaphysics, or ethics.

To illustrate (since I won't discuss every extant thought experiment that's ever been propounded by philosophers to establish my claim), consider a popular example originally due to Gettier (1963, 122) and that's presently treated as paradigmatic in the literature on intuitions (what follows is my distillation of the case in Gettier's article).[64]

> Smith and Jones have applied for the same job. Smith has strong evidence Jones will get the job and has ten coins in his pocket. Smith infers that the man who has ten coins in his pocket will get the job. But Smith gets the job and also has ten coins in his pocket (although he doesn't realize this). Smith is *right* that the man who gets the job has ten coins in his pocket, Smith is *justified* in thinking this, but Smith doesn't *know* it. Therefore, the generalization: *S has a justified true belief that p iff S knows p* has a counterexample.

Why is *S has a justified true belief that p iff S knows p* a language generalization? Isn't this, rather, a refutation of the claim that justified true belief is necessary and sufficient for knowledge? That's certainly what Gettier thought he'd established. And he *had*—provided that the applications of the words "justified," "know," and "true" in this example are as Gettier took them to be—that is, they're *not* being used here as words are sometimes used, as metaphors or as exploiting pragmatic factors in ways that aren't typical of what they mean. If they are being so used, then, in this example, "know" doesn't refer to the know(s) relation and/or "justif(y/ies)" doesn't refer to the justification relation, and so on. There are also tacit assumptions about the role of reasoning (and the kind of reasoning allowed) to sustain knowledge or justification, as well

anthologized in Knobe and Nichols (2008; 2014). For a fairly recent survey of the controversy, with references, see Gao, Gerken, and Ryan (2017, 88–90).

[64] I analyze additional (famous) examples of philosophical thought experiments in Azzouni (forthcoming d).

as assumptions about when testimony suffices for justification and the like—assumptions that are needed to enable the example to unwind the way it does. I'm not challenging *any* of these assumptions (I find the example compelling); I'm pointing out that they're there, but I'm also pointing out that none of this cuts against the evident facts that (1) there is a language-generalization in the neighborhood of *S has a justified true belief that p iff S knows p*; one which connects the words "justified," "true," "belief," and "know" together in a particular way that enables a purported definition of "know(s)"; (2) this generalization is, first and foremost, the target of Gettier's discussion; and (3) the example he gives purports to be a counterexample to this generalization. Of course, *corresponding to* this generalization are substantial claims about how knowledge, justification, belief, etc., are related, but that shouldn't obscure the fact that a relation between words is simultaneously posited. *Every* generalization ("All humans are mortal") simultaneously tells us something general about the world and about how we should use certain *words* if that generalization is true.

I'll put the Gettier-refuted language generalization this way: The phrase "*A* has a justified true belief that *p*" applies to an agent *A* iff "knows *p*" applies to *A*). It's this language-generalization that the Gettier case is a counterexample to. *Language generalizations* about several words, notice, are under scrutiny in the telling of Gettier's anecdote. (My thanks to Florence Bacus for pointing out an infelicity in my earlier discussion of this.)

Perhaps it's rash to characterize all philosophical thought experiments as doing *something* similar, if only because, as both Williamson (2007) and Deutsch (2015) stress, philosophers usually make all sort of judgments about the thought experiments they present. Deutsch points out that these thought experiments (Gettier's in particular) invariably involve *arguments*. Nevertheless (so I claim), there are always language propositions that are presumed by these thought experiments: words (or phrases) *P* apply to *p*—or words (or phrases) *P* don't apply to *p*—in the situations given, real or imagined; and (usually) some targeted language-generalization (as a result) is taken to have a counterexample. None of the propositions about phrases involved here is a priori, epistemically special, or *epistemically* ground-floor (pace Ichikawa and Jarvis (2009), Malmgren (2011), and others). Rather, they're mostly common-ground presuppositions about words. So they're epistemically challengeable.

As I've already noted, the idiolects of individuals *do* deviate on particular phrases and words—they deviate even on *syntax*. Massive agreement is compatible with *some* disagreements. So, this commitment to ground-floor language presuppositions being part of the common ground (of science) is compatible with a methodology of empirically *spot-checking* claims about usage (perhaps by questionnaires) *on occasions*.[65] However: The spot-checking role of empirical studies of usage isn't the (modest) view that many xphilosophers take toward their empirical methods. Instead, as I mentioned, they see promoting empirical studies of the philosophical "intuitions" elicited by "the method of cases" as a global challenge to the philosophical use of thought experiments. Swain, Alexander, and Weinberg (2008, 153) write:

> intuitions about the Truetemp Case vary depending on whether, and which, other cases are presented before it. Such variability calls into question the legitimacy of using the intuitions generated by the Truetemp Case as evidence against reliabilism. But it is unclear what about this case makes it susceptible to these effects, which raises questions about the reliance on intuitions about thought experiments more generally, especially given that this is not the only case called into question by empirical research. We take the growing body of empirical data impugning various intuitions to present a real challenge for philosophers who wish to rely on intuitions on evidence.

The study mentioned involves the presentation of a thought experiment and the question of whether the word "know" applies to the described protagonist; the answers statistically vary depending on which of two other anecdotes (and questions about whether protagonists in those cases "know") is presented to those surveyed.

The problem with a global requirement of "empirical research" (read: questionnaire surveys) directed toward "intuitions" (read: presuppositions of common word usage) is that scientific methods—certainly of the questionnaire sort, but more generally—themselves require common-language presuppositions because of the words that occur in the studies *themselves*.

Consider, for example, the thought experiment (and posed question) from a study (Swain, Alexander, and Weinberg [2008, 154-155]):

> Suzy looks out the window of her car and sees a barn near the road, and so she comes to believe that there's a barn near the road. However, Suzy doesn't realize that the countryside she is driving through is currently being used as the set of a

65 Questionnaires are *still* the primary tool of "experimental philosophers," pace claims to the contrary in the preface of Knobe and Nichols (2014, vii). I should stress—but cannot pursue further now—that any empirical tool poses epistemic risks due to the details of the methods used; statistical methods are especially fallible. For discussion of this, see, e.g., Deutsch (2015). I detect a modest interpretation of the philosophical role of survey methods (similar to the one I've expressed) in Pinillos and Simpson (2014, 10–11): "What we think is warranted . . . is a pluralism of methods—where the new methods we devise aim to get around some of the shortcomings of traditional philosophical methodology. This doesn't mean that the new methods are better than the old methods. In fact, they may even be less reliable overall. But even if this is the case, it does not mean that [they] cannot give us philosophically important information in certain cases."

film, and that the set designers have constructed many fake barn facades in this area that look as though they are real barns. In fact, Suzy is looking at the only real barn in the area.

Please indicate to what extent you agree or disagree with the following claim: "Suzy knows there is a barn near the road."

__Strongly agree __Agree __Neutral __Disagree __Strongly disagree

Notice the many words the usage of which is part of the common ground presumed by this study. Notable are the complex words "agree" and "indicate," as well as many words and phrases in the description of the case ("see," "look as though," "fake," "real") that philosophers have long argued over the meanings of—e.g., Austin (1962).[66]

I'm here raising the challenge of *idiolectical scepticism*, that demanding "empirical" (i.e., questionnaire-survey) tests of what are called "philosophical intuitions" (i.e., presuppositions of common word usage) leads to a complete undercutting of the common-ground assumption that we speak a language in common; this, in turn, undercuts the empirical methodology of xphilosophy to begin with.[67] Remaining standing, of course, is the modest position that massive agreement on word usage is compatible with *some* disagreements—ones that can be verified by empirical questionnaire studies, although not by those alone. One can, as linguists routinely do, informally check the usage impressions of colleagues and others.

If no principled distinction (like the one I've drawn) exists between ground-floor language propositions and the other judgments made in the course of presenting philosophical thought experiments, then we're threatened with *judgment scepticism* (Williamson (2007, 220–225)): Global epistemic challenges to the "philosophical method" of thought experiments yields (collective) cognitive suicide. My challenge isn't this one.

Xphilosophical studies, it seems, are best used to (defeasibly) recognize idiolectical differences between speaker-hearers, like the one hypothesized (in note 44) with respect to "remember(s)" and "remember(s) that." But such studies should be well informed by established results from lexical semantics (and

[66] One imagines pushing the global requirement of verifying philosophical word-usage claims consistently by requiring empirical tests, along the lines of the one just quoted, for "meat," "dog," "chair," "the," or, nearly enough, any *other* word. What justifies, after all, philosophers relying on their "intuitions" about *these* words? If anecdotes are presented in which one-legged oddly shaped pieces of furniture are used as chairs, or in which lab meat (that's nevertheless genetically indistinguishable from beef) is grown in glass tubes and then avidly eaten, I predict that the surveyee's applications of the words "meat" or "chair" will be sensitive to appropriately chosen thought experiments that are presented first.

[67] Also raised by claims that speaker-hearers can't trust their "intuitions" about their own usage is the sceptical challenge of *idiolectical obtusity*—that one's "intuitions" aren't even accurate about one's *own* idiolect.

linguistics, more generally), especially because within-population questionnaire studies that search for statistically significant differences in usage are (as currently designed) poor indicators of idiolectical differences that aren't due to obvious demographic confounders that can be independently studied.[68]

It's worth comparing disputes over the purported "intuitions" used by philosophers with the purported role of "intuitions" in mathematics—I'll only sketch the comparison, which is quite rich. Informal rigorous mathematical proof, as the form of professional mathematical proof that appears in journals and textbooks is called, is distant enough from formal derivation that their relationship is controversial.[69] There is enough epistemic distance between ordinary mathematical proofs and formal derivations, for example, that a grasp of formal methods seems unable to explain the ability of mathematicians to distinguish valid from invalid informal rigorous proofs. Mathematicians, generally, "intuit" the links between steps in ordinary mathematical proofs, steps that are—from a formal point of view—"gappy." This is apart from the many examples of mathematicians "intuiting" results that they haven't yet proofs for.

Similar to the emergence of xphilosophy, a major project of translating ordinary mathematical proofs to computer-checkable derivations has arisen. The results of computer-checking ordinary mathematical proofs, however, have proven to be quite conservative: nearly enough, only *one* informal rigorous mathematical result has been corrected on this basis.[70] It's not implausible to think that what are recognized in the transitions of the steps of ordinary mathematical proofs are semantic/conceptual connections between the propositions established;[71] if so, apart from the fact that mathematical concepts are artificial constructions, the resemblance to philosophical thought experiments is very close. Mathematicians, of course, must be initiated into an understanding of their specialized terminology—but once this happens, agreement among mathematicians about successful (informal rigorous) proof is *very* good.

Regardless of the source of mathematical facility in informal rigorous proof, this is another case (other than the one of speaking natural languages) where an extensive common ground is established on which an epistemic practice of pattern recognition can flourish. Talk of "intuitions" has long occurred with respect to mathematical insight—especially among philosophers—but the word is as useless here as it is in the case of philosophical thought experiments: it covers

[68] One can hypothesize that idiolectical differences are always going to correlate with obvious demographic differences such as geography, age, gender, and the like, but this is implausible with something as developmentally intricate as language mastery: demographically independent individual eccentricities always emerge.

[69] For a mild taste of the substantial literature on this, see Rav (2007), Azzouni (2009), Tanswell (2015), Azzouni (2017a), and the citations in these articles.

[70] See Bueno and Azzouni (2005) for discussion.

[71] This is argued for by Rav (2007). Azzouni (2009) opposes the view.

up a complex epistemic phenomenon that's best described directly rather than through the lens of a piece of shortcut jargon.

One indication of the complexity of the phenomenon is something that manifests in both facility with ordinary language and facility in theorem proving. This is that both language abilities and mathematical abilities are strikingly varied and graded. Mathematicians differ greatly in their facility in specific subject areas, and in how "good" they are in those areas—they range from incompetence to "workmanlike" to "sheer genius." What seems, in part, involved are quite different kinds of pattern recognition that mathematicians can possess: it isn't one sort of pattern-recognition skill set that's manifested by all mathematicians.

Ordinary-language facility similarly varies both in degrees of skill and in kind. Although all speaker-hearers, nearly enough, manifest the same ease with—and mastery of—usage, this mastery isn't usually accompanied by a grasp of the patterns exemplified by speaker-hearer usage. And it's *those* patterns that linguists (and philosophers) draw attention to—because they're otherwise likely to be overlooked.[72] We most differ in languages abilities in this way, and here also is where variations in "expertise" among otherwise same-language speakers arise: Some are talented at seeing these patterns and conveying knowledge of them to others, e.g., J. L. Austin; others see them once they're pointed out, but not otherwise; and some don't see them, regardless. There is much more to say about this—but this isn't the place. I'll just mention that one way I try to mitigate these differences in languages skills—so that they don't affect the recognition of evidence for philosophical claims—is by spelling out examples of usage in fuller detail than is usually done.

[72] Chomsky (2000, 35) writes:

> that a brown house has a brown exterior, not interior, appears to be a language universal, holding of "container" words of a broad category. In addition . . . [i]f I see the house, I see its exterior surface; seeing the interior surface does not suffice. . . . If Peter and Mary are equidistant from the surface—Peter inside and Mary outside—Peter is not near the house, but Mary might be, depending on current conditions for nearness.

These pattern facts (which Chomsky draws our attention to) usually go unnoticed unless attention *is* drawn to them; they're not "common knowledge."

1
Knowledge Attributions to Minimal Epistemic Agents

1.1 First Remarks

Hume got it right. He tells us that (1977, 70):

> It seems evident, that animals as well as men learn many things from experience, and infer, that the same events will always follow from the same causes. By this principle they become acquainted with the more obvious properties of external objects, and gradually, from their birth, treasure up a knowledge of the nature of fire, water, earth, stones, heights, depths, &c., and of the effects which result from their operation.

Hume again applies "knowledge" and "learn" to animals a little later in the same section, writing (1977, 72), "But though animals learn many parts of their knowledge from observation, there are also many parts of it, which they derive from the original hand of nature."

His evidence for his claims is equally important (1977, 70):

> The ignorance and inexperience of the young are here plainly distinguishable from the cunning and cleverness of the old, who have learned by long observation to avoid what has hurt them in the past, and to pursue what gave them ease or pleasure. A horse that has been accustomed to the hunt comes to know what height he can leap, and will never attempt what exceeds his force and ability. An old greyhound will leave the more tiring part of the chase to the younger dogs, and will position himself so as to meet the hare when she doubles back; and the conjectures that he forms on this occasion are based purely on his observation and experience.

I establish in this chapter (and rely on it later in the book) that Hume's attributions of knowledge to animals aren't metaphorical (despite the oddity of the expression "parts of their knowledge"). They are straightforwardly natural applications of "know" and "knowledge"; the contrasting "ignorance" and "inexperience" are as well. As importantly, this is so of other words—what, along with

Attributing Knowledge. Jody Azzouni, Oxford University Press (2020). © Oxford University Press.
DOI: 10.1093/oso/9780197508817.001.0001.

the words just mentioned, I'll call "epistemic words" and, sometimes, "cognitive words." Hume applies many of these other words to animals, as I noted with "learn(s)." Because these *third-person* applications of epistemic words are apt, we (that is, observers of animals—among them, importantly, cognitive ethologists) *attribute* various cognitions and concomitant cognition abilities to animals on the basis of behavioral (and, increasingly, neurophysiological) evidence. We take animals to know, recognize, see, remember, and so on, *in the same ways that we take ourselves to know, recognize, see, remember, and so on.* Hume (I dare say) was the first cognitive ethologist, and he relied on this ordinary practice of similarly applying these words to ourselves and to animals; contemporary cognitive ethologists continue to do the same.

What I'll call *rich epistemologists*, those who argue for tight semantic, conceptual, and/or normative relations among epistemic, cognitive, and semantic terms—*knowledge, belief, justification, truth, understanding, concepts*, etc.—often refuse to credit animals with knowledge.[1] Rich epistemologists think that for an epistemic agent to know that there is something green in front of her is to know a great deal else (about obligations of justification, for example, or about one's "authority" in thinking something is green, and so on). Much of this additional knowledge—so rich epistemologists claim—is too much to attribute to animals or small children. For the same reason, they deny the strict suitability of applying notions related to knowledge—belief, justification, etc.—to anything other than adult humans. It's become almost a cliché of this literature to treat parrots and thermostats as epistemically alike. Parrots and thermostats are both described as having—in Brandom's deliberately machinery-flavored language—"reliable differential responsive dispositions," but not genuine knowledge, beliefs, concepts, etc.

This chauvinistic demand about when these words are to be correctly applied is, unsurprisingly, usually coupled with an opposition to externalist/reliabilist views of knowledge. As I noted in the introduction, Williams (2001, 32), writes, "It may be that externalist attributions of knowledge, say to children and animals, are less than literal." Despite his claim that this nonliterality claim isn't obvious, Williams develops a perspective on knowledge in that book that rules out literal attributions of knowledge to children and animals; he does this, however, without supporting evidence for how speakers use these natural-language

[1] I previously used the nomenclature "Sellarsians," to describe those philosophers I'm here describing as "rich epistemologists," but Ram Neta protests strongly that this is misleading both in implying Sellars's influence, on philosophers like C. I. Lewis and Davidson, who also hold the views I'm targeting, and as implying the holding of these views that others, who otherwise explicitly defer to Sellars in certain respects (such as McDowell), don't. Like all labeling, "rich epistemologist" is poor as a description of my targets. My citations and in-text characterizations must be the ultimate guide here.

words, and without a theory of literal meaning. He doesn't provide, that is, empirical grounds to think that attributions of knowledge to children and animals are either nonliteral or even recognized (i.e., experienced) by speakers to be nonliteral.

Brandom (1995, 899–900, n. 3), as I've already indicated, has similar views about animals (and toddlers too). He writes:

> Non- or prelinguistic animals do not have status or standing in the space of reasons. So according to the idiom being recommended here, they neither deploy concepts, acquire beliefs, nor count as having knowledge. Nonetheless, it is common to talk about them loosely as though they were capable of some version (usually admitted to be degenerate cases) of these accomplishments. The informational states most closely resembling genuine beliefs that they *do* have (call them *beliefs**), when they both correctly represent how things are and are acquired by a suitable reliable process may be called *knowledge**. An externalist account of *this* sort of state is all that is to be had. This status has in common with the genuine article what the parrot has in common with the reporter of red things: reliable differential responsive dispositions.

Many philosophers immunize their theories against empirical refutation by claiming the usage data that contradicts those theories is "loose," "less than literal," "metaphors," or even "pretense." This dubious strategy is rampant everywhere in contemporary philosophy where ordinary usage would otherwise be relevant (and damaging) to a theorist's favorite position. It should be recognized, however, that without both substantial empirical data *and* fairly robust theories of literal/precise speaking as well as supposedly contrasting metaphorical language, this is a weak position. (Recall my discussion of this in part 2 of the introduction.) As for the cases under consideration here—applications of the words "know(s)," "recognize(s)," "anticipate(s)," "understand(s)," and so on, to animals (and artifacts)—these claims lack even prima facie support from the language practices of speaker-hearers.

It's tempting to describe attributions of "knowledge," "recognition," "anticipation," "seeing," and the like, as attributions of "cognitive" or "mental" *states.*[2] For reasons forthcoming in this chapter, a non-pleonastic construal of these "mental states" goes far beyond the roles these words play. I'll either use the noun "mental state" without committing myself to any structural requirements on its use or avoid it altogether (as too dangerous), instead usually describing these attributions as "cognition attributions" or "attributions of cognitions" and

[2] As Williamson (2000), especially chapter 1, does. Many researchers similarly assume that knowledge is a mental state. Turri (2015, 308) gives a long list.

staying neutral about what metaphysical conditions (on the psychology of the agents) their correct use imposes.[3]

I make the case, in this chapter, that these epistemic words are straightforwardly applied to animals by careful scientists (of many sorts, but especially evolutionary or cognitive ethologists) and by popular writers, and that these attributions aren't understood by their users as "loose," or "metaphorical." What *is* true is that more sophisticated observers worry about whether certain cognitive attributions are genuine or instead involve an "anthropomorphism" overreaching beyond available data.[4] This is an issue about the *evidence* for attributional claims; it's not about whether these words are correctly applied. That is, it's a question on a par with the question of whether someone seen from a distance is over five feet tall; it's not the worry that the phrase "over five feet tall" is here applied "metaphorically" or "loosely." These attributions are, often, embedded in subtle arguments about what animals are (and aren't) aware of, what they know (and don't know), when they've made errors, etc. Scientific observers, that is, are sensitive as they should be to questions of *which* cognitions should be attributed to animals on the basis of the available evidence. A straightforward word search on animal-study articles for words like "know" and "evidence," therefore, only reveals some of the grounds for what I'm claiming here: knowledge attributions are often embedded in substantial discussions in which "know(s)" or its cognates don't appear—although it's clear that knowledge and other cognition attributions are being made to animals. (I'll give examples later in the chapter.)

One of the reasons for this linguistic complexity is identified by Williamson (2000, chapter 11) and codified in his "knowledge account"; it's also noticed by

[3] For the record, however, I suspect these attributions impose nothing more metaphysically beyond a minimal cognitive agency. (I discuss this further in chapter 6.) We may, of course, empirically discover additional metaphysical constraints on what a "nervous system"—or any other kind of organized structure—must be like in order for it to possess the needed competencies. We may also succeed in characterizing a functional description of the relationship between such a specified kind of nervous system and the world in order for there to be these needed competencies. How any of this turns out doesn't affect how third-person attributions of knowledge, perception, and the like appropriately apply.

[4] Studies of animal cognition have dramatically taken off in the last two decades, fueled by two factors. First, an ongoing development in the knowledge of (and the tools to study) neurophysiology: this enables interspecies comparisons. The second is substantive improvements in the observation of animals in the wild (both technically aided and unaided—see, e.g., Uetz and Clark (2014), Smith and Evans (2014, 186–187)) and in experimental design (see, e.g., Snowdon (2014, 215–216)). Relevant is the current freedom of practitioners from behaviorist presumptions. Behaviorism—in this context a refusal to attribute non-behavioristic psychological traits to animals in "scientific settings"—only slowly loosened its hold on animal studies after the 1960s. See de Waal (2016, especially chapter 2) for a historically informed and methodologically sophisticated discussion. See Grandin and Johnson (2005, chapter 1) for an otherwise sympathetic description of its impact (on Grandin and on Grandin's education). For far less sympathy, see Safina (2015). It's orthogonal to this chapter that animal researchers (for a certain period of time) withheld psychological attributions to animals (and, indeed, from themselves and other humans) for currently discredited methodologically based reasons.

Unger (1975), Slote (1979), DeRose (2009, chapter 3, and, earlier, by Moore. We often use indicatives to implicitly characterize their own content as known by the speaker (or as known by the narrator—in the case of attributions to others). When this happens "know(s)" and its cognates aren't used. (I discuss this phenomenon, and significantly restrict its scope, in chapter 4.)

Not only are there widespread (ordinary and natural) attributions of knowledge and other cognitions to animals, but there are also widespread (and again, ordinary and natural) attributions of such to *artifacts*: drones, robots, etc. This bears on how the various cognition attributions are (semantically/conceptually) linked. It also bears on the earlier point about mental states. At least as far as usage is concerned, to attribute epistemic cognitions to agents needn't be to concomitantly attribute an internal subjectivity to those agents, a "what it's like to be me" experience—one accompanied with "qualia." Even "aware" and its cognates, when used to indicate an agent's responsiveness to something in its environment, as in "S is aware of A," aren't conceptually/semantically linked either to the experience of qualia or to internal experiences of "what it's like to be me." It can be said of a robot, for example, that it's aware of such-and-such items in its environment (although it's not aware of certain other items in its environment) without the attributor simultaneously (or necessarily) claiming that the robot is conscious or has experiences. This may be surprising, but usage is clear on this, as I'll show in this chapter (and, indeed, as should already be obvious).

This is typical in ontology, epistemology, and other philosophical fields. A common—although not exclusive—application of a philosophically important word is singled out as the "literal" application of it, and other uses—although occasionally noticed—are sidelined as metaphorical, nonliteral, or applied only in "special circumstances." Such views are often held despite the absence of supporting principled linguistic-science reasons. For example, the phrase "There are *A*s," because it's often used by speakers who take *A*s to exist, is characterized by philosophers as *requiring* *A*s to exist for its correct application to *A*s—and this is despite the fact that "There are as many Greek gods as goddesses" is an ordinary and straightforward locution easily uttered by individuals who don't believe in either gods or goddesses.[5] The same is true of "I see *A*s": In the philosophical tradition—especially in philosophy of perception—the literal truth of this phrase is widely taken as requiring *A*s to exist, although hallucinations and other sorts of nonexistents (holes, etc.) are often indicated by ordinary uses of such locutions. Contrary to views that take these words to be ontologically laden, these words, strictly speaking, are neutral about ontology: sometimes their usage presupposes ontological commitments and sometimes it doesn't. Similarly,

[5] I've discussed this ubiquitous phenomenon often, most recently in Azzouni (2017b, part 1).

although the agents we most often attribute knowledge (and other cognitions) to have "inner lives," the possession of an inner life, nevertheless, is no requirement of these words. It's notable that the opposing viewpoint—that attributions of knowledge can only be to agents taken to be conscious—has never been argued for; it's only been assumed. It's hard to see however, what argument for this is even possible, apart from the claim—impossible to establish—that *all* the usages that contradict the view aren't literal.

I turn to this topic in section 1.4, specifically the concern of determining what it is that third-person cognition attributions reveal about "knowledge" and knowledge, as well as other cognitions. This won't provide a full characterization of "knowledge" and knowledge—that's for later chapters. But I'll partially evaluate externalist and reliabilist proposals about knowledge, and other cognitions, when applied to animals, artifacts, and small children. One important point made here is that many of these externalist/reliabilist characterizations of knowledge originally arose as attempts to handle Gettier counterexamples; and so they were often intended to enable necessary and sufficient conditions (a definition) for knowledge. Some objections to these proposals fail if that program is treated as bankrupt, as many philosophers now urge.[6] Pure externalist approaches, however, inadequately characterize the knowledge of agents with rich cognitive resources. This will emerge in section 1.8. That, nevertheless, the very same word "know(s)" applies correctly along purely externalist lines to one sort of epistemic agent but doesn't apply along purely externalist lines to others will be illustrated by straightforward applications of the lexical tools I described in the introduction, e.g., the conjunction-reduction test. My primary task in this chapter, however, is illustrating how we apply "know," and related epistemic words, to animals, artifacts, and children.

Other important fallout from this chapter (as I've already indicated) is how cognition attributions come apart in ways that oppose rich epistemic views about the conceptual/normative interconnections of these words—in particular, correctly attributing "knowing" to agents doesn't seem to require much by way of subsidiary "knowings" of those agents, if any.[7] There are, nevertheless, *some* linkages among cognition attributions: a metaphysically deflated version

[6] See, e.g., Zagzebski (1994) or Williamson (2000).

[7] It's interesting, and possibly significant, that we have "belief" but nothing corresponding to "knowledge" (no "believeledge" or "beliefledge") and that we have "knowledge" but nothing corresponding to "belief" (no "knowings" or "knowals"). I sometimes use "knowing" and "knowings" to correspond to "beliefs," as in the sentence this note is appended to, and later too; but of course this isn't English—it's Jargonish. (I don't know whether a noun phrase like "knowing" exists in other languages; it doesn't in French, German, or Icelandic—see the discussion of this in section 2.2.) This is why we need "items of knowledge" or Hume's "parts of knowledge." "Knowledge" as in "knowledge frameworks" is often used nonfactively; that means it's functioning the way "beliefledge" or "believeledge" would, if we had such words. I discuss these differences in usage in chapter 2.

of Williamson's "most general factive mental state" claim about "know(s)"—that, for example, *A perceives that B* entails *A knows that B*—still garners support from Williamson's examples despite the falsity of his claim about the differences between *perceiving B* and *perceiving that B*, *knowing B* and *knowing that B*. I discuss this in section 1.4.[8]

Apart from this, the upshot of this chapter is a fundamental disagreement with traditional coherentists and other rich epistemologists, because they require epistemic agents to have substantial conceptual competencies. Very little, actually, is required of epistemic agents. What *is* true is that the cognitive competencies of sophisticated epistemic agents aren't layered so that the knowledge-gathering properties of their underlying competencies are unaffected by this layering. Even if two agents have similar sensory faculties, the differences in their other faculties (in their capacities to reason, say) affect what they know by means of the shared sensory faculties. I discuss this briefly at the end of this chapter, but the topic can only be fully discussed—as it deserves to be—in a later book.

1.2 What Animals Know

They know a lot, apparently. And crucial to the numerous discussions of, and experiments designed to reveal or elicit, what animals know are descriptions of *what* they know, recognize, remember, foresee, and so on—*in just those words*. Consider, for example (Safina (2015, 2)):

> When a poacher kills an elephant, he doesn't just kill the elephant who dies. The family may lose the crucial memory of their elder matriarch, who knew where to travel during the very toughest years of drought to reach the food and water that would allow them to continue living.

Safina (2015, 17) quotes Katito Sayialel, a longtime elephant observer: " 'When I first arrived here,' Katito recalls, 'they heard my voice and knew I was a new person. They came to smell me. Now they know me.' " Molnar et al. (2015) write:

> In wolves, the loss of one or both of the dominant individuals creates important perturbations in the group. . . . Adult wolves provide important stability to a

[8] Williamson's views about the relations of "know(s)" to other words must also be qualified because certain verbs—"infer(s)," for example, and "remember(s)" and "remember(s) that," for many speakers—can have both factive and nonfactive usages, although "know(s)" is always factive. Recall note 44 in the introduction, as well as the discussion of the factivity of "know(s)" in the introduction itself.

> pack through their knowledge of the territory, experience, and long-established social bonds.

Next, consider a description of elephants at play (Safina (2015, 50–51), his italics):

> Even full-sized adults sometimes play games against imaginary enemies. They might start running through tall grass, thrashing it, the kind of behavior they might actually use to chase away lions. "But the elephants are playing," declares Vicki [an animal researcher,] "they know there are no lions." . . . But . . . isn't it possible they're just making a mistake or being extra careful? . . . "It's easy to tell," Vicki explains. A serious elephant faced with a real threat pays steady attention. Playing elephants run in a loose and "floppy" way, shaking their heads to let their ears and trunk flap and flop around. "They are not making mistakes or giving false alarms. They're running around as if highly alarmed but doing what we call 'play-trumpeting.' They all know they're playing."

In an important survey article of studies of chimpanzees, Call and Tomasello (2008, 191) write, "Chimpanzees understand both the goals and intentions of others as well as the perception and knowledge of others." Here (and in the articles surveyed), not only is knowledge attributed to other chimpanzees, but cognitive states like "understanding" are attributed to them as well.[9]

A lot of the evidence for what animals know arises from observations of animals deceiving one another. Call and Tomasello (2008) allude to several of these results from studies of chimpanzees. Holekamp, Sakai, and Lundrigan (2007, 530) describe sophisticated deception among spotted hyenas that compares well to the cognitive sophistication of higher primates. They write:

> [W]e once observed a low-ranking male, which was travelling with several higher-ranking hyenas, spy a leopard with a young wildebeest it had killed only moments before. The leopard had not yet had time to move its kill to a safe place and was crouching in a creek bed beside the carcass. The group of hyenas crossed the creek bed just upwind of the kill, and none of the other hyenas appeared to note the leopard or its prey. However, four different human observers saw the low-ranking male hyena look directly at the kill as he crossed the creek, but continue past it with the rest of the group until he was well over 100

[9] Much of the animal literature is concerned with what sorts of cognitions can (and can't) be attributed to different sorts of animals. (I discuss this further, in relation to metacognition, in chapter 6.) Different kinds of knowledge are attributed to animals—ones that otherwise differ greatly in their cognitive capacities. This is part of the evidence that cognition attributions needn't be applied cohesively.

> m beyond the creek. At that point, he turned and loped directly back to the kill and wrangled it away from the leopard without having to compete for it with any higher-ranking hyenas.

This is a knowledge attribution to an animal (along with speculation about the absence of that same knowledge from the other animals—"none of the other hyenas appeared to note the leopard or its prey")—*without* the word "know(s)" or cognates. As I mentioned, this is ubiquitous. Here, the evidence for the knowledge attribution is the behavior of the animals—specifically, behavior that shows the animal has noticed (or not noticed) something.

With regard to primates hoarding food, Kummer and Goodall (2003, 225) write:

> To hoard food in a cache is one form of storage, but the hoard is vulnerable to decay, to parasitism and to plundering by observant conspecifics. . . . Nonhuman primates do not use hoards. . . . By far the most elegant form of storage is new knowledge or skill in communication or ecological techniques.

The phrase "observant conspecifics" officially notes that conspecifics (the animals) know things by observing. A standard way of justifying that animals know something, as the quotation about hyenas illustrates, is to indicate they've *recognized* something by their senses—often something that's fairly higher-level. The abstract to Holekamp, Sakai, and Lundrigan (2007, 523) reads:

> As in cercopithecine primates, spotted hyenas use multiple sensory modalities to recognize their kin and other conspecifics as individuals, they recognize third-party kin and rank relationships among their clan mates, and they use this knowledge adaptively during social decision-making.

The epistemic word "recognize" supports knowing attributions to spotted hyenas; notice also the appearance of the higher-level cognitive verb phrase "rank." In addition, a capacity for singular reference is attributed to spotted hyenas—as it often is to various social animals—by the phrase "recognize their kin and other conspecifics as individuals."

The word "know(s)" and its cognates often explicitly (or implicitly) arise in descriptions of how knowledge is transferred from one party to a second, or how knowledge is deliberately induced in an epistemic agent. I won't dwell on these cases in this book, but they also occur widely in the animal literature. When describing the practice of collecting semen from Brahman bulls, Grandin and Johnson (2005, 103) write (their italics):

> Brahman bulls are so affectionate that when you collect semen from [them] you have to pet them a *long* time first. They'll refuse to give the semen for twenty minutes because they want twenty minutes of throat and butt scratching; that's the stuff they really care about. . . . They'll delay the sex in order to get some good, serious stroking. With some of them you have to walk away and leave or they won't give you the semen at all. You have to let them know that if they don't give the semen they're not going to get stroked.

This is a straightforward and common use of the phrase "know that" to describe a method of getting an epistemic agent to *know* something.

Unsurprisingly, there is a *great deal* published about knowledge transfer: animals taking something they've learned in one context and applying it elsewhere. Cooper et al. (2003, 240–241), describing the "social cognition" of domestic dogs, write, "the preference for the Knower in the first trial suggests that the dogs had transferred knowledge from previous situations (e.g. the home) when exposed to a new problem." And (242), they write: "animals may be more likely to use transfer of knowledge from another situation (i.e. thinking) when exposed to a new problem." The jargony flavor of "transfer of knowledge" is easily corrected. In the first quotation, replace "had transferred knowledge" with "applied what they'd learned in previous situations" or "applied what they knew from previous situations." In the second, replace "use transfer of knowledge" with "apply what they've learned." (Jargony writing shouldn't raise doubts about the naturalness of these knowledge attributions.)

"Know(s)" and "knowledge," aren't applied in isolation to animals, as the foregoing quotations illustrate. Any epistemic word that applies to humans can be straightforwardly applied to nonhuman animals too—this is carefully done by researchers to avoid going beyond the data.[10] Researchers often carefully delineate what the evidence they give shows the animals they're studying to know, and they distinguish it from the cognition attributions the evidence doesn't establish; they also usually make it very clear what the evidence is on the basis of which they're making these distinctions. Speculation is flagged to distinguish it from facts in the standard ways we all use. For example, Mech (2009) is titled "Possible

[10] Sloppy applications of epistemic words to animals, on the other hand—genuine "anthropomorphism"—occur in popular discussions of pets. Contemporary animal researchers are *so* careful about avoiding this—in particular, designing careful experiments that avoid gratuitous cognition attributions by ruling out simpler explanations that don't involve such attributions—in part because of the behaviorist traditions in their fields that they remain aware of. See, e.g. de Waal (2016), who gives many examples throughout his book of the empirical challenges of cognition attribution on the basis of behavioral evidence, and how those challenges have been (and are being) cleverly circumvented by researchers. Great care in this respect is compatible with substantial confusion about cognition and metacognition—because it's so easy to get confused about the latter. See chapter 6 on this.

use of foresight, understanding, and planning by wolves hunting muskoxen." Here, the various attributions of knowledge to wolves are provided by words like "expect" and "understood." Mech explicitly uses "It is even possible" to mark speculation, writing (2009, 148):

> This waiting-in-ambush behavior implies that the wolves expected the muskoxen to become available eventually and that they understood that waiting in hiding would improve their chances of getting nearer to the muskoxen. It is even possible that the wolves chose a hiding place that was near a meadow they expected the muskoxen to visit.

"Learn," the other epistemic word notably used *factively* by Hume, occurs *quite* often—and unsurprisingly—since many cognitive differences between types of animals turn on what they can and can't learn. It's a truism in this literature (as it is with Hume, and generally) that what animals learn they then *know* (the factive use of "learn" is thus presupposed). Abramson et al. (2012, 18) write, "The short training period that killer whales required to learn the copy command compares quite favourably with that observed in great apes and even dolphins." Foote et al. (2006, 511), write, "The mimicry data strongly indicate that killer whales are capable of vocal production learning." Safina (2015, 43) writes (italics his), "Elephants have to *learn* everything about how to be an elephant from other elephants, who protect them." Box (2003, 201) writes:

> Moreover, experiments by Rapaport (1999) with captive golden lion tamarins have shown that, compared with obtaining foods independently, immature animals were more likely to accept new foods acquired from other members of the social group. Further, adults transferred to immatures food that was known to adults, but new to immatures, and foods that were new to all, was transferred more frequently than foods that were familiar to both adults and immatures. Hence, she suggests that adults change their behavior in ways that result in the facilitation of learning about food.

Now consider the important word "recognize(s)." It has appeared in earlier quotations already, but Palagi and Cordoni (2009, 984) write about wolves: "During their third-party contacts, the Pistoia wolves were able to recognize specific group members as more valuable partners than others." Topál et al. (2009, 104–105) write:

> In another study, one dog has been shown to base his performance not on human behavioral cues but on previous knowledge about the names of other familiar objects (Kaminski, Call, and Fischer (2004). Although there is some

disagreement on the interpretation of the underlying cognitive processes (see Bloom (2004)), this dog, knowing the names of about 200 different objects, was able to recognize that a novel utterance indicates the name of the novel object among a set of familiar objects with known names.

Beynon-Davies (2011, 312) writes, using the epistemic words "recognize" and "discriminating":

> colour vision experimenters have shown that [prairie dogs] can recognize easily differences between humans wearing blue and yellow T-shirts but have trouble discriminating between green and yellow T-shirts.

Kummer and Goodall (2003, 227) write:

> Peripheral females readily learned to discriminate between nails painted different colours that were used as markers for food buried in the ground. They also remembered the location of underground water several hours after being allowed to watch its burial. Central females seemed unable to learn these tasks, perhaps because their attention was almost totally absorbed in social interactions.

Notice that "discriminate(s)," "learn(s)," and "remember(s)" naturally occur together to describe what animals know (and don't know). Next is a case where "know(s)" is used (and, strictly speaking, correctly) but where "remember(s)" would have fit better. Topál et al. (2009, 105) write that "In these tasks, dogs could see a human 'Hider' placing a toy object or piece of food in one of three identical boxes. Dogs could always know the location of the reward."

Other examples of "remember(s)": Bearzi and Stanford (2008, 255) tell us chimpanzees remember the locations of "hundreds or thousands" of fruit trees, keeping track of their ripening progress over weeks while the band patrols its large territory. Safina (2015, 314) quotes Brunk (2013): "Dolphins have the potential for lifelong memory for each other." (Again, poor writing shouldn't leave the impression that memory attributions to dolphins are metaphorical.)

Lastly, a potpourri of epistemic/cognitive words applied to animals, including "comprehend(s)" and "understand(s)." Hare and Tomasello (2005, 439) tell us: "Domestic dogs are unusually skilled at reading human social and communicative behavior." Kaminski et al. (2011, 222), write, "Domestic dogs comprehend human gestural communication in a way that other animal species do not." Researchers often use "comprehend(s)" or "understand(s)" to focus on differences between what animals know (and on explaining why certain animals know things others don't). Kaminski, Schultz, and Tomasello (2011, 231), write:

> When young children from 18 months of age see gestures directed to others as still being informative for themselves (Gräfenhain et al. (2009)), dogs do so much less. This might reflect young children's understanding of the communicative act as informative—so that anyone may take advantage of the information being communicated—whereas dogs may understand the communicative act as imperative—in which case the individual being addressed is the most relevant one.

Huber (2016, 339) writes: "In recent years, researchers have become increasingly interested in how dogs understand us humans," and "Our knowledge of how dogs perceive the human environment and use this information to solve their everyday problems is important for understanding why they fit so well into the human environment." Here "understand" occurs twice, once as an attribution to dogs and once to us; the word isn't ambiguous, polysemous, or otherwise different in the two cases. A sentence like "Researchers have become increasingly interested in how dogs and humans understand one another" is natural.[11]

1.3 Insects and Non-biological Things Know a Lot Too

The important objection to make to rich epistemologists, of course, isn't that they deny literal attributions of knowledge to parrots and small children—this could be (at worst) a failure to realize how cognitively sophisticated these agents are. The important objection is that epistemologists who deny this do so because they falsely presume literal attributions of "observe(s)" and other cognition words to epistemic agents require those agents to have a lot of subsidiary knowledge. Many of the recent animal-study articles and books, however, that attribute knowledge to animals are studies of primates, spotted hyenas, orcas, elephants, and wolves, all of which live in complex societies. It may be thought, therefore, that this literature shows only that Brandom, Williams, and others were overhasty in denying to certain animals (including parrots) this subsidiary knowledge and accompanying cognitive abilities. This would sustain the idea that knowing attributions require the attributions of a great deal of other knowledge and cognitions to epistemic agents.

It's hard, however, to discern any minimal cognitive limit on the agents to which knowledge is attributed from animal-observation usage or from our ordinary cognition attributions. On the basis of sheer usage, anyway, even

[11] Further quotations illustrating animal knowledge, and other cognitive attributions to animals from the cognitive ethology literature are in Kornblith (2002, especially sections 2.1 and 2.6).

"consciousness" (whatever *it* is) isn't required of an epistemic agent to attribute knowledge or other cognitions to her.[12]

I'll establish this by first illustrating attributions of knowledge, memories, etc., to insects, and then with additional attributions to *mechanisms*.

Franks et al. (2002, 1575) write:

> A second . . . mystery is this: how does the swarm [of honeybees] as a whole know where to find the new nest-site given that, at take-off, only a tiny proportion of the bees have visited it or monitored dances advertising the chosen site?

And later (1581) we read:

> although one scout may discover a particular site, and initially advertise it because it is the best site she knows, if a second scout finds a better site, the first scout will eventually shift her allegiance to the superior alternative.

Baddeley et al. (2012, 1–2) write (italics theirs):

> Upon first leaving the nest, a new forager [ant] performs a series of short *learning walks* where a carefully orchestrated series of loops and turns allow her to inspect the visual surroundings from close to the nest entrance (Muser et al. (2005); Muller and Wehner (2010); Wehner, Meier, and Zollikofer (2004)). The knowledge gained during these special manoeuvres means she will be able to use visual information to pin-point the nest entrance after future foraging trips.

And a few lines down (2), we read, "Routes have a distinct polarity; knowledge of a nest-food route does not imply knowledge of a food-nest route." The bits of knowledge that these insects do and don't have, that is, are carefully distinguished by these researchers. They write (2, italics theirs): "Route knowledge defines a *visual corridor* as opposed to a narrow ridge, so the overall shapes of routes are stable but ants do not have to recapitulate them with high precision," and "The visual knowledge used to define routes can be used independently of any odometric information that the ant may possess." Lastly, they (6) write, "ants do not just use a single training run but will continue to develop their knowledge of the surroundings during multiple runs." Wehner (1990, 404) tells us that:

> while searching for food, bees and ants always know their position relative to their starting point (home) through path integration. During their circuitous

[12] In section 6.3, I discuss legitimate knowledge attributions to virtual beings that have an extremely minimal grasp of their environments.

> outwards journeys, they continuously monitor the angles steered and the distances traveled and integrate these data, so that they are always informed about the vector pointing from their current position towards home.

Notice the complexity of this attribution, in particular what is and isn't being described as known. The insects know their position relative to home; it's *not* being suggested that they know path integration.[13] They're *using* path integration, however, similar to our use of the modularized anatomy of our brains to handle numerical calculations. It's a mistake to take *us* to know anything about how our brains enable knowledge of some numerical relations—unless we're specialists in that area of study.

Other epistemic words are routinely applied to insects as well. Safina (2015, 22) writes that "with about one million brain cells, honeybees recognize patterns, scents, and colors in flowers and remember their locations." He quotes Sacks (2014): "It is increasingly evident that insects can remember, learn, think, and communicate in quite rich and unexpected ways."

Here is an example where researchers describe a case of ants learning something, and subsequently possessing knowledge of it (Collett and Collett (2002, 548)):

> Naïve and experienced ants will then behave differently when given competing information from chemical and visual cues; naïve ants follow the scent trail, whereas experienced ants ignore the scent trail and follow visual landmarks instead. The scent trail provides a means of stabilizing the route of an ant over several trips. It might also aid learning by providing a training signal, so that the ant knows to learn landmarks while it can detect the scent.

I suggested earlier that "know(s)" attributions don't require a simultaneous attribution of experience or consciousness when this is understood in the sense of an inner life or the experience of "what it's like to be me." Some writers infer consciousness, in this sense, from the evidence of an appropriate attribution of knowledge (see, e.g., Safina (2015, 22)). In a popular article, we read (Jabr (2017)):

> There is now a consensus that numerous species, including birds and mammals, as well as octopuses and honeybees, have some degree of consciousness, that is,

[13] A formalization of this passage would codify explicitly what's within and without the scope of a "know operator." Natural language benefits from flexibly indicating this tacitly and by context—that's valuable, of course, except for the dangers of syntactic ambiguity. I thank Otávio Bueno (personal communication, July 2017) for pressing me to clarify this.

> a subjective experience of the world—they feel, think, remember, plan and in some cases possess a sense of self.[14]

Whether or not Jabr is concluding that birds, mammals, octopuses, and honeybees are conscious from the cognitive/epistemic qualities attributed to them (as opposed to their "feelings"), what shows any such inference via the attributed cognitive/epistemic qualities to be mistaken, I think, are widespread applications of "know(s)" (and other epistemic words) to *mechanisms* that we (most of us) would deny have inner lives (are "conscious"). This observation doesn't rely on the premise that such mechanisms *aren't* conscious; I'm not arguing for this one way or the other. I'm instead relying on the fact that someone can consistently attribute knowing (and other cognitions) to such entities without simultaneously being required to claim that those entities experience qualia or have "this is what it's like to be me" experiences.[15]

Lauer et al. (2010, 288) tell us about autonomous soccer-playing robots:

> The robots get their commands by wireless communication from an external computer that is connected to a fixed camera above the field which yields an eagle-eye-perspective of the situation. This way of sensing ensures that all agents share the same, complete knowledge of their environment.

They add (294):

> The key idea of visual self-location is to use landmarks, significant objects that can be recognized easily, and to measure the distance and angles at which the landmarks are seen in the camera image.

[14] Many are trying to establish the presence of consciousness in (certain) animals on the basis of comparative neurophysiological evidence. See, for discussion of this, Rowlands (2019), especially regarding the Cambridge Declaration on Consciousness (19–20).

[15] A striking case: There's been a lot of philosophical debate (over the years) on whether anyone knows *anything* when asleep—the claim is that such a person's cognitive faculties are so diminished that even if he dreams about such and such memories (that he actually has), it's not true that he's really remembering. But suppose someone opens her refrigerator while sleepwalking (noctambulism). "Wow," it's observed, "she still knows exactly where the ice cream is." This person is taken to know things even though she's not conscious. In particular, this knowledge attribution (which seems straightforwardly correct) is compatible with massive irrationality and massive (in the moment) cognitive incapacities. Sellars (1956, 169) writes: "in characterizing an episode or state as that of *knowing*, we are not giving an empirical description of that episode or state; we are placing it in the logical space of reasons, of justifying and being able to justify what one says." This kind of view is *widely* held despite, as this and the many other examples in this chapter indicate, fitting so badly with how we ordinarily attribute knowledge.

But (294):

> The soccer field does not provide an adequate number of landmarks. Therefore, we are using the white field markings instead. Although white lines can be extracted easily in the camera images, they are not uniquely identifiable, the robot does not know which line segment it actually sees.

The robot is described as *seeing* a line. But Lauer et al. aren't claiming the robot is *having* an experience. I'll develop this point further toward the end of this section.

A couple more quotations from this article: "It is also possible to distinguish situations in which the robot knows where it is (low value) from those situations in which it [has] lost track of its position (high value)" (295), and "The catadioptric camera has a very limited field of view. Objects of the size of a ball can be recognized only up to a distance of 5 m"(302).

Driverless cars (unsurprisingly) need to know *a lot*. Mcbride (2016, 179) tells us that:

> Such driverless cars will internally integrate many different inputs to analyse their environments and issues such as road conditions in order to make decisions about where and when to drive. Using learning algorithms, they will build knowledge bases of road conditions and learn to [manage] unusual and exceptional conditions such as plastic bags blowing across the road, or obstructions in the road.

These are attributions of knowing (of "road conditions" and of "unusual and exceptional conditions"—but not necessarily of recognizing an exceptional condition *to be* a plastic bag blowing across the road)—*as well as* descriptions of the mechanisms that make this knowing possible ("learning algorithms") that *aren't* being described as known by the car.

Drones know a lot too. Pullen (2017) tells us that "an altimeter lets the drone know what altitude it's at." Rosenberg and Markoff (2016), in an ominously titled article, write:

> Armed with a variation of human and facial recognition software used by American intelligence agencies, the drone adroitly tracked moving cars and picked out enemies hiding along walls. It even correctly figured out that no threat was posed by a photographer who was crouching, camera raised to eye level and pointed at the drone, a situation that has confused human soldiers with fatal results.

To correctly "figure something out" is, of course, to come to know that something.

Maney (2016) writes:

> Let's say you name your drone Rover. You could tell it, "Rover, go pick up Daddy's medication from CVS." (If CVS is smart, it will have a drone takeout window tomorrow.) It would know where to go and how to get back to you. Or an AI drone could operate as a watchdog. Hear a noise outside, and you say, "Rover, go check it out." It could zip around the perimeter and know that the person peeking in your window is a stranger, not your mother-in-law.[16]

What about something as simple-minded as a floor-cleaning robot? Consider Palladino (2015) on what the Roomba 980 can learn to recognize, and thus come to know:

> The 980 will actually learn the floor plan of your home with all your furniture in it. It uses a vision localization sensor and a low-res camera to search for "landmarks" where it cleans—think a chair or a coffee table—and then recognizes its shape and memorizes it. Combine that knowledge with tracking sensors, which help the machine know how fast it's moving in your home's space, and the Roomba has the power to map every space in your home that it touches.

Furthermore:

> iRobot claims this knowledge helps the Roomba 980 be more efficient in its cleaning—once the robot knows where to go, it can avoid obstacles that get in its way of collecting dirt and terminating dust-bunnies.

Every reader should be able to hear the difference between "the robot knows where to go" and "terminating dust-bunnies." "Terminating" *is* metaphor—the word is being used in a mild *joke*; but the robot knowing where to go and recognizing the shapes of things it has memorized is no joke—that's straightforward. This straightforwardness is *relied on* by the company's claims about what this "knowledge" is good for. Similarly, although Palladino puts "landmark" in

[16] Despite the jokey flavor, the knowledge attributions to "Rover" are neither metaphors nor jokes—no more than the numerous attributions of this sort published everywhere today. Notice, in particular, that the use of "actually learn" in the next quotation functions to *avoid* metaphor or pretense. "Jimi Hendrix was actually on fire" is nearly impossible to not hear as a pointed avoidance of metaphor: he's *really* burning alive. The characterization of CVS as "smart" or not "smart" isn't metaphor, pretense, or an application of "smart" outside standard usage either—but that's to be discussed in another book, not this one.

quotation marks—presumably because it's odd (or metaphorical) to describe chairs or coffee tables as landmarks—she doesn't do this with "knowledge."

Mechanisms can be quite minimal in both what and how they cognize. One can say, naturally, "The cash machine doesn't recognize who I am; it won't take my card" or "The thermostat is broken; it no longer knows that it's too hot if the temperature goes above 80."[17]

I'll close this section by making official with examples that several words—"see(s)," "aware," "recognize(s)," "identif(y/ies)" "scan(s)," "fail(s) to recognize," and so on, as well as slang like "spot(s)," or "tell(s)"—are *all* used to attribute visual cognitions to things that *aren't* taken by attributers to be conscious or have experiences. Bilger (2013) writes of the self-driving car that:

> It never gets drowsy or distracted, never wonders who has the right-of-way. It knows every turn, tree, and streetlight ahead in precise, three-dimensional detail. Dolgov was riding through a wooded area one night when the car suddenly slowed to a crawl. "I was thinking, What the hell? It must be a bug," he told me. "Then we noticed the deer walking along the shoulder." The car, unlike its riders, could see in the dark.

Boudette (2016b) writes:

> Google and other companies hope more precise laser-based sensors, known as lidar, and other technology will make it easier for driverless cars to spot potholes—as opposed to shadows—and avoid them.

Boudette (2016a, B1), quoting Elon Musk, writes:

> The new version of Autopilot, with its improved radar, "would see a large metal object across the road," and be able to determine that the object is not an overpass or overhead road sign that poses no threat, he said. "Impact probability would be assessed as high and it would probably brake."

[17] Dennett describes "the intentional stance" as one that can be adopted even toward *lecterns*. (They "want" to stay where they are—forever.) What makes Dennett's view not sound absurd on the face of it—the way that a philosopher's suggestion of "a circular stance," applying "circular" to squares, would sound absurd—is that ordinary usage already allows literal and sincere applications of cognition attributions to mechanisms. See especially Dennett (1987, 21–23). The lectern is the minimal (and pretty unacceptable) possible target of the intentional stance—something Dennett acknowledges. The unacceptability of applying the intentional stance to the lectern, he suggests, is because doing so adds nothing to predicting its behavior beyond what we have already. I suggest a different reason is at work, as far as cognition attributions are concerned, in section 1.7.

Here's why "seeing" and "being aware" are appropriately attributed to these mechanisms even though they're not assumed to have experiences. The mechanisms use light the way we do to see, or if not, they use other tools to see that exploit electromagnetic radiation that we aren't sensitive to. But this doesn't require the mechanism to experience or be conscious of what it sees. All that's needed is that it can locate items visually, and, being aware of them, it can respond appropriately. We, however, have experiences, and we use "seeing" and "being aware" not only to describe how our visual faculties enable us to navigate, but also to characterize the special experiences we have when we do so. But this is a different use of the same word: it's not a necessary condition of all uses of "see" or "be aware of" that to see, or to be aware of something, requires having a certain experience.[18]

As I've said, without powerful evidence that the usages I've discussed are deviant, knowing attributions (and other cognition attributions) to animals, insects, and mechanisms can't be dismissed as metaphorical or nonliteral.[19] But treating such attributions as legitimate uses of our concept of knowing (and related concepts) raises a number of pressing questions about the conceptual contours of those notions. I turn to exploring these in later sections and, indeed, throughout the rest of this book.[20]

[18] Recall from introduction section v Jackendoff's suggested sufficient conditions for "see(s)." The words "conscious of" or "experience(s)," however, *do* seem to require an inner life of an agent. To ask if a driverless car is conscious of pedestrians whom it avoids hitting sounds like a question about whether driverless cars have an inner life. Uses of "experience(s)" are similar.

[19] Evidence for nonliterality are admissions by attributers that their words are *meant* metaphorically or nonliterally. These admissions are common in the popular literature on quantum mechanics, where descriptions are often characterized as "not precise" or "metaphorical," e.g., "electrons are waves." Furthermore, these admittedly metaphorical descriptions don't occur in the technical literature. In cognitive ethology, on the contrary, cognition attributions aren't described as nonliteral; instead, the suitability of such attributions is carefully argued for and against in professional articles, as well as in the popular literature. In the case of cognition attributions to things, attitude-attribution language is utilized, as I've indicated, in both popular and technical literature. Not only are knowing attributions made, but important implications of the possession of knowledge by artifacts are drawn (e.g., about their economic viability). This is why someone with Brandom's or Williams's views about these attributions is at an argumentative disadvantage. I don't deny that speakers often use (and often recognize they're using) these words nonliterally. Consider Stewart Cohen's example, "The underdog is the guy that everyone knows is going to lose" (Hawthorne (2004, 70 n. 53)). Is this an example of "know(s)" that's nonfactive (as Hawthorne suggests)? No, people routinely withdraw the knowing attribution when pressed on it, usually replacing "knows" with "thinks that he knows"; the remark is recognized by everyone as an often-repeated (old) joke. Recall the discussion of Hazlett's (2010) supposed examples of nonfactive uses of "know(s)" in the introduction. What about (Hawthorne (2004, 70 n. 53)), "The car knows when it is out of gas," when speaking of an ordinary car with an ordinary gas gauge? Here too, *most* people are likely to treat the usage as metaphorical, although see the discussion on this in section 1.7.

[20] I can't resist: while doing the final preparation of this book, I came across another article exhibiting the lessons I've drawn in this section: Quain (2019). In particular, a tagline from the article: "Autonomous Cars Are Still Learning to See."

1.4 The Flexibility of Cognition Attributions: Φing that *p*

I'll start with a supposed distinction between attributions of cognitions with and without "that." In the foregoing (except in one case), I've not been explicit about whether it's "knowledge *that p*," "perceiving *that p*," etc., that's attributed to animals and mechanisms in the quotations I've given, or instead, "knowing *p*," "perceiving *p*," and the like. I've implied by this omission that the distinction isn't particularly important. According to Williamson (2000, 36), however, the distinction between these two locutions is very important to acknowledge because "know(s) that," "remember(s) that," "perceive(s) that," and so on, have a significant epistemic condition of application that's absent from "know(s)," "remember(s)," and "perceive(s)":

> [Such phrases ascribe] an attitude to a proposition to the subject. Thus 'S Φs that A' entails 'S grasps the proposition that A.' To know that there are infinitely many primes, one must grasp the proposition that there are infinitely many primes. . . .
>
> Thus, given that "see(s)" and "remember(s)" [are as above], one can see that Olga is playing chess or remembers that she was playing chess only if one has a concept of chess.

The suggestion isn't that these phrases sometimes so ascribe having concepts and grasping propositions; the claim is that they *always* do.[21] If so, the attributors of such "attitudes" have substantial empirical promissory notes due to the conceptual content of the propositions following "that." To claim a hyena *knows that* his conspecifics haven't noticed a leopard with a freshly killed wildebeest requires attributing the concepts "conspecific," "wildebeest," and so on, *to* the hyena. To say a driverless car has *noticed that* there is an obstruction in the road presumes that the driverless car "has" the concept "obstruction in the road." Not only are such additional attributions of having concepts and grasping propositions implausible in most of the cases I've described, but empirical researchers are unaware of such conditions. They never acknowledge that there are such conditions on their knowing-that attributions to animals, nor do they try to meet them.

Williamson is wrong about these conditions on "S Φs that *p*" locutions. These locutions require context—both verbal and non-verbal—in order to indicate what concepts (if any) are had by the agent the propositional attitude is attributed

[21] Brandom (1995, 897) and Dretske (1993) seem to have even stronger positions: any belief or knowledge attribution of *p*, regardless of the presence of "that" in the attribution locution, requires a "grasp" of the concepts appearing in *p*. This is wrong too. See section 5.4 on this.

to; they also need context to indicate what "proposition," if any, is grasped by that agent. Correspondingly, anyone who uses "S Φs that *p*" has broad latitude in asserting which concepts, if any, are had by S. Consider this example (due, but in an earlier form, to Williamson (2000)):

> Olga gives Rover—her dog—treats whenever she plays chess, but never when she plays other board games. This isn't deliberate; the reason she does this isn't discernible (by the dog, by her, or by others); it's just a subpersonal habit she's fallen into (as we so often do). As a result, though, Rover gets excited whenever she plays chess. This is something that never happens when she plays other board games. Rover, of course, doesn't know how to play chess—he doesn't know what chess *is*—but nevertheless Rover does *see that* Olga is playing chess (whenever she plays chess in front of him).
>
> "Rover knows that I'm playing chess," Olga can say to someone as Rover jumps up and down, waving his tail, "that's why he's so excited." She can explain (quite naturally), and with that typical pride commonly exhibited by pet owners: "Rover can always tell that I'm playing chess when I am!"

It would be tone-deaf to respond to Olga (either sarcastically *or* seriously) with "Um, Rover plays chess, does he? Has he ever . . . *won*?" This isn't because this context is peculiar and special, and the phrases "knows that" or "can always tell" have been wrenched from their normal patterns. Rather, the phrases, "know(s) that," "see(s) that," "remember(s) that," etc., are flexible and open-ended in exactly what kind of knowledge they can be used to attribute to an agent. They're neutral with respect to which concepts and/or propositions, if any, S, the agent, supposedly has and/or grasps.

It's useful to describe these phrases as "template phrases": what the agent knows *about* the event being described by the proposition *p* following the phrase "S Φs that" may be filled out in many ways all of which are compatible with its truth. "S Φs that *p*" operates (in context) in relation to options that are being excluded. We can be—on the basis of what we've said before, or after, the attribution—precise about what we claim an agent sees (or knows) and doesn't see (or know), by qualifying our attribution to that agent. Olga can say, "It's amazing that Rover always knows that I'm playing chess since (of course) he has no idea what chess even is." She can say (attributing more knowledge to three-year-old Sofia than to Rover), "Sofia knows that I'm playing chess, although she hasn't learned its rules." Sofia, presumably, already knows a lot about board games, although perhaps not much about *chess*. Rover, however, knows almost nothing about *any* board game. It suffices for him to know *that* Olga is playing chess, nevertheless, merely because he *distinguishes* her playing chess from her playing the six or so other board games that she also plays.

Notice that in attributing correctly to Rover that he knows that Olga is playing chess, or that he sees that Olga playing chess, no one need be able to say *how* he distinguishes chess from the other board games Olga plays. One may know (or have speculations about) how he's managing it—Olga's particular body language when she decides to play chess, the shapes of the pieces she takes out (or the box she keeps them in), where on a shelf she keeps her chess set, the particular look of the pieces arranged on the board . . .—but of course, one may have no idea whatsoever how Rover is managing the trick; *knowing how* the agent manages the trick of knowing that *p* isn't required for a correct attribution of knowing that *p* to that agent.

1.5 Knowledge, Belief, Action, and Consciousness

Epistemic *agents*, all things being equal, *act on* their knowledge. This truism, when hedged *explicitly*, is dangerously close to having no content. As a first rough attempt to give it content, we can say, about humans, that they act on what they know because, if they know something *p*, then they believe *p*, and their beliefs (generally) determine how they consciously (with full awareness) *take action*. This rough characterization, notice, links "believe(s)," "know(s)," "act(s)," and consciousness in ways that seem required if attributions using "believe(s)," "conscious," and "know(s)" are to make sense. I turn to undercutting this impression. I show that this first attempt is only a rough regularity with many exceptions; it isn't an infallible guide to the applications of these words. There is, I suspect, no such infallible guide.

Belief attribution has at least two connected roles in cognition attribution. (It may have more, but set that aside.) I described one role in the last paragraph: we often attribute beliefs to agents to explain/describe the contours of their actions. Because Lance believed the gun was in the desk drawer, he moved toward the desk; because Lance believed he was being watched, he moved stealthily; because Lance thought he only had a few seconds, he moved quickly (etc.). With respect to this use of belief attributions, we standardly although not invariably presuppose the (human) agent is conscious of the ascribed beliefs. The second role of belief attributions is used to contrast *false* beliefs with what that agent knows. We often attribute an absence of knowledge to agents; an agent, for example, has failed to see (or notice) an object in her vicinity. An attribution of ignorance to an agent is often although not invariably accompanied by a description of particular false beliefs that are instead attributed to her. The agent hasn't noticed the predator lurking nearby; so the agent *believes that* she's safe; the agent—we can say this too—*thinks that* she's safe. "Think(s) that" also attributes beliefs to agents.

Although these two roles are closely linked—false beliefs are used to describe/explain behavior just the same way that true beliefs (determined by what the agent knows) do—these two uses of "belief" are nevertheless in some tension, at least when it comes to attributions of cognitions to artifacts. To attribute knowing something to artifacts (that aren't omniscient) is to allow that such artifacts can also fail to know things, and consequently (at least in some cases) to allow that such artifacts can have false beliefs. Rover the drone, described by Maney (quoted in the last section), might "know the person peeking in your window is a stranger, not your mother-in-law"; but Rover could also "think the person peeking in your window is a stranger, despite being your mother-in-law" because your mother-in-law has disguised herself. If drones know things, they can also get things wrong—they can also have false beliefs. At one stage in their development, for example, driverless cars confused the red taillights of the cars in front of them with stoplights. Pretty straightforwardly, however, to *confuse* A with B when in the presence of A is to *think* one is in the presence of B when one isn't.

But to describe drones and driverless cars as things without consciousness, which is natural, is to describe them as *without beliefs*—at least in one common way that we use "belief." For many philosophers as well, to describe an agent as "having beliefs" requires that these beliefs be ones the agent is conscious of.

What considerations move philosophers to think that if beliefs are attributed to an agent, that agent *must be* conscious of them? I don't think what's at work is an explicit (or implicit) characterization of "belief"—semantic or conceptual—that has as a corollary or yields as a condition on belief attribution that the agent is *conscious of* those beliefs. Rather, one consideration is the tendency to sometimes (perhaps often) disavow that an agent has particular beliefs if the agent isn't conscious of them. In the case of humans, and in standard cases of those humans, if a human has particular beliefs, the human can express them, and humans do so consciously. Further, an epistemic agent, in this case (and this is a widespread practice), is often the final court of appeal about whether she has a particular belief. "I don't believe in elves," Ahmed can say sincerely. It's scarcely credible to challenge Ahmed's claim on the grounds that Ahmed might unconsciously believe in elves but be unaware of this. Ahmed can be challenged about his sincerity, of course—but that's another matter.

If true, this doesn't follow from a definition of "belief"; it's reasonable to think that the word hasn't got a definition—like nearly all our words outside of mathematics, specialized scientific nomenclatures, jargons, or kinship vocabulary. The concern here, instead, is whether speaker-hearers experience an entailment of "belief" to be that the beliefs attributed to agents are ones that agents are conscious of. Relatedly, the issue is whether there are circumstances in which it's reasonable (admissible) to attribute beliefs to agents that those agents are taken to be unconscious of. It certainly seems like there are such circumstances. The impression, to the contrary, of "belief" (belief attributions) entailing "consciousness" (of those beliefs) would manifest as the impression that talk of an agent being unconscious of her beliefs is an oxymoron or (more dramatically) an outright contradiction. One would scarcely know how to take sentences in which this talk appeared. Imagine, for contrast, the introduction of *square circles* into a discussion of kinds of shapes—where the suggestion is made that this too is a type of shape. Try to imagine what sort of sense we could make of sentences in which this phrase appeared (for example, "Some square circles are quite pretty to look at").

No similar problem arises in the literature on "repressed memories" or, more generally, in cases where someone's actions are explained by beliefs attributed to him that he's unaware of. Similarly, that our knowledge of the grammar of our native language is knowledge we're unconscious of may be a controversial use of the word "knowledge"; but that hardly makes it inconsistent or semantically/conceptually inappropriate—which is all that's at issue here.

There is an important distinction between someone deciding to obey a law—to drive a car for a few hours in an elliptical orbit around a central object, let's say—and the orbits of planets in our solar system. Some may worry that attributing grammatical knowledge to us because of our effortless ability to speak grammatically doesn't take account of this important distinction. In speaking grammatically, some may think, we're more like planets (or like people falling from windows) than like people who consciously act. It may be further thought that the required dividing line (between what planets do and what we do) can only be drawn by conceding the border between conscious and unconscious action. I don't think this is correct (for one thing, we often willfully produce ungrammatical sentences); but at the moment, all that matters is that this hasn't anything to do with how we use the words "believe(s)," "know(s)," and related expressions. A substantial (philosophical) position may be established by a subtle argument that shows that this important distinction—between an agent choosing to act according to regularities and an agent's behavior being governed by regularities—must be grounded in the border between conscious and unconscious behavior. As a result, this quite subtle and sophisticated argument may show that belief attribution therefore requires consciousness. It won't show, however, that consciousness is a conceptually/semantically necessary condition on our understanding of the word "know(s)," or that our usage reflects this condition. The result of this subtle and sophisticated argument would instead be a revision in usage, or the introduction of a new scientific/technical word "know*" that deviates from our ordinary one.

1.6 Knowledge and Belief (and Consciousness Too)

I've suggested in the foregoing that our usage shows that consciousness isn't required for knowledge or even belief. Recall the rough characterization I opened the last section with: humans act on their knowledge by means of the conscious beliefs they have as a result of that knowledge. I've pushed back on the supposed requirement that the agent be conscious of the beliefs in question (or the supposed knowledge). It seems, correspondingly, that no epistemic agent is required to be conscious at all. In describing/explaining behavior, therefore, there is space for the attributions of beliefs and/or knowledge that the agent isn't conscious of. But what about the connection posited in the rough characterization between knowing something and believing it?[22]

We often describe certain cases as ones where people know things without believing them. This has led some philosophers to suggest that belief isn't a necessary condition for knowledge, contrary to the traditional tripartite set of conditions on knowledge: belief, justification, and truth. Williamson (2000, 42) writes, against those philosophers:

> When the unconfident examinee, taking herself to be guessing, reliably gives correct dates as a result of forgotten history lessons, it is not an obvious misuse of English to classify her as knowing that the battle of Agincourt was in 1415 without believing that it was. But intuitions differ over such cases; it is not very clear whether she knows and not very clear whether she believes. . . . We have no clear counterexamples to [If S knows that A then S believes that A].

And Williamson follows these remarks with references to some of the philosophical discussion of these cases.[23]

We can do better than this. That "intuitions" aren't clear about certain cases indicates what lack of clarity about certain cases *sometimes* indicates: those cases are under-described. It's worth developing them further (that is, characterizing a *range* of such cases, and evaluating the usage impressions they elicit) because this reveals constraints on belief attributions that aren't shared by knowing attributions. Because of these different constraints on belief and knowing attributions, these attributions can and *do* come apart.

[22] Hawthorne (2004, 70 n. 53) says there are examples of uses of "know" that "clearly don't require belief: I say of the quiz contestant that he knows the answer when he knows what answer people want to hear but does not believe it himself." But "knows the answer" is short for "knows the answer the judges want to hear" where he *does* believe the proposition knowledge of which is attributed to him.

[23] He refers to: Radford (1966). Armstrong (1973, 138–149), and Shope (1983, 178–187).

Let's consider, first, a straightforward case. The examinee, Mary, says: "Yeah, the last time I looked at this stuff was about seventy-five years ago, early in high school, actually; but I'm sure I still remember most of it." And when she's queried, the examiner says, clearly impressed: "Yes, you do still remember quite a bit—almost everything, actually." As "remember(s)" is used here, it entails "know(s)": to remember that the battle of Agincourt was in 1415 is to know that it was. We (third-person attributers) would also describe Mary as believing she knows, for example, that the battle of Agincourt was in 1415, as well as believing that the battle of Agincourt was in 1415. (These aren't the same beliefs.) One may imagine that Mary is unsure of this particular fact, saying instead, "I think it was in 1415, but I'm not positive." And then, when she gets it right, both she and the examiner will agree she has proved she *did* know it. This is especially the case if she answers a significant number of the other questions correctly.

Did Mary *believe* that the battle of Agincourt was in 1415 as she tentatively gave that answer? She was unsure, and it's not unreasonable in this case to say that because she was unsure, she didn't believe it—although, as it turned out, she did know it.[24] When, on the other hand, she says firmly, "I know that one," it's clear she also believes it—even if she discovers afterward that she got it wrong. (She might say, in this case, "I was *so sure* of that one.")

In these kinds of cases, therefore, we do seem to require surety of beliefs although we don't similarly require surety of knowings. Let's switch to a case more like the one Williamson alludes to. The only difference, imagine, is that Dorothy (unlike Mary) remains uniformly unsure of her answers; she continues to think she's only guessing, and (sincerely) expresses great surprise that she continues to get the answers right. Here too, we, from a third-person position, will treat her as knowing the facts that she got right—even though Dorothy doesn't think this herself, even after getting the answers right several times.[25]

Why not presume, in these timidity cases, that because the examinee knows these things, she *does* believe them? She doesn't *believe that she believes*

[24] Radford (1966) stresses the link between being sure and believing. I explore this purported linkage momentarily, coming (pretty much) to the same conclusion as he does about it—at least with respect to the reading of "believe(s)" in play here.

[25] An important subtlety: Guessing *particular* dates correctly is hard. If questions have answers that are easy to guess, we might think that even though the examinee did learn this stuff back in high school, she's still guessing. The antecedent implausibility of guessing right answers, coupled with a mechanism for why she can know the right answers (because she's recalling what she learned in high school), is crucial to the attribution of knowing being sensible in this case. This is part of why, if Dorothy claims she only guessed the answers even after she's told she got them right, we disagree with her: Dorothy is being irrationally cautious about attributing knowledge to herself, especially given the background fact about how hard it is to guess these answers correctly. A different case, where Dorothy isn't being irrationally cautious, is where she's asked to answer a series of questions—thirty, say—but not told how she's doing. She can doubt, and sensibly, *all* her answers even though (the examiners see) she gets every one of them right. Here, if she's not irrationally cautious, she will agree with the examiners afterward that she knew all the answers. Compare my examples with Reynolds's (2017, 76):

them—but that's different. There are certainly cases where we—from the third-person point of view—*will* attribute beliefs to someone who sincerely disavows those beliefs. And in those cases it's right to describe the person as not believing that she believes what she does believe. But those cases aren't like the timid-examinee cases. One of those different cases is where an agent's actions are more compatible with a set of beliefs the agent denies she has than with the ones she avows. If a sincerely expressed belief doesn't impact appropriately on the agent's actions, we doubt the agent has that belief, despite what she claims. "You believe he's untrustworthy, even though you say you think he's trustworthy," we assert, "because you always recalculate his receipts after he's given them to you even though you don't recalculate anyone else's." A pattern of behavior, that is, can betray that an agent's beliefs aren't what he says they are, and if the agent is sincere, they aren't what he thinks they are either. In this case, someone doesn't believe what he thinks he believes. And the agent owes an explanation to anyone who challenges his belief on the basis of his behavior. He has to "explain that behavior away." An honest agent even has to do that for himself, if he compares his actions with the beliefs he ascribes to himself.[26]

The diagnosis is this. Belief attributions are very closely linked with behavior. And with humans, a great deal of the relevant behavior is verbal utterance.

> Imagine a game show contestant who once learned in some respectable way that *p*. In answer to a question she decides to say that *p*, but in the pressure of the game she experiences feelings of doubt whether *p*. These feelings are usually taken to imply that she doesn't believe that *p*, or at least doesn't fully believe that *p*. So let us assume for the sake of argument that she doesn't (fully) believe what she says. When her answer is acceptable she may say, perhaps with some surprise, "I knew it!" Even on the hypothesis that she doesn't believe, some of us agree with her that she knew; others say that she didn't really know.

Reynolds is certainly right about his case, because (after all) who can say for sure where a single guess is offered about something the contestant "once learned in some respectable way": hardly a convincing display of knowledge regardless of how confident the contestant is. Reynolds falsely suggests this is typical of cases where belief seems to separate from knowledge: intuitions will clash. No: They won't clash when Dorothy answers correctly thirty questions about exact dates in French history although she thinks she's just guessing because she learned them long ago! I should add that we can distinguish different cases where Dorothy's phenomenology differs. Imagine she answers correctly thirty questions, but she isn't told she's answered them correctly until after she answers all the questions. One case is where it feels to her like she's guessing each answer (although we would say she isn't; and after she's told, if she's not irrationally modest, she'll agree). Another is where she feels she's remembering but because she learned these facts so long ago she thinks she's guessing. In both cases, she's wrong about her own mental state, but for different reasons. In the second case she mistakenly distrusts her own phenomenology, but in the first case her phenomenology misleads her. In both cases, notice, Dorothy doesn't believe she knows these things nor does she believe her answers. (My thanks to Tianyi Zhao for discussion here.)

[26] Williamson's (2000, 25) example: Someone believes that the world is going to end soon. But he doesn't cash in his pension, or do the other things someone who really thought the world was going to end soon would do. We (or many of us) would deny he really believes the world is going to end soon—and we can do this consistent with claiming this person sincerely thinks he believes the world is going to end. Not everyone (we realize) is insightful about themselves. A generalization of this fact is key to understanding the subtleties of cognition and metacognition. See chapters 5 and 6 on this.

In addition, the "logic" of belief attribution is confining: we either attribute a belief to an agent or we don't. The agent either believes *p*, or he doesn't believe *p*—these are our options. If the agent doesn't believe *p*, maybe he's unsure or maybe he disbelieves it. But we generally don't undercut an agent's self-attribution of a belief unless either (a) we doubt the agent's sincerity, or (b) there is too much of a mismatch between the agent's avowed belief and his relevant behavior. All of this turns on systematic patterns of behavior. An agent who regularly lies about all sorts of things that he really thinks are true is someone whose sincerity we're likely to doubt. And here, as well, we're unlikely to suggest the agent is unaware of his real beliefs unless we have independent reasons for doing so. When there is one pattern of (verbal) behavior and another conflicting pattern of non-verbal behavior, we make a decision about which beliefs (if any) to attribute to the agent by seeing which attributions make the most sense of his (overall) behavior—given our background understanding of how behavior is supposed to be influenced by beliefs.

It may seem that in cases where the agent is presumed to be unaware of her real beliefs, questions of surety are irrelevant; if the agent disavows believing *p* (although we think the agent does believe *p*), it makes no sense to say that the agent is nevertheless sure of *p*. This isn't so. Confidence is something we can and do recognize non-verbal behavior to exhibit as much as we detect it in verbal expressions. Surety or confidence is manifested, often, in sheer non-hesitancy. The animal straightforwardly reaches for the food item, or instead, hesitates, looking around first, or it blinks and rubs its eyes before reaching for the food item, or the animal reaches out tentatively, touching it slightly, before grasping it, etc. What beliefs are being acted on, confidently or not, is determined by how different sorts of beliefs interlock with different sorts of behavior. So we can describe beliefs—both conscious and unconscious ones—as required to be items that an agent has confidently.[27] And, correspondingly, we can attribute confidence to an epistemic agent whether or not the agent is conscious of the beliefs in question or even conscious at all. A drone that relentlessly tracks someone down (and kills him) can be described as confident that what it tracked down was (say) an enemy agent. And we can (and do) say this even though we don't think drones *experience* confidence, or, indeed, experience *anything*.

Knowing things, although as closely conjoined with behavior as beliefs are, doesn't require confidence. We allow agents to know things that they aren't at all sure of, or even that they believe they don't know. And so, related to this, we also allow agents to remember things that they aren't at all sure of. An amnesiac may still remember where his home is even though he doesn't believe he does. If he invariably manages to get home every time he tries, always by the correct route, his

[27] Nearly a year after I wrote this, I was delighted to stumble across the same suggestion in Russell (1948, 132) also with respect to animals and their beliefs.

sincere claim that he's guessing will be disallowed. In so describing the amnesiac, we're saying both that he doesn't believe he knows his home is at such-and-such an address and that he doesn't believe his home is at such-and-such an address, even though he *does* know his home is at that address.[28] (A variant is this. Imagine the amnesiac has lost his capacity for episodic memory. So he doesn't remember that he has got home on many occasions by the same correct route, although he always does (although he always feels like he's just guessing). He knows where his home is although he doesn't realize this, nor does he believe it.)

1.7 Mindless Knowing

To allow that knowledge and true or false beliefs can be attributed to entities not even *susceptible* of an inner mental life threatens us with a *reductio*.[29] It seems crazy, frankly, to attribute knowledge or beliefs to tables or chairs. I agree. That *does* go too far. And we can see that it goes too far by recognizing that some sort of cognitive process is required of a knower: to bear a knowing relation to proposition requires some sort of "grasping"—some sort of cognitive process, or result of a process. This much excludes tables, chairs, and lecterns. They don't do *anything*, and so they don't do anything cognitive either. It may seem that the "this much" requires consciousness (of *some* sort). Thermostats, gas gauges, drones, driverless cars, and robots, most of us think, don't have minds of any sort. Describing these things as knowing or believing things, therefore, *must be* metaphorical.

Call this the threat of "mindless knowing." What global conditions govern "believe(s)," "know(s)," and the like, that prevents knowing or belief attributions to things that lack minds? It's tempting to think that even without definitions there ought to be a global necessary condition (of *some* sort) that makes it inappropriate to apply these words to thermostats, drones, driverless cars, and even robots.

[28] Craig (1990) acknowledges timid-student cases but complains that taking seriously such cases as faulting belief as a necessary condition on knowledge is a mistake. Craig (1990, 14) writes: "anything not strictly a necessary condition simply vanishes without a trace. Of all [belief's] deep centrality nothing whatever remains." Recognition of the violation of necessary conditions can have this effect because the violator of such a condition can be one "outlier." Craig thinks this happens in the case of belief and knowledge because the function of "know(s)" is to flag good informants and so belief is central because good informants usually believe what they inform us about. Craig is wrong: As I hope is already indicated by my discussion, and to be shown in detail throughout this book, there is a whole continent (as it were) of knowers who don't believe what they know. Characterizing the "role" of "know(s)" the way Craig attempts is simply too crude and obscures our routine use of this propositional attitude in conjunction with the presence or absence of other propositional attitudes to categorize all *kinds* of knowers.

[29] I thank Otávio Bueno for pressing me on the topic of this section. Like most philosophers I've talked to about this, he vehemently disagrees with the conclusions I draw. (Sigh.)

One can then try to formulate what this condition is. I've already mentioned a "mental-life" condition: any agent must have an inner life—*experiences*. But there are other possible conditions. Perhaps the cognitions attributed to agents must be grounded in a nervous-system-like structure with a certain minimal complexity. Or perhaps there must be a certain minimal richness to the cognitions attributed to agents. A fourth possible condition is that there must be a minimal richness to the behavior appropriately associated with the beliefs and knowledge attributed. How might one or another of these conditions be established?[30]

We need to leave aside what should be labeled "a priori outrage," or the "sputter response" to the suggestion that a thermostat has beliefs or knowledge. These responses show only what can't be denied, that in fact we largely don't attribute knowledge or beliefs to thermostats—this much is shown by sheer usage alone.[31] But *this much* only provides us with local necessary conditions for the application of these terms—we don't apply the words in *these* cases. This is far from a global necessary condition that can guide usage in new cases. And that's the problem. We notice a number of cases in which we attribute knowledge to agents and a number of cases in which we don't; we additionally notice that the affirmative cases have something in common that the non-affirmative cases lack. Nevertheless, we need an argument that turns this "something in common" into a global necessary condition. Only then can the resulting condition be used against other applications of the words that don't satisfy the condition; only then can we describe those usages as "deviant," "degenerate," or, more mildly, "metaphorical" or "not literal."

We *do* recognize some global necessary conditions on "know(s)." I've already mentioned that an object, to be a knower, has to do *something* cognitive—and that the something it does must coordinate (more or less) correctly with the something that the object is attributed knowledge *of*. Tables and chairs don't meet this condition, although thermostats and gas gauges do.

It also seems, for another pertinent example, that we don't allow anything to know things that are false.[32] That this is a global necessary condition is indicated

[30] As the repeated use of the word "minimal" indicates, we're running up against *vagueness*. This is a genuine aspect of "know(s)" attributions, as well as the attributions of other cognitions to agents. See chapter 10 on this.

[31] All I think is *actually* shown by usage is that most of us will withdraw knowledge or belief attributions to thermostats. One might say of a thermostat, "it doesn't realize anymore that 85 degrees is too hot," but under pressure one is likely to say, "I didn't mean to say that thermostats realize things, of course." Many—but not all of us—are also likely to try to deny that Roombas have knowledge. As I said, this is a vagueness issue.

[32] I continue to avoid a complication: "knowledge" is a gradable mass term; knowledge of a subject area allows someone to "know a lot" about that subject area even though she's wrong about some (or even many) things. The way that "S know(s) that *p*" or "S know(s) *p*," which are factive, interacts with the mass term "knowledge," which isn't, is complex and causes misunderstandings. It may be a source of the misapprehension that "know(s)" is contextually infiltrated; "knowledge" *is* contextually

by the two ways that usage marks a global necessary condition on the meaning of a word. First, speakers will (pretty uniformly) withdraw or qualify uses of that word that violate the condition as "not literal" or "metaphorical" when pressed. Consider a sarcastic claim that John knows that the Civil War occurred in the twentieth century. Someone will point out that the remark is sarcastic if someone else attempts to read that use of "know(s)" as literally implying that something known can be false. Second, when one use of a word obeys a condition but another doesn't, the condition is perceived as a necessary global condition on the word if the standard test for ambiguity is successfully passed when a usage that violates the perceived necessary condition is used in the same sentence with a usage that obeys the perceived necessary condition: e.g., we can't combine these uses into one occurrence of the word.[33] Both these conditions seem at work with the jargon "knowledge system" where the phrase is used in a way that allows that much or most of what's "known" can be false.

Perceived global necessary conditions on words are quite rare. In the particular case of "know(s)," "believe(s)," and the like, it's easy for philosophers to imagine different global necessary conditions for these words (that disagree on the disputed cases) and, even worse, there seems to be no crisp lower limits—apart from either sheer inactivity on the one hand or completely uncoordinated responses to the environment on the other—on the kinds of agents that can be excluded given the correct application of these words. This seems to show that ordinary usage dictates no global necessary conditions of the sort needed to adjudicate cases of drones, robots, and thermostats. That there are some sufficient conditions for these words (cases, that is, that we all more or less agree on) and some local necessary conditions (cases that we also all more or less agree the words shouldn't be applied to) isn't in doubt. And, of course, the global necessary condition that one knows only what's true is perceived as well. Without definitions for these words, however, the foregoing is completely compatible with there being no global necessary conditions that exclude the application of these words to thermostats or equally simple mechanisms.

I'm not urging us to *allow* these words to so apply; I'm only pointing out that there is no reason to think there are general constraints on our words "know(s)" and "believe(s)" that prevent these applications. (This is why philosophers can get into arguments about this.) It's compatible with the foregoing usage data to explain why we're disinclined to apply these words to

infiltrated, of course, but the "S know(s) that *p*" and "S know(s) *p*" locutions aren't. I discuss this in detail in chapter 2.

[33] Recall the discussion of the conjunction-reduction test in part 2 of the introduction. We similarly can't combine metaphorical and literal uses of a word.

thermostats by noting we're inclined to deny that thermostats *act* on the basis of their attributed knowledge or beliefs—we similarly won't claim that a piece of litmus paper knows that a particular liquid it's been dipped into is an acid. What undercuts attributions of knowledge to litmus paper, I therefore suspect, is that we would deny that litmus paper is an *agent*, let alone a cognitive agent. It's unclear that we would deny agency to a thermostat. Agency attribution, however, raises some complications I can't pursue now. For example, a free-standing device is more likely to have agency attributed to it than one being used by a larger mechanism—than one that's perceived as a "part" of a larger mechanism. A driverless car, we might think, *does* know it's low on gas via a gas gauge it's using, although we wouldn't say this of the gas gauge itself (at least not if it's being used by a car). As I noted, further analysis goes beyond what's appropriate to say about this now.

In any case, the factivity of "know(s)" signals the presence of something I've suggested is unusual: a *sharp* global necessary condition on a word. I'll show in chapter 10 that this factivity is the source of a lot of mischief (misunderstanding) about the word "know(s)"—in particular, it generates the impression that "fallible knowledge" is contradictory. But, in addition, factivity is a key to understanding the distinctive role of "know(s)" in our discourse. I'll discuss this in chapter 10.

1.8 Final Lesson from Knowledge Attributions to Animals: Methods of Knowing aren't Modular

We *can* say, as certain externalists do, and relying on the traditional tripartite characterization of knowledge, that a global necessary requirement on an agent knowing something is that the agent be justified, although that "justification" needn't be something the agent has psychological access to. The question looms, however: what is it for an agent to be justified, and relatedly, what is it for an agent to know? (As I mentioned earlier, these concerns have been linked by the project of providing a definition of "knowledge.")

Philosophers have many suggestions.[34] A belief is knowledge if it is true, certain, and obtained by a reliable process; S knows *p* just in case it is not at all accidental that *S* is right about *p*; a non-inferential belief qualifies as knowledge if the belief has properties that are nomically sufficient for its truth; a belief *p* of S qualifies as knowledge just in case S believes *p* because of reasons he possesses that would not obtain unless *p* were true—that is, S's reasons are a reliable indicator

[34] I follow Goldman and Beddor (2016) closely here. What follows are characterizations due, respectively, to Ramsey, Unger, Armstrong, Dretske, and Goldman.

of the truth of *p*; lastly (but hardly the last formulation in this tradition), S perceptually knows that *p* just in case (roughly) she arrives at a belief in *p* based on a perceptual experience that enables her to discriminate the truth of *p* from all relevant alternatives.

These suggestions have all been developed in complex and sophisticated ways. In going forward, I set aside certain concerns that have animated many of these approaches, some of which are transparently built into the formulations I've quoted. First, in light of section 1.6, I leave aside characterizations of knowing something in terms of believing it. Second, I leave aside any concern with defining "know(s)" or "knowledge." Instead, what's attempted are—at best—characterizations of some necessary conditions and some sufficient conditions for the correct application of "know(s)," as well as similar sorts of description for when attributors are warranted in their knowing attributions. Third, I leave aside attempts to characterize knowledge in terms of logical possibility. The gloss on knowledgeable agents being "non-accidentally right" isn't anything in the ballpark of: The reasons for why S knows *would not* obtain unless *p* were true. I'll expand briefly on this important point now, although this is the topic of later chapters, especially chapter 11 (and, actually, a later book, *Challenging Knowledge*).

A central paradigm of knowledge is that gained through perception. This is a source of knowledge, nearly enough, that every epistemic agent shares with us, although (of course) the details of perceptual sensitivity and range vary greatly. However, although perception is surely a source of knowledge—if anything is—it's, nearly enough, never the case that perception provides reasons for why S knows that *p* that would not obtain unless *p* were true. Perception doesn't do this simply because all perceptual knowledge is based on physical mechanisms in agents that enable those agents to interact with their environments in certain ways. But physical mechanisms in agents *always* allow various forms of subversion and failure. We attribute knowledge to all sorts of creatures, knowing full well that, pretty much, anything they know on the basis of perception is something (given extreme enough circumstances) they could be wrong about.

It's a bad idea to build into the analysis of the "justification" for what animals know (for example) safeguards against sceptical scenarios (like the possibility that the animal is a brain in a vat). That issue comes in at a different point, I claim: in the ways that knowledge is challenged. Instead, we need to ask, on what basis do we attribute knowledge to agents? The answer to this question is clear. We do so on the basis of our recognition of the agent's capacities for actual contact with the world. Here "capacities for actual contact" stands in for a number of epistemic tools available to the animals: perception, reasoning, forms of communication, and so on. We also concern ourselves with how the knowledgeable agents can be misled: A monkey hears an eagle call from his conspecifics, but that call is (deliberately) deceiving. There is a question, of course, of the range of cases in which an agent can "get it wrong," but our primary focus arises from our understanding of the cognitive faculties of that agent. We don't worry about possible cases, unless they are based on the mechanics of how agents actually know things.

There is a distinction here between challenging possibilities—in general—and challenging possibilities that arise because of the agent's (limited) powers. Putting this in third-person terms may seem cogent; but sceptical scenarios—one might think—can erode any knowledge of one's own faculties that any such distinction is based on. I'm not dodging a discussion of this now; I'm pointing out that the distinction is made, and that making it is what allows our knowing attributions to other agents to be non-empty. Justifying this distinction to keep it safe and non-empty—despite sceptical threats—is set aside for future work (in a future book): it requires analyzing the notion of possibility relevant to challenges to knowledge.

That said, a rough gloss (not a definition!) of third-person knowing attributions is this:

> An epistemic agent S knows *p* is true if S has used method *M* that yields *p*, and S acts according to *p*, when so acting is appropriate. Furthermore, *M* is reliable in the sense that *M* yields a true outcome in a sufficiently large number of cases. Lastly, *p* is true.

This formulation needs substantial filling out before it has a chance at being adequate. Here are two of the details needed.[35] First, how are methods individuated; second, what's "sufficiently large"? I take on these important questions later, especially in chapter 9 and section 11.3. As should be already clear, however, one way of individuating methods has to be excluded at the outset. Ruled out, that is, are modular characterizations of capacities so that "methods" of knowing can be shared by individuals who otherwise greatly differ in their other capacities. A kind of nonhuman primate, let's say, has the same sensory capacities as humans but largely lacks human inferential capacities. In a case like this, if sensory knowledge was characterized modularly, humans and these primates would know the same things on the same sensory basis. Humans could certainly know more (let's say) on the basis of inference; but particular knowledge items would be on a par insofar as their sources lie in our senses—we'd know them on a sensory basis if and only if these nonhuman primates also knew them that way.

[35] Also needed is an explication of "appropriate." Reasons for thinking that this rough gloss *can't* be analytically nudged into a definition occur throughout the book and become explicit in chapters 10 and 11.

But if knowledge were thus characterized modularly, doubts about sensory knowledge, entertained by human agents, would all fit the timid-student model. An individual, for example, whose senses and mental state were in normal working order looking appropriately at an orange would know that there was an orange in front of him, regardless of his background beliefs and background knowledge. That most of us take sceptical challenges seriously, however, doesn't fit with this characterization. For, if these challenges *are* taken seriously, an individual can *fail to know* there is an orange in front of him even though his senses *are* working perfectly, he's awake, he's looking appropriately in the right direction, and there is an orange he sees and he's aware of. Descartes concludes that he doesn't know whether he sees a piece of paper and a pen in front of him on the basis of the *mere possibility* that he might be dreaming. He doesn't draw the apparently weaker conclusion that he *doesn't know whether he knows* there is a piece of paper and a pen in front of him; something compatible with his knowing there is a piece of paper and a pen in front of him, despite this possibility.[36]

That we don't—generally—individuate our methods of knowing things modularly seems to follow, therefore, from the fact that timid-student cases look rare; instead, we seem to assume that an individual's doubts, in a large number of cases, successfully undercut what otherwise that individual would know on the basis—say—of her senses or her memory. This is something to be looked into, in detail, in subsequent work (not in *this* book).

But this much can be said in a preliminary way now. "Methods," as characterized here, seem to be procedures that it makes sense to individuate in such a way that the doubts of an agent can (often) undercut what she would otherwise know. Imagine two epistemic agents. The first agent, S_1, simply uses his visual senses to see the colors around him. His "method" is to follow the dictates of his senses to categorize colors according to how they appear to him. The second, S_2, instead, uses her senses plus a finite number of additional considerations about background conditions *that she explicitly and consciously checks*—e.g., about the ambient light around her. S_1 knows that a certain color is red once he has looked; S_2 knows (and takes herself to know) that a certain color is red once she has looked *and* verified that certain background conditions are in place. Their "methods"

[36] Or, if he does draw this conclusion, it's intermediate: he then infers from his not knowing whether he knows there is paper and a pen in front of him that he doesn't know this. There is no textual evidence that Descartes reasons via the KK thesis, although since he apparently accepts the KK thesis, he *could* have. KK, in the form of: *If I know p, then I must know that I know p* looks friendly to scepticism. Indeed, Stroud (1984) at times uses KK—or more complex K-iteration principles—to support scepticism; Adler (1981) treats the emergence of KK—because of attempts to legitimate knowledge against counterpossible scenarios (a process that leads to scepticism)—as a symptom of an unavoidable tension in our epistemic practices. More recently, Greco (2014), in his defense of KK, denies that the iterated knowledge KK justifies is knowledge requiring ever-higher standards. The general non-modularity of the knowledge methods of an agent can be established, regardless of the status of KK. I discuss KK, and other iterated propositional attitudes, in chapters 5 and 6.

aren't the same; and in addition, their methods don't always give the same answers. S_1's methods mislead him more often than S_2's methods do her. Nevertheless (let's say), S_1's methods are reliable enough that we'll attribute the knowledge to him that a certain color is red when it *is* red and he thinks it is because of his (pretty reliable) method of looking. In the same way, we'll also attribute the knowledge to S_2 that a certain color is red. However, there are circumstances where S_1 will know that something is red whereas S_2 doesn't know this even though they are both looking at the same thing in the same circumstances—even though, as we might say, they have the same evidence. S_1 knows it's red because he has applied his method, gotten the answer that the something is red, and it is. S_2 doesn't know because she hasn't verified her needed background conditions. It's *possible* the item isn't red even though it looks (to her) like it is.[37]

Notice that on certain readings of the methods of S_1 and S_2, pure externalist and pure internalist characterizations of knowledge are ruled out. For S_1, the method of knowledge can be read purely externally; this isn't possible for S_2, whose method requires her explicit evaluation of whether certain conditions are in place—e.g., background lighting conditions.

One last point about this: I'm saying that we often reject modularizing our methods; this isn't to say we always do. That depends on how modularized the agent's methods actually are (and here I'm using "modularized" in the sense of Fodor (1983)). Again, I apologize for putting this off for later work. (But, really, isn't *this* book long enough?)

1.9 What's Been Done and a Look Ahead

Apart from remarks in the last section that involve some promissory notes I can't redeem in this book, the project of this chapter has been to strip from our understanding of the word "know(s)" a (large) list of entailments that have

[37] It may sound like I'm here echoing the idea that the evidence sets that S_1 and S_2 use are different insofar as S_2 is considering certain alternatives that S_1 isn't. In turn, this may seem to be introducing a form of evidence contextualism (see, for very different versions of this, Neta (2003) and Williams (1996)). Or, perhaps, knowledge is being characterized as semantically invariant—without contextual parameters—although relative to the "situation" an agent is in. An agent knows *p* if she can rule out all the alternatives to *p* that are reasonable from her point of view (see Lawlor (2013)). I'll here deny both suggestions briefly (because I expand on my objections in chapter 3). Contextualisms *of all sorts* (including evidential ones) are ruled out by usage facts. Those same usage facts also rule out Lawlor's subtle invariantism. Apart from this, any analysis of knowledge in terms of excluded *reasonable* alternatives is backward. "Reason" and "reasonable" are complicated notions dependent, in large part, on the cognitive methods agents are *capable of.* A dog can't reasonably entertain certain alternatives (and exclude them) because he's incapable of it. In this respect, "reasonable" is like most normative terms. The cognitive methods used by agents are determined in large measure by their cognitive capacities: My use of "methods" closely tracks agential capacities. (See chapter 10 on this.)

traditionally been associated with the word. Attributions of knowledge to cognitively minimal agents supplement Radford's early recognition that belief isn't a necessary condition on knowledge; neither is consciousness. Minimality also excludes the necessity of metacognitive attitudes accompanying instances of knowing, e.g., knowing that one knows, believing it, or even other more tentative attitudes—not being sure if one knows or not. These will be the focus of two later chapters, 5 and 6.

But there is a lot more to say about the contours of our knowledge concept that its minimality doesn't dictate answers to (and that have been hotly contested in recent epistemology). For example, is the verb "know(s)" contextual or is it sensitive to the pragmatic needs of knowing agents (or attributors of knowledge); is the notion fallibilist or infallibilist? Most of the conceptual contours of our notion of knowledge encapsulated in the meaning and use of "know(s)" remain shrouded. I turn in the next few chapters to exploring its supposed contextuality and impurity; in later chapters its fallibility is explored.

As important are questions of conceptual engineering. In particular, one might argue (as Corey Dethier has urged, without necessarily endorsing; email April 25, 2019) that there is a scientifically licensed distinction between human knowledge and nonhuman knowledge, one that vindicates an account of human knowledge in which we only are capable of "knowing"—in this modified sense—when we're able to recognize that *p* is a reason, etc. This clearly involves metacognition, and so *that* might be the dividing line between distinctive kinds of knowing. Even if the ordinary notion doesn't license the significance of this distinction (as, say, this chapter seems to have shown), perhaps we should change our notion of knowledge to accommodate it—as we have changed many of our ordinary concepts, e.g. heat, to accommodate scientific discoveries. I take this challenge up explicitly in chapter 11. In the meantime, I continue with the descriptive project of getting our (actual) ordinary notion of "know(s)" *right*.

2
Knowledge and Knowing that *p*; "Knowledge" and "Knowing that *p*"

2.1 First Remarks

"Knowledge" and its relatives, historically and still today, are central to epistemology. That these words have no definitions, and that many of the other important words they're entwined with in our usage—"belief," "conscious," "aware of," "see(s)," and the like—are without definitions as well, would perhaps not be troubling if continued misunderstandings of these words (and the concepts associated with them) didn't bedevil so much else in philosophy and, frankly, so much else well beyond philosophy. I've suggested that crucial to getting clear about knowledge is getting clear about how we use the verb "know(s)," the noun "knowledge," and so on. Once we recognize no guiding definitions are to be had of these words (at least as they're employed by the folk), we have no other way—apart from the evidence of usage—of studying what knowledge and the like come to for those of us who use these words responsibly. In particular, we have no alternative approach to determining the conceptual contours of such words. So that's the task of this chapter and the next one: to get clear enough about our usage of these words to illuminate the issues this book is grappling with.[1]

In section 2.2, I describe the contrasting properties of the noun phrase "knowledge" and a central use of the verb "know(s)." The former, I show, is a gradable mass noun that's context-sensitive. "Knowledgeable" is a related gradable

[1] I'm *not* saying that a definition of one or another of these words might not be possible at the *conclusion* of the analysis I'm engaging in here, as I've indicated in the introduction. Sometimes the empirical world is sweet to us: what we've more or less settled on as the targeted scope for a set of words is amenable to empirical (de facto) definitions. This, for example, has been the result of the scientific study of certain elements and compounds in chemistry. But *things* (as it were) needn't be so friendly to our terminological hopes. Biological kinds, for example, still resist definition, and they look like they will do so forever because of the *subject matter*—in particular, genetics and the like (as opposed to, say, the electromagnetic interactions of charged particles). Our (intricate but ordinary) concepts needn't be so nice to us either—recall the complexities of our otherwise humdrum notion of truth that were raised in introduction section x. Notice, however, the crucial point: Even if we managed (at the conclusion of this analysis) to produce workable definitions of certain epistemic words, it would be because of the analysis of *usage*; it wouldn't be because definitions came first, and the (successful) analysis of usage piggybacked on those definitions.

Attributing Knowledge. Jody Azzouni, Oxford University Press (2020). © Oxford University Press.
DOI: 10.1093/oso/9780197508817.001.0001.

adjective that's similar in its properties to other standard examples of gradable adjectives that occur in both the linguistic and epistemic literature, e.g., "flat," "bald," "rich," "happy," "sad" (but it's also similar to the less often mentioned "sandy," "bloody," and "dirty"). The verb phrase "know(s) about" is related to these as well and has the same properties—in particular, gradability and context sensitivity.

On the other hand (section 2.3), at least one major use of "know(s)," when attributing the knowing attitude to oneself or others with respect to *particular* propositions, e.g., "John knows that the trains are running on time" or "I know the trains are running on time," has *none* of these properties. When these results are coupled with a close look at the variations in our knowing judgments—which follows in chapter 3—we're in an awkward position. No systematic position about know(s) attributions looks right. The variation in judgment data seems to cut directly against pure (traditional) invariantist positions that treat know(s) attributions as context-insensitive (provided those agents are otherwise the same in their abilities to appreciate the bearing of evidence on knowledge). Traditional invariantist positions treat know(s) attributions as insensitive to changes in contexts of use and variations among agents in their pragmatic goals (or in other non-epistemic respects). The popular (and popularly discussed) contextualist positions, that allow "know(s)," in one way or another, to be sensitive to contextual factors, face that fact that "know(s)" must be contextual in some new way unlike well-understood contextually sensitive words; and further (as I show in chapter 3), these views don't explain our usage practices with respect to comparison and retraction judgments. Impure views—positing sensitivity of know(s) attributions to pragmatic needs—take the know(s) relation to be partly constituted by non-epistemic factors; such views also don't account for much of the usage data.

The result is a logjam where plenty of usage evidence shows know(s)-judgment variability but apparently rules out any systematic theory that *explains* how know(s)-attribution variability works. This puts us in a good position (humorously enough) to move to a solution—which I attempt in later chapters. After all, once all the dead ends have been clearly labeled, one way (out) is left.

I'll stress that one point of the study of the usage of "know(s)" and "knowledge" in this chapter is to contrast a word where usage *obviously* indicates contextual infiltration and a word where usage, without exaggeration, indicates nothing of the sort (despite so many philosophers trying to show otherwise). That the two words "knowledge" and "know(s)" are closely related is at least ironic. It may also be a source of misunderstandings.

A terminological wrinkle. Because of these hitherto unacknowledged differences between "knowledge," "knowledgeable," and the like, and (a particularly central use of) "know(s)" and "know(s) that," the widespread practice of using the phrases "knowledge attribution," "knowledge attributing," "knowledge ascribing," and the like[2] to cover indifferently both the attributions to agents of (amounts of) knowledge and attributions of knowing specific propositions is misleading. Strictly speaking, "knowledge attributions" *and* "know(s) attributions" (or "knowing attributions"), "knowledge ascriptions," and "know(s) ascriptions," and so on, should be distinguished because these have different properties. They don't (generally) attribute the same things to agents, although, of course, they're intimately related: "knowledge," as I've said, is a mass noun that attributes more or less well-specified collections of "know(s) that *p*," for a range of *p*s. It's notable that this difference can't be expressed easily—this is because there are no noun phrases like "knowals" or "knowings" in English (or, for that matter, in related languages like French and German). I discuss this in section 2.2.

I could distinguish the usages with the purportedly contrasting labels "knowledge attributions" and "propositional knowledge attributions"; but "Isaac knows that the trains run on time" and "Isaac has a lot of knowledge about trains" are both "propositional-knowledge attributions," if either is. One attributes a particular proposition as known; the other does the same with a *group* of propositions. So I'm staying with the contrast labels, "knowledge attributions" and "know(s) attributions," and the clumsy expedient of mentioning both when I need to, despite the shortcomings of these choices. (Or, as I did in earlier chapters and I'll do again in later chapters, I'll just resign myself to the standard usage, or even on occasion help myself to the nonexistent noun phrase "knowings.")

2.2 "Knowledge"

I'll start with a certain oddity of usage that I first mentioned in passing in note 7 of section 1.1. The plural noun phrase that accompanies the verb "know(s)" is "knowledge," although there are no single nouns cognitively connected to "know(s)" that stand for single or multiple *items* of knowledge. Oliver, let's say, knows that Santa Claus doesn't exist. "Santa Claus doesn't exist," therefore, is an *item* or *piece* of his knowledge—a "*part* of his knowledge" (as Hume might say). We can't say that "Santa Claus doesn't exist" is a *knowing* or a *knowal* of Oliver's; correspondingly, we have no plural nouns such as *knowings* or *knowals*.

[2] E.g., as in the titles and contents of chapters 2 and 3 of Stanley (2005); in Ichikawa (2017, 11 n. 1), where a definition of "knowledge ascription" is given; throughout DeRose (2009); in the many articles in (and the title of) Brown and Gerken (2012); and in the title of this book. (Peter Ohlin, my editor at Oxford University Press, would *not* let me title the book "Attributing knowings.")

Although we can speak of a *system* of knowledge or a *body* of knowledge, we can't speak of a collection of, or a body of, knowings or knowals; nor can we speak of a system of knowings or knowals. A comparison with "sand" (and other mass nouns, modified or not, "water," "blood," "clotted blood," "dirt," "sewage," "meat," "tainted meat," "ice," "cream," etc.) helps. We can talk about a *pile* of *dirt*, a *cup* of *water*, a *lump* of *ice cream*, a *package* of *tainted meat*, a *cube* of *ice*, or a *particle* of *sand*; we similarly have no single-word cognates to "sand," "water," "clotted blood," "meat," etc., that are count nouns.

The noun phrases that accompany the word "believe(s)" have complementary omissions. That is, there is no mass noun (such as "believeledge," or "beliefledge," say), although we do have the count nouns "belief" and "beliefs"—a singular and a plural that pick out single (and multiple) items of belief. So, although we can't say that Oliver has a lot of beliefledge, we can say that he has a lot of beliefs, and "Santa Claus doesn't exist" can be one of them. Notice that we can barely speak of an "item of belief" or of "items of belief" (although I just did); it sounds, nevertheless, weird or awkward, because to do so, a word ("belief") that's a count noun is being impounded as a mass noun. We *can*, of course, speak of a system or body of beliefs (or a collection of beliefs) quite naturally.[3] It's notable that other propositional-attitude-ascription words, "hope," "long," "desire," "wish," and so on, are similar. We have "hopes," "longings," "desires," and "wishes," but no "hopeledge," "longledge," "desireledge," "wishledge," etc.[4] "Opinion" is like

[3] "Belief" and "knowledge" somewhat dovetail in coined jargon: "belief system" and "knowledge system" are virtually interchangeable—perhaps only if someone is quite deluded do we avoid attributing a "knowledge system" to him instead of merely a "belief system."

[4] My thanks to Sigrún Svavarsdóttir for reminding me of hopes, longings, desires, and the like on September 3, 2017. She assures me that Icelandic, despite complications (primarily due to there being more subtle distinctions among "knowledge" phrases than in English), nevertheless sustains this distinction between beliefs, wishes, and so on, on the one hand, and "knowledge" on the other. German (apart from a "know phrase" that translates roughly as the count noun "acquaintances") is similar; so is French.

Here is the Icelandic usage evidence (from Svavarsdóttir, email, September 4, 2017).

"know":

1. "að vita"—to know (know that): e.g., "vita að hann veit allt" (know that he knows everything), "ég veit ekki hvað gerðist" (I do not know what happened).
2. "að kunna"—to know (know how), to master: e.g., "að kunna ensku" (to know English), "að kunna að hjóla" (to know how to bike).
3. "að þekkja"—to know by acquaintance: e.g., "að þekkja Jody" (to know Jody), "að þekkja bara með nafni" (to know by name only), "að þekkja margar plöntur" (to know many plants), "að þekkja svæðið vel" (to know the terrain well).

"knowledge":

1. "vitneskja"—knowledge (being aware of): e.g., "ég hef enga vitneskju um þetta" (I would translate this as "I have no knowledge of this" or "I know nothing about this"; in some contexts, it might even be appropriate to translate this as "I was not aware of this").
2. "kunnátta"—skill-based knowledge, mastery: e.g., stærðfræðikunnátta (mathematical knowledge), enskukunnátta (knowledge of English).

"belief" in these respects; but, although we have the count nouns "opinion" and "opinions," as well as an adjective, "opinionated," there isn't a verb: "opine" is a philosophical coinage, or a jokey extension of the word. There aren't "opinion systems" or even "systems of opinions," although that's probably just a contingent fact about academic jargon. On the other hand, the adjective "believable" isn't about the agent, in contrast to "opinionated"; it's about whether something—a proposition—is something agents *should* believe.

The robust mass/count differences between "believe(s)" and "know(s)" and their linguistic relatives are exhibited by numerous words. "Marble" when used to describe a small spherical toy (often made from glass, clay, steel, plastic, or agate) is a count noun without a corresponding mass noun. There are the count plural and singular words, "marbles" and "marble"; but we can't say "that's a lot of marble" when speaking of a large collection of marbles. "Marble," however, when used to describe the metamorphic rock composed of recrystallized minerals, is an entirely different word that's a mass noun; here there is no corresponding count noun that takes singular and plural form. (We cannot say of a lot of marble tables in a room, "that's a whole lot of marbles"—it's not even funny as wordplay!) This difference extends to the metaphorical uses of these words: to describe someone as "having lost their marbles" is to metaphorically extend the word "marble" as applied to the small spherical toys; it's not to extend the word "marble" as applied to the metamorphic rock.

3. "þekking"—knowledge, a body of knowledge: e.g., "ég hef enga þekkingu á þessu" (I would translate this as "I know nothing about this" or "I am not at all knowledgeable about this"), "hann hefur mikla þekkingu á bókmenntum" (I would translate this "he is very knowledgeable about literature").

These all function as mass nouns. They're not used in the plural; they're not used with numerals. We don't have an indefinite article in Icelandic, so that test cannot be used for whether a noun is being used as a count or a mass noun.

"believe":

Some verbs that would be translated with "believe that": "trúa því að," "halda að" (no corresponding noun), "telja að" (no corresponding noun), "álíta að."

Then, there is the verb phrase: "hafa þá skoðun að" (have the belief that, or have the opinion that), which might be the best translation of "believe."

"belief":

There are several candidates, but probably the most common ones are:

1. "álit" (pl. "álit")—count noun: e.g., "við ættum að fá fleira en eitt álit á þessu" (I would translate this as "we should get more than one opinion on this").
2. "skoðun" (pl. "skoðanir")—count noun: e.g., "hann hefur sterkar skoðanir á öllu" (I would translate this as "he has a strong opinion on everything" or "he is extremely opinionated"), "ég hef enga skoðun á þessu" ("I have no opinion on this"). This is probably the best word to use as a translation of "belief."

We use fewer nominalizations in Icelandic than in English. For example, I would translate the claim "all his beliefs are true" as "allt sem hann telur satt er satt" (lit.: everything he takes to be true is true) but "allar skoðanir hans eru réttar" (lit.: all his beliefs are correct) is also a possibility.

"Faith" operates similarly to (although not exactly like) "knowledge."[5] To have a lot of faith isn't to have a lot of "faiths." This latter use of "faith" is different (like the case of "marble"): to speak of "faiths" is to speak of various different religions—as in "different religious faiths." Thus, there are two uses of "faith," one as a mass noun and one as a count noun. "Meat" is like "faith" (and like "marble") in this respect. A lot of different "meats," "deli meats," for example, are a lot of different *types* of meat: bologna, salami, ham, and so on.[6] The mass noun "faith" does allow us to talk about *aspects* of a person's faith; we don't, however, often speak of items of faith—in the mass-noun sense of "faith"—although the phrase occurs. "Knowledge" has no count-noun homonym; there are no "knowledges" in any sense (except, perhaps, in recent poorly written academic prose).

Let's focus more closely on "knowledge." This is a standard gradable mass noun, like "meat," "sand," and so on. Oliver can have a lot of knowledge ("lots of knowledge") or, instead, only a little bit. He can have lots of knowledge about trains, but almost no knowledge about cars. Having no knowledge about cars does allow him to have *some* knowledge about cars, nevertheless. His knowledge of trains can be pretty good, although his knowledge of cars may be pretty shoddy. In the same way, Itay can have a lot of meat (or only a little); Itay can have a lot of meat in the refrigerator, although only a small amount of meat in the microwave. Still, a small amount of meat in the microwave is *some* meat in the microwave. And many other words are similar to "meat," "sand," and "knowledge" in these respects.

Next, Oliver's knowledge of trains can be good for an amateur, but inadequate for an Amtrak engineer. Oliver having lots of knowledge about trains can be true if Oliver is an obsessive child with a train hobby, but false if Oliver is an engineer with the same amount of knowledge just hired by Amtrak (because of, say, a fraudulent CV). Thus, context affects whether Oliver knows "a lot" about trains or not. Similar remarks apply to whether Oliver knows a lot, in general, and not with respect to a specific subject matter. If Oliver is a dog, for example, it's OK to say, "Oliver knows a lot," although that's sarcastic or weird (or at least insensitive) if Oliver—with exactly the same knowledge—is a seven-year-old child.

Mass nouns of this sort allow various degrees of "impurity" in what they're applied to; in the case of "knowledge" this yields that someone's knowledge can (nevertheless) involve falsehoods. "That's a lot of sand" can be said of a mound of sand that also contains (mixed up with it) some gravel, and other impurities like

[5] I owe the reminder that "faith" is a mass noun to Mark Sullivan, who mentioned this to me at the bar at the Heights Café on August 13, 2017.

[6] I remember, as a child, often hearing the phrase "that's baloney," or "that's full of baloney" used to describe claims regarded as ridiculous (even claims by highly placed officials). It seems to have disappeared from the vernacular; see section 8.6 for descriptions of contemporary ways we have of making the same point.

rat droppings. *How much* there can be of something other than sand in what's nevertheless a pile of "sand" depends (again) on context, and on other factors of usage. "There's the sand," someone can say of a pile of stuff, even though it's not pure sand. The same is true when describing something as "sandy": something else can be involved besides sand (say, some dust). In the same way, we can describe someone as "knowledgeable," even though some of what's involved in what's being indicated is false. It's hard to find usages like "There's the knowledge"—"knowledge" isn't like "sand" in this way; but someone can say (proudly, perhaps) tapping his head, "there's knowledge in here," or perhaps, "here's the knowledge about that," if, say, we were wondering who knew how a particular set of bureaucratic procedures worked. Again, this is true even if some of what that person thinks about these procedures is wrong. Similarly, A might pass on his knowledge to B, even though a number of falsehoods are being passed on as well. Similar things can be said about "water," as *many* philosophers have noted. (Thanks to Florence Bacus here for disagreement.)

As I've just mentioned, this property of the mass noun "knowledge" is why "knowledge" isn't *factive*. Oliver's knowledge of trains being "really good" is nevertheless compatible with his not knowing quite a bit about trains, and getting a lot wrong. How much he can get wrong, again, depends on what may broadly be described as "context." A child with an obsessive train hobby can get a lot wrong and still be described as having "a lot of knowledge" about trains; the same number of mistakes by an Amtrak engineer isn't compatible with the claim that *he* "has a lot of knowledge" about trains. Even a lot of knowledge about something, nevertheless, is never perfect; to have a lot of knowledge about a subject area isn't to know everything about that subject area; knowledge comes in degrees. How little knowledge can someone have about something to be described nevertheless correctly as having knowledge? That depends. "Well, he has *some* knowledge of the Civil War, but not enough to pass the course," we might say about a student who got several answers right.

Some cognates of "knowledge" are also gradable, notably the adjective "knowledgeable." Stanley (2005, 37) describes two linguistic tests for "the gradability of expressions."[7] The first is that any such expression should allow for modifiers. We have, for example:

[7] Stanley's examples aren't of gradable "expressions" but only of gradable adjectives. What *about* gradable verbs? Well, some verbs are gradable—that means they can be modified by various degree adverbs. Some examples: We very much enjoyed the vacation; I agree completely; His attitude kind of gets on my nerves; I was greatly annoyed by her comments; I half believed her story. Natural comparative constructions are available in these cases too: We enjoyed the vacation much more this year than last year; I agree with you more than I do with Jason; I was annoyed a lot more by your tone than by your words. Some verbs fail both tests (so they aren't gradable, according to Stanley): "fully boiling" and "completely ridiculous" are examples: *That's completely fully boiling; *That's fully boiling more than this is; *That's very much completely ridiculous; *That is completely ridiculous more than this is completely ridiculous. Although "fully boiling isn't context-sensitive, "completely

John is very tall.
John is really tall.

Similarly, we have:

John is very knowledgeable.
John is really knowledgeable.

Stanley's (2005, 36) second test is that a gradable expression should be "conceptually related to a natural comparative construction." For "flat," "tall," and "small," there is "flatter than," "taller than," and "smaller than." We *don't* have "knowledgeabler than."[8] But that's because it's *phonetically* easy to modify "flat," "tall" and "small" to "flatter," "taller," and "smaller." (*Knowledgeabler* or *knowledgeableer*?) Let's switch to examples of adjectives that are derived from gradable mass nouns, like "blood," "sand," and "water." We can (and do) say "bloodier than" and "sandier than." We can't quite manage "wateryier than" or "waterier than." (Try it sometime.) That doesn't make "watery" less of a gradable adjective than "sandy" or "bloody" (or "knowledgeable"). We often use, instead, the natural comparative "more . . . than," as in "that drink is more watery than this one" or "Jazmin is more knowledgeable than Haruto." So with this phonetic caveat, "knowledgeable" passes Stanley's second test.

The gradable adjective "knowledgeable" also occurs in "about" constructions. "Leilani is very knowledgeable about trains," we can say. What's required of Leilani for this isn't complete knowledge about trains (omniscience about trains,

ridiculous" *is* context-sensitive; so lack of gradability doesn't necessarily show context insensitivity, as Stanley seems to assume. Incidentally, *propositional* "believe(s)" seems to fail the two tests: *Ismael believes that Peter is tall more than Jiali believes that Peter is tall. *Ailsa completely (totally) believes Peter is tall. Similarly, *Benedict believes God exists more than Peter believes God exists; but (interestingly) "Benedict believes in God more than Peter believes in God" seems acceptable. On the other hand, "hope(s)" seems to pass these tests: Callum hopes the Royals will win the game more than Peter hopes they will win the game. Callum totally hopes the Royals will win the game; Callum really hopes the Royals will win the game. On the other hand, *Callum completely hopes the Royals will win the game. The data is complicated.

Anyway, consider "sufficiently tall" (see Halliday (2007), Stanley (2004, 43–44), DeRose (2009, 169 n. 8)). "Sufficiently tall" is context-sensitive, but not gradable: *Santiago is very sufficiently tall; *Santiago is really sufficiently tall; *Santiago is more sufficiently tall than Mary. "Totally ridiculous" is similarly context-sensitive, but not gradable. More accurately (Halliday [2007, 390]), "modified comparatives" (e.g., "sufficiently tall") are gradable$_1$ (their extensions can alter due to changes in standards) but not gradable$_2$ (they can't apply in different degrees to different objects). Halliday hypothesizes that "know(s)" is similarly gradable$_1$, but not gradable$_2$; and that gradability$_1$ is the only form of gradability relevant to contextualism. In sections 3.3 and 3.4, I give examples that show that "know(s)" isn't gradable in *any* sense.

[8] My spellcheck *and* grammarcheck both indicated disapproval when I typed this in. (Of course, "grammarcheck" was rejected too.)

as it were), nor is it required that all her "knowledge" about trains be true. Even being "very knowledgeable" or "completely knowledgeable" is compatible with getting things wrong—maybe many things wrong.[9]

There are also the verb expressions "know(s) . . . about" and "know(s) . . ." that are derivative from "knowledge" and inherit its properties; that is, they too are gradable, contextually sensitive, and applied on the basis of the amount of knowledge that the agent has. Oliver, for example, can know a lot about trains; again, knowing a lot about trains may be true if Oliver is a child with an obsession about trains, although false if Oliver is an Amtrak train engineer. We can also say, "Oliver doesn't know that much about trains" or even "what he knows about trains isn't very good." (Imagine we're judging two candidates for a job and discussing their answers after an interview.) Oliver, of course, can also know a lot, without specifying any subject area at all. (Some annoying people are like that: they know *a lot*—that is, they know a lot about *everything*.)

It's relatively unnoticed (in the epistemic literature) that "knowledge," "knowledgeable," and the usage of "know(s)" and "know(s) about" related to these words are *straightforwardly* context-sensitive.[10] Stanley (2005, 38) *almost* realizes this when he discusses these examples:

> John knows Bill better than Mary does.
> Hannah knows logic better than John does.

He describes these, however, as expressing

> the acquaintance relation, what would be expressed in German by *kennen* rather than *wissen*. It is only the gradability of propositional knowledge ascriptions that is at issue in contextualism in epistemology.

[9] Stanley (2005, 36 n. 1) observes that gradable "expressions . . . can often occur with measure phrases." "Knowledgeable" doesn't. But gradable "expressions" can also often *not* occur with measure phrases. "Sandy" and "bloody" are examples. That's apparently because all these adjectives are derived from mass nouns. (I'm guessing here.)

[10] Another thing (that's weird) about this literature—as I already intimated in note 7—is that contextualists (and their opponents, e.g., Stanley and Hawthorne) largely debate the contextualist properties of the *verb* "know(s)" along the model of gradable *adjectives*. DeRose (2009, 169 n. 8) writes: "I am not—here nor anywhere in this volume—attempting an indirect positive argument for contextualism that takes as its premiss that some other term, like 'tall,' is context-sensitive, and then argu[ing] that because 'know(s)' is so similar to 'tall,' 'know(s)' too is context-sensitive. As I admitted, such an indirect argument would be very insecure, in my opinion, because, while there are very important similarities between the behaviors of 'tall' and 'know(s),' there are also many important differences. (We are, after all, comparing a verb with an adjective!)" That's what DeRose *writes*, but-but-but . . . *why* are we comparing a verb to an adjective? Shouldn't the discussion in this literature focus directly on gradable *verbs* and the like? And why (similarly) isn't the gradable adjective "knowledgeable" consequently compared to other gradable adjectives like "tall," from which its behavior *is* (largely) indistinguishable?

This, it should be clear from the foregoing discussion, is an inadequate description of the examples I've given, for example, "Hannah is more knowledgeable than John"; it's similarly inadequate as a description of "Hannah is more knowledgeable about logic than John is" and "Hannah knows more about trains than John does."[11] It isn't completely absurd on the face of it to suggest that "Hannah is very knowledgeable about geography but John isn't that knowledgeable" is about Hannah being more *acquainted* with the subject of geography (although it sounds pretty off *to me*); but saying that "Hannah is very knowledgeable, but John isn't" is about Hannah being "more acquainted" (with something) than John does look palpably wrong. Is the subject that Hannah is acquainted with supposed to be *everything*?

Let me conclude this section by stressing a couple of notable properties of "knowledge" that are directly due to its being a mass noun—and that distinguish it from the verb "know(s)." The first is that, like "meat," it's open to subcategorizations: there can be different kinds of knowledge even though there aren't, as a result, different kinds of specific cognitions of knowing. A particular instantiation of this is how "knowledge" often separates from understanding. Someone can know something without understanding it, the way someone can know the economy is crashing without really understanding what that means. The same knowledge (the same items known) can be accompanied by different varieties and degrees of understanding; someone can know a lot of calculus while understanding very little of it. That's because understanding what one knows involves recognizing implications of what one knows, or, at a minimum, having other knowledge the agent (who lacks understanding) doesn't have, or it involves global recognitions of how what one knows is internally connected or connected to other areas of knowledge. None of this intrudes into "S knows *p*," for specific *p*; in this respect sheer syntax is a useful guide.

[11] The German is more complicated than Stanley acknowledges; it does *not* illustrate the simple topic-neutral distinction between acquaintance and propositional knowledge that he wants to import into English to sideline these counterexamples against his case. "Kennen" can only quite awkwardly render "Hannah knows logic better than John does" into German. "Hannah kennt Logik besser als John" reads awkwardly (because "Logik" is a mass noun, not a count noun). To handle this, Germans have to say, instead, "Hannah kennt sich mit Logik besser aus als John" ("Hannah knows herself with logic better than John"). It's far more natural to use the verb "weiss," as in "Hannah weiss mehr über Logik als John" ("Hannah knows more about logic than John") or to fall back on noun-phrase transliterations of "knowledge" and say in German, "Hannah hat mehr Logikkenntinsse als John" ("Hannah has more logic-knowledges than John"). Part of the problem is that, depending on the context or topic, German is less forgiving than English about describing people as "knowing logic" or "knowing mathematics" (*weiss*); for example, "Hannah kann mehr . . ." is a matter of knowing *how to do* more logic—this is quite natural, whereas "Hannah kennt mehr . . ." is about knowing more *countable items* and doesn't work with "Logik." I thank Yvonne Raley and Michael A. Schmidt, both native German speakers, for these details.

2.3 "Knowing *p*" and "Knowing that *p*"

Let's turn to the "know(s) that *p*" locution, as in "Oliver knows that Santa Claus doesn't exist." The properties of *this use* of "know(s)" are different from the properties of the usages derived from the mass noun "knowledge." Let's start by observing (again) that it's acceptable to say that some people know certain subject areas better than other people: Grace, for example, can certainly know *more about* Napoleon than Albert. Albert, let's say (Aikin (2014, 19)),

> knows that Napoleon lost the battle of Waterloo, because he once dressed as Napoleon for a dinner party and people kept making jokes about his "meeting his Waterloo" when he lost at the party games. He inferred [correctly] that Napoleon must have lost some battle called "Waterloo." Grace, on the other hand, is a real history buff. She's not only watched a few PBS-type history shows about Napoleon, but she's even read a book about him, and when a famous historian gave a talk at the university, she went to see the presentation.

We can say that "Grace knows her Napoleonic history a lot better than Albert"; we can say that "Grace knows more about Napoleon than Albert"; we can even say that "Grace knows a lot of Napoleonic history," although we might temper this accolade if we were comparing her to, say, the writer Andrew Roberts.[12] In that case, we might say instead that Grace is "knowledgeable about Napoleon—for an amateur, anyway." All of these are claims about the amount of knowledge about Napoleonic history Grace has compared to the amount of knowledge Albert has about the same subject. But we can't say this:[13]

> *Grace knows that Napoleon lost the battle of Waterloo better than Albert does.

If someone *does* say this (odd thing), we can figure out what he means—of course. Our capacity to provide interpretations for even quite mangled English is very good. Or we can ask, "what on earth did you just mean?"—and if the person tells us the kind of story I'm quoting from Aikin, we can "get it"; although we can still complain about "Grace knowing that Napoleon lost the battle of Waterloo better than Albert." After all, he knows *that* (at least), and so he knows *it* just as well as Grace does.[14] It's *everything else* about Napoleon that he doesn't know.

[12] I.e., the writer of Roberts (2015).

[13] Oddly, Aikin (2014) thinks we *can* say this. Stanley (2005) simply observes without argument that we can't say things like this, as he should.

[14] The concluding sentence of the passage quoted from Aikin (2014, 19) is: "Grace knows that Napoleon lost the battle of Waterloo better than Albert." As often happens in philosophy officially written in English, this sentence simply *isn't* English. Aikin (2014) gives several examples (that

Similarly (and perhaps more obviously), we can't say of Grace that she knows Napoleon lost the battle of Waterloo a lot more (or better) than Albert does. We also cannot say that Grace knows *p*, generally, if *p* is false; e.g.:

> *Grace knows that Napoleon lost the battle of Waterloo, although he didn't.

Contrast this with:

> Grace knows a whole lot about Napoleon although she thinks his birth name was "Napoleon."[15]

This usage of "knows a lot," however (section 2.2), derives from the mass noun "knowledge."

Stanley (2005, chapters 2, 3, and 4, but especially chapter 2) makes a sustained—but ultimately unsuccessful—case that the needed contextual sensitivity of "know(s) *p*" or "know(s) that *p*," if it exists, isn't like the contextual sensitivity of any of the uncontested examples of context-sensitive expressions. In particular, he stresses that it flunks the two earlier-mentioned linguistic tests for gradability—allowing for modifiers and being "conceptually connected to a natural comparative construction" (Stanley 2005, 36). These are tests, notably, that the verb "regret(s)" that is in the same syntactic category as "know(s)—and which takes exactly the same sorts of direct objects—nevertheless *passes*. We can say, as Stanley (2005, 41) points out, that:

> Hannah very much regrets that she is unemployed.
> Hannah doesn't regret very much that she is unemployed.
> Hannah regrets very much that she is unemployed.
> Hannah regrets that she is unemployed very much.
> Hannah regrets that she is unemployed more than she regrets that she is unpopular.

These constructions—and others like them that are possible with "regret(s)"—aren't possible with "know(s) that *p*":[16]

similarly fail to be English) to motivate his suggestion that, with respect to a specific sentence *p*, one person can know that *p* better than another person. Since my only point is that none of this is English, I'm passing over the details. I should add that Aikin can certainly coin specialized philosophical terminology, "S_1 *kcnows p* better than S_2 does," and attempt to define *it*. But that's another matter entirely.

15 It was, actually, "Napoleone," as Napoleonic aficionados know (as well as people like me who are constantly searching for examples).

16 Actually, many of these *are* acceptable but not as indicating gradability—rather as an emphasis of just how aware Hannah is of her unemployment. (My thanks to Eric Dean, email, May 25, 2019.)

*Hannah very much knows that she is unemployed.
*Hannah doesn't know very much that she is unemployed.
*Hannah knows very much that she is unemployed.
*Hannah knows that she is unemployed very much.
*Hannah knows that she is unemployed more than she knows that she is unpopular.

Notice also the following contrasting pair:

Hannah regrets that she is unemployed more than John regrets that he's unemployed.
*Hannah knows that she is unemployed more than John knows that he's unemployed.

So, it looks like if "know(s)" is context-sensitive, it must be context-sensitive in a way that's quite different from how other verbs in its syntactic class are context-sensitive. Stanley (2005) canvasses many possible analogies with all the well-understood context-sensitive expressions (indexicals, gradable adjectives, verbs) and finds them all wanting. Consider, however, "sufficiently regret(s)" or "completely regret(s)" (recall the second paragraph of note 7):

*Hannah very much sufficiently (completely) regrets that she is unemployed.
*Hannah doesn't sufficiently (completely) regret very much that she is unemployed.
*Hannah sufficiently (completely) regrets very much that she is unemployed.
*Hannah sufficiently (completely) regrets that she is unemployed very much.
*Hannah sufficiently (completely) regrets that she is unemployed more than she regrets that she is unpopular.

And:

*Hannah sufficiently (completely) regrets that she is unemployed more than John sufficiently (completely) regrets that he's unemployed.

If "sufficiently regret(s)" or even "completely regret(s)" are context-sensitive (I think they are), then gradability isn't a very good test for context sensitivity; and Stanley hasn't made the case that the verb "know(s)" doesn't act like other context-sensitive *verbs*.[17]

[17] Or, anyway, "modified comparatives," as Halliday (2007) calls them. Other examples: "totally hate(s)," "really like(s)," "naively believe(s)," and so on. All of them fail Stanley's tests although all of

Regardless, Stanley (2005, 73) then says:

> A complete case against the contextualist would involve canvassing every kind of context-sensitive expression, and showing some clear disanalogy between the behaviors of expressions of that kind and instances of "know that *p*." This is obviously a task that cannot be accomplished here. However, the above arguments are not thereby rendered idle. Before such a task is undertaken, one might think that there are surely some context-sensitive expressions that behave like knowledge ascriptions. But the above discussions show that there is no familiar kind of context sensitivity upon which to base the alleged context sensitivity of knowledge ascriptions. The burden of proof is therefore on the contextualist to produce one.

Stanley understates the task by saying "it cannot be accomplished *here*"; after all, still not ruled out (and impossible by these tools *to* rule out) is the possibility that "know(s)" is *uniquely* context-sensitive.[18] Stanley *can't* rule out this annoying position because he takes the thought-experiment evidence seriously that contextualists rely on to confirm their claims about the context sensitivity of "know(s)": cases in which we have different "intuitions" about what the participants in these cases know, and in which these intuitions seem driven by factors irrelevant to the apparent epistemic standards in play. The contextualist invokes differences in context to explain these differing "intuitions"; Stanley, and other anti-intellectualists (e.g., Fantl and McGrath (2009)), instead invoke differences in the practical costs to the participants that they conclude must be among the factors that determine the know(s) relation; and knowledge relativists, finally, invoke differences in contexts of assessment. We must look closely at the cases that motivate these positions, and I do so in the next chapter. Because of the uniqueness possibility for "know(s)," it can only be on the basis of these cases that debates over correct systematic positions on know(s) attributions will be won or lost.

them are context-sensitive. All of them seem gradable$_1$ in Halliday's sense (as described in the second paragraph of note 7); we'll see in sections 3.2 and 3.3 that the relevant uses of "know(s)" aren't gradable$_1$; and, correspondingly, the word isn't context-sensitive. "Hate(s)" and "like(s)" pass Stanley's two tests (and also look context-sensitive); but "believe(s)" seems to fail the two tests, and, anyway, doesn't look context-sensitive (see the examples in note 7). So it looks like modifiers can sometimes yield a context-sensitive modified comparative from a verb that isn't context-sensitive, as "naively" applied to "believe(s)" does.

[18] A uniqueness view is held by many philosophers about the semantic properties of "exist(s)"—the word, many philosophers think, is uniquely different from all the other verbs in its syntactic class. Furthermore, DeRose (2009, 169 n. 8), cited here in note 10, just about *does* embrace the uniqueness claim for the verb "know(s)."

3

The Variability of Know(s)-that Judgments

3.1 First Remarks

This chapter focuses on the primary items of empirical evidence that (have been used to) support epistemic contextualisms of many kinds (including "knowledge relativism," so dubbed by MacFarlane (2005; 2014)) as well as the various anti-intellectualist positions. These are various "cases" or "thought experiments" presented by philosophers that seem to show that our applications of "know(s)" to agents are sensitive to various contextual/agential variables. Controversy arises because these variables aren't the traditional "epistemic" ones—differences in the evidence an agent has, what an agent believes, or how sure that agent is—nor, like tense, are they epistemically innocent. Instead, they're related to the "pragmatic needs" of the agent or even to the pragmatic needs of ascribers or assessors of the knowledge of that agent.

Following the literature, let's describe the traditional invariantist foil position for contextualist and anti-intellectualist positions as a "purely insensitive one." This nomenclature is misleading because traditional positions can be "sensitive" too: the view I like takes know(s) attributions to be sensitive to certain cognitive (epistemic) virtues and vices of the knowing agent.[1] Terminology aside, according to "sensitivity" positions, there are many things that know(s) attributions—at least in principle—can be sensitive to, apart from the pure epistemic qualities of agents; and enough of the possible options have been explored in the contemporary literature that the discussion space has become quite cluttered.

As mentioned, the traditional invariantist position supposedly keeps knowledge standards fixed across all contexts, agents, attributors, and assessors. Furthermore, it doesn't allow salience (or similar psychological factors) to filter content that bears on knowing attributions by excluding (for example) what agents aren't conscious of or what isn't salient to them. Sensitivity positions, by

[1] Recall the discussion, in section 1.8, of the non-modularity of our knowledge tools: the two agents with the same visual senses, a nonhuman S_1 who sees something blue and a human S_2 who sees the same thing the same way, but hasn't checked the background lighting to determine whether the item is really blue. S_1 knows the item is blue; S_2 doesn't.

Attributing Knowledge. Jody Azzouni, Oxford University Press (2020). © Oxford University Press.
DOI: 10.1093/oso/9780197508817.001.0001.

contrast, can allow such psychological factors to affect standards for knowledge and in this way to function as filters.

Contextualist positions are examples of sensitivity positions (DeRose (2009, 2)) "according to which the truth conditions of [knowing ascriptions and knowing-denying ascriptions] vary in certain ways according to the context in which they are uttered."[2] In the case of self-ascribers/assessors, the truth conditions for knowing attributions are sensitive to variables from the context of use. When ascribers or assessors are third parties, *three* pure forms of context-relativity emerge, one in which the variables affecting truth conditions are from the context of the knower, a second where those variables are from the context of the user of the knowing ascription, and a third where they're from the context of the assessor of that ascription. (Not all of these are described as "contextualism" by proponents of epistemic contextualism.) Mixed views have presumably principled conditions on when and how relevant variables are drawn from one or another context.

Pure anti-intellectualist positions focus on individuals rather than on contexts; this is why they can be described as invariantist (or as involving *agential* variables). The standard anti-intellectualist view takes the invariant knowing-that-*p* relation of the agent to be (at least partially) infiltrated by the practical interests of that agent. That is, although the knowing relation itself is invariant across contexts, it depends, in part, on non-truth-conducive (non-epistemic or "impure") factors.[3] The agent's practical goals, her personal stake in the truth of the matter (e.g., what she personally stands to lose or gain), and other "practical interests" help determine, according to this version of interest-relative

[2] DeRose credits Unger (1984) with the idea of contextualism. The main progenitor figure for the view *has* to be J. L. Austin. See DeRose (2009, 47–48 n. 1) for observations and misgivings about this; also see DeRose (2009, 81–82 n. 1).

[3] Stanley (2005, specifically p. 179). DeRose (2009, 25 n. 25) credits Stanley with "isolating" and "labeling" the position "intellectualism" (as well as its opponent position "anti-intellectualism"), although I detect a long-standing anti-intellectualist presence in the American pragmatist tradition, along with an alertness to the (traditional) intellectualist position about knowledge that it was consciously opposing. See, for a contemporary example, Aikin (2011, 21), especially his discussion of his "Principle of Worthwhile Justification." That there are pragmatic encroachments on knowing attributions—that "knowledge is not simply a matter of truth-related factors (evidence, reliability, etc.)" (Fantl and McGrath (2007, 558))—is believed by proponents of a family of positions with a fairly long history even in the analytic tradition—it dates back to the last century at least. "SSI" ("subject-sensitive invariantism") is recent nomenclature, however; so is "IRI" ("interest-relative invariantism"), a term which Stanley (2005) prefers and Wright (2017) uses, and which strikes me as better. Fantl and McGrath prefer "purism" to "intellectualism." (See Fantl and McGrath (2007, 561 n. 5) for some discussion of the tortured terminology in this area. I should add, however, that "impurism" as they define it is compatible with no pragmatic encroachment—see my discussion of this in section 10.2, note 8.) Recent opponents of intellectualism are Fantl and McGrath (2002; 2007; 2009), Hawthorne (2004) (tentatively), Hookway (1990), Owens (2000), and Stanley (2005). I'll sometimes shift on the available nomenclature here—often because of whom I'm quoting or commenting on.

invariantism, when agents know and don't know certain things in certain cases. The position is nicely described this way (Fantl and McGrath (2007, 559)): "a subject's stakes in whether p can be relevant to whether she is in a position to know [p]." In third-party cases, we again have three possible variants, where the knowledge relation can be infiltrated by the practical interests (or salience conditions) of agents, attributors, or assessors; and as before, mixed views (where the interests or salience conditions of assessors, attributors, and epistemic agents become relevant in some systematic and principled way, depending on the cases).[4]

One last kind of theory variation is possible. Nothing (in principle, anyway) rules out various combinations of contextualism *and* anti-intellectualism. (Lewis (1996), for example, is such a case.) It can be, that is, that certain impure factors infiltrate the knowing relation—certain sorts of pragmatic needs or salience conditions of certain individuals—while at the same time (in other respects) the knowing relation is relative to one or another context.

I'll make it clear—if it isn't already—that I'm both anti-contextualist and intellectualist: I reject *all* the positions just canvassed. This might sound like I'm what DeRose describes as a "classical invariantist." According to DeRose (2009, 26):

> On CI [classical invariantism], regardless of the speaker's conversational situation and regardless of the subject's situation, one set of epistemic standards comprise the relevant truth-conditions that govern all knowledge-attributing and knowledge-denying claims.

If CI, as so described, implicitly ranges over agents—one set of epistemic standards goes for all of them—then I reject the position. (DeRose's formulation is open to more than one interpretation.) I'll show later in the book that standards of knowing can differ, due to the differing cognitive properties of agents; these aren't differences in the agents' "practical aims," nor do they involve other "pragmatic encroachments"—instead, it's that the agents' epistemic *capacities* determine the knowledge standards appropriate to them.

There's also a more important reason this formulation of CI doesn't correctly characterize the invariant-insensitivity position I think we're forced to. The words "know(s)," "knowledge," and the like (but *not* "justified," "justification," and the like) are criterion transcendent. This means these words can't, *on the basis of their perceived meanings*, be characterized (defined) once and for all as having a fixed set of standards of application. In section 11.2, I explain criterion transcendence; it will be clear then why criterion transcendence implies neither

[4] Wright (2017, 17) also analyzes the space of possibilities; and see Fantl and McGrath (2009, 34–37) for their taxonomy.

some version of contextualism nor any version of interest-relative invariantism (IRI)—although (to some) it may look like it should. Characterizing "know(s)," and certain other words, as criterion-transcendent exploits a perceived analogy between such words and what are called "natural-kind terms"—"gold," "zebra," etc.—instead of (as contextualists do) attempting to exploit a perceived analogy to context-sensitive words such as indexicals, gradable adjectives, and so on.[5]

Lastly (but this is *very* important), "standards of knowledge" are *vague*; this impacts on our epistemic practices and pronouncements in a number of easily misunderstood ways if the wrong perspective is taken on *vagueness* itself—e.g., that either it's a semantic phenomenon (to be handled in certain semantically specific ways) *or* (along the lines of Williamson (1994)) that it's a metaphysical illusion—because in reality all applications of epistemic words are bivalently sharp, whether we can realize it or not. How to avoid this false dilemma and its bearing on our "know(s)"-ascription practices are explained in section 9.4.

The empirical evidence I spoke of some paragraphs back are the ubiquitous thought experiments (or imaginary cases) that epistemologists use and that are meant to elicit what are commonly described as "intuitions" about whether the agents described in these cases know or don't know certain propositions, and whether we agree that various knowing attributions do or don't apply to those agents. As I indicated in introduction section xi, these thought experiments should instead be characterized as based on common-language presuppositions, and as tests of language generalizations. This is how I'll treat them in what follows.

The most relevant point to stress now about thought experiments is that an easy way to fool ourselves and others about what our judgments about them are is by underdescribing them: failing to provide enough details or supplementary facts in our characterizations of them. (I illustrated this in section 1.6 with timid students.) In such cases, those judging the cases implicitly fill them out in different ways, or they (again implicitly) focus on very different cases that conform to the insufficiently determinate characterizations. No amount of detail or supplementation, of course, will help those with "tin ears" to appreciate what such thought experiments actually show. Supplementing such experiments with actual (published) cases of usage can help a little with this problem.[6] But I stress again: as with all empirical studies (and in science everywhere), evidence is always a subtle and difficult matter.

[5] I discuss the criterion transcendence of the word "exist" and its effect on metaphysics in Azzouni (2017b, chapter 2). The analogy between "natural-kind" words and "know(s)" is also exploited by Williams (1996) and Kornblith (2002), although the lessons for "know(s)" that they draw aren't mine.

[6] But only up to a point, because people with tin ears talk too, and the results of their chatter can be found, for example, everywhere on the web! Simple surveys of usage always introduce false positives—e.g., the "result" that "know(s) that" isn't factive.

In any case, in section 3.2, I present (some of) the cases that are the evidence for contextualism/subject-sensitive invariantism (SSI); in sections 3.3 and 3.4, I undercut their value for contextualism; in section 3.5, I do the same for SSI; in section 3.6, knowledge relativism is undermined, and in section 3.7, I evaluate (negatively) attempts to save classical invariantism by pragmatic explanations. In section 3.8, finally, I point us toward the additional analysis of "know(s)" and its linguistic relatives that needs to be undertaken in later chapters in order to provide a coherent description of the semantics of "know(s)" and of the roles of knowing attributions.

An underlying theme of this chapter is that the thought experiments that both contextualists and anti-intellectualists rely on don't show what they claim they show. This is because crucial to our usage practices are *comparison-case judgments*—how speaker-hearers react to comparisons *between* scenarios. Many contemporary contextualist and anti-intellectualist proponents have underappreciated the evidential force of these user judgments against their own positions. As it turns out, native comparison-case judgments robustly illustrate how speaker-hearers insist on imposing pure truth-conducive *uniformity* on their knowing attributions: speaker-hearers try to *eliminate* attribution variations when comparing cases where only pragmatic or contextual factors are what are perceivably different—differences in understanding or other variations in cognitive competence, however, acceptably infiltrate knowing attributions.

That is, although when focusing on individual cases (or being *in* them) speaker-hearers shift in their judgments of knowing attributions in various ways that appear superficially compatible with some version of contextualism/anti-intellectualism (as contextualists and anti-intellectualists recognize), they refuse to do so when the cases are compared.

In this respect, judgments about knowing attributions are very similar to the recognition of inferential fallacies: just about anyone can recognize that a piece of reasoning (that they otherwise have a tendency to accept) is fallacious when it's compared to similar pieces of reasoning with conclusions they recognize shouldn't be accepted on the basis of the premises they start with. Usage results about comparison cases, as a result, undercut both contextualism and anti-intellectualism. They do so by showing that a focus on immediate judgments about individual cases fails to take account of our *full* knowing-attribution practices. (So, in my view, most of this literature theorizes on the basis of an only partial account of the relevant data.)[7]

[7] None of the comparison-usage results described in this chapter—including conditions on when speaker-hearers retract—has been investigated (as far as I know) as of this date by xphilosophical studies. Such studies—so that they avoid confounders and other artifacts of sociological survey tools—will be even harder to design than the current kinds of cases now studied (the design of which is very hard already, as the controversies in the field indicate).

3.2 Some Thought Experiments that Are Problematic for Classic Invariantists

Here are four cases.[8]

Low Stakes. Hannah and her wife Sarah are driving home on a Friday afternoon. They plan to stop at the bank on the way home to deposit their paychecks. It is not important that they do so, as they have no impending bills. But as they drive past the bank, they notice that the lines inside are very long, as they often are on Friday afternoons. Realizing that it isn't very important that their paychecks are deposited right away, Hannah says, "I know the bank will be open tomorrow, since I was just there two weeks ago on Saturday morning. So we can deposit our paychecks tomorrow morning."

High Stakes. Hannah and her wife Sarah are driving home on a Friday afternoon. They plan to stop at the bank on the way home to deposit their paychecks. Since they have an impending bill coming due, and very little in their account, it is very important that they deposit their paychecks by Saturday. Hannah notes that she was at the bank two weeks before on a Saturday morning, and it was open. But, as Sarah points out, banks do change their hours. Hannah says, "I guess you're right. I don't know that the bank will be open tomorrow."

Low Attributor–High Subject Stakes. Hannah and her wife Sarah are driving home on a Friday afternoon. They plan to stop at the bank on the way home to deposit their paychecks. Since they have an impending bill coming due, and very little in their account, it is very important that they deposit their paychecks by Saturday. Two weeks earlier, on a Saturday, Hannah went to the bank, where Jill saw her. Sarah points out to Hannah that banks do change their hours. Hannah utters, "That's a good point. I guess I don't really know that the bank

[8] I quote Stanley (2005, 3–5) verbatim. As he notes, these cases "have largely been made famous by others." And in his second note, he writes, "In particular, most of the examples have been discovered by Stewart Cohen and Keith DeRose." DeRose (2009, 2 n. 1) describes their history (in relation, specifically, to him and Stewart Cohen). See, however, Rysiew (2001, 507 n. 1) for references to similar cases designed by other authors. DeRose (2009, 59 note 11) criticizes Stanley's characterization of these cases because Stanley has some of the characters say the word "really," as in "really don't know": "This becomes problematic because the function of the 'really' is quite unclear." Stanley's ear is better about this, frankly, because "really" is just the word people would use in such circumstances (the dialogue exchange is completely natural). Whatever role "really" is playing is simply something the contextualist is required to analyze and deal with! (I also note that "really," so used, has posed complications for xphilosophical studies; see, for example, Weinberg, Nichols, and Stich (2001), Starmans and Friedman (2012), and Cullen (2010).) I'm not saying that sorting out the role of "really," here and elsewhere, is easy; Austin's (1962) work indicated otherwise long ago. But puzzles about the ordinary use of some words shouldn't be used to "cook the data" by illegitimately excluding cases. (I should add that, in any case, "really"—as used by speakers in cases like this—ultimately doesn't, in my view, cut one way or the other against contextualism.) See Wright (2017, 15–16) for very nice alternative presentations of Stanley's first, second, and fourth cases. I've left out a fifth case Stanley gives ("High Attributor–Low Subject Stakes") that involves a cell-phone call to "Bill." I discuss this case in Azzouni (forthcoming d). It's irrelevant, given my current purposes.

will be open on Saturday." Coincidentally, Jill is thinking of going to the bank on Saturday, just for fun, to see if she meets Hannah there. Nothing is at stake for Jill, and she knows nothing of Hannah's situation. Wondering whether Hannah will be there, Jill utters to a friend, "Well, Hannah was at the bank two weeks ago on a Saturday. So she knows the bank will be open on Saturday."

Ignorant High Stakes. Hannah and her wife Sarah are driving home on a Friday afternoon. They plan to stop at the bank on the way home to deposit their paychecks. Since they have an impending bill coming due, and very little in their account, it is very important that they deposit their paychecks by Saturday. But neither Hannah nor Sarah is aware of the impending bill, nor of the paucity of available funds. Looking at the lines, Hannah says to Sarah, "I know the bank will be open tomorrow, since I was there just two weeks ago on Saturday morning. So we can deposit our paychecks tomorrow morning."

Stanley (2005, 5), writes:

> Suppose that, in all [four] situations, the bank will be open on Saturday. Here, I take it, are the intuitive reactions we have about these cases. In Low Stakes, our reaction is that Hannah is right; her utterance of "I know the bank will be open" is true. In High Stakes, our reaction is that Hannah is also right. Her utterance of "I don't know that the bank will be open" is true. In Low Attributor–High Subject Stakes, our intuition is that Jill's utterance of "she knows the bank will be open on Saturday" is false. In Ignorant High Stakes, our reaction is that Hannah's utterance of "I know the bank will be open tomorrow" is false.

These examples, in this case of bank hours, in other cases of when planes or trains are scheduled to leave or arrive (e.g., Cohen (1999) or Fantl and McGrath (2002; 2009)), of what itineraries for trips describe as their trajectories (as opposed to what might actually happen, or is even planned to happen by airlines, bus companies, or railroad companies), of when restaurants are open (and what's on their menus), and so on, are a large and broad class of examples of what we may describe as "ordinary knowledge." (They aren't, of course, everything that ordinary knowledge comes to, but they do amount to an awful lot of it.) We commonly rely on what we take to be knowledge of schedules, itineraries, menus, and the like, to guide our actions, to advise each other, and to evaluate each other's knowledge about these things—all in pretty much the ways that Sarah and Hannah in these (and other) scenarios do.

More importantly, we (largely) *shift* in our knowledge and knowing attributions in just the ways that Stanley (and other anti-intellectualists as well as contextualists) take these cases to illustrate—although, as Wright (2017) shows, when enough cases are laid out, it seems that the specifics of the shiftiness don't clearly support contextualism, IRI, *or* knowledge relativism because it's not obvious that the shiftiness exhibited in *all* these cases can be systematically explained by any of these views.[9]

That very same shiftiness of the judgments exhibited across the cases, however, is the primary threat that these cases pose to classical invariantism. And this challenge remains even if the fine structures of the "invited intuitions" are disputed.[10] That is, even if someone's "intuitions" about these cases—specifically one's impression of what we (or that person) would say about who knows what and who doesn't know what—aren't as sharp as (or quite in accord with) what Stanley or Wright (or others) suggests about these cases, it should be realized that nevertheless Stanley is right (and so are the contextualists, in particular, DeRose and Cohen, who use examples like these) that our know(s)-attribution judgments *do* shift, and that the shifts are roughly along the lines illustrated. The examples, that is, are specific encapsulations of a broader observation that contextualist and anti-intellectualist arguments *start from*: that our claims about what we know (and what others know) change under various sorts of pressures that are recognizably not relevant to truth conduciveness.[11]

[9] Consider Wright's case 5 (2017, 17–18):

> [Ashley and Bobbie's mortgage lender will foreclose unless the cheques are in the account by Monday to service their monthly repayment. Ashley and Bobbie know this.] They ask Chris, another customer who is leaving the building, whether the bank will be open tomorrow. Chris says "yes, I happen to know it will—I was in here a couple of weeks ago on a Saturday." Ashley says to Bobbie *sotto voce*, **"Hmm. That person doesn't know any better than we do.** We had better join the queue." *Invited intuition*: Ashley speaks truly even though—as we may suppose—there is nothing at stake for Chris, the subject, in whether the bank will open on the Saturday or not. [italics and boldface are Wright's]

This looks like a win for ascriber contextualism. But Wright's case 6 (2017, 17) supports IRI. In case 6, case 5 continues as follows:

> Chris is puzzled that Ashley and Bobbie have joined the queue again notwithstanding the advice [he just gave them. He] asks them about this. They explain their concern about the risk of foreclosure of their mortgage. Chris says, "OK, I understand now. I guess you guys had better not assume that the bank *will* be open tomorrow." *Invited intuition*: Chris speaks truly. But since "You know that P but had better not assume that P" is some kind of conceptual solecism, Chris's remark is presumably a commitment to **"You do not know that the bank will be open tomorrow"** (italics and boldface are Wright's).

Wright gives yet another case (5*) that supports knowledge relativism, although that position also faces a problem with case 6, just given. I'll return to the question of what position(s) can be supported by judgments elicited by *all* these cases in section 3.6.

[10] I'll add that shiftiness of judgments in some such spread of cases appears to be something being established (although with some controversy) via xphilosophical studies as well. See Pinillos and Simpson (2014) for discussion.

[11] The "intuitions" elicited by these examples aren't the "evidence" for these knowing-attribution judgments—at least as I see it. Rather, we have widespread tendencies to shift our knowing attributions in these kinds of cases—these are tendencies that *everyone* shares; and this should be easily recognized by alert observers of our common-world sociology (not to mention relatively sober self-observers), even *before* thinking about (or being introduced to) these examples. That is, these philosophical scenarios should, ideally, function as *reminders* of what all of us already know we do, and not as *proofs* of this.

One point about descriptions of these examples should be stressed. Stanley writes (and I quoted him) that "In Low Stakes, our reaction is that Hannah is right; her utterance of 'I know the bank will be open' is true. In High Stakes, our reaction is that Hannah is also right. Her utterance of 'I don't know that the bank will be open' is true." Some contextualists separate the Hannah-is-right judgment from Hannah's-utterance-is-true judgment. DeRose (2009, 49, n. 2), when speaking of such cases, writes that his "intuitions" about the "object-level question" about whether characters in a story know or don't know something "would be far more wavering and uncertain than are my intuitions that the claims made in the cases are true." Cohen (1999, 58ff.) similarly distinguishes between whether speakers in the cases use "know(s)" correctly and whether they know or not. Pynn (2017, 34) also supports this distinction in judgments. It's important to notice that the impression that these judgments come apart, that one judgment, say, is more "wavering" than the other, is *not* intuitive—despite what DeRose (especially) says. They are however exactly what the intuitive judgments of speakers *would be* if (i) contextualism were true, and (ii) if speaker-intuitions reflected the fact of contextualism. It's data against contextualism, therefore—although only prima facie data—that apart from theorists like DeRose, speaker-hearer judgments about Hannah being right versus Hannah's usage being right don't separate the way contextualism requires. So, Stanley is right to treat these judgments alike in his attribution of the judgments "we" make about the cases: if we think the speakers in the story speak truly about what they know, then we think they truly know what they speak of knowing. The particular versions of contextualism that Cohen and DeRose support (agent-relative contextualism) must explain away these impressions of usage somehow or other.[12]

With respect to these examples, Stanley argues that the judgment shifts about what the agents (Sarah, Hannah, and so on) know, is directly due to the various agents' practical stakes in the outcomes (in this case, how costly mistakes about the bank's hours will be to the agents involved). Other examples offered by contextualists—notably, examples derived from classroom discussions of the standard sceptical scenarios—seem to support a far thinner factor inducing shifts in judgment (at least at times): mere salience of certain possibilities that we're (otherwise) not thinking about. An agent merely being made to focus on

[12] Kompa (2002, 82) treats this as an "unpleasant consequence" of contextualism; Cohen and DeRose—as cited—seem to just to accept the counterintuitiveness, but I don't see how they can do so without at least trying to explain it away. Bach (2005, 60) suggests it can only be handled if "the relevant standards are made explicit" and indicated verbally as differing, as in (Bach's example) "Martha said something true in uttering 'George knows [relative to D_2] that he has hands,' but George does not know relative to D_1 that he has hands." That is (according to me), this is intuitively acceptable only because in such examples our ordinary talk of "know(s)" has been replaced with a specialized know(s) jargon. I discuss this further in section 3.4. (My thanks to Florence Bacus for pressing me about flaws in my earlier discussion of this.)

certain unrealized possibilities, because they've been mentioned in a conversation the agent is participating in, can also apparently shift his (and our) standards for knowing things, as Lewis (1996) suggests.

I stress again the one inescapable conclusion from the foregoing discussion. When thinking about (or being in) various situations, we self- and other-attribute knowings and knowledge in ways that shift in the ways these examples illustrate. And so, this is prima facie bad news for classical invariantism.

Contextualists (and anti-intellectualists) don't merely draw this minimal conclusion. They draw stronger conclusions, utilizing other considerations, that some more specific position—a version of contextualism, anti-intellectualism, or knowledge relativism—is right (and, with some work, can handle *all* the cases). I show why individual cases are bad evidence to focus on *at all* because (in effect) they're designed to leave out a significant aspect of our knowing-attribution practices; they only induce *case-isolated* responses.[13]

3.3 Hawthorne's DSK Principle

I've intimated that a closer look at how non-professional philosophers respond to trans-context knowledge and know(s) attributions reveals that epistemic contextualisms and anti-intellectualisms are prima facie implausible. It's time for that closer look. Let's start with a case where someone (in an arbitrary context and with arbitrary interests) describes what someone else (who may be in another context—of whatever sort—and with possibly quite different interests) believes that he knows. DeRose (2009, 162) offers (for subsequent rejection on the basis of a counterexample) a version of a principle that Hawthorne (2004, 101) originally offered:

> (*Disquotational Schema for "Knows"*—DSK) If a speaker S1 sincerely utters a sentence of the form "A knows that p" where "A" is a name that refers to a subject, then a speaker S2, who is using "A" with the same meaning as S1 and to refer to the same subject S1 refers to, and who is using "p" with the same meaning as S1 and to designate the same proposition that S1 designates, can truthfully assert a sentence of the form "S1 believes that A knows that p," where "S1" is a name that refers to S1.

This principle isn't in the most general form possible (pronouns or descriptions could be employed instead of names). Nevertheless, as it stands, it looks plausible.

[13] Strangely, a case-isolated methodology is used—rather uniformly—in the literature to evaluate the bearing of these cases on epistemic positions; Fantl and McGrath (2009), for example (but typically), never mention retraction phenomena or "going to extremes" (see my section 10.6) although this is extremely important evidence against their position.

Under a broad range of circumstances, that is, speakers deduce straightforwardly (in their *own* contexts) the *beliefs* of a speaker, based on that speaker's know(s) attributions (that occur in his *different* context).[14] This threatens contextualism (although not definitively), as DeRose (2009, 162) notes, because

> it can seem if "knows" were context-sensitive, then no . . . schema like this would govern its use, because if the epistemic standards that govern S2's context are different from (and especially if they are higher than) those that governed S1's context, S2 will seem to be ascribing to S1 a belief—that A knows according to the higher standards—that S1 may well not hold.

DeRose (2009, 163, italics his), however, claims that as far as "*the best and most relevant test cases*" for contextualism are concerned, DSK fails. The best and most relevant test cases are pairs of them where, according to the contextualist, the standards in the two cases are very different, and in which it can be seen that DSK fails. Let's see how this goes—I crib this specific counterexample, and somewhat modify it, from DeRose (2009, 164–165):

> Thelma and Louise have just left their workplace. They can always tell that their weird and reclusive boss, John, is in his office whenever his old discolored (and quite unique) bright blood-red hat is hanging on the hat rack in the hallway outside his office, as it was today. John's employees check that hat rack regularly because he's in his office far less than he should be (and everyone parties at the workplace when he's not there). Furthermore, before Thelma and Louise left, they overheard other coworkers talking about John in a way that strongly indicated he was in his office. Thelma and Louise then go to their local bar (the setting for low epistemic standards), where they talk with other coworkers about who has to pay up the $2 bet on whether John showed up for work that day (his employees often make small bets about this). Thelma and Louise both claim to "know" that John was there. They explain why they "know" this (the notorious hat and what the other coworkers said), and everyone agrees: Thelma and Louise have won the bet. Thelma continues to hang out gossiping with her coworkers. Louise leaves, and just before she gets home, she's stopped by the police. They're investigating a string of gruesome murders that John might be involved with, and so they question her about whether John was at work that day. (The cops are taking careful notes—which scares her.) They clearly already have some reason to think John was at work, and no reason to think that's false (other than that John is often absent from work, which Louise already knows).

[14] For reasons given in sections 1.5 and 1.6, it's unwise to draw from the appropriateness of DSK any principle like: An agent A knows p implies that A believes p.

> Louise, of course, admits that she doesn't "know" whether John was at work today, but she tells them all her reasons for thinking he was: his long-standing habits, the hat, and what she overheard her coworkers saying. The police now ask Louise whether Thelma might "know" whether John was at the office. Louise, of course, knows that Thelma has only the same evidence Louise has about whether John was at the office. She also knows that Thelma is still at the bar drinking (and so Thelma is still in a low-standards epistemic context, according to the contextualist). Nevertheless, she denies that Thelma knows any more than she does about John's whereabouts.

According to DeRose (2009, 165), we need only pose this question about this case to make it into a counterexample to Hawthorne's DSK:

> [While talking to the police], will Louise say, "Thelma believes that she knows that John was at the office yesterday"? [The claim that she will] seems to me at least somewhat clearly wrong. Yes, as Louise heard, Thelma said, "I know John was at the office yesterday." But Louise too made just such claims about herself while she was at the [bar]. And now Louise is telling the police that she "doesn't know." And it seems quite wrong for Louise to say, while [in a high-standards case, talking to the police,] that either she or Thelma "believes"/"believed" that she "knew"/"knows."

DeRose's presentation of this case is quite long (and, as a result, so is my condensation of it); despite this, it's still very much underdescribed. In particular, by spelling out details about the case, we can see both that it doesn't pose a counterexample to Hawthorne's DSK and that it doesn't support the contextualist gloss of how these know(s) attributions go.

Consider this variation. Suppose the police know that Thelma (and Louise) said that they knew John was at the office when they were at the bar. So one of the cops says testily, "Wait a minute, when you guys were at the bar, Thelma said she knew John was at the office. So how do you get off saying she didn't believe that she knew that John was at the office?"[15] That is, the natural thing for the cop to say is—using DSK to draw an inference on the basis of what Thelma said—"Thelma believes that she knows." The one thing Louise *can't* say in response to this challenge is "She did say that, and sincerely, but, after all, she didn't believe it." She *has* to say something like the following:

> Look. We were both drinking. *A lot*. We were in *a bar*. We were trying to collect on *a $2 bet*. So Thelma said she knew John was at the office even though she'd only seen

[15] The cop could also naturally say this in the present tense: "So how do you get off saying she doesn't believe that she knows John was at the office?" The result is the same.

> his hat, and overheard some coworkers saying things about him that made it sound like he was in his office. And me too. You shouldn't hold this against us. We really didn't know where John was, and of course we didn't really believe we did either.

One imagines an irritated cop saying, "You said you *knew* he was at the office to win a $2 bet?!"[16]

So, one conclusion that possibly follows is this: DSK needs a supplemental (and constructive) caveat of some sort. Here's one:

> (DSK*) Suppose a speaker S1 sincerely utters a sentence of the form "A knows that p" where "A" is a name that refers to a subject. Then a speaker S2, who is using "A" with the same meaning as S1 and to refer to the same subject S1 refers to, and who is using "p" with the same meaning as S1 and to designate the same proposition that S1 designates, can truthfully assert a sentence of the form "S1 believes that A knows that p," where "S1" is a name that refers to S1, *provided that* S2 doesn't instead (on behalf of S1) deny that S1 thinks that A knows p.

Questions about how to fix Hawthorne's DSK aside, a more significant and ominous fact is intruding that threatens contextualism (and ultimately all forms of anti-intellectualism too). This is that speakers have a widespread practice of making their judgments consistent (by *withdrawing* one or another knowing attribution). Indeed, this is something they invariably do when faced with pairs of cases like the ones section 3.2 opened with.

3.4 Comparing Knowing and Knowledge Attributions Across Contexts

So, let's return to the cases from section 3.2. What happens when native speakers consider *pairs* of these, for example, High Stakes and Low Stakes, after having considered them individually? DeRose (2009, 55 n. 7) writes, "Of course, we may begin to doubt the intuitions above when we consider [the cases] together," wondering, in particular, whether Hannah's claim to know in the first case and her claim not to know in the second case "can really both be true."

[16] This extension of the case has Louise suggesting that she and Thelma were being insincere or at least disingenuous. Another possibility has Louise suggesting they were being sloppy in their thinking. They were thinking they knew—but under pressure, even in the bar, they would have withdrawn the claim. Or, perhaps, they even kind of knew they didn't *really* know. But since everyone was going along with it, who cares? ("Who cares?" . . . until cops show up, that is, and start questioning witnesses.) The crucial point is that Louise *has* to say something along one or another of these lines; and that's bad news for DeRose's purported counterexample to DSK.

That minimizes the almost universal reaction. Instead, what invariably happens is that one of the "know(s)"/"do(es)n't know(s)" attributions is *withdrawn*. What also happens quite often—although *not* invariably—is that the knowing denials are accepted over knowing attributions. That is, people commonly exhibit a sceptical shift in their self- and other-knowing attributions in order to resolve what they experience as an exposed inconsistency in judgment.[17]

Withdrawing one of the attributions after contemplating pairs of cases is a systematic, widespread, and robust phenomenon; I'll illustrate this in the rest of this section. But let's first observe that people don't invariably react this way to similarly structured clashes involving context-sensitive words. Instead of withdrawing one or the other of their claims using a context-sensitive word, they usually discuss (or argue about) what they *meant* by the use of their words.[18]

Consider the word "tall." Imagine I overhear a bit of conversation as I'm passing by the participants in a hallway. Frank (whom I know) says, "Mary is tall." As DeRose (2009, 169–170) notes, in a later conversation,

> I'll be pretty quick to say, "Frank believes that Mary is tall," even though it seems I should consider it very possible that the standards governing the true use of "tall" in Frank's conversation were slightly lower than are those governing the new conversation I'm presently engaged in.

We attribute beliefs to others about whether someone is tall, although we'll make ourselves more or less explicit about the standards involved when a misinterpretation is possible, or when a misinterpretation has been brought to our attention. Suppose, for example, that Lucius says of the 6-foot-5-inch-tall Reeves that "he's tall" to explain why he's such a great high school basketball player. If in a later

[17] DeRose (2009, 178–179 n. 21) is aware of this. These kinds of sceptical shifts are *very* important and must be explained. I do so in section 10.6. I'll also point out that, often, nonphilosophers are *already sceptical* about the supposed knowledge in question even *before* any considerations of stakes (high or low) are brought up; nonphilosophers, that is, often quite quickly deny that "anyone" knows that a bank will be open on a Saturday just because she knows it was open on a Saturday two weeks before. Indeed, I rarely get past the bank setup—when giving these examples to nonphilosophers—before an objection like this comes up. (The examples can be changed to make the evidence stronger.) I think, however, that people reading (or hearing) these examples are always more careful in their knowing attributions than they are in practice. One reason for this is that investigation of any sort involves "costs." People, therefore, are motivated to treat the standards of knowing as lower if they're *in* the situation—in a rush, for example—than when they're contemplating cases. (It's also worth noting that these examples are dated: some people have wondered aloud to me why anyone needs to go to the bank to deposit checks, and some have even wondered what "checks" are. The examples are easily updated.)

[18] That is, nonphilosophers *semantically ascend*. They don't call it "semantic ascent," of course, or (much of the time) realize this is what they're doing. Thus, in the quotations to follow I don't put quote marks around the words people in the examples are talking about; this makes the quotations realistic. Our various tendencies to shift to metacognition and back again without noticing are among the topics of chapter 5 and later chapters.

conversation, we're instead discussing whether Reeves would make a good NBA center, and I say (sarcastically), "Well, *Lucius thinks* Reeves is tall," someone familiar with the earlier conversation, can say, "Wait, that's unfair. Everyone knew Lucius was talking about being tall for high school basketball players, not NBA centers." In contrast, Louise can't say (about Thelma) to the cops, "She meant know for someone sloppy drunk in a bar and trying to collect on a bet."[19] Louise *can* say that Thelma was "being sloppy. She didn't really know." It's not appropriate to say of Lucius, "Well, he was being sloppy in his use of tall. He didn't really mean tall." Lucius would be annoyed if someone said that about him, and he could easily challenge the claim if he was articulate enough.[20]

DeRose, nevertheless, claims our behavior with "know(s)" is like that with "tall." He (2009, 172) writes of the Louise/Thelma case, considering the modification I introduced earlier:

> But now suppose the police officer questioning her has been in radio contact with another police officer who has arrived at the [bar] since Louise left it, and challenges her as follows: "Hey, but didn't you say at the [bar] that you *did* know that John was at work today?" It isn't obvious how Louise might best answer, but one thing that is fairly clear here is that it would be wrong for her to reply, "I didn't say that" or "I never said that." I should stress that by claiming that this response would be clearly wrong, I'm not asserting that it's clear that Louise would be saying something false if she were to say that. *No* verdict about the truth-value of such a problematic claim seems *clearly* correct.

This last sentence is *wrong*, and importantly so. (Recall note 12 and the discussion around it.) Louise would be perceived by everyone to be *lying*. And she would be in a *lot* of trouble with the police if she did say, "I didn't say that" or "I never said that." She could be charged with a crime! This is because these statements *are* (universally, except, apparently, for DeRose and similarly thinking philosophers) perceived as straightforwardly *false*.[21]

DeRose is right that "know(s)" and all recognized context-sensitive expressions are similar in one respect. If an agent *says* the words "he's here," "I'll arrive about now," "This is a mess," or "That animal is tall," she can't subsequently

[19] All the ways you might try to modify this to make it work are absolutely horrible—for example, "She meant know as drunks use the word" or "She meant know by the typical low standards operative in bars" (one imagines the cop saying "huh?" at this point). Or, "she meant know as pretty much everyone uses it when you're not being questioned by cops." I'll return to this shortly.

[20] The context-sensitive word "rich" is similar insofar as we articulate explicitly talk of standards, and either concede shifts in what nonphilosophers would describe in meanings or instead push back. See Richard (2004) and Stanley's response (2005, 55–56).

[21] Exactly this necessary condition on when people are lying or not about what they claim(ed) to know or not to know is applied, on almost a daily basis (during the course of this writing, in 2016, 2017, 2018, 2019, and 2020), by critics *to* Donald Trump and his enablers!

deny she said these things. Where a word seems (to speakers) to have standards that have shifted, what speakers can do—as I've already indicated—is explain "what was meant" by the use of the expression, and in this way show why it's *not* what one would say in the current context (with the current conversational standards). For example:

> When I said, "he's here," I didn't mean in the room with us; I meant in the house.
>
> When I said, "I'll arrive about now," I meant within twenty minutes—as anyone would![22]
>
> When I said, "this is a mess," I didn't mean to claim that there's dirt all over the place, I was talking about the organization of the files . . .
>
> When I said, "That animal is tall," I meant (obviously!) tall for a pygmy elephant. Why would I be talking about *giraffes*?

But these sorts of responses aren't available for "know(s) that *p*." No one can say:

> When I said, I know that John was in the office, I meant I knew that according to low bar standards.
>
> When I said, I know that the theory of human-induced global warming is false, I only meant that I know that according to the typical standards of American politicians (but not according to the standards of ordinary scientists).

DeRose (2009, 210) denies this. He notes that in the Reeves case, Lucius can say in his own defense:

> No, what I was claiming before was that Reeves is tall for a high school player, and that was and still is true. But he certainly isn't tall for an NBA center.

DeRose (210) then asks (rhetorically):[23]

> What could [Louise] say instead in the case of "know(s)"? How could she use "clarifying devices" to correctly express something along the lines of the somehow incorrect ["No, what I said—'I know John was in his office'—was

[22] Imagine a typical fight because someone arrived late. People often argue over whether "about now" can mean "around twenty minutes." They'll argue over, that is, what the standards *held in common* are (in that cultural setting) for "about now": what's the commonly recognized acceptable temporal penumbra.

[23] In this context, DeRose is speaking of the problem in general: that affirmations or denials that oneself (or others) "know(s) *p*" in earlier circumstances sound completely incompatible with denials (or, respectively, affirmations) that oneself (or others) know(s) such. I'm applying the concern to DeRose's "best case," but the inappropriateness reaction always arises if an "explaining away" speech act is contemplated as said instead of the standard thing that speakers do, which is to *retract* the earlier know(s) or knowledge attribution. I turn to the philosophical debate of "now you know it, now you don't" statements right after discussing this case, and illustrate again the lessons I'm drawing here.

> true. But now I wish to add this: I didn't know John was in his office"]. I think there are many locutions by which speakers clarify what they meant and mean by "know(s)," and many of them would work fine here.

He then refers us to a list from earlier in his book (and also to other examples in Ludlow (2005)). Here are some of the examples of "clarifying locutions" DeRose (2009, 182) gives:

> All I was claiming before was that [I know/she knows it] . . .
>
> quite well
> beyond any reasonable doubt
> by ordinary standards
> by any reasonable standard
> with a high degree of precision
>
> I never meant to be claiming [to know it/that she knows it] . . .
>
> for certain
> with absolute certainty
> beyond all possible doubt
> perfectly
> as God would know it

None of this works (and none of the additional examples in Ludlow (2005) works either). The easiest way to see this is to plug any of these into the Louise/Thelma case. We get, for example:

> Suppose the police actually know that Thelma (and Louise) said that they knew John was at the office when they were at the bar. So one of the cops says testily, "Wait a minute, when you guys were at the bar, Thelma said she knew John was at the office. So how do you get off saying she didn't believe that she knew that John was at the office?" Louise says, "I never meant to claim that Thelma knew John was at the office *for certain*."[24]

[24] Ram Neta protests: "I hear nothing wrong with the response 'Well, she didn't believe that she knew it for certain.'" I think he should (or, at least, I urge him to be *very* careful if he ever has to talk to a *cop*). A cop could say. "*Wait a minute*, she either knew it or she didn't." The problem, again, is that Neta's suggested response sounds "mealy-mouthed" ("not speaking frankly or straightforwardly"). And cops often get responses like that, which (by the way) *really* irritates them. Furthermore, a response like this opens the person, who is qualifying the knowledge attribution, to the "well, you should have said so" response, which—when available—is a symptom that a qualification to a knowledge attribution *has to be stated at the time the knowledge attribution is made*: qualifications of in what sense what a person (oneself or others) knows can't be assumed as they *can be* with genuinely contextual expressions, such as "tall." See the discussion of this that follows.

> Or:
> Suppose the police actually know that Thelma (and Louise) said that they knew John was at the office when they were at the bar. So one of the policemen says testily, "Wait a minute, when you guys were at the bar, Thelma said she knew John was at the office. So how do you get off saying she didn't believe that she knew that John was at the office?" Louise says, "I never meant to claim that Thelma knew John was at the office as God would know it."
> Or . . .

That is, substitute any of the items of the second list. The resulting statements either sound like *lies* (because they are), or prevarications (to mildly understate things), or just *weird* (like the last one). Why do they sound like this? Because if someone claims to know *p* (or that someone knows *p*), she isn't understood as claiming to know *p* (or that someone knows *p*) with "qualifications." Such qualifications have to be *stated* to be understood as operative. The reason for that—unlike in the cases of genuine context-sensitive expressions, like "tall"—is that, as we understand "know," "know something beyond a reasonable doubt," and "know something by any reasonable standard," or "perfectly," are recognized as explicit qualifiers *that must be stated because otherwise they can't be assumed.* In particular, they're qualifications of the nature of the *evidence* for a person's claim (in a court of law, for example). Other purported qualifications of "know(s)" either apply naturally only to cases where the mass noun "knowledge" instead is what's involved (but *knowledge* attributions *fit* contextualism, as I illustrated in section 2.2) or are (this is important) coined philosophical terminology that nonphilosophers wouldn't use at all (and, by the way, neither would *philosophers*—certainly not if they were being questioned by the *police*).[25]

I'll *again* go through this disanalogy of "know(s)" with context-sensitive expressions, but using other examples that DeRose gives. Yourgrau's (1983, 183) unnatural dialogue seems to pose a challenge to any contextualist view:

> A: Is that a zebra?
> B: Yes, it is a zebra.
> A: But can you rule out its being merely a cleverly painted mule?

[25] See Hawthorne (2004, 105–106 nn. 120, 121, 122) for valuable details. In general, "clarifying" or "hedge" remarks are more available for some context-sensitive expressions than for others, and more for them than for "know(s)." Hawthorne nevertheless entertains the thought that the differences between "know(s)," "flat," and "empty" are matters of degree. No, because there are resources for speakers to push back with "flat" and "empty," saying of a field that someone else has pointed out a couple of bumps on: "Oh, come on, that's just what we mean by flat!" This kind of pushback isn't available for "know(s)"—and so this isn't a matter of degree.

B: No, I can't.
A: So, you admit you didn't know it was a zebra?
B: No, I did know then that it was zebra. But after your question, I no longer know.

Consider, also, a third-person version of this (due to DeRose (2009, 201)):

A: Does Mary know that that's a zebra?
B: Yes, she knows.
A: But can she rule out its being merely a cleverly painted mule?
B: No, she can't.
A: Ah, so you admit now that she didn't know it was a zebra?
B: No, she did know before your question that it was a zebra. But after your question, she no longer knows.

DeRose (199–200) notes that the last lines of these dialogues sound absurd, but it seems that

> because contextualism will hold that B [or Mary] no longer counts as knowing the animal is a zebra after A raises her question, that last line is what B should or least could say if contextualism were correct.

DeRose (204–206) responds (correctly) on behalf of contextualism that context-sensitive terms don't usually operate the way that the objection presumes a context-sensitive "know(s)" would have to operate in these dialogues. If I say, for example, "When I was in Houston last year, David was here," "competent speakers of English know that by 'here,' I mean New Haven (my present location), not Houston (my location at the time I'm talking about)" (DeRose (2009, 204–205)). DeRose claims this is true of other indexical expressions as well, and he illustrates it with "possible." I'll concede his claim for these dialogues because more threatening ones can be designed.[26] For example, there is DeRose's (206) "fortified first-person dialogue":

A: Do you know that that's a zebra?
B: Yes, I know it's a zebra.
A: But can you rule out its being merely a cleverly painted mule?
B: No, I can't.
A: Ah, so you admit now that you were wrong when you said you knew?

[26] But I'll complain about something I complained about earlier, in chapter 2, note 10: Shouldn't DeRose make his case by examining context-sensitive *verbs*?

B: No, what I said—"I know it's a zebra"—was true. But now I wish to add this: I didn't know that it was a zebra.

A similar, third-person "fortified" dialogue can be constructed:

A: Does Mary know that that's a zebra?
B: Yes, she knows.
A: But can she rule out its being merely a cleverly painted mule?
B: No, she can't.
A: Ah, so you admit now that she didn't know it was a zebra?
B: No, what I said—"She knows it's a zebra"—was true. But now I wish to add this: She didn't know that it was a zebra.

These dialogues honor how DeRose immunizes contextualism against the earlier dialogues: current usages always obey current standards, but *descriptions* of earlier usages characterize them (as contextualism requires) as obeying earlier standards. The result is still unacceptable.

DeRose tries to save contextualism by showing that "is tall" and other context-sensitive expressions operate the same way as "know(s)" does with respect to fortified dialogues. I've already explained why this won't work using the Thelma/Louise case, but I'll spell the problem out (again) explicitly in terms of DeRose's dialogues. Consider the following:

A: Is Reeves tall?
B: Yes, he is.
A: But would he be taken seriously as an NBA center?
B: No, he would not.
A: So you now admit that he's not tall.
B: No, what I said—"Reeves is tall"—is true. But I now wish to add this: Reeves isn't tall.[27]

DeRose is right; this—flatly stated—is weird (wrong, really). Speakers explain or make explicit ("clarify" is the expression DeRose uses) shifts in words. So instead, what's natural is:

A: Is Reeves tall?
B: Yes, he is.

27 DeRose (2009, 209) uses the past tense instead in his version of this dialogue: "Reeves wasn't tall." But that makes an already bizarre remark unnecessarily even worse. It's still problematic when put in the present tense.

A: But would he be taken seriously as an NBA center?
B: No, he would not.
A: So you now admit that he's not tall.
B: No, when I said, "Reeves is tall," I meant tall for a high school student; but that isn't good enough to be an NBA center. He certainly isn't tall by their standards.[28]

Recall from the discussion of the Thelma/Louise case that DeRose thinks we can introduce a similar dialogue for "know(s)." But he's wrong:

A: Do you know that that's a zebra?
B: Yes, I know it's a zebra.
A: But can you rule out its being merely a cleverly painted mule?
B: No, I can't.
A: Ah, so you admit now that you were wrong when you said you knew?
B: No, when I said, "I know it's a zebra," I meant "know for someone who isn't thinking about painted mules." I certainly didn't know it was a zebra by ruling-out-painted-mule standards.

Someone defending DeRose might complain: "Of course no one is going to talk about ruling-out-painted-mule standards for knowledge. *That's just absurd.*" Response: Right, it is absurd. But formulating sharp-grained "standards" on the spot *is* how people speak with respect to "tall," "rich," "flat," and so on, as the previous dialogue illustrates (and as other easily invented ones show as well). I've deliberately crafted this second dialogue analogously; and the failure of "know(s)" to function analogously to "tall" is the only reason the dialogue sounds so bad.

We don't naturally talk about different standards for knowledge *at all*; that's one problem.[29] We certainly don't do so to excuse our failure to consider a challenge to our claim to know something. But in addition, it's acceptable to notice a tacit use of "tall" where "tall for a high school student" is meant, and argue that one is currently being misinterpreted; that's why it's natural to say "tall for a high school student," or "rich for someone living in New Zealand," or "flat for a floor tile," or the like. We do have the expressions "with absolute certainty," "beyond all possible doubt," "perfectly," or "as God would know it" (as DeRose notes), but injecting any of these into a dialogue would yield something equally bizarre:

[28] Or, more succinctly: "No, when I said, 'Reeves is tall,' I was talking about high school students, not NBA centers. He certainly isn't tall by their standards."

[29] Schiffer (1996, 326–327) writes: "no ordinary person who utters 'I know that *p*,' however articulate, would dream of telling you that what he meant and was implicitly stating was that he knew that *p* relative to such-and-such standard."

A: Do you know that that's a zebra?
B: Yes, I know it's a zebra.
A: But can you rule out its being merely a cleverly painted mule?
B: No, I can't.
A: Ah, so you admit now that you were wrong when you said you knew?
B: No, when I said, "I know it's a zebra," I didn't mean "know beyond all possible doubt." I didn't know it was a zebra beyond all possible doubt.
A: Huh?[30]

Qualifying "tall" and other context-sensitive expressions is something speaker-hearers do all the time—that's why "changing the standard dialogues" sounds natural with context-sensitive words like "tall," "rich," and the like. But this is *not* something we do with "know(s)."

The primary reason is that one important thing we *often* do with knowing attributions and, more important, knowing denials is *criticize* one another. We do so while presupposing that the (epistemic) contexts, situations, or whatever, between the critic and the person criticized are *the same*. We do so, very often, by pointing out alternatives that the criticized agent has overlooked, is unaware of, or even is incapable of entertaining (because of lack of knowledge).

Lawlor (2013, 89–90) defends DeRose's analogy between the behavior of "know(s)" and "tall" by denying this. It's instructive to see why her suggestion fails to accommodate what we do with knowing attributions and denials. She claims, to begin with (89), that "there are cases where speakers are fully aware of there being a difference in the situations of their utterances (and they may even be fully aware of the nature of those differences)." She's thinking of cases where experts criticize (or can criticize) amateurs on the basis of the knowledge gaps between experts in an area and those amateurs. So imagine that there's a significant (biological) difference between chain and Pike's pickerels (kinds of fish), and imagine the following scenario (Lawlor 2013, 89):

> Aware: Dav's lab assistant reports that he heard Ben say that he knew the fish is a chain pickerel. Dav knows that Ben is a layperson—he's a local fisherman, who supplies the lab with fish. Dav knows that Ben doesn't know anything about the difference between chain and Pike's pickerels, although he does know that Ben is a knowledgeable lay fisherman.

30 Ram Neta suggests substituting for B's last remark in this dialogue to get something that "doesn't sound nearly as bad": "No, when I said, 'I know it's a zebra,' I DIDN'T mean 'know beyond all possible doubt.' I just meant that I know what zebras are, and I recognized that thing as at least seeming to be a zebra. Of course I didn't know it was a zebra beyond all possible doubt." I don't see why this helps. It's definitely open to the "well, you should have said so to begin with," objection—at best, therefore, it sounds like a (defensive) retraction of the earlier knowledge claim.

Lawlor (89) writes:

> In the Aware scenario, Dav refrains from uttering the overtly metalinguistic "Ben's claim is false."[31] What will he say, then, to clarify for his lab assistant, who is in the dark about Ben and what he knows? When the lab assistant reports "Ben says this is a chain pickerel," Dav knows that they shouldn't take this claim into their conversation. He is aware of the fact that Ben isn't even considering the alternatives that he, Dav, is reasonably concerned with. So Dav will find other ways to resist letting Ben's knowledge claim enter his dialogue with his lab assistant. Dav may focus on the *target* of knowledge, i.e. the proposition *that the fish is a chain pickerel*, or he may focus on the fact that there are open questions concerning its truth. So he may reply, for instance, "Well, that's not so clear" or (with amusement) "I guess he also knows it's not a Pike's pickerel then!"

She generalizes this behavior:

> Observation: When a speaker is fully aware of a difference in epistemic situation, he or she will resist allowing a knowledge claim that concerns the different situation to have any role in his or her own conversation, about his or her own situation.

Lawlor claims, that is, that the speaker won't (directly) deny the knowledge claim but will (merely) exclude it from having a role in "his or her own conversation, about his or her own situation."[32]

[31] She claims, in fact, that Dav will refrain from an overtly metalinguistic denial of Ben's claim because—like all of us—(93) "we sense that something is wrong about [Dav saying Ben's claim to know is false.]" I do not sense any such thing. Presumably, Ben doesn't know what he thinks he knows (notice, *I'm* making a metalinguistic claim here about Ben's remark—completely naturally), and Dav can naturally point this out too. This is an absolutely ubiquitous feature (of our knowing attribution and denial practices) that the contextualist is apparently committed to denying is cogent. Lawlor, in particular, has to redescribe this feature as one in which speakers must endeavor to isolate knowing attributions—ones that they'd normally straightforwardly contradict—from their own discourse contexts. Such discourse contexts are individuated—on Lawlor's view—by the different alternatives speakers are reasonably entertaining.

[32] Lawlor invokes a form of metalinguistic negation where one can object to a "feature of the utterance," instead of denying the utterance itself—see Carston (1996) for discussion—and claims that this is operative in *all* cases where the "situations" of agents differ (that is, where the alternatives that agents are reasonably considering differ) as they often do between experts and amateurs. She writes (90–91): "We have to be quite careful, as theorists, to bear in mind the complicated nature of denials of other's claims. When a speaker is sure there is a difference in contexts, she will resist employing the overtly metalinguistic claim. On that score, contextualism is in the clear—ordinary speakers who are aware of the difference in situations or contexts do not employ the overtly metalinguistic claims that, according to contextualists, are false." This is wrong; see what follows.

It's true that Dav may sneer at the fisherman, as in "I guess he also knows it's not a Pike's pickerel then," or say (as experts so often do) politely, "that's not so clear."[33] It's extraordinarily common, however, to just be blunt about the matter: in this case, to instead make any number of *straightforward* remarks about what Ben claims and what Ben thinks he knows, such as "Ben doesn't know what he's talking about," "Ben is wrong," "Fishermen like Ben don't know the difference between a Pike's pickerel and a chain pickerel—I wish they wouldn't be so stubborn," and so on.[34]

We should give up on contextualism.

3.5 Comparing Knowing and Knowledge Attributions Across Agents

DeRose (2009, 276) writes:

> One natural way to view the difference between SSI [subject-sensitive invariantism] and contextualism is that, while both views allow that different epistemic standards govern knowledge-attributing sentences in different situations, SSI rules that the subject's context sets the standards, while, as Hawthorne writes [2004, 59], according to contextualism, "It is always the ascriber's standards that call the semantic shots, so to speak."

This needs refinement. SSI isn't supposed to relativize knowing attributions to the subject's *context*; it's supposed to relativize knowing attributions to the *subject's* stakes, pragmatic goals, and so on.[35] This is important because two agents in the *same* context can have, of course, very different stakes in what the truth is, and this allows a whole family of straightforward counterexamples to SSI. Imagine, for example:

[33] This kind of understatement—"Well, that's not exactly so," "That's not so clear"—is so widespread a verbal practice among academics when speaking down to nonprofessionals as to be a cliché. One should be able to hear the (slight) presence of condescension in it. (I always avoid using it unless I fear the person I'm talking to is likely to be defensive if I'm blunt, and so I'm trying to be reassuring while simultaneously avoiding being dishonest about that person being wrong.)

[34] There is a large popular literature, by the way, that points out—with various degrees of glee—how most of us don't know what we think we know about watermelons (and other berries), or avocados, bananas, coral, and so on. (See, e.g., Spar (2015) or Spiegel (2014).) Experts (and science popularizers such as journalists) often correct "laypersons" about what they think they know by pointing out that there are alternatives laypersons have overlooked or don't know about. This is pretty straightforward evidence that alternatives themselves—even all the "reasonable alternatives"—that an agent may consider don't insulate that agent's "epistemic situation" from epistemic criticism the way Lawlor's particular brand of contextualism requires.

[35] Although alternatives are possible: Recall the space of possibilities described in section 3.1.

> Jacob is playing Russian roulette with a device like a revolver, but with 6,000 chambers instead of the usual six. There is a bullet in only one of the 6,000 chambers. John, who is watching Jacob play this game (once), has no stake in the outcome. He doesn't care whether Jacob lives or dies (and because John is mildly sociopathic, he doesn't even have a stake in wanting to avoid feeling bad because he's just witnessed a death). Jacob, despite being the possible progenitor of his own death, has an enormous stake in the matter. According to SSI, very-concerned Jacob doesn't know he will live; but because the gun has so many empty chambers, indifferent John does know that Jacob will live.

We generally *do not* think that two agents in the same context and with exactly the same evidence about *p* can be described, respectively, as simultaneously (but respectively) knowing and not knowing *p* on the mere basis of having different stakes in whether *p* is true.[36] Two agents in the same context with the same evidence for a proposition *p* (and with exactly the same capacities to evaluate *p*) are always seen as either both knowing *p* or as both not knowing *p*. That's a very bad problem for SSI, one that contextualism apparently doesn't face since contexts are assumed to be *shared* by speakers.[37] SSI is motivated by the thought that each agent's personal stakes matter with respect to whether he or she knows *p*, or not. If this were right, we should have different knowing-attribution practices from those we actually have; we'd be required to think people differ in what they

[36] Wright (2017, 16) writes: "IRI [interest-relative invariantism—i.e., SSI] allows, apparently, that a pair of subjects may both truly believe that P on the basis of the same evidence or cognitive achievements yet one knows that P, and the other fails to know that P if they suitably differ in pragmatic respects." Nothing stops, of course, subjects suitably differing in pragmatic respects from being in exactly the same context and talking to one another. Worse, nothing stops *one subject* suitably differing in pragmatic respects vis-à-vis two items that we'd otherwise think the subject either both knows or both doesn't know. Consider this clever example due to Neta (2007): S sees two street signs "Main" and "State" at an intersection. It very much matters whether S is on Main Street but not at all whether she's on State Street. So does this mean she does know she's on State but doesn't know she's on Main? Fantl and McGrath (2009, 201–208) attempt to formulate impurist principles that allow intrasubjective purity (although intersubjective impurity). Although I have no doubt such principles can be cobbled together, I think Neta's example indicates there is something fundamentally wrong with the suggestion that interests—in any way—infiltrate our epistemic evaluations. For if that were right, we *would* experience agents, in his cases, as knowing things like being on State but not Main (because, in so many ways, different *aspects* of the *same* things that we can come to know on the basis of pure epistemic considerations differ in their importance to us). The same thought sinks the motivation for epistemic contextualism: If our practical aims don't affect us differently based on pragmatic needs, in Neta's cases, why should contextual variables be involved in epistemic evaluations *at all*?

[37] Imagine, though, bank cases like the ones section 3.2 opened with, but where Hannah and Sarah (or Ashley and Bobbie) have different pragmatic aims (one couple's mortgage check will bounce although the other's won't). They're arguing with each other, given the information about the bank being open two Saturdays before, about whether *they* know it will be open or not. Same context, presumably . . . but what are the "intuitions" here? My prediction is that knowledge relativism does best: *the person to whom the case is being presented* (the knowledge assessor) will decide whether there is knowledge or not on the basis of her own (operative but tacit) standards. I discuss knowledge relativism in the next section.

know even when they are in the same situation, talking to one another, have the same evidence (and capacities), but merely have different stakes in the outcome. We clearly don't think this. When two people are arguing with each other, no one ever says: "Well, whether *p* is true or not matters to you a whole lot more than it matters to me, so it's obvious why you wouldn't know that *p* is true, although I do."[38] Notice that outsiders viewing the case don't say anything analogous either.

If we step back from specific cases, we can notice a general practice we have with knowledge that directly conflicts with the SSI positions. This is that we routinely transfer knowledge to one another.[39] We *do* recognize that a person's interests may preclude their caring about what we have to tell them; we *don't* recognize that a person's interests may preclude what we have to tell them from being knowledge for them as a result. This is striking. I can fail to learn from someone because I don't trust him or because I don't understand him. I can fail to learn from him because my interests prevent me from even *listening*. It's also on the list of failings that he might not provide me with enough evidence to satisfy me, if I ask for it. But that failing is *not* recognized to be due to my practical interests.

Wright (2017, 21) points out, relatedly, another aspect of SSI deeply at variance with our ordinary notion of knowledge—it seems to allow us to change what we know by changing our practical interests (or by having them change). He writes that "it seems absurd to suppose that a thinker can acquire knowledge without further investigation simply because his practical interests happen to change so as to reduce the importance of the matter at hand."

DeRose (2009, 194) gives a number of straightforward statements that look very problematic for SSI:

> She does know, but she wouldn't have known if more had been at stake.
>
> She doesn't know now, but she will know tomorrow, when less will be at stake.
>
> She knows on the weekends when she isn't on duty and is only wondering out of idle curiosity; but on weekdays, when much rides on whether she's right, she doesn't know.

That is, when we articulate the supposed practical considerations that the knowledge relation is supposed to be partially constituted of, we get statements that

[38] We *do* say, ". . . so it's obvious why *you* wouldn't think *p* is false, although I do."

[39] A step in the (tacit) reasoning that allows this involves accepting shifts like that from Hannah's utterance of "I know the bank will be open" being true to Hannah being right (in the cases noted in section 3.2). I make a big deal of knowledge transfer in section 11.4.

people reject.[40] These same sorts of statements, however, equally undermine contextualism; more dramatically, they cast into doubt the evidential value of isolated judgments directed toward the kinds of cases illustrated at the beginning of section 3.2:

> She does know the bank is open on Saturday, but she wouldn't have known if more had been at stake for her.
>
> She doesn't know the bank is open on Saturday, but she would have known if less had been at stake for her.

Even this sounds unacceptable, or (at best) sarcastic:

> She doesn't know the bank is open on Saturday, but she would have if her standards for knowing things had been (a lot) lower.

This *is* acceptable (although sophisticated):

> She doesn't know the bank is open on Saturday, but she would have if her standards for "knowledge" had been lower.

Despite acceptability, this last example doesn't support contextualism: We can take this sentence seriously only by treating "knowledge" as labeling *whatever* the person willingly claims she knows—that is, by making a joke. In fact, this *is* a common sort of mean-spirited joke: "You must have pretty low standards for knowing things, if you're willing to say *that*." It works as a joke precisely because, apparently, we recognize that the standards for knowledge—whatever they are—aren't supposed to shift under these kinds of pressure.

Additional unacceptable statements can be generated by bringing in any of the various pragmatic factors that an anti-intellectualist philosopher might think affects the knowing relation. The conclusion is: For better or worse, our ordinary usage of "know(s)" is clearly understood by us to be context-insensitive and "pure": only factors of "evidence" that affect truth conduciveness seem relevant (as far as usage is concerned) to whether someone knows something or not.[41]

[40] It's important, as DeRose points out, that these are third-person know(s) attributions. First-person attributions can be explained away compatibly with anti-intellectualism, as in Hawthorne (2004, 159–160).

[41] DeRose (2009, 190–191) thinks that the agent's confidence is a factor in whether an agent knows something or not that's *independent* of that agent's appreciation of evidence. This isn't true either, as we can already see from the timid-student cases discussed in section 1.5. I discuss this further in section 9.3.

Anti-intellectualism and contextualism are positions that were "born refuted" by the usage evidence that was available in our attributions practices all along.

We should give up on all forms of epistemic impurity, invariant or otherwise.[42]

3.6 Knowledge Relativism Denied

Perhaps my conclusion is premature. Two kinds of counterexamples bear against SSI and contextualism. First, trans-case judgments show we require our judgments about knowing to be consistent; second, in cases where agents have differing practical goals when together in the same contexts, the agents nevertheless are never seen as differing in knowledge on that basis alone. These are "judgment-and-practical-consistency requirements" (JPC requirements). It looks like there is still one contextualist view left standing that's compatible with JPC requirements—one or another version of MacFarlane's assessor-relative contextualism. When a judgment is withdrawn (retracted or rejected), the meta-judgment in question is relative to the context of the *assessor*—whether that context is of the agent herself (at a later point) or someone else.

Two possible views look compatible with JPC requirements. The first is some version of classical invariantism. On this view, the judgment is, of course, relative to the assessor—but only in the always-trivial sense that the assessor is making a knowing attribution: there is no claim that either the knowing proposition expressed is relative to the context of the assessor, that its truth value is relative to that context, or that the proposition is infiltrated by the pragmatic needs of that assessor. But classical invariantism faces the difficulty—stressed by contextualists, anti-intellectualists, and knowledge relativists—that our judgments about knowing attributions shift. The second view is that there is, indeed, an unnoticed contextual variable influencing either the knowing attribution expressed or its truth value—it's the standards (that shift) of the assessor.

Is there any evidence against assessor contextualism—or, as MacFarlane prefers to call it, knowledge relativism? As Wright (2017, 25–28) points out, there are many retraction cases that seem to refute this family of positions—ones in which an agent has realized he has overlooked a possibility. To evaluate this evidence, it's important to consider the subtle retractions of those who willingly admit their mistakes. (Many people, it must be said, do *not* admit their mistakes—ever.) One way, for example, that an agent can retract a knowing attribution is to say, "Because of a possibility I overlooked, I didn't know *p*, although

[42] I'm not done arguing against this (family of) positions. Fantl and McGrath (2009) mount a sophisticated argument that fallibilists should be anti-intellectualists. I take up their important arguments in chapter 10.

I thought I did." But another acceptable way is to say, strongly and explicitly, "I should not have claimed to know *p*. *I made a mistake*."

Assessor contextualism handles "I didn't know *p*," because current assessor standards govern *current* past-tense knowing attributions even if assessor-knowing standards were different in the past. But on what grounds are current assessor standards supposed to govern what one *should have said* in the past? To admit to a *mistake* is to admit to failing to meet the standards operative *at the time*. On any reasonable construal of epistemic responsibility—or a notion of responsibility, more generally—one should make knowing attributions according to the standards governing those attributions at the time the knowing attribution is made. So this is evidence that the standards for knowing attributions *don't* shift over time.[43]

More accurately, this is evidence that speaker-hearers *don't think* standards for knowing attributions shift over time. Always open to the knowledge relativist is attributing a kind of "semantic blindness" to speaker-hearers: Assessor-relative knowing standards do shift—and in a way that's reflected in the semantics of "know(s)"—but speaker-hearers aren't aware of this.

Wright (2017, 25) is dismissive of this strategy of falling "back too readily on the idea that aspects of that practice which fail to accord with the theory may be discounted as misuses." If, however, we're comparing assessor relativity to classical invariantism, Wright's objection fails. After all, it's an undeniable fact that our knowing attributions shift; and it's also a fact that speaker-hearers, in general, don't realize this unless case comparisons are explicit.[44] It may be that this failure of insight into our own verbal practices is enough to explain the misuse of "I should not have said." I discuss this in a broader framework in what follows.

3.7 What Speaker-Hearers Can Reasonably Be Taken to Be Confused About with Respect to their Own Usage

I've already noted that, regardless of the status of the various contextualist/interest-relativist positions—vis-à-vis usage data—a classical invariantist position seems unable to handle judgment shifts. It's been suggested (Rysiew (2001),

[43] Some philosopher or other will argue that "mistakes"—just like "know(s)"—is governed by current conditions, not past ones. Frankly, pushing this move as far as it needs to go seals the objectivity of the past off from contemporary contemplators of it. I think even to concede, as Wright does, that "I didn't know *p*" is governed by contemporary standards (and not the ones holding at the past time in question) is a mistake; it's a mistake about whether tense or "know(s)" (and consequently its standards) takes broad scope in statements of this sort. I forgo giving more details about this.

[44] In part, what the emergence of these examples into the discussion space, by Cohen, DeRose, and others, amounts to is the belated recognition *in the philosophical literature* of this fact.

Rysiew (2005), Brown (2006), Rysiew (2007), with other references found in Rysiew (2017, 208)—that a "pragmatic" explanation of these shifts can protect classical invariantism against judgement-shift counterexamples. Rysiew (2005, 45, and elsewhere) calls an invariantist position that helps itself to pragmatic explanations of judgment shifts "sophisticated invariantism."

The idea is simple and straightforward (although detailed implementation is always complicated—and there is more than one way to go). Assume that some classical invariantist position or other is right—one according to which shifts in judgment about knowing attributions in pairs of cases reveal that one (or both) of the cases involves false claims about knowing attributions (rather than true ones that shift somehow or other because of context). This is explained by one or both of a pair of knowing attributions not being literal—where this phrase is understood quite broadly, anything from making an exaggerated claim to one that's metaphorical, or loose in some Gricean sense because it conveys (additional) content that's not semantic but pragmatically conveyed.[45] Exactly what's (speaker-)meant depends on the specifics of the approach being taken.[46]

We *often* experience utterances as saying more than (or something different from) what we can be brought to recognize is what they literally say. There are many standard examples of these sorts of utterances in the literature: "I have eaten," "It's raining (here)," "Everyone [in this course] got an A," "Howard is too old [to be leader of the Tory party]" (Brown 2006, 417), as well as "I've had [/ haven't had] breakfast," "You won't die" (Rysiew 2017, 206), and "There's an [open] garage around the corner" (Rysiew 2017, 205). "I have eaten," for example, conveys (literally) that one has eaten at some time in the past; it doesn't literally convey that one has eaten at some contextually relevant point earlier in the day, which is what's usually conveyed by its utterance. The others are similar.

Applying this pragmatics-of-literality/nonliterality apparatus to the paired cases contextualists have focused on, we have—depending on exactly what invariantist position (moderate or high standards) is presupposed—a characterization of the knowing attribution in one of the scenarios as nonliteral. Consider, for example, a moderate invariantist position (one according to which knowledge standards moderately allow the evidence most people have in most circumstances to suffice to make knowledge what they and others claim they know) and consider *High Stakes*, here repeated:

> Hannah and her wife Sarah are driving home on a Friday afternoon. They plan to stop at the bank on the way home to deposit their paychecks. Since they have

[45] Bach (2001): "sentence nonliterality."

[46] Rysiew and Brown offer Gricean approaches using, e.g., Grice's maxims; Schaffer (2004) treats ordinary knowledge claims as "hyperbole." See Rysiew (2017, 208) for further references.

an impending bill coming due, and very little in their account, it is very important that they deposit their paychecks by Saturday. Hannah notes that she was at the bank two weeks before on a Saturday morning, and it was open. But, as Sarah points out, banks do change their hours. Hannah says, "I guess you're right. I don't know that the bank will be open tomorrow."

Pragmatist strategists deny that Hannah speaks truly. She speaks falsely because she does know that the bank will be open tomorrow. However, the nonliteral (conveyed) content of Hannah's "I guess you're right. I don't know that the bank will be open tomorrow" is claimed to be (something like) "I'm not in a strong epistemic position vis-à-vis this claim."[47]

Crucial to this strategy is that the impression that "know(s)" is being used literally by Hannah is because she's confused about the line between semantics and pragmatics. This "confusion" explains the "intuition" that Hannah speaks literally; and, relatedly, this is taken by proponents of this position to explain why Gricean cancellations in these sorts of cases fail.[48]

For example, the implicature that the speaker had breakfast that morning can be canceled by saying "I've had breakfast, just not this morning." In the right context (e.g., having traveled for a long time on a red-eye flight), this will be a natural thing to say. But Hannah can't say in the earlier scenario "I still know that the bank will be open, although I'm not sure." As I mentioned, what makes the utterance of this cancellation uncomfortable for speakers (despite its being quite comfortable in normal cases of implicature) is a presumed confusion about the line between what's literally said and what's implicated.[49]

A focus on *comparison judgments*, however, will dispel the idea that speaker-hearer confusion explains the impression that Hannah is speaking literally. The

[47] Where, given moderate invariantism, a strong epistemic position vis-à-vis *p* can easily go beyond what's required to know *p*. See Rysiew (2017, 211; 2005, 58). Other common nonliteral conveyed content will be "I'm not sure"—when the speaker says "I don't know" or an emphatic "I believe" when saying "I know" (Rysiew (2007, 636)).

[48] Rysiew (2017, 211), for example, quotes Borg (2012, 15) that "[s]peech act content is, in the jargon, a massive interaction effect." Rysiew adds, "i.e., that what's communicated by a given utterance is the product of multiple factors (syntax, semantics, pragmatics, etc.). And, to the extent that our intuitions are attuned to the total message communicated, rather than just the semantic features of what is said, certain cancellations are apt to feel uncomfortable." Similar remarks explaining away speaker-hearer impressions of literality in these cases are offered by Rysiew in other work (e.g., 2001; 2007), as well as by Brown (2006) and Bach (2005 and elsewhere). In particular, Rysiew (2005, 47) writes: "our 'semantic intuitions'—our intuitions about the truth conditions of sentences—are generally insensitive to the semantic/pragmatic distinction (we often read things into what is literally said, even by ourselves, without realizing we're doing so." As I indicate in what follows, this claim, which Rysiew repeats often, dramatically overstates the facts.

[49] Rysiew (2007, 639). He notes there something that's true: some Gricean cancellations are apt to be uncomfortable—as Grice also noted. Uncomfortable cancellations, however, are (so I claim) always special cases that need specific explanations. A one-size-fits-all "speakers confuse pragmatic and semantic factors" won't do.

problem is straightforward. *All* examples of pragmatic enrichments of "what is said," although not necessarily visible to speaker-hearers at "first glance" or "in the moment," become quite visible "at second glances." Consider "I've had breakfast." This, of course, is usually understood as "I've had breakfast [this morning]"; but speaker-hearers can recognize the "sentence nonliterality" of this utterance either because it's exploited in bad jokes ("Yes, I've had breakfast. I've had other meals as well. *Many times* by this point in my life") or because of the presentation of scenarios in which the literal meaning of the utterance is required to understand the utterance.[50] We need, therefore, to make a distinction between a pragmatic enrichment of a literal remark being noticed by a speaker-hearer in the moment of utterance and its being *accessible* to that speaker-hearer. The problem, for pragmatic approaches to cases in which knowing attributions shift, is that pragmatic maneuvers are generally accessible to speaker-hearers, but the purported pragmatic enrichments aren't ever accessible to speaker-hearers in the cases of knowing attributions. That "know(s)" and its cognates *all*, generally, make Gricean cancellations uncomfortable, and must be *all* be explained away by speaker-hearer confusions about the line between semantics and pragmatics, suggests that this isn't the right analysis of these usages.[51]

The difference between all the standard cases mentioned by proponents of the pragmatic strategy and the proposed application of it to the cases of knowledge-judgment shifts that we see between *High Stakes* and *Low Stakes* is that there is no accessibility to speaker-hearers of the supposed pragmatic (as opposed to literal) interpretation of the statements in question. This is why speaker-hearers—when faced with the apparent inconsistency of their judgments—don't make jokes or grimace at a belated recognition of the "unintended" interpretation (as they do in all the standard cases) but instead retract one of the knowing attributions. If we continue to focus only on judgments about single cases, and don't take into account how speaker-hearers react to perceived inconsistencies in knowing attributions across different cases, we won't see how much pragmatic approaches fail to accommodate usage evidence.

[50] For details and refinements about the notion of "literality" in play here, as well as many examples, see Azzouni (2013b, chapter 5).

[51] Other nonliterality approaches to these cases face the same problems—for example, attempts to treat them as hyperbole or metaphors or Bach's (2005) claim that the judgment shifts in such cases are due to thresholds of confidence on the part of the attributors. None of these purported forms of nonliterality is visible to speaker-hearers—even with careful inspection—as they should be if such views are right.

3.8 Making Progress? (Where We Are and Where We're Going)

After establishing a preliminary minimal characterization of the semantics of "know(s)," it was natural, in continuing my exploration of the contours of the word to evaluate the popular thesis that pragmatic factors somehow affect epistemic valuations. Unfortunately, although the subsequent analysis undercuts the usage evidence apparently supporting contextualist/SSI positions, traditional invariantism didn't seem to emerge unscathed. Indeed, the situation looks as bad as situations ever look in philosophy. *Nothing* (canvassed) seems to work. That is, granting the impressions of knowing attributions in the cases that have been focused on in the literature, neither an invariantism (with standards of any sort) nor any candidate contextualisms or anti-intellectualist positions work. They all fail—pretty much—when we take comparison judgments of cases into account. Contextualist positions fail because the variations in epistemic judgments are rejected as unacceptable when comparisons are made; the traditional invariantist positions fail because—nevertheless—there are such variations in judgments; but sensitivity-invariantist positions fail because we reject the acceptability of variations in judgments being due to pragmatic factors. Notably, assessor-relative contextualism fails because, as Wright (2017) has made clear, we recognize that current standards don't govern current descriptions of *past* know(s) ascriptions.

I've also rejected, along the way, methodologically suspicious attempts at special pleading—for example, trying to rule out the relevance of user data on the grounds that it's methodologically not "straightforward" (recall the discussion of DeRose's version of this maneuver in introduction section v) or by arguing that speaker-hearers are naturally "confused" about the (semantic) status of what they're saying, e.g., they think it's not metaphorical when it is. By no means am I denying that this is (often) the case. But to avoid tainting the data with presumptions about that data that favor one theory over another, we need to recognize that claims about speaker-hearer confusions are claims that shouldn't be offered as *general panaceas* for mismatches between theories and data. In particular, if a claim is made that speaker-hearers confuse something (in a systematic way), this claim needs to be exhibited (and justified) fairly explicitly. Just claiming, for example, that speaker-hearers often confuse pragmatics with semantics won't do; they don't *always* do this. What shows that, with care, they see the distinction are their ability to make jokes (that others get) that exploit the (second) impression that a pragmatically enriched interpretation isn't literal and their ability to be conscious (and explicit about) Gricean mechanisms (e.g., the maxims and how they allow, e.g., cancellations) that are operative in speech. Given this background competence of speaker-hearers, a specific reason for why, in a particular case, a confusion should be posited as operative is needed; I submit that proponents of the pragmatic approach to knowing attributions haven't managed this.

As I mentioned earlier, I intend to support (a version of) CI; and as I've also mentioned, I intend to argue that the judgment shifting is due to vagueness. My approach clearly faces obstacles. First, to some extent, the explanation requires that the vagueness in question be somewhat invisible to speaker-hearers. I need, therefore, to show that the respect in which the vagueness in question is invisible is both typical and more general—extending beyond the special context of "know(s)" and its cognates, and also that it's not like the kind of vagueness that speaker-hearers are aware of. After all, speakers often recognize when their attributions are vague (as Schiffer (1996, 328) notes), but these judgment shifts are cases where we don't seem to know this.

I'll return to this in later chapters—starting in chapter 9. But first another aspect of knowing attributions must be described in the intervening chapters. This is in what ways we take account of and fail to take account of metacognition. It's important that this material intervenes here because, in general, metacognition is the source of misunderstandings about how knowing attributions work, and as importantly, it's a source of misunderstandings about justification.

4
Assertion Norms

4.1 Introduction; Preliminaries About Assertion

Analysis of the "know(s)" locution and its relatives, as I've promised, is intricate. This intricacy continues to be exhibited in this and the next two chapters, although the focus changes to knowing and iterated knowing assertions. Preliminary to this topic a discussion is needed of assertion norms and the like. Recent epistemology has explored the idea that the knowledge relation is important because it functions as a norm for verbal activity—specifically assertion—and for action. Related ideas have been around for a while; many philosophers, for example, have thought that knowledge is a norm for belief.

The specific claim that knowledge is an assertion norm is the topic of this chapter. Chapter 10, in turn, will evaluate the related idea that knowledge is a norm for action. My background concern, I should note now, is determining what the indispensable role of "know(s)" in natural language is—a role that, along with its various syntactic/semantic properties, will help explain the form it takes. I'll show that although it's very natural to think that knowledge is a norm for belief, assertion, or action, it's not needed for any of these—and it's not a norm for them either. I'll eventually argue (in chapter 11) for a quite deflated (but indispensable) role for "know(s)": as an inferential linchpin for the transferring of propositions (without an accompanying transferring of the justifications for those propositions).

I've already indicated in earlier chapters that because of a widespread failure to appreciate the sheer range of usage practices, and because of a tendency to hunt for definitions, philosophers often elevate local sufficient conditions into global necessary and sufficient conditions. I've suggested in section 1.3 that this tendency gives rise to the just-about-universal (but false) view that consciousness is required to know or see things. A more recent mistake (similarly due to insufficiently appreciating full usage) yields norms-of-assertion claims—specifically, the claim that there is a knowledge norm of assertion.

Some have argued that an agent knowing *p* is a "constitutive requirement" for that agent asserting *p* (e.g., Williamson (2000, chapter 11)). Although there are disputes about exactly what this condition *requires* (or even what it *means*), the empirical evidence available for it (if any) is clear: expectations that speakers and hearers have when assertions are made. These expectations are revealed by how

Attributing Knowledge. Jody Azzouni, Oxford University Press (2020). © Oxford University Press.
DOI: 10.1093/oso/9780197508817.001.0001.

listeners criticize assertions (these criticisms show that listeners have expectations that have been violated); expectations are also revealed by the oddity of certain locutions, which—because they're not semantically or grammatically incorrect—also illustrate that listeners have expectations that have been violated. Corresponding to the expectations that listeners have when assertions are made are responsibilities speakers have apparently undertaken by virtue of making assertions—*commitments* that they undertake by asserting.[1]

I show that when our full range of assertion practices is canvassed, listener expectations don't correlate with assertion as proponents of assertion norms need them to; instead they vary concordantly with the beliefs that speakers (and listeners) have about the circumstances of the assertions. The reality about the experience of assertion, therefore, is much closer to how Cappelen (2011, 21) characterizes "sayings": these "are governed by variable norms, come with variable commitments, and have variable causes and effects." Close, but this isn't right either, in part because of what Cappelen says next (italics his):

> *What philosophers have tried to capture by the term "assertion" is largely a philosophers' invention. It fails to pick out an act-type that we engage in and it is not a category we need in order to explain any significant component of our linguistic practice.*

On the contrary. *Assertions, what is said, demands, questions, guesses*, and so on, are phenomenological categories. They're aspects of *language experience*—of how we experience language when language events take place. Language experience is part—but an important part—of the data for the language sciences. The robustness of language experience, that theories of language must rely on that experience as part of their data, and that asserting, in particular, is part of language experience, suffices to rule out Cappelen's eliminativist attitude toward assertion.

Brown and Cappelen's overview of the various possible answers to the question *what are assertions?* doesn't include the answer "assertions are sayings experienced in such-and-such ways." Instead (apart from Cappelen's "no assertion" view), Brown and Cappelen (2011, 3) describe there being four options that the contemporary literature on this topic exemplifies:

[1] Williamson (2000, 257, emphasis his) writes: "One can think of the knowledge rule as giving the condition on which a speaker has the *authority* to make an assertion. Thus, asserting p without knowing p is doing something without having the authority to do it, like giving someone a command without having the authority to do so. Characteristic standards of authority thus play a constitutive role in the speech act of assertion, as they do in other institutions."

(i) Assertions are those sayings that are governed by certain norms—the norms of assertion (e.g., Williamson).
(ii) Assertions are those sayings that have certain effects (e.g., Stalnaker).
(iii) Assertions are those sayings that have certain causes (e.g., Bach and Harnish).
(iv) Assertions are those sayings that are accompanied by certain commitments (e.g., Brandom, MacFarlane, Rescorla).

Mixed views are possible, e.g., Kölbel (2011), who gives necessary and sufficient conditions for sayings to be assertions that involve both norms and Stalnaker effects on the common ground.

The literature, as Brown and Cappelen's four options indicate, uniformly presupposes that "sayings" are speech acts, and that assertions are a specifiable class of sayings. (So the debate is over the nature of this specification.) I significantly modify these assumptions, as I indicate next.

The distinctive difference between the semantic-perception view (that I'm committed to) and this Gricean perspective turns on my claim that any analysis of language experience can't restrict itself to *speech acts*.[2] According to the semantic-perception view, the experience of *language entities*—sentences, words, etc.—is a central experience of language. These aren't perceived as *actions* but *are* perceived as things with properties, *being meaningful, grammatical*, and so on.[3] (They're experienced as the things that we act *with* when our actions have speech as a core or even a constitutive part.) Being an assertion, as well, is experienced as a property of a language entity—a kind of sentence—which is different from the event of a human being asserting a sentence. The peculiar complexity of human-language experience, involving both language objects with perceived properties and the actions of people using these language objects, rules out simply categorizing "assertion" as a specifiable kind of "saying." I discuss this further in section 4.2. It's *not* part of language experience that language entities and their properties are reducible to human speech actions; these entities are experienced as independent of human action.[4]

[2] I've already raised this issue in section ix of the introduction.

[3] Azzouni (2013b) is a general approach to language based on the experience of speakers and hearers of apparent language *objects* and their properties. (I don't presume these objects are real—I think they're not.) Chapter 3 of that book analyzes the experience of *what is said*, but doesn't explicitly discuss the experiences of *assertion* and *asserting*, the topics that matter here. So, in the course of this chapter, I extend the analysis of Azzouni (2013b) in what I hope is a self-contained way.

[4] Although no such reducibility of language objects and their properties to human action and intention is experienced, that doesn't mean that, subpersonally, a reduction isn't possible—human experience (alone) dictates no answer to this. For example, the meaning (and syntactic) qualities of sentences that we perceive as properties of those sentences are often contextually cued in ways we do *not* perceive. This makes them relations in ways we don't perceive them to be. See Azzouni (2013b) for further discussion of this and of issues of reducibility.

Shifting from theories that centralize speech acts to those that centralize the experience of language objects yields surprising predictions. If the experience of language is solely that of speech acts of humans (where propositions and their properties are derived from speech acts), then the action of a speaker asserting *p* is essential to the sentence asserted being an assertion. If, that is, an utterance of a sentence is an assertion, then it's so because that utterance is essentially tied to asserting—it's essentially tied to something a speaker *does*. If, however, the experience is of language objects with properties that humans use to make assertions (but which human intentions and the like don't create), then, in principle anyway, it's possible—it's within the possibility of human experience—to experience a language object, a sentence, for example, as an assertion and even as being asserted (having the *property* of being asserted), *without* there being an asserter. The striking fact (see section 4.2 and the sections that follow) is that this indeed is a *common* experience.[5]

The experience that a particular verbal utterance (or written token) is asserted is cued, of course, by environmental factors—so assertions certainly have certain causes; and similarly they have effects. But they aren't—generally—governed by particular norms, nor do speakers accompany their utterances of assertions with assertion-specific commitments. Instead, assertions (and acts of assertion) are experienced as taking place against a background of presuppositions, as Stalnaker (1974; 1978; 2002) describes the "common ground." Speaker-hearer expectations are due entirely to what those presuppositions are in particular cases—or, more accurately, to what speaker-hearers *take* those shared presuppositions to be. Call this the "common-ground expectation view" of assertion. *Shared* expectations among the speaker-hearers in a group are optimal; the reality is that, often, speakers and hearers have different presuppositions, and therefore they can have different expectations, which can lead to misunderstandings (e.g., "why are you saying that?"). I allow the terminology "common-ground expectation view" to cover these kinds of cases, and I'll allude to them when necessary.

According to the common-ground expectation view, there are no knowledge, belief, or other norms that uniquely or specifically govern assertion; speakers-hearers, instead, have expectations *in many contexts* that asserters believe or know (or have other propositional attitudes toward) the uttered propositions they've witnessed; having these attitudes, nonetheless, isn't required,

[5] This is weird—but there are compelling reasons to think it's true. A human shouts a word. That's an action of a human: shouting. But the experience of a word being a shout can be an experience of the word having a property, being a shout, without it being shouted by someone—the experience of a shouted word doesn't require there to be a shouter, or that the shouted word is related to a shouter. The experience of a word being a shout is the experience of the word itself having a one-place property: *being a shout*. (A necessary condition on this is simply that the sound of the word is *loud*.)

conventionally or otherwise, nor are such attitudes entailed by norms.[6] Neither, as suggested by Unger (1975) and Slote (1979), do utterers (always) "represent themselves" as knowing (or believing) their utterances. *Sometimes* they do, and *sometimes* they don't.

Contributing to the usage data that rules out norm views of assertion is the widespread phenomenon of "spokespersons" (sections 4.3 and 4.4): salespeople or "industry spokesmen," purveyors and representatives of official views of institutions or individuals (like presidents), who assert on behalf of those institutions or individuals during, for example, press conferences. Spokespeople are understood as *asserting* what they say—that's their *job*—despite being neither required nor expected to know, believe, or understand what they're asserting. Other counter-evidence against assertion norms are sentences that are experienced as occurring *without* there being asserters to whom those assertion norms can apply. I'll also show that the common-ground expectation view better explains the apparent oddity of what I'll call "Moorean remarks" (statements like "It's raining, but I don't believe it" or "It's raining, and I don't know that") than norm views do. The impression of the intrinsic oddity of these propositions is due to overlooking many cases where they're acceptably uttered. Lastly, I'll expose a methodological danger that norm views face: it's easy to immunize them against empirical refutation by a priori stipulating the properties of assertions or by deeming the norm operative regardless of the facts of verbal behavior, or of the expectations that accompany that behavior.

Even without there being norms governing generally characterized practices, such as *all* meals, there still are restricted norms governing special occasions, such as formal dinners. Perhaps there are specialized assertion norms too. In section 4.8, I consider contexts where we expect a lot from asserters: face-to-face chats with close reliable friends and assertions made in reputable venues, such as during the lectures of experts or in articles from respectable newspapers. Even in these cases, where background expectations of knowledge or sincerity are in place, there is nevertheless no good reason to think that *norms* of assertion are operative.

This chapter-length discussion—of norms of assertion—is necessary not just because there is (now) a large literature on the topic but also to prevent false claims about knowledge norms from confounding an analysis of KK. In addition,

[6] So, despite my disagreements with Cappelen, I agree with him when he writes (2011, 25): "Speech behavior, like other kinds of behavior, is evaluated by a range of rules, norms, and constraints—some moral, some norms of etiquette, some having to do with the practicalities of cooperation and information exchange." I'd only add something to the letter of what he states (which he probably also agrees with), that the specifics in particular cases of this range of rules, norms, and constraints are presupposed by conversants (and nothing, of course, prevents the awkward discovery by conversants that they don't have the common ground they thought they had).

philosophers use the purported existence of assertion norms to support contextualism, subject-sensitive invariantism, and significant planks of Williamson's "knowledge-first" program. The purported existence of knowledge norms of assertion also threatens cogently *asserting* sceptical claims. Thus, that there actually are no such norms dramatically reconfigures contemporary arguments in epistemology.

4.2 Semantic Perceptions

The assertion-norm literature in epistemology is voluminous.[7] Most of it presupposes a *pure speech-act phenomenology*, as I indicated in the last section. An assertion, according to (most of) this literature, is an *event* that speakers-hearers experience as an *action* of speakers (a "speech act"); it's necessarily accompanied by communicative intentions. This is fundamentally wrong; it doesn't, for one thing, make sense of our experience of assertion when we know there are no asserters. There is, in fact, an experienced distinction between things, sentences that can be assertions or indicatives (or both) on the one hand and *events* like speaker actions of asserting on the other. Only the experience of the second is, properly, described as an experience of a speech act. I'll now give an overview of how we experience assertions and asserting (that is, what we experience assertion and asserting to be). Then, in the sections to follow, I'll turn to the specific roles that the knowledge and beliefs of speakers play in our understanding of their assertions.[8]

The first point is that native speakers (with standard language-learning upbringings) involuntarily experience auditory and written sentences and words as *objects* intrinsically possessing their meanings. These meanings, in turn, are experienced the way functional properties of tools are: we experience pliers not just as shaped metal and plastic but additionally as *pliers*—as having specific powers. These powers are experienced as differing from those of other tools (screwdrivers, hammers, nails . . .) and differing, yet again, from the powers of other artifacts (lamps, chess pieces, cars, drones . . .).[9]

Because we experience the meanings of sentences (and words) as intrinsic to the sentences (and words) themselves, we don't *experience* meanings as derivatively imposed on sentences by public conventions or as due to the

[7] Pagin (2016) is an excellent survey and discussion; also see the overview in Brown and Cappelen (2011).

[8] What follows in the next few paragraphs is summarized discussion from Azzouni (2013b).

[9] This experience of functional properties goes beyond artifacts, of course, as, for example, *hands*, *fingers*, and *feet* (and "superheroes") make clear.

communicative intentions of their utterers.[10] That is, although we infer the propositional attitudes of speakers *from* the sentences they utter, we experience this inference as we do our inferences of people's intentions from the tools they use—pliers (say) instead of screwdrivers. We don't see the tool user's attitudes or intentions as *constituting* or *causing* the properties *of* the tool he picks up; we instead see him as using the properties of the tool—properties it's experienced to already have. Our experience of sentences and words is the same. The meanings of sentences and words are surface properties that utterers and hearers normally experience those sentences and words to have—for example, that "she" in the utterance "She is running," when uttered in a context with a unique mutually perceived female runner, is about that runner. Or, if there is someone female standing in the vicinity and the speaker points to her and says, "She's running," the *sentence* uttered is perceived as false.

The semantic-perception view—because it focuses on the *objects* we experience ourselves to utter— reconfigures the application of Gricean communicative intentions and other Gricean apparatus, maxims, common ground, etc., to language experience and to the pragmatics of language; it doesn't exclude them. A speaker who utters a sentence that's obviously false is up to something (she's not trying to express a truth); and our usual (Gricean) interpretative practices allow us to recognize what that something is. *Real* communicative intentions, that is, presuppose the meaning properties uttered sentences are experienced to have independently of those intentions. It isn't, therefore, the "speech act" (the fleeting physical event of the person speaking) that's perceived to be meaningful—no more is *how* someone *uses* a screwdriver (the "tool act," as it were) perceived to have the properties of the screwdriver. We're always aware, generally, of a tool *that's being used* and its properties. This is in addition to seeing that (and how) the person is using the tool. So too, we experience the uttered *sentence* as having properties, but we're also aware of how the person is using that sentence. (The analogy is *exact*.)[11]

[10] This is a point about experience, not about *reality*. It's also not about what we may know about this matter, contrary to our experience. (Compare this to the Müller-Lyer illusion.) I *know*, and I think you do too, that the meaning properties and, for that matter, the grammatical properties that we experience sentences to have aren't properties physically had by *anything*. They're involuntary psychological projections by speakers and hearers onto physical objects (ink marks on paper) or events (utterances). That is (depending on one's theory), they *are*—contrary to our experience of them—due to language conventions, the propositional attitudes of speakers, or other aspects of speaker and hearer psychology (depending on particular theories of this).

[11] We have a good grip on the properties we attribute to tools and sentences, to what we perceive as *objects*; we have a shaky grip on the properties we attribute to tool and speech acts, to what we perceive as *events*. This generalizes: we always have a good feel for what we experience as properties of objects; we have less of a feel for what we experience as properties of events. In the case of sentences and speakers, however, we do have a good feel for the psychological states of those *speakers*—much of our recognition of the properties of speech acts amounts to (as with all human action) the intentional qualities of the individuals engaged in those actions.

We experience written and spoken sentences and words as *public* items; we understand them as things that can be seen, and their properties grasped, by anyone who "understands the language." (This is part of the common ground that conversants speaking the same language to one another presuppose.) It's because of this experience that communicative intentions make sense to us: as speakers and listeners, we rely on the grasping of the meanings of uttered sentences for irony or sarcasm, to enhance (or undermine) what we've actually said—more generally, to *imply* (as it's put by nonphilosophers) things that we haven't said. While doing so, we recognize ourselves as exploiting the meanings of sentences in contexts, where both those meanings and (the salient aspects of) the contexts are mutually perceived.

To claim that *the speech act* is the basic phenomenological unit that speaker-hearers experience to have meanings badly mischaracterizes the language experience. Again (yet again): I'm not making an *ontological claim*; I'm *not* saying that there *are* sentences the way that there *are* screwdrivers.[12] It's true (I think) that there *really are* only actions (speech acts) that occur when speakers and hearers transact; there *aren't* these things, sentences, that we pass around to one another. But this isn't how language transactions are experienced; and to adopt the speech act as the basic meaning unit, and to understand the language experience and the language psychology of speakers and hearers (the actual intentions they have, communicative and otherwise) on this assumption distorts the actual intentions and attitudes speakers and hearers *do* correctly attribute to one another. It distorts the real psychology of communication. And to distort the real psychology of communication is to distort the real psychology that underlies our epistemic practices. (Epistemology *really is* a special science.)

This dramatically changes our view of the experience of *assertion*. On pure speech-act views, assertions are seen as actions of speakers—and so they must operate via the intentions of speakers. On the semantic-perception view, there is a more complicated set of categories. There certainly is the "asserting" by speakers when they *use* a sentence assertively—that *is* an action—but this is seen by speakers and hearers as the utterer exploiting a property that some indicative sentences *already have* of *being* assertions. Indicative sentences, that is, are (usually) experienced, in addition, as asserting truths or falsehoods *all by themselves*—even if no speaker of the sentences exists. Odd as this sounds (to trained speech-act theorists, anyhow), it really is the speaker-hearer experience as "meaning illusions" reveal. Here are some examples (from Azzouni (2013b, 72–80, 92–93, 107–108).

[12] That's false, and it's the source, in particular, of interesting confusions people have about types and tokens—see Azzouni (2013b), chapter 1. People don't experience sentences as *types*—which is how philosophers (formally) analyze sentences—they experience them as *objects*.

Should we see a beetle, by sheer accident, creating shapes in sand that look like the printed words BARACK OBAMA, we'll nevertheless (involuntarily) experience those shapes as Barack Obama's *name*. Should an avalanche—equally improbably—generate the clear articulation of what sounds like words shouted by a human voice full of concern, I'M COMING; PLEASE WATCH OUT; I'M COMING; PLEASE WATCH OUT . . . even knowing how these sounds are being produced, it's impossible not to hear them as meaningful—and, indeed, as a warning! Should the beetle trace out (instead) I'M COLD, even knowing that the event is a sheer accident, we'll experience the pattern as expressing the thought that *the beetle* is cold. Similarly, should we notice (or become aware of) an erosion-induced pattern on a cliff wall above a path, where the pattern reads: SHE'S RUNNING, and where, on that path, a female runner happens to be jogging, we'll involuntarily experience the sentence as *about her*; if she's walking, we'll experience the sentence as false. If you're paging through a book in a foreign language that you don't know (but with an English alphabet), and you find "She is running," an accidentally orthographically similar expression of this language, next to a picture of a woman running on a bumpy road, even if you're told by a native speaker that the sentence means "That's a bumpy road," you'll still involuntarily experience the English interpretation (in addition, with "she" as referring to the woman running in the picture).

These examples illustrate how we experience propositions as meaningful independently of communicative intentions. The "sentence" is experienced as having properties independently of its origin (whether people, erosion, or beetles); it's, regardless, seen as meaningful, true or false, "about" things, and as *asserting something all by itself.* (Sentences, even indicatives, aren't *always* experienced as assertions or as asserting things, as I'll illustrate in the next section.)

These thought experiments may seem improbable (although it's not obvious what sort of objection the improbability of a thought experiment is supposed to be). So here are some real cases, anonymous postings on the web.[13] People often communicate with one another on "social media"; they read (or hear) what others have written or said "on the web." Although many electronic communications are from recognized sources (like your friends), many aren't. Quite common are blog postings that are effectively anonymous. The names

[13] Goldberg (2013) discusses the impact of the existence of anonymous postings on views about assertion norms. Pagin (2016) notices that "If utterances in these circumstances are still recognizably assertions, there seem to be assertions without, or with hardly any, speaker commitments. . . . [This phenomenon] seems hard for a commitment account to accommodate." It's a position along the lines of Pagin's insight that I'm articulating here—although I'm using tools (from the semantic-perception view) that Pagin is unlikely to accept, and I'm drawing conclusions that fault far more than commitment accounts of assertion.

accompanying the posts needn't reveal who's posting—or even that he or she exists.

"Even that he or she exists." One thing we've recently learned, in the aftermath of the peculiar election of Donald Trump, is that the credentials of Facebook account holders are easily fabricated.[14] That is, there needn't be a (single) person posting to the account despite appearances; it can be a crowd of Russian hackers. Due to advancing programming technology, furthermore, it's now possible for electronic programs to *themselves* post items on the web—items *no human agent* has written. If programs randomly produce and post propositions on the web, we have electronic variants of my earlier (Azzouni (2013b)) thought experiments: propositions we experience as meaningful and as asserting truths or falsehoods. We'll experience these propositions as having these properties even when we suspect (or, in fact, know) them *not* to be postings of human beings.

These propositions can be *criticized* by readers despite those readers' knowledge that these are postings (even random ones) "by a program." It can be complained of a posting that "that's not true" or that "no one is going to believe anything like *that*" or that "no one knows that." These are remarks about *propositions*: it's the *proposition* that isn't true, that no one will believe, or that no one knows. Only derivatively are criticisms lobbed at a program—that *it* isn't doing a good job if it produces and posts propositions that aren't true, that no one will believe, or that no one knows. But that these criticisms will (or can) be made at all turns on context: they aren't *automatically* reasonable criticisms. A program, for example, may be designed to produce propositions that no one will believe. The program can't then be (appropriately) criticized for doing this. The other point to stress is that regardless of what's known about the origins of these postings; and regardless of whether there are *asserters* of them, they're experienced as *asserted*. I develop this point further, using these cases and others, in the next few sections.

If the foregoing is right, however, this already shows assertion norms to be in trouble: our experience of assertion, not just that certain indicative sentences all by themselves are assertions but that the sentences themselves are in, as it were, asserted mode, is something we *can* experience without experiencing agents as doing this.

Let me conclude this section by discussing two objections that have been raised to the claims I've made (in an earlier version of this book). Neta (comments sent anonymously to me on June 24, 2019) describes seeing an IKEA video (that

[14] This, I hope, will be much more difficult to do by the time you read this. (As of 2018, anyway, it's *claimed* to be much more difficult to do.) A careful assessment of the 2016 election, with respect to anonymous postings, may be found in Shane and Mazzetti (2018), at least as far as what we know as of that date (September 20, 2018).

gives instructions for putting together the parts of a desk) in which an animated screwdriver goes

> in a screw and [turns] it so that it fastens two pieces together. But though I experience the animated screwdriver as being used to turn a screw and so fasten two pieces together, I know that there is nobody actually turning the screwdriver. . . . Perhaps we could say that the experience presents me with a screwdriver being used, but not with the agent using it. But this is a familiar feature of experience: it presents me with what I know full well can only be a partial view of reality. And if I experience a sentence as asserted (even if I don't experience anything at all about the asserter, and know full well that there is no asserter), then could I not also experience that same sentence as spoken in a way that clearly indicates knowledge of its truth (even if, again, I do not experience anything about the asserter)? And to the extent that we cease to experience them as said in such a way as to indicate knowledge, can we continue to experience them as assertions, rather than something weaker?

First a small but relevant point about what Neta has written: I don't think we—I don't, anyway—*experience* the video as one in which the screwdriver *is being used.* I experience the screwdriver itself as moving independently of any user of it.

Compare: If certain corner-shaped figures move in unison, then we experience them as part of a figure, a triangle, for example, most of which we don't see. I *don't* experience, correspondingly, an invisible hand as moving the screwdriver—although I would if a ghostly hand shape were holding it. I might *infer* such a thing. For example, if I knew about those new devices that can be controlled by an agent's mental states, I might then infer that the screwdriver in the video is being controlled this way. But I don't *experience* this. Importantly, I don't experience the screwdriver as acting either. I simply experience it as moving through space. (I could experience it as acting, but that would be different too: I'd need cues for this, like its having little wings that it's flapping, or an animated face, and perhaps also the contours of the body of the screwdriver shifting in some way.)

In the same way, I don't *experience* an agent as uttering or as having written sentences on walls or anonymously on the web. And so, I don't *experience* such agents as having knowledge either. Nor, lastly, do I experience the sentences themselves as *doing* anything; they're experienced instead as just possessing certain properties.

My observation about our experiencing certain two-dimensional angles when seen as moving together in a certain way as triggering the experience of there being a larger invisible figure (e.g., a triangle) that they're part of has a correlate in the case of anonymous sentences on the web. Corey Dethier (email, May 1, 2019) writes (italics his):

> I think the phenomenology [of anonymous postings] is . . . complicated. . . . In at least some online communities, the posters are pseudonymous and long-term users can come to identify patterns in other long-term users' behavior related to assertions. Some users are patient, or wordy; some are terse. There are experiences akin to "where have I met *that* person before?" and though (as with all textual exchanges) it can be hard to distinguish between assertions made with different tones, the assertions are absolutely experienced as having tones. The upshot of all of this is that those assertions are *experienced* as having asserters. Perhaps more importantly, they're experienced as involving speech acts in much the same way that an email is. One can berate or harass or console or encourage over email or via pseudonymous posting.

Dethier is absolutely right. But this doesn't detract from there being many cases as I've described them, where no experience of an asserter (or speech acts of an asserter) occurs. Just as if animated visual images are given enough (moving-in-unison) structure, we then experience them as part of a larger visual image most of which we can't see, so too, certain patterns of anonymous postings will induce the experience of the psychology of a particular asserter along with that (invisible agent) engaging in certain speech acts and the like. This doesn't exclude the experiences I'm focusing on, where experiences of anything agential are absent, just as the fact that animated visual images with enough structure induce the experience that they're part of something we can't see doesn't exclude the experiences of visual images without an accompanying experience that such items are part of something larger that can't be seen.

4.3 Experiencing Asserting, Assertions, and Their Differences

To start, we can *use* indicative sentences without asserting them. If I want to *demonstrate* the existence of an indicative sentence with six words, I can display one or say it aloud:

> I am hungry at this moment.

If I'm lecturing and I assert there are sentences with six words, I can then say the above. The sentence, despite being demonstrated and not asserted, is experienced as having a truth value and is also experienced as *an* assertion, but not as an assertion that's being asserted. I repeat: the above sentence is *experienced as an assertion that's not being asserted by the speaker.*[15]

There are other ways to use sentences, apart from demonstrations, where they're not asserted—although they nevertheless *have* truth values and *are* assertions. Consider an actor in a movie who says: "George Washington chopped down cherry trees"; he's *pretending* to assert this sentence—more accurately, he's performing, where to "perform" in this way involves pretense. Nevertheless, despite this, the sentence has a truth value and *is* an assertion.[16]

This shows the experience of assertion isn't supervenient on the appreciation of the referential properties of the words in a sentence or on its truth value. That makes it tempting to explain those experiences of propositions-as-assertions as due to the experiences of their utterers *uttering them*; after all, nothing perceivably semantic about the sentences seems relevant. Not so, as the examples in the last section indicate. An anonymous sentence on a uniform background on a website,[17] for example, or as graffiti, *will be* experienced as an asserted assertion, not as a demonstration of an assertion (or of an indicative sentence); it also won't be experienced as the mere *appearance* of an indicative sentence. Furthermore, it will be experienced as an asserted assertion even with the knowledge that it's a random product of a program.

This is striking. Shapes we experience as sentences are often experienced as *asserted* sentences unless framed otherwise; see the example of framing a demonstration in the next paragraph. We *could have* been psychologically constituted

[15] Let not terminology trap us in nomenclatural tiffs on which nothing philosophical turns. Cappelen (2011, especially 36 n. 16) notes that the English word "assertion" isn't used as widely as philosophers use it (and as I'm using it here); neither, of course, is "say" or "utter" as he (and speech-act theorists generally) use these words. The point, above, is that if I demonstrate "I am hungry at this moment," the sentence uttered is experienced as an indicative—but it's experienced as having a property, one I'm calling "being an assertion," that goes beyond that grammatical property. Some sentences are experienced as grammatical indicatives but not as assertions, e.g., "You'd better not close that door" is experienced as a, possibly threatening, *demand*—and it's so experienced even if it appears as a piece of graffiti on a wall. What a sentence *means*, on the other hand, is experienced as a property it has regardless of whether it's an assertion or not. The experienced meanings of sentences come closest to what Cappelen (2011, 22) calls a "speech-act neutral saying" the existence of which he claims is a shared assumption of the assertion literature. Contrary to Cappelen (and the rest of the literature, if he's right), we don't have an experience of anything like *that*. "Speech-act neutral sayings" are theoretical posits driven by the attempt to characterize language experience only in terms of speech acts. Doing so makes the experience of the "content" of a sentence elusive—something that can be captured only by positing a speech act of this peculiar sort. Actions, however, even language actions, are always *doings*. There is no doing that's—as it were—a "neutral" doing that's always being done when something else is being done too. "Saying," as Cappelen (and others) need it to be, is experientially incoherent; we do experience "what is said," but that's an experience of the property of a sentence that's being uttered.

[16] If someone utters indicative sentences to practice elocution, these are also experienced as assertions that are nevertheless not being asserted. Practicing elocution isn't engaging in performance. (I owe this example to Sigrún Svavarsdóttir, communicated on October 13, 2017.)

[17] Imagine that upon landing on a particular website, a light blue background fills your screen (along with some white clouds) against which the following black shapes appear: **God exists.**

to experience naked appearances of sentences without utterers as only that: mere appearances *of* sentences, indicative, interrogative, and so on. But that's not the experience. It *is* the experience we have with single words, provided those words aren't commonly used to give commands or to express single-word sentences (e.g., "Leave" or "Exit"). Advertisements *often* exploit our experience of unframed indicative sentences as asserted: poster advertising regularly takes the form of isolated uttererless sentences.

For a sentence to be experienced as a *demonstration*, it must occur within a demonstrative context, as "I'm hungry" does in what follows:

> The following sentence has two words: I'm hungry.

The sentence "I'm hungry" is experienced as an assertion that's nevertheless not being asserted. I speculate that our default experience of presentations of indicative sentences is as asserted unless a sentential framing indicator short-circuits this or they're typically used in some other way (as "You'd better not close the door" is).[18]

Sentences exhibited in absent-speaker cases are experienced as asserted—even when they're *known* to not have asserters. Consequently, they're also experienced as without asserters who know, believe, or understand *what's asserted*. But there are other cases—what I'll call spokespersons or spokespeople—where asserters are experienced as present, and those asserters experience themselves, as their audiences do, as asserting. Nevertheless, there is no expectation (by anyone) that asserters believe, know, or even understand their assertions. The asserted propositions, that is, are experienced as meaningful, with truth values, and as asserted; but nevertheless, their asserters aren't (usually) expected to know or believe these things. In addition, the propositions themselves that the spokespersons assert, although experienced as meaningful and with truth values, needn't be items that their audience expects to be rational, justified, informative, or even sensible. The propositions themselves can be "crazy."

Spokespeople publicize "information" about the products of their companies, or about the "positions taken" of other individuals or institutions on various issues. Those spokespeople, however, aren't expected to necessarily believe what they say; *they* aren't expected to know that what they assert is true, nor (with

[18] So one disanalogy between our experience of assertions and that of screwdrivers is that we can't experience screwdrivers as being used without experiencing individuals using them (recall my earlier discussion of Neta's animated-screwdriver example), but we *can* experience assertions as being asserted without asserters. Pagin (2011), in the course of arguing for "prima facie informativeness" being a necessary condition on asserting, describes a psychologically rich set of speaker cues—some cultural—among groups of speaker-hearers as inducing the experience of asserting. On the contrary, as my examples indicate: speakers and their properties needn't come into the experience at all.

respect to technical aspects of certain products, e.g., new software or drugs) are they expected to even *understand* what they're telling others—what they're nevertheless *asserting*.[19] We can criticize the asserted *propositions* as false, as things that shouldn't be believed, or as not known. Sometimes these criticisms *do* take the form of criticizing the spokesperson—but (usually) criticism of propositions is primary. Consider:

S: Taking this drug will make you *a lot more* attractive.
A: That just isn't true. *You* know that isn't true.

The criticism of the proposition comes first; it's then *supported* by the subsequent point that the spokesperson doesn't know (or shouldn't think) it's true.

Or, consider:

S: There are no bugs in this new software.
A: No one can know anything like that.

Or:

S: Cigarette smoking doesn't cause cancer.
A: Even you don't believe that.

Here, "even" implicates: This *proposition* is so absurd that not even *you* believe it.

In each of these cases, and generally, the criticism is directed toward the proposition. The *proposition* isn't true, or it's obviously not true, or it's something no one should believe; and *derivatively*, the spokesperson is criticized for asserting a false proposition, or one that's obviously false, or something that no one should believe. It's not that the spokesperson, having asserted something, is violating an expectation that (of course) what she asserts will be true, or something she believes or knows.[20]

[19] Brandom (1994, 214) doesn't require understanding for assertion. He says, "An assertion, even if true, is not taken to express knowledge unless the one making it *understands* the claim being made." Brandom's understanding condition on knowledge is false. We can fail to understand claims we nevertheless know to be true. For example, a close friend of a mathematician can know that a certain result (that the close friend can *state*, say) is true on the basis of his never-lying friend telling him that she has *proved it*. It's then possible for this close friend to tell other mathematicians what he knows without knowing what the result he's conveying to others *means*.

[20] If someone believes a salesperson and purchases something that turns out different from how the salesperson described it, that *someone* is often criticized. "What did you expect?" is typical. This is an accusation of gullibility: he should *not* have *expected* the salesperson to have asserted something true, or known (by the salesperson), or even something the salesperson believed. (The following was added while checking the copyediting, March 22, 2020—under stressful circumstances.) Let's distinguish "deontic" and "epistemic" uses of the word "expect." (Thanks to Florence Bacus, February 13, 2020, written comments, and David Owens, February 29, 2020, personal communication, for this;

(The following paragraph was added while checking the copyediting of this book, March 22, 2020.) Florence Bacus complains (February 13, 2020—written comments; I'm paraphrasing her thought fairly, I hope): We don't criticize *propositions*. She writes (not necessarily exactly endorsing the sentiments she expresses here): "Strictly speaking, a proposition can't be criticized; a proposition doesn't have any inherent teleology in it according to which it ought to be true, i.e. a proposition is not in itself defective or deserving of criticism just because it's untrue; that would be crazy." *Response*: Yes, you're describing the reality correctly. These things—propositions—*given what they are* (things with meanings) aren't the sorts of things that can be criticized this way. But that's not the phenomenology, and how we speak, given that phenomenology. We *do* criticize propositions, and in just this way, as the examples sandwiching this parenthetical paragraph indicate.)

Sean Spicer briefly had the job of asserting things (on behalf of the elected Donald Trump) that were *clearly* false, and (therefore) *clearly* things he neither believed nor knew (that is, he either didn't know these things or—worse—he knew them to be false because they were *blatantly* false). Nevertheless, *he* wasn't criticized for asserting that *he* knew these things or for saying that he believed them; he was criticized for saying things that were obviously (and laughably) false.[21]

I'm paraphrasing their concerns—faithfully, I hope.) Then to merely note that one "expects" or even "should expect" flakes, known liars and salespeople to say falsehoods doesn't all by itself undercut assertion norms. And to criticize someone who fails to expect flakes, known liars and salespeople to lie doesn't undercut the existence of an assertion norm either. After all, what the criticism of the person who expects a salesperson to tell the truth could amount to is criticism of his failure to realize that such people routinely violate some norm or other of assertion, say, the truth norm; that is, the criticism isn't of the person's deontic expectations but of his epistemic one. *Response*: Distinguishing these "uses" of "expect" doesn't help the assertion-norm proponent. Consider the case of a tardy student. And suppose the teacher criticizes the student for being late. If someone says to the teacher, "why'd you bother to criticize him; you *knew* he was going to be late," the teacher can respond with: "he's *supposed* to arrive on time." But responses like these aren't apt in the cases I give. Consider again someone saying, "You expected the salesperson to tell you the truth?" To respond with, "he's *supposed* to tell the truth," strikes my ear as *still* naïve—that is, *expecting a norm of assertion* (like truth or sincerity or knowledge) to be in place with salespeople is *also* naïve. The classroom is different since, to some extent, *the teacher* stipulates the norms that are operative. Compare this case with an expert giving a talk: You and I listen to an expert lecturing on a topic (in her area) and you notice it's all wrong and complain; and I say: "What did you expect?" (Because I'm someone, say, who thinks "experts" are often "bullshitting.") You can respond with: "But she's *supposed* to know what she's talking about." This does suggest a norm is in place—but it's a norm, notice, that's coming in because the speaker has *professional* credentials. (And so it's not that any sort of norm of assertion is operative here.) Compare: I ask someone on the street what time it is, and as that person rushes past me he blurts out a time that's obviously wrong. I *can't* complain: "He was *supposed* to tell me the right time," although I *can* mutter under my breath, "asshole." Clearly: no norm of assertion is in place here.

[21] He was also *morally* condemned for continuing to *assert* what he knew was laughably false. He wasn't condemned for not believing or not knowing what he was asserting; *that* was assumed. Spokespeople for chemical companies (such as Dow) or for tobacco companies are also often morally condemned for what they assert. This isn't because they know the things they are asserting to be false

Notice: a spokesperson doesn't "represent" herself as knowing or believing what she asserts. She doesn't even represent it as true. She does represent it as an assertion appropriately attributed to the person or institution she's asserting it on behalf of. But that doesn't require her representing it as known by that person or institution or as something that person or institution believes or even thinks is true (or reasonable).

It might be argued that spokespeople aren't asserting anything. They are, instead, conduits (or "loudspeakers") for another individual's (or corporation's) assertions; those are the only entities making assertions—although indirectly—in these cases.[22] No: The spokesperson is making assertions *on behalf of* someone else—but that's not to be a conduit or loudspeaker. Spokespersons rarely quote or even paraphrase. Contrast Spicer making assertions that represent Trump's position (as Spicer always did) with a case where he instead reads aloud a prepared set of short ungrammatical bullet points that everyone knows that Trump has *written*. In this case, Spicer isn't asserting anything (in the first case, he is, although, as mentioned, on behalf of another person: Trump). Nor is he making a *report*. That's different too. Is to report something to assert it? It seems so; it's certainly not to *demonstrate* it. Quiz-show contestants also (sometimes) assert what they say in order to win; sometimes they've memorized formulas from physics or sophisticated scientific facts, and they don't know, believe, or even understand them. These are cases where—in one sense—we'll describe such contestants as "knowing the answers" while simultaneously describing them as "not knowing what they are talking about." I forgo further discussion of this interesting kind of case, except to observe that we allow that someone can know things in one way but not in another. This characterization of this someone *isn't* (and doesn't have to be) expressed in a contradictory way, e.g., by saying that A knows that *p and* A doesn't know that *p*. Recall the discussion of "knowing that" in section 2.4.[23]

(although they do); it's because these false things are dangerous to assert; and these spokespeople (should) know *this*: they're doing something wrong by *asserting* these things (because some people might believe them). We shouldn't confuse moral outrage with outrage over the violation of an *epistemic* assertion norm. Most people don't become outraged over the (mere) violation of epistemic norms. For the most part, only academics (and certain journalists) become outraged over the violation of epistemic norms.

[22] I owe this suggestion to Vassilios Pipis, October 5, 2017, personal communication.

[23] One last point. Dethier (email, May 1, 2019) suggests that spokesperson cases really are cases of *pretending*, that "we pretend as though the words uttered by the spokesperson are the words of the company or the individual that they represent." I strongly disagree with this description of the experience. (We must be careful not to bloat the rather special case of pretense beyond its proper place.) Spokespersons are *speaking for* the companies or individuals that they represent; that isn't for them (or us) to experience pretense as taking place. I even think that describing spokespersons as "performing" is misdescribing what they're doing. "Reporting" comes closer, although that too isn't right. They're speaking for someone—that all by itself is neither to perform nor to pretend nor to report. It's not to act either, as one does in movies (where pretense does take place). All these are different kinds of speech acts with very different properties.

4.4 The Assertions of Spokespersons and Moorean Remarks

Sean Spicer was a spokesperson for Donald Trump. The phenomenon of spokesperson assertion is an important part of our assertion practices if only because it shows that many claims philosophers have made about assertions fail to capture the phenomenon accurately.

To illustrate this, consider a family of propositions (some of which) Moore claimed to be quite odd—when asserted by speakers:[24]

It's raining out; but I don't know this.
It's raining out; but that's not true.
It's raining out; but I don't believe this.
It's raining out; but that might not be true.
It's raining out; but I don't understand what I've just said.

I'll now show that these "odd-sounding" remarks can be successfully and naturally asserted in a number of contexts; spokespersons, in particular, can easily utter them. To begin with, notice that speakers can change their minds after saying something because they've realized that what they said isn't true or might not be true, or it's something they don't believe. After saying, "it's raining," the speaker can, for these reasons, *withdraw* or *retract* the statement. But she can't use a Moorean remark to do this; she can't say, "It's raining, but I don't believe it," "It's raining, and that's not true," or "It's raining, although I don't believe that." She *can* say, "It's raining—no, I'm wrong" or "It's raining—oops, I don't believe that." So the cases that I intend to describe, of acceptable Moorean remarks, can't be cases of *speaker retraction*.[25]

They also can't be cases of *demonstrations*. None of the above Moorean statements is odd if "It's raining out" occurs demonstratively. Suppose I demonstrate the following sentence (as I actually am):

It's raining out.

I could add afterward, "By the way, it's not" or "I don't know if it's raining out or not." These are OK but not because they're Moorean remarks. The second clause

[24] Cappelen (2011, 38) gives other examples that seem equally odd, ones along the lines of "It's raining out, but 'it's raining out' doesn't answer the question you asked." I should add that variants of all these Moorean remarks, using "and," "although," or a semicolon instead of "but," are possible. This doesn't make any difference, except in tone.

[25] I thank Samia Hesni for raising the issue of speaker retraction (personal communication, October 15, 2017).

is a comment on the assertion properties of the first clause—but the first clause isn't asserted. Spokespeople, on the contrary, aren't *demonstrating* the thoughts of the institutions or individuals they're representing. It's *possible*, of course, for them to do this, but that's different. I may list several statements on the blackboard that I attribute to Descartes. I'm not, by virtue of that, a spokesperson *for* Descartes; to do *that*, interestingly, a necessary condition is my *asserting* those statements, not simply listing them.

These preliminaries aside, consider the last item on my list of Moorean remarks, and notice it's acceptable *in certain contexts*. Consider a spokesperson saying this:

> The notorious Supercooling Effect has been solved. (*smiling self-depreciatingly*) I really don't understand what that means. Our lab techs can explain it, though, if you're into details like that.

Moorean remarks in the family of "It's raining, but that's not true" are also acceptable in *many* contexts. It's common for a lecturer discussing a complex phenomenon to say something and then add: "but that's an exaggeration. Let me now try to be more accurate" or "that's right, but only sort of." It's also common to add, instead: "but that's not quite right" or "but that's only a first inaccurate stab at the matter" or "but that's not exactly true." A speaker could also add bluntly, instead: "Sorry. That last remark was flat-out false, although it helps as a first attempt at a characterization." This is even true of the classic Moorean remark about rain exhibited above. Imagine a meteorologist (with sophisticated descriptions of rainfall at her disposal) saying: "It's raining, although not really. What's really going on out there is . . ."[26] Notice that these *aren't* cases of speaker retraction. If what followed the first clause, in these cases, were simple retractions, experts couldn't use the first clauses the way they do, as a basis for refinement. That's why these corrections and refinements—they should be called this rather than "retractions"—can take the form of Moorean remarks, although, as I indicated earlier, speaker retractions don't.

What about the other forms of Moorean remarks? Generally speaking, spokespeople can utter them in the right circumstances. Suppose (contrary to

[26] Why are these sorts of Moorean remarks so common? And why is their *commonality* largely unnoticed in the literature *on* Moorean remarks? I can't answer the second question, but here's an answer to the first. Putting sophisticated points *very accurately* (so that they're *true*)—philosophical observations, for example, or subtle scientific points—can make the resulting discourse very hard to understand; sometimes the caveats and qualifications (by their sheer numbers) are confusing. So, to get people to see a point clearly to begin with, one often puts the point falsely and refines it after: a Moorean remark results. Melia (2000) calls this "weaseling," and his observation has been taken up in some of the philosophy of mathematics literature, but no one to my knowledge, including Melia, connects "weaseling"—so called—to Moorean remarks.

actual history), Sean Spicer had become fed up with what Donald Trump was requiring him to assert during news conferences; suppose, as a result, he took to asserting things like the following:[27]

> Donald Trump's inauguration was the biggest in history; but I don't know this.
> Donald Trump's inauguration was the biggest in history; but that's not true.
> Donald Trump's inauguration was the biggest in history; but I don't believe this.
> Donald Trump's inauguration was the biggest in history; but that might not be true.
> Donald Trump's inauguration was the biggest in history; but I don't understand what I've just said.

Spicer would have lost his job immediately.[28] For this reason alone, these aren't remarks Spicer would have been *expected* to assert in normal circumstances; but, given the bizarre circumstances of someone like Donald Trump being a president, these are perfectly acceptable things for Spicer *to* assert. Spicer would have been recognized as being in the unenviable position of having to *assert* statements that he (and everyone else) recognized were *embarrassingly* not true. He would, in addition, be engaging in the rare act of publicly asserting this—being (unusually) honest and brave. This is unexpected but only because people almost never have the (moral) capacity to pull off such things.[29] Spicer would have asserted the first clause in each sentence above because that's his job; he would have asserted the second clause in order to indicate that he, personally, doesn't believe, know, etc., the first thing he has nevertheless (had to) assert. With the right tone of voice, Spicer could have asserted *contradictions*. He could have said: "It's raining . . . but it's not raining!"—the first in a tone of voice indicating he's asserting the false claim about rain on behalf of Trump (false claims

[27] One of the earliest things Spicer was required to assert at news conferences on Trump's behalf were absurd lies about the size of the crowd at Trump's sparsely attended inauguration. This set the tone of Spicer's subsequent tenure in his job—in particular, the ways he was repeatedly ridiculed in public.

[28] He could also have said "and" instead of "but," or he could have juxtaposed two sentences, or spoken in a way that conveyed a semicolon. He would have still lost his job. He could also have said (along the lines of an example due to Pagin (2011, 133)), "Donald Trump's inauguration was the biggest in history; but I personally don't believe this." Yes, he would have lost his job then too. A spokesperson's *job* is to assert the company line—and not follow it with one's own personal views. Naturally, and depending on the background beliefs of the listeners, they'll take the first clause of a Moorean remark by a spokesperson as true, false, informative, and so on—and so evaluate the second clause similarly or differently.

[29] Here is something more likely (this could easily have happened): Spicer afterward is watching on film—with a close friend—himself asserting various false things on behalf of Trump. Imagine him saying, after each remark: "And I didn't [or don't] believe that *either*." These are *quite close to* Moorean remarks. (I owe an example like this one to Sigrún Svavarsdóttir, October 12, 2017.)

about *weather* are ones Trump could easily have made)[30] and the second in a tone of voice indicating he's asserting a truth on behalf of himself. (Again, instead of "but," he could have used "and," a semicolon, or even a period.) Unlike the expert refining a previous remark, Spicer wouldn't be modifying his previous assertion. He'd be disowning the appearance of a personal commitment to what he (nevertheless) continued to publicly assert.[31]

An individual is often assigned the task of reporting the views of a committee. This person may therefore be required to assert things that she nevertheless doesn't personally believe or know to be true. This is universally recognized as a requirement of the task. It can also, in certain cases, lead to Moorean remarks.

Let me summarize the points made here. A straightforward assertion norm would require an asserter to assert what she knows or (more weakly) believes she knows. Moorean remarks seem to be evidence for assertion norms: they're experienced as weird (so this take on them goes) because an assertion of them seems to undercut the speaker's knowledge of what he asserts. I'll eventually show (in section 4.8) that where Moore remarks *are* experienced as bizarre—if uttered—this can't be the explanation. But, so far, this has been shown: Spokespersons *assert*, but they don't have to believe, know, etc., what they assert—that's why their making Moorean remarks is acceptable. So either an assertion norm allows exceptions, e.g., "unless the speaker is a spokesperson" (we'll soon see that there are *too many* exceptions for this to be plausible), or there are no such norms.

4.5 Assertions: Of Journalists, in Advertisements, by Cartoon Characters and Flakes

Let's return to the expectations that hearers have of asserters and look at additional cases. Consider journalists. Our expectations about journalists vary—some of them we think are no better than spokespersons; but others we hold in higher esteem. We do expect *certain* journalists to believe what they are saying, and to know these things as well; we expect *those journalists* to do the appropriate research to give themselves the authority to make their assertions.[32] This isn't

[30] I'm *so* annoyed because Trump subsequently ruined the light witticism this note is appended to. (I wrote it about a year and a half before Hurricane Dorian.)

[31] Suppose reporters took to asking Spicer himself: "Do you believe this?" Spicer could have said, "Stop asking me what *I* think. It's not my job to assert what *I* think." (I think he would have lost his job under these circumstances as well: Trump wouldn't have understood a subtlety like this and would instead have regarded Spicer as being disloyal. Indeed, it's my view—I'm writing this sentence on March 21, 2020 while reviewing copyediting—that Mick Mulvaney *did* lose his job for pretty much saying this.)

[32] Once upon a time, certain journalists were held in *very* high esteem. I'm thinking of Walter Cronkite or—even more so—Edward R. Murrow. This public esteem could hardly have occurred if

true of most "talking heads" on television. These people aren't even expected to necessarily understand what they're asserting—let alone believe or know it.

Now consider assertions in *advertisements*. We (currently in the United States) live in such *advertising-saturated* environments that perhaps most of us (in the United States, anyway) hear or see language events in ads far more often than we hear or see them in face-to-face interactions with real human beings like our friends, lovers, or family members. (I'd like to think the previous sentence is an exaggeration, although I've come to doubt it.) And, despite the fact that the language events in ads range widely from stand-alone exhibits of sentences on posters (without named sources), to utterances by nameless spokespeople (who are only heard) as well as to utterances from official actors and (occasionally) from real people (who believe or know what they are saying), nevertheless these utterances are mostly *asserted*.[33] Unlike in the movies, actors in ads are *not* experienced as "pretend asserting." Actors *pretend to assert* in movies—just as they pretend to command, to be kings, and so on; what they pretend to assert, but *do* utter, however, are assertions. But in ads, even when scripted, actors nevertheless assert things about products (and the—often unwilling—recipients of ads know this). There is no expectation, however, that actors in ads know what they're talking about or believe it; there is no expectation that the things they assert are true, informative, or even sensible. (If the audience has background information about the actors, about the advertising agencies, or about the companies making the products, this changes: beliefs of the recipients determine their expectations about these things.)

Unreal *cartoon characters* often assert things in ads.[34] Nevertheless, *they* are the asserters in these ads; it's not that the ad creates a context within which assertions are only pretendedly asserted. There are no expectations that cartoon characters (!) know or believe what they assert—although, depending on the case, there may be expectations that what they're asserting is nevertheless true or justified. Such expectations always arise from specific background knowledge about the companies that purchased the ads or designed them.[35] On the

the public (generally) had had the expectation at the time that journalists (or anyone, really) who assert something know it or even believe it. *These people obviously stood out.*

33 More accurately, ads also have plenty of rhetorical and genuine questions, commands, and all the other "speech acts" we make. I need attend to only assertions for current purposes.

34 Three cases from my childhood: Smokey Bear, Tony the Tiger, and Charlie the Tuna. All of these "beings" would assert things about, for example, the dangers of not putting out campfires, the great taste of various foodstuffs, or the quality of StarKist tuna. Tony the Tiger, some of you recall, described the taste of Frosted Flakes as "Grrrrreaaat!!!"

35 People differ in their responses to (and expectations about) "truth in advertising." Some are highly critical—always suspicious of what's asserted—others are gullible; these reactions differ depending on the qualities of the spokespeople appearing in the ads, as well as (unfortunately) on epistemically irrelevant factors such as production values. That said, notice how odd the following reaction is to someone who, after seeing an advertisement for a product, decides that he needs to find out

semantic-perception view, this otherwise odd experience of unreal asserters is easy to understand: if indicative sentences are experienced as objects with assertion properties independent of asserters, then they can be experienced as having these properties in a context that's otherwise pretense. A pure speech-act phenomenology that restricts our experience of assertions to speech acts of *asserters* can't accommodate the experience of recognizably unreal beings uttering real language objects.[36]

Let's return briefly to anonymous postings. If an anonymous posting occurs on a website that carefully vets its content, those who know this *expect* the assertion to be true and there to be evidence. They may not expect the individual who posted the anonymous remark to know or believe the post—although they may believe this of the website's fact checker or, more vaguely, of those who "run the website." The same is true of anonymous articles in the *Economist* or anonymous editorials in the *New York Times*. Those in authority at these publications and/or the editor(s) and/or the reporter(s) and/or the writer(s) of the pieces are expected to believe, know, and think true what's been written. But this clearly isn't a *generally held expectation* of anonymous (or any) assertions. There is also, notice, often a specific requirement in cases like the *Economist* or the *New York Times* that the writer be accurate, have verified what she asserts, etc. Again, this isn't generally required of asserters—as I'll discuss further in section 4.6.

Consider, for contrast, "flakes." These individuals are quite sloppy in their assertion practices because they're quite sloppy about supporting what they know. Whereas moderately responsible people would normally take some care to verify their claims, flakes instead assert things they don't know, and often (worse) things that *no one* can know. Gossip columnists are examples; and what these people write or broadcast is almost always based, to put it mildly, on shaky "evidence." Flakes are common in ordinary life too: individuals who are recognized by their friends not to be relied on for facts or (for that matter) anything informative or even interesting. *Some flakes* can't be relied on to even know what they *believe* because they're either poor at introspection, or too glib, or . . ., and so on. During a momentary epiphany, however, such an individual may recognize this about herself and say:

whether the product is good: "You don't have to do that—didn't you hear the ad?" Naturally enough, a great deal of (expensive and ongoing) research is directed toward determining what qualities an ad (or a spokesperson in an ad) needs to successfully convince its targeted audience that what's asserted in the ads is true. None of this variability in expectation affects the experience that nevertheless ads are largely composed of asserted statements.

[36] Notice the complex nature of our (ordinary) response to cartoon characters making assertions: (1) What cartoon characters utter are (sometimes) assertions. (2) Cartoon characters don't exist. (See Azzouni (2010; 2017b) for discussion of how this goes.)

He didn't commit the murder. (*pause*) Oh, wow, even I don't believe that.

Imagine, for example, a trial lawyer, during a conference on a case (but off the record) saying this. He's simply noticing aloud that he doesn't believe the first assertion he made, nor does he think it's true. The "even" indicates that he (at least at this moment) recognizes himself to often believe the outlandish things he says even though one (generally) shouldn't believe such things. But his assertion that he doesn't believe what he's just said is nevertheless an assertion (and the whole utterance is a Moorean remark that's perfectly acceptable and, actually, *not all that uncommon*). Trial lawyers are specialized spokespeople: they "represent their client's best interests." But some lawyers can lose sight of—during the flows of rhetoric that such individuals (professionally) engage in—what they actually believe; and (more rarely) they can acknowledge this. Such acknowledgments will take the form of sensible Moorean remarks. Notice that the above remark isn't—or needn't be—a retraction. The lawyer can continue to assert the outlandish claims, on behalf of his client, "on the record." Indeed, "on the record" and "off the record" are ways of distinguishing the *kinds* of assertions being made—it's *not* a matter of scorekeeping retractions or a (consequent) drawing of a distinction between what's (still) asserted and what's been withdrawn.

The last group I should mention is a set of individuals that has been noticed in the assertion literature: known liars. Our current president (2017, 2018, 2019, 2020 . . .), alas, is a good example. In known-liar cases, expectations also vanish that what a person asserts is true, known, and, often, if we think the liar is chronically insincere, things he believes.[37]

To recapitulate, the full range of cases—anonymous postings, ads, and assertions by liars, flakes, and spokespeople, in addition to face-to-face conversational interactions philosophers focus on—reveals that only *sometimes* do we expect what's asserted to be true, reasonable, informative, or sensible; only sometimes do we expect what's asserted to have an asserter; only sometimes do we think that what's asserted is believed or known by the asserter; only sometimes do we think an asserter has taken on commitments *of any sort*. Expectations vary widely depending on the common ground presupposed that the recipients of the assertion are aware of, or depending on background beliefs that they don't share with asserters—in many cases, asserters needn't be aware that they're liars or flakes. This is all bad news for views that there are norms of assertion (of any sort).[38] I turn to this after the next three paragraphs.

[37] There is a lot of mystery, notoriously, about whether Donald Trump believes his lies. That's not uncommon with chronic liars; they can fail to know when they're lying.

[38] Richard Moran (2005, 11) writes (italics his): "the speaker, in presenting his utterance as an *assertion*, one with the force of *telling* the audience something, presents himself as *accountable* for the truth of what he says, and in doing so he offers a kind of guarantee for this truth. This shows up in

Some of the phenomena I've described have been noticed (and acknowledged in the literature); cases are also discussed that I don't think involve assertion. I'll comment briefly. Cappelen (2011, 42) describes trying out ideas in a philosophy seminar—making claims that one doesn't believe. This isn't a genuine example of assertion, however. Professors don't assert the things they're trying out in front of a class; they're *performing*. (Only sometimes are these professors pretending, by the way.) The statements, of course, *are* assertions (the situation is similar to the case of actors in film, as mentioned), but only those committed to a speech-act phenomenology have to claim that someone who is uttering what are experienced to be assertions is *therefore* asserting them.

Lackey (2007) describes cases where neither belief nor knowledge is required to assert. One of her well-known examples is a fourth-grade teacher who's a creationist, but who nevertheless accurately teaches her students the facts of evolution as they're portrayed in textbooks. These are good cases.[39] Like a spokesperson, the fourth-grade teacher asserts claims she neither believes nor knows to be true. She can also, under the right circumstances, utter Moorean remarks.

Cappelen (2011, 43) suggests guesses and hunches are assertions, e.g., "It's behind Door No. 2" or "The restaurant is on 4th Avenue." Pure-speech-act phenomenological assumptions, I think, are distorting impressions: the statements themselves *are* assertions, but no one who's clearly guessing is themselves asserting anything by uttering them. Imagine this reproach: "You asserted that the restaurant was on 4th Avenue" or, more weakly, "You claimed it was on 4th Avenue." "No, I didn't; I was just guessing" is an acceptable defense. Recall the quiz-show contestants at the end of section 4.3. I mentioned that such contestants (sometimes) assert things they've memorized and don't understand (or believe). Sometimes contestants guess answers to win; in those cases they're *not* asserting anything although they *are* uttering assertions.

the fact that if we are inclined to believe what the speaker says, but then learn that he is *not*, in fact, presenting his utterance as an assertion whose truth he stands behind, then what remains are just words, not a reason to believe anything." Given the preceding cases, this wrongheaded overview of assertion (and our experience of it) is due to elevating quite special situations—and our expectations in those—to the status of *default* ones. Moran's quotation, however, is regarded by rather many philosophers writing in this area as a litany of *truisms*.

39 And they overlap to some extent with the ones I've given. Although Lackey recognizes her "selfless assertion" cases pressure knowledge norms of assertion, she thinks they don't pressure a weaker "reasonable to believe norm of assertion." My spokesperson, flake, and other cases together pressure any norm whatsoever (even a consistency norm!) because they establish that we have only background-specific expectations about assertions, what's asserted, and asserters. Relatedly, there are no conditions on asserters, asserting, and assertions, such as an asserter's assertions being informative, consistent, true, and so on.

4.6 Assertion Norms

Assertion norms are empirically elusive.[40] Their evidence isn't verbal behavior in accord with them, nor explicit statements of the norms—something that occurs with the norms of many games and those governing other social practices. Proponents of assertion norms admit that verbal behavior is (even usually) not in accord with their purported norms; furthermore, there are no explicit statements of these norms that asserters recognize (or take themselves to be governed by).[41] As Williamson (2000, 240) describes assertion norms, which he takes to be "constitutive rules":

> Constitutive rules do not lay down necessary conditions for performing the constituted act. When one breaks a rule of the game, one does not thereby cease to be playing that game.[42] . . . Likewise . . . when one breaks a rule of assertion,

[40] Williamson (2000, 238–239) writes: "That assertion has [constitutive rule(s) of assertion] is by no means obvious."

[41] There are many social norms governing special meals and how one dresses (both generally and in specified circumstances)—to choose two salient examples. It's notable that there is a *lot* of popular literature about this—in the form of explicit guides to appropriate behavior. This has been so for *centuries*. Characterizations of purported norms for assertion, in contrast, occur only in (relatively recent) articles in philosophy. This is an ominous fact for proponents of assertion norms—it surely is if they're hoping for empirical confirmation of some sort.

[42] There is some acknowledgment in the literature of the problems this claim faces. Such "constitutive" rules don't exist in games or in other rule-governed activities that aren't games, such as (logical) inference or grammatical utterance. Williamson's remark is oddly put, is undeveloped, and collapses under analysis. As Johnson (2018, 55) points out, lots of ways of breaking the rules of a game (using a racket in a soccer game, carrying the football out of bounds and claiming that nevertheless one has scored a touchdown, etc.) certainly *are* ceasing to play the game. There *are* things one can do in certain games, like "fouling" in basketball, that are spoken of as breaking a rule; but clearly they're not, *strictly speaking*, breaking the rules of the game, since (i) what a foul is, is stipulated, (ii) there are penalties for fouls, and (iii) there are stipulations for how the game continues after a foul is made. (Fouling *is* a move in basketball—one that can be used deliberately in a strategy to win.) This isn't true if one uses a racket in a basketball game or pulls out a gun to prevent others from taking the basketball (notice the absence of rules in basketball stipulating penalties if one player shoots another in the leg during the game). When an action is governed by conditions like (i)–(iii), that makes the action part of the game. (And this is true regardless of whether we informally speak of "breaking the rules.") Similarly, if one breaks the rules of logical deduction, one *ceases* to deduce—at that point, anyway. (This isn't to say that, therefore, one has become unreasonable or irrational. That calls for more.) We do sometimes say instead that one is "inferring badly"—but this is a "casual use" similar to when we take amateurs to still be playing a game although they've allowed themselves to nevertheless break certain rules (Johnson (2018, 54 n. 6)). Grammar is a different matter: a large and indeterminate number of ungrammatical sentences are still described as "English"—although not *all* are. Is the grammatical case enough to support Williamson's claim that a "constitutive rule" for assertion can be broken and yet the resulting item nevertheless remain an assertion? No. The mechanisms that determine the syntax of English tell us what the grammatical sentences are, and that tells us what *English* is. We then tell a pragmatic story about how speaker-hearers are able, in a context, to decode utterances that *aren't* English, and recognize what's meant—that is, what (grammatically correct) English sentence is meant by a particular ungrammatical utterance. Derivatively, utterances for which this can't be done aren't considered "English" in this broader loose sense of "English." (That there are "constitutive" rules for assertion that aren't part of the individuation conditions for assertions is a nice example of trying to have one's cake and eat it too.) My focus is on the evidence for various positions on assertion, and not directly about the cogency of Williamson's framework, so I've restricted these remarks

> one does not thereby fail to make an assertion. One is subject to criticism precisely because one has performed an act for which the rule is constitutive.

Furthermore (Williamson (2000, 240)):

> The normativity of a constitutive rule is not moral or teleological.[43] The criticism that one has broken a rule of a speech act is no more a moral criticism than is the criticism that one has broken a rule of a game or language.

These two quotations describe what's empirically available to support assertion norms. Not widespread adherence to them—as I've already indicated, that's not an option—nor, as with games, are there explicit codifications of rules. Rather, as Williamson (2000, 243) puts it (on behalf of the knowledge account), "if the account is correct, ordinary speakers are implicitly sensitive to the knowledge rule, for they must have implicitly grasped it in mastering assertion."

How does this so-called implicit sensitivity manifest? It can only be by the recognized appropriateness of criticism on the non-moral grounds that a speech act (that's nevertheless an assertion) has failed to meet the norm—or the recognized peculiarity of certain assertions because they blatantly violate the proposed norm.[44] That is, the evidence from usage is (and only is) violated expectations; if these expectations are instead traced to assumptions and presuppositions of speakers and hearers, ones that recognizably change along with recognized changes in context, that undercuts the evidence for assertion norms.

Let's look at this evidence from usage. Here are six norm candidates.[45]

to a note. (My thanks to Asa Lukas Zabarsky and Shayan Koeksal for discussion on this in the spring term of 2018; my thanks to Asa for bringing Johnson (2018) to my attention.)

[43] Here is a second complaint about Williamson's framework that I'll also confine to a note. Williamson (2000, 239) writes: "Constitutive rules are not conventions. If it is a convention that one must φ, then it is contingent that one must φ; conventions are arbitrary and can be replaced by alternative conventions. In contrast, if it is a constitutive rule that one must φ, then it is necessary that one must φ. More precisely, a rule will count as constitutive of an act only if it is essential to that act; necessarily, the rule governs every performance of the act." He writes later (2000, 266): "The knowledge rule is a constitutive rule; it is not a convention," and uses that to strike an attitude, as at (2000, 267): "It is pointless to ask why the knowledge rule is the rule of assertion. It could not have been otherwise." This last remark is relying on a *metaphysical* claim: Because the knowledge rule is a constitutive rule, and because these are *essential* to assertion acts, of course it could not have been otherwise. But this metaphysical claim is based on sheer stipulation (Williamson *asserts* we should individuate the concept of "assertion" so that it's an essential property of it that the knowledge rule holds of it). Stipulations like this shouldn't be allowed to do philosophical work; it's a matter of no (metaphysical) consequence whether we individuate assertion speech acts so the knowledge rule supposedly governing it is essential to it or a contingent fact that holds universally.

[44] Williamson (2000, 243) writes that "Much of the evidence for the knowledge account comes from the ordinary practice of assertion." This is misleading: What *other* evidence is there supposed to be? (See, however, the forthcoming discussion on Burge's a priori entitlements.)

[45] I draw the formulations of these rules, except one, from Williamson (2000, 242–243, 260–261). Two points about Williamson's intricate argument for the knowledge norm. Although, at the

(The truth rule) One must: assert *p* only if *p* is true.
(The warrant rule) One must: assert *p* only if one has warrant to assert *p*.
(The belief rule) One must: assert *p* only if one believes *p*.
(The knowledge rule) One must: assert *p* only if one knows *p*.
(The BK rule) One must: assert p only if one believes that one knows *p*.
(The RBK rule) One must: assert *p* only if one rationally believes that one knows *p*.

The many cases from earlier sections show why none of the above is a *general* norm of assertion—for the expectations implied by one or another of these assertion norms *don't* occur in many cases of assertion. Spokespeople assertions, to begin with, are *assertions*; but it's usually inappropriate to challenge the asserter on her knowledge of what she's just asserted. It *can* be appropriate to challenge the knowledge of the individual or institution on behalf of which the spokesperson is making her assertions. (It could have been said to Sean Spicer more than once, for example, "Does *President Trump* know this?") The truth of the *proposition* uttered can often be challenged in spokesperson cases. ("Is *this* true?") But this isn't to challenge either the asserter or the agent on behalf of which the asserter is making assertions; it's to challenge the statement *itself*. As for the assertions in ads, any of a number of challenges may (or may not) be appropriate. That the propositions asserted are false or aren't known is a criticism often directed *at the propositions*, and not at asserters; it's often not directed at asserters because there aren't any, or the asserters are fictional (or actors). Apart from that, it may simply be recognized that the assertions in an ad are (unsurprisingly) not true.[46] Criticism is therefore sometimes directed back at the person criticizing the propositions in an ad: A: "That's not true." B: "*No kidding*? You're *surprised*?"

moment, I'm focusing only on usage evidence, crucial to Williamson's argument are two other important considerations (and in this matter, his discussion has a lot in common with other defenses of one or another norm of assertion). First, there is a crucial reliance on the lottery paradox—in particular (and in agreement with many other philosophers), he relies on the assumption that it's intuitively robust that one never knows that one is going to lose a lottery (no matter how high the probability is that one will lose—as long as it isn't 1). I challenge this assumption in section 10.5. The second point is a strong assumption about justification being required for knowledge (and consequently for assertion). Williamson (2000, 245), for example, writes: "Assertion obviously has some kind of evidential norm. It is somehow better to make an assertion on the basis of adequate evidence than to make it without such a basis." Flakes directly show that although it's true that it's "somehow better" to make an assertion on the basis on adequate evidence than otherwise, this doesn't indicate the existence of an evidential "norm." That, apart from this, justification—in the sense of being able to give a justification—is required for knowledge has already been shown false in chapter 1. I revisit this in chapter 8.

46 Notice that sentences like "None of his assertions is true," "He doesn't believe anything he says," and so on, aren't odd *in any way at all*. They ought to be—at least in some way—if there is some kind of assertion norm.

In cases of known liars, it can also be inappropriate to challenge the liar's knowledge or even the truth of what he asserts. Imagine that a known liar (in authority) is holding forth. "Is that true?" she can be asked. "Of course not," she can respond (while laughing). And lastly, it's just *silly* to ask flakes if they know (or believe) or have any warrant for the statements they're asserting. And after doing so, people can challenge the challenger: "What was the point of that? You know he never has any idea what he's talking about."

The other (the only other) usage evidence for norms is based on apparently violated expectations that Moorean remarks seem to exemplify by their perceived oddity.[47] But, as I illustrated in section 4.4, Moorean remarks are often sensible—and, indeed, Moorean remarks *are* made. Should a spokesperson feel the need to separate herself from assertions she has just made, either because she doesn't understand or believe them or because she hasn't good reasons for thinking they're true, she may engage in the (rare) speech act of saying so. (And in most cases, I'd imagine, she'll lose her job.) Flakes or chronic liars, on the other hand, can occasionally engage in frank and honest avowal of the facts: "Oh wow, even I don't believe that," said after a remark that he (and the audience) find epistemically unacceptable. There are, finally, the very common cases of lecturers—experts in their fields—grappling with putting a point accurately. The standard move is to assert something false and then immediately qualify it—by describing it as inaccurate, misleading, or exaggerated.[48]

Given the empirical usage evidence I've described, the primary competitor with one or another norm view is the common-ground expectation view of assertion which traces the legitimacy of criticism when it exists, and the experienced oddity of Moorean remarks, when that exists, to the common-ground expectations of asserters and their witnesses. Support for the common-ground view turns on appropriate criticisms of the assertion of what's asserted, and the assertion itself, concomitantly varying with background assumptions; further support arises from Moorean remarks *not* being uniformly experienced as odd—but only in specific cases.

Proponents of assertion norms can circumvent these counterexamples to their views by stipulating that they *aren't* examples of assertion. At this point (if not before), the non-empirical flavor of the assertion-norm thesis emerges into full light. Another (more promising) way to defend assertion norms is to restrict

[47] See, e.g., chapter 3, section 5 of DeRose (2009).

[48] Another kind of verbal evidence against a truth norm for assertion: Consider this ad I heard recently, "What if we told you [equally good: "said," "asserted"] that there is a quick and easy way to eliminate contact lenses? And what if we told you it's cheap and safe? Well, it's all true . . ." Notice that the cogency of the ad trades on the fact that speakers asserting something true (equally: knowing that something is true) goes beyond their asserting it. (I'm grateful to Ram Neta for pressing me to provide more discussion of this example.)

their ranges. It's not assertions per se that are governed by norms—it's specific kinds of assertions. Perhaps sincere assertions among reliable friends or those of experts are governed by the knowledge norm. I explore this in section 4.8.

A last way to circumvent the counterexamples, apart from denying that assertion behavior is (or needs to be) in accord with these purported norms (as Williamson asserts), is to further deny that the assertion norm need even be in accord with (most) people's *expectations*. This would immunize norm views from empirical refutation altogether. I assume this is bad.[49]

4.7 Burge's Acceptance Principle

I turn to Burge's *acceptance principle*, a different (and independent) approach to establishing a normative property of assertion—one that proceeds by directly establishing entitlements for the witness of an assertion instead of directly establishing responsibilities for the asserter (as Williamson and others do). Burge's acceptance principle purports to be an epistemic "entitlement" to take things presented (by others, verbally and otherwise) as true. The acceptance principle, "to a first approximation" is (Burge (1993, 238)):

> A person is entitled to accept as true something that is presented as true and that is intelligible to him, unless there are strong reasons not to do so.

He immediately glosses the principle this way (238):

> As children and often as adults, we lack reasons not to accept what we are told. We are entitled to acquire information according to the principle—without *using* it as justification—accepting the information instinctively.

Burge isn't offering an empirical argument for this principle;[50] he's also not trying to establish, on empirical grounds, the epistemic entitlements he takes this

[49] But, again, see the discussion of Burge's approach that immediately follows.

[50] He writes (1993, 238, italics his):

> The general form of justification associated with the principle is: *A person is apriori entitled to accept a proposition that is presented as true and that is intelligible to him, unless there are stronger reasons not to do so, because it is prima facie preserved (received) from a rational source, or resource for reason; reliance on rational sources—or resources for reason—is, other things equal, necessary to the function of reason.*

My subsequent discussion of his argument is simplified; I push back (here) against only one of its weaknesses. The other important threads of his argument turn on a view of the content of expressions that derives from the Gricean tradition and from Davidson's views on interpretation. I omit discussion of these additional assumptions—although I've challenged them as well. (I'm thinking specifically of remarks like Burge (1993, 240): "I think that one is apriori prima facie entitled to presume

principle to license.[51] The argument, rather, is this: speaker-hearers (to a first approximation) have a priori entitlements to believe (to take to be true) propositions that are presented to them as true, and that they find intelligible. That this is an "entitlement" and not a "justification" is based on (Burge (1993, 230)) a distinction between "justification" and "entitlement":

> Although both have positive force in rationally supporting a propositional attitude or cognitive practice, and in constituting an epistemic right to it, entitlements are epistemic rights or warrants that need not be understood by or even accessible to the subject. We are entitled to rely, other things equal, on perception, memory, deductive and inductive reasoning, and so—I will claim—the word of others.

Thus, animals and children only have entitlements, not justifications.[52] That Burge intends the acceptance principle not to be empirically established is clear given, first, that he allows it to be defeasible. (One can decide to distrust what one hears for good reasons.) It's also not to be based on general empirical facts about human behavior—e.g., that most humans are honest and sincere in their utterances;[53] nor is it to be based on the fact that—as Burge suggests—children can only acquire language from their parents to begin with by relying on the acceptance principle.[54] It's not even to be based on the fact that—as Burge (1993, 242) claims—it's unnatural to adopt a general attitude of scepticism toward whatever people assert.[55]

that the interlocutor is a rational source or resource for reason—simply by virtue of the prima facie intelligibility of the message conveyed. . . . In understanding language we are entitled to presume what we instinctively do presume about our source's being a source of rationality or reason. We are so entitled because intelligibility is an apriori prima facie sign of rationality." Not so, as the examples in section 4.2 indicate.)

[51] Burge (1993, 241 n. 13) writes: "I think that empiricism cannot possibly explain all our justified acceptance of what we read or hear. The idea that we should remain neutral or sceptical of information unless we have empirical grounds for thinking it trustworthy is, I think, a wild revisionary proposal. I also think that empiricism cannot account for norms for children's relying on others in the acquisition of language or knowledge."

[52] Burge (1993, 230) writes later: "The unsophisticated are entitled to rely on their perceptual beliefs. Philosophers may articulate these entitlements. But being entitled does not require being able to justify reliance on these resources, or even to conceive such a justification. Justifications, in the narrow sense, involve reasons that people have and have access to." I should add that this distinction of Burge's is a refining of an ordinary distinction between being justified and being able to express or articulate a justification that many philosophers (myself included) accept. See note 12 of section 8.3 for a list. Burge builds on this distinction in ways I don't accept. (See the discussion that follows.)

[53] Burge (1993, 241–242) writes: "Just as the Acceptance Principle does not assume that truth is in a statistical majority, the justification of the Principle does not assume that most people are rational. We could learn empirically that most people are crazy or that all people have deeply irrational tendencies—not just in their performance but in their basic capacities."

[54] Burge (1993, 238) writes: "Acceptance underlies language acquisition."

[55] Burge (1993, 242) writes: "Apart from special information about the context or one's interlocutor, neutrality (as well as doubt) is, I think, a rationally unnatural attitude towards an interlocutor's

To explain what the justification of the acceptance principle *is* based on, I'll first indicate the reasons (I think) that Burge has for thinking these entitlements are a priori. First, we're to assume that the child (for example) is *entitled* to the acceptance principle. It's not the mere fact that a child has no choice but to use it. The latter may be true (Burge thinks it *is* true) but pragmatic necessity isn't sufficient for epistemic justification.[56] Since the child is justified, and since empirical facts can't provide epistemic entitlements, we're left with such entitlements (and the principle such entitlements are based on) being a priori.

That said, how does the a priori justification of the acceptance principle go? The argument Burge recommends[57] turns on noticing a "teleological aspect" or function of reason. Reason is intrinsically truth-seeking. Although "lying is sometimes rational in the sense that it is in the liar's best interests . . . lying occasions a disunity among the functions of reason. It conflicts with one's reason's transpersonal function of presenting the truth, independently of special personal interests."[58]

This is supposed to be a nonobvious constitutive function of *reason* that we recognize a priori (Burge (1993, 242 n. 14). The first point to make is that there is little reason to think that a human (or any animal, for that matter) has anything even resembling a (unified) "faculty" of reason. Our reasoning capacities have been revealed by cognitive-science research to be a hodgepodge of restricted (localized) cognitive (and noncognitive) abilities—"kludge" is the word that captures the quality of our internal "software" and "wetware" perfectly. To the extent (and for a time) that we resemble anything like a successful idealized reasoner (e.g., a Turing machine) while executing a task (or, more usually, *part* of a task), we're successfully *simulating* the unified exercise of reasoning with a

presentation of something as true. (Compare: lying for the fun of it is a form of craziness.)" I doubt any of this is true—especially the bit about lying for the fun of it being a form of craziness. As much as decent people everywhere would like to think that cruelty—at least wanton cruelty—is "crazy," it's just not so. In any case, with respect to Burge's justification of the acceptance principle, these empirical disagreements about human psychology don't matter. They do matter, of course, to whether humans can adopt a systematic sceptical attitude—as ancient Pyrrhonians (and their contemporary proponents) attempt—an important question I can't take up in this book.

[56] I don't see that Burge here—or anywhere—defends himself against those who simply refuse to see the child as epistemically entitled (Brandom and Williams are two examples). Burge (1993, 236) writes: "Though ontogenetically later than perception and memory, reliance on others for learning language and acquiring beliefs is deeply ingrained in our evolutionary history. Acquiring beliefs from other seems not only psychologically fundamental, but epistemically justified. We do not as individuals justify this reliance empirically, any more than we justify our use of perception empirically. But we seem entitled to such reliance." I agree we seem entitled: reliabilists, of course, explain why in a way that doesn't require anything a priori. I do the same—as I'll show in a later book.

[57] He writes (1993, 242), honestly: "This issue is more complex than I can see through now."

[58] This doesn't just have a *Kantian* flavor, as Burge and, for example, Fricker (2006) recognize; it should remind knowledgeable readers of Plato's analysis of the soul in *The Republic*—in particular, Plato's picturesque characterization of the dysfunctional soul of the *tyrant*.

sequence of applications of quite topic-specific gerrymandered abilities. Apart from this, there is a long history (dating backward to Plato, forward from Kant[59] and continuing into the contemporary setting) of trying to show the irrationality of selfish behavior (e.g., the "craziness" of systematic lying). We haven't gotten anywhere with this project; indeed (and here I'll be blunt), that's because there's nothing particularly irrational or defective about selfish behavior.[60]

Since I've wandered (almost against my will) into a discussion of an ethical topic, let me say this to conclude this section. People can say to one another (whenever they're planning—as a group—about how to "spin something"): *Here's what we're going to assert about this*: . . . This remark isn't redundant, or weird, or intuitively a violation of any sort of norm on assertion.[61] It *does* sound unsavory. But that's a moral judgment; and it's also clear that our disapproval reactions range widely when faced with these sorts of cases. I stress again: these are reactions about the *ethical consequences* of making (or presenting) assertions that aren't true (or aren't justified or known). In some cases, it doesn't matter much—and so few people will be outraged by lies; in other cases, it's a very big deal. Often, the mere fact of how many people will hear an asserted lie is relevant to the ethical evaluation of the assertion. This is because publicized assertions have more impact.

4.8 Expectations in Special Cases

Consider the following examples:[62]

> Whether President-elect Donald J. Trump knows it or not, nuclear weapons policy has a meticulous language, meant to signal clearly to allies and adversaries.

[59] I'm thinking especially of Kant (1934), and specifically his discussion of the will and "radical evil in human nature."

[60] Just the opposite: There isn't much in recent psychological literature that shows that sociopaths, for example, are irrational, cognitively disunified in any way, or even particularly *unhappy*.

[61] People are more likely to describe what they're going to "say" than what they're going to "assert." But that's because "assert" and "assertion" as used by philosophers (as semi-technical jargon) abstracts from a flavor of "assert" that's always present as we ordinarily use it: to assert something is to say it *strongly*. ("Say," however, is sometimes similar in import, as in the locution "I'm tempted to say *p*," a locution of which includes a saying of *p*. Here, what's meant by "say" is the stronger "assert.") In any case, the result is that the philosophical use of "assertion" covers more speech acts than those which nonphilosophers—in most circumstances—would naturally label "assertions." (Recall note 15.)

[62] First quotation from Max Fisher, *New York Times*, December 23, 2016, A17; second and third quotations from Editorial Board, *New York Times*, December 23, 2016, A22.

> It's unclear what Mr. Trump means by this, or if he understands the threat that a breakdown in relations would pose for Taiwan, an American partner, as well as broader American interests in Asia. Or maybe he understands and just doesn't care.

> Mr. Kabila and his family have looted the nation's resources, including diamonds, to amass a fortune worth hundreds of millions of dollars while doing little to alleviate widespread poverty. This has not been lost on Congo's citizens.

The most straightforward interpretation of these statements is that their declarative contents are presented as known. That is, "nuclear weapons policy has a meticulous language, meant to signal clearly to allies and adversaries," "It would be a threat to Taiwan, an American partner, as well as to broader American interests in Asia, if there were a breakdown in relations to Taiwan," and "Mr. Kabila and his family have looted the nation's resources, including diamonds, to amass a fortune worth hundreds of millions of dollars while doing little to alleviate widespread poverty" are presented in these quotations as known facts. Known to whom? To the writers and readers of these sentences—and perhaps, in the case of some readers, by virtue of reading these sentences. The last statement of the last quotation, in addition, indicates that it's known that Congo's citizens know the preceding sentence in the quotation as well.

That indicative statements (in this context) are represented as known is also shown by a widespread practice of using what I'll call *contrasting-ignorance expressions* that reveal that someone doesn't (or may not) know what's nevertheless being represented as known by the sentence. In the first quotation above, a neutral stance is explicitly taken about what Trump knows, by the use of the phrase "whether President-elect Donald J. Trump knows it or not"; "if he understands" in the second quotation is similar. Here are some more examples of words used contrastively to straight indicative expressions in order to restrict "what's known":[63]

> Mr. Trump's statement, in a midafternoon Twitter post, may have been a response to President Vladimir V. Putin of Russia, who in a speech to his military's leadership in Moscow earlier on Thursday vowed to strengthen Russia's nuclear missiles.

The phrase "may have been" modulates what otherwise, indicatively, would be a presentation of knowledge. That Trump tweeted midafternoon is presented as known. A headline:[64]

> Experimental Ebola Vaccine is Said to Be 100% Effective

[63] From Michael D. Shear and James Glanz, *New York Times*, December 23, 2016, A1.

[64] Donald G. McNeil, Jr., *New York Times*, December 23, 2016, A1. Interestingly, in the archived electronic edition, the title read: "New Ebola Vaccine Gives 100 Percent Protection."

Here, "is said to be" is used instead of "is" to indicate that someone (we aren't told who in the headline) is claiming something the narrator is neutral about. (The narrator isn't neutral that it has been said that an experimental Ebola vaccine is 100 percent effective; that's presented as known.) The words "perhaps," "if," and "could" are similar:[65]

> Idealistic and perhaps overconfident, Mr. Obama arrived in the White House certain that he would be the president who would finally resolve the decades-old dispute between Israelis and Palestinians.

"Idealistic" is treated as known fact; "overconfident" is demoted to speculation by "perhaps." That Obama was certain (etc.) is also presented as known.

> If it is the last word—and there are still 27 days left in the Obama presidency—it will serve as a coda to a relationship that never clicked.

Here "if . . . will" functions to mark a prediction as not known. Lastly, the role of "could" is illustrated by this headline:

> With Nuclear Threat, Trump Could Set World on a Scary Path

Two more examples:[66]

> If President-elect Donald J. Trump meant what he said, then the world may one day look back to recall that the first superpower nuclear arms race since the Cold War was announced by two pajama-clad talk show hosts.

"If" and "may" demote indicative representation of knowledge to informed speculation. Were "may" replaced by "will," then what follows the antecedent would be represented as a known consequence of the not known antecedent. Another way of doing the same thing:

> Mr. Trump has a history of bluster and his declarations may turn out to be bluffs. But should he follow through on instigating a nuclear arms race, the consequences could be severe.

[65] First two quotations from Peter Baker, *New York Times*, December 24, 2016, A7; third quotation from Max Fisher, *New York Times*, December 24, 2016, A12. Interestingly, the digital edition headline reads: "Trump, Promising Arms Race, Could Set World on a Scary Path."

[66] Quotations from Max Fisher, *New York Times*, December 24, 2016, A12.

And of course, "don't know"/"know" and "is true"/"is not true" are explicitly used in these contrastive roles.

One thing that follows from these examples is that in *certain* contexts, unadorned indicative sentences present knowledge; and concomitantly, certain words and phrases, "don't know," "if," "may," etc., contrastively indicate what's not known. We can thus say that *in these contexts*, asserters "represent themselves" as knowing, believing, and taking to be true what they assert. The linguistic markings for these representations are contrasting-ignorance expressions. This is the first needed step to empirically establish specific-case assertion norms.

So: Are certain contexts—passages in a respectable newspaper (as above), conversations between trustworthy friends, and so on—ones in which a restricted norm of assertion is operative, a knowledge or belief norm or some other norm? It's clear that, *in these cases*, Moorean remarks are bizarre; and one reason for this could be that unqualified assertions play a contrastive role with certain words, "if," "perhaps," etc.

But this much is compatible with the common-ground expectation view of assertion. Indeed, that there are no popular-literature discussions of assertion norms (of any sort) is strong evidence that there are *no* local assertion norms governing assertions in special cases. For if expectations are generated by background knowledge or beliefs about agents or circumstances, why would asserters need anything *explicit* as guides? The point of the popular literature on norms is to alert people (or warn them) of local norms (that they may not otherwise know about) that demand behavior that they wouldn't otherwise expect on the *mere basis* of their knowledge of background circumstances. Thus, when it comes to assertion, common-ground knowledge or beliefs suffice to explain our expectations (with the qualification, of course, that the knowledge or beliefs in question need not always be commonly held).[67]

And indeed, this seems, anyway, right. If I *expect* a person to tell me something true, then I expect him to know these things or (at least) to believe them. If I think he's trying to do something else, then I expect something else. (I overhear someone asserting things to himself—*talking* to himself. Should I expect him to know or believe what he's saying? It depends.)

Williamson (2000, 252) claims that "conversational patterns confirm the knowledge account." No, they *don't*—not if we consider the full range of "conversational patterns." That's already been established earlier in this chapter. The ways we normally criticize or challenge assertions don't even confirm the idea

[67] Pagin (2011, 101) points out, in general terms, how our assertion practices don't seem governed by conventions or norms. Johnson (2018, 56–57) points out how what she calls "intuitions of criticism" don't seem particularly connected to assertion norms as opposed to a broader backdrop of ethical and epistemic concerns.

that, in special cases—say, when asserters are close trustworthy friends engaged in what they mutually regard as sincere expressions of what they believe—it's expected that asserters know what they're asserting. We *can* criticize someone, as Williamson states, by asking directly: how do you know? But it's normal for criticisms of asserters to take forms *other than* direct challenges to their purported knowledge. These are common: "You don't believe that," "You have no good reasons to think this is true," "You have no justification for that," "There's no way you can be sure of something like that"—as well as the many kinds of criticisms that can be directed toward the proposition itself (and indirectly toward the asserter), as I indicated earlier in this chapter: "That's not true," "No one believes that," "That's off the wall," "That's unreasonable," "You're nuts to assert *that*,"[68] and so on. We can also say: "Are you certain of this?" or "Is this *true*? It's hard to believe." Attention to how we do challenge assertions (and push back against inappropriate challenges to those assertions) doesn't reveal those challenges to particularly single out the knowledge of agents: the propositions themselves can be attacked, or instead the agent's rationality, justification, certainty, and so on. Indeed, it seems clear that a critic (depending on what that critic is presupposing about the asserter and the assertion) can criticize any of a broad number of things.

That Moorean remarks are (often) bizarre looks like better evidence that, at least with normal face-to-face interactions with certain individuals, we *expect* assertions to be of the asserter's knowledge, or at least of what the asserter thinks is knowledge. We also seem to similarly expect (in those same contexts) asserters to believe their assertions. Perhaps, though, even if these aren't general expectations of assertions, there's still a norm (of some specialized sort) that it can be hoped explains these experiences of Moorean remarks being bizarre.

Notice: *If* our experience of Moorean remarks in certain cases is evidence for a norm of a specialized sort or (more weakly) for certain general expectations in those cases, then the presence of those norms or expectations ought to explain our experience of Moorean remarks in these contexts. But they don't. First consider the explanatory role of purported expectations. People often don't know what they're asserting, they often know they don't know this, they often don't believe what they're asserting, and they commonly don't know if they believe it or not. But even in those cases (of face-to-face interactions with those with good character) where the listener knows one of these things about the asserter (and so doesn't expect knowledge or belief), an uttered Moorean remark is still experienced as bizarre. *But an expectation can't explain an intuition of bizarreness if*

[68] This last one, as earlier, involves a criticism of the speaker that piggybacks on criticism of the *proposition*. Several philosophers (e.g., Kvanvig (2009) and McKinnon (2012)) have observed that there are many natural and proper responses to assertions.

the intuition is still in place without the expectation being there. Second, to suggest that an expectation can be absent, but that nevertheless the presence of the norm (of knowledge or belief or whatever) explains this, also misfires as an *explanation*. This is because, normally, when a norm is violated by an action, we experience the action as a *violation*; we don't experience it as bizarre.

Compare: someone puts a napkin on the wrong side of a plate. We don't usually experience this as bizarre. *If*, however, someone breaks the plate into pieces, arranges the pieces in a weird pattern, pours hot soup over them, and *then* invites us to enjoy a meal, we *will* experience this as bizarre. We *understand* the first action—the person violated a norm out of ignorance or deliberately. We don't understand the second action—what's he *doing*? Our response to Moorean remarks—when we have them—is like the second response. We don't understand why she asserted them; what's she *up to*?[69]

That's the key to understanding our reaction to Moorean remarks. Consider first, "It's raining, but I don't believe it." If someone asserts this sincerely, we're puzzled. If we expect sincerity, then we expect the assertion to be of the asserter's beliefs: that's what sincerity *means*. But this Moorean conjunction can't convey anyone's *beliefs*. If, however, someone asserts this insincerely, we're also puzzled. If someone deliberately doesn't express her belief, she has a reason: she's motivated not to express what she really thinks. Why, then, draw attention to the utterance of the first clause being insincere? We can't make sense of why someone would utter this Moorean remark *in either case*.[70]

The same form of explanation applies to "It's raining, but I don't know this." Let's say A is asserting *p* to B. Assertion is *often* aimed at convincing the hearer of what's asserted. Therefore, for B to accept that A knows what he's asserting suffices to convince B. But this purpose is defeated if A adds: "But I don't know this." If A *doesn't* know *p*, then A, by asserting *p*, is engaged in subterfuge. To reveal that he doesn't know *p* defeats this purpose. In cases where we recognize that

[69] As Cappelen (2011, 38) notes, and as I sketch in the next paragraph, Gricean maxims and the like are relevant to when we, and when we don't, find Moorean remarks bizarre. (I should add: they're *sometimes* relevant.) Thus, in this way, our expectations affect whether we do or don't find Moorean remarks bizarre. This, however, is not the same thing as a truth, knowledge, or rational belief norm being in place and as a result generating a general assertion expectation that the assertion be true, or the asserter know or rationally believe the assertion. The suggestion by Pagin (2016) that a condition of truth or informativeness be placed on assertion in general is faulted for the same reason: it fails to explain impressions of bizarreness for Moorean remarks, when we have them.

[70] This is why, as I suggested in section 4.4, we don't have the same reaction to Sean Spicer uttering Moorean remarks. Our recognition of the peculiar—if not pathological—circumstances he's in enables us to make sense of what he's doing—"what he's up to." Pathology, I should add, can take us pretty far. Suppose S is hallucinating and both S and Q know this. S can look out the window (onto a sunny day) and say to Q, "It's raining out, but I know it's not." S speaker-means, "I'm hallucinating that it's raining out," but that's not what he *says*, and what he says is clear to Q and works.

A intends to convince B of something, we can't make sense of what A is up to if he asserts a Moorean remark.

Here's the point in phenomenological terms. A speaker asserting a proposition is perceived as using *it* as a tool for a certain purpose she *has*. It can certainly happen that someone can attempt something with a tool that we can't make sense of. ("What on earth are you trying to do with that *fork*?") Our response to a Moorean remark—when we find it puzzling—is like this: we can't make sense of what someone is up to when he says it. Thus, the common-ground-expectation-view-of-assertion explanation of Moorean remarks is sensitive both to cases where we react to those remarks with puzzlement and to cases, like flakes, liars, experts, and spokespersons, where we needn't find their utterances puzzling. That is, the common-ground expectation view of assertion offers better explanations of our *overall* responses to Moorean remarks than its norm-assertion and general-condition-on-assertion competitors do.[71]

4.9 Concluding Remarks

My focus on language experience as the determiner of when we do and don't assert, and when we do and don't utter assertions, might seem to have theoretical gaps when it comes to characterizations of *assertion* and *asserting*. Leave aside the demand for a characterization that gives necessary and sufficient conditions for these things (something most of this literature is concerned with). Although it should be clear how the foregoing descriptions of our assertion practices refute norm and commitment views of assertion, it may not be clear what the status is of what are described as "certain effects" and "certain causes" views. This labeling is a bit vague, but the extant views these labels are used for *have* been ruled out by the counterexamples given in this chapter. Stalnaker's view of assertion, for example, characterizes assertions as contributing to changes in the common ground. But that's wrong as a general characterization of assertion: changes in the common ground are made only if it's part of the common ground that the speaker is someone (e.g., not a flake) who can do such a thing. I omit further discussion of how the discussion in this chapter undercuts extant views on assertion.

[71] That said, there are, nevertheless, *some* constitutive conditions on assertion, although I doubt they're *norms*. The obvious one is: you *can't* assert sheer gibberish. (You *can* pretend to assert sheer gibberish.) Notice that this is constitutive in the normal sense of the word. It isn't *possible* to assert sheer gibberish; you'll fail to assert at all.

I turn instead to taking up other aspects of the "know(s)" and "knowledge" locutions. The results of this chapter have been primarily prophylactic—to prevent an overreading of acts of asserting as all by themselves generating knowledge claims or requirements of knowledge (or other sorts of requirements) and, in this way, distorting our understanding of other aspects of how we attribute (and deny) knowledge to ourselves and others.

5

Usage Traps in the Language of Iterated Knowledge Attributions

5.1 Introductory Remarks about KK and K¬K and About Metacognition

KK and K¬K: If an agent knows something, she always knows that she knows it; if she doesn't know something, she always knows that too.[1] An aim of this chapter (and the next one too) is to illustrate the falsity of these theses in fresh ways: (i) by, in this chapter, describing those aspects of how we ordinarily use epistemic words that make it easy to confuse claims to know with

[1] KK, sometimes called "epistemic transparency" and sometimes called "positive introspection," is currently in a strange place. Some contemporary epistemologists think it's largely rejected by contemporary epistemologists ("has seen better days" is how Greco (2014, 169)) puts it; Antony (2004, 12) describes it, exaggeratedly, as "the principle, roundly rejected by epistemologists of almost every stripe"). Many earlier major philosophers (Plato, Aristotle, Augustine, Schopenhauer, etc.) defended it, as Hintikka (1962, chapter 5), who also defends it, points out. In any case, whether it's taken seriously or not by any particular "contemporary epistemologist" often corresponds to how much she is an externalist or internalist about justification and how strong she requires "justification" to be: externalists will tend to reject it, and internalists tend to say things that seem to support it—even if they don't embrace it officially. Those who rely on the Lewis/Schiffer notion of common or mutual knowledge to support a notion of public convention or for other purposes also accept it. On the other hand, Williamson's (2000) attack on it has been very influential. I should add that some recent supporters of KK aren't *genuine* supporters. McHugh (2010, 231), for example, defends not KK but this principle: "For any subject S and proposition p, if S knows p, and S grasps the proposition that she knows p, and the normal conditions for psychological self-knowledge are in place, then S is in a position to know that she knows p." Regardless of how "the normal conditions for psychological self-knowledge are in place" is understood (and in my view, McHugh understands it quite strongly), this is a qualification Q of the principle, in the form that is, not $(p)(Kp \rightarrow KKp)$, but instead $(p)((Kp \,\&\, Qp) \rightarrow KKp)$, which isn't KK. So too, Dokic and Égré (2009) don't defend $(p)(Kp \rightarrow KKp)$, but instead a much weaker $(p)(K^*p \rightarrow K^*K^*p)$, where K^* is a restricted "right sort of knowledge." Their "modularized" knowledge view in effect drops the ordinary notion of knowledge for something else. Greco (2014; 2015) seems to defend the genuine article—but his (2015) fragmentation of epistemic attitudes into "subattitudes" doesn't support the original KK principle either. I discuss Williamson's attack on KK in section 9.5: although KK fails, it doesn't fail for Williamson's reasons. I should add that I'm much less interested in KK itself than I am in a family of metacognitive principles: the thought that knowing *p* requires additional metacognitive attitudes or that knowing *p* is governed by a norm to the effect that one can (or should) engage such metacognitive resources. None of this can be true—as we should already see from the knowing attributions I described in chapter 1. Nevertheless, such views are often presupposed by philosophers and by psychologists (of various sorts) not only when discussing knowledge but when discussing concept attribution and the like, as I'll show in this chapter, in chapter 6, and in chapter 8.

Attributing Knowledge. Jody Azzouni, Oxford University Press (2020). © Oxford University Press.
DOI: 10.1093/oso/9780197508817.001.0001.

claims to know what one knows, and (ii) by, in the next chapter, conceptually connecting the truth or falsity of the *instances* of these theses (with respect to specific agents and specific propositions *p*) to the varying understandings of those agents of how they know that *p*. Instances of *iterated knowledge* or *iterated knowings*—instances, that is, where an agent S knows that she knows *p* or knows that she doesn't know *p*—are ones where that agent grasps enough of the specifics of how she knows or doesn't know *p* to suffice for her to have this knowledge. *Ground-floor knowledge* is the knowing of *p*, for proposition *p*, where the content of that *p* isn't (or doesn't include) that agent's own knowing of *q* for some proposition *q*.

Iterated knowledge is a particular species of what has come to be called *metacognition*, an agent's knowledge of her own cognitive processes.[2] It's sometimes treated as a specification of an agent's capacity to know about (or monitor) others' cognitive processes, or with "theory of mind" (ToM): the capacity to understand other minds, their beliefs and emotions. Byrne (2016, 84) writes, "Cognitive psychologists describe information in the mind as 'representations' of reality, and since theory-of-mind knowledge is a representation of other representations (of the world), they use the term meta-representation as synonymous with theory of mind."[3]

[2] Some characterizations of "metacognition": Beran et al. (2012, 7) write: "Metacognition is often defined as 'knowing what one does (or does not) know.' " Beran and Smith (2011, 90) write, "Humans' abilities to assess confidence and to manage uncertainty adaptively are collectively called metacognition. Metacognition can be informally defined as 'thinking about thinking,' but it also refers to the monitoring of other, more basic 'first-order' cognitive processes such as the processes of perceiving and remembering. . . . Whenever humans reflect on what they know, monitor their thought processes, judge their confidence, or seek additional information, they demonstrate their metacognitive abilities." Thompson, Prowse Turner, and Pennycook (2011, 109) characterize the metacognitive process of "monitoring" as the "subjective assessment of one's own cognitive processes and knowledge." (This is from Koriat, Ma'ayan, and Nussinson (2006, 38).) Basile et al. (2014, 85) write: "Metacognition refers to the ability to monitor one's cognitive processes, the ability to take action to control those processes, and general knowledge about how one's cognitive processes function." (This, they point out, is taken from Flavell (1979) and Nelson (1996).) These characterizations aren't the same, and they cover a wealth of cognitive phenomena: this reflects the current state of the literature; there is real controversy about how metacognition should be characterized and, related to this, how it can be (empirically) recognized.

[3] I mean "mental representation" (which I'll treat as synonymous with "concept") more specifically than Byrne does. Mental representations aren't merely information in the mind that's about the world; they're mental items—with entailments—that often refer (e.g., the concept *house*), but sometimes don't (e.g., the concept *phlogiston*). *Sometimes* these concepts are successfully characterized by *our* words, "house," "water," etc. On some views (see the above-cited Beran et al. (2012) for discussion), it's possible for an agent to have "information in the mind" about the world or her own mind without having concepts. Esken (2012, 135) calls nonconceptual information about the mind "procedural metacognition"—and he suggests it results in "epistemic feelings," such as "feelings of knowing," "feelings of uncertainty," and "feelings of confidence." See Koriat (2000); Proust (2006; 2007); also Brandl (2012, 161). I comment on this hypothesis in section 5.5 and in chapter 6, e.g., note 26 of section 6.3.

There is a lot of controversy in this rapidly advancing interdisciplinary literature about what metacognition is and how to characterize it—in particular, what cognitive resources it requires. One view takes metacognizing agents to possess rich representational resources along with an understanding of those resources. For an agent to metacognize her mental states—to realize, e.g., that she remembers something or that she doesn't remember that something—she must possess concepts (or "mental representations") of the somethings remembered as well as of her remembering itself; she must be aware *of* those concepts, and be aware *of* their properties (she must know that concepts have semantic properties, for example, that they refer, and perhaps she must grasp some of their entailments as well). Dretske (1999) and Dienes and Perner (2001) characterize metacognition in this strong way. Across the spectrum are various denials of the requirement that the metacognizing agent need possess and/or understand her possession of these resources—from denials that the metacognizing agent must be able to cognize her mental-representation resources all the way to denials that metacognizing requires any concepts at all.[4]

To a large extent, this is a difficult *empirical* question. To an equally large extent, therefore, "metacognition" is a scientific term-in-the-making: what "metacognition" will eventually come to mean turns on what will be discovered to be the best way of terminologically contouring (and best enabling scientific theorizing about) what's currently characterized as "metacognitions"—in part, this will be a discovery about what kinds of cognitions are naturally studied together and with similar methods. I dwell on this for a few paragraphs. (My discussion of this complements some of what I've said about language in part 2 of the introduction.)

In the sciences, often, ordinary words are adopted: their entire extensions are initially studied. As a science develops, it's invariably found that these extensions are heterogeneous phenomena not suitably studied together—because, for example, they don't obey the same regularities or laws, or because the same scientific tools don't apply to all of them, or because they simply aren't the same sorts of things. A commonly cited illustration: there is no suitable (unified) scientific study of what's ordinarily understood as "heat"—this includes boiling water, cayenne peppers, and decaying organic material. The original word merely classifies together phenomena that (kind of) feel similar to us—that classification role doesn't require the word to interact very much with other words of the vernacular or with scientific terminology, either semantically or otherwise. Thus, the specialized terminological refinements of "heat," that place specific conditions on what in these refined senses is "heat," can unproblematically coexist with

[4] See Beran et al. (2012, 5–6) for brief characterizations of these options and for citations.

the original word in the same language. The word "heat" is like other ordinary "natural-kind" expressions—"water," "insect," "magnet," "coral," and so on.

An expression, "gene," say, coined (at the beginning of a scientific investigation) to name an entity that's theoretically posited to have a certain functional role can similarly evolve. It can be discovered that no particular entity plays that role (and in the case of "gene," it *has* turned out this way). The word can then vanish altogether (as "phlogiston" did), or its meaning can deviate from its original use (as many scientific words did when relativity replaced Newtonian theory, "space," and "time," for example, which had already been refined in Newtonian physics), or the word can splinter into many different words in use (as happened to "gene"). These various fates of coined expressions can cause disputes among specialists, as Kuhn noted long ago, but those specialists, or descendant practitioners, eventually do adopt the new terminology.

It might be hoped that, under pressure of discovery "metacognition," a coined expression like "gene" will also mutate into a family of terms corresponding to various cognitive abilities that differ both in function(s) and with respect to their psychological and neurological resources—for example, into "conceptual metacognition," "procedural metacognition," "metacognitive knowledge," "metacognitive regulation," etc. The close ties of "metacognition," however, with the family of ordinary-language epistemic locutions that include "know(s)" complicate matters (so say I). Some have thought otherwise because (they claim) the word "know(s)" isn't important. Chomsky (1980, 82) writes that "it is not at all clear that the ordinary concept of 'knowledge' is even coherent, nor would it be particularly important if it were shown not to be." Williams (1996) presses hard on the analogy he perceives between "knowledge" and "witchcraft" or "heat," and suggests there is no reason to think that "epistemology" characterizes a suitable subject area of sustained study. These positions take "know(s)" and "knowledge" as like "heat"—easily supplanted by descendant scientific coinages.

Unfortunately for these views, it's neither straightforward nor obvious that the family of ordinary-language epistemic locutions that "know(s)" belongs to can be easily replaced or modified. Their semantic intricacy resembles that of "house" more than "heat"; and their roles in our lives, indicated by the mere fact that the family in question includes "knowledge," "evidence," "justification," "aware," "infer," and "see" (among others), makes it look like there are semantic entanglements among these words *as they're ordinarily used* richer than what's usually exhibited by ordinary words that are typically co-opted (and adapted) to scientific needs. That remains to be determined.[5] Currently, however, "know(s)"

[5] Two points: First, one aim of this book is to understand enough about how these words *are* used to evaluate the cost of doing without them. A way to investigate this, ironically, is to explore the possibility of coherently living one's life as a sceptic. I intend to do so in a subsequent book. Second, in the foregoing chapters, I've argued that many of the simple *semantic* entailments among "belief,"

and related words—*as they're ordinarily used*—are central to the metacognition sciences. The studies in these fields (as the definitions in note 2 indicate) are framed almost entirely in ordinary language. Among these, for example, are studies of what animals experience through their senses: the ordinary words "see," "hear," "aware," and so on, are therefore necessarily used. These studies are often of what the animals in question can infer: the ordinary words "realize(s)" and "recognize(s)," as well as "infer(s)" and "deduce(s)," are thus also used; and, to put the point plainly, the word "know(s)" comes up a lot.

Perhaps *all* these words will be eventually replaced with specialized terms; I doubt it. In any case, "know(s)" and the other words in its epistemic family aren't like "heat": "heat" not only has few or no attachments to other words; its role in our non-scientific lives is limited too. We could replace it even in the vernacular (if we chose) without much effect. Ordinary epistemic words, however, are everywhere in our discourse. It's unclear what the vernacular, or even scientific language, could look like without them.[6]

Related to this is the tangled question of what the word "know(s)" means (and how it can be used); this directly bears on the topic of metacognition. One point to make immediately: It has become a truism of much of the metacognition literature that metacognition is a major psychological achievement calling for substantial cognitive resources above and beyond ground-floor knowledge. Human children, in particular, apparently come quite late to recognizing when they're ignorant ("knowing that they don't know")—around age six or seven.[7] On the other hand, what might be called "the logic of 'know(s)'" treats metacognition as mere terminological iteration: John knows *p*, John knows that he knows *p*, John doesn't know that he knows *p*, John knows that he sees *p*, and so on.[8]

Furthermore, as I discuss in section 5.2, we effortlessly slide in speech (and thought!) between what knowing expressions are used to convey and what they (literally) express. This makes it still easier to confound iterated knowings with

"justification," "consciousness," and "know(s)," presumed by previous epistemologists, don't exist. This may allow transplantation of "know(s)" and its family of epistemic terms to cognitive-scientific contexts without requiring significant modifications. I touch on this point shortly and later in this chapter.

[6] See Wierzbicka (1996).

[7] See Kloo and Rohwer (2012). Also see Carruthers and Ritchie (2012, 79) for the ways the psychological literature shows us to be so much better at mind reading than at metacognition, in particular, that "human metacognitive capacities are fragile and cue-based, late to develop in childhood, and are heavily dependent on individual differences in personality and local cultural mores for their effectiveness." Those who think that there are metacognitive nonconceptual *feelings*, however, think that certain forms of metacognition arise extremely early.

[8] Some practitioners, e.g., Perner (2012, 97), taking notice of this, call it "recursive cognition"—"cognition about cognition." Esken (2012, 138) uses the phrase "recursive consciousness" to describe iterated characterizations of subjects' awareness of one another, e.g., John sees that Sally sees that John is . . .

ground-floor knowings, and metacognition with ground-floor cognition. These usage facts provide part of the diagnosis for what's actually a pretty strange state of affairs: that there is, until recently, a quite dominant trend in epistemology and philosophy of mind, one that, nearly enough, treats metacognition (or at least knowing that one knows) as required for ground-floor knowledge. Alongside this is (or was, anyway) a long-standing commitment to KK and K¬K in epistemology, as well as similar metacognitive theses about justification and perception and/or deduction.

A goal of this book is to establish that our knowledge and knowing-attribution practices have quite modest presuppositions. One thing this means is—at least as far as ordinary knowing attributions are concerned—the knowledge of agents, including their knowledge of their own cognitive processes, can, in general, be fragmentary and piecemeal. That is, it's important to separate cases of specific knowings of *p* from knowings of closely related *q*s: an agent may have knowledge about his own cognitive processes but not knowledge about what he knows, or an agent may have limited knowledge about certain aspects of her cognitive processes without knowledge of other aspects of those processes. It's important, as well, to separate an agent's knowledge of other agents' cognitive processes or what that agent knows about what other agents know from that agent's knowledge of his own cognitive processes or knowledge.

These potential uncouplings of the individual knowings (of an agent) from one another arise because there is no requirement that if an agent knows *p*, she therefore knows *q*—regardless of how close (semantically or otherwise) the propositions *p* and *q* are. As far as the semantics (and use) of "know(s)" is concerned, there is no contradiction in saying of an agent S that she knows *p* but doesn't know *q*. So, if *p* is "Mark Twain wrote books" and *q* is "Samuel Clemens wrote books," it isn't a contradiction to say that S knows *p* but doesn't know *q*; so too if *p* and *q* are logically equivalent, or even if *p* and *q* mean the same things but have (slightly different) linguistic forms.[9]

Many philosophers concerned with cognition and/or knowledge, in contrast, think attributing metacognitive, and, indeed, ground-floor cognitive, abilities to agents are necessarily "all or none" packages. Relatedly, they—as Dretske

[9] "S believe(s)," "S see(s)," and other propositional-attitude expressions are similarly modest. There is a large literature on the individuation conditions of propositions, one that focuses on how these (semantic) properties of propositional-attitude expressions block straightforward characterizations of the individuation conditions of propositions—e.g., Millian ones. A recent development (see Greco (2015) and other citations therein) is the exploration of dropping the notions of "belief" and "know(s)" as "too crude" and replacing them with a refined family of scope-restricted notions. This raises two issues. First, whether the ordinary notions *are* too crude to take account of phenomena Greco discusses, such as inconsistent beliefs or the failure to manifest knowledge in all contexts. As I'm already indicating (and see section 10.7 for more details), they can already accommodate these things. Second, and still remaining, is the issue of whether, despite this, these notions should be replaced *anyway* with "fragmented" successor notions. No (say I); see section 11.4.

believes, for example—require rich conceptual resources of agents. According to a dominant epistemic tradition dating back to Kant and earlier—one that includes philosophers influenced by Sellars, such as Brandom, Williams, and Aikin, as well as C. I. Lewis, Davidson, and others—agents with any capacity for knowledge *at all* have, necessarily, substantial metacognitive abilities and knowledge. Most in this tradition think (therefore) that for agents to believe, see, or know, they must also be aware of their own possession of the concepts of *belief*, *sight*, and *knowledge*; they must be able to recognize (that is) that these concepts have conditions of application, and they must be able to recognize what those conditions are.

Such positions sometimes arise from antecedent views about logic (or, more grandly, "Reason"): epistemic agents must be "reasonable," and to interpret agents as reasonable (or capable of reasoning) requires attributing a great deal of knowledge to them. Agents, as a result (on these views), have lots of knowledge about their own cognitive processes. Sometimes a position like this arises from antecedent views about justification—that agents must possess justifications of knowledge in a strong (introspective) sense, and that these justifications presuppose a lot of background knowledge. Sometimes the views seem to arise from sheer claims about the semantic entailments—or the normal use—of the words "aware," "know(s)," "see(s)," and so on.[10]

I illustrate in this chapter (and the next) that our ordinary epistemic attribution practices aren't "total packages" and that empirical studies of metacognitive abilities in animals and humans illustrate this. The ordinary words "know(s)," "believe(s)," "see(s)," etc., can be applied to agents whose knowledge is fragmentary, gerrymandered, and/or limited in scope. Correspondingly, it's empirically possible that nonhuman (or possibly human) epistemic agents exist with only quite fragmentary/gerrymandered/limited knowledge or metaknowledge.

If this is right, then (contrary to the concerns raised earlier) there is no tension between empirical studies of the cognition and metacognition of humans, animals, or artifacts and the ordinary epistemic notions that (still) frame these studies; that's apart from the fact that it's easy to confound cognition and metacognition, knowledge and iterated knowledge. These confusions, however, can't be mitigated by judicious specialized vocabulary. We confound cognitions and

[10] Dretske (1993, 265) seems to take the following as a series of truisms about words, how they're used, and what they're about: "Seeing, hearing, and smelling *x* are ways of being conscious of *x*. . . . Seeing a tree, smelling a rose, and feeling a wrinkle is to be (perceptually) aware (conscious) of the tree, the rose, and the wrinkle. It may be that thinking or dreaming about Clyde is a way of being aware of Clyde without perceiving him. . . . I do not deny it (though I think it stretches usage). I affirm, only, the converse: that to see and feel a thing is to be (perceptually) conscious of it."

iterated cognitions of all types because of deep aspects of language use we can't easily escape.[11]

5.2 Exclamation and Redundancy Uses of "Know(s)"

I discuss counterexamples to KK, as I said, and I give a sketch of kinds of iterated knowledge (and when they arise) in chapter 6. Before doing that, an important cluster of usage traps must be described first. These usage traps make the analysis of iterated and ground-floor know(s) attributions hard. This contributes to the appeal of KK: we—philosophers and nonphilosophers alike—often think we're saying less by uttering iterated knowledge claims than we actually are (or that we're saying *more* than we actually are by uttering ground-floor knowledge claims). It also (I surmise) contributes to the appeal of Cartesian views about the transparency of mental states. Indeed, an entire fabric of interconnected epistemic misconceptions—about Moorean "paradoxes," the transparency of mental states, the mistaken KK and K¬K theses themselves, can *all* be blamed (in large measure) on these usage traps. I'll illustrate, here and in chapter 6, how these usage-induced confusions affect modern empirical work on metacognition as well as philosophical epistemology.

I adopt the usual speech-act nomenclature: What speaker-hearers perceive sentences to (literally) convey by virtue of their syntax and the meanings of their words is their "contents." Following Grice, what the *speaker* means to convey, to "speaker-mean," is often perceived as very different from an uttered sentence's content. The syntax of a sentence conveys "grammatical mood": the sentence itself, that is, is an indicative, an interrogative, a command, and so forth. Lastly, "illocutionary force" is what's conveyed, sometimes by speakers, sometimes by the grammatical forms of sentences, although it's seemingly independent of these forms because a command or question can be conveyed by an indicative sentence, and an assertion can be conveyed by a (rhetorical) question. Illocutionary force seems independent of speakers and their intentions as well.[12]

[11] The sources of the troubles, that is, show up in *all* natural language: (i) illocutionary-force/content distinctions; (ii) some members of the epistemic family of locutions, "know(s)," specifically, are lexical universals. I suspect "see(s)" is as well. I should add that, for the most part, our "stumbling" over these things doesn't occur among nonphilosophers who shift over the relevant distinctions without noticing them and without it leading to much in the way of problems of communication. It shows up everywhere, however, in philosophy (specifically, in epistemology—but not just *there*) and in cognitive-science thinking about knowledge and metacognition.

[12] E.g., as I indicated in section 4.2, the appearance of "Save the whales now!" on a cliff wall will be experienced by viewers as a command or a plea despite their knowledge that it's due to erosion, and so there's no utterer of it, neither one who is commanding nor one who is pleading.

I'll occasionally represent force with "force indicators"—"!" "?" "??"—as *prefixes*, as opposed to punctuation at the ends of sentences, where they're already understood (in English) to be part of the (written) grammar. I'll also sometimes use the word "literally" to describe the content of a sentence that's speaker-meant to convey something other than that content, as in "*p* literally means *q* although it speaker-means *r*." Similarly, what a proposition "literally implies" is "what its content implies."[13]

The key point is this. Sentences are perceived as possessing illocutionary force along with a content.[14] When a speaker utters a statement with that force, witnesses experience an illocutionary-force relationship of the speaker *to* that content; force, thus, isn't perceived as *part of* that content. Speaker-meaning, however, exploits the force and contents of utterances so effortlessly that what's speaker-meant by an utterance often invisibly deviates from the content of the uttered sentence. This affects our understanding of "know(s)" locutions. I illustrate this ubiquitous phenomenon next.

"S knows that *p*" *literally* describes the knowing relationship between S and *p*. "I know that *p*" or "I know *p*" describes knowing relations between *p* and first-person utterers. These statements have contents that refer to the agent, refer to the proposition (or the content, the sentence, or whatever) *p*, and contain a locution holding of the knowing relation between the agent and *p*.[15] Despite this (and confusingly), in the first-person case we regularly use "know" to speaker-mean emphatic "exclamation-mark" assertions of *p* that aren't about the agent's (the speaker's) relation to the targeted *p*. I assert that snow is white, and I'm challenged. I then assert: "I *know* snow is white, I *really* do." I *may* be asserting more than the mere statement that snow *is* white; I may be communicating that I can *back up* what I've claimed. Where I'm expected to know what I assert (when, furthermore, I recognize I have that responsibility), I'll usually therefore speaker-mean that I know enough about the relationship between me and the proposition "snow is white" to *know* that I know snow is white: the evidence I have proves that.

[13] Although I break with the Gricean tradition in many respects, as I indicated in chapter 4 (and in detail in Azzouni (2013b)), I still accept the important distinction between sentences and the utterances of those sentences that's central to much of that literature. I accept the crucial distinction, in particular, between illocutionary force and linguistically mandated content—one that largely includes various classifications of illocutionary forces, as in, e.g., Searle and Vanderveken (1985). (See Green (2014) for a nice overview of the nomenclature and review of contemporary discussion.) The main point of disagreement relevant to present concerns is that I deny that our experience of speech acts essentially joins them to communicative intentions—as indicated in note 12.

[14] This statement can be taken to be true if, for example, we allow that a demonstrated statement is accompanied by "demonstrative force."

[15] Millian views of propositions take the content to *contain* the agent, the proposition, and the knowing relation. Nothing I say here forecloses on any *particular* metaphysics of propositions.

But often, the assertion "I *know* that snow is white, I *really* do" is only an enthusiastic replaying of my already-articulated commitment to snow being white. I speaker-mean *Confidence: Snow is white.* (Or *!Snow is white.*) I thus don't convey or intend to convey (I don't speaker-mean) a *statement about myself,* that "*I* am confident that snow is white." A statement with *that* content would be like "I know that snow is white" about the agent (myself) and the relation I have to a proposition—that *I'm* confident of *it*. Contrary to this, for me to literally utter (or speaker-mean) a proposition *p* with an illocutionary force (confidence, say) isn't for me to state that *I* am confident of that statement.[16] Expressing *p* confidently, and asserting (sincerely) "I'm confident that *p*" are *not* the same thing although they're usually interchangeable.[17] In the first case, *p* is asserted accompanied with the force: confidence. In the second case, that the first-person agent is confident of *p* is in the *content* of *p*.

I've dwelt on these speech-act truisms about illocutionary force and content because they cause confusions in epistemology. To repeat: despite the (common) exclamation-mark usages of "know," the *meaning* of "I know snow is white" *isn't*: Totally confident about this: Snow is white ("!Snow is white"). So I'm distinguishing *three* kinds of utterances of statements, ones that can be either literally conveyed or instead speaker-meaning conveyed, and varying in their meaning and/or in the illocutionary force with which they're uttered: "!Snow is white," "I know that snow is white," and "I'm confident that snow is white." *None* of these should be identified; in particular, identifying exclamation-mark usages of "know" with genuine "knowing that" claims helps confuse literally understood "confidence that" claims and "knowing that" claims.[18]

Closely related to this exclamation-mark usage of "know(s)" is a common redundancy usage. We often say "S realized that she knew *p*," for example, while not

[16] Adding to the mess is that it's, in addition, easy to confuse a (first-person) speaker *bearing* an attitude relation to a verbal locution she's uttering with that speaker (self-referentially) *describing* her relation to that locution. (This is closely related to use/mention errors; it's *not*, itself, *a* use/mention error since it's a contrast between the force conveyed with a content and talking *about* that force while simultaneously conveying it, rather than a contrast between using an expression and talking about that expression.)

[17] Eric Dean (email, May 25, 2019) writes: "I think they're not quite interchangeable in institutional settings in which, for example, person A is being challenged about an assertion he made, person B is assessing the challenge, and person C is being asked about a fact of the matter relevant to the challenged assertion. If person C were to say 'I'm confident that p,' person B could say, 'Your confidence isn't relevant here. The question is whether p obtains.' C's emphatic 'yes' in reply would mark the distinction between expressing p confidently and sincerely asserting 'I am confident that p.'"

[18] Wittgenstein (1969, 3e) falsely writes: "The difference between the concept of 'knowing' and the concept of 'being certain' isn't of any great importance at all, except where 'I know' is meant to mean: I *can't* be wrong." No: "I know" doesn't *mean* (and so never *means*) "I can't be wrong." That it's so *used* by speakers (at times) to assert (to speaker-mean) that they can't be wrong is just like the fact that "I'm cold" is often used to *ask* someone else to close a window—despite windows having nothing to do with the meaning of "I'm cold," being cold having nothing to do with the meaning of "Close the window!" and declaratives not being questions.

intending to speaker-mean the literal implication of this statement, that "S came to know that she knows *p*." It instead—perhaps most often—describes the *instantaneous onset* of S's knowledge that *p*.

Sarah plays hide-and-seek with her daughters. We can say, "Sarah realized where the girls were hiding." We can also say, "Sarah realized that she knew where the girls were hiding," while speaker-meaning only what the first statement expresses. Sometimes (rarely) we *do* mean Sarah realized she *already knew* where the girls were hiding. In these cases, we mean: Sarah *metacognized.* (Hearing rustling in the closet, she thinks, "I'd forgotten the girls were in the closet!") More often, the statement just speaker-means: Sarah had a realization event—an instantaneous occurrence of knowing where the girls were. In this case, the statement isn't *used* to speaker-mean an iterated knowing statement although it literally is one—that's its content.[19]

Another way that illocutionary force is sometimes grammatically conveyed enforces the naturalness of redundancy usages. This is how we, in the first person, describe indecision about a proposition. An unsure agent may wonder: "*p* or not—*which* is it?" In doing so, the agent needn't be thinking (even tacitly) about *her own indecision.* She *is* undecided—she's *feeling* undecided—although she's not thinking about that.[20] Nevertheless, *describing* indecision about *p* with an *indicative* expression requires her to say: "*I don't know* whether *p* or not."[21] Even quite unreflective (English-speaking) agents say in such cases, "I don't know if *p* or not," even though they aren't aware of, thinking about, or otherwise trying to convey anything about themselves. This arises directly from how our language resources allow us to describe illocutionary force; in the first person, we can't do so *without* simultaneously conveying it. Some illustrations follow.

Consider commands. "Close the door!" isn't grammatically an indicative. Its subject matter is only the door—that it should be closed. Perhaps a term indicating that the recipient is tacitly present, although not syntactically visible—perhaps the command (literally) is "*You there*: close the door!" Regardless, a term indicating the speaker isn't present. But if we put the command in indicative form, we can say: "I command you to close the door," or "I'm commanding you to close the door."[22] These two imperative speech acts simultaneously characterize the imperative three-way relation between the (first-person) agent, the

[19] A *test* for redundancy: after someone utters, "S realized that she knew *p*," say: "You mean that S knew that she knew *p*?" If the speaker is surprised, the redundancy usage was speaker-meant.

[20] I revisit this possibly controversial claim in further depth in the next section.

[21] Or, "*I* wonder whether *p* or not." She has to include a term referring to herself in the statement. "It's being wondered whether *p* or not" is grammatical but sounds *off.* "It's not known whether *p* or not" is the claim that it's not known by anyone (in our knowledge group) whether *p* or not.

[22] We don't *have to* say these things; we can say instead: "You're commanded to close the door." That this can be said by someone other than the person who is commanding shows this locution doesn't (implicitly) contain a term referring to the speaker. "The King commands you to kneel" conveys illocutionary force due not to the speaker but to the King. Furthermore, the King needn't ever tell the recipient (or anyone) to kneel for the command to nevertheless be apt. "Promise(s)" is

person being commanded, and the proposition describing what's commanded. These locutions are grammatically similar to indicative descriptions of previous commands (which, consequently, aren't simultaneously commands): "I commanded you to close the door earlier today."

Questions are similar. "Is that door red?" isn't grammatically in indicative form, and a first-person indexical isn't part of its content. If the question is put in indicative form, however, a first-person indexical must occur in the content, as in: "I'm asking you whether that door is red."[23] A content that indicatively conveys indecision, therefore, involves a speaker engaging in semantic ascent and talking *about* his attitude toward the proposition he's indecisive about: "I don't know whether *p* is true," "I don't know about *p* one way or the other." ("I don't know about snow being white, one way or the other.")

We can introduce an illocutionary-force indicator that conveys puzzlement. This isn't an illocutionary-force indicator for interrogative force because interrogative force is often conveyed despite a speaker not conveying puzzlement. A teacher asking a student a question that she knows the answer to is nevertheless asking a genuine question (and conveying this): her speech act involves interrogative force although not puzzlement. That's not asking a rhetorical question, which doesn't convey interrogative force even though its grammatical mood is interrogative. So, let ?*p* stand for the conveying of *p* with interrogative force. And let ??*p* stand for the content of *p* accompanied by the force of (genuine) puzzlement.[24]

As I said, some assertional forms describe the force of interrogatives or commands while simultaneously conveying interrogative or imperative force but without containing a term that refers to the agent in the content. These do sound weird (although not improper) when uttered. An agent can say, for example (and rather archly): "Whether that door is red is being asked." This is off because it's a description of a speech act of an agent (e.g., the one speaking) without an indication of who that agent is. For an agent to speech *act* doesn't require a term designating that agent either in the content or (of course) in the force-operator term. The agent, when there is one, *is* the speech-act utterer—but that's no reason to take such speech acts as intrinsically reflexive (or metacognitive). To fully *describe* the speech act, however, does require a term referring to the utterer (when

different. To be apt, "The King has promised to give you much gold" requires the King's promise to have been speech-enacted to *someone* by the King. I can't analyze these differences any further now.

[23] There are two cases. The questioner may have previously asked, "Is that door red?" When this question isn't answered, the questioner confronts the answerer by pointing out what the original question *was*. A second case is where the question was only tacitly implied to begin with, and the answerer missed the implication. "I'm asking you whether that door is red," in this case, may be the first time in the conversation where a question about the door is explicitly posed.

[24] If ??*p*, then ?*p*, but not the reverse, as the teacher case indicates.

he exists) in the description. That's why, in third-person descriptions of speech acts (questions or commands), the natural form is: "S asked *p*," "S commanded of Q that he *p*." First-person assertional forms that simultaneously convey interrogative (or imperative or . . .) force have two jobs. Their descriptive job requires including whatever is needed for a *full* description—including a term that indicates the speaker. Their second job of conveying interrogative (or promissory or . . .) force doesn't require such a term.

Nevertheless, the grammatical similarity of first- and third-person locutions is striking: "I command you to *p*," "he commands you to *p*," "I'm asking about *p*," "he's asking about *p*." It seems that the first-person versions of these are assertional versions of statements with interrogative or imperative force; concomitantly, these locutions have a redundancy role (one where the first-person indexical isn't speaker-meant). Whatever the diachronic reasons for this linguistic state of affairs, the upshot is an intricate usage practice that confuses us about iterated knowledge, and about metacognition more generally. In particular, the above usage facts help explain why it's easy to overlook acceptable cases of Moorean "paradoxes," and they also explain the intuitive plausibility of KK.

I'll close this section with an example of how our practices enable speaker-meaning and literal content to confusedly mingle redundant know(s) attributions with genuine iterated knowledge attributions. A standard question is "Do you know the way to 14th Street?"[25] The literal answer to this question (treating it as one about the stranger's *knowledge*) is the tired joke: "Yes, I do." (And then silence, because, after all, the question has been answered.) The usual positive answer is to give directions, but, strictly speaking, that doesn't answer the question (although it *is* an answer to what's speaker-meant if the speaker-meant question isn't what the recipient of the question *knows* but instead the ground-level: "Which way to 14th Street?"—which is what's *usually* speaker-meant). A negative answer, however, is invariably: "I don't know—I'm sorry." Thus, the positive answer is usually not literally about the speaker's knowledge, although the negative answer invariably *is*. Perhaps a shrug (which is a little rude) conveys a pure topic-focused: "??Where 14th Street is," but we have no such speech act in English—despite our rarely thinking about our own knowledge (states) or ourselves when we tell someone we don't know something.[26]

Notice the ambiguity in ". . . a question to a stranger about her knowledge." It can mean a question about the stranger's *knowledge state* or one about the *content*

25 This example is dated because people now mostly use their cell phones for directions instead of asking for help. The same for "Do you know the time?" "Do you know who that is?" is still used.

26 We have no such "speech acts" in English, but we (now) have plenty of "text acts" of this sort. If puzzled by what someone has texted you, you can text back a "puzzled" emoticon or a freestanding question mark. Or, if you prefer, you can send other punctuation (exclamation marks) or (many different) emoticon responses.

of that knowledge state—about the thing the stranger knows. This is also true of phrases like "I have questions about what John knows." Williamson (2000, 252), recall, describes "How do you know?" as a standard response to an assertion. This *looks* like a question like "How is it that you're in a knowing state?" But the level confusions I've been describing should make us distrust this characterization. It may really be: "What justification is there for this?"—a question that isn't directly about knowledge.

The redundancy phenomenon that confounds ground-floor knowledge with iterated knowledge runs deep and broad in how we speak—it infects, nearly enough, all epistemic words; I'll illustrate its effect on "aware" in the next section. Yet another important illustration of the scope of the redundancy phenomenon is how we (both philosophers and nonphilosophers) run together "justifying *p*" and "justifying that one knows *p*." These aren't the same. I discuss justification and iterated knowledge attributions in section 5.5.

5.3 Redundancy Usages for "Aware" and the Puzzling Case of Pain

It's tempting to claim that if someone (a human animal, a nonhuman animal) has a feeling, then she's *aware of* having that feeling.[27] To have a feeling just is to be aware of feeling a certain way. Pain looks paradigmatic and typical: I'm in (terrible) pain. So, of course, I'm aware I am. All these questions, therefore, look on a par: "Are you in pain?" "Do you have a pain?" "Are you aware of any pain?" It's a short path from this to the idea that, at least with certain (mental) states M, awareness of M and being in M come to the same thing. And so, being in M and knowing that one is in M come to the same thing too. This impression goes nicely with the thought that we can't be wrong about certain experiences—pains, in particular.[28]

Let's explore the idea of pain and other basic feelings being mental states that require being aware of being in those states.[29] For the moment, I grant this for pain and these other feelings, and explore whether it leads to cases where certain epistemic phrases, "aware of," and perhaps even "know(s)" have only

[27] Wait! Isn't it possible to have *feelings* one doesn't experience or isn't aware of? Yes, and I talk about that later in this section. But I first explore how assuming there are certain states that are intrinsically awarenesses affects the meaning of iterations of "I'm aware that . . ."

[28] Still, there are considerations that drive these two ideas apart. Pains shade continuously into itches; so there looks to be a blurry area where it's hard to say whether a sensation is a pain or an itch. See Williamson (2000, 24). I won't pursue this line of thought now. I examine the effect of vagueness on epistemic locutions in chapter 9.

[29] I'm not here focusing on complex layered emotional states such as pride or shame that (structurally, as it were) involve iterated (self-)awareness.

redundancy uses. To start, it does look like pain is (intrinsically) an *awareness* of pain. That's why (one might think) "I'm aware of pain" and "I'm in pain" are the same. Relatedly, if I feel terrible about *p*, this awareness seems to necessarily go beyond just awareness of *p*: I feel terrible, and I'm (necessarily) aware of *that*. So here too, we might think that *Terrible: p*, and *I feel terrible about p* should be identified because a sensation of feeling terrible is intrinsically an awareness of that sensation "feeling terrible."

Here's a second consideration that apparently leads to the same place: To be aware is to be aware of *something*. But . . . if you're in pain, there's nothing else (relevant to the pain) for you to be aware of. So, to be in pain (or to have a pain) *just is* to be aware of that pain. Phrases like "an experience of pain" invite this interpretation by apparently amounting to no more than "a pain" despite a literal meaning that allows (at least in principle) that one could have a pain distinct from an experience of it.

The foregoing treats these mental states as intrinsically *metacognitive*. And indeed, that looks like a corollary of the common view that one always knows when one is in pain. But, nevertheless, it looks implausible because pain seems too basic to be intrinsically metacognitive. Feelings and simple emotional/bodily states (fear, hunger) are similar—surely they aren't metacognitive all on their own; having them can't imply all by itself that we know we have them.

A fallacy lurks in the reasoning I called "the second consideration." I'm aware of a rock (let's say). There isn't anything metacognitive about *that* state of awareness—all by itself, anyway. But in the case of pain, there isn't anything external for the awareness to be an awareness of.[30] So then one thinks that the awareness is of the state itself—but this is a *fallacy*, because an awareness doesn't have to be awareness of *something*. It's better, therefore, to say that pains are *sensations* with properties of various sorts.[31] That is, if someone is in pain, then he's aware, of course, but this awareness needn't be an awareness of *something*. If right, then we're not forced to treat pains as intrinsically metacognitive states by the second consideration. We *can* metacognize our pains, of course—inspect them mentally. But that goes beyond being in pain and being aware that one is in pain, as I discuss next.

Let's provisionally grant the *conclusion* of what I described as fallacious reasoning, that pain and awareness of pain are phenomenologically joined—after

[30] It's tempting to suggest that pain is always an awareness of a specific body-part state. This misses the point because the phenomenology of pain doesn't require pains to be localized: "a pain in my leg" or "a pain in my arm." Pain can be phenomenologically nondescript in its location: just *pain*. (We sometimes say, during a fever, "Everything aches.")

[31] Do we want to say, instead, that pains have *contents*? We could do this (I guess), although we should be careful. In any case, my forthcoming points—about how much we can fail to know about our pains—hold regardless of whether we speak of pains as having properties or instead as having contents.

all, that looks (to many) to be true on experiential grounds. It still doesn't follow that an awareness of (aspects of) a pain amounts to being in that pain. The experience of a pain needn't be accompanied by an awareness of the specific properties of that pain—the recognition that it's a throbbing pain, for example, or a pain that's relatively constant, or burning or itchy. Pains can be described in detail, if one can attend to them carefully. No one does this if the pain is bad enough; bad enough pain prevents focusing on the details of *anything*, even on the details of the pain itself that's so distracting to one's ability to focus. A pain can be so bad that I'm attending to *it* completely *without* taking in its properties. Being in pain (having a pain) therefore is completely compatible with that pain having lots of properties that I *overlook*.

So, even assuming that pains (and other feelings) are *intrinsically* self-referential experiences doesn't mean that a particular awareness of a pain can't be an awareness of it that's over and above the awareness of the pain that arises from the self-referential qualities of the pain experience itself. That means that pain experiences (although themselves awarenesses of those pain states) aren't the same as other awarenesses of those pain states that we could have.[32]

But *should* we assume that pains (and other feelings) are intrinsically metacognitive experiences? After all, we can have pains that we don't attend to *at all*—or so it seems. If a pain is slight enough, I can ignore it (I can forget I have it), and only later notice that I've been in mild pain or discomfort all along. This happens with certain dull chronic aches, for example. So, we *can* distinguish paying attention to a pain as opposed to just having it.[33]

Interim conclusion: Cases of iterated constructions of "is aware that" or "knows that" reducing to ground-floor usages are quite special. This is both in the sense that the states of mind that this is true of are nowhere near as many as we're prone to think, and in the sense that even when it's the case that "S is aware that he's aware of *p*" follows from "S is aware of *p*," for a certain *p* (e.g., "pain"), this will not be true for very closely related *q* (e.g., "burning pain"). In general, therefore, these iterated usages shouldn't be identified with ground-floor ones. This is all the more so for feelings other than that of pain. Even if feelings are to be treated as intrinsically self-experiential, there is a great deal about them that we can fail to be aware of.

32 Relatedly, to describe pains as intrinsically "transparent" mental states is seriously misleading.

33 Objection: "How can we remember we've had that pain all along without having consciously experienced it all along?" I demur: I can recognize that if I had had a certain experience (a sudden vanishing of the pain), I would have noticed it. I recognize that I don't remember any such thing and realize (therefore) that I've been in (very mild) chronic pain all along. This is certainly the case with bodily sensations that aren't painful. I feel a light pressure on my arm for a while, for example—even though I haven't been aware of it most of that time. I'll notice immediately if it ceases; I can realize that I *haven't* noticed this light pressure all along. This is, by the way, a metacognition of some of my own memories.

But should all "feelings," in general, be described as *intrinsically* self-experiential? No: it's clear that we often have feelings we're *not* aware of *at all*. Pain, despite the considerations I've raised (especially in note 33), isn't the best model for these cases, perhaps, but anger and other emotions are. Even being hungry is something we can miss—and only belatedly realize we're experiencing. (People often "forget to eat.") Apart from that, we're often in complex emotional states that we wrongly characterize when we become aware of them.

What about what some practitioners have come to call "epistemic feelings" (Koriat 2000), ones like "feelings of knowing," "feelings of uncertainty," "feelings of confidence"? A view taken about these is that they are (i) nonconceptual but, otherwise, (ii) metacognitive. I'll discuss them a bit further in section 5.5 and in chapter 6, but it seems, introspectively, that one can *have* feelings that should be described as feelings of confidence, feelings of uncertainty, and even feelings of knowing *without* being aware or knowing that one has them.[34] Epistemic feelings, therefore, are *not* intrinsically metacognitive. This isn't to exclude the possibility that they sometimes are metacognitive; it's to deny that they must be.[35]

Consider, finally, my feeling terrible about something (a dead bird I'm looking at). Here, there are both metacognitive and non-metacognitive attitudes in the same neighborhood; and along with this, the same pattern of usage confusions like those about "know(s)" described in section 5.2. I can be in a state, *feeling terrible*, that's directed toward something I see. It takes the form *Terrible: dead bird*. Or I can make this metacognitive judgement about myself: *I feel terrible about that dead bird*. The second (but not the first) is a judgment about a relationship (feeling a certain way) that holds between me and a dead bird. In the first case, I have a feeling and see the bird, but I needn't be thinking about myself or my feelings at all. In the first case, as with "know(s)," to describe (in first person) what I'm going through with a declarative sentence, I must use an expression that refers to me, to my feelings, and that characterizes them. But that's not the same as a metacognizing thought. I can *say* "I feel terrible about that dead bird" without thinking about myself or my own feelings at all. I'm simply expressing what I say using a declarative in the only way allowed in English, apart from adopting a childish way of speaking—an interjection while pointing at the dead bird: "Terrible! Dead bird!"[36]

We have quite primitive feelings, fear, hunger, and so on. These are primitive in the sense that we uncontroversially share them with most members of

[34] A says to B because of B's tone of voice and other ways that he's been acting, "You're feeling pretty cocky about the answer you've just given." B says, surprised by what A has just said: "Yes, you're right. I didn't realize how sure I felt about this until you brought it up."

[35] It *is* to deny, however, that behavioral signs of surprise and confidence, for example, are prima facie evidence of metacognition. See section 5.5 and chapter 6.

[36] Again, "text acts," however, allow this (recall note 26).

the animal kingdom. These feelings are often (maybe usually) directed toward targets that fearful agents are conscious of. For example, *Fear: Tiger there.* We're aware of the tiger, and we *are* fearful. But being fearful shouldn't intrinsically include self-experiential elements—fear shouldn't be treated as intrinsically metacognitive. When we're *frightened*, the experience can be all-consuming. We act on the fear—we run for our lives (for example). While doing that, we're not thinking about our fear; we're just experiencing it (and acting on it). In this case, like that of enormous pain, our experience is quite close to the experience of many animals, such as rodents and reptiles (but maybe not insects), as well as close to the experience of human babies. There is no metacognition whatsoever.

5.4 Iterated Knowledge and an Agent's Command of Her Concepts

There are a number of related theses (held by many philosophers) which, although not strictly implying KK or implied by it, nevertheless mutually support it and one another. These theses interrelate (i) knowing that one knows that *p*, (ii) grasping that one has the concepts exhibited in the characterization of *p* (as well as being aware of some of the properties of these concepts), and (iii) being able to justify *p*. It's commonly thought that to know *p* requires being able to justify *p*; that, in turn, to justify *p* requires grasping the concepts involved in *p*, in the strong sense referred to in (ii); and (lastly) that a necessary condition for the foregoing is that one knows what one knows. There are other ways these notions have been argued to interconnect; I've just given one sketch of how it can go. In fact, however, although epistemically sophisticated agents exhibit all the abilities these theses interrelate, these abilities can come apart in ways that can bear on the structure of the knowledge of *any* epistemic agent.

What contributes to thinking that (i), (ii), and (iii) are mutually entailing is that our ordinary ways of talking about "concepts" obscure a three-way distinction in how we ordinarily think agents can be related to their concepts. I therefore have to introduce special terminology to mark these distinctions out. There is, first, *having* a concept C and, second, *grasping* it. Third, third parties can use concepts in *their* description of what someone knows or believes without attributing either the having or the grasping of those concepts *to* that agent.

Recall Rover, the dog who recognizes when his owner, Olga, plays chess (section 1.4). Rover distinguishes Olga playing chess from Olga playing checkers. Although Olga can say correctly, "Rover knows when I'm playing chess" (or "Rover knows that I'm playing chess"), she wouldn't (nor would we) claim that among the concepts (if any) in Rover's mental repertoire is *chess*. She'd deny that Rover has the concept *chess*. (She'd deny that he knows what chess is.)

If an agent *has* a concept C, then that concept is in that agent's mental repertoire—the agent *uses* it, for an inference or to apply it to something that falls under it. However, if we say that an agent knows ("can tell") the difference between red things and blue things, we *may be* attributing the concepts of *red* and *blue* to her; we *may* think that those concepts in her mental repertoire explain certain capacities she exhibits. The agent can, for example, distinguish red things from blue things.[37]

Rover's abilities indicate that the phrase "may be" in the above paragraph is essential. Agents aren't required to have the concepts *we* use to describe what they know, believe, or see. Rover knows the difference between Olga playing chess and Olga playing checkers, but that's not to say Rover *has* the concepts of chess and checkers. Rover can see that Olga is playing chess (because he can see that she isn't playing checkers). If Rover mistakenly thinks that Olga is playing chess because she's set out the game to meditate on its look preliminary to sketching it in a drawing, he'll *believe* that she's playing chess even though she's not.

So, *having a (particular) concept* calls for more than discrimination. In the case of Rover and chess, what's additionally called for are inferential connections between the concept of chess and other concepts—*games, checkers, game pieces*, and so on—inferences beyond Rover's capacity. For sure, Rover has mastered *some* inferences: "She's playing chess, so now she's going to give me a snack." But Rover can't manage other crucial inferences—that playing chess is playing a board game with a game piece that moves in an L shape, for example; if *those* inferences were within his capacity, we would allow that he had the concept of chess.

Suppose we decide that Rover *does have* the concept of food because he's capable of all the relevant inferences necessary for having *this* concept; we can further say that Rover knows that because Olga is playing chess, he's going to get some food; nevertheless, we can deny that Rover has the concept of chess. Our "knows that" locution allows that some, all, or none of the words occurring in the proposition p known by the agent correspond to concepts the agent can be said to have. Although it's reasonable to say that Rover has the concept of *food*, it's not reasonable to say that he has the concept of *snack*.

Knowing-that attributions, thus, uncouple from having-concept attributions. The same is true of believing-that, seeing-that, and other propositional-attitude

[37] Discriminative capacity is sometimes taken as the sole criterion for concept possession. See Fujita et al. (2012, 50) for an attribution of the concepts of *humans, trees, fish, artificial objects, paintings of a particular school, Baroque music*, etc., to pigeons on the basis of sheer sensory discrimination. I'll suggest momentarily that this isn't sufficient for an ordinary understanding of concept possession—but this is nomenclature. We can always operationalize (coin) a thin notion of "concept*," an agent's possession of which turns solely on discriminative capacities.

attributions. In turn, having-concept attributions uncouple from iterated-knowing attributions. Having certain concepts, having certain mental representations, and therefore being able to carry out inferences of certain kinds don't imply that the agent is aware *that* she's engaging in inferences. To infer *q* from *p* doesn't require one's knowledge *that* one is inferring *q* from *p*. (I'll discuss this further in section 7.3.) Thus, having certain appropriate mental representations (that enable certain inferences) doesn't require one to know that one has these mental representations.

Consider the case of Sultan, a chimpanzee studied by Wolfgang Köhler during World War I. Byrne (2016, 1–3) writes:

> Köhler had presented chimpanzees with a range of tasks, including the use of a rake to get foods that were out of reach even to the long arm of a chimpanzee. Sultan was good at raking, but he was stumped when Köhler gave him several short sticks, none of them long enough to reach the food. After a while, Sultan gave up and simply sat next to some of the sticks. Then insight dawned. While fiddling with the sticks for no apparent purpose, Sultan happened to push two sticks together—and they held, making a long stick. Sultan suddenly became animated, took the sticks across to the out-of-reach food, and used his new, combined tool to reach it, with immediate success!

This looks like Sultan *has* mental representations of aspects of the problem situation that he was concerned with—perhaps *stick, food, reaching acts*, and so on. As Byrne (2016, 3) puts it, had Sultan "remained at the food site, fiddling with the sticks and constantly re-trying the objects at hand, no mental representation would have been necessary to explain sudden success: trial and error might just have given him a useable tool." Byrne suggests that his suggestion is (still) controversial. But Byrne's motive for this interpretation is easy to see: Sultan, away from the food site, makes an inference about his food problem from what he has just discovered about the sticks; the medium for those inferences has to be something mental that he's manipulating (call this medium "concepts" or "mental representations"). Were he engaged with the food and sticks at the site, Byrne suggests, there would be no need to posit his having made inferences via his mental manipulations of representations—or of his having made any inferences at all.

So, this suggests a second consideration for attributing the having of a concept to an agent: being able to employ it *apart from* the circumstances in which it directly applies—in this case, being able to exploit inferences using it apart from the circumstances in which it applies. Sultan draws certain implications of "stick" using the concept "stick" that he has, and then applies those results to a circumstance in which they can be applied.

We shouldn't assume that Sultan is *aware that* he's manipulating mental representations; furthermore, we don't need to assume that he knows he's drawing inferences or anything like that. We don't need what might be described as metacognition to explain his behavior. Such an attribution to Sultan is easy, however, if we imagine ourselves in Sultan's place: I'm thinking about food that isn't in front of me—in contrast to when the food *is* in front of me. So too, Sultan is imagining (let's say) the food; furthermore, *he knows that* he's imagining this—he's not confused, after all, thinking he's perceiving out-of-reach food when he's only imagining it. As soon as he realizes the solution, he gets up and *goes over* to the food site (he doesn't reach out in front of him). So that's one route to an illegitimate metacognitive attribution to Sultan.

Here's a second. It's quite natural to describe Sultan's "aha!" moment this way: Sultan suddenly realized that he knows how to get the food! Or: Sultan realized that he now knows how to get the food! (Compare this to Sarah playing hide-and-seek with her daughters, as described in section 5.2; the same redundancy locution arises in both cases.)

Both these routes to an attribution of knowledge of his own knowledge to Sultan go beyond what he exhibited. (They even go beyond what we need to attribute to humans exhibiting the *same* behavior as Sultan did.) It does seem clear that Sultan carried out an inference of the form $p \rightarrow q$, where p describes a set of physical movements (*Do this*, then *do that* . . .), and q describes a desirable result. Sultan's reasoning doesn't require Sultan to think about himself or his mental representations. He need only infer a conclusion *using* his mental representations, and then act on the basis of that conclusion—without once thinking *about* those mental representations or *about* himself or *about* what he's doing. For an agent to move to a place and then reach out in a certain way doesn't require him to be aware that *he's* doing so; no more does thinking of reaching out or moving to a certain place require thinking: *I* can move, and then reach out . . .[38]

Next notice this: To attribute the mental representations "food" or "stick," etc., to Sultan isn't to necessarily attribute *our* concepts of "food" or "stick" to him. I made this point earlier about Rover. We may require of the possession of our notion of "food" or "stick" a capacity for certain inferences involving other concepts or mental representations that Sultan can't make. Our description of what Sultan knows or realizes, even when we use our own words "stick" or "food," doesn't require us to attribute *those* concepts to Sultan. We can say that Sultan realized that

[38] I'm therefore characterizing these inferences as in the form of command rules that don't refer to the agent himself. I discuss this assumption further in section 6.3.

he could use the longer stick to get the food; but we can add that he didn't realize that the stick is made of metal, or plastic, or . . . That is, our knowledge, realization, belief, and seeing attributions to a subject allow qualifications that modify even the semantic properties of the concepts we use to describe what that subject knows so that those resulting concepts better fit how the subject thinks. We can even, after using certain concepts to characterize an agent's thought, deny that the agent *has* those concepts. (Said admiringly, "Rover always knows when Olga is playing chess even though he doesn't know what chess is.")

Consider, now, *grasping a concept*: a subject being *cognizant of* the concept *itself* that's had by her. Grasping a concept calls for more skills than the mere possession of concepts or mental representations does. It's tempting to say: grasping a concept calls for the agent, in addition to having that concept, being capable of being aware of that very concept (and his possession of it).

Sheer metaphor. Someone aware of his concepts doesn't mentally *contemplate* them. What on earth is *that*? The closest thing many of us do to contemplating a concept is visualizing a *word*. But words have meanings, and it's the "meanings" that are relevant to (or are) the concepts these words correspond to. Unfortunately, it's quite hard to say what visualizing or (more vaguely) contemplating *a meaning* is supposed to be like. It's no solution to say that contemplating a concept is contemplating an image (in one's mind) of the thing the concept is of. Even if we keep clear the distinction between thinking of an apple by means of an image in one's mind as opposed to contemplating the *image* itself, it's no solution. A concept goes beyond any mental *image*. (This is a famously old problem with image characterizations of concepts—most associated with Wittgenstein.)

To understand what's being attributed to an agent when it's claimed that she grasps (some of) her own concepts, we need to characterize what abilities that agent has because of her awareness and/or what it is that agent recognizes about her concepts that we're attributing to her by saying that she grasps her concepts; only in this way is the metaphor of "being aware of a concept" given determinate content.

For example, an apparently necessary condition on grasping a concept (in addition to having that concept) is recognizing that the concept has a certain *scope* beyond its immediate application. Grasping that a concept has a certain scope, in turn, isn't to mentally encompass all the specific items that fall within that concept's scope—that's too much. (Grasping the concept of "everything" can't be an ability to think, specifically, of every single thing there is, and to recognize, of *each* thing, that it falls under the concept of *everything*.) But it does require apprehending a property had by any concept—that it applies beyond any particular case being thought of. A *sufficient* condition on grasping a concept is being able to discuss the properties of that concept—being able to *talk about* it.

This isn't a necessary condition. Perhaps some nonhuman animals grasp some of their concepts; if so, they don't talk about this!

This three-way distinction between "having" and "grasping" concepts, as well as attributing knowledge or beliefs to an agent without ascribing to her either having or grasping the concepts used in those attributions, isn't concisely marked by how we ordinarily speak about agents' concepts—not even by "having a concept" and "grasping a concept." There are no ordinary locutions that straightforwardly make these distinctions. For example, it's natural to understand *all* the locutions "John has the concept of *number*," "John possesses the concept of *number*," "John grasps counting," "John understands how to count," "John can count," etc., as attributing the grasp of the concept "number" to John rather than the mere capacity to deploy the concept—to be able to count. But, equally naturally, "to grasp counting," "to understand how to count," and even "to *possess* the concept of number" can be understood as characterizing someone as merely capable of counting—for example, a small child will be described as now grasping counting *once she can count* even if she is incapable of saying anything about (or thinking about) her ability *to* count. "She now has the concept of counting" might even be reported of her to indicate only that she's now confident of her counting.

We might describe the child as confident of her counting ability or her counting skills. But this isn't to necessarily say that she ever thinks: "I have good counting skills." It may not even mean that she's *aware of* her feelings of confidence. It may only mean that when we give her a counting task, she handles it quickly without hesitation: she *manifests* confidence.

Recall (section 1.4), Williamson's claim that "Rover sees *that* Olga is playing chess" requires Rover to know what chess is, although Rover isn't required to know what chess is by "Rover sees Olga is playing chess." Williamson, thus, claims a *possession condition* for concepts is codified in English by the verbal distinction between "see(s) *p*" and "see(s) that *p*."[39] But, as I've indicated, Rover can see *that* Olga is playing chess even if Rover lacks the concept of chess. That an agent "sees that *p*" is suitably said when there is (sometimes implicitly or contextually) a contrast class of options that the agent is capable of distinguishing from *p*, and regardless of which concepts among those utilized to express *p* are had, grasped, or neither by the subject.

[39] *Which* possession condition? Grasping concepts? Having concepts? Williamson doesn't say; most likely it's grasping concepts, in light of his discussion of an agent following rules that agent can't formulate (Williamson (2000, 40–41)). Dretske (1993, 265) writes: "One cannot be conscious that the toast is burning unless one understands what toast is and what it means to burn—unless, that is, one has the concepts needed to classify objects and events in this way." No—that's not required of "conscious that" either: Rover is conscious that Olga is playing chess and not checkers. Dretske's other remarks (here and elsewhere) suggest that he would regard grasping a concept as a necessary condition on *having* a concept. I discuss Dretske's views further in section 5.5.

Imagine now that an agent C has the concepts of an agent desiring *p*, seeing *p*, or knowing *p*. These are concepts we claim humans have. Does it follow *from this* that C grasps these concepts, e.g., the concept of an agent knowing *p* or the concept of seeing? Why would it? Our inference that C *has* these concepts can happen on the model of Sultan—that C makes inferences (the way Sultan did) about agents when not face-to-face with those agents, that C has certain "aha!" moments, and so on. None of this, or so it seems, requires C to grasp these concepts, or to manifest awareness of the concepts themselves. What about C *having* the notion that an agent has the concept of seeing? Does this require C to *grasp* the notion of seeing?[40] It seems so because C needs to understand what *an agent having a concept* means—for example, that such an agent can make inferences using the concept when not dealing in "real time" with situations that the concept applies to. This means that C understands that concepts apply to cases, and that sounds like C is focusing on concepts and their properties and representing *these*. Does this, however, require C to grasp the notion of an *agent*? It seems *not*. C has the notion of an agent, and uses it, but doesn't have to think about her own concept of agent.

What about metacognition, metarepresentation, or metaknowledge—specific iterations of A φs that B ψs? It doesn't seem required that any *specific ones* need *necessarily* come into a characterization of the above competencies. In particular, C—as described in the last few paragraphs—needn't be required to be able to think about herself, her own concepts, or what she herself knows. To repeat the point I made earlier about the concept of *everything*, to have a concept (or to grasp it) can't mean one can recognize explicitly *all its applications*. That means that one isn't required, by having or even grasping a concept, to be able to apply that concept to oneself (if it applies)—to thus have the concept of *the knowledge of an agent* or of *an agent having concepts* doesn't require (logically speaking) the recognition that *oneself* has knowledge or concepts. To repeat: To have a concept doesn't require the ability to recognize that the concept in question applies to something in particular; one can have the concept of an apple while being unable to recognize that a particular apple *is* an apple. So too (unless an additional argument is available that establishes this—which I doubt), because someone has the concept of a self doesn't *require*—all by itself anyway—that one recognizes that oneself *is* a self.

That said, I'm not making claims about cognitive development—neither of children nor of animals. It may be that as a child develops and acquires certain concepts—the notion of a self or that of belief, and so on—she acquires certain applications of those concepts (to herself or to others) as well. The "ontogenesis"

[40] I have to confess: these questions—as the cliché goes—"make my head hurt." Everything is *so* much more straightforward, of course, if (i), (ii), and (iii) are mutually entailing!

in a species of concepts, metacognition, and the like needn't directly reflect the logical structure of these concepts.[41]

5.5 Davidson, Dretske, Esken, and Malcolm on Metacognition, Cognition, Belief, and Metabelief

Malcolm (1972–1973) and Davidson's (1982) discussion of Malcolm (1972–1973) illustrate further the absence of any explicit markings in English of distinctions between different kinds of concept possession—despite attempts by philosophers to show that these exist, and to draw empirical results from them.[42] After discussing these, I turn to Dretske's attempt to show that metacognition requires the grasping of concepts, and show how it turns on assuming that ground-floor belief attributions require the grasping of concepts (contrary to what has been shown in the foregoing).

If a dog barks up an oak tree he's chased a cat into, we can say subsequently, "He thought that the cat had gone up the oak." Malcolm (1972–1973, 13) adds: "We should, in contrast, feel reluctant and embarrassed to say, 'He had the thought that the cat went up the oak tree.'" This *does* sound off. Malcolm (14) claims this is because we can't attribute having a proposition *in mind* to a dog. Although dogs (and other non-verbal animals) can think, Malcolm claims, they don't think of (or with) *propositions*: their thinking is intrinsically nonpropositional. Furthermore (and quite surprisingly), our attribution usage *exhibits* this; Malcolm thinks the exhibition of this distinction in ordinary language *licenses* a strong conclusion about non-verbal animal minds.

The argument overreaches. Leave aside the obvious option that if Malcolm were right about usage, this might only show that ordinary propositional-attribution language requires revision in the light of science. Our reluctance (and "embarrassment"), if any, is because we've attributed a *specific* propositional content to the dog. It doesn't follow from *this* being inappropriate that our attribution practices require (or presuppose), that dogs aren't capable of propositional thinking. Suppose a Frenchman (who doesn't speak English) was staring up the

[41] The points I make here and elsewhere in this book also don't require any specific structural views about concepts (e.g., "the prototype theory," "the theory theory" view, pluralist views, etc.)—apart from my denial of the traditional view of concepts (that concepts have definitions—necessary and sufficient conditions).

[42] Why do I keep qualifying the point to English, rather than to natural languages generally? Because, as notes 4 and 11 in chapter 2 indicate, foreign languages, even ones similar to English (like German), draw distinctions, with respect to epistemic locutions, that aren't drawn in English except by writing a paragraph about the distinction (as, in effect, I'm doing here). See note 11 (in this chapter), however, for my reasons for thinking the phenomena I've exposed in this chapter occur in every natural language.

oak, trying to see a cat he saw run up that tree. It would be just *as embarrassing* to say, later, that "he had the thought that the cat went up the oak tree." No one should be convinced, of course, of Malcolm's original claim: that it *is* embarrassing (or even just odd) to say of a dog that "he had the thought that the cat went up the oak tree." Whether the locution *does* sound odd turns on whether "He had the thought that *p*" requires *p* to be a close *paraphrase* of the dog's thinking. If so, the usage is bad for both Frenchmen (who don't speak English) *and* dogs; otherwise it's fine for both.[43]

Davidson (1982, 102) misinterprets Malcolm; he attributes to him a distinction between "having a belief and having the concept of a belief," and not the distinction between propositional and nonpropositional thought Malcolm actually argues for. Davidson next claims that in order for an agent to have beliefs at all, that agent must have the concept of a belief. Davidson is also explicit that, according to him, this comes to: when one believes *p*, one knows that one believes *p*. So, an agent having any beliefs at all requires iterated knowledge, as well as the requisite concept of belief. Davidson argues that if an agent believes *p*, that agent can only be surprised at discovering that *p* isn't the case if she believes that she believes *p*.

Davidson's argument is refuted by simple examples:[44] Facing not *p* contrary to one's previous belief (e.g., there's no apple in the refrigerator) can induce surprise all on its own. It can induce more than surprise; it can induce shock or annoyance. This depends on the agent's expectations *about p*—for example, if the agent was hoping for certain implications of *p* (e.g., "there's some good edible fruit in the refrigerator"). The agent doesn't have to be thinking about herself or her internal states to be surprised or shocked by the discovery of *p* not being the case. Actually, *any* of an agent's beliefs being falsified can induce surprise—unless that agent is wrong *so often* that she's become numb to being surprised at all.[45]

[43] Well, *which is it*? Does "S had the thought *p*" require *p* to be a close paraphrase of what S thought? This is indeterminate in two senses. First, some people will think it's bad, and some won't (that's my experience when I run the example by nonphilosophers); second, for some people, in some cases the expression passes muster, and in some cases it doesn't. This is because in some cases those individuals understand it as a close paraphrase of the purported thinking, and sometimes they don't. As data, the usage in question has another drawback: it's arch and somewhat dated. So, it's hard for contemporary listeners to interpret. This, therefore, is poor evidence for the strong hypothesis that our attributions of thoughts to non-verbal animals require (or presuppose) that those animals can only think nonpropositionally. Furthermore, and in any case, this bit of usage doesn't exhibit the distinction Malcolm needs.

[44] See Carruthers (2008, 62) for similar objections to Davidson's remarks about being surprised.

[45] The widespread "staring test" is used by cognitive scientists (of all sorts) to determine whether small babies (and animals) are surprised or not. This is widely understood to be a test of expectations; it's not widely understood to be a test for metacognition. Nor should it be. See Proust (2012, 238 n. 10).

Esken (2012, 135) offers the following contrast:

Surprise I:
The dog is surprised about the new garden seat in its well-known surroundings and starts barking.

Surprise II:
I am surprised that I only have 5 Euros in my pocket, because I thought it was much more.

Surprise I, Esken (2012, 135) tells us,

> can simply be based on a perceptual mismatch between a stored representation in the dog's memory and the dog's current perceptual experience of its well-known surroundings. . . . This mismatch does not mean that there is a mismatch between the dog's expectation and his current perception, which the dog *recognizes* as a mismatch. It is just a mismatch between two cognitive states (i.e. a first-order mismatch) which leads to a certain reaction and may involve a certain feeling.

That is, the dog can have the feeling, and act on the basis of that feeling, without being aware *of* that feeling. The dog isn't thinking: "Oh, wow, look at that: *I'm* totally surprised by that garden seat." It's rather, *Surprise: Garden seat there.* Surprise, although an "epistemic feeling" doesn't have to have a metacognitive component.

What, however, makes Surprise II metacognitive?[46] The answer is complex. It isn't that it has to *describe* a metacognitive judgment: It *needn't*, because what may have happened could be like what happened, according to Esken, to the dog. I pull out all the coins in my pocket and find only 5 Euros.[47] I'm surprised because of the mismatch between my expectation and my current perception—this is a first-order mismatch.[48] But for a sentence to *describe* this mismatch event (recall from section 5.2), it has to mention the agent and that the agent is surprised. I can't say in English, (*Surprise: q*) *follows* (*Expectation: p*), or (*Surprise: q*) *because* ((*Expectation: p*) and (*Perception: r*)). So, my sentence has to be (literally) a metacognitive one.[49]

[46] Esken (2012, 135) writes: "Surprise II surely is a metacognitive ability. It entails a metacognitive judgement ('I thought that I had more than 5 Euros in my pocket') which is connected or leads to a special feeling of being surprised ('I feel surprised')." I don't analyze Surprise II as required to take the trajectory Esken describes: I deny the *necessary* connection in humans between the metacognition and the surprise. See what follows.

[47] I don't bark as a result—that's true. But I might utter several loud obscenities.

[48] Borrowing the idea of "implicit" metacognition from Proust (2006), one might think the emotion "carries the information of a conflict of emotion and expectation," and so is metacognitive in this sense. (I owe this suggestion to Carruthers [2008, 62], who doesn't endorse it.) No; as Carruthers observes, "implicit metacognition" so described is trivial: it's everywhere.

[49] Carruthers (2008, 62) explains our "so naturally" reporting surprise in metacognitive terms as due to "humans" being "inveterate mind-readers." Maybe, but I think it's just grammar.

Of course, what happened to me *needn't be* what happened to the dog. Esken's description *can be* true of me: I had a metacognitive perception of only 5 Euros plus the recognition that that's what I'm perceiving; I'm, that is, in a state of perceiving *p* but expecting *q*, along with an awareness of all that. In turn, that awareness leads directly to my surprise. In this case, the analysis Esken gives would be the right one. But it needn't have gone that way.

More should be said. Compare "I am surprised that I only have 5 Euros in my pocket, because I thought it was much more" with "I am surprised that I only have 5 Euros in my pocket, because I expected it to be much more" and with "I am surprised that I only have 5 Euros in my pocket, because I expect it to be much more." Even though *only* the last thought might accurately describe what happened: a presently felt expectation undercut by the perception of 5 Euros, we naturally put the consequent into the past tense. This makes the mental state metacognitive-sounding because it looks like I'm remembering an expectation I earlier had. That needn't correspond to the psychological state being described: it can be a current active expectation that's defeated, not *the memory* of a previous expectation that's defeated.

Things change, of course, if I then ruminate, "Why *am* I surprised at what I've just done? After all, I make this kind of mistake all the time." *These* thoughts *are* metacognitive; they're compatible with my earlier thought also being meant literally (i.e., metacognitively) *or* with my transitioning to metacognitive thinking only with the later thoughts. Either can happen. I'll look at other examples in chapter 6 that illustrate how difficult it is to keep clear between metacognitive and non-metacognitive thinking. Part of the reason is that we (adult humans) are capable of either sort of thought in similar epistemic circumstances—like when we're surprised by something. Our thinking/emoting is (unsurprisingly) far more variable than the language we typically use to describe it.[50]

I now briefly discuss Dretske's claim that metacognition requires the grasping of concepts. His argument relies on a claim he makes about the ordinary expression "aware of the fact that *p*," so let's look at that first. I claimed in section 5.4 that ordinary propositional-attitude talk doesn't require agents to either have or grasp the concepts described in the proposition *p* their attitude toward which is attributed. But what about the phrase "S is aware of the fact that *p*"? Does *it*

[50] Metacognitions are run together with cognitions in speech and thought outside epistemic contexts—with respect to desires, for example. "I want a cookie," I say petulantly—this can express a mental state *solely* directed at the cookie. I have a desire, and what's represented (if anything) is just the cookie. What about when I don't know which cookie I want? Metathinking? Monitoring my own indecisive state? Why? Why not just: *Polar-Bear Cookie* or *Mountain-Lion Cookie*? Then an evaluation takes place (and even substantial reasoning). But why does there need to be any representation or cue monitoring of my own indecision? I *am* indecisive—that's triggering the whole thing, but no *awareness of* this is needed. Perner (2012, especially 198) stresses this by distinguishing "BEING in a state versus KNOWING that one is in this state."

require that S grasp the concepts expressed in *p*? We can say that the Frenchman was aware of the fact that the cat was in the tree. But we can say the same about a dog too! I say to my friend that we can leave the house for an hour without Rover getting into trouble. My friend says, warning me, "Rover is quite aware of the fact that there's food in the kitchen cabinet." This doesn't require Rover to either have or grasp the concept *kitchen cabinet* or *fact*.

Dretske (1999, 106) distinguishes between "*o*-awareness (for *object*-awareness . . .), *f*-awareness (for *fact*-awareness) and *p*-awareness (*property*-awareness)."[51] One can be aware of the fact that a cat is in the tree without being aware either of the cat or of its properties (because one has, say, inferred that a cat is in the tree from a dog's barking at the base of that tree—which it only does when a cat is up there). Dretske claims anyone's metacognitive knowledge, Sarah's knowledge (for example) that she's having a pumpkin experience, must be *f*-awareness because it must be based, not on a direct awareness of the experience of a pumpkin and *that experience's* properties, but instead on an awareness of what the experience is of—namely the pumpkin.[52] However (and this is why, according to Dretske, metacognition requires grasping concepts):

> One cannot be *f*-aware that *o* is an apple without understanding, at some conceptual level, what an apple is. If a child (or an animal) doesn't know what an apple is, this does not prevent it from being *o*-aware of apples or *p*-aware of their properties (this presumably happens when the child is a few months old), but it prevents it from being *f*-aware that the apples (she is *o*-aware of) are apples.

The example may be convincing: small children (or animals) don't know that apples *are* apples[53]—but why should this be true of *f*-awareness generally? Why *must it* be false that Rover is aware of the fact that there is food in the kitchen cabinet? Dretske's argument for this is in a note which I quote in full (Dretske [1999, 123–124]):

> I take *f*-awareness (of the fact) that *o* is *P* to imply knowledge (of the fact) that o is P, and the latter to imply belief that *o* is *P*. Belief, in turn, requires possession of concepts corresponding to the (obliquely) occurring expressions (i.e., "*P*") in

[51] Also see Dretske (1993, 265) on "perceptual awareness of facts."

[52] Dretske (1999, 112) writes: "One is made aware of what a pumpkin experience is like . . . not by an awareness of the experience, but by an awareness of the pumpkin and an awareness of its (the pumpkin's) properties."

[53] What *is it* to know that apples are apples? I'm not sure—this sounds really . . . "deep." That may be why the example is (rhetorically) so convincing. Or . . . it's utterly trivial, and then of course children and animals *do know* that apples are apples.

> the factive clause that specifies what is believed. Hence, one cannot be *f*-aware that *o* is *P* without possessing the (or a) concept corresponding to *P*.

No. Belief attribution is like knowledge attribution in its agential concept requirements; to say "S believes *p*" is compatible with S having, grasping, or neither all, some, or none of the concepts characterized in *p*. Dretske's strong representationalism about metacognition relies on a premise about ordinary ground-floor belief attributions (and on other ground-floor attributions as well)—one that deviates from how we ordinarily attribute beliefs to agents.

5.6 Iterated Knowledge and Belief, and Justification

I've suggested, so far, that neither knowledge, nor belief attribution, of *p* to an agent requires that agent to grasp or, more weakly, have the concepts used to convey *p*. Rover can know or believe that Olga is playing chess, without having or grasping the concept of chess. For Rover to know or believe that Olga is playing chess only requires his ability to distinguish Olga's chess playing from her playing the other board games she typically plays. He may be able to recognize this because of a special—but fairly subliminal—way that she moves when she gets out the chess board, as opposed to when she sets up other board games. Sheer iteration of knowledge doesn't change this: if an agent knows that he knows *p*, there is no reason we've seen (so far) for why that agent must grasp or even have the concepts of know(s) or knowledge.

Given this, it shouldn't surprise that ordinary talk of justification crosscuts possession (or not) of iterated or ground-floor knowledge as well as the grasping and/or having (or neither) of concepts. In addition, a justification can involve metacognitions without iterated knowledge. That is, a justification of a piece of knowledge *may* involve some iterated knowledge used to justify what's (purportedly) known, or it may just be some further knowledge of some other kind that's so used. As I indicated at the end of section 5.2, ordinary talk of justification is tainted by confusing slippages between iterated and ground-floor knowledge attributions—and this contributes to a presupposition, among philosophers, that agential knowledge has strong justification requirements.

Consider "That's an apple on the table." One justification for it is: "That thing is a fruit that looks and tastes just like apples do." A different one is: "I *see* that it's an apple." These justifications can be motivated by differences in how the agent has been asked to support his claim to know. The first justification is an inference from details about the fruit on the table. It's not iterated or metacognitive knowledge because the agent's justification focuses only on *apples* and their properties—merely carrying out an inference doesn't, all by itself, require iterated knowledge, or any other sort of metacognition.

For the agent to justify that there is an apple on the table by saying that *she sees* the apple is different. She has explicitly brought her own cognitive relationship to the apple *into* the explanation by speaking explicitly of her own seeing of the apple. This differs from the first case where the agent infers one fact from another, but it doesn't bring a reference to that inference *into* the explanation. The justification, in this case, takes metacognitive form: "I see that's an apple. Therefore, that's an apple," although it doesn't involve iterated *knowledge*. The inference directly relies on the factivity, in this case, of seeing. Because *I see* that's an apple, it *is* an apple. Although the agent uses the facticity of seeing *to* infer, *that's* not *in* the explanation either; only a term labeling the seeing state is there. The factivity of seeing isn't (even implicitly) something that (all by itself) connects seeing to knowing. So—at least in principle—an agent who doesn't have (let alone possess) the concept of knowledge can still give a justification like this one.

Consider, now, a third justification that runs, roughly: "I see an apple on the table. But if I see an apple on the table, then I know there's an apple on the table. So there's an apple on the table." This is a justification via (a bit of) iterated knowledge. The agent makes the explicit inference from seeing an apple on the table to knowing that the apple is on the table; from there he infers—using the facticity of "know(s)"—that the apple is on the table.

These are *different* justifications relying on different cognitive resources; metacognition isn't involved in the first case; there is metacognition in the second, but not iterated knowledge; iterated knowledge occurs only in the third. There are other, many other, justifications for the same conclusion, some (for example) that invoke explicit metacognition about the inferences the agent is employing (rather than about what he's seeing).

Do these justifications come (pretty much) to the same thing? No. However: suppose you (a certain philosopher, say) hold a certain view about propositional-attitude ascriptions, that a necessary condition on an agent knowing certain things (or anything) requires that agent to possess a great deal of metacognitive knowledge—about her own sensory and inference faculties—as well as a great deal of iterated knowledge. Or suppose you accept KK and K¬K. Then you (that particular philosopher) *will* take these justifications to amount to the same because knowing agents can run any one of them at will, and for those agents, each one easily implies the other ones.

The reality is that these justifications come apart: agents may only be capable of providing (or agents will only have) certain justifications for their beliefs without the other ones.

5.7 Level Confusions in Epistemology

The usage traps discussed in this chapter predict "intuitions" about iterated "know(s)" locutions that are borne out. First, they cause a cleavage between "know(s)" and "know(s) that one know(s)" locutions, and higher-order "know(s)" attributions. A cleavage is otherwise unexpected because one naturally thinks that "I know that I know that I know *p*" shouldn't raise interpretational issues beyond "I know that I know *p*." This cleavage occurs because redundancy usages are common on the ground floor; these give the impression that second-order "know" iterations make (trivial) sense. Third- and higher-order "know(s)" locutions require a focus on the evidence and reasons (if any) we have for our (claims of) knowledge that we (ordinarily) have little awareness of. That alone makes an expression like "I know that I know that I know *p*" hard to understand.[54]

On the other hand, the same confusion (fueled by redundancy usages) can make it easy to slip between requiring justifications for the knowledge of *p* and justifications for the knowledge that one knows *p*. This especially matters in philosophical contexts—and especially in contexts where KK itself is under scrutiny. Does this happen in philosophy? Sure it does, as Alston (1980) pointed out forty years ago. Alston's litany of sinning philosophers is somewhat mixed: although many of the cases are genuine "level confusions," in some cases, the "conflation" looks to me to be only an (implicit) acceptance of KK along with an acceptance of related iteration principles of other members of the "know(s)" epistemic community—including "justification." Rather than discuss these cases, I prefer to indicate how difficult it is to keep clear on the distinctions even when one is completely aware of the importance of doing so, and even when one is (for example) aware of Alston's paper.[55]

Greco (2014, 190) argues that he can "appeal to the phenomenon of abominable conjunctions to motivate KK." Consider a reliable chicken sexer, Jimmy, with a reliable chicken-sexing faculty, but (172) "no information about [his] reliability." Does Jimmy know that the chicken is female? Greco tells us that in some contexts, "this may seem perfectly reasonable." But, maybe, he doesn't know that

[54] Proust (2007, 276, and what follows) notices the phenomenon of seeming to grasp second-order know iterations, but not higher ones, and offers a different explanation for it in terms of a clash between an easy grasp of recursion coupled with a "*limited ability to engage first-personally in a self-directed n-order recursive thought for n greater than one*" (her italics); Greco (2014, 196) explains the same phenomenon via contextualism. I reject both explanations. Hintikka (1962, 103) suggests iterated know(s) expressions lack sense, and thus theorists are free to stipulate their properties (an easily rejected claim).

[55] I shouldn't rule out the possibility, therefore, that *I've* exhibited confused usage *even in this chapter* . . .

he knows the sex of the chicken, because he can't rule out his having no reliable chicken-sexing faculty, and is merely guessing. Greco (190) tells us:

> it is a bit awkward to insist that he nevertheless does know that the chicken is female—if Jimmy cannot rule out the possibility that he is just guessing, then how can he rule out the possibility that the chicken is not the sex he thinks it is? That is, how can he know what sex the chicken is?

To bring "out the tension" that's supposedly here, Greco urges us to "consider the following abominable conjunction":

> (AC′) Jimmy does not know whether he knows the sex of the chicken or is merely guessing, but he knows that he is not guessing incorrectly.

Why must the opponent of KK (who accepts closure in the form: S knows *p* and *p* entails *q*, entails S knows *q*; Greco (2014, 176)) have to accept that Jimmy knows that he is not guessing incorrectly? Because, we are told (Greco (2014, 191 n. 47)), closure gets us from *Jimmy knows that he believes that the chicken is male* and *Jimmy knows that the chicken is male* to *Jimmy knows that he is not guessing incorrectly.*

Of course, Jimmy needn't know that he believes that the chicken is male. That's *metacognition.* Perhaps he just knows that the chicken is male and he just believes that it is; for him to know that he believes it calls for more. Or so the denier of iteration principles will claim.

Well, fine. Let Jimmy metacognize this much. Now what?[56] Greco (2014, 191) writes:

> If we deny KK, then we will accept that one sometimes knows that P without knowing whether one knows or is merely guessing. But then we cannot explain why conjunctions like (AC′ are abominable—we cannot explain why there is a tension between acknowledging that for all Jimmy knows, he might be guessing (that is, he does not know that he knows the sex of the chicken), *and* insisting that he nevertheless does know the sex of the chicken.

Stop right there! There is no tension between Jimmy not knowing that he knows the sex of the chicken and insisting that he nevertheless does know the sex of the chicken. Not to the KK denier, anyway. But, of course, everyone is going to feel a tension between *acknowledging that for all Jimmy knows,* he

[56] My thanks to Patrick McKee and for Tianyi Zhao for recognizing my earlier version of this wasn't right.

might be guessing and insisting that he nevertheless does know the sex of the chicken. After all, "for all Jimmy knows" isn't limited in scope: it includes anything Jimmy knows, including the sex of the chicken. That is, Greco's gloss on "he does not know that he knows the sex of the chicken" obliterates just the level distinction that's supposed to be respected (and is respected by the phrase, "Jimmy does not know that he knows"). (AC′), that is, isn't abominable—not to the KK denier, and so there is nothing here to explain.

Diagnosis: Despite the admirable care about avoiding level confusions in a polemical context that requires being clear about this—something that Greco exhibits throughout the article—he has, nevertheless, level-confused knowing *p* and knowing that one knows *p*.

5.8 Conclusion and Transition to the Next Chapter

Our propositional-attitude locutions allow many options vis-à-vis the intersection of knowledge, the role of concepts, metacognition, and, more broadly, metarepresentation—at least in principle. My analyses about usage haven't yielded any empirical theses about any of this—not even about humans who speak English. And they *shouldn't have*. That, indeed, is the point of sections 5.4 and 5.5: I've tried to show that epistemic locutions in ordinary language, contrary to widespread claims, are flexible—"neutral," if you will—and don't dictate or presuppose empirical options. This nicely contrasts with physics, for example, where ordinary notions of space and time have presuppositions that preclude their inclusion (without substantial modification) in scientific theory.

Consider the logical space of complete sets of items of knowledge of possible epistemic agents. (Call this "the landscape of possible extensions—in the model-theoretic sense—of the predicate S-know(s)-*x*," or, for short, "the epistemic landscape.") If KK and K¬K are true, then this landscape isn't rich, because if certain items are known to an agent, then all know(s) iterations of those items are known to that agent as well. Similarly, more generous closure principles—e.g., $(Kp \& (p \rightarrow q)) \rightarrow Kq$—impoverish the epistemic landscape more than stingy closure principles do—e.g., $(Kp \& K(p \rightarrow q)) \rightarrow Kq$. Impoverishment vs. enrichment of the epistemic landscape involves trade-offs. The more impoverished the epistemic landscape, the more principles there are that govern it—e.g., KK and K¬K; that $p \rightarrow q$ implies $Kp \rightarrow Kq$. That's nice for philosophers who like to *prove things*. But the richer the epistemic landscape, the more descriptive resources it provides for characterizing different kinds of knowledgeable epistemic agents.

(The more different kinds of epistemic agents there can be.) That's nice for cognitive ethologists, and psychologists, generally, who want to *describe things*.[57]

If I'm right, that these theses are false of our ordinary knowing attributions, then the epistemic landscape is intricate and rich. I've indicated this already: There are many kinds of justifications—some of which some agents have access to and some of which they don't. There are many more ways that agents can be piecemeal knowledgeable and ignorant both of their own faculties and of the world. I continue to explore this epistemic landscape in the next chapter.

But we must proceed carefully, as this chapter has shown. This is because, although our knowing attributions, and, more generally, all our propositional-attitude attributions, aren't governed by KK and K¬K and other members of the metacognition family (as I've illustrated already in this and earlier chapters, and will illustrate further subsequently), there are usage traps that make it easy for us to attribute (meta)knowledge and other metacognitions to agents that we have no good evidence they actually possess.

[57] My hypothesis about natural languages is that such languages usually optimize descriptive resources over general principles, although there always are some general principles (of *some* sort) governing most ordinary words. A preference for descriptive resources on the part of natural languages, however, is good, because any general principles that *are* presupposed in those languages are always the result of special cases. Despite this, as I mentioned, there are always some general principles, and often they're empirically restrictive (given later scientific discoveries). So . . . it's perhaps surprising that our folk talk of knowledge and belief hasn't (so far) been shown to be as inadequate as the way our folk talk of space and time is. (I fear I'm overlooking something—always a danger, especially in epistemology, where there is *so much* to watch out for.) I should add that we've seen this trade-off tension already in a related but different subject area. Recall that according to me (in section 4.2), we must treat language experience as (potentially) involving the experience of speech acts, of assertion, say, as well as involving language instruments which themselves can exhibit the property of being asserted (without the presence of a speech act). The result is a richer classification system for language experience than would be available otherwise.

6

Iterated and Ground-Floor Cognition, KK and K¬K Arguments and Empirical Studies

6.1 Introduction

Consider KK—namely, $(p)(Kp \rightarrow KKp)$.[1] If someone knows that p, she *knows* that she knows it. And, conversely, $(p)(KKp \rightarrow Kp)$: if someone knows that she knows that p, she knows that p. Both claims once struck philosophers as truisms and, when stated straightforwardly, they *sound like* truisms. The converse of KK *is* a truism—as much a truism as the factivity of "know(s)," since the latter guarantees it. If, *for all p, if an agent knows p then p*, then S knowing she knows p guarantees that she knows p. Because of factivity as well, the converse is also an instantiation of a general truism about knowing attributions about others: For all agents, S and Q, if S knows that Q knows that p, then S knows that p too.

But KK, like I said, sounds truistic *too* (at least with respect to a proposition p that's not about an agent's propositional attitudes) although it's independent of the factivity of "know(s)." Redundancy-usage phenomena (section 5.2) are the culprits: Kp and p in these cases seem interchangeable in meaning, and if so, K iterations innocently follow. Joelle says, "I know that p" ("I know that John is out running.") And she's challenged with, "Do you *actually* know this?" "Of course I do," she responds (as we all would if we were challenged this way). Consider Silvia who says, more simply, "John is out running"; imagine she's challenged: "Do you *know* this?" "Of course I *know* this," she'll likely respond as well (because echoing a know-challenge with a know-response is typical). And there are many other ways challenges and responses commonly interchange know-claims with what those claims are of. Apinya asserts, "Divya is out running," and he's challenged by "That's implausible." "I know it's true," Apinya responds. Claims of fact and claims to know those facts, thus, sound the same; challenging presumed facts and

[1] For a brief characterization of KK's current state of play, see note 1 of chapter 5.

Attributing Knowledge. Jody Azzouni, Oxford University Press (2020). © Oxford University Press.
DOI: 10.1093/oso/9780197508817.001.0001.

challenging a speaker's presumed knowledge of these facts look like the same—although put slightly differently.[2]

Only if we ignore the evidence about redundancy usages, and how they enable confusions between ground-floor and iterated knowledge claims, can our verbal practices, as just described, be regarded by philosophers as "intuitively supporting" KK. Our "intuitions" about usage have been shown to be untrustworthy—at least in this respect. So, iterated know(s) theses must be established on other grounds. Philosophers have certainly *tried* this—but the arguments turn (at crucial stages) on misreading the ordinary "know(s)." One strategy, for example, is to find semantic entailments that govern "know(s)," and that yield these theses as corollaries, e.g.: If knowledge requires justification, and all justifications, in turn, come in certain strong forms, these theses follow. The Cartesian project is a version of this strategy, as I'll illustrate in section 6.2. An alternative approach (among those I call "rich epistemologists") is to argue that ground-floor knowledge is only possible if it's accompanied by iterated knowledge, along with the grasp of the relevant epistemic concepts; again, the iterated know(s) theses emerge as corollaries of this claim.

I know of no successful arguments—of either sort. Strong-form justification arguments mischaracterize our notion of justification: they treat required justifications as stronger than ones we actually give—or that we need to. I discuss justification in chapters 7 and 8, and (a bit) in this chapter as well. The problem with rich-epistemic arguments, on the other hand, is almost always typified by the arguments I exhibited in section 5.5: they misconstrue ordinary usage practices as requiring attributions of ground-floor belief or knowledge to agents to have as conditions that those agents in addition grasp certain epistemic concepts. But such competence, in turn, entails iterated cognitions, and knowledge.

I haven't undercut KK (and K¬K) and other related metacognition theses by merely shifting the burden of proof against their proponents. So, with the above considerations are also a number of counterexamples, cases—for example—where we attribute knowledge to agents without attributing any iterated knowledge to them.[3] In chapter 5, I showed that the properties of "know(s)" (and how we use it) allow there to be such cases; I've discussed some details of some of these

[2] This is true of other propositional-attitude attributions. Evans (1982, 225–26) writes, "whenever you are in a position to assert that *p*, you are *ipso facto* in a position to assert 'I believe that *p*.'" Actually, this depends on "you." Yes—if "you" have the cognitive resources characterized by "believe" and "I," and the resources to draw that inference. No, otherwise. Humans, generally, have these resources; when they don't, if they can nevertheless talk, they *sound like* they have these resources. (As people do who have Williams syndrome.)

[3] "Counterexample," although literally correct, understates because there are many epistemic phenomena—about humans, animals, and artifacts—that are poorly describable (indeed, in some cases, can't be captured at all) if we attempt it with epistemic locutions governed by iterative K-principles, and other iterative metacognitive theses. Recall section 5.8.

counterexamples in earlier chapters, e.g., the timid-student case. In this chapter, I'll go further, exhibiting ways in which, in ordinary life and scientific studies, we unjustifiably presuppose or attribute iterated knowledge. I'll also illustrate, however, how iterated knowledge can arise similarly to how ground-floor knowledge arises—not a lot of subsidiary knowledge (or iterated knowledge) is needed in either case.

A well-known argument against KK, originally due to Williamson (2000, chapter 4) connects its falsity to vagueness—my impression is that this argument is widely accepted. I show it fails in section 9.5; I thus need to establish the falsity of various iteration theses about knowledge (and cognitions, generally) in other ways—as I've been going about it in this book. Nonetheless, there are important effects that vagueness has on our epistemic practices that are the main topic of chapter 9.

The demise of KK and K¬K, and their other family members, complicates the epistemic landscape—the logical space of possible epistemic agents—because instances of these principles only hold when agents engage (or can engage) in specific kinds of thinking about their own thinking. In addition, it's already been shown in chapter 5 that there is nothing straightforward or easy about establishing that an agent has iterated knowledge—any iterated cognition, really; in part because our talk about this confuses us. I'll illustrate this with additional cases from the empirical metacognition literature.

Relevant to that literature, and to the terminology I'll adopt when discussing it, are the results of the last chapter; and so, despite my previous use of "metacognition," I'll largely avoid that word from here on. I'll call cognitions with repetitions of propositional attitudes (φing that one ψs p)—e.g., thinking that one knows that p, remembering that one knows p, believing that one knows that one remembers p, and so on—*iterated cognitions*; singled items like "remembering p" and the like I'll call *ground-floor cognitions*. (Later in this chapter, I'll rely on similar nomenclature for desires.)

The having/grasping-of-concepts distinction introduces additional complications. Iterated cognitions (and correspondingly iterated propositional-attitude expressions) are "coarse-grained"—involving only "propositional-sized" *relata*; this is indicated by propositional variables p in formulations like "she φs that she ψs p," and no (noun)-term variables. Without further argument, we can't attribute to an agent—on the mere basis of an iterated cognition—a grasp of *either* the concepts φ or ψ, or the concepts that occur (are expressed) in p. If an agent knows that it knows p, and p is "there is a cat over there," we can't assume—without further argument—that the agent *grasps* the concepts of know(s), cat, or something over there. The grasp of one's concepts involves a focus of the agent on more than the cognized proposition-sized thoughts during iterated cognitions: an agent grasping concepts is scrutinizing (aspects of) the structure of those cognitions. As I showed in chapter 5, grasping concepts—grasping "representations," as it's often put—goes strictly beyond iterated cognition.

The reason, thus, I avoid the label "metacognitive"—although I'm inconsistent about this—is that the current literature is in flux, specifically with how "metacognition" is itself used, and so various characterizations of "metacognition," and how various theorists, psychologists and philosophers alike, deploy the word, cut across mental phenomena that must be distinguished. The characterizations I quoted of "metacognition" in section 5.1 (note 2) show this. "Knowing what one does (or does not) know" is iterated knowledge. "Humans' abilities to assess confidence and to manage uncertainty adaptively," though (so I'll argue in section 6.6), may involve iterated cognition, the grasping (or not) of some concepts in those iterations, or it may only involve ground-floor cognitions. "Monitoring thought processes," and "judging confidence," may similarly involve only ground-floor cognitions. "Access to one's states" is ambiguous between a proposition-sized "accessing" of one's states (and thus iterated cognitions) and a richer access to those states by grasping concepts of them. Correlatively, as I'll indicate in section 6.6, studies of what's officially regarded as metacognition, and the skills that animals (and children) exhibit in such studies, only sometimes show that the agents in question cognize iteratively or grasp their own concepts.[4]

6.2 The Cartesian Perspective: *Full* Metacognition About the Self

Some think KK is a truism because they hold a transparency view about mental states—Williamson (2000) calls it "luminosity": we always know when we're in the mental state we're in (and, as important, we always know we're not in mental states we're not in). Applied to knowledge states (assuming, that is, knowledge states are—pure—mental states, as Descartes evidently did), luminosity amounts to both KK and K¬K: we could—and perhaps should—define the luminosity of knowing states *as* these theses. Williamson (2000, chapter 1) argues that knowledge *is* a mental state, but denies the general transparency of mental states: he argues for a modest non-transparency with respect to *all* mental states—even pains. With respect to "know(s)," specifically, he notes that circumstances that

[4] The way iterative cognitions come apart from the grasping of concepts complicates debates over whether and when an experimental result shows "metacognition." Carruthers (2008, 59), for example—like Dretske, and like other philosophers mentioned in chapter 5—treats iterated cognitions as requiring the grasp of the concepts involved in what's cognized. This makes "metacognition," on his view, a rich cognitive capacity; Proust (2012), by contrast, believes in "nonconceptual" metacognition. I'll give indications later for thinking that the notion of nonconceptual cognition, in any case, isn't needed—that the distinction between having and grasping concepts, and possible subdivisions of this distinction, does all the needed taxonomic work.

we're knowledgeable about can change quickly without our recognizing this. Thus (Williamson (2000, 23)), a "well-informed citizen N.N." can know that Lincoln is president until he's assassinated. N.N. will continue to think she knows Lincoln is president even though he's not; she doesn't know that she doesn't know that Lincoln is president although she thinks she does. This counterexample, if it works, refutes the transparency of knowledge by refuting K¬K; it doesn't refute KK: if KK is true, then N.N. knows that she knows that Lincoln is president as long as she knows that Lincoln is president. Once the latter knowledge is gone, so is the former.

Does this counterexample work? Claim: As soon as an agent no longer knows that *p*, he knows that he doesn't know it—whether he realizes this or not. Counter: If "S realizes that *p*," then "S knows that *p*"; and, further, if "S hasn't realized that *p*," then "S doesn't know that *p*." But if N.N. doesn't realize she no longer knows that Lincoln isn't president, N.N. doesn't know that she knows this. KK and K¬K, that is, involve other words that "know(s)" is entangled with: "realize(s)," "recognize(s)," etc. If someone recognizes that *p*, then he knows that *p*; if someone realizes that *p*, then she knows that *p*. These words are factive, as "know(s)" is; but in addition, "knowledge" seems comprised, in part, of recognitions, realizations, and the like.[5]

This counterexample to K¬K is a nonstarter for philosophers who are stringent about what justifies knowledge—e.g., those who allow only present-tense introspectively transparent "clear and distinct" mental states to confer knowledge. This constraint on acceptable justification immunizes K¬K against these potential counterexamples by instead denying, for example, that N.N. ever had knowledge about Lincoln being president to begin with.

Let's explore "the Cartesian perspective" to make visible the necessary conditions on knowledge we have to deny to desert that perspective. To know something, according to Cartesians, is to be (at that moment!) mentally alert to that something's "clarity and distinctness." Whatever the paired conditions—clarity and distinctness—exactly are, they constitute a mental state we're supposedly concurrently and transparently aware of. If this is *all* that (justified) knowledge is, that implies KK and K¬K: I can mentally encompass everything involved in the knowing relation that I bear to a thought at the moment I'm having that thought. I transition from the thought that I'm thinking to the thought that I exist while (simultaneously?) appreciating the clarity and distinctness of that very transition of thought. Thus, KK. Similarly (according to Descartes), I can always avoid mistaken self-knowledge attributions: I can always realize I'm *not* experiencing clarity and distinctness when I'm not: this (if true) establishes K¬K.

[5] See Williamson (2000, chapter 1). Williamson draws conclusions about the metaphysics of knowing mental states by means of these entailments; I won't go this far.

These claims together give a *decision procedure* for knowledge—as well as for iterations of that knowledge: Descartes is explicit that he thinks this is a *rule*, one among his other "rules for the direction of the mind."[6]

A distinction between tacit and explicit knowings is needed to make sense of there being a *rule* we can disobey, and that it makes sense for Descartes to urge us *to* obey; and this anyway is a distinction that makes good sense here. KK and K¬K are understood to *tacitly* hold: I always know that I know *p* because I *can* always explicitly bring the thought that I know that I know *p* to mind; it needn't *automatically* accompany the thought that *p*. It doesn't refute these theses, therefore, to notice that we don't (generally) explicitly think the iterated knowing proposition, although that's true and relevant; what does refute them is that we often *can't*—either because we're congenitally incapable or because circumstances make it impossible.

If this is the right interpretation of Descartes's approach, there seems a phenomenological incoherence at its core. It requires of any knowing agent an ability to bring to mind *any* instance of iterated knowledge, for example, the seventeenth iteration of knowing that one knows that one knows that . . . that one knows that *p*. Consider the first three stages of an iterated seeing clearly and distinctly, starting with a ground-floor base thought: "I think, I am"; I see this [I think, I exist] clearly and distinctly; I see that [I see this [I think, I exist] clearly and distinctly] clearly and distinctly . . .[7] It seems any such thought, at any such stage, to be successfully thought must be thought through *thoroughly*: all the previous thoughts must occur in one's thought *explicitly*. But we can't do this *at all* after a small number of iterations, possibly at most three—so it seems. We can *allude* to the earlier thoughts—but this isn't to bring the iterated know-thought containing those earlier thoughts to mind. To deny that iterated know-thoughts need to be explicit involves making these many different thoughts similar in the sense that appreciating the clarity and distinctness of a thought becomes ineffably and automatically available to one's thinking (rather than as a distinct thought with a distinct subject matter—which is how it appears). But this undercuts the suggestion that Descartes's rules for the direction of the mind are *rules*.

The Cartesian perspective is one extreme foil to the correct moderate characterization of sophisticated knowing minds: they possess limited amounts of knowledge and iterated knowledge. Call these *modest minds*. Claim: Humans, or most humans, have only modest amounts of iterated knowledge. Call minds without iterated knowledge *ground-floor minds. Cartesian minds*, in contrast, have knowledge and sources of that knowledge entirely accessible to them.

[6] Perhaps, however, this isn't *Descartes*. See note 28 of chapter 11.

[7] The "this" and "that" in these formulations are directed to the immediately following bracketed thought.

But a Cartesian mind isn't a reasonable model (even as a "regulative ideal") for *any* epistemic agent. That is, even if you attempt to follow Descartes's epistemic advice—even if you faithfully follow his rules for the direction of the mind and deliberately circumscribe your beliefs to fall only within what you perceive "clearly and distinctly"—you still won't be a Cartesian mind; there will be iterated cognitions, infinitely many, outside your ken. The incoherence argument given here is one route to this conclusion. Another route is to concretely look at specific cases of genuine knowledge—such as our grasp of our own reasoning (which I do starting in section 6.4) and show explicitly the non-necessity of iterated knowledge.

6.3 A *Very Minimal* Ground-Floor Epistemic Agent Who Cognizes and Knows Without Iterated Knowledge or Cognitions

Ground-floor minds introduce possibilities actually exhibited by certain animal minds, by most artifacts that have knowledge—so far, anyway—and perhaps newborn humans as well. These have knowledge without iterated cognition—in particular, they have knowledge without knowing it. What's that *like*? These minds aren't best described as having "nonconceptual" knowledge; to attribute concepts of some sort or another to a mind is a lightweight affair—although *which* concepts should be so attributed as had is delicate. In any case, the possession of concepts by a mind isn't relevant to whether it has iterative cognitions or not, although a mind doesn't *grasp* any of its own concepts if it doesn't have some accompanying iterative cognitions.[8] In describing a particularly limited ground-floor mind, I'll also be illustrating the important theme of chapter 1—that the amount of knowledge had by an epistemic agent can be minimal (and fragmented), and this is allowed by the semantic/usage independence of various epistemic notions: "conscious of," "conscious that," "see(s)," "aware," "aware of," "know(s)," and so on.

One obstacle to recognizing the possibility of minimal ground-floor minds is that it's automatic to attribute to those minds things *we* know about them but that it's illegitimate to claim *they* know. Part of the solution is to recognize, in line with the point of the last paragraph, that certain characteristics we take to be linked, such as being conscious and having knowledge, or having memories and being aware of time, needn't be linked: an agent can have certain of

[8] I'm speculating here. I've argued already (at the end of section 5.4) that no *particular* iterated cognitions need be involved; that's not to say that some iterated cognitions (although no specific ones) aren't required.

these characteristics but not others. Related to this is that when describing the concepts that minimal ground-floor minds have, we mustn't carelessly employ *our* ways of conceptually grasping the situation those minds are in—we need instead to craft concepts that fit how those minds think. The extended example I now give illustrates these lessons.

Let B.B. be a ground-floor mind. We can—from a third-person perspective—describe B.B.'s knowledge explicitly by a list—*B.B. knows p, B.B. knows q*—where the variables *p, q*, etc., range over propositions, and regardless of whether B.B. has the concepts (or doesn't) exemplified in those propositions. A full description of B.B.'s range of cognitive states, I'll illustrate, includes the concepts we take B.B. to have; it's the particulars of the ground-floor mind, its behavior, and the world that mind lives in that determine the legitimacy of attributing certain concepts as had to that mind.

Despite B.B. being a "toy" example, attributions of knowledge, perception, etc., to B.B. are genuine; furthermore, issues that arise in complicated cases of knowledge and concept attributions—to animals on the basis of sophisticated experiments (or observations of them in the wild), for example—arise with B.B. too. B.B., however, is perhaps the most basic epistemic agent possible. Although B.B. has memories, it lacks awareness that its memories *are* memories or that they're memories of things it once saw; B.B. moves in space and in time, but it lacks a notion of movement over time, or of the passage of time, or of the space it moves through. B.B. has no grasp of memory or perception—despite having both faculties. Although it's a puzzle to say when an animal has a notion of itself or of its own agency, we can be sure that B.B. has neither idea. Despite all this (or rather, despite being without all this), knowledge attributions to B.B. are coherent and arise naturally (and, I'll add, rather indispensably).

Imagine that B.B. is a colored shape in a two-dimensional space of squares where other colored shapes are as well—and where only one shape can occupy a square at a time. B.B. perceives colored shapes at various distances from itself and B.B. remembers (some of) what it has seen. So we can say (as a first pass): *B.B. perceives a blue square directly in front, B.B. perceives a green triangle left front*, or *B.B. remembers that a blue square is directly behind a red circle that's left front*, etc.[9] Suppose that certain rules govern B.B.'s behavior on the basis of what it sees and remembers, for example: *Approach the blue square that's directly in front. Orient left, Orient right, Move*, etc. In other words (but somewhat inaccurately—I'll fix this later), B.B. is aware of colored shapes and is aware

[9] We can, instead, and synonymously, describe B.B. as "aware" of the blue square in front of it, or as "seeing a blue square."

of orientations toward and away from those shapes, as well as changes in the locations of those shapes.[10]

The background scenario is a typical (1980s) arcade game, designer Toru Iwatani's PAC-MAN, for example. "Cells" eat their targets by moving into their locations; they approach eatable targets when they see them, and retreat from cells that will eat them—when they see those or remember where they are. Such creatures aren't aware of "eating"; their perceptions and memories encompass no more than what I've described—I'll give additional details momentarily. So, although B.B. eats blue squares and is eaten by red circles, B.B. doesn't know *this*. What B.B. *does* know, one might think, is that when it sees blue squares, it approaches them; when it sees red circles, it avoids them; when it sees green triangles (which are obstacles), it moves around them.[11] As the rules are, B.B. can't see that a red circle is behind a blue square directly in front of it, but it *can* remember this. It will, for example, orient (and move) away from a blue square that it sees if it remembers a red circle is behind that square; it approaches the square otherwise.

Before describing B.B.'s knowledge in more detail (and more accurately), here's a fuller characterization of the framework of B.B.'s memory and perception. The memory/perception/action space for B.B. is an infinite grid of "places"; its memories are limited to the objects located in any of a finite number of places around it (say, of no more than a radius of ten places in any direction). Its perception is more restricted: It sees to a depth of three places directly in front, two places deep from the squares to the immediate left and right of the place in front of it, and only one place deep to the left and right places of those places. (So, B.B. lacks peripheral vision, but has pretty wide visual scope otherwise.)

B.B. moves (and thinks) in segmental stages (like a Turing machine head) and updates what it sees and remembers at each stage after it moves; it also updates what it sees after a stage in which it doesn't move. Perception updating is straightforward: B.B. replaces all its perceptions at an immediately previous stage with what it sees now. Beyond its perceptual range (but within its memory range), B.B. retains the location of the objects it has seen to radius ten in all directions but modifies those positions according to its pure memory-state rules. How B.B.'s memories are updated: the locations for green objects are shifted to accommodate B.B.'s own movements (except when those locations fall outside a radius of

[10] Perhaps B.B. has no pure orientation rules, although B.B. has a pure move rule; orientation rules, instead, are always relative to seen or remembered objects, e.g., *Orient left from a front perceived object; Orient front from a right remembered object*; and so on. There is, of course, more than one possible set of rules. (If the rules are set up as I've just described them, then B.B. will continue to move straight ahead if there are no objects that it sees or remembers.)

[11] I'll soon deny B.B. knows even this much—at least as I've put it. Describing accurately what B.B. does and doesn't know, purely with concepts that B.B. has, is difficult. It's similarly hard to state, only in terms of concepts that B.B. has, what B.B.'s thinking looks like.

ten from B.B.—then they're deleted from B.B.'s memory). Blue or red objects are different. As long as one of those is within B.B.'s perceptual range, their locations are updated according to the perception rules. Once blue or red objects move (or B.B. moves) so that B.B. can't see them, either because they're behind objects that block B.B.'s vision of them or because they're now outside B.B.'s perceptual range, B.B.'s memory treats them like green objects—updating their positions only in terms of egocentric location changes from B.B.'s own movements. Once their locations fall outside B.B.'s memory range, they're deleted from B.B.'s memory.

B.B. can exhibit—by means of what it sees and remembers, and using the rules governing its behavior, perception, and memories—what look like (fairly sophisticated) examples of *reasoning* about its world: its reactions to the dangers it faces and the opportunities it sees can be intricate and "clever." For example, B.B. will flee the location of a blue square if it remembers that a red circle is directly behind that square. Thus, we can introduce a (large) number of orientation and movement rules that guide the behavior of the cell given what it sees (and remembers). There is a finite upper limit on these rules, just as with pure memory updating rules—if they are deterministic—because of the limitations of B.B.'s senses and memory.

Nevertheless, if there are enough rules of this sort, B.B.'s behavior will simulate flexible responses to complex situations.[12] The rules governing B.B.'s behavior, in particular, *exhibit differences* between remembering and perceiving—they may exhibit *generalizations* about those differences in B.B.'s reactions to what it sees versus what it remembers. For example, B.B. always orients away from a red circle that it perceives; it doesn't orient away from a red circle it remembers except coincidentally when other conditions prompt such an orientation; it just endeavors to keep the distance between it and that circle the same.

I've described B.B., its world, and the rules governing its memories and perceptions enough to fruitfully answer questions about what B.B. *knows*. A preliminary question first: Is it legitimate to talk about what B.B. knows or is aware of? After all, B.B. isn't just not conscious, B.B. isn't even a real artifact—B.B. is a virtual "being." So isn't it metaphor (or pretense) to describe B.B. as knowing that, or being aware that, a red cell is in front of it? No, it's not.

Recall the discussion of metaphor in part 2 of the introduction. It's difficult to show that a usage of "know(s)," or of any word, for that matter, is metaphorical. I take it as established (section 1.5) that knowledge doesn't require consciousness; it doesn't even require a *capacity* for consciousness. I'll agree (for the sake

[12] I call what B.B. does (no matter how many rules are introduced, and how detailed they are) "simulating flexible responses"; I suspect something like this can be scaled up to capture what *we* call "flexible responses"—this is especially the case if new rules can be introduced over time into B.B.'s repertoire—because of, say, cognitive "maturing." I won't pursue further details.

of argument) that it's anthropomorphic to attribute desires to B.B. on the basis of B.B.'s behavior (that is, I'll agree it's anthropomorphic to say that B.B. doesn't want to get eaten, or that B.B. is scared of red circles, or that B.B. is hungry).[13]

More significant, however, is the absence of semantic or use conditions on epistemic words so that perception and/or knowledge *requires* an agent to be capable of desire or other emotions.[14] It can even be argued (but I won't pursue this now) that legitimately applying "know(s)" to entities like B.B. drives subsequent (and illegitimate) anthropomorphizing: attributing emotions to B.B. We often assume—fail to imagine the opposite, really—that creatures who know things also desire things because the creatures we almost always attribute knowledge to have desires. The same points hold of "aware." Although there are uses of "aware" that are, concomitantly, applied to conscious creatures, there are also legitimate applications of "aware" to creatures that either aren't conscious of what, nevertheless, they're described as aware of, or to creatures who aren't capable (as far as we know) of consciousness at all. For example (section 1.3), one naturally, and non-metaphorically, can describe a drone as suddenly becoming aware of an enemy combatant crouching low against a wall.

What also supports the legitimacy of attributing knowing states to B.B. is how hard it is to deny that B.B. *perceives* and *remembers* objects. This is especially so in light of further programming details of B.B.'s perception and memory. For exactly the same reasons (section 1.3), it's impossible to deny that a drone "really" sees you when it's (for example) shooting right at you or following you. In part, this is because the mechanisms of how a drone sees don't obviously make "seeing" attributions to drones metaphorical—nor does the mechanisms of its memory do this.[15] Similarly, it's hard to deny, given B.B. sees or remembers that a red circle is located at such-and-such a place, that this is something B.B. *knows*.

Let's turn to the details of what we can say B.B. knows and doesn't know—equivalently, what B.B. is and isn't aware of. I'll first talk about the rules that govern B.B.'s behavior and memory on the basis of what it sees and remembers; I'll focus, in particular, on the predicates and relations in those rules. I'll then turn to the background context these rules operate within—e.g., the properties of the perception/memory/action space the rules presuppose. This must be

[13] Although it's certainly metaphor to talk of B.B. "eating," I'm not sure this is true of B.B.'s "desires"; alas, I can't pursue this any further in this book. (One thing at a time.)

[14] One could argue that B.B. doesn't exist *at all*, and that's why it can't be said that B.B. has knowledge. This *doesn't* falsify knowledge attributions to B.B.—at least, not because of the semantics of "know(s)" or how we use it. There is no requirement: An agent said to know is *real*. We can utter *truths* about what fictional beings know or don't know. See Azzouni (2017b) on this.

[15] As we learn more about the neurological mechanisms of our own senses and memory, nothing seems to be emerging from the details of these discoveries that *requires* consciousness. (Because, or so it seems: How could there be such details? How would they arise?) This is why the problem of consciousness continues to be the hardest problem in philosophy of mind—nothing we can ever discover about neurophysiology, so it seems, will ever bear on the question.

examined to determine what we may legitimately describe B.B. as aware of or knowing.

The first point is that these rules can be formulated purely in terms of the property descriptions of the perceived or remembered objects ("blue square," "green triangle"), and their spatial egocentric content locations (e.g., "immediate front," "left immediate front one back," etc.). These labels, however, contain more spatial information than what's needed to frame rules in terms of concepts B.B. has. Not only can, e.g., adjacency facts, distance metrics, and other spatial properties be left out, but relational facts involving B.B.'s own position can be left out too. This is because the locations B.B. remembers or perceives are both egocentric and finite. Only brute labels, "a," "b," "c," etc., are needed to play spatial roles in the rules governing B.B.'s perceptions, memories, and movements/orientations; the rules so formulated exhaustively and explicitly describe everything pertinent to B.B.'s memory, perception, and movements/orientations.

In addition, whether B.B. remembers *or* perceives objects needn't be coded into the rules. The differences between memory and perception, rather, are embodied in *how* these faculties of B.B.'s operate—in particular, in *how* B.B.'s knowledge of locations shifts, given how B.B. moves, as well as the differences in B.B.'s responses to what it perceives as opposed to what it remembers. These differences are concomitantly due to the nearness of the spatial locations of objects to B.B., rather than anything intrinsic to B.B.'s remembering (or perceiving) these things.

Describing B.B. as remembering that a *green triangle* is at such-and-such a *distance from itself* misleads if this is interpreted as indicating concepts, *green, triangle, distance, itself,* that *B.B.* has. B.B. isn't remembering (or perceiving) a green triangle being in a particular spatial relation to itself. B.B. isn't even remembering, instead, something like "green triangle left front one back"—that too misleads if as a result we misattribute to B.B. the possession of the concepts "in front of B.B.," etc. B.B. lacks *those* concepts. If we only use formulations with concepts B.B. has, we should label all the color-shape qualities with subscripts, e.g., "G_1," "G_2," R_1," "B_{33}, . . ., to distinguish same-colored shapes at different locations.

The meanings of these labels *for B.B.* (if any) are encapsulated in both the movement and orientation rules utilizing these labels as well as in the updating mechanisms for perception and memory governing each stage of B.B.'s cognizing. The same holds of the color and shape terminology I've framed the example in terms of. Only needed are rules that determine B.B.'s movements on the basis of what it sees or remembers by distinguishing the different items B.B. sees or remembers—thus the subscripts. What's crucial to realize is that only the rules governing B.B.'s reactions supply content to "how" B.B. sees or remembers what it sees or remembers.

Now consider the orientation and movement rules. I've formulated these so that neither "B.B." nor any term coreferring with "B.B.," e.g., "I," appears as a term *in* them: the rules are pure commands. One issue is how B.B. executes these rules. Here are two possibilities. (1) B.B. is a deterministic Turing machine—each action of B.B. follows mechanically from what B.B. perceives and remembers.[16] (2) B.B. has more than one possible response to a configuration of objects it sees and remembers. In both cases, we can describe B.B. as "making choices."[17]

There's an important distinction between how B.B.'s perceptions change because of *B.B.'s* movements and how they change because of the movements of the objects near B.B. These differences are exhibited by explicit updating rules on what B.B. remembers that partially determine B.B.'s execution of movement and orientation rules, but no other updating rules—except insofar as what B.B. perceives (at a stage) supersedes and replaces what B.B. saw earlier.

But is B.B. *aware of* these differences in the rules governing its memory and perception? No more than *we're* aware of aspects of the rules governing the grammaticality of our native languages. We know, of course, *those languages*; we're also (pretty naturally) described as knowing the rules of those languages; but we're not explicitly *aware of* these rules. This is crudely captured by saying that we know the grammatical rules of our language "tacitly." Similarly, B.B. "tacitly" knows the rules governing its memory and perception, but that doesn't require it to have the concept of a memory, a perception, or a *rule*. So too, a native speaker can know the rules of her language without having (or grasping) the notion of a *rule*. These ways of speaking about knowledge are licensed by our epistemic words. B.B.'s cognitions are governed by the rules I describe, but B.B. neither knows nor iteratively knows anything about this.[18]

B.B. exhibits generalizations when responding to what it remembers and perceives. These can be proved to follow from the rules B.B. obeys, but they aren't represented *in* those rules. On one view, it's mistaken, on the basis of B.B.'s behavior, to assume that because B.B. exhibits differences in behavior between remembering the location of an object and seeing it, B.B. has the notions of

[16] Because of B.B.'s limited senses and memory, an explicit finite set of rules suffices to determine what B.B. does, given any configuration of objects within B.B.'s ken. B.B.'s behavior is finite-state-machine computable.

[17] There is much to argue with here; but I can't do it now. Knowledge, memory, and perception attributions don't require "free will"—that's perhaps easy to establish (the burden of proof is on the opponent, if only because, for any purported semantic/conceptual connection between words, it's more likely it doesn't exist than that it does). It takes more to establish that the autonomy of movement, or, anyway, the experience of autonomy, doesn't require genuine "free will"—there is a gigantic literature on this that I can't engage with now.

[18] I can't escape the feeling, however, that it's inaccurate to say we "know" the rules of our languages. If they have rules, we know their *outputs*: we know which utterances (up to certain lengths and subject to other restrictions too) are grammatical and which aren't. That's different from saying we know the rules themselves. The same is true of B.B.

percept and *memory*, and that B.B. can tell these apart (because it acts differently in each case). On the other view, B.B. does have these notions. Here, "having the concept *percept*" and "having the concept *memory*" look determined (purely) by B.B.'s behavior. Which is right? The answer may involve genuinely different notions of "having concepts."[19] I'll discuss this a bit more, later in this section, and try to provide a principled characterization of "having concepts."

A much stronger case can be made that B.B. doesn't understand or know anything about the past, time's passing, memory, or itself. This is because B.B.'s knowledge is fully captured by phrases like "Object o is at location l"; this knowledge changes over time (in stages) according to what B.B. perceives, what B.B. remembers, and how B.B. orients and moves; but B.B. has no cognizance of *this*. (B.B. can't recollect its previous states of knowledge; it doesn't know it *had* previous states of knowledge—no more than it knows it has a current one.) B.B.'s cognitions are always in the present tense—not that it knows *that* either. So B.B. doesn't know anything about how its perceptive faculties work; it doesn't know about any of the properties of the spatial grid; it *sees* none of this, nor has B.B. any awareness of its own place in the grid, and the importance of that to what it does or thinks. The rules take account of B.B.'s position, of course, but that's different from *B.B.* knowing anything about this.

Pertinent is that although the rules are commands *to B.B.*, this needn't be stated *in* the rules. Being a command doesn't, all alone, make executing that command iterative cognition. What seems required for *that* is an essential term *in* the rule that refers to the agent. That is, if a term referring to B.B. did appear essentially in the formulation of a command rule, we would say that B.B. had the concept of *its own self*; that wouldn't be enough to claim that B.B. *grasped* the notion of its own self. B.B., in such a case, would, however, have knowledge about itself (although not necessarily knowledge about its own knowledge—having knowledge about its knowledge would call for further rules within which terms about B.B.'s own cognitions appear).

This "occurrence in the rules" condition, independently of specific considerations about B.B., looks sensible as a necessary condition for having a concept. We shouldn't want to say that movements—even sophisticated movements that are sensitive to the situation around the moving entity—are, because of that alone, iterative-cognitively structured. Consider two entities, A and B, with different move rules because one is bigger than the other. The rules "take account" of this difference insofar as the rules governing B's movements aren't as optimal

[19] The case of Sultan, discussed in section 5.4, intimates yet a third notion of "having a concept": to show possession, the agent needs the ability to employ the concepts—in reasoning—apart from contexts of their immediate applications. But that additional requirement makes no sense for concepts characterizing *memory* or *percept*.

for A as the rules that actually govern A's movements are. But those facts aren't—by themselves—enough for these rules to reveal cognition of size differences. One might argue that there has to be evidence that the entity, when moving, uses a representation of *aspects of itself* (e.g., its size) to do so. This requirement is hard to characterize further because sheer movement rules that fit an entity well can be detailed and sophisticated—and yet still not involve iterative knowledge or the grasping of any of that entity's concepts.[20]

There are theoretical considerations in play here—I'll sketch them. First, B.B.'s possible and actual behavior underdetermines B.B.'s program. Different programs—using different concepts—can yield identical (actual and potential) behaviors; and there may even be no "rules" at all.[21] The result seems to be choices in criteria for "having concepts" that the notion of "having concepts" doesn't dictate decisions for. One way to go is to demand program instantiation in the cognition mechanism—in some sense (see note 22)—as a necessary and sufficient condition. Two entities with different programs thus have different concepts (instantiated in their programs) even if their actual—and possible—behavior is identical. On this view, certain finite-state machines don't "have" the concept of addition even though they add perfectly (note 21). We can soften the criteria for "having concepts" by allowing "tacit concepts" that are definable (in some sense) from the concepts actually instantiated in a program. Depending on the conditions on definability, some finite-state machines that can do certain tasks are described as having the relevant concepts.[22] Another set of approaches

[20] If we show that an animal computes ahead of time the effect of some of its own properties (e.g., its body weight and size) on what it's moving through (e.g., branches), that may show that it *has* a representation of its own body (in these respects). but this won't show that it *grasps* this representation. See Byrne (2016, 93–94) for discussion of this kind of case, with respect to great apes and monkeys. I discuss grasping concepts starting in section 6.4.

[21] A finite-state machine (or a simple finite McCulloch-Pitts net) that adds needn't represent in the mechanisms of its operation the concept of "plus," or corresponding rules for addition. See, for example, the finite-state diagram of a binary adding machine (Minsky (1967, 23, figure 2.3-5)) or the diagram of a McCulloch-Pitts net that adds (Minsky (1967, 45, figure 3.2-15)); in both examples, a representation of "carrying" perhaps occurs—see note 22—but that's pretty much it. Nevertheless, some will think it's reasonable to claim such a machine "has" a representation of addition, although it needn't have all the notions we traditionally take an agent having the concept of "plus" to *also* (necessarily) have, like the compositionally connected notions of number, successor, etc. ("Carrying" isn't essential to the notion of addition!) Perhaps we should only say such machines *exhibit*—perfectly—addition behavior without having the representation of addition. I explore this shortly.

[22] If a finite-state machine has a subroutine that's always executed when the machine adds, we can say, pretty naturally, that it has the concept of addition—one represented by that subroutine. This isn't true of a minimal finite-state machine that only adds. The idea is that if the *entire* finite-state machine table is always involved in the same way in executing a task, we don't describe it as having a representation of that task; we do this only if a distinguishable subroutine executes the task. Similarly, if we consider a device that multiplies, we may be able to distinguish subroutines it always engages in to carry out certain tasks (e.g., remembering summands). Those, and only those, will correspond to concepts it "has." This is to treat representations as episodically instantiated. Suppose a complex finite-state machine executes two tasks, utilizing the same subroutines—but in a different order; each time it's "accessing" a different representation. I suppose, then, that even a minimal finite-state

to agents having concepts uses behavioral criteria. The least demanding of these attributes a concept to an agent whenever that agent can distinguish what falls under that concept from what doesn't. This is weak as it allows, for example, sheer capacities to distinguish items as sufficient (recall note 37 of chapter 5). Stronger behavioral criteria require the agent to exhibit *certain kinds* of behavior with the purported concept—for example, the kind of reasoning behavior Sultan manifested. There seems no way to privilege one or another criterion for "concepts" being had—on the basis of the meaning of "having concepts"; a family of concept notions may result (one that goes beyond my simple distinction between having and grasping concepts) as well as a concomitant recognition that possessing these different sets of concepts amounts to distinctive differences in cognitive capacities.

Here's what I suggest, though. Generalize the "subroutine" characterization to fit whatever cognitive mechanisms are at work in an agent (finite-state machine, Turing machine, nervous tissue), and characterize an episodic notion of representation via those routines as described in note 22, including the degenerate case where the entire mechanism exhibits one concept. Interpret behavioral criteria (using pertinent background theoretical assumptions) as *symptoms* of the presence of concepts had. Thus, Sultan's additional representational powers (being able to think about items without being in their presence) don't necessarily show he has representations that pigeons, say, lack. Rather, it's that he can manipulate the representations he has in ways pigeons can't.

This is weak—even apart from the degenerate case. As long as an agent cognitively does *different things* to make distinctions, that agent has the relevant concepts because of the different cognitive subroutines she uses. This is true even if the entire cognitive apparatus is used each time, provided the episodic uses of that apparatus differ. Pigeons that distinguish different groups of visual objects must be using different cognitive routines to do this.

This *isn't* a book on concepts (one book at a time)—so I'm stopping the analysis now and returning to characterizing what B.B. knows in terms of a set of minimal concepts crafted to appear in rules that fit B.B.'s behavior. Denying that B.B. has certain concepts C turns on: (i) a certain set of minimal concepts without C sufficing to characterize what B.B. knows via their explicit appearance in rules governing B.B.'s behavior, as well as (ii) those concepts not implying (e.g., by definitions) tacitly richer conceptualizations including C that can be claimed to be had by B.B.

Does B.B. have any knowledge (or concepts) of identity within time or across time? We might say, because of the subscripts for different green triangles at

machine that uses its entire routine the same way to execute a task can be described as having the representation of that task. (This sounds weird—but is that an *objection*?)

different locations, that B.B. distinguishes objects-at-a-time from one another. (I'll accept this.) We might claim, further, that these rules embody a distinction between a new entity appearing in B.B.'s perceptual field as opposed to a memory-updating of the movements of an object from one location to another. No; the rules, as described, needn't identify objects across moments. Rules adequately characterizing B.B.'s behavior need only have variables sufficient to distinguish objects *at a time*. An arbitrary renumbering of the subscripted names of the entities at each new stage won't negatively affect B.B.'s behavior. Since the rules governing B.B.'s behavior, perception, and memory do need to distinguish objects at a time in order for B.B. to function successfully, we can, correspondingly, say that B.B. knows that a specific green object is different from another green object. But this isn't to say, of a green object that B.B. remembers at one location, that B.B. *knows* that it's the same object that B.B. remembers (or sees) at a later location.

"Knowing the same object remembered at a later location" can be iteratively interpreted, or not—I reject its application to B.B. *either* way. The ground-floor-cognition interpretation is that the item b that B.B. remembers at the location l_1 is known by B.B. to be the item c that B.B. knows or remembers at location l_2. This takes B.B. to identify b and c in two tensed judgments about the locations of b and c. The second iterated-cognitive interpretation includes *in B.B.'s judgments* that B.B. remembers the location of b and remembers or perceives the location of c. (So, this distinction is, formally, "scoped"—what falls within the B.B.'s judgment *itself* as opposed to what we say about that judgment.)

There is a general lesson to draw from B.B.'s case that I haven't mentioned yet (and that will matter later—especially in section 6.5). This is that relations between a cognitive agent and the target of that agent's cognition needn't be cognized by that agent *as relations* to that agent. Being vigilant about this helps avoid inadvertent characterizations of cognitions of agents as iterated cognitions. B.B. is aware, we might (rashly) say, that a particular green triangle is three spatial units away from B.B. itself; indeed, since B.B. cognizes all spatial relations egocentrically—in relation to itself—we might think that B.B. must be aware of its own egocentric spatial relations to objects and therefore must have an awareness of itself. No, because we can replace explicit characterizations of spatial relations in the rules governing B.B.'s perceptions, memories, orientations, and movements, with the brute characterizations "a," "b," . . . It's concomitantly clear that B.B. needn't be thinking (in any sense at all) of itself when it changes its "mental states" and/or its movements/orientations in terms of these rules.

The point, as I've just mentioned, is a general one. To experience something as sweet is to have an intrinsically relational experience of that something.[23] What

[23] Perhaps *every* experience is relational in the sense I mean here; but the importance of this point, if it's important, isn't what I'm in pursuit of now.

makes, in fact, that experience "subjective" is that the relations between different agents and the same aspect of the cognized object (the taste of a fruit) can be different. But this intrinsic relation-ness of the agent's experience mustn't be included as part of the experience itself (I'm again making a "scope" point: the *experience* is relational, but the content *of* the experience isn't.) The agent experiences the taste of anything as a property *of the object*; the agent doesn't experience that taste *as a relation* between the fruit and the agent's own taste buds. Experiencing sweetness doesn't all by itself, therefore, require iterated cognition. To recognize that the sweetness of a fruit is "subjective," of course—that one's own sensation of its flavor needn't be shared by others (because, say, one's taste buds are different)—*does* require an iterated cognition.

What's it *like* to be B.B.? Or: What would it be like for B.B. if B.B. were conscious? (What are things like from the perspective of a conscious B.B.?) This is a good question if only because it deflects the objection some may have that describing B.B. as *thinking* is a mistake because thinking *requires* consciousness.[24] For us humans, introspection seems to offer a lot of iterated cognitions and the grasping of one's own concepts; we seem (most of the time) able to distinguish between our own memories and our concurrent perceptions, for example. Imagine that we *can't*; instead, spontaneous judgments arise: *p*—without *p* being accompanied with what might be called "a cognitive pedigree." Although *many* of *our* thoughts usually come *stamped*, as it were—that's a memory, this is an inference, that's a percept—B.B.'s thoughts don't. B.B. has *naked* thoughts; they're accompanied by other thoughts, but just, as it were, in a list with no distinctions among them. *That's* what it's like to be B.B.[25]

One last point. As long as an agent can make distinctions, there are reasons to think the agent has concepts to do this with. There is, therefore, no minimal case where we need to attribute knowledge to an agent but deny the agent possession of concepts; there is no need to attribute "nonconceptual content," of any sort, to agents.[26]

[24] We can *meet* the objection, however. As chapter 1 showed, we can (and do) describe drones or driverless cars as thinking *p*, especially when *p* is wrong—e.g., the car thinks that the something ahead is a pothole it must swerve to avoid, although it's only a shadow. We can do this without believing—even for one second—that these things *are* conscious.

[25] B.B.'s state of mind (when B.B. is imagined as conscious) may be the endgame state of mind for all of us after the onset of certain dementias. (I'll let you know . . .) Apart from this speculation, see, e.g., Bentall (1990), where hallucinations are hypothesized as due to impaired "reality monitoring," the ability to discriminate between real and imagined events. (An additional cognitive mechanism is posited as enabling discriminations between real and imagined events—nothing intrinsic to the content of experience does this, according to this theory. Specifically, auditory hallucinations are one's own inner voice—but not stamped *as* one's inner voice.)

[26] Certain philosophers claim nonconceptual content is valuable in psychology and philosophy of mind (see, e.g., the essays in Gunther (2003)). The natural distinction between having and grasping concepts provides everything needed. One reason for this is that "having concepts" (as B.B. illustrates) is flexible and doesn't have strong constraints. Concepts of an agent that enable

I turn now to empirical studies of ground-floor and iterated cognitions—human and nonhuman. The B.B. case warns us against over-interpreting the data. In particular, B.B. foils the idea that a creature that reasons or explores its environment perceptually in certain sophisticated ways can be assumed—because of *that*—to be engaging in one or another form of iterated cognition or as exhibiting the grasp of its own concepts.[27]

6.4 The Non-transparency of Knowing States

Chapter 5 was about the language of iterated knowledge and how we insensibly run it together with ground-floor knowledge. This theme was revisited in section 6.3, in illustrating attributions to B.B. of knowledge and not iterated knowledge. But there's something else it's important to be explicit about. Recall from section 5.6 how justifications take many forms—ground-floor cognitions or iterated cognitions. That different kinds of justifications can be given for the same proposition corresponds to the fact that a human agent can engage in a particular epistemic behavior (searching for food in a refrigerator) compatibly with *any* of a number of *different* psychological processes, where exactly which processes an agent goes through are constitutively related to the ways in which (if at all) an agent iteratively cognizes.

According to the Cartesian picture, to cognize my knowing relation to a proposition, I needn't consider anything outside my own mental states.[28] That's why,

distinctions in perception (and thus account for how rich the perceptual experience of that agent is), for example, needn't be ones the agent utilizes in other ways—e.g., puts into words. Humans make distinctions among colors, for example, that they can't articulate; but articulation isn't a requirement for having concepts, as I understand them. Neither must concepts be "compositional." See the essays in Gunther (2003) for contrasting viewpoints.

[27] Figdor (2018) may seem to be arguing for a parallel thesis: Literal uses of psychological concepts are (now) occurring in the sciences—specifically the application of such concepts to plants and bacteria. I think the differences (in method) and in our views are more important than any apparent resemblances. Two remarks about this: First, as Figdor's study of the cases makes clear (chapters 2 and 3), these aren't uses that are already in place: they're recognized by scientific practitioners as extensions of the previous usage of psychological/intentional terms, and the scientific practitioners are currently involved in debates over whether these usages are literal or not. This—as I hope my book makes clear—isn't a debate that's fruitful if evaluated about *all* the psychological concepts being applied at once (along the model, for example, of an "intentional stance"). Each concept—word or phrase—must be evaluated *separately*—if only because the meaning properties of these words are so different. Second, in many cases, the debate over whether these usage extensions are literal or not is likely to be moot: as in law, whether an extension of previous usage is in accord with the word's previous meaning, and so whether the word so extended is being used literally or not, may simply be indeterminate.

[28] It really does help to pause a moment and savor how *bizarre* this view is: how clever and innovative Descartes was in convincing generations of philosophers (and himself) of this otherwise profoundly implausible view.

on that view, iterated knowledge is always available to a knowing agent. This (I suggest) isn't our ordinary understanding of knowing relations (when we think about them at all, I mean). For an agent to have a knowing relationship to a lizard that's just crawled in front of him (that "there's a lizard in front of me"), one thing we all recognize that's needed (not *everything* that's needed) is that he be in one or another class of sensory states vis-à-vis that lizard. It won't do for that agent to hallucinate the presence of a lizard in front of him; it won't do even if the hallucination he's having matches perfectly the scene before him that he would have experienced if he hadn't been hallucinating. In these sorts of cases (but not necessarily always), the knowing relation is, in part, *externally constituted*: to have knowledge, the agent has to be in a sensory relationship with the lizard the proposition he consequently knows is about: he has to be (to put it simply) *looking at* the lizard.

Descartes replaces the ordinary route to knowledge via senses with a pure *inferential* one. He exploits our intuitive recognition that there's more than one kind of justification route to propositions. Most straightforward justifications for sensory knowledge claims directly rely on sensory routes; the Cartesian replacement involves inferences from a proof of God.[29] More generally, Cartesians restrict suitable justifications for propositions *only* to inferences. As I show in section 6.5, the supplementary Cartesian thought that the capacity for inference intrinsically involves iterated knowledge—that all knowledge based on inference obeys KK—is false.

This aside, by broadening acceptable knowing relations, and their support, beyond Cartesian strictures, it becomes virtually certain that knowing that *p* and knowing that one knows that *p* require different resources—different capacities. These differences arise from the different ways agents come to know the propositions in question. The contents of the propositions can (sometimes) be a guide here: To know about *p* requires knowledge pertinent to whatever it is that *p* is about. To know about my knowing-that-*p*, therefore, requires *additional* knowledge about me or about the particulars of my cognitive relationship to what *p* is about. This truism indicates that, at least prima facie, KK *can't* be right. Instances of it can only hold when I do have knowledge about myself or my cognitive relationship to *p* and/or to what *p* is about (in addition to whatever knowledge I have that's required to know that *p*).

Can we be more specific (in the form of illuminating generalizations) about what *is* called for to have iterated knowledge—to know that one knows *p*? No.

[29] There isn't *one* possible justification route to knowledge (of a lizard) that relies on the senses, of course. Nor is there just one possible justification route to knowledge (of a lizard) via deduction. *Any* of these justifications, purely deductive, partially deductive and partially sensory, or purely sensory, may be ground-floor or iteratively cognitive.

For reasons related to the fact that "know(s)" evades definition, I can't give a full characterization of iterated knowledge, apart from the purely formal "knows that one knows," let alone any "necessary and sufficient conditions." Case studies are all that's available, ones that explore "paradigms" of knowledge and determine how and when iterative knowledge arises (and doesn't arise): reasoning, perceiving, testimony, etc. I'll illustrate this in the next section with deduction.

But first a warning: let's revisit what I'll call "Cartesian mental states"—introspective recognitions that one is in certain mental states simultaneous with being *in* those states. Severe pain *isn't* the best example, as I illustrated in section 5.3—because what's required to know that one is in pain is simultaneous processing: one is *aware of* the mental state simultaneously with being *in* it. If pain is severe enough, second-order awareness is impossible: I can't be aware of anything *but* that pain. Mild pain—and other states, like mild discomfort—leave room (introspectively) for us to also be aware that we're in them—and if we *also* focus on knowing we're in such states, these really are states of mind that can be accompanied by the knowledge that we're so knowledgeable about the state we're in.[30] What seems involved in these cases is that agents not only grasp the propositional targets *p* of their knowing relations—that they're in pain (or happy, etc.)—but that they also bear knowing relations to a *something* that enables them to know that *p*. What this something comes to in various cases depends, of course, on specifics.

The Cartesian model (and Cartesian examples of knowledge) can distort an evaluation of what's needed for an agent to know that she's in a knowing relation to a proposition. In general, complete visibility to her of her knowing relations is too much to demand—*cues* are often sufficient. That is, we don't need to know *everything* that constitutes a knowing relationship—everything that's involved in the knowing relationship—to know we're in it. I'll illustrate this in the next section with knowledge by deduction. But notice, first, that it's an illusion that when we introspect (successfully) our being in one or another mental state (desirous of something, say, or angry, or . . .), the introspected knowing *relationship* between ourselves and the mental state we're knowledgeable about is itself completely (or even obscurely) transparent to us. We don't grasp (by introspection, or at all) the psychological-neurophysiological mechanisms that enable introspective access to our psychological states (when we do). That we don't facilitates the common misimpression that we can't be wrong about our own psychological states. (Without a grasp of how we know what we know about our own psychological

[30] More accurately, "*part* of the state we're in"—because, of course, included in the complete "state" we're in (in this case) is our *knowing* that we're in pain. To think we're thus aware of the entire mental state we're in would be to force KK for all cases of self-knowledge. (There are so many *different* ways to mistakenly think KK is true; no wonder philosophers did it for so long.)

states, we won't have an introspective grasp of how we can go wrong about this.) Nearly everything going on in us—even nearly everything going on in us that can be described *folk-psychologically*—is invisible to us.[31]

6.5 Iterated Knowledge About Deduction

Let's take up deduction. I make, let's say, a short inference. I recognize, because certain premises are true, that a particular conclusion is too. (I infer q from p & q.) I can (or so it seems to me) be aware both that q follows from p & q *and* that I know all this: I know q follows from p & q because q *does* so follow. (I *realize*—nonredundantly, that is—that I *know q must be* true if p & q is true). Now, as I'll spell out in detail in section 7.3, an agent doesn't *have* to be able to have the simultaneous experience of drawing the conclusion q from p & q as well as being aware that in doing so she's exploiting an implication relation between these propositions in order to infer (correctly) q from p & q; nor (I confess) do I always have this experience when I infer.[32] But when this simultaneous experience *is* being had, it isn't required that the agent know of (or be aware of) all the antecedent requirements of being able to infer correctly—that there are

[31] Folk-psychological attributions—as I stressed in chapter 1—don't entail requirements of consciousness; that's why such attributions can be made to artifacts that we simultaneously deny are conscious; that's why the "Freudian" discovery of unconscious desires and attitudes wasn't perceived by the public as an oxymoron. Ram Neta protests *strongly*: "If 'invisible' to us means nothing more than 'unknown by us,' then I agree, and I don't know who would disagree. But if it means something stronger and more controversial—for instance, if it means something like: cannot be known by us even if we perfectly exercise our capacity for reflective self-knowledge—then I disagree, and I don't see how any of the considerations that precede this claim actually support it." Let me, therefore, moderate my claim and make explicit the considerations behind it. I suppose, to begin with, that "reflective self-knowledge" can only be various self-directed metacognitions (perhaps a group of them is required). Necessarily, therefore (since we are not and cannot be Cartesian minds), the mental states we're in when reflecting self-knowingly are ones not included in that reflective self-knowledge. (I assume that explicit distinctions between the various metacognitions we can entertain is part of folk psychology.) I lastly assume that no matter how much we try, that's a situation we remain in: we can bring some further self-reflective states to consciousness by consciously reflecting upon them—but this process isn't iteratively easy. So there is no such thing as "perfectly exercising our capacity for reflective self-knowledge"; I table, however, the stronger claim that (as a result) "nearly everything . . .," although I suspect (nevertheless) that it's right.

[32] I mostly *don't* have this second-order awareness (it, in any case, developed only *many* years after I refined my abilities to deduce). When, for example, I'm listening to a president's utterances, and I hear inconsistencies, I'm focused on the whole topic. I'm not aware, that is, of *exactly which* (or how many) fallacies are in his spiel—I'm not aware *in detail* of his assumptions, and the different implicational roles of those assumptions. So, without some careful and focused thinking, I may not know exactly when and where the fallacies are. I'll simply recognize: Oh, wow, *that* doesn't follow *at all*. Many people listening to such a president who recognize he's uttered fallacies are like me: they can work out which fallacies the president has uttered (if they want to spend time on it). Many, however, who are otherwise *equally aware* that the president has uttered fallacies *aren't* capable of working out the details: these abilities come apart. Frankly, any view on which they *don't* come apart is in trouble. (This is why courses in "Critical Reasoning" *do* teach valuable skills.)

requirements on her successfully inferring that she understands the language the inference is couched in, that she be mentally intact, etc.; and she needn't know what's psychologically/neurophysiologically supporting her optimal inferential mental states. Just as knowing any *p* is necessarily accompanied by massive ignorance about many other things that are nevertheless in the neighborhood of, or even intimately related to, *p*, so too, knowing that one knows that *p* is similarly necessarily accompanied by massive ignorance about many other things that are nevertheless in the neighborhood of, or even intimately related to, knowing that one knows that *p*.

To illustrate, let's ask: What does iteratively cognizing an inference look like? Philosophers are very likely to think of a flow of thought somewhat like this:

> I'm now applying modus ponens to p and $p \rightarrow q$ and that gets me to q. I know that modus ponens is a valid rule of inference that justifies my drawing q. OK, so therefore q.

No. On pretty rare days, a well-educated somebody or other *might* iteratively cognize her inference this way—especially if she's reviewing work (in logic or mathematics) that she's just done, and checking for errors. For the vast majority of us all of the time (and for all of us most of the time), the "rules" we use to reason (if we *do* use rules), and even that rules are involved, are introspectively invisible. It might be thought that the rules that reasoners reason by are "tacitly" available. No—this isn't true even of reasoners who, say, are capable of explicitly transliterating their arguments into first-order logic, and then mechanically checking them for validity. What happens is that, when reading an argument—even one that's in quasi-formal form like a syllogism written in plain English[33]—we read each sentence and then have a reaction: *OK, that's right; um, not sure about this one; totally not valid; I'm pretty sure it's valid*; etc.

Our reaction should be described this way: *Confidence (to degree n): That's a valid piece of reasoning*. Or: *Dislike (to degree n): That reasoning*.[34] That is, the experience is a *roughly graded feeling* accompanying a proposition or a set of propositions; there needn't be anything iteratively cognitive about it. That is, that the feeling is roughly graded is *not* a matter of the gradation (degree *n*, say) being directed toward the feeling like so: Degree *n*: Feeling. That treats the gradation of the feeling as iteratively cognitive: a degree-edness directed at a feeling.

[33] For example:
All dogs are pets.
All pets are pampered.
All dogs are pampered.

[34] The phrase "to degree *n*" is idealization: These feelings are intrinsically—but only *roughly*—linearly ordered; nevertheless it's clear they're experienced as graded (as differing in strength).

Rather, the feeling is itself intrinsically a certain strength. So too, that the feeling is directed toward (or about) a proposition or a set of propositions doesn't make the possession of that feeling *by* an agent iteratively cognitive either. The agent *has* the feeling *about* the content of a proposition; the agent, that is, is reacting *to* the proposition.

I should dwell on this because it allows confusedly seeing iterated cognition where it's not. Notice first that, in exactly the same way, the agent could be reacting to a rock ("that's a cute purple rock"). Although it's a set of propositions, and not a rock, that the feeling is directed toward when we're deducing, I repeat: we shouldn't describe *the experience* as iteratively cognitive or as "metarepresentational." Compare: The agent experiences a purple rock. Thus, the agent's mind (let's suppose) must contain a representation of the rock. The *constitution of the experience* the agent has, therefore, is a certain directionality of a feeling toward a rock. But what the experience is of *isn't* of what it's constituted of; the experience isn't of: a feeling directed toward a representation—neither is it an experience of: a feeling directed toward a rock; it's of—and only of—the *rock* being a certain way (of the purple rock being cute).[35] It's one thing to experience *myself* feeling a certain way about a rock; it's another to (simply) feel a certain way about a rock.[36] We mustn't confuse what the experience *is of* from what the experience *is constituted of* mentally; that's a scope error. Describe the experience (in textspeak) this way: Experience: Content. The scope error confuses the part *Content* with the whole: *Experience: Content*. The experience is constituted of a relation—it *is* a relation. But its content isn't of a relation.[37]

The experience of the feeling of confidence (to degree n) toward a piece of reasoning, similarly, need only be of propositions, not of the constitutive fact that the feeling of confidence is degree-edly directed toward propositions. To experience a certain proposition as likely, or unlikely, etc., isn't intrinsically metarepresentational; it isn't an experience *of* representing the proposition(s) and experiencing the feeling as degree-edly directed toward representations. The propositions are there—being read by the participant—and the content of the experience is the rightness to a degree of (a property of) the propositions being read. That is, the feeling is an experience of propositions having certain properties to certain degrees (but it's not a feeling of that).

Call this feeling of confidence, following the psychological literature, a *Feeling of Rightness* (FOR). I've just argued there's no reason to describe this feeling as

[35] "Experience" is ambiguous about the point at issue. "An experience is . . ." can mean either "The content of the experience is . . ." or "What (kind of thing) an experience is is . . ."

[36] As chapter 5 indicated, we mustn't confuse "I feel that purple rock is cute" with "That purple rock is cute," even though, in practice, these are often used interchangeably.

[37] Or, not necessarily, since I might experience the spatial relation between a purple rock and a green rock—that's an experience of a relation but not one between me and something else.

iteratively cognitive or metarepresentational.[38] If, however, the experiencing person is then asked about it, only *at that point*, by responding to the question, *may* the person be iteratively cognizing. (She may not be even then, or so I'll argue.) Saying in response: "I feel this syllogism is valid," is to *literally* utter an iteratively cognitive *statement*: the statement is literally about the agent's very own feelings—that is, in the content of this statement, "I" and a word indicating the feeling itself explicitly occur. But (section 5.2) even this statement when expressed by an agent needn't correspond to an iterative thought the agent is having because all the agent may be doing is expressing iteratively (in English) a reaction that's directed solely toward a subject matter: *Confidence (to degree n) of validity of that.*[39]

This, however, isn't how many of the psychologists studying this area of "metacognition" see things. For example, Thompson, Prowse Turner, and Pennycook (2011, 108–109) write:

> the metamemory literature . . . has long acknowledged the distinction between the processes responsible for retrieving information from memory and the processes responsible for monitoring that information (see Dunlosky and Bjork (2008) for an overview). Monitoring refers to the "subjective assessment of one's own cognitive processes and knowledge" (Koriat, Ma'ayan, and Nussinson (2006, 38)). This assessment can be derived inferentially from implicit cues, such as the ease with which a memory comes to mind (Benjamin, Bjork, and Schwarz (1998); Koriat and Ma'ayan (2005)), or based on explicit cues, such as beliefs about one's skills at a task (e.g., Dunning et al. (2003); Prowse Turner and Thompson (2009); see Koriat (2007) for a review).

The notion of "monitoring," widely used in these studies, bundles ground-floor cognitive processes together with iteratively cognitive ones. Consider, "subjective assessment of one's own cognitive processes and knowledge," due to Koriat, Ma'ayan, and Nussinson. An agent, experiencing a feeling of rightness, can act or not act *because of* the degree of that feeling—and in the case of inferences, regard the conclusion as valid (or not). This can be characterized as a "subjective

[38] Contrast Proust (2007, 272–273), for whom a "metarepresentational" experience involves an epistemic or conative attitude directed toward a representational content: By merely having an attitude about a proposition, one metarepresents. I reject this construal of metarepresentation because it confounds different cognitions. It's acceptable, of course, to terminologically distinguish an attitude toward a rock from an attitude toward an intensional object—but by calling the latter attitudes "metarepresentational" in contexts where that word also stands for iterated thinking is misleading: it invites the scope confusions I'm dwelling on here.

[39] Carruthers (2008, 69) also stresses that a "meta-cognitive report" needn't correspond to a "higher-order awareness." Even if an agent subvocalizes—imagines the words in his mind—"I suspect that . . .," it doesn't follow that his thinking is truly iterated, that he's contemplating the suspects-that relation between himself and a proposition.

assessment of one's own cognitive processes and knowledge." But it needn't be a "subjective assessment" in any sense of *thinking about* one's own cognitive processes and knowledge—not even, really, of any sort of "self-monitoring"—it can be behavior causally induced by having the feelings, and thus, of course, it's sensitive to (correlated with) one's own cognitive processes and knowledge. Only if one thinks about or (literally) makes a subjective assessment *of the feeling itself*, is there an iteratively cognitive thought—not otherwise.

Let's look at the experiments of Thompson, Prowse Turner, and Pennycook (2011), and the conclusions they draw, to see why nothing iteratively cognitive is relevant. This discussion, I claim, is illustrative: it generalizes to much of this literature—including the work on metamemory.[40]

The theoretical notions Thompson, Prowse Turner, and Pennycook (2011) rely on are (i) FOR (characterized above) and (ii) Type 1 and Type 2 psychological engagements in tasks—the latter two notions drawn from (the family of) dual process theories.[41] Type 1 processes are "fast" and "automatic"; Type 2 processes are "deliberate," "analytic," and "difficult." One thing Thompson, Prowse Turner, and Pennycook aim to show is that the degree of FOR accompanying the result of an agent's application of Type 1 processes in deduction triggers whether and how an agent brings Type 2 processes to bear—the weaker the sensation of FOR, the stronger the subsequent use of Type 2 processes.[42] Their experiments additionally show that the degree of FOR an agent experiences doesn't correlate, as a philosopher might have presumed (or hoped), to genuine recognitions of the *validity* of the deductions in question (i.e., by appreciating the *formal properties* of these deductions) but instead to cues such as the fluency with which the initial answer is produced.

How is FOR operationalized in these studies—how is it measured? Thompson, Prowse Turner, and Pennycook (109) write:

> we sought to measure the FOR explicitly, rather than by using a proxy such as consensus. This allowed us to make a direct link to the metamemory literature,

[40] I'll again mention Perner's (2012, especially 198) distinction, "BEING in a state versus KNOWING that one is in this state." Carruthers (2008) makes the same point. The diagnosed source of misunderstanding: being *in* these states is bearing a relation to something—usually a "content"; but being in these states *isn't* by virtue of that an *experience* of oneself as *in* a relation. Knowing one is in such a state *is*, however, generally to experience oneself as being in a relation.

[41] E.g., Evans (2006), Kahneman (2003), Sloman (2002), Stanovich (2004). For the record (but this doesn't matter here), though I take Type 1 processes seriously—insofar as I think they're neurophysiologically genuine (and neurologically specialized), I worry about whether this is true of Type 2 processes. Type 2 processes, instead (or so I speculate), are heterogeneous—and often individually idiosyncratic—sets of psychological processes that are triggered under certain circumstances (e.g., by the feeling that "something isn't right").

[42] Specifically, low FORs generated "longer rethinking times," as well as "greater probability of answer change" (Thompson, Prowse Turner, and Pennycook (2011, 111)).

where metacognitive constructs such as the Feeling of Knowing or Judgments of Learning are solicited directly from participants.

That is, the participants were *asked* how they felt (this is what "solicited directly from participants" means). Thus, the first point: As far as I can tell, neither in the experiments Thompson, Prowse Turner, and Pennycook describe in their article, nor in the experiments in the metamemory literature their results are linked to—all the ones that utilize *this way* of measuring FOR—is a distinction being experimentally drawn between what they describe as a "direct measurement" of the FOR (via what the agent says about it) or, instead, a measurement of the (possibly quite different) agent's *cognition of* her FOR. Second: If the idea that FOR is itself metacognitive is challenged, these experiments won't help because the measurement assumptions presuppose this fact of FOR; they don't establish it.

I don't claim that asking participants in the experiment how they feel about a presented inference *isn't* to measure FOR—the psychological act of iteratively cognizing one's FOR may not introduce a divide between the feelings one *actually has* and those *one thinks one has*. But this is something to be empirically determined (*somehow*; the control Thompson, Prowse Turner, and Pennycook used, see note 45, doesn't do this). I'm also pointing out that nothing in their experimental setup shows that degrees of FOR are iteratively cognitive—even though such feelings of an agent "monitor" (according to the definition of Koriat, Ma'ayan, and Nussinson (2006, 38)) that agent's own cognitive processes and knowledge by being correlated with their outputs.[43]

Let's turn to what these experiments *do* establish. They establish (i) a relationship between FOR and Type 2 thinking and (ii) a relationship between answer fluency[44] and FOR. That is, the hypotheses (with refinements) they take the experiments to confirm are (Thompson, Prowse Turner, and Pennycook (2011, 112–113)) that:

(1) Answers accompanied by a low FOR should promote more Type 2 thinking relative to answers accompanied by a strong FOR, and

[43] I repeat: iterated cognitions needn't arise *even when elicited*, and even when participants answer the questions about their FORs. The participant may not be cognitively looking at her FOR but only responding *to it* to answer the question. In this latter case, my first point amounts to asking whether such verbal responses always *correlate with* FOR in the way this measurement technique presupposes. Where the participant does cognize her FOR, the issue amounts to whether her cognition of her FOR is accurate.

[44] *Answer fluency* (Thompson, Prowse Turner, and Pennycook (2011, 12) stress) should be distinguished from *processing fluency*. The latter is how handling a task *feels* (e.g., reading a word problem in a difficult font, as opposed to an easy one). Answer fluency is the speed or ease with which a purported answer comes to mind.

(2) The FOR, in turn, should be higher for fluently generated answers than their less fluent counterparts and for conclusions that were accepted as opposed to rejected.

I'll focus on the first experiment.

The task was to evaluate examples of conditional reasoning for validity or invalidity. The participants were told: "If a car runs out of gas, then it will stall." Next, they were asked to determine which of these follow validly:

The car has run out of gas. Therefore it will stall. (Valid inference)
The car has not stalled. Therefore it did not run out of gas. (Valid inference)
The car has stalled. Therefore it ran out of gas. (Invalid inference)
The car has not run out of gas. Therefore it will not stall. (Invalid inference)

Participants were first required to give (113) a response quickly, and a FOR was also elicited from them (by asking). Afterward they were "allowed as much time as needed to generate a final conclusion."[45]

Validity is independent of content. What each conditional says doesn't matter; only their form does; so the questions can be answered via truth tables or by formal rules—if there is sufficient time. Thus, these tools can be used (if one knows about them) only on the second go-around; one must answer too quickly the first time.[46]

Tested for in these experiments (and in others) are various deductively irrelevant factors that affect a FOR. First (Thompson, Prowse Turner, and Pennycook (2011, 112)), "reasoners tend to accept a provided conclusion more often than warranted by chance (or by other task-relevant features, such as the validity or believability of the conclusion)." In addition, at least as far as tasks of determining *validity* are concerned, degrees of believability are irrelevant since they are linked to the content of the sentences. Thus, believability can be manipulated independently of validity, and Thompson, Prowse Turner, and Pennycook (114) do so

[45] A control group was required only to give an intuitive response and to provide a FOR. This was to rule out the "possibility that differences in thinking times and answer changes were produced by having participants make FOR judgments" (113).

[46] The distinction between participants using Type 2 thinking instead of Type 1 thinking, in these experiments, isn't drawn by characterizing the different kinds of thinking that participants bring to bear on the tasks. Rather, the two-stage participants are given unlimited time in the second stage of the task (and so, they *can* engage in Type 2 thinking). This is why Thompson, Prowse Turner, and Pennycook have to hypothesize about what kind of Type 2 thinking is occurring—e.g., that in some cases, the participants are rationalizing their first answers (117), rather than employing superior time-consuming methods of reasoning.

> by changing the relationship of the p and q propositions. To the extent that occurrence of p is sufficient to bring about the occurrence of q . . . the valid inferences are believable. When p is not sufficient for q, the valid inferences are less believable. . . . Similarly, to the extent that p is a necessary condition to bring about q, the invalid inferences are believable.

Some results (Thompson, Prowse Turner, and Pennycook (117–118)): First, as mentioned, FOR is positively correlated with answer fluency. That is, there is a strong negative correlation between "FOR judgments and the time taken to produce the initial response." Second, FOR is positively correlated with acceptance bias; it's also positively correlated with both the believability and the validity of the conclusion, as is also the probability of acceptance. (The latter is *not* correlated with the validity of the inference.)[47]

Although these results do show interesting and important correlations between FOR and Type 2 vs. Type 1 thinking, they don't bear on iterated cognition; nothing about these results establishes that FOR must correspond to an experience of iterated cognition—that, I repeat, is assumed. Also, although the experiment only presupposed the FOR to be "metacognitional," nothing here shows that the more analytic and careful nature of Type 2 thinking requires such thinking to be iteratively cognitive either. Ground-floor cognition can be quite intricate, careful, and analytical, without that requiring it in any way to involve an awareness or thought about the very process of Type 2 thinking itself.

There is an important issue these experiments raise. Given that FOR strongly correlates with answer fluency and with the apparent truth of the conclusion (and *not* with formal validity), it can easily be thought (by those familiar with what Thompson, Prowse Turner, and Pennycook (110) call "relevant normal standards") that these participants are all reasoning invalidly. Therefore (according to this way of thinking), iterated thinking about one's FOR should be ruled out as capable of yielding iterated *knowledge*. Answer fluency, relatedly, is highly correlated with *thinking* one's memory is veridical.[48] Philosophers are tempted to think that even if (for certain epistemic agents) answer fluency correlates well with veridical memory or valid reasoning, such agents don't remember or recognize validity in such cases. Or that if they do, they don't *know* they remember veridically or *know* that they have recognized a valid result.

No. Iterated knowledge, like ground-floor knowledge, is "cue-driven"; this is related to the fact that iterated knowledge, like ground-floor knowledge, can be

[47] "The longer participants spent rethinking their answer, the less likely they were to get it right at Time 2" (117).

[48] Some of the psychological literature on this: Benjamin, Bork, and Schwartz (1998), Jacoby, Kelly, and Dywan (1989), and Whittlesea and Leboe (2003)—further results are cited at Thompson, Prowse Turner, and Pennycook (2011, 111).

"piecemeal" and involve "bits"—and also that iterated knowledge, like ground-floor knowledge, can occur without the epistemic agent grasping the relevant concepts involved in the content of that knowledge. In particular, an animal (or human) may know that he's remembering (veridically) without having the relevant concepts—that is, he may know that he's remembering *p* on the basis of cues (such as answer fluency), rather than by a deeper grasp of the mechanisms of his memory.[49]

We can see that the cue-driven-ness of knowledge is the mechanism behind the possibility of ground-floor knowledge (of *p*) without a corresponding grasp of concepts (in *p*). Rover the dog (from section 1.4) knows that Olga is playing chess because he's sensitive to cues that correlate with Olga playing chess. He can grasp those cues without grasping what chess is. Iterated knowledge is no different. So, similarly, someone who takes fluency as an indication that a deduction is valid, and whose appreciation of fluency correlates nicely (enough) with validity can know that she knows a proposition is valid without grasping the notion of validity![50]

6.6 Nonhuman-Animal Studies in "Metacognition"

There are now many studies of nonhuman animals where certain behaviors of those animals (while executing certain tasks) are taken by many—but not all—practitioners to show "metacognition." I claim they don't—as they stand—show this. At least, they don't show this if "metacognition" is understood as iterated cognition, or iterated cognition accompanied by the grasp of relevant concepts. I'll turn in section 6.7 to one result I've found in the literature that, in my view, is a quite promising indication of a nonhuman animal iteratedly cognizing.

Given that "metacognition" is understood either as iterated cognition or as iterated cognition accompanied by the grasp of some or all the relevant concepts,[51] the problem this literature faces is what I'll call *the apparent*

[49] Thompson, Prowse Turner, and Pennycook (2011, 109) put the point well: "[An assessment of one's own cognitive processes and knowledge] can be derived inferentially from implicit cues such as the ease with which a memory comes to mind, or based on explicit cues, such as beliefs about one's skill at a task." When *really* engaging in iterated cognition, one can know that one knows *p* by means of background beliefs about how one knows *p* or by means of one's explicit (and justified) trust in the ease with which one's memory emerged, or in other phenomenological accompaniments of that memory.

[50] The great mathematician Ramanujan, notoriously, didn't quite grasp the notion of proof; he relied on feelings of rightness to *know* his results. See Hardy (1941). Many mathematicians similarly rely on feelings of rightness—the proofs often follow later, if at all.

[51] As I've already indicated, it's not a requirement for the value of these psychological studies that "metacognition" be characterized this way. The results may show the presence of "metacognition"

ineffability of iterated cognition (hereafter, "apparent ineffability"). This is that a sequence of (non-verbal) behaviors of an agent that are open to attributions of iterated cognition are also (often? always?) open to attributions of ground-floor cognitions. One thing that contributes to apparent ineffability is that, often, a human agent's awareness of her own mental states *causally idles*: being in the state suffices for the behavior manifested despite the iterated cognitions. If, for example, I'm running from a polar bear (an activity, in practice, that's apparently futile), that I'm aware I'm frightened isn't doing any additional work (to affect my behavior) beyond my fear itself.

The way that an attribution of ground-floor desires and beliefs can mimic iterated cognitive reasoning, however, can be much more subtle; and this is why apparent ineffability is a challenge to experiments designed to show behavior indicating iterated cognition. Suppose S is running from a black bear, and only when cornered does S confront the bear by yelling and waving his arms. This can be characterized in terms of ground-floor cognitions and ground-floor desires. S is afraid, and when cornered, S shifts in behavior not because S is aware of his own fear (even if he is) but simply because the fear state itself (along with perceptual awareness) generates complex responses, like, when cornered, confronting bears.

Imagine, however, S stops running suddenly (without being cornered) and confronts the bear. S's thinking might be: I'm running because I'm afraid of this bear; but I've just remembered that the best way to survive a black-bear attack isn't to run fearfully but to confront it.[52] Thinking this is *why* S stops running and confronts the bear. This reasoning (involving knowledge of S's own fear state) may seem to be the most plausible construal of S's behavior because S changed his behavior in mid-run (without this being triggered by perceptual cues). But S's fear state (all by itself) might still be the source of S's behavior because it might generate the following complex timed-behavior and (ground-floor) cognitions: First run, and only while running evaluate the animal giving chase. If it's amenable to being scared off, change to confrontation behavior. This second bit of reasoning *doesn't* involve iterative cognition.

We may think introspections, and verbal expression of one's introspections, are available (in the case of humans) to distinguish iterative vs. ground-floor

in the sense in which the authors of the studies use the word, and "metacognition" so defined may label important abilities some species of animal have that others don't. My focus on iterated cognition accords, however, with how *many* practitioners implicitly and explicitly understand "metacognition"; in addition, it connects to the broader epistemological and philosophical issues this book is about.

[52] The example doesn't require the agent to be *right* about this.

cognition cases.[53] But this approach isn't available for nonhuman animals. Let's turn to the question of how the distinction is to be managed in *that* case.

Carruthers (2008) denies that any of the studies he discusses (as of 2008) shows the presence of metacognition. His strategy for determining what these studies actually show about animal cognition is to illustrate how the behavior of the animals in these cases is compatible with belief/desire reasoning, where both are ground-floor and come in degrees—"world-directed" rather than "self-directed" (59). He shows—correctly, in my view—that the patterns of ground-floor cognitions and desires he posits suffice to explain every behavioral result elicited from nonhuman animals in these studies. My conclusion is that what he shows this way is that—empirically speaking—we're currently at an impasse. Although the various patterns of reasoning Carruthers hypothesizes are complex enough that some animals (and not others) can carry them out, in none of these cases is it definitive that iterated cognitions of any sort must be involved.

Carruthers does *not* draw an impasse conclusion. He invokes Morgan's Canon instead: "Roughly: don't attribute to animals cognitive processes more complex than is necessary" (59). On the interpretation of this canon that Carruthers uses, if we can tell a ground-floor cognitive/desire story about how an animal manages a task, we should reject any iterated-cognition hypotheses about its reasoning. That is *not* my view. In such cases, empirically speaking, iterated cognition is possible unless we rule it out either because we've operationalized iterated cognition in a way that distinguishes it from ground-floor cognition or because of background theoretical considerations. Such considerations, for example, allow us to attribute knowledge to spiders and drones, but we rule out iterated knowledge because of the simplicity of their neural structures (spiders) or because we haven't—so far—designed them to have iterated knowledge (drones). "Operationalizing" iterated knowledge to distinguish it from ground-floor knowledge is another matter. Much of the psychological literature I discuss and

[53] Not, however, if we go as Carruthers (2008, 69) urges: humans are often wrong about which internal states of theirs are actually why they engage in the behaviors they engage in. Carruthers (60) writes, "There is good reason to think these Cartesian, or quasi-Cartesian, conceptions of self-knowledge are false." One, however, can accept the value of introspective reports without adopting Cartesian or quasi-Cartesian conceptions of self-knowledge. Regardless, apparent ineffability coupled with systematic denials of the value of introspective reports is yet another route to treating iterated cognition as "cheap"—always amounting to one or another ground-floor pattern of cognitions and desires. I reject "blanket rejections" of introspective reports. For one thing, we're not that far (technologically speaking) from neurophysiological studies of brains to determine when and whether introspective reports of iterated cognitions (with or without the grasping of concepts) are accompanied by different activation patterns from ground-floor cognitions. If these are found in humans, they could be postulated as operative in those nonhuman animals where similar activation patterns are found. (This would be further evidence, not a definitive confirmation.) So in no sense (I've just argued) should apparent ineffability be taken either as a sceptical hypothesis or as an underdetermination-of-theory-by-(all-possible-)data claim. It's a problem facing animal studies—given tools *currently available*.

allude to (and that Carruthers discusses) involves experimental attempts to do this. These attempts (in my view) have so far failed.[54]

Let's look at some results.[55] Consider, first, a series of experiments (Smith et al. (1995; 1997)); Shields, Smith, and Washburn (1997)) where animals were trained to press a symbol ("D," say) in response to a dense visual pattern or high-pitched auditory tone and another symbol ("S," say) for patterns less dense or tones less highly pitched. The animals received typical food rewards for correct responses and had brief "time outs" for incorrect ones (delays before opportunities to get more food). A third symbol ("DK," say) allowed them to opt out of the current test and go immediately to another without a time out. The discrimination tasks were made increasingly difficult to see whether (and when) the animals would utilize DK to avoid time outs.

All the animals in question (humans, monkeys, and dolphins) under circumstances in which they would make errors (if DK wasn't available) made use of DK—individual animals even displayed differences in when they made use of DK. Humans told experimenters that they were aware of being uncertain whether they knew; Smith (2005) argues that the animals should be similarly described as being aware of being uncertain. Notice the intuitive simplicity of the iterated cognitive explanation Smith offers (iterated cognitions are often intuitively simple in this way): Is the pattern dense or sparse? *I* don't know (understood as iterated, not redundant); but if I guess wrong, I'll get a time out. So I'd better push DK.

Carruthers (2008, 64–65) offers an alternative way of thinking (and desiring): Is the pattern dense or sparse? Believes (weakly): dense. Believes (weakly): sparse. Don't want (strongly): time out. Weak desire: push D; weak desire: push S; strong desire: push DK. (Animal, as a result, pushes DK).[56]

[54] Hampton (2009, 18), discussing the same experiments Carruthers discusses, importantly distinguishes between private and public mechanisms for metacognition ("Private mechanisms are those by which cognitive control is contingent on the privileged access the subject has to their own cognitive states"), but this doesn't capture distinctions between iterated cognition, ground-floor cognitions, and the grasping of the concepts involved in the cognitions, since both public and private mechanisms for "metacognition" may involve any of these—in particular, "privileged access" doesn't distinguish between iterated and ground-floor cognizing unless it is understood as the grasping of the relevant concepts. Similarly, Carruthers (2008, 64 n. 8) writes: "Our topic is not to delineate the precise concepts that the animals deploy, but more broadly to determine whether they are entertaining higher-order concepts of some sort, or merely first-order ones." As often happens in this literature, ambiguous locutions are being used: "entertaining higher-order concepts" can be a matter of grasping them or merely having them. Carruthers, however, intends the "grasping concepts" interpretation, as I've already mentioned. I'm here exploring the weaker possibility of iterated cognition without the concomitant grasping of the concepts in question.

[55] I rely somewhat on Carruthers's (2008) careful discussion of these experiments. See his paper, Hampton (2009), or the (cited) reports of the original results for further details.

[56] Carruthers (2008, 64–65) lays out the entire ground-floor inference/desire pattern; it's, of course, more complicated than what I've written. If, similarly, the entire inference/desire pattern for the iterated cognition is written out, it's also more complicated than what I've written—but still more

So far, Carruthers's approach only manages cases where animals experience four-way ties between pressing or not pressing S or D, along with an unopposed desire to press DK. But threshold effects (where the desires for pressing S or D are slightly different in strength) must be accommodated to handle animals pressing DK in (some of) these cases as well. A posited "gatekeeping" mechanism handles this, as well as the fact that different animals respond differently to the same degrees of not knowing. Carruthers (2008, 67) writes:

> [W]here different goals are competing with one another to control behavior [the gate] would only initiate one of the desired behaviors if the degrees of desire involved are sufficiently far apart. . . . Otherwise the animal becomes motivated to pause, engaging in information-seeking behavior or searching for another alternative. Since conditions of uncertainty are also inherently dangerous in various ways, one might expect a series of bodily changes to take place in the animal that it will experience as a form of aversive anxiety.

Carruthers (67) notes the ground-floor nature of such a gatekeeping mechanism (italics his):

> It doesn't *represent* the fact that two desires are very close to one another in strength. Rather, it responds differentially depending on whether or not the desires it receives as input are in fact close to one another in strength. It is a mechanism that is sensitive to one *property* of desire (strength) without needing to represent that it is a *desire* that has that property.

This apparatus, it should be clear, provides models of desire/inference for the behavior of animals in *many* animal studies. Consider studies of "meta-confidence" involving betting that were introduced by Son and Kornell (2005). Here is Carruthers's (2008, 71–72)—slightly rewritten—description of the task:

> The animals had to judge which one of nine lines presented on a screen was longest, and then touch it. Then they had to choose between a high-confidence symbol (which gave greater gains if the initial choice was correct but an equivalent loss otherwise) and a low-confidence symbol (which yielded a small reward). On the screen throughout the trials was a reservoir of tokens, to which won (and lost) tokens were added (and removed) with a salient sound. Monkeys got a food pellet once the reservoir exceeded a certain level (after which the

intuitively simple than the ground-floor inference/desire pattern. Built into Carruthers's notation is the absence of referents to the animal engaging in the reasoning and having the desires—e.g., no first-person pronouns. This contributes to the ground-floor inference/desire patterns being unintuitive.

reservoir was reset). Monkeys were more likely to take the "high-risk" gamble where they correctly chose than when they erred.

Despite the plausible attribution of iterated cognitions to the monkeys navigating this task, Carruthers (2008, 72–73) can provide a ground-floor reasoning and desire pattern that equally well explains their behavior. He replaces iterated-cognition patterns of reasoning/desire with ground-floor patterns of such for a number of further experiments, including (transparent and opaque) hollow-tube tests (Call and Carpenter (2001), Hampton, Zivin, and Murray (2004), and Kornell, Son, and Terrace (2007)) as well as ones designed to test memory and meta-memory in animals (Hampton (2001)). We may justly fear that Carruthers's strategy is always available to rewrite metacognitive characterizations of behavior purely in terms of ground-floor cognitions. There is a way out of the logjam, however, in terms of generalizations about the transfer of knowledge that the animals can be postulated to grasp;[57] these generalizations can be tested in subsequent experiments.

Monkeys (Son and Kornell (2005), Kornell, Son, and Terrace (2007)), for example, can transfer what they've learned in gambling tasks (about when to press or not press buttons given the confidence they have) to new cases: they seem, that is, to have acquired a *generalization* they can apply immediately in new contexts. Kornell, Son, and Terrace argue that the generalization the monkeys have acquired is something like (Carruthers's numbering):

> (32) Strong belief: If I am certain that I have chosen correctly and the "high risk" symbol on the next screen is touched, then three tokens will result.

This generalization involves an iterated cognition. Carruthers (2008, 74) substitutes for this generalization two others without iterated cognitions:

> (33) Strong belief: Within each array there is a target symbol, touching which achieves three tokens if the "high risk" symbol is pressed thereafter.
>
> (34) Strong belief: If the target symbol hasn't been touched and the "high risk" symbol is touched on the next screen, then three tokens will be lost.

Number (32) contains a reference to the mental state *being confident*. It's also couched as first-person—but that's not essential to it. What *is* important, however, is that although (32), on the one hand, and (33) and (34) on the other, do the same work with respect to the experiments *under discussion*, they generalize

[57] Recall the discussion of the results of Cooper et al. (2003) in section 1.2.

differently. Number (32) generalizes to *whatever* cases involve an animal's confidence—regardless of whether target symbols need to be touched or not; (33) and (34) don't.

This reveals Carruthers's use of Morgan's Canon to be an overreach: he claims that one should assume that no metacognition is taking place on the basis of a substitution of one kind of generalization for another. Instead, these differing generalizations must be teased apart empirically in subsequent studies; and this is why apparent ineffability is *apparent*. It can be circumvented (in principle) by further studies.

I'll illustrate this point further with a very interesting result that has emerged recently.

6.7 A Possible Case of Nonhuman-Animal Iterated Cognition?

A recent study apparently not only reveals the mind-reading of one chimpanzee by another but the apparent recognition by a chimpanzee that another chimpanzee can learn facts about the world by seeing where the first one is looking.

Before giving the details of this study, let's consider a sadly typical human (or American) case. My gun is hidden in a desk drawer. An intruder, I realize, will recognize (or suspect) I've got a gun hidden there if I look toward that desk *in a certain way*. Not only does this involve "mind-reading," but more important for our purposes is the iterated cognition: I know that I know something, along with: I know that looking in the direction of that something will betray to someone else where *it* is. I consequently engage in "gaze-averting behavior."

Can this these inferences and desires (which lead to my behavior) be characterized via ground-floor cognitions and desires? Not without losing significant generalizations *I'm* entirely capable of. I can (and do) avert my eyes to avoid betraying what I know, where what I know are things I see, ones I'm aware of, indeed, where what I know can be *all* sorts of things—ones located where my gaze would reveal them to be, but also elsewhere, where someone would learn their locations from my gaze coupled with some reasoning (e.g., about a key I'm looking at).

I'm aware of this: I control my behavior deliberately so that *something I know* isn't revealed to another. And this is generalizable just the way the phrase "something I know" shows, by quantification into an "I know" context. Describing this as ground-floor cognitions and desires loses this quantification in terms of what I *know*. So the fact that, under a very broad range of circumstances—not just with a gun in a desk drawer—I will avert my gaze requires an iterated-cognition generalization as an explanation.

Now consider the following background facts about chimpanzees established by numerous studies. (I've cribbed what follows from Hall et al. (2016) but omitted the citations; I've also shortened—excerpted and combined—the passages):

> Chimpanzees have been found to follow the gaze of their conspecifics, even in the absence of head movement cues. Chimpanzees can use others' gaze direction to gain information about their attentional states and their focus of interest: for example, the presence of food or predators, and social interactions between others. Following gaze is not merely a response to a stimulus, as individuals appear to understand that gaze conveys information; for example, all great apes follow gaze around barriers to a target, and often refer back to the face of a human experimenter after following their gaze to the ceiling where no target is present. If chimpanzees are able to use others' gaze as a source of information, then countermeasures to this ability may have also developed. Specifically, chimpanzees may be able to deceive a competitor by omission (averted gaze) or by commission (deliberately gazing at the "wrong" place).

Hall et al. (2016) carried out two studies to investigate a subordinate's ability to remain one step ahead of a dominant's exploitation. A dominant chimp can brazenly take food from a subordinate; a dominant chimp can (Hall et al. (2016, 4)) "follow her and steal food from [a hidden location] once the subordinate has uncovered it." In both experiments, the dominant chimpanzee would trail after the subordinate and follow her gaze. The two experiments differed in that in the first one, there was only a tasty foodstuff that had been hidden; in the second case, contrasting tasty vs. not as tasty foodstuffs were hidden in difference places—bananas vs. cucumbers.

Among the results was that, in the first experiment (4),

> in response to the dominant directly approaching her, the subordinate was likely to pause walking for 5 consecutive seconds. . . . Additionally, when the subordinate stopped walking for 5 s, she was slightly more likely to stop gazing toward the banana for 5 s than expected by chance. . . . Put simply, when the dominant approached her, the subordinate stopped walking and gazing in the direction of the hidden banana.

In the second experiment (6),

> the subordinate approached the two baits differently: by pausing and alternating gaze with her ignorant competitor, she may have revealed the

> location of the cucumber to her, whereas she moved swiftly to retrieve the banana. . . . While we expected the subordinate to lead the dominant toward the cucumber, we additionally found an unexpected pattern (alternating gaze between the partner and the cucumber—but not the banana—while pausing) that functioned to recruit the dominant to that location, indicating that chimpanzees are highly flexible in their use of gaze direction and movement to both conceal and reveal information to manipulate a foraging partner.

The following detail about the subordinate's use of gaze is worth noting (7):

> In approaching the cucumber in particular, the subordinate looked at her competitor in an ostensive manner, that is, she looked directly at her partner in order to get her attention . . . and then used her own gaze (head orientation) as a social cue to point toward the location of the cucumber, and was then likely to pause her movement for 5 s. . . . The subordinate, however, did not behave this way while approaching the banana.

Notice what the use of the phrase "highly flexible" *does*: it indicates generalizations the chimpanzees are taken to grasp; among the implicit generalizations, in this case, are ones about the chimp's *own* gaze. I'll stress out loud what I've just intimated. Although I'm willing to claim these results *reveal* iterated knowledge, I won't claim the chimpanzee in question *has* the concept of *knowledge*; a more restricted (but, crucially, factive) concept of *gaze*, or something similar, is more likely to be what the relevant generalizations are couched in terms of.[58]

As with gambling experiments (section 6.6), only further experiments will sustain or disconfirm generalizations (ground-floor or iterated) that the animals are posited to know. But the two experiments of Hall et al. (2016) *together* suggest

[58] Richard Byrne (email, December 14, 2017) writes: "we were quite careful not to talk in terms of awareness of others' knowledge, but rather in terms of tendencies that were reliably evoked by particular recurring situations—which might not be the same thing! I think it is a moot point: and of my co-authors, my colleague Mike Oram is pretty sure the chimpanzees are not computing with mental states, Katie [Hall)] herself is totally convinced they are. I shall sit on the fence! (but then, I wonder how much of our own behavior (apparently in the consciousness of other people's knowledge) is really routine and automatic . . ." (The final ellipses are his). It may tame (although not eliminate) the disagreement to note, as I have repeatedly throughout this chapter, that "computing with mental states" needn't involve a *grasp* of mental-state concepts. Indeed, this is true, generally, of the possession of a theory of mind: animals need only grasp generalizations couched in terms of mental-state concepts, without grasping the concepts themselves—a much more arduous requirement. Knowing appropriate generalizations only requires animals to flexibly perform in a way that can't be captured by ground-floor generalizations of the sort Carruthers offers.

that ground-floor cognitive/desire characterizations of the chimpanzee's reasoning/desire patterns won't be sustained.[59]

6.8 Conclusion

Once we distinguish iterated knowledge from ground-floor knowledge, and iterated cognition from ground-floor cognition, epistemology becomes hard in an unexpected way. We must avoid confusions too easily introduced by how we talk; and we need to engage in subtle (empirical) maneuvers to recognize when we (and others) are iteratively cognizing and when not. I've illustrated this in this chapter and in chapter 5. One important "take-away" of this chapter is that we must focus not so much on whether animals (or ourselves) use mental-state concepts (which is a disturbingly ambiguous concern), but instead on the nature of the generalizations (couched in mental-state concepts, of one sort or another) that can be justifiably attributed to these animals (or to ourselves). Transfer of knowledge and the accompanying generalizations will prove important to the question of the function or role of "know(s)" in the vernacular (section 11. 4).

I turn in the next two chapters to justification, and I show how the same issues with iterated and ground-floor cognitions bedevil our understanding of that concept as well.

[59] That said, Richard Byrne (email, December 14, 2017) has warned me that "[i]t was only in a second experiment, and indeed only one pair of chimpanzees, that we (Katie Hall was my PhD student) were able to show that the subordinate averted her gaze from the hidden reward when the dominant was in a position to see her."

7
Inferential Justification

7.1 First Remarks

I examined cognition attributions to relatively unsophisticated epistemic agents including nonconscious mechanisms in chapter 1, and I showed a number of surprising facts about how these cognition attributions uncouple when we apply them (e.g., how "awareness" attributions uncouple from consciousness attributions). I also showed in that chapter that the notion of knowing that we use on animals and artifacts is the same notion we apply to *our* conspecifics (e.g., to our knowing friends, and to ourselves). Some philosophers who take "know(s)" attributions to animals seriously (although not Hume) have instead thought the word "know(s)" bifurcates: we don't mean the same thing when we describe an animal as knowing something as when we describe a human as knowing something.[1]

[1] Brandom and Williams can take the bifurcation line on "know(s)" if they decide to drop their implausible denial of the application of "know(s)" to animals being literal, although this alternative is *also* implausible because of the conjunction-reduction test. We (using single instances of the words "see(s)," "know(s)," etc.) simultaneously attribute such cognitions to animals, to nonconscious artifacts, and to ourselves (e.g., "Me and the two Rovers realized right away that an intruder was in the house," where one Rover is a dog and the other is a drone). An alternative, that respects the linguistic facts about "know(s)," is to instead bifurcate knowledge into *kinds*—something a mass term like "knowledge" allows. We might require certain intellectual virtues of "human knowledge" but not "animal knowledge," where such intellectual virtues include additional metacognitive knowings directed toward some of the knowledge. Sosa (1991, 240), for example, distinguishes between animal knowledge and reflective knowledge, which in addition to direct responses to environmental items, manifests an "understanding" that includes "one's belief and knowledge . . . and how these come about." We may also, more specifically, take "inference" or deduction to require certain additional metacognitive knowings (e.g. the understanding and/or grasping of certain additional metacognitive meanings) and/or attitudes that must be (consciously or unconsciously) adopted. A commitment to *p* yielding *q* (where *q* follows from *p*) would be such a thing. Boghossian, Hlobil, Malmgren, and Neta have argued for such views. Also, see my quotation of Turri and Klein (2014b, 9) in chapter 8, note 2. I will argue against such additions being *necessary* for inference in sections 7.2 and 7.3 and later in chapter 8, especially in section 8.7; but I won't presuppose my opposition to these enrichment positions, vis-à-vis deduction, when raising my objections to infinitism in section 7.4. My objections to infinitism are independent of issues of whether certain psychological conditions or norms govern inference, in addition to, say, formal properties. I should add that one way of bifurcating knowledge turns on (as Turri and Klein (2014b) do) distinguishing between "fully justifying" as we do and mere brute justification as animals do. No such distinction occurs in natural language, although as I indicate here (and discuss in chapter 8), a distinction between having a justification and being able to give one does occur. Aikin (2011, 22) reconciles "know" attributions to animals and babies with a strong interpretation of "possessing justification" by treating third- and first-person justifications differently. First-person justification requires intellectual integrity, as well as additional knowledge and cognitive capacities; third-person justification doesn't, and "is fine for cats and babies." This isn't tenable (as

Attributing Knowledge. Jody Azzouni, Oxford University Press (2020). © Oxford University Press.
DOI: 10.1093/oso/9780197508817.001.0001.

One sympathizes with bifurcaters. A problem is the apparently close connection of articulated justifications with knowings—at least, apparently, for humans. That's what Brandom stresses (in the quotation in section 1.1): animals, he thinks, aren't "justified" in what they know. If you insist that they "know" things, all you can mean is that they have reliable differential responsive dispositions. And that's not *justification* regardless of whether you want to say animals know things or not.

What's needed to rebut this charge is to show that, just as the same notion of "know(s)" is attributed to animals and human, so too for "justification." I'll make a useful point immediately: It's unproblematic to describe animals as justified (or not justified) in what they believe—those of us who observe animals do it regularly. If Rover smells the odor of his food in a particular place (although unbeknownst to him I've moved the food), he's justified in thinking that's where his food is. We can also describe Rover as not justified in thinking *that's* where his food is if he still thinks it's there even though there is no odor left, and furthermore, he *saw* me move it.

It's perhaps worth saying a little about why talk of justification naturally arises, when it does, when describing what animals know.[2] The reason is straightforward and related to how Gettier cases arise among animals just as they arise among us—and sometimes at the same time and for the same reasons. Consider a case where a monkey makes fake eagle calls to scare other monkeys into hiding (so he can get food he knows about without interference from them). His fellow monkeys are justified in thinking there is an eagle about (just as human observers are who haven't realized yet that this monkey is a deceiver). Should there, unbeknownst to this monkey, actually be an eagle about, we have a Gettier case: the other monkeys (and the human observers) are justified in believing there is an eagle about, there *is* an eagle about, but neither the other monkeys nor the human observers know this.

In just the way we do, animals come to know things through certain processes—in particular, by using their senses and, in some cases, by drawing inferences as well. They also have memories they rely on, and in the case of highly social animals, they communicate information to one another—as social monkeys do. In all these cases, an animal's sources of knowledge justify what she knows just as our sources of knowledge do. And in all those cases, just as with us, animals can fail to know, but still be justified in believing what they believe, as

I've already indicated) because, often, justifications are described as (or assumed as) *shared* by third-person attributors of knowledge with the agents they're attributing that knowledge to.

[2] Especially because some philosophers will resist the idea. My thanks to Ram Neta for pressing me on this.

I illustrated with the monkey/eagle case. In carefully designed experiments, rats (for example) will exhibit frustration when a process that they've learned leads to food doesn't—when, that is, what they're now justified in expecting doesn't turn out. It's not only natural to use talk of "justification" in these cases, as those studying animals do; there seems no good reason to withhold this kind of talk.[3]

[3] Ram Neta writes: "My cat knows various things and thinks various things. Some of its thoughts are true, and others false. But are these thoughts justified or unjustified? I don't find it natural to give any particular answer to this question." I think it becomes more than natural—it's indispensable to talk this way—when describing a situation where a cat's reasonable expectations are foiled. This is especially the case should the cat's caretaker share those reasonable expectations. (Imagine a case where you're opening a can of cat food right in front of the eager—and hungry—cat, and when you do, what's in there smells really, really weird and doesn't even look like food. *Both of you* were justified in thinking that the cat's meal was "around the corner.") This said, I do want to note the following about the relation of "justif(y/ies)" and its cognates to "know(s)." "Justif(y/ies)," unlike "know(s)" is, in my view, jargon (even though it's jargon that was introduced into English centuries ago). By contrast, "know(s)" is—I've claimed—a lexical universal. One result of this is that, as I show in subsequent chapters, especially chapter 11, the properties of "know(s)" are fairly rigid. The word isn't open to linguistic negotiation, as it might be put. This isn't true of "justif(y/ies)"—we might want to restrict and/or change its scope in various ways, and nothing (I suspect) about how its semantic properties are entrenched in the languages it occurs in need stop us. Tianyi Zhao tells me, in particular, that "justif(y/ies)" doesn't occur in Chinese, and so there is something of a debate about how this notion, and its relatives, are to be translated to Chinese. In any case, it's no surprise that it sometimes feels awkward to attribute being justified to an agent that we have no trouble attributing knowledge to. Is B.B., for example, justified in thinking there is a triangle in front of it? There is certainly a reliable process by which B.B. comes to know this; but it's not entirely natural to ride talk of being justified on the basis of this process. Once, however, we find it natural to attribute to an even unconscious agent—such as a driverless car—the thought that something is an obstacle although it's not, Gettier cases become possible. It's then natural to say, in certain cases, that the car was justified in thinking there was an obstacle although the car didn't know this because how it came to know of the obstacle was misleading in a way typical of Gettier cases. Part of the problem has to do with cases where an agent knows things that agent isn't aware of or consciously thinking about, although that agent is capable of consciously thinking about those things or, worse, *is* thinking (consciously) about them. In these cases our two acceptable attributions of "think" or "believe"—to conscious or unconscious agents—clash. To see this, first note that it's hard to directly speak of being justified as a necessary condition on knowing because we don't say, "*John is justified in knowing *p*." We need an intermediate belief or thought that's justified and connected to what's known: It *is* natural to say to say, "John is justified in believing/thinking p." To the extent therefore that we can say, of an unconscious agent, like B.B., that it thinks *p*, we can say that it's justified in thinking *p*, and that it knows *p*. Consider, though (section 1.6, especially n. 25), Dorothy, who answers thirty questions about the French history right—exact dates—although she studied the subject many years ago and has no reason to believe that she still remembers this stuff. In the case where the examiners don't tell her that her answers are correct until after she gives them all, she reasonably believes she doesn't know these things and reasonably doesn't believe the dates she's answered the questions with. Two cases: she feels like she's guessing; she feels like she's remembering, but she—reasonably—doesn't believe she's remembering. In both cases, her *answers* are justified because her memory is operating and is good—unbeknownst to her. But we don't want to say she's justified in *believing* her answers because she *doesn't* believe them. We don't want to say she's justified in *thinking* her answers are true because she *doesn't* think this. We have no natural-language way of expressing the mental state she's in, one that's justified but isn't one of (conscious) belief or thinking. We need to coin a new expression—a new piece of jargon—("subpersonal thinking," or something awful like that). Lexical negotiation, of this sort, can happen, I speculate, whenever we try to wed lexical universals to jargon that's been introduced into natural language. (This material on the relationship between "justif(y/ies)" and "know(s)" has been added during copyediting, on March 24, 2020; my thanks to Florence Bacus, Shao-An Hsu, Monika Greco, Patrick McKee, Yingsa Zhang, and Tianyi Zhao for pressing me about this.)

Kornblith (2002, 92, n. 38) says Williams's suggestion that ordinary talk of "justification" is ambiguous is "very reasonable," and he also writes, "it is noteworthy that talk of non-human animals as justified in their beliefs does seem to be simply at odds with ordinary usage." Both claims are wrong as I've just illustrated. And the conjunction-reduction test when applied to justification locutions is fatal to the first suggestion: animals, humans, and nonconscious artifacts can be described as justified in thinking the same *p* for the same reasons, with the same instance of "justified": "We were all justified in thinking an intruder was upstairs because he was so loud," where "we" includes me, my infant, our drone, and the growling cat.

To a very large extent, debate over "justification" and "justif(y/ies)" tracks closely the same debate about "know(s)" that played out in earlier chapters. Like with "know(s)," a contextualist position for justification is tempting;[4] so too, the rejoinders that I've made to the contextualist position about "know(s)" apply here, and, as we've just seen, the same responses can be made to those who are tempted to distinguish genuine "justification" from "lightweight" or pleonastic justification.

Nevertheless, there are important differences between the two words. One important difference is that, as many philosophers have recognized, there is an ordinary distinction between describing an agent as *having* a justification—being able to articulate a justification—and *being* justified. I've already alluded to (and relied on) that distinction, but I'll discuss it in more detail in section 8.5 and in later sections. It's an ordinary distinction that's applied not just to non-human animals (who have justifications without being able to give them), but to humans too. What allows it into logical space (so that we can regard the distinction not only as indicated prima facie by usage but as centrally rooted in our understanding of justification) is the antecedent distinction between ground-floor cognitions and iterated cognitions: in short, that some agents can metacognize and others can't. If an agent is justified, that's—in part—a fact about the agent's cognitive state; as we've seen in earlier chapters, such a fact by no means has to fall within the ken of that agent; if it doesn't, the agent won't be able to correctly articulate her justification, or articulate it at all. If an agent can articulate what justifies her belief, she's capable of metacognition. I'll illustrate many examples of humans who can and can't correctly articulate their justifications in section 8.5.

Let me, however, preliminarily show how the blending of metacognition with belief and justification plays out with an example I've given already. Distinguish

[4] More than tempting; because such a position can essentially be found in Austin's work, it, historically speaking, precedes the forms of knowledge contextualism I discussed in chapter 3. I speculate this is because, unlike "know(s)," as I mentioned in the previous note, "justif(y/ies)" isn't a lexical universal; rather, it's jargon introduced long ago—centuries ago, actually. (This makes it "intuitively" more open to philosophical manipulation.)

(following Neta (2014, 153–154)) *strong* and *weak internalism* about justified beliefs. Strong internalism requires that a "belief can be justified in light of some factor or other only in virtue of the believer's being somehow aware of that factor, and of its serving to justify the belief." Weak internalism (which Neta, and others, support) is the thesis "that a belief can be justified in light of some factor or other only in virtue of the believer's *being capable, by means of reflection, of becoming aware* of that factor, and of its serving to justify the belief" (Neta's italics). Importantly, the weak internalist claims that "whatever justifications we possess cannot be beyond our reflective reach, even if they are not currently within our reflective grasp." This means that whatever justifications are available for what we know cannot be beyond our reflective reach either.

Neta (2014, 153) describes weak internalism as plausible. It's a metacognitive capacity condition on believing agents. It's compatible—at least on a literal reading of my quotation from Neta—with the claim that knowing doesn't require a capacity for metaknowing (of any sort) *provided* this occurs only when such knowing is unaccompanied by belief.

Nevertheless, the animal cases and B.B., discussed in section 6.3,[5] cause trouble for both strong and weak internalists precisely because they're cases where belief is unaccompanied by any awareness (or even capacity for awareness) whatsoever of the factors that justify these creatures' beliefs—because this requires metacognition. But an agent can be unable to metacognize in any way at all the psychological processes by which she's justified (or can be justified) in believing things; she may be utterly incapable of being aware of "a [justifying] factor, and of its serving to justify [her] belief." Consider deduction (which I describe in some detail shortly). What weak internalism seems to require of a deduction of q from p—in order for an agent to be justified in believing q—is that the agent can be aware of the deductive process itself. But even when an animal deduces a result from something it hears (there is an eagle about), it's an additional cognitive requirement for the animal to be aware of this deductive process. It's a subtle empirical question whether an animal that's able to carry out certain primitive deductions is also capable of reflecting on those processes of deduction. One doesn't seem to require the other. I've already discussed this in

[5] Weak and strong internalism also face trouble with humans who have become incapable of the metacognitive processes that these internalisms require. An amnesiac who nevertheless knows his way home (but doesn't know, and is incapable of knowing this) violates both internalisms. So does the blind-sighted individual who nevertheless can guess—where guessing is how her experience feels—correctly whether or not a pencil or a rubber ball is in front of her—within sight. (Such individuals aren't conscious of the visual information that their eyes are nevertheless picking up.) In these cases, knowledge occurs even though the processes by which this knowledge is justified aren't within reflective reach of these agents—not even in principle. Notice that an agent might believe his or her "guesses"; doing so would be justified, although the agent couldn't justify doing so. (So, here, the distinction between having a justification and being justified comes into play: these agents are justified but don't have justifications.)

chapter 6. (My thanks to Florence Bacus, Monika Greco, Shao-An Hsu, Patrick McKee, Yingsa Zhang, and Tianyi Zhao for discussion of an earlier version of my discussion of weak and strong internalism that led to deletions.)

Weak internalism rules out what I'll describe as *episodic deducers*. An episodic deducer is incapable of reflecting on the process of (his own) deductions because he simply can't keep in mind the process of deduction: he deduces *q* directly from *p* and then *moves on*. He doesn't think about the process of deduction at the moment *or* later. It's nontrivial to claim that episodic deducers aren't justified in believing what they believe. I not only think it's false; I think it's empirically refuted.[6]

I've been exploring a significant difference between "justify" and "know"—that metacognitive factors underwrite a distinction between being justified and having justifications that isn't echoed in "know(s)." There's another important difference between the two words, however. This is that—as I show in this chapter and the next one—characterizations that yield necessary and sufficient conditions for the words "justification" and "justif(y/ies) are within reach, given an analysis. It's true that being justified and being justified sufficiently to know—characterized *in general* for epistemic agents—remain currently elusive, as the long frustrating history of epistemology indicates. An obstacle is that the words in this family—"justif(y/ies)," "evidence," "reason," "belief," and so on—like "know(s)," are (among nonphilosophers) without definitions *too*, and this makes them treacherous. Without definitions, it's easy (as the first chapter illustrates), to overlook or sideline crucial uses. The result is premature generalization about what such words "mean."

The words in the justification family, however, *can* be definitively characterized by teasing out from a necessary condition governing justification an exhaustive categorization of possible justifications (although I won't bother with the minutia needed to write it out explicitly). One aim, here and in the next chapter, is, in light of this, to show that previous philosophical presuppositions about conditions on justification (and even "adequate justification")—like previous philosophical presuppositions about knowledge—require too much. Justifications can be (and are) much "thinner" than most have realized.

As I mentioned, it isn't *always* possible to tease out necessary and sufficient conditions for an otherwise valuable word and in this way derive a definition. It can't be done for "know(s)" and "knowledge." It's fascinating that "knowledge" and "know(s)" aren't open to necessary and sufficient conditions—even with a sophisticated analysis of them—and yet words so intimately related to them, like

[6] I'm not done arguing with proponents of positions in the neighborhood of weak internalism. I discuss, in section 8.7, arguments that can be brought to support the position due to Kaplan, Leite, and Neta.

"justification" and "evidence," are. In section 11.3, I'll hazard an explanation for this—it turns on special facts about "know(s)," although it should be pointed out (again) that a word's value—and even its indispensability—in ordinary usage (and in ordinary life) doesn't require a definition.

I frame my approach to the analysis of justification in this chapter and the next via Agrippa's trilemma: A justification for a claim itself needs justification. This threatens agents with justification scepticism: no one's purported knowledge can be justified because doing so derails either in an arbitrary stopping point, a circular repetition of justifications, or a vicious infinite regress. Epistemologists can be classified by their responses to this trilemma,[7] and in *some ways*, my response resembles foundationalism or reliabilism—agents can know things without that knowledge in turn needing to be "justified" by agents. After my full story is told, however, it will be clear it isn't either of these—see my next book, *Challenging Knowledge*, on this.

The kinds of things we speak of as "justified" are several. We speak of cognitive agents being justified or not justified ("the cat was justified to think his meal was about to arrive"), but we also describe actions as justified or not justified ("Bill's firing John yesterday was completely justified"), as well as certain targets—let me call these "contents"—of an agent's thinking as justified or not justified. ("The belief that there are men on Mars has never been justified," "The claim that inflation is always a bad thing, despite what many people think, isn't justified.") In some of these cases, we use other words to stand in for "justified" or "unjustified," such as "out of line" or "wrong"—"It was out-of-line for Bill to fire John yesterday," "the cat was wrong to think his meal was about to arrive"—where "wrong" in the second sentence isn't simply being used to convey that the thought the cognitive agent had was false. In some settings, that is, instead of "justified," or "not justified," we can and do use other words. We also describe certain items—that at first glance are elusive—as justified, as in "That attitude is completely unjustified." Let me briefly describe these various uses of "justify," "justified," and the like, and sort all this out a little.

I'll start with what I called "contents." We certainly do seem to describe beliefs, thoughts, claims, and similar items as justified. ("You think that investing in gold is sensible; that thought isn't justified." "Your belief in God isn't justified," "You claim that 2 plus 2 is 4, but is this claim justified? (really justified)?") What are these "contents"? I chose the word "content" deliberately because what's being described as justified or not justified in these cases are (so I claim) proposition-like—or sentence-like—items to which truth values can be attributed and which

[7] Aikin (2011, 46) describes the challenge as a "hexalemma"; he mentions seven options (apart from blends of positions): justification scepticism, "foundationalism, contextualism (unjustified justifiers), externalism, circularism, coherentism, and infinitism."

are the targets of propositional attitudes. These are also items that we describe cognitive agents as sharing, as in "having the same thought" or "making the same claim." Apart from contents, we also, as I indicated above, treat *attitudes*—using that very word—as justified or unjustified. If attitudes are seen as aspects of human actions (as aspects of speech acts, in particular), then these are cases where the psychological state that accompanies an act (or, linguistically speaking, the force that's part of a speech act) are described as justified; in any case, aspects of actions also seem to be items that we describe as justified or not justified.

Can it be claimed that we never (really) claim that contents are justified or not justified? To support this claim, notice that we don't speak of "contents" being justified (although, after all, that's no surprise since "content" is recently introduced philosophical jargon), but we really don't speak of propositions being justified either. We don't say, pointing to the proposition "2 + 2 = 4" written on a blackboard, that "The proposition '2 + 2 = 4', is justified," or (pointing) "That proposition is justified." We *will* say of a sentence written on a blackboard that, "That's justified," and when pressed with "what's justified?" we will add (while pointing), "that sentence" or "what's written on the board."

This shows, I think, that "proposition" as philosophers use it—to refer to any "content"— has been stretched by philosophers of language in need of terminology; otherwise, as an ordinary word of English, it's used fairly restrictedly, or in only fairly special circumstances. (I'll illustrate where in a moment.) But we do speak quite regularly of beliefs, claims, and the like being justified or not justified. Aren't "beliefs" and "claims" and the like particular kinds of what I'm calling contents? Aren't beliefs and claims, for example, what's expressed by linguistic items (sentences) and aren't they, therefore, the sorts of things that (sometimes) have truth values?

Against this last suggestion would be the counter that, no, what's really being claimed to be justified or unjustified in these cases are *thinking- or uttering-actions of particular contents* (actions of thinking particular things or of asserting them), "believings," "claimings," and so on. Notice I've just fallen into *nonEnglish*, as philosophers often do: a form of speaking that philosophers are sometimes legitimately pushed to because they're trying to describe what no one ordinarily ever talks about. I was slightly unfair in doing this: the ordinary word "claim" in particular, already does double-duty. We can mean by it the very act of "claiming," as in "Your claims are annoying!" where, anyway, it's not obvious that the contents are being described as annoying; but we can instead indicate the target of the claim when we say, "that claim simply isn't true; you should stop claiming that." (Notice: "that" anaphorically refers to "that claim" but "claiming," which appears in the same clause, doesn't; "that claim" refers to a content but "claiming" indicates the claiming-action.) "Belief" doesn't quite do double-duty, but similarly to "claim" and "claiming," we have the closely related "belief" and "believing": "Stop believing such silly things," is a criticism of the act of believing by virtue of a criticism of what's believed. "They both have the same beliefs about this but some of them aren't justified," however, describes unjustified contents that are shared, not psychological states.

Notice that we don't speak, for example, of shared states of anxiety or fear or believings. If we say, "we have the same fears," that stands for, "We fear the same things." We *wouldn't say that* if we were both in a fearful state—that kind of state people sometimes are in—where there's no object of fear, but just a generalized experience of a certain sort. We don't say, similarly, when we're both hungry, "We have the same hunger," nor do we say, "We share hunger," nor "We share the same hunger." Similar psychological states, identical psychological states, aren't described as shared in the way that contents are described; neither are similar actions.

Apart from this, speech acts (generally speaking) are items no one normally talks about. For consider: the *act* of saying "John is running," is best—although still awkwardly—captured by "utterance" ("John's utterance was loud"). This is awkward because it's also philosophical coinage—"utterance" is being used to describe an act of saying a sentence and not the physical item—the noises that a speaker makes—nor the contents, although both of these are items that "utterance," which does multiple-duty, *can* refer to. (See Azzouni (2013b) on "utterance" and "utter.") Utterances, when describing speech acts, *aren't* items we describe as "true" or "false," nor, usually, do we describe them as justified or not justified. We will (in rare circumstances) say things that amount to saying that a speech act wasn't justified, e.g. "Mary shouldn't have said anything while John was still angry"—where this means, "Mary shouldn't have spoken *at all*."

Consider the sentence, "John's belief that extraterrestrials exist isn't justified." *What* is being claimed not to be justified? Is it the psychological standing condition that John is in that's not justified? (It's a bit odd to describe a belief as an action, especially because beliefs can be long-standing or tacit, but let's not worry too much about that now.) Or is it the proposition-like item that's believed that's not justified? How do we distinguish these? It's clear that the psychological standing condition should be described as a "believing" not as "what's believed" and notice that we don't—normally—speak of "believings" at all, let alone as "justified" or "not justified." I indicated earlier why the same is true of "claim." That's one piece of evidence that it's an expression that refers to a content-like item that's what the phrases "justified," and "not justified" are modifying. Notice: we can say, "Although John's belief was true, it wasn't justified." We're speaking of contents here.

Notice that, often, the "force" expressed may be described as unjustified (for example), while at the same time the content associated with that attitude is differently described as justified. One can say, for example, "That attitude isn't justified, although what you think is fine," where what's meant, for example, is that you shouldn't convey your claims as ironic questions.

Notice also that although "proposition" is fairly restricted in how it's used in the vernacular, it's not particularly unnatural to offer the following gloss in terms of "proposition" for "belief" and "claim": "A belief is a proposition that someone believes," and "A claim is a proposition that someone claims." Relatedly, a bit of speech like this is possible. "You claim that the Riemann zeta function has its zeros only at the negative even numbers and complex numbers with real part ½. But this claim isn't justified. For this proposition hasn't been proven yet." It's even natural to substitute "proposition" for "claim" in the second sentence. "Claim," as I mentioned above, does double-duty. So, we need to be careful. A "claim"—used one way—is an utterance with a certain force. That's an action. But a claim—used as the content-target of a claim-action is another use of "claim." This doesn't come with a force, it's a content, of course, that someone has claimed. That someone has claimed a content is a possible *property* of that content; that's not for it—the claim-as-content—to *itself* have a force. It shouldn't be thought that a belief or a claim (when these words are used to describe the content of what is believed or claimed) has both content and force. That's only true when these words are used to describe speech-acts.

In the last paragraph, I pointed to an important fact about "proposition," as it's used in the vernacular. It's quite unnatural to use it with short and simple sentences; but it's quite natural to use it with complex, controversial sentences or ones in dispute (as I did with the Riemann hypothesis). Consider the sentence, uttered during a lecture, "The primary drivers for climate change in the modern era are the greenhouse gases emitted by human activities." It would be natural—although ill-advised—to follow that utterance with, "This proposition isn't justified," or "The proposition just uttered isn't justified."

The foregoing is a *sketch*—of some of the usage data—for the claim that when we speak of beliefs or claims or thoughts as justified (or unjustified), we're often, if not usually, focusing on the proposition-like content that is the target of our psychological states of belief or our claiming-utterances, and so on, and not the action-vehicle (the mental states/actions or the utterance-action) or the cognitive agent. Let me turn next to some necessarily brief observations about the relationships between talk of justification/lack of justification of contents, actions and agents.

First notice that attributions of "justification" to contents and to agents or actions are *not* synonymous. This is shown by applications of the conjunction reduction test: That is—for example—it isn't natural to say, "John and what he believes are justified." Indeed, I think that "justify" when applied to contents is dyadic: a proposition is always justified by something else (what else can justify a proposition is the topic of this chapter and chapter 8). This is important and explains the interesting phenomenon I described in section 5.6, that there are many justifications possible for any proposition. Indeed, the same proposition can be justified (is in a justification relation with) many sorts of things.

Next, cognitive agents who believe something *p* are themselves justified in believing it, so I claim, when what they believe—*p*—is itself justified in some way (by something, a proposition or something else) and the agent bears an appropriate justificatory relationship to that proposition and whatever proposition (or whatever) that justifies it in the dyadic sense. What that relationship amounts to is, in specific cases, different neurologically complex processes that involve perception, reasoning shifts and whatnot. These processes are to be empirically characterized—and at the moment we understand very little about them. Importantly, though, we don't use a dyadic notion of justification when we talk about agents being justified, or being justified in what they believe, think, etc. We simply describe them for example, as being justified in believing *p full stop*.

The way we effortlessly and naturally shift talk of justification (and lack of justification) between agents and contents illustrates the observations of the previous paragraph: Generally, I'm justified in believing *p* (I'm justified in being in a particular mental state) because I cognize (in some way) the justification of my belief *p* (a content). Recall that I wrote, earlier in this section, that "In all these cases, an animal's sources of knowledge justify what she knows. And, in all those cases, just as with us, animals can fail to know but still be justified in believing what they believe." (The first "justify" targets a content: what she knows; the second targets that animals as being justified in what they believe.)

As I also mentioned before, explicit talk of justification often doesn't occur because it's replaced by something else that in fact does the justifying: seeing a proof of *p*, for example, or seeing that *p*, where *p* describes an event that's witnessed. Actions, on the other hand, are often spoken of as justified or not justified in ways that don't always turn on talk of content itself being justified or not justified. If we say, "John wasn't justified in shooting the intruder," we needn't have contents—thoughts or beliefs of John's—nearby that we need to say John wasn't justified in thinking or believing. (He may have fired the gun unjustifiably without thinking of or believing anything specific.) But these *are* connected in the case of mental states/actions, thoughts or beliefs, and speech-acts, utterances; we can say: "John's belief in God isn't justified"; where we mean: what John believes, i.e. the target content "God exists" itself isn't justified.

The last point to make about contrasts between talk of justification, when applied to agents and when applied to contents, is that the grasping/having distinction is live with agents, but not with contents. The distinction turns, as I've suggested, on the particulars of an agent's relationship to a proposition believed, thought (etc.), the item that justifies that proposition, and the relationship between them. Metacognitive elements among these, I believe, enable an agent to grasp and not merely have such a justification.

Because of the foregoing, I'll subsequently not only focus in this book on "justification" as used when we describe the items that agents believe, think, and so on, as justified, I'll also presume that talk of justified or unjustified *agents* derives from an antecedent usage where content-bearing items believed, thought, etc. by those agents are themselves are taken to be justified or unjustified. (I'll slide naturally between applications of "justified" to agents and to contents, as I think we're justified by the foregoing in doing.) A definition, I think, of a "justified cognitive agent," where that agent is justified in having the propositional attitude she has towards a content is available in terms of what it is the agent has a propositional attitude *towards* and that she bears the appropriate relationship (has/grasps) the latter's justification relation to what justifies it. However, because of some of the cases I've given above, I *don't* assume this is true in general of our talk of justified and unjustified actions.

Furthermore, in going forward, I'll help myself to "proposition," as a philosophical piece of jargon, to cover all content-bearing items, beliefs, claims, thoughts, and so on; and I'll focus—as I've suggested I can—on the justification of "propositions," so described, by other propositions, mental states or ways that the world is. I should repeat that what I've said about the justification of propositions, speech acts and agents is sketchy; further, in filling it out I'd also discuss other closely related words and phrases that we ordinarily use, such as "evidence," and the like. I can't now. (My thanks—April 6, 2020—to Florence Bacus, Patrick McKee, and especially to Shao-An Hsu, for challenging my centering my chapter 7 discussion of justification on "propositions"; the class discussion yielded a response to this and the previous eighteen paragraphs into the copyedited manuscript.)

That is, in both this chapter and in chapter 8, I use "propositions" as terminological stand-in-jargon for the targets of agents' cognitions that we normally speak of as justified, "beliefs," etc. And I use the widely accepted linkage of justification to truth to give the promised categorization of the possible ways an agent's "thinkings" can be justified. In this chapter, I focus on the general property of propositions that they can be deduced from other propositions—and how that underwrites justification; in chapter 8, I focus on the general fact that propositions are related to ways the world is (either directly or indirectly) represented—this is one thing that's meant by attributing content to propositions—and the accompanying fact that the "representational content" of propositions can be used to help underwrite justification as well.

I thus endorse the widespread practice (illustrated in chapter 1) of attributing propositional knowledge, and other propositional attitudes, to animals and artifacts. Many philosophers deny the cogency of such attributions because they've thought that "S ϕs that *p*" attributions require the agents to grasp the proposition *p* or the concepts exhibited in *p*. Not so (section 1.4 and chapter 5). The relationship between an agent and a proposition so attributed to that agent is more subtle and flexible than that—propositions are *tools* we use to express the intentional contents in an agent's mind.[8]

The representational and deductive sides of justification face distinctive issues encapsulated in Agrippa's trilemma to justification. On the deductive side, there's the leg of the trilemma involving an infinite sequence of justifications. This has given rise to contemporary infinitist and coherentist responses, which attempt to show that the regress isn't vicious. I undercut infinitist and coherentist responses to Agrippa's trilemma in this chapter. On the representative side, there is Sellars's dilemma for the myth of the given; I tame this dilemma in chapter 8 without sustaining the myth. In section 8.5, I turn to the role of justification in knowledge claims; I also focus on the earlier-mentioned ordinary distinction between "being able to give a justification" and "being justified." Usage allows the latter as an attribution to agents even when the former can't be applied—e.g., in the case of animals and nonconscious mechanisms; these are usually perceived as justified in believing or thinking what they know without ever being able to give what we would call "justifications." In section 8.6, I illustrate how our justification practices allow (and even applaud) our sometimes rejecting demands for justification. In many cases, we think this is *rational*. We understand it as *rational*, that is, to stop the justification regress in many ordinary cases where we do so. I revisit weak internalism in section 8.7, and deepen my objections to the position. Section 8.8 briefly summarizes the two chapters' results on justification, and prepares the reader for the last three chapters of the book.

One point about the methodology of this and the next chapter: Cohen (2016) worries that we don't know what the philosophical term "epistemic justification" means. He's right, although I'm trying to change that by providing a characterization that relies on what it is that we ordinarily do to legitimately justify our knowledge claims. (I assume that philosophers have meant this term to characterize an ordinary already-in-place practice.) Cohen evaluates whether a "theory-neutral" account of this notion is possible—where that means: an account neutral among competing *philosophical* views. I reject the need for an account like *that*: theory-neutral definitions, in the sciences (for example),

[8] Thus, the properties of propositions that my analysis relies on are easily generalized beyond "propositions" as they're typically understood (i.e., as what are expressed by linguistic items like sentences) to pretty much any kind of "intentional" object. Representational properties and deductive properties are all that are needed here (regarding the generalization of deductive properties beyond linguistic items, see my later observations in note 22 of this chapter). As I've already stressed—perhaps at length—no one should put particularly much metaphysical weight on "proposition" as used in this book.

aren't considered virtuous. One motive Cohen has for a theory-neutral definition of "justification" is to make sense of philosophical *disputes*: a theory-neutral notion for the dispute to be over. But really (and this is "good sense"), someone who thinks her own view is *right* should craft notions appropriate to her *view*. If that makes mush of a dispute with some other philosopher whose views are—anyway—wrong, so what?[9] To make sense of a philosophical debate (where one side is wrong), one explains how that side has gone wrong—doing so may involve explaining the inadequacy of a set of concepts that side is using. If it's unclear who's wrong, then (correspondingly) it's not clear what's causing the dispute: searching for a theory-independent set of concepts won't help. Of course, the dispute can involve both sides being wrong (or worse, the dispute can be based on misunderstandings shared by both parties). Even still worse, something may make the dispute irresolvable—a stipulative element, for example, that neither party recognizes is stipulative. None of this requires theory neutrality.

7.2 Justification and Truth

Being justified seems intuitively crucial to having knowledge. Some philosophers, though, mention perception, memory, and testimony as sources of knowledge; and claim that genuine justifications for the knowledge originating from those sources are either absent (or circular). Others disagree.[10] Mostly to blame for this disagreement is the wide application of these words which it's (therefore) hard to see the proper scope of—as well as the similar intricacy and scope of "evidence" and its cognates. Also complicit is that philosophers have modified these words for semi-technical purposes and/or to support theoretical presuppositions. The way, therefore, to avoid the resulting talking-past-each-other debates that discussions in this subject area often end up in is to get clearer about when we apply these words, and how we use them.

So . . . what *is* justification? Philosophers seem to know far less about it than they should. Are there, for example, justificational stopping places? (Are there statements which are either self-justified or not in need of justification?) Many say yes and just as many say no.[11] Another example: consider an infinite chain

[9] Imagine a similar claim: theory-neutral notions of space and time are needed for Newtonians and Einsteinians to debate. Thanks to Megan Entwistle for alerting me to Cohen (2016).

[10] E.g., Lewis (1996, 421–422), Cohen (1998, 290 n. 6), Burge (1993).

[11] The term "stopping place" is Chisholm's (1964, 86). He accepts the existence of these and expresses indifference about whether they "justify themselves" or are "neither justified nor unjustified." Traditional candidates for justificational stopping-place statements are logical and mathematical truths, certain self-ascriptions, and statements about experience.

of statements, . . ., J_{n+1}, J_n, . . ., J_1, C, where C is justified by J_1, each J_i is justified in turn by J_{i+1}, no J_i is a justificational stopping point, and no other justifications for these statements are had by the agent. Call such an infinite justificatory chain *successful* if C is justified by its presence in this chain. *Can* C (and, for that matter, any other statement in the chain) be justified by its mere presence in such a justificatory chain? That is, are there successful (infinite) justificatory chains? Some say yes; others say no.[12] Philosophers apparently don't know enough about how justification works to settle either of these questions in ways that convince opponents.

A third question: Can knowledge be justified by something lacking propositional content? For example, can an agent's knowledge that there is an apple on a table be justified by an apple on the table? Again, some say yes; others no.[13] As twice before, we seem too ignorant about "justification" to settle *this* either. I'll try to show, on the contrary, that we *can* discover enough about how justification works to get answers to *all* of these questions.

Consider the constitutive link between justification and truth. BonJour (1978, 113) writes:

> Knowledge requires *epistemic* justification, and the distinguishing characteristic of this particular species of justification is, I submit, its essential or internal relationship to the cognitive goal of truth. Cognitive doings are epistemically justified, on this conception, only if and to the extent that they are aimed at this goal.

Something like this is right, as other philosophers have also noted.[14] It's hard to put the point precisely, however; and I'm unhappy with BonJour's

[12] E.g., Klein (2003), Sosa (1980), Foly (1978), Post (1980), Gillett (2003). See Aikin (2011) for an excellent discussion and for citations. Also see Turri and Klein (2014a) for recent papers on the topic, and especially Atkinson and Peijnenburg (2017) for a sophisticated (and masterly) presentation of the technical and philosophical issues probabilistic regresses give rise to.

[13] E.g., Williams (2001), Sosa (1980), BonJour (1978). Fogelin (1994, 146) describes the following as a "justificatory principle" adopted by coherentists: "The only thing that justifies a belief is a belief." Williams (2001, 98) asserts that "only that which can be true or false—thus propositionally contentful—can confirm or refute." The primary argument for this is in the influential Sellars (1956). Apart from the question of whether apples can justify knowledge about apples, there is also the question of whether certain *experiences* (especially "raw" ones without propositional content) can do so. I should add that most epistemologists focus on the experiential question rather than on "the apple question." "Sellars's dilemma," as it's widely called, is about the justificatory role of the experiential "Given." I take up this tangled issue in chapter 8.

[14] Burge (1993, 239) writes: "An epistemic reason for believing something would not count as such if it did not provide some reasonable support for accepting it as *true*" (italics his). Aikin (2011, 11) writes: "Justification is truth-directed. . . . Justifying reasons count in favor of a belief's *truth*, not its preferability or other non-truth-directed concerns" (italics his). At the end of Stanley (2005), he speculates that non-truth-directed concerns affect justification relations. Widespread views connecting justification to truth in this way are described by Berker (2013) as "epistemic

characterization, because he uses "essential or internal relationship" and "cognitive goal of truth." (But I'll admit, I don't particularly like my use of "constitutive" either.) In any case, one thing is clear: justifications for our beliefs, in the sense of "justification" relevant to knowledge claims ("epistemic justifications"), put us in a better position to think those beliefs are true. The same seems true of "evidence." If a purported justification or piece of evidence did the opposite—made us less sure of a belief—or if it couldn't change our attitude toward the belief it was supposed to support (because, say, it was irrelevant), we'd reject its status as a *justification* or as *evidence*. ("Why did you bring *that* up?" it'd be natural to complain. "It didn't help one bit.") Some think this apparent truism explains what's wrong with "begging the question": arguments that beg the question don't increase our confidence in the truth of something beyond what we had initially.[15] Let's call this "the truth condition on justification" or "the truth condition." Let's call a justification form "truth-conducive" if it provides either a full or partial justification of the item it justifies—that is, if it either entails the item it justifies or increases its probability above what it would be otherwise.

I called the truth condition a necessary condition on justification; but isn't it sufficient too? Dunno. Some (in certain religious traditions) suggest that faith is a reason to believe—a reason to think *p* is true. Faith in *p*, they also say (some of them say this, anyway), isn't justification or evidence for *p* (and this second point is right).[16] In any case, if the truth condition is a necessary and sufficient condition, it can function as a definition for justification—and given that, I can categorize forms of justification by teasing these categories out from that definition. If it's only a necessary condition, I can derive the same categories. Regardless, the truth condition looks substantial (it has, I mean, a *lot* of content). This isn't because "true" has a lot of content (it *doesn't*); it's because how propositions are made true helps to characterize how propositions can be justified, and what justification is.[17] I turn to this now.

consequentialism." He attempts to undercut them with a family of counterexamples (cases where we're supposed to deny the beliefs in question are justified despite acquiring such beliefs yielding a greater number of true beliefs). Versions of these counterexamples are originally due to Firth (1981). I argue in section 11.4 that these counterexamples *aren't* counterexamples. That is (contrary to what Berker and Firth claim), epistemic consequentialism isn't undercut by these cases. (My thanks to Corey Dethier, on May 14, 2019, for drawing my attention to Berker (2013).)

[15] Sanford (1972, 198).

[16] I owe the suggestion that faith can be a reason to think *p* is true without being a justification for *p* to Asa Zabarsky (communication on February 12, 2018).

[17] See Azzouni (2018) on the distinction between a theory of "true" and a "theory of truths"—it's a theory of *truths* that's needed here—a theory of how truths are made true.

7.3 Justifications Based on Truth-Preserving Deduction

I distinguish "strict deduction" (truth-*preserving* deduction) and weaker truth-increasing deduction.[18] The truth condition directly explains why we can (and do) often use strict deduction for justification. If we know *p*, *q*, *r* are true, and we know *s* strict-deductively follows from *p*, *q*, and *r*, then we can use our knowledge of the truth of *p*, *q*, and *r* to justify our knowledge of the truth of *s*. During discussions of any ordinary sort (*not* philosophical debates with sophisticated epistemic-closure deniers like Robert Nozick or Fred Dretske), if someone retains the negation of a recognized implication *q* and the premises *q* follows from, this is seen as either confused or as trying to cheat.[19] Being sure of the truth of a set of premises *usually* enables surety of the truth of conclusions we *recognizably* strict-deduce from those premises.[20]

"An agent being justified about *q* being true on the basis of a strict deduction of *q* from *p*" is a cognitive process that goes roughly like this. An agent knows that *p* is true and knows that *q* follows from *p*. Then the agent *uses* that knowledge to realize that *q* is true. Here's a simple (but absolutely crucial) question about this process. Is it that *p* is true, and that *p* strict-deductively implies *q*, that (in turn) justifies (for the agent) that *q* is true, or is it the agent's *knowledge* that *p* is true, and her *knowledge* that *p* strict-deductively implies *q*, that justifies (for her) that *q* is true—or, perhaps, justifies her knowledge that *q* is true?

Both ways of speaking are natural (and *seem* interchangeable). This is because we can stress either "knowing that" or "that *p*" when saying "knows that *p*"[21]—we can focus on the cognitive event/state of the knowing agent *or* the target of

[18] I mean both notions to cover what might be called "inferential deduction" where the weaker notion is, for example, probabilistic entailment (an inference from *p* to *q*, where *p* makes *q* more likely than otherwise).

[19] Or it's recognized as a kind of vicious bullying, as when someone in authority—a president, say—tries to force you to agree to a collection of visibly inconsistent statements for his own fun or profit.

[20] The "recognizably" and the "usually" are important. The importance of "recognizably": Humans don't *have* truth-preserving procedures of deducing truths from other truths (e.g., mechanical tools like truth tables) in the sense that they can physically and psychologically embody (perfectly imitate) such procedures. What they *have* are methods of simulating such procedures and/or recognizing that truth-preserving procedures have been simulated successfully. That is, they can get this wrong. This is one reason the "possession" of methods, or the being in the state of having "learned" such methods, of truth-preserving inference tools (for purposes of justification) is nevertheless compatible with fallibilism about knowledge. The importance of "usually": Related to the above, knowledge closure *fails*—that is, not even hedging formulations of the principle in some careful way (e.g., spelling out "recognizably") will save a closure principle from counterexamples. Those *instances* of it, however, that knowledge-closure deniers have tried to deny (e.g., inferences from "I know I have hands" to "I'm not a handless brain in a vat," or from "That's a zebra" to "That's not a donkey cleverly disguised as a zebra") are *fine*. So the failure of (principles of) knowledge closure can't be used as insurance against scepticism. (See section 10.8 on both important points.)

[21] This isn't the whole story of why these locutions seem interchangeable. See chapter 5 for details on the large verbal *mess* that's behind this conflation.

her knowing. These aren't the same, and we shouldn't slide from the first to the second, or vice versa, because of slippery language. Specifically, it's that *p* is true, and that *p* implies *q* is true, that justifies (for the agent) that *q* is true; it's not the *knowledge* that *p* is true and the *knowledge* that *p* implies *q* that justifies either that *q* is true or that justifies the agent's knowledge of *q*.

Suppose the agent talks to himself. "Oh, wow," he says, "*p* is true. Oh, wow, *p* implies *q* too. *That's* why *q* is true." Or, instead: "Oh, wow," he says, "I know *p*. Oh, wow, I know that *p* implies *q* too. *That's* why *q* is true." The second formulation is *wrong*. That the agent knows *p*, and knows that *p* implies *q*, *isn't* why *q* is true. We might say: Sure, but that he knows *p*, and knows that *p* implies *q*, is why he *knows* that *q* is true. Yes; but this focuses on why the agent can know what he knows, not on what it is *about* what he knows that enables him to know it. If the agent didn't know *p*, or didn't know that *p* implies *q*, he wouldn't (of course) know *q*. But if we're focusing on the *something* that the agent knows, and why he knows *that*, then we must focus on the target of the knowing attribution, not that it's what's known.

The upshot: formulations using "know(s)" are parasitical on formulations without "know(s)." That is, that coming-to-know statements are true by deduction relies on those *statements* being implicationally truth-linked. *In turn* (and specifically), an agent's knowing that *q* is true is justified by the deduction she has just completed—a deduction of *q* from *p*. *Because* she knows *that p is true*, and that *p implies q* (that is, because she knows that if *p* is true, *q* must be true), she's justified in thinking that *q* is true. But it's *what* she knows (*p*, and that *p* implies *q*) that's why she knows *q*. *We* describe her as knowing *p*, as knowing that if *p* is true, then *q* is true; and as therefore knowing *q*. She, however, has only to go from *p* and that if *p* is true, then *q* is true, to *q*. She *never* has to cognize that she knows that *p*, and knows that *p* implies *q*. For purposes of successful inference, she doesn't need the concept of "know(s)" at all. That is, it's wrong (for us) to think her *knowing that p is true* primitively justifies *her knowing that q is true*. Instead, it's the if-*p*-is-true-and-*q*-deductively-follows-from-*p*-then-*q*-is-true relation among statements, coupled with the truth of *p*, that justifies (for her) *q*'s truth.

Those who learn something by deduction, therefore, know it by a cognitive process that "piggybacks" on deductive relations between statements. I've spoken of "statements," but I could have used "thoughts," or other vehicles of inference.[22] I'll continue to use "proposition" to stand for any of these.

So, accompanying the distinction between *using* vehicles of cognition (as a reasoning agent does) and *talking about* those vehicles, as we do when we discuss

[22] I *mean* it. Maybe certain animals use *imagery* to make inferences. That diagrammatic proofs in mathematics exist (that Turing computable systems of the manipulation of diagrams—of *pictures*—exist) shows that such psychological mechanisms for representation and reasoning are possible. Given that we're so cognitively adept with diagrams, these mechanisms are surely operative in us and (consequently) in other animals too. (See Azzouni (2017a).)

knowing agents, is the distinction between items of knowledge and what those items are knowledge *of*. To repeat: John knows *p* (let's say). *That John knows p* is one thing, and the *p* (which John knows) is another. These are linked, of course, but shouldn't be conflated as it's easy to do. We often speak of *John's knowing p* as a piece of knowledge that John has; strictly speaking, the piece of knowledge that John has is *p*, not his knowing *p* (that is, one of the things John knows *is* p).[23]

To keep clear on the **knowing-that-***p*/knowing-**that-*p*** distinction, notice that in the way that *knowing* piggybacks on deductive relations, other cognitions also piggyback on these relations. If an agent is *very sure* of *p* and she knows that *p* deductively implies *q*, then she'll (usually) be *very sure* of *q*. Or, if she thinks *p* is *somewhat likely*, and she knows *p* deductively implies *q*, then (given she knows nothing else that bears on the likelihood of *q*) she'll at best think *q* is *at least as likely* as *p*—and consequently that *q*, too, is only *somewhat likely*. (Similar points hold if she is only *very sure* of the deductive link, or thinks such a link is only *somewhat likely*.) And if she's quite sure *q isn't* the case, then because of the deductive relation between *p* and *q*, she can be quite sure *p* isn't the case either. Deductive relations among sentences support many cognitions of agents, apart from knowing. It's a mistake to think justifications based on deductive inferences involve primitive relations among knowing states, e.g., that an agent's *knowing that p is true* primitively justifies her *knowing that q is true*. If so, there are similar primitive relations among many cognitive states, *opining that, thinking that*, etc.

A second point: We mustn't overestimate what an agent *knows* in knowing *q* by an inference from *p*. Although semantic ascent is needed to characterize the cognitions of epistemic agents, those agents needn't engage in (or have the ability to engage in) semantic ascent themselves. Philosophers not only *use* an enriched set of concepts—including "know(s)" itself—to characterize what an agent knows in knowing *q* because of an inference from *p* (something necessary), but also often *attribute* that enriched set *to* the agent (which *isn't* necessary). There is a tendency, specifically, to think that when an agent infers, she also grasps the *notions* of *inference, truth, knowing*, and *proposition* (or *sentence*)—in the sense of *being aware of* these notions, that is, of *knowingly employing* them. But this isn't required for successful inference.

"The semantic ascent fallacy" is an attribution of an enriched set of concepts (that *we* use to describe what an agent knows) *to* an agent solely on the basis that she knows something.[24] It's no fallacy to *argue* that agents must grasp these

[23] Knowings and iterated knowings are being distinguished here.

[24] Chisholm (1964, 90) accuses unnamed philosophers of this; he writes: "Logicians now take care to distinguish between the *use* and *mention* of language. . . . As we shall have occasion to note further, the distinction has not always been observed in writings on epistemology." To some extent, my discussion of the semantic-ascent fallacy is my gloss on Chisholm's (brief and somewhat obscurely described) charge.

notions to engage in correct inference—unless those arguments *trade on* that fallacy. I'll discuss, in this section and in chapter 8, arguments for the general claim that in order to know *p*, agents must have many accompanying concepts—among them ones that arise by semantic ascent. But let me illustrate now why it's clear both that we don't have to attribute semantic-ascent concepts to successfully reasoning agents and that in fact we don't, in practice, attribute such concepts to such agents.

Someone deduces "This reptile is cute," from "All turtles are cute" and "This reptile is a turtle." This cognitive process *uses* three propositions—or thoughts. The *agent* doesn't have to think *that* these propositions are true, nor does she have to think *that* the second and third propositions imply the first. All she needs for inferential success is to cognitively move (deductively) *from* the second and third propositions *to* the first. She's justified, of course; but her being justified doesn't require an ability to articulate to herself *that* she's justified by explicitly cognizing that the second and third propositions imply the first. Most average adults *can't* do this; even acute above-average adult reasoners can't justify themselves this way unless they're appropriately trained in *logic*; only those who possess concepts like *proposition, implication*, and so on, and *know how to use them* can give this kind of justification.

I'm relying on a simple fact. To think, "Turtles are cute," doesn't *require* thinking anything about *the proposition itself*, either during (or after) thinking it. An agent, of course, *might* think, "I don't have much evidence for thinking that turtles are cute," or he *may* realize, "The sentence that I'm thinking of, 'turtles are cute,' has three words," or he may even think, "The proposition 'turtles are cute' isn't just meaningful, it's true too!" But none of these thoughts is required for successful deduction. *An argument is needed* that any agent who has thoughts and infers using those thoughts must have the enriched capacity to think *about* his own thoughts and their relationships to other thoughts.

Along the same lines, an agent who can execute turtle/reptile inferences needn't be able to articulate to herself that "All turtles are cute" and "This reptile is a turtle" are *propositions* containing *words* (or *concepts*) structured so that those propositions have *implication relations* among one another. To draw inferences, she needn't even realize she's using thoughts (or sentences) to think what she's thinking. She need only actually *do this* regularly and correctly; she needn't be able to *describe* (or understand) that she's doing this.

Here's notation to distinguish inferences *of* propositions from thinking *about* inferences between propositions. An inferring agent S bears a certain complex relationship R to the vehicles he uses to infer.[25] Call *p* the set of items he bears this

[25] He's *thinking that*..., for example.

relationship to. So this epistemic agent is in a certain relation: SR*p*. Nothing so far requires that for SR*p* to hold, S must grasp facts *about p* or R. Nothing requires him to recognize what *p* is, that it *is* a certain vehicle (of thought, say) or certain concepts structured in a certain way, or whatever. Nothing requires him to recognize what R is. R is complex, and in the case of animals encapsulates, among other things, badly understood sensory/cognitive processes the agent goes through—e.g., comprehending something read. This involves a successive sequence of experiential states underwritten by various neurological changes, and the sensory interfaces between that agent and the world, and so on. Included in "R," therefore, is the *cognitive support* an agent S has that enables his inferences, whatever an agent uses to manage this. For example, someone may follow a syllogism (and realize the conclusion is justified) by reading and understanding what she's reading.[26] To *describe* a reasoning process SR*p* (one's own or another's), of course, necessarily requires "semantic ascent"—talking *about* R and *p*. We bear, that is, a different relationship R* to *p**, where R* and *p**, respectively, involve R and *p* as targets.

To repeat the essential point with examples: Small children reason successfully; so do animals. But small children and (most) animals can't reason about, describe, or think about their own reasoning processes or their vehicles. A position that overlooks (or explicitly denies) how little is conceptually required for agents to reason from one thought to another, and to be justified in that reasoning, treats reasoners as (potentially) possessing a metalogical grasp of their own reasoning mechanisms. This is overreaching. In saying this, I'll repeat again that I'm not denying the possibility of *arguments* for such a claim; I've only argued in this section that as far as the sheer *phenomenology* of reasoning is concerned, an ability to reason (successfully and with justification) doesn't require metalogical competence.

The phenomenology of reasoning that I've just described is in serious tension with the earlier-mentioned (section 7.1) weak internalism. On that view, it's important to distinguish a genuine inference of *q* from *p* from a mere causal movement in the agent's mind from *p* to *q*. This is to be managed by (as Hlobil, Malmgren, and Neta argue) the agent having a commitment to *p* supporting *q*, whether this commitment is something the agent is conscious of or not.

[26] Reading, I claim, like listening, doesn't require one to attend to and be aware *of* the physical/semantic structure of the sentences so apprehended (or even be *capable* of this): one can just *use* them, and "see through them" to what they're about. Indeed, this experience is the normal state of affairs when reading or listening to sentences. This is just a specific illustration of my claim that if an agent is in the relation R to a *p* (that enables the agent to be justified in the conclusion of a piece of reasoning), that agent isn't required to apprehend R or *p*, make R or *p*, or what they come to, the target of her thinking. I'll return to this later in the chapter.

Correctly excluding certain kinds of "causally induced" cognitive movements from the category of inference (e.g., blows to the head that induce a belief in *q* from believing *p*) doesn't mean that every kind of cause must be excluded. Indeed, this is impossible because carrying out an inference *is* a neurophysiological causal process of a very specific sort: one that we call "inference." Whether this inferential process induces a "commitment" or not—and to what—turns crucially on what such a commitment is supposed to amount to. The phenomenology of one's experience of inference—especially that it's the *same*, phenomenologically, when one is a child and later—militates against this commitment having any sort metacognitive component *whatsoever*.[27] It also militates against such a commitment being "subconscious," and yet being additional to the mere deductive movement (however that's neurophysiologically realized) from *p* to *q*. Lastly, it militates against the *capacity* for metacognizing one's deduction being a condition of one's inferences being genuine inferences. If "internalism"—weak or strong—requires this, than internalism so called faces a heavy burden. *Why* should we regard successful ground-floor inference as requiring so much?

I'll return to this form of overreaching in chapter 8.[28]

[27] The point I'm stressing—illustrated in my own case by my cognitive development from a capacity, in early childhood, of being able to engage in quite sophisticated inferences, although without any metacognition whatsoever, to the case, much later in life, of publishing research logic that involved substantial metacognition—is that early childhood inferences are phenomenologically indistinguishable from most of the inferences that the subsequent adults still carry out—this includes the kinds of inferences that I'm engaging in right now as I write this. Seeing, that is, that *q* does or doesn't follow from *p*, where I'm thinking from *p* to *q* is often unaccompanied by any thoughts about *p* or *q* themselves—in a word, "using" them but not "mentioning" them. And, in the case of many adult humans, I think, there can be successful reasoning without any capacity for metacognition of this sort.

[28] Neta (2019, 183) requires accounts of what's come to be called "the basing relation," "the distinctive kind of explanatory relation that holds between a belief and the reason for which it is held," to be able to address two issues. The first is to distinguish the precise explanatory relation from the broader reasons an agent may have a certain belief (e.g., S believes *p* because she's carried out an appropriate deduction vs. S believes *p* because she's psychotic). I'm unconvinced this demand can be *met*. (My reasons are complex and can't be given in this book—but they involve the rule-following problem; see Azzouni (2017c).) The second reason is, essentially, that an explanation is needed for why an agent's current justification for *p* can be challenged by misleading evidence against it that she's concurrently aware of and takes seriously, although this misleading evidence doesn't challenge her having been justified if she *later* becomes aware of it and subsequently takes it seriously. Nor is her being justified challenged from the perspective of a third party who is aware of (and takes seriously) that misleading evidence if the third party knows she isn't aware of this misleading evidence. Neta cleverly uses this phenomenon to argue for weak internalism. I undercut this (and provide a different explanation for the phenomenon in section 8.7.)

7.4 Infinite Chains of Justifications

7.4.1 Infinite Deductive Sequences of Justifications

The foregoing analysis of the strictly deductive side of justification is enough of a basis to evaluate the prospects of an infinitist response to Agrippa's trilemma. *This is the most technical part of the book.* Those allergic to technicalities (of this sort) or convinced on other grounds that an infinitist response to Agrippa's trilemma is a non-starter can go straight to chapter 8. (I don't recommend this, however, because these technicalities are extremely interesting, and reveal quite a bit along the way about inferential justification—in particular, significant differences between truth-preserving deductive inferences and inferences that aren't truth-preserving.)

An infinitist responds to Agrippa's trilemma by suggesting that an ω-sequence of justifiers, $J_0, J_1, \ldots, J_n, J_{n+1}, \ldots$, where each J_i is justified by J_{i+1}, no J_i is a justificational stopping point, and where no other justifications for any of these statements are available to the agent, can nevertheless *by its properties as a whole* justify J_0.[29] I'll first consider ω-sequences of propositions, $J_0, J_1, \ldots, J_n, J_{n+1}, \ldots$, as above, where each proposition *strict-deductively* implies the one before it.[30] Call these *deductive ω-sequences.* If justification piggybacks only on strict deduction in standard logic, as I'm initially assuming, then this brand of infinitism is easily ruled out by the considerations that follow.

It's a *theorem* (in standard classical logic) that if an agent can be justified in her belief that S is true *on the basis of an ω-sequence*, as above, then there is a specific J_k that the agent *knows* to be true; and therefore all but a finite number

[29] ω is the smallest infinite ordinal, the one that corresponds to the natural-number ordering. What I'm here calling "ω-sequences" are often instead called "chains" in the infinitist literature. My reasons for avoiding "chain" nomenclature are alluded to later in note 35. I'm describing what Aikin (2011) calls "pure" infinitism. His "impure" infinitism allows experiential stopping points in justification—but only when accompanied by additional reasons that, in turn, need justifications (see especially Aikin (2011, 133)). This alternative infinitism avoids *some* of the objections I raise in this section to infinite sequences of justifiers because there need only be an infinite *braid* of justifications without any particular justificational thread in that braid being infinite. Aikin shares with rich epistemologists the assumption that any capacity for knowledge *requires* subsidiary cognitive capacities and (this is the second key step I reject) a lot of other subsidiary knowledge all of which (on Aikin's view) needs justification. I discuss this in section 8.4. My denial of this assumption, however, plays no role in the objections to infinitism that I raise here.

[30] What are called for, more accurately, are infinite branching justificatory ω-*trees*, because deductive implication allows statements to be justified by two or more propositions, as with modus ponens. I'll continue restricting myself to the case of ω-sequences, here and in what follows, suppressing explicit discussion of justificatory trees except when it matters to the argument. (See Atkinson and Peijnenburg (2017), 174 n. 8)—hereafter "A&P"—for a list of philosophers who have discussed justification trees.) I should add that although I'm only focusing on the deductive tissue connecting the justificatory relations here, there may be additional conditions on the relations for them to be justificatory. This doesn't make any difference to the subsequent discussion.

of the J_is are justificatorily *redundant*. This is because, in standard logic, deduction is *warrant-transferring* but not *warrant-originating* (to borrow the warrant talk some epistemologists like); the entailment relations themselves don't contribute any warrant in addition to the warrant they convey from the premises. So deduction in classical logic functions purely conditionally: *If* the premises are true, the conclusion is too. This points to the fundamental distinction between soundness and validity—in particular that we *cannot deduce soundness from mere validity* (except in the case of logical truths). I've stressed that this is a fact about standard classical logic because logical principles, or, more generally, principles of entailment, *needn't* be pure justification transmitters; and as we'll see shortly, probabilistic entailment *isn't* justification-neutral; it contributes additional justification—and this is significant.

Notation: I'll use "$\Rightarrow$" for the "material conditional" of classical first-order logic and "$\models$" for its metalanguage cohort "implies." In first-order logic, and in many other useful logics where an analogue of the material conditional appears, we have the metamathematical "deduction theorem": for sentences p and q, $p \models q$ iff $\models p \Rightarrow q$; that is, $p \models q$ iff $p \Rightarrow q$ is a validity.[31] When I speak of justification, however, even when justification is taken only to be formal deduction, I follow A&P in using a reverse arrow, and in also reversing the order of implications, like so: $q \leftarrow p$ ("q is justified by p"). Finally, for readability, I'll sometimes enclose ω-sequences of propositions in brackets, like so: $\{p_1, p_2, \ldots, p_n, \ldots\}$; when we push the Agrippan regress systematically enough, these brackets will be valuable.

In classical logical settings, modus ponens is needed to escape premises continuing to be conditions on the truth of the conclusions drawn. That is, to justify q by means of a logical inference from p, p itself must be justified *full stop*. Otherwise we're stuck with: $p \Rightarrow q$. If q is only conditionally justified in a sequence by further propositions that are only conditionally justified, that's insufficient for a deduction of q—for a justification of it. Even an infinite number of conditionals without anything given *full stop* outside a conditional won't help. That is, the justificational content of the above deductive ω-sequence: $J_0, J_1, \ldots J_n, J_{n+1}, \ldots$, is completely captured by transforming it into an ω-sequence of the conditional statements, $J_1 \Rightarrow J_0, J_2 \Rightarrow J_1, \ldots, J_n \Rightarrow J_{n-1}, J_{n+1} \Rightarrow J_n, \ldots$, i.e., $J_0 \leftarrow J_1, J_1 \leftarrow J_2, \ldots, J_{n-1} \leftarrow J_n, J_n \leftarrow J_{n+1}, \ldots$

But *this* means that if we know J_k is true, for some k, and we know this only because of other J_is in the sequence, we must know it because of some J_{k+r} that we *know* to be true. Otherwise, the truth of J_k remains promissory: we don't know that it's true; we only know that it's true *if*. . . That is, we know that each finite sequent of reasoning, $J_i \Rightarrow J_{i-1}$ is valid; we don't know further, at least on the basis of

[31] See, e.g., Kleene (1971, 90–98) for a general statement of the result and for proofs in classical and intuitionistic logic.

validity, that *any* of these are sound (that any of their consequents is true). This is *bad*; what the deductive infinitist needs is a deductive ω-sequence of justifiers for J_0 that confers justification on J_0 that no finite subsequence of such justifiers manages. This won't happen on the basis of pure (truth-preserving) deduction—at least in standard logics.[32]

Aikin (2011, 79), following Klein (2007), distinguishes between "transmissive infinitism" and "emergent infinitism." The first requires J_0 to be justified by virtue of each member of the sequence justifying the one before it. This is insufficient for strict-deductive sequences, as I've already explained, because of the conditional nature of strict deduction (unless logical-truth stopping points are acknowledged—and then in the linear case J_0 is a logical truth). Emergent infinitism allows a conclusion J_0 to be justified by the sheer *existence* of the entire justifying ω-sequence itself. For purely strict-deductive sequences, this deserts first-order logic because first-order logic has the compactness property.[33]

More than noncompactness is needed. *A* sequence of propositions of the form, $J_1 \Rightarrow J_0, J_2 \Rightarrow J_1, \ldots, J_n \Rightarrow J_{n\text{-}1}, J_{n+1} \Rightarrow J_n, \ldots$, must exist, where $\{J_1 \Rightarrow C, J_2 \Rightarrow J_1, \ldots, J_n \Rightarrow J_{n\text{-}1}, J_{n+1} \Rightarrow J_n, \ldots\} \models J_0$. Although this is *allowed* by a failure of compactness, it doesn't specifically follow from its absence. Furthermore, it must be that only *certain* ω-sequences (not all of them) imply their initial proposition, J_0.[34] Klein and Aiken, as well as others, when offering infinitism, don't acknowledge they're deserting compactness, introducing a new (infinitary) argument form, and apart from all this, changing logic dramatically. Doing so is a *big deal*, and deserves official notice. Of course, they could (and probably *should*) argue that I've inappropriately narrowed the suggestion; it's not the strict truth-preserving deductive

[32] Klein (2003, 86) argues that—all things being equal—we have more justification for *p* than we have for *q* if we have an *r* such that $r \Rightarrow q$ when we don't have a corresponding *s* and similar conditional for *p*. He asserts this, apparently, for all forms of justification. But it's impossible to take this seriously with respect to truth-preserving justification. Klein (I assume) doesn't mean to rely on the fact that $r \Rightarrow q$ is strictly weaker than *q* because *r* could be false. But then no value—provisional or otherwise—is introduced by mentioning an unjustified *r* and noting it implies *p* since this amounts to (leaving aside the possibility that *r* is false) *r* & *q*, which is stronger than *q* alone. Perhaps things change when we consider probabilistic entailments since the entailments themselves provide confirmation. I take up whether this can help the infinitist in section 7.4.2.

[33] That is, if any infinite set of propositions implies a conclusion, then a finite subset of that set does too. (See any standard logic textbook.) Consider, alternatively, a substitutional-quantifier language where, if P is any formula with *x* free, and $a_1, a_2, \ldots, a_n, \ldots$ are all the constants of the language, then we have: $Pa_1, Pa_2, \ldots, Pa_n, \ldots \models (x)Px$, although for no finite subset of statements $Pa_i, Pa_{i+1}, \ldots, Pa_{i+m}$, (where $a_i, \ldots, a_{i+m}$ are—not necessarily consecutive—constants from the sequence $a_1, a_2, \ldots, a_n, \ldots$) is it the case that $Pa_i, Pa_{i+1}, \ldots, Pa_{i+m}, \ldots \models (x)Px$. A number of publications discuss the implications of the loss of compactness, given the substitutional interpretations of the quantifiers. See Dunn and Belnap (1968) for one of the earliest discussions.

[34] Why *some* and not all? Because, as it's been noted in the literature, a sequential regress of this sort can be (in principle) constructed for *any* proposition. This has been labeled, in the infinitist literature, the "reductio argument." Not all of these ω-sequences can imply their first proposition on pain of the resulting logic being trivial. See in particular Post (1980) and the discussion of the literature on this in A&P, 128–131. See A&P, 120 n. 3 for further citations.

core of justification that allows emergent infinitism, but the truth-likelihood-increasing aspect of justification that does this. A&P, nearly enough, do argue this way. Fair enough; I turn to this suggestion in the next subsection.

Before doing so, however, I need to make some points about the deductive case that generalize to the probabilistic case (and that I'll need). Imagine, as suggested, that we understand the offer of the deductive version of infinitism as *revisionist*. The infinitist is taken as arguing this way: all that matters to justification is the truth condition: Any form of argument (finite *or* infinite) is acceptable if it's truth-preserving (or truth-likelihood-increasing). If we change the deductive logic as above, then what results are *new forms* of infinitary inference that satisfy the truth condition because *some* deductive ω-sequences, of the form: $J_1 \Rightarrow J_0, J_2 \Rightarrow J_1, \ldots, J_n \Rightarrow J_{n-1}, J_{n+1} \Rightarrow J_n, \ldots$, imply their initial propositions, J_0; these should be added to our stock of justifiers.

So, notice first that the notations, $J_0, J_1, \ldots, J_n, J_{n+1}, \ldots$, or $J_0 \leftarrow J_1 \leftarrow J_2 \leftarrow \ldots \leftarrow J_n \leftarrow J_{n+1} \leftarrow \ldots$ are misleading, at least as initial descriptions of the arguments that Agrippa's trilemma is based on. Sextus says (quoted in A&P, 4):

> In the mode deriving from infinite regress, we say that what is brought forward as a source of conviction for the matter proposed itself needs another source, which itself needs another, and so on *ad infinitum*, so that we have no point from which to begin to establish anything, and suspension of judgement follows.

The Agrippan challenger starts from what arguments ordinarily look like, and his challenge generates an ω-sequence of *finite* arguments, where, for each premise in any argument in the sequence, there is an argument later in the sequence justifying that premise, where the entire sequence begins with a finite argument for J_0, the proposition to be originally justified.[35] Thus (in the linear case, where each argument is a one-line deduction), $J_1 \Rightarrow J_0, J_2 \Rightarrow J_1, \ldots, J_n \Rightarrow J_{n-1}, J_{n+1} \Rightarrow J_n, \ldots$, is correct.[36] Characterizing the Agrippan challenge this way explains the infinitary option not being taken seriously (until the twenty-first century). That such a sequence of arguments doesn't justify J_0 is obvious because each argument itself is as provisional as the unjustified premises it starts with. The right way to picture the infinitist deductive proposal, therefore, is (as I've argued) as introducing a new (infinitary) argument form that's supposedly truth-conducive. That is, we have now introduced new arguments of the form:

[35] This is why I avoid "chain" to describe the infinitary option, and instead use "sequence."

[36] Replacing implication arrows with reverse justification arrows: $J_0 \leftarrow J_1, J_1 \leftarrow J_2, \ldots, J_{n-1} \leftarrow J_n, J_n \leftarrow J_{n+1}, \ldots$

$$\{J_1 \Rightarrow J_0, J_2 \Rightarrow J_1, \ldots, J_n \Rightarrow J_{n-1}, J_{n+1} \Rightarrow J_n, \ldots\} \Rightarrow J_0$$

Call these *ω-sequence validities*; call infinitary propositions of this form—ones that needn't be validities—*ω-sequence-antecedent propositions*. (I promise: I'll only use this second awful bit of nomenclature *twice* more.) Klein (2003, 87–88) distinguishes between pessimistic and optimistic infinitism. The pessimistic infinitist worries that ω-sequence validities don't exist; the optimistic infinitist hopes they do. Sosa (1980, 10–13), similarly, distinguishes between "actual" and "potential" regresses, where the former are the desired (truth-conducive) ω-sequences, and the latter aren't. Both philosophers are noticing something they aren't fully explicit about. Although finite (first-order) arguments can be (finitely) *tested* for validity,[37] this is false of *ω-sequence-antecedent propositions* without a *prior* description of them that strongly restricts the forms their finite arguments can take. We need, that is, enough of a grip on the pattern of sentences in an ω-sequence: $J_1 \Rightarrow J_0, J_2 \Rightarrow J_1, \ldots, J_n \Rightarrow J_{n-1}, J_{n+1} \Rightarrow J_n, \ldots$, to know whether it validly implies J_0 or not. That is, that *the ω-sequence* itself implies J_0 needs a further justifier JJ_1; we need:

$$JJ_1 \Rightarrow \{\{J_1 \Rightarrow J_0, J_2 \Rightarrow J_1, \ldots, J_n \Rightarrow J_{n-1}, J_{n+1} \Rightarrow J_n, \ldots\} \Rightarrow J_0\},$$

where JJ_1 provides a reason (a justification) that the ω-sequence itself, $J_1 \Rightarrow J_0$, $J_2 \Rightarrow J_1, \ldots, J_n \Rightarrow J_{n-1}, J_{n+1} \Rightarrow J_n, \ldots$, implies J_0 as opposed to not doing so. In the case of purely deductive sequences, what this amounts to is that JJ_1 must deductively entail:

$$\{J_1 \Rightarrow J_0, J_2 \Rightarrow J_1, \ldots, J_n \Rightarrow J_{n-1}, J_{n+1} \Rightarrow J_n, \ldots\} \Rightarrow J_0.$$

Putting the entire thing in reverse justification arrows, what's required is:

$$\{J_0 \leftarrow \{J_0 \leftarrow J_1, \ldots, J_n \leftarrow J_{n+1}, \ldots\}\} \leftarrow JJ_1$$

Let's suppose we can get this.[38] Given the infinitist dialectic, however, JJ_1 *isn't* a stopping point either—because there are no stopping points! Let $\{J_0 \leftarrow \{J_0 \leftarrow J_1, \ldots, J_n \leftarrow J_{n+1}, \ldots\}\}$ be J^1. The regress generates a second ω-sequence like so:

$$J^1 \leftarrow JJ_1, JJ_1 \leftarrow JJ_2, \ldots JJ_n \leftarrow JJ_{n+1}, \ldots$$

[37] That is, there is a *decision procedure* for the recognition of (first-order) proofs.

[38] That is, let's suppose we can design a logic that enables us to deduce results about *ω-sequence-antecedent propositions*.

We now need a justification that this new ω-sequence implies J^1. *And so on.* If we let $J^i \leftarrow \omega$, for any J^i, as above, stand for the infinite argument, $J^i \leftarrow K_1, K_2 \leftarrow K_3, \ldots K_n \leftarrow K_{n+1}, \ldots$, where the K_i are the propositions of ω-sequences as constructed above, then the full regress (with appropriately placed ellipses) looks like this:

$$\ldots\{J^n \leftarrow \ldots\{J^1 \leftarrow \{J_0 \leftarrow \omega\}\} \leftarrow \omega\}\}\} \ldots \leftarrow \omega\}\}\}\ldots\} \leftarrow \ldots$$

Being consistent (and true to the spirit of infinitism) with regard to the infinitary regress that's required by repeated demands for justification has driven us to argument forms far beyond ones that infinitists have imagined (or, anyway, dared tell us about). By pushing the position the way I have (in perhaps annoying detail), I've illustrated a point Fumerton (1995, 57) makes, that justification challenges, even in the case of deductive inference, can't be restricted only to premises: the deductive links themselves can (and should) also be justified.[39] But infinitists can't simply take these additional demands for justification on board and treat them the same way as they hoped to treat demands for justifications of premises. The regress generated by doing so is impossible to deal with (at least in the pure deductive case considered so far). I'll make a few further points about this in the next paragraph.

The infinitist hopes the infinitist leg of the Pyrrhonian challenge, which until the twenty-first century was only employed to facilitate scepticism, can instead reveal other forms of truth-enhancing justification (that have been hitherto overlooked). But for these justification tools to be cogent, certain conditions must be met. First, these new tools of truth-enhancing justification must be ones that are technically *well defined*. I've been primarily focused on this issue in the foregoing; considerations about compactness and the like have been seen to be relevant.

But second, the new argument forms introduced by the infinitist must be ones that *we can use*. This issue already arises in a muted form in the current literature on infinitism—namely, the widely mentioned finite-minds objection.[40]

[39] Fumerton focuses only on probabilistic inferences—not deductive ones—and it's this version of his "mushrooming" that A&P consider. But in post-Quinean times, it ought to be obvious that deductive inferences are similar to probabilistic ones in this respect. If logical principles are open to revision, as Quineans claim, then all the more so they're open to needing *justifications*. I consider probabilistic entailments in the next section.

[40] See A&P, 15–16, and chapter 5 for discussion, and for citations of its use by other philosophers. Notice that the argument I've given here isn't really an example of this (somewhat vague) objection. For one thing, I've tacitly accepted the initial idea that an infinite sequence of arguments *can be* surveyed, at least in the sense that such sequences of arguments can be given global constraints that indicate properties all the members of such a sequence must have (just as, by analogy, the sequence of numbers 2, 4, 6, . . . can be in a sense fully surveyed, and certain properties of all of them recognized,

But the concern takes a far more vicious form (as I've just shown) when we push the need for justifiers more consistently than infinitists have heretofore. Leaving aside the fact that the justification patterns in question are structurally intricate (not mere ω-sequences of finite arguments, but involving the embedding of ω-sequences within other ones), it's also clear that as soon as we turn to questions of the justification of the *logic itself*—of the entailment relation—we're in danger of losing the technical well-definedness of the inferential rules in play. We can't pretend that's no issue by letting the infinitist simply take some logic or other for granted—for by doing that, the infinitist is treating those logical principles foundationally, contrary to the infinitist spirit which accepts *no* foundations. But even waiving considerations of infinitistic spirituality (adopting to this extent, that is, an impure infinitism), the infinitist is still in trouble, as we've seen, because by introducing infinitary forms of argument, she has already deserted standard logic—at least with respect to *deductive* ω-sequences, and faces the burden of showing that arguers can grasp the generalized ω-sequences of arguments that arise when demands for justifiers are consistently pursued.

7.4.2 Probabilistic Infinite Sequences of Justifications

Probabilistic inferential chains are a very natural generalization of deductive ω-sequences because ordinary justification surely involves more than deduction. It's a serious mistake, however, to think that the introduction of probabilistic inferential steps doesn't change much. It changes, actually, a lot; and what's interesting is that the changes aren't particularly obvious either to ordinary reasoners or to professionals. One difference is that transitivity fails. Another, more important difference (for current purposes) is that the entailment relation *itself* provides confirmation independently of the premises the entailment is from. Both these changes, as I mentioned, are counterintuitive. I'll take up transitivity first, and then turn to the second point.

The vast majority of our inferences are mixed, involving both deductive and non-deductive steps.[41] And, although strict implication obeys transitivity

e.g., that they're all divisible by 2). The problem, despite this concession, is that we're being asked by the infinitist to do much more than that. I discuss this further, in particular the finite-minds objection, after I generalize ω-sequences to include probabilistic entailments.

[41] This is true for two reasons. The first is that we're often inferring in ways that are obviously not truth-preservingly deductive (e.g., drawing conclusions that are only more likely given the assumptions). But second, even when engaging in what we officially take to be "formal deductions," we're always using methods of recognizing these strict deductions that *aren't* strictly deductive—or, more accurately, aren't "everywhere truth-preserving." I discuss this further in section 10.8.

(unless we change the logic), because probabilistic inference (in general) doesn't, this means that mixed sequences won't obey transitivity either (unless we constrain the probability links with special Markov conditions). Here's a simple illustration from Black (1988, 431):

P1: Paul is a logician who has forgotten Zorn's Lemma.
P2: Paul is a logician.
P3: Paul can state Zorn's Lemma.

P2 follows strict-deductively from P1. P3 follows from P2 because of the high likelihood that any logician can state Zorn's Lemma. P1 justifies P2, and P2 justifies P3, but P1 won't justify P3. This is related to a common observation about probabilistic reasoning (and confirmation, generally) that contrasts with strict deduction.[42] Strict deduction is locally constrained this way ("$\models$" stands for "follows from," and "$\cup$" for union): For any two set of propositions, Γ and Ξ, and for any proposition, τ, if $\Gamma \models \tau$, then $\Gamma \cup \Xi \models \tau$, as well. That is, what follows strict-deductively from a set of propositions still follows if that set is augmented. This is valuable in deduction because we can combine sets of propositions without disallowing any statements we've already deduced from those statements.[43] Likelihood inferences are different. Paul's being a logician increases the likelihood he can state Zorn's Lemma; but it doesn't do so in company with Paul having forgotten the lemma. Because likelihood inferences are sensitive to what's left out, it's rational to draw those inferences from as large a class of one's beliefs as possible, and update the non-deductive inferences in light of new acquired beliefs.

In the rest of this section, I'll focus on non-deductive inferential links providing confirmational content; in the next section, I'll evaluate whether this enables the sustaining of infinitistic inference patterns, as A&P hope. I'll rely closely on A&P's discussion in what follows.

To this end, I first introduce the notion of *probabilistic support.* Let $P(A|B)$ stand for the probability of A given that B. We say that B raises the probability of A if the probability of A given B is higher than the probability of A given $\neg$B, that is, if:

[42] Again, this is a fact about strict deduction *as we currently view our deductive logic,* not if we change it. But these would be nontrivial and unappealing changes, as I indicate in a moment.

[43] Thus we can augment empirical theories with mathematics and not worry that results (that follow deductively from the individual theories) *don't* follow from the combination. For that matter, we can pool *empirical theories* and not worry that what follows deductively from the individual theories *doesn't* follow from their combination. (Imagine how bizarre the practice of science would be if we couldn't so combine scientific theories with one another or with mathematical theories.)

$$P(A \mid B) > P(A \mid \neg B),$$

Or, equivalently,[44]

$$P(A \mid B) > P(A).$$

An ω-sequence of purely probabilistic justifications, therefore, $J_0 \leftarrow J_1 \leftarrow J_2 \leftarrow \ldots \leftarrow J_n \leftarrow J_{n+1} \leftarrow \ldots$, is one where we have, instead of logical entailments, probabilistic support relations, $P(J_i|J_{i+1}) > P(J_i)$, for all J_i. That is, each item in the ω-sequence is probabilistically supported by the item after it. It might seem like we have the same situation we have with purely deductive ω-sequences: call it the *modus ponens problem*. J_0 has a greater probability than otherwise *if* J_1. J_1, in turn, has a greater probability than otherwise *if* J_2, . . ., and so on (forever); but these conditionals are insufficient to yield a probability for J_0; they only yield a probability for J_0 *if*. . . In other words, as in the deductive case, it seems that it *isn't* the case that:

$$\{P(J_0 \mid J_1) > P(J_0),\ \ldots, P(J_n \mid J_{n+1}) > P(J_n),\ \ldots\} \Rightarrow P(J_0) = p,$$

where $0 < p \leq 1$.

On the contrary. A&P show that under a wide range of circumstances ω-sequences of probabilistic justifications *do* yield specific values for the target probability $P(J_0)$. In classical logic, ω-sequences of deductive justifications of finite arguments aren't truth-conducive. But in the *standard* probability calculus, ω-sequences *are*—at least (as I said) they're so under a wide range of circumstances.

It's important to see why (and when) this happens—if only to evaluate whether it really does supply the lifeline infinitism needs. Consider, first, that any finite n-subsequence of a deductive ω-sequence, $J_1 \Rightarrow J_0, J_2 \Rightarrow J_1, \ldots, J_n \Rightarrow J_{n-1}$, can be put in the logically equivalent form, $(J_n \,\&\, (J_n \Rightarrow J_{n-1}) \,\&\ldots\&\, (J_1 \Rightarrow J_0))$. This form makes it obvious how, at each stage, the truth-conduciveness of the entire (finite) sequence up to that point is entirely dependent on the last member J_n.

In the probability case what corresponds to modus ponens are the principles of total probability;[45] for every J_i:

$$P(J_i) = P(J_i \mid J_{i+1})P(J_{i+1}) + P(J_i \mid \neg J_{i+1})P(\neg J_{i+1}),$$

[44] See A&P, 38 n. 39, for the proof of this.

[45] This is the "rule or law" of total probability, 2.4, of A&P, 54. It's due originally to Andrey Kolmogorov.

and (of course),

$$P(\neg J_i) = P(\neg J_i \mid J_{i+1})P(J_{i+1}) + P(\neg J_i \mid \neg J_{i+1})P(\neg J_{i+1}).$$

By starting with these rules for $P(J_0)$and $P(\neg J_0)$, and substituting successively in each J_i and $\neg J_i$ instance of them, the right-hand side of the instances of the rules for J_{i+1} and $\neg J_{i+1}$, A&P rewrite finite subsequences of $J_0 \leftarrow J_1 \leftarrow J_2 \leftarrow \cdots \leftarrow J_n \leftarrow J_{n+1} \leftarrow \cdots$, that is, $J_0 \leftarrow J_1 \leftarrow J_2 \leftarrow \cdots \leftarrow J_m$, in terms of the conditional probabilities $P(J_{i-1}|J_i)$ and $P(J_{i-1}|\neg J_i)$, $1 \leq i \leq m$ which are treated as the probabilified entailment relation (corresponding to modus ponens), and $P(J_m)$ and $P(\neg J_m)$, which are treated as premises. Then, relying on the fact that $P(J_i|J_{i+1}) > P(J_i)$, for all *i*, $P(J_0)$ is evaluated as $m \to \infty$. Following A&P, first consider the case where, given an ω-sequence, $J_0 \leftarrow J_1, \ldots, J_n \leftarrow J_{n+1}, \ldots$, the conditional probabilities $P(J_i|J_{i+1})$, for all *i*, are the same, and the conditional probabilities $P(J_i|\neg J_{i+1})$, for all *i*, are the same as well. Letting $\alpha = P(J_i|J_{i+1})$, and $\beta = P(J_i|\neg J_{i+1})$, for all *i*, and after a finite number of substitutions[46] that mimic the deductive form $(J_m \& (J_m \Rightarrow J_{m-1}) \& \ldots \& (J_1 \Rightarrow J_0))$, we find (A&P, 71, equation 3.15, rewritten to fit my notation):

$$P(J_0) = \beta + \beta(\alpha - \beta) + \beta(\alpha - \beta)^2 + \cdots + \beta(\alpha - \beta)^m P(J_m).$$

Because this ω-sequence is one of probabilistic support, $0 < \alpha - \beta < 1$, and so $\beta(\alpha - \beta)^m P(J_m)$ goes to zero as $m \to \infty$. The result (A&P, 72, equation 3.17) is that

$$P(J_0) = \beta / (1 - \alpha + \beta),$$

which, for $0 < \alpha, \beta < 1$, is well defined (and not zero). That is, the contributions of the "premises" $P(J_i)$ and $P(\neg J_i)$ to the probability of J_0 vanish in the limit—unlike with deductive ω-sequences.

A&P (73) then generalize this result to where the conditional probabilities—$P(J_i|J_{i+1})$ and $P(J_i|\neg J_{i+1})$—vary for *i*. In this case, let $\alpha_i = P(J_i|J_{i+1})$, $\beta_i = P(J_i|\neg J_{i+1})$, and $\gamma_i = \alpha_i - \beta_i$, where, because of probabilistic support, $0 < \gamma_i < 1$.

Then, proceeding as they did in the first case, the result is (A&P, 73, formula 3.20, rewritten in my notation):

[46] That is, after a finite number of substitutions, starting with J_0, of the form, given, e.g., (1) $P(J_i) = P(J_i|J_{i+1})P(J_{i+1}) + P(J_i|\neg J_{i+1})P(\neg J_{i+1})$, (2) $P(J_{i+1}) = P(J_{i+1}|J_{i+2})P(J_{i+2}) + P(J_{i+1}|\neg J_{i+2})P(\neg J_{i+2})$, and (3) $P(\neg J_{i+1}) = P(\neg J_{i+1}|J_{i+2})P(J_{i+2}) + P(\neg J_{i+1}|\neg J_{i+2})P(\neg J_{i+2})$, substituting for $P(J_{i+1})$ and $P(\neg J_{i+1})$, respectively, $P(J_{i+1}|J_{i+2}) P(J_{i+2}) + P(J_{i+1}|\neg J_{i+2})P(\neg J_{i+2})$ and $P(\neg J_{i+1}|J_{i+2})P(J_{i+2}) + P(\neg J_{i+1}|\neg J_{i+2})P(\neg J_{i+2})$.

$$P(J_0) = \beta_0 + \gamma_0\beta_1 + \gamma_0\gamma_1\beta_2 + \cdots + \gamma_0\gamma_1\cdots\gamma_{m-1}\beta_m + \gamma_0\gamma_1\cdots\gamma_m P(J_{m+1}).$$

A&P show that the term $\beta_0 + \gamma_0\beta_1 + \gamma_0\gamma_1\beta_2 + \cdots + \gamma_0\gamma_1 \cdots \gamma_{m-1}\beta_m$, always converges as $m \to \infty$. The other term, $\gamma_0\gamma_1 \ldots \gamma_m$, however, goes to zero (or not) depending on how the conditional probabilities, $P(J_m|J_{m+1})$ (that is, α_m) and $P(J_m\neg|J_{m+1})$ (that is, β_m) act as $m \to \infty$. If (as $m \to \infty$) $\alpha_m \to 1$ at least as rapidly as $1/m \to 0$ *and* if $\beta_m \to 0$ at least as rapidly as $1/m \to 0$, then it's not the case that $\gamma_0\gamma_1 \ldots \gamma_m \to 0$.[47] That is, the value of $P(J_{m+1})$ continues to matter to the probability of J_0 in the limit.

These results are importantly further generalized to cover the additional justification challenges that I argued are required by the infinitist view of justification, with respect to the "entailment" relations—in this case, the conditional probabilities. Notice that the results just reviewed treat the conditional probabilities, $P(J_i|J_{i+1})$ and $P(J_i|\neg J_{i+1})$, as merely given (without justification), in analogy with the treatment of deductive entailment relations as just given (and without justifications).[48] If these, in turn, generate regresses of justification (as they must), then we must introduce justificational trees (or nets, if you will); and corresponding results must be given for conditions of convergence similar to the results A&P have for the cases I've described—which they do.[49]

7.4.3 A Failing Grade for Infinitism, Nevertheless

These results don't transparently salvage infinitism. I now argue that, in fact, infinitism fails as a response to the original Agrippa's trilemma *despite* these striking mathematical results.

[47] Or, as A&P, 99, state "formally," $\gamma_0\gamma_1 \ldots \gamma_m \to 0$ if $\exists c > 0$ & $\exists N > c$: $\forall n > N$, $1 - \gamma_n > c/n$.

[48] A&P somewhat underplay this by writing, for example (95–96): "It is perfectly possible to unpack the conditional probabilities and consider them as targets that are themselves justified by further probabilistic chains." They also write (96), with respect to a specific (imaginary) case that they give about reproducing bacteria and that I discuss at the end of the next subsection, that "conditional probabilities arise from observation and experiment. Research on many batches of bacteria have established the relevant conditional probabilities, α and β. These conditional probabilities are typically obtained by repeated experiments: they are measured by counting how many 'successes' there are in a given number of trials." It should be perfectly obvious, given the Agrippan dialectic, that of course the conditional probabilities *must be* (in turn) justified—and that in the imaginary case A&P are describing, the empirical processes used to establish the conditional probabilities α and β *are* forms of justification. I discuss this in the next section.

[49] See A&P, section 8.5. The results are established via an isomorphism to results established about higher probabilities. There are intricate mathematical constraints under which these results are established. A&P sketch (e.g., 180–181) results that show that when some of these constraints are dropped, there are still domains of convergence.

I'll start with a constructive point. Neither of the two cases in the last two sections is a natural one. This is because the first involves pure deductive regresses and the second involves pure probabilistic regresses. But as I mentioned at the beginning of section 2, justifications—both in ordinary life and in the sciences—involve a mixture of *both* sorts of inference.[50] It's easy, however, to extend the convergence results described in the last section to mixed cases. Consider a justificatory ω-sequence,

$$J_0 \leftarrow J_1, J_1 \leftarrow J_2, \ldots, J_{n-1} \leftarrow J_n, J_n \leftarrow J_{n+1}, \ldots.$$

where each "←" may either be deductive or probabilistic. Call these justificatory sequences "mixed" justificatory sequences; and call any successive deductive subsequence, $J_{i-1} \leftarrow J_i, J_i \leftarrow J_{i+1}, \ldots$, of a mixed sequence a *deductive block*. As long as all the deductive blocks in a justificatory sequence are *finite*, A&P's convergence results follow nevertheless. This is because—in brief—blocks can be replaced with single propositions, and the resulting (infinite) probabilistic sequence converges iff the original one does. So that's the good news.

The bad news will take time to explain because it isn't about a fault in A&P's technical results; it's about how these technical results bear on our already-in-place notion of justification. What A&P offer by way of supporting infinitary inference patterns is actually a finite justification of an infinite sequence of justifications—one that itself generates new sequences of justifications. Thus, even if there are ordinary argument patterns that A&P's convergence results apply to (which I'll argue at the end of this section isn't true), they nevertheless don't actually establish what's needed, which is the introduction of new infinitary justification patterns. We have, instead, an illustration of our ordinary finitary justification patterns being applied *to* an infinite sequence of arguments—which isn't the same thing at all. To think it is confuses reasoning *about* a pattern of arguments with reasoning *with* that pattern of arguments.

To show this, begin with the "Carl the Calculator" case that Podlaskowski and Smith use to try to bring the finite-minds objection against A&P. Podlaskowski and Smith (2014, 216) write (italics theirs):

> [I]magine Carl, whose impressive talent in calculating conditional probabilities is strangely at odds with his ability to grasp various concepts. Carl has no problem solving all manner of complex equations, including those involving conditional probabilities. . . . Yet there are various concepts which he is entirely

[50] A&P 2017 don't take account of this anywhere in their book, although, as I immediately argue, it doesn't affect their technical results.

> incapable of grasping, some of which might feature in reasons whose probabilities of being true are conditional on other reasons. Suppose that Carl is given two lists, an infinite list of conditional probabilities and an infinite list of reasons. Unbeknownst to Carl, the two lists correspond perfectly: the list of probabilities . . . capture(s) the probability of each reason being true, conditional on its predecessor. Moreover, some of the members of the list of reasons are comprised of those concepts that Carl is incapable of grasping. Even if Carl were capable of working through some infinite list of reasons, at some point on the list at hand, Carl would fail to comprehend the concepts deployed. But he would have *no problem* doing the corresponding calculations. Does merely calculating the probability of the chain make Carl justified in holding any of those beliefs, when Carl is incapable of understanding the concepts on which those beliefs depend? Surely not. If an agent *cannot* understand some of the reasons in the infinite chain, it is difficult to see how those reasons can do any justificatory work for him.

In the process of crafting a response to this, A&P (116) claim, "for us, as for Podlaskowski and Smith, Carl fails to justify."

Contrary to both A&P and Podlaskowski and Smith, Carl has *completely* justified the target proposition J_0. He has done so, however, in a way that neither party to this debate recognizes.[51] Suppose, first, that Carl is dealing with an ω-sequence of probabilistic justifiers,

$$J_0 \leftarrow J_1, J_1 \leftarrow J_2, \ldots, J_{n-1} \leftarrow J_n, J_n \leftarrow J_{n+1}, \ldots.$$

There are two cases. For the first, imagine Carl doesn't understand many or most of the J_is, for $i > 0$, although he understands J_0. If he relies on some of the J_is he doesn't understand to carry out his probabilistic reasonings, and justify J_0, he's engaging in a form of justification that's very common in ordinary (research) mathematics. It's *often* that mathematicians engage in what may be described as "blind calculation" where a piece of reasoning crucial to a proof is mechanically checked for validity without grasping its content, or how that content shifts under syntactic manipulations. Knowing that a set of calculational rules are validity-preserving and applying those rules to a statement or formula often lead

[51] Given the setup of the example, in particular, that "unbeknownst to Carl the two lists correspond perfectly," *Carl* doesn't recognize he's justified the target proposition J_0 either. Notice, however, that the key point Podlaskowski and Smith try to establish, "If an agent *cannot* understand some of the reasons in the infinite chain, it is difficult to see how those reasons can do any justificatory work for him" (italics theirs) *doesn't turn* on this aspect of the case. My objections don't turn on it either. (Carl is *justified* in either case: in one he knows he's justified; in the other he doesn't.)

to a sequence of intermediate steps that one doesn't recognize the meaning of. This doesn't induce a failure to have justified the result.[52]

What I'm here calling "blind calculation," it's important to realize, is what's normally called rule-governed inference in mathematics. We recognize the validity of the steps of an argument by recognizing it fits certain inferential forms. If "internalist" views of justification—recall my discussion of them at the end of section 7.3—require denying that inference on this basis is genuine, that's a real problem for such views: they deviate from our ordinary understanding of much of ordinary mathematical practice and (arguably) all of our logical practices. It doesn't change the case if, instead of recognizing the validity of steps in a proof, we are instead recognizing probabilistic entailments.

Imagine now that Carl doesn't understand J_0. Does this mean it's not possible for him to justify J_0 or know that J_0 is true? No. In addition to calculational methods of recognizing the truth of J_0 that I just mentioned (and which Carl can use to recognize truths, even without premises), if we can know things on the basis of testimony—because we've read them in books we can independently verify are trustworthy—we can learn that formulas are true, and know this without understanding them. $E = mc^2$ is probably the most famous equation in all of physics; if it's right, it's known to be true by more people than any other equation—and it's known to be true by a great many people who don't understand it. All the more so, these people (who don't understand it) are nevertheless justified in thinking it's true.[53]

In any case, what Carl does to understand J_0 is closely related to what A&P do to establish their results about probabilistic sequences (indeed, the Carl example has been designed by Podlaskowski and Smith for just this purpose), and this fact reveals something else that seems to have been overlooked by all the parties to this debate, namely that Carl has engaged in a piece of *finitistic* reasoning that's roughly of the following sort. He has recognized that

$$J_0 \leftarrow \{J_0 \leftarrow J_1, J_1 \leftarrow J_2, \ldots, J_{n-1} \leftarrow J_n, J_n \leftarrow J_{n+1}, \ldots\}$$

But *how* did he do this? He did it by recognizing that the sequence $J_0 \leftarrow J_1$, $J_1 \leftarrow J_2, \ldots, J_{n-1} \leftarrow J_n, J_n \leftarrow J_{n+1}, \ldots$, has a certain property, in particular, that the conditional probabilities $P(J_i|J_{i+1})$ and $P(J_i|\neg J_{i+1})$, for all $0 \leq i < \infty$, obey the

[52] When changing variables or using other computational/algebraic shortcuts to manipulate integrals and the like—especially when the formulas are complex—mathematician aren't keeping the meanings of all the intervening formulas generated clearly in mind, or even *at all* in mind. The same is true in logic when, for example, many quantifiers are embedded in a complex formula. The advantage of mechanical computation in mathematics and logic is precisely that meanings can be left behind without damaging proof (i.e., justification).

[53] Internalists about justification, I think, must accept this.

conditions that imply convergence. Call this property Y. He has realized, that is, that $Y\{J_0 \leftarrow J_1, J_1 \leftarrow J_2, \ldots, J_{n-1} \leftarrow J_n, J_n \leftarrow J_{n+1}, \ldots\}$, and he has also realized that $Y\{J_0 \leftarrow J_1, J_1 \leftarrow J_2, \ldots, J_{n-1} \leftarrow J_n, J_n \leftarrow J_{n+1}, \ldots\} \Rightarrow J_0$. What we have here, therefore, is a mixed justification (assuming Carl has probabilistic truth-enhancing reasons to think $Y\{J_0 \leftarrow J_1, J_1 \leftarrow J_2, \ldots, J_{n-1} \leftarrow J_n, J_n \leftarrow J_{n+1}, \ldots\}$) coupled with some deductive reasoning. Carl has, in short, a finitary justification of the form: $J_0 \leftarrow J^{meta}$. J^{meta}, notice, isn't any of the J_is in the sequence Carl is reasoning about.[54] That's because the justification Carl has engaged with is about the entire series of justifications. That's legitimate, and similar to the reasoning mathematicians engage in when proving results about, for example, transfinite arithmetic. To show that $1 + \omega = \omega$, one needn't survey ω in the sense of having available "in one's mind" every number in the ω-series. One must have in mind certain properties of the whole series—properties sufficient to establish results about the whole series—but that doesn't require a detail-grasp of every item. The same is true of the justification J^{meta} that Carl has for J_0. He needs to grasp ("understand") *that* the series of arguments, $J_0 \leftarrow J_1, J_1 \leftarrow J_2, \ldots, J_{n-1} \leftarrow J_n, J_n \leftarrow J_{n+1}, \ldots$, has certain properties (that force convergence); he doesn't have to, as a result, understand every J_i. This shows that debates about whether Carl has to "have available" or "understand" the J_is misses the point—it betrays a failure to see the nature of the justification Carl has for J_0.

There is a fundamental distinction between reasoning *through* an infinite (or finite) sequence of steps in an argument, and reasoning *about* that sequence—this distinction can be used *against* the infinitist. Reasoning *about* an ω-sequence of arguments is meta-reasoning: it's reasoning *about* that sequence. Reasoning *through* an ω-sequence isn't meta-reasoning: it's the step-by-step reasoning from one sequent in the ω-sequence to another. The Sextus quotation (and challenge) is concerned with "reasoning *through*," and not reasoning *about*. Furthermore, reasoning *through* plausibly requires understanding each sequent reasoned through—although I've argued against this interpretation of the process above. *Regardless of what I've argued*, reasoning *about* doesn't require this; it only requires grasping whatever properties of the sequents necessary to carrying out whatever inference one's trying to carry out. Analogously, I can reason about "p_1 & p_2 & . . . & p_n" by deriving some result based on the fact that at least fifteen &s appear in the formula; this needn't require understanding *any* of the p_is.

Notice what I'm (ultimately) claiming here. A&P's technical results don't show what they think they show. They don't show that infinite sequences of arguments are justifying as *wholes*. What they show, instead, is that if we, in a situation, recognize *that* an infinite sequence of propositions—starting with J_0—has the properties they describe, then we can (finitistically) reason *about* that infinite

[54] Notice also that, according to the infinitist, J^{meta} isn't a stopping point—it can be used to generate another regress.

sequence of propositions and in that way extract a finite probabilistic justification for J_0. It does *not* show that infinite argument forms are among our stock of justifying arguments.

Could A&P concede what I've claimed but argue that they've at least shown the revisionary possibility of adding to our stock of justifiers infinite sequences? No—not if we distinguish "reasoning through" from "reasoning about." Anyone who recognizes a target probability on the basis of convergence reasoning about the sequence *isn't* reasoning through that sequence, as the infinitist imagines, but reasoning about the sequence, just as I've depicted Carl as doing. Reasoning *through* the sequence remains the impossible task it has always looked like it is (especially to the ancient Greek sceptics): forever reasoning *from* one sequent to *another* and never coming to an end . . .

One of the results A&P celebrate (section 5.3) is that the difference between the limit probability of a convergent ω-sequence and finite subsequences of it can be calculated, so that reasoners can decide when it's appropriate to stop carrying out inferences—and in doing so, they can calculate how inaccurate their having stopped where they've stopped is (and play that against how many reasons they must keep in mind). This process is clearly one of reasoning *about* the ω-sequence and thus seeing how much of it is needed to reason *through*.

We could take this last idea and, focusing on it, deny that the infinitist project is one of introducing whole infinitary pieces of reasoning. Instead, leaning heavily on probabilistic justifying sequences, we can treat the process as one of introducing "provisional" justifications on the basis of a calculation of how close to the probability of the whole we've reached. But thinking of justification this way is *foundationalist* in spirit—not infinitist. We are now considering introducing finitary arguments that confer a certain probability on the conclusion—not provisionally but absolutely. We *show* that they do this by an evaluation of their relations to infinite sequences of justifiers, but we don't reason through these infinite sequences; rather, a finite argument is given.

Although the considerations I've just given are damaging enough to the infinitistic leg of Agrippa's trilemma to give up on it, it's worth taking a moment to notice something else: how artificial the cases are in which we actually *do* have enough access to the conditional probabilities of an ω-sequence in order to know about the *entire series* that it obeys the mathematical conditions for convergence.[55] I'll start with A&P's opening illustration (2), meant to motivate the infinitistic take on justificatory regresses:

[55] All the more so, therefore, for the generalized cases where we're to know this about the infinite regresses generated by justifying, in turn, the conditional probabilities *too*.

> What would count as a good reason for believing that a snake has escaped and installed itself in my bedroom? Here is one: an anxious neighbor knocks on my door, agitatedly telling me about the escape. But how do I know that what the neighbor says is true?... My friendly neighbour shows me a text message on his cellphone, just sent by the police, which contains the alarming news.... [H]ow do I know that the police are well-informed?... I call the head of police, who confirms the news, and says that he was apprised of it by the director of the zoo; I call the director, who tells me that the escape has been reported to her by the curator of the reptile house, and so on.

Two points about this purported piece of ordinary reasoning: First, the reasons raised as justifiers are *quite* open-ended and varying in their properties. Anything, from intricate deductive reasoning, to probabilistically justifiable claims, based on common-sense induction, to scientific facts (all differing greatly in what probabilistically supports them, *and to what degree*), may be invoked. We can see this, in part, because we can imagine that the very sequence mentioned above could have gone differently: perception (on the part of the director) could have intruded, and justifications exploring whether and how much she has used hallucinogens (during therapy, for example) could have intruded instead. There is *no telling* what kind of reasons and what sort of probabilistic entailments might arise. The nature of the challenges to be made to reasons that have been given (at any stage) makes it seem quite unlikely that any probabilistic constraints can be placed on the ω-sequence being generated.[56]

The artificiality of the kinds of cases that *do* obey these conditions deserves further scrutiny. Here is a case that A&P (61) describe as a "real-life probabilistic regress"—I've changed their notation for ω-sequences to fit mine (79–80):

> From our experiments we know that the probability that Barbara [a bacterium] has [a trait] *T* is considerably greater if her mother has *T* than if her mother lacks it. So if J_0 is "Barbara has *T*" and J_1 is "Barbara's mother has *T*," then we can say that J_1 probabilistically supports J_0. [Assume that experiments have shown that] the probability that a bacterium has *T* if her mother has *T* is 0.99, and the probability that a bacterium has *T* if her mother lacks it is 0.02.

Using A&P's results given here in section 7.4.2, it follows that $J_0 = \beta/(1-\alpha+\beta)$, that is, 2/3.

How *representative* is this case? Very, if we're *not* thinking of it as an example of an infinite regress of *arguments* that infinitists are concerned with—but

[56] In particular, that the condition described in note 47 is even *likely* to be satisfied.

instead as an empirical argument about bacteria. In that case, probabilities of this sort can *definitely* be calculated; and the calculation—as I indicated in the discussion of Carl the Calculator above—is a *finite* argument *about* a sequence of probabilities of events (a sequence, actually, that, as A&P admit, isn't infinite but ceases when tracing back Barbara's ancestry by leading either to a non-bacteria ancestor, or to a mutation in one of Barbara's ancestors which resulted in the first appearance of *T* in her ancestry). If we're thinking about the example as an infinitist should, however, then the sequence of justifying reasons traces back from the conditional probabilities (justified by such-and-such considerations about lab experiments) as well as the other sorts of regresses I've described. The result instead is one where we rapidly lose touch with general constraints on the mathematical properties of the (infinite) regress.

7.5 Conclusion

I'm finished exploring one branch of justification—the inferential branch. The "take home" result is that the sheer presence of transmission steps for a justification never—on its own—suffices to provide a stopping point for justification. In this sense, transmission links for justifications are well named; calling them "transmission links" indicates they're provisional, even if they add probabilistic support, because they're based on something else that provides the stopping points for justification—if there are any stopping points, of course. In the next chapter, I complete my analysis of justification by exploring the tangle of issues surrounding the question of "stopping points" for justifications.

8
Representational Justification and Challenges to "the Given"

8.1 Representational Justification Characterized

The study in the last section, of strict-deductive and likelihood transitions in justification reasoning, is an application of the truth condition (section 7.2). Are there other models of justification similarly connected to that condition? One other, so it seems. The cogency of the ordinary practice of justifying (some of) what we cognize—thoughts, beliefs, etc.—on the basis of what we see (for example) turns on the truth condition too, but in a way that's different from how (truth-preserving or likelihood-increasing) inference turns on the truth condition; in this case, a cognized item's truth is justified by what that item is *about*.

Let's start by assuming that the correspondence theory of truth holds of certain statements, such as "The apples in Room 221 are red." Suppose, further, there are only red apples in Room 221. "The apples in Room 221 are red" is true *because of* these red apples. It seems, therefore, that those red apples can be used by an agent who sees them to justify "The apples in Room 221 are red." Let's call this "representational justification."[1]

For deductively based justifications, my *use of* a deductive relation, the one between "All apples are fruit" and "Those apples are fruit" (say), is what justifies my conclusions, e.g., that *those apples* are fruit. Similarly, my *use of* a representational relation between red apples and the proposition "Those apples are red" is what justifies my thought that those apples are red.

During deductive justification (section 7.2), the agent cognitively *travels along* the deduction to knowledge (or to another epistemic cognition, e.g., "pretty sureness") of a conclusion. The agent's justification for knowing q on

[1] Perfectly suitable terminology eludes me. "Semantic justification" and "referential justification" fit specialized cases, where a sentence, "Some roses are red," say, is true because "is red" applies to the things that "roses" refers to. What a sentence expresses, and that it's true, is due to word meaning, its compositional structure, and, crucially, how the world is with respect to what the words in that sentence refer to. An agent's relying on this is what enables her to "semantically justify" her knowledge that some roses are red. See the discussion that follows. At the end of this section I generalize "representational justification" to cases where "semantic" or "referential" sounds wrong because the relevant truths aren't correspondence truths.

Attributing Knowledge. Jody Azzouni, Oxford University Press (2020). © Oxford University Press.
DOI: 10.1093/oso/9780197508817.001.0001.

the basis of another proposition *p*, for example, depends on the implication relation between *p* and *q* that the agent employs. The same is true of someone who justifies "some apples are red" by means of red apples—someone who engages in representational justification, as I call it. In inferential justification, a relation between propositions ("truth enhancement") is used justificatorily. In representational justification, a semantic relation—between a proposition and what it is that makes that proposition true—is instead what an agent uses justificatorily.

In both cases, the agent is justificatorily enabled to believe because of her capacities to exploit inferential (or representational) relationships; but she needn't be aware of those capacities to *understand* the inference that justifies the proposition she knows or to *understand* the proposition itself, and to know *it*. The agent needn't understand or be aware *that* she has to be in certain sensory/cognitive states in order to understand and know what she understands and knows, nor does she have to understand that these sensory/cognitive states enable her to go through a certain relational process to what she understands—via a proposition, say, that describes a state of affairs. In the deduction case, the agent must acquiesce in the correctness of the deduction (the agent must *draw the conclusion*). That *sensory/cognitive process* (and what goes into it) is part of what makes the relation R possible that the agent bears to something—a structured something that enables her conclusion to be justified. But, as I indicated, *none* of that needs to be targeted by her thinking.

In the representation case, the agent recognizes a certain state of affairs is true. To do so, she's in a certain cognitive state (or process) and she utilizes a certain proposition representing that state of affairs. But here too, neither that cognitive state (or process), nor the proposition itself, nor the semantic relation the proposition bears to the state of affairs need be a target of her thinking. She needn't know anything about these things. She's justified, of course, in what she thinks (thinking that *p*) because of the state (or process) she's in, and because *p* represents a certain state of affairs. Part of this justification is a semantic relationship between the proposition in question and the world that the agent relies on. The agent can *see* the red apples in Room 221, and then justifiably think: "the apples in Room 221 are red." The agent initiates (and undergoes) a complex sensory/cognitive process that involves both her competently *thinking* the proposition (e.g., the thought) coupled with her sensory/cognitive interaction with the world that bears on what she thinks. But *this* process, although crucial to determining that *the apples* justify her belief, needn't itself be in the scope of her thinking. She needn't be aware that she's *seeing* apples. In the case of deductive justification, as I've just indicated, something similar occurs: there is an understanding of propositions but there is also a sensory/cognitive engagement with the world—for example, if someone is reading a sequence of sentences in a press release purporting to give an argument; but the agent needn't be aware that she's seeing/cognizing those sentences.

Exactly as in deductive justification, representational justification piggybacks on representational relations between propositions and the world. And, just as with deductive justification, the agent can be in cognitive states other than knowledge. The agent may only be very sure that the thing in the distance is a predator, or she may think that it's somewhat likely. These cognitive states turn on her more-or-less confidence in the representational relationship between the propositions she's thinking and the world—that they do, indeed, represent the world as it is, just as her cognitive states vis-à-vis inferences can turn on her more-or-less confidence in the truth-conducive nature of those inferences. This is *me* saying this: she needn't be aware that she's having a thought and that her confidence turns on its truth-veridical relationship to the world. She can be worried (and only worried) about whether that thing over there is a predator.

That is, the semantic-ascent fallacy (section 7.3) looms again, threatening to turn what's only a cognitive *option* for some knowing agents into a necessity for all of them. It's natural to use "grasp" and write, for example: "The agent, on the basis of understanding a proposition, must recognize it's true because of a state of affairs—her justification turns on her *grasp* of a particular semantic relation holding between the proposition in question and the world." But "grasp" dangerously sounds like more than the characterization of an agent as only having a thought (and thus *using* that thought's relation to the world), but in addition *thinking about* the relation she's using. That is, it's tempting to think that on the mere basis of an agent having a thought about the world that's justified (because of what she sees), she must grasp *that* her thought has a semantic relation to the world that determines that it's true, as well as grasp that her *seeing* her particular locale of the world justifies that thought via its semantic relation.

The latter thoughts, however, are sophisticated. An animal seeing a predator in the distance has a justified thought as a result. (And so she runs away.) She doesn't *have to* think: "This thought I'm having is made true by something in the world—something I'm seeing." Nor does she have to think: "Whoa! Look at that big scary thing I'm *seeing* over there. Seeing experiences (come to think of it) are usually veridical, so I'd better start running." We, who describe the sensory/cognitive process the animal is going through, one that helps justify her thought, of course must invoke *thoughts*, how they're *structured*, and whatever *relationship* those thoughts have to the world. We also have to include the sensory/cognitive relationship the animal is in *with* the world.

But without an *argument*, it's hard to see why the animal, justified in what she thinks, needs to be able to do *any* of this. She only has to *be in* these relationships—she only has to *appropriately have the thought*, that is, with her senses working correctly, her cognitive faculties operating correctly, and so on. She doesn't have to cognize that *any of this is the case*, or pat herself authoritatively on the back for being in an optimal cognitive/sensory state. The relationship her thought has to the world, and the cognitive process/state she's in, does all the work for her.

The same for us: When I'm in a meditative (cognitively sophisticated) state of mind, I entertain my sensory/cognitive relationship to the world, the semantic relationships of my thoughts, and enjoy how everything in me is optimal (or rue that I'm under par). When I'm having a thought, I can *simultaneously* (or so it appears) contemplate the relationship of that thought to the world. But *most of the time*, when I'm in such relationships—when I'm thinking about this, or noticing that—I don't engage in *self-reflection* at all. What makes (certain branches of) philosophy arduous is that students need *to learn* semantic ascent—to *practice* thinking *about* the justificatory relationships their thinkings and sensings in the world induce—something most of us don't find particularly natural otherwise.

The last thing to point out about this is that restricting the representation justification model to *correspondence truth* is unnecessary. (I did it only for ease of exposition.) Consider, alternatively, any non-correspondence characterization of truths (any alternative characterization of the truth-making process for truth)—for example, coherence with some set or other of propositions, the satisfaction of a set of pragmatic conditions, etc. Let SEM be the relationship that a proposition must satisfy (to whatever it must be related to on this view of truth-making) to be true. As with the correspondence model of truth, the truth of a proposition is justified by its satisfaction of SEM. The agent, as earlier, by using this relationship, is justified in her knowledge that the proposition is true. It may be that these alternatives aren't correctly described as "semantic" models of justification because (on global coherentist views, for example) the truth-makers for a proposition are deductive relations that proposition has to other propositions. If so, the semantic model of justification reduces to the deduction model of justification. Given current purposes, this doesn't matter.

8.2 Representation and Deduction Exhaust Justification

Apart from suggesting that the semantic-ascent fallacy *is* a fallacy, I've also suggested in section 8.1 that the truth condition on justification implies that there are, at most, two ways that a proposition can be justified. One is deductive—broadly construed to include truth-increasing inferences and truth-preserving ones—and the other is representational, how the world makes propositions true or false by virtue of their content.

Perhaps, however, this dichotomy is insufficient for understanding justification. Aikin (2011, 165) claims that a "more restricted semantic conception of good argument (soundness as a gold standard) is very thin, indeed, compared to what is necessary for properly run argumentation." Consider an agent. We can regard *that agent* as justified in thinking a predator is nearby because she sees paw tracks and draws an inference. Her mind and senses are working properly, and that's why she's justified. But this justification, one may think, is more than a correct inference of q from p, where q in turn is recognized to be true. What *justifies* the agent is more, we realize, if we notice how an agent (who has the capacity to do so) can challenge herself. *Am I seeing what I think I'm seeing? Does it really follow from seeing these paw tracks that a predator is nearby? Am I clear-headed about this, or did I drink too much last night?* That the agent *is* clear-headed, knows how to infer, and is in a situation where her vision isn't misleading, among many other things, *justifies* her conclusion. But doesn't this "justify" go beyond what I've (in sections 7.3 and 8.1) characterized justification in terms of?

No, despite how rich it is. Suppose that everything alluded to contributes to an agent's justification (but leave aside whether agents must, in principle, *grasp* all this—*make* all this the target of their thinking). What does *all this* come to? Only additional propositions—as I understand "proposition"—that in turn are justified either by what is represented by those propositions or by truth-supporting deductions from other propositions. "I am clear-headed about this" might be justified by the agent's ability to introspect the representational target of the proposition—that she *is* clear-headed. Or "I'm really seeing what I think I'm seeing" might be justified (in part) by an inference from, in effect, the proposition "I'm in broad daylight." That is, when focusing on the *agent* being justified instead of justifications of the particular propositions that she purportedly knows, a different kind (a "richer" or "thicker" kind) of "justification" doesn't emerge; it's just different propositions being focused on—but ones that are justified the same ways that I've already described.

What's commonly called "inference to the best explanation," it may be thought, is a *different* form of justification from either deductive or representational justification. We explain $p, q, \ldots, r$ by hypothesizing s, because on the basis of s, the items $p, q, \ldots, r$ are more likely than otherwise, or we hypothesize s because we can deduce $p, q, \ldots, r$ from s. In this case, we may describe s as justified by $p, q, \ldots, r$.

There is plenty to say about inference to the best explanation (and indeed, about likelihood-increasing inferences generally—more than I said in chapter 7), but I can't now. The main point is that we *are* engaging in an inference to s, because we find s more likely. The hypothesis s (the "best explanation") is selected from a range of competing hypotheses, or (sometimes) it's a lonely option (because we haven't got others). In either case, we accept s only because, *given* $p, q, \ldots, r$, *it* has greater likelihood than otherwise: a hypothesis providing an explanation for something else (that we already accept) does increase that hypothesis's likelihood—all other things being equal.

To summarize: An agent's justification requires an agent's competent *use* of justificatory relationships. If the truth condition *is* a necessary condition on content-justification, then this seems to follow: Justifications can only arise by an agent's cognitive/sensory use of inferential or representational relations. Given that it's always something with propositional content that's justified, these are the only ways that the truth of a proposition expressing that content is increased/established, and justification must track this. Thus, the truth condition for justification results in a *full characterization* of what justification (for us) is. Justificational relationships are either inferential or representational. Competent uses of these relationships, in both cases, require agents to be in certain relationships to both propositions and the world; the agent (in particular) has to be in certain sensory/cognitive states.

That said, we haven't seen (yet) that for an agent to use these representational and deductive relationships, to know (for example) that a predator is approaching her (and to be justified about this), she *has to* grasp the particulars of the representational relationship she's exploiting between her thought and the world, or the particulars of the inferential relationship between the propositions she uses. In the next section I explore the reasons many philosophers have for thinking that any agent must be able to do this to *really* know a predator is approaching her, or at least, to know this in a way that's not "brute" or "mechanical."[2]

That is, many philosophers disagree with the claims of this section and the last one. Many have objected strenuously, specifically, to the idea that something nonpropositional, like a bunch of apples, can justify a proposition or belief or whatever. As it's sometimes put, "only that which can be true or false—thus propositionally contentful—can confirm or refute" (Williams (2001, 98)). The *argument* for this (or rather, the *family* of arguments) occurs in Sellars (and perhaps originates there), although a version of it occurs in Kant's *Critique*.[3] In any case, different versions of these arguments have been plied by lots of twentieth- and twenty-first-century philosophers—BonJour, Brandom, Davidson, McDowell (1996) and Williams (1999), among others. The various considerations and

[2] Turri and Klein (2014b, 9) write: "A calculator might know that 2 + 2 = 4, and a greyhound might know that his master is calling, but neither the calculator nor the greyhound reasons in support of their knowledge. Their knowledge is merely mechanical or brute. Adult humans are capable of such unreasoned knowledge, but we are also capable of a superior sort of knowledge involving full justification, due to the value added by reasoning."

[3] Kant raises a concern with the "heterogeneity" of concepts and intuitions, at A137/B176, where he writes: "Pure concepts of understanding on the other hand, are quite heterogeneous from empirical intuitions (indeed, from sensible intuitions generally) and can never be encountered in any intuition." But also relevant are Kant's discussions of apperception.

arguments, I'm afraid, are complex enough that an extended discussion of them beyond what I've written in this and the last section is called for.[4]

Before turning to this, I'll describe how characterizing content-justification via the truth condition sinks coherentism *too*. Circular reasoning is ruled out because it doesn't increase surety beyond what we had initially.[5] Consider, alternatively, a coherentist emergentist view—one, say, that takes the justification of a proposition as due to its coherence (in some sense) with background propositions, ones in turn justified solely by their coherence with one another.[6] This faces the same mismatch problem with our actual justificatory practices that infinitist emergentist views face. We don't justify our beliefs by evaluating their "coherence" with background beliefs (which in turn are evaluated by *their* coherence with other background beliefs—or, even harder, by evaluating their "coherence" with *all* of our background beliefs *at once*); instead, we justify them by using the background beliefs, *assumed outright*, to evaluate, and to accept or reject them.[7] It will be ultimately relevant to questions of debate over sceptical challenges that, intuitively speaking, we reject circular justifications, but we accept the rejection of a challenge because of burden-of-proof considerations.[8]

[4] Aikin (2011, section 4.7) gives an excellent discussion of the dilemma and a description of its history. I don't agree with his response to it, as emerges in due course; my discussion, nevertheless, owes a lot to his sharp insights.

[5] Quine (1969) thinks of his "naturalized epistemology" in coherentist terms, and so he embraces circular reasoning. Verhaegh (2017, 321) writes: "It is characteristic of Quine's naturalism that he has no problems with such circularity; since there is no extra-scientific perspective we cannot but presuppose science in justifying our prima facie acceptance of science." Hylton (2014, 150) writes, "How do we know that the methods and techniques of natural science are our best source of knowledge about the world? Quine's predecessors within the analytic tradition . . . might at this point start . . . invoking philosophical ideas. . . . Quine, by contrast, insists that the naturalistic claim . . . too must be based on natural science. (If this is circular, he simply accepts the circularity.) This is the revolutionary step—naturalism self-applied, as it were." (I'm quoting Hylton from Verhaegh (2017, 321 n. 18).) Revolutionary? *At best*, this is the coronation of a hitherto nonjustificatory form of argument, one we (still) don't recognize as valid. The move is insufficiently supported by proclaiming that some examples of circular reasoning are now deemed "virtuous" because they're unavoidable (because we're now "naturalists").

[6] These sorts of views, Fogelin (1994, 147) says, are often described as "positive coherence theories." Fogelin writes (146–147): "In place of such linear conceptions of justification, the coherentist pictures justification using such metaphors as a network, a mesh, a system, or an organic totality of beliefs. The fundamental idea is that the items in coherent systems of beliefs must stand in relationships of mutual support." He cites Blanshard (1939) and BonJour (1985) as examples. As has been pointed out before, any sense of justificatory "emergence" *beyond* these metaphors (including the metaphor of "mutual support") has yet to be offered by anyone; Quine is no exception. This is in evident contrast to strict deduction (now explicated in terms of algorithmic systems) or the various competing formalizations of likelihood reasoning. (On the other hand, see Neta (2019) for an insightful and detailed attempt to give "coherence" content.)

[7] As is well known, and regularly noted in the psychological and philosophical literature, this justificational practice introduces biases: powerful (truth-likeliness-increasing) evidence against something that's only been previously established to a certain degree of truth likeliness may fail because that evidence isn't brought against that something together, but only piecemeal. The most famous article on this, and other related heuristic biases, is Tversky and Kahneman (1974).

[8] I'll this take up in my subsequent book, *Challenging Knowledge*.

This matters. A philosopher could bolster a coherence theory of justification with a coherence theory of truth, and treat coherence considerations as genuinely truth-preserving or (more likely) genuinely truth-likelihood-increasing. The problem, to repeat, is that we don't understand the justification of propositions as working through coherence in this way: we have no recognizable coherence emergentist justificatory practices. When we use background beliefs to evaluate if we should adopt or reject a new belief, we employ inference—both strict-deductive and truth-likelihood-increasing. But this requires treating these beliefs not conditionally (by virtue of their coherence with other propositions) but, as I've described it, *full stop*.

The problem for the coherentist is this: If background propositions need in turn to be justified, we can, perhaps, probabilistically increase the epistemic status of groups of propositions by connecting individual propositions in those groups to one another using truth-enhancing justifications—but nothing beyond this is gained by sheer "coherence" alone. That's distinctive only in introducing circularity, which recognizably doesn't help. And, again, if mere (emergentist) coherence is all the coherentist offers, we don't recognize this as "justification."

This echoes an objection I raised in chapter 7 against the infinitist. There is a bit of discussion in the literature about whether the coherentist's circular justifications are vicious. But they're not; they're *irrelevant*: we don't recognize sheer coherence as *justifying*. What's needed to understand the role of our background knowledge in justification isn't the invocation of a new (and unanalyzed) notion of circular or emergent justification, but to see that "being justified" as we understand it doesn't always require agents to *provide* what we take to be justifications. I develop this point further in sections 8.5 and 8.6.

It's been suggested to me that, "intuitively," someone with a very large coherent set of beliefs *is* more justified than someone with a relatively small coherent set of beliefs.[9] That intuition is what's behind the impression that emergent coherentism does offer a distinctive form of justification that we recognize. Against this reading of this supposed intuition, I think, is this decisive point. We *don't feel* that increasing the size of a set of consistent beliefs increases their emergent warrantedness (toward 1, say). This is evident because no one feels that if a conspiracy theorist's consistent set of sentences is made large enough almost all of us will be convinced by it.[10] We may be impressed (or appalled) by the ingenuity of the conspiracy theorist in retaining consistency among his crazy views—but we aren't tempted to believe he's right; we're not tempted to think that he's

[9] I thank Alex Sarappo and Asa Zabarsky for pressing me on this on February 22, 2018.

[10] Related to this is the famous and old problem of nonuniqueness that coherentist views face: Given *any* finite set of consistent propositions, there are many, infinitely many, different maximally consistent sets of propositions containing it.

more likely to be right the more he works at increasing the set of propositions that fit together with his conspiracy theories.

The last point to observe about coherentism is that it faces a problem infinitism doesn't. This is the sad fact that every agent's beliefs are inconsistent.[11] Any characterization of knowledge must accommodate this by enabling agents to know things *despite* inconsistencies in their beliefs. Characterizing justification by the coherence of an agent's background beliefs prima facie fails to do this because it seems to result in *none* of any agent's beliefs being justified. I describe how despite possessing inconsistent beliefs, agents can know things in chapter 10, especially section 10.9.

8.3 The Given-Dilemma for Nonpropositional Justification

A nonhuman animal facing a predator thinks, "Oh, man—*this isn't good*." She's justified in thinking this, even though it would be wrong to say that she *has* a justification for her thought. That an agent *has* a justification for a thought sounds like she can *give* such a justification; in this case, let's say, to do so, she needs to be able to talk about how reliable her sight is—something she evidently can't do. This distinction (as I said) will be spelled out further in section 8.5.[12]

Meanwhile, what has to be said now is that the animal's thought isn't justified by any of its *further* thoughts, but by something else. *What*? The natural suggestion ("natural" insofar as it's regularly offered by philosophers) is that the animal's *experience* or *intuition* or *immediate apprehension* of a certain state of affairs justifies its thought. The claim that any such experiential item—widely called *the Given* in the literature—can provide justification leads to a "fundamental dilemma." BonJour (1978, 11) writes:

[11] Well, I'm not sure. This is *definitely* a sad fact about humans—but maybe not about certain animals. Wolves might not have inconsistent beliefs (this isn't to say that they don't have *false* beliefs). In particular, it doesn't look like wolves have beliefs about *their beliefs*. This isn't the only way, of course, to induce inconsistency in a set of beliefs. Humans have *lots* of ways of being inconsistent. Sheer complexity and the sheer *number* of their beliefs will easily do it because there is no test for inconsistency—but the beliefs of nonhuman animals may not be complex or numerous enough for this. I discuss the inconsistency of human belief—with respect to preface paradoxes—in section 10.7.

[12] Leite (2004, 220) describes adherence to this distinction as "quite orthodox." Not only is it explicitly supported by Alston and Audi, but "this tendency," he notes (246 n. 4), is exhibited by otherwise strange bedfellows (his list): BonJour, Goldman, Kornblith, Haack, Plantinga, Chisholm, Pollock, and Pryor. And, despite Sellars's opposition to the distinction, Leite notes that Brandom and Williams also accept it. Using "quite orthodox," as Leite does, indicates he intends to reject it (and that this is a *big deal*—a "reconceptualization of the basic framework for understanding epistemic justification" (220)). I discuss his attempt in section 8.7.

> If [these] intuitions or immediate apprehensions are construed as cognitive, then they will be both capable of giving justification and in need of it themselves; if they are non-cognitive, then they do not need justification but are also apparently incapable of providing it. This, at bottom, is why epistemological givenness is a myth.

This needs unpacking.[13] To start, what work is the adjective "cognitive" doing? One widely held view is that a valid deduction of one proposition from another supervenes on the *structural properties* of those propositions. These properties are semantic and/or syntactic ones; but, regardless, what's crucial is that propositions are structurally *contentful*. That's why one proposition can imply another, and why justification relations can supervene on deductive structure. If this is what "cognitive" means, then the idea is that nothing can be self-justifying because nothing can be true on the basis of its intrinsic structural properties.[14] The other limb of the dilemma is that if something isn't cognitive, then it can't provide justification.

What's the move, given *this* horn of the dilemma? Perhaps that the inferential model of justification is being assumed as all that justification can amount to (note the use of "logical" in Aikin's item III quoted in note 13). If justification runs solely along inferential lines, then (given the structural-property-of-propositions view of inference) something without "cognitive content" can't justify because—here's how to put it—such a thing has no *implications*.

I challenged this suggestion in section 8.1 with *representational* justification. This doesn't require the item that justifies a thought to be propositional although it does require the item to be structured so that confirmation can occur. The thought that the cat is in the hat is justified by the hatted cat—but that hatted cat is a (structured) way that the cat and the hat correspond to the thought (it's a fact about the cat and the hat, if you will).

[13] Here's a version that unpacks the assumptions somewhat. Aikin (2011, 139) writes (italics his): "(I) If there is a Given that plays a justificatory role, it has propositional content or it does not. (II) If the Given has propositional content, then that proposition, if it is to provide support requisite for justification, must be *justified*. So a further proposition is required, which means the regress problem is not solved. (III) If the Given has no propositional content, then the Given, if it is to provide support requisite for justification, must be capable of standing in a *logical relation* to the proposition it justifies. But only propositions may stand in logical relations, so the Given cannot justify. *Therefore*, there is no Given that plays a supporting justificatory role."

[14] But . . . *really*? Even if first-order logical truths—as a group—are only recursively enumerable (because a proof method is needed to *generate* them), that doesn't show that some of them aren't structurally immediately true; after all, proof methods commonly begin with a core set of logical truths with a recognitional decision procedure. (Most views of the a priori start *here*.) My suspicion is that Sellars's dilemma builds into justification a *recognizing* or *apprehending* requirement. I explore this shortly.

Presupposed by (most) proponents of Sellars's dilemma (and by those—foundationalists, for example—who think they have a response to it) is that the hatted cat doesn't justify the thought that the cat is in the hat. Rather, it's an *experience* or *apprehension* (of some sort) that justifies the thought—in this case, perhaps, the *experience of seeing* the hatted cat.[15] This presupposition viciously mutates the dilemma: my second limb for justification is set aside. Whatever an experience is, and whatever it has to be like to justify the thought that the cat is in the hat, it can't provide justification by representation. This is because whatever the thought "the cat is in the hat" is about, it's not about anyone's *experiences*. That leaves only one approach to justification: deduction; and then the "cognitive or not" dilemma has bite. If there is no cognitive content in experience, after all, how is its justificatory relationship to the thoughts it justifies supposed to fit the only model of justification we have left—one that relies on semantic/syntactic structural properties?[16]

What motivates the almost universal replacement of the contents of *propositions* being what indicates what representationally justifies those propositions with the contents of the *experiences* of agents instead doing this? I'm not, of course, denying that an agent's experience (when pertinent) is a component in the description of an agent's justification. When an agent *does* rely on her experience to know something, those experiences are part of what justifies that agent. But this, all by itself, doesn't (or shouldn't) sideline that we justify our claims—often—by pointing at something because it's that *something* that justifies our claim.

Avoiding scepticism is one motivation—perhaps the main one—for this replacement strategy. Premise (*sic*): We're *more sure* of the contents of our experience than of anything else. If so, then (*sic*) ultimately, what directly (representationally) justifies our beliefs *can only be* the contents of our experience. The hatted cat has to be set aside as representationally justifying our belief (or knowledge or opinion) that the cat is in the hat; the *actual* cat being in the hat must come in at a later stage of justification, as something we infer our way to, as something to be justified, not as something that justifies.

[15] Siegel (2017, 29 n. 11), for example, describes Sellars's dilemma in just this way, and gives a list of philosophers who argue for and against experience being able to provide "immediate justification." She ties the issue to whether experiences have "accuracy conditions." Aikin (2011, especially his chapter 4) is dedicated to explaining how experience, "being appeared to thusly," can function in a justificational role (although, on his view, necessarily accompanied by an interpretational context that amounts to many other items that need to be justified—so that a form of justificational regress continues).

[16] This isn't quite how the traditional presentation of the given challenge goes; instead, experience is often described as an unconceptualized morass that thus can't confirm *anything*. This is much closer to the original Kantian move than what I've suggested. We end up in the same place, nevertheless—one which I can challenge in the same way.

This is why Sellars's dilemma is officially a dilemma for "the Given." The Given is, for those epistemologists who take it seriously, a justificational stopping point that's *experiential*. I'm, therefore, leaving aside the question of how *those epistemologists* are to handle the dilemma. I'll make the case, in section 8.6, that justificational stopping points take no particular form: they aren't, in general, experiential. The only question now, therefore, is whether the supplementary considerations, raised by Sellarsians, show that representational justification, as I've described it, *must be* restricted to experiential justifiers. I criticize these supplementary considerations in section 8.4, and I raise a fresh one on behalf of the proponent of the necessity of justification stoppers (if they exist) being experiential, and then criticize it too.

8.4 Why Representational Justifications Needn't Be Experiential

I've already mentioned one reason some give for why representational justifications have to be experiential: No agent directly uses facts about external-world objects to justify her claims. Sensory and/or judgmental routes to such objects are always there. This is a truism about knowing agents.

So what? The truism *does* show what's already conceded in section 8.2: the agent, to be justified in drawing an inference, must be in one or another sensory/cognitive relationship to the world—included in this is that she must be clear-headed, be appropriately exercising the right capacities, and so on. This doesn't mean that we have to replace the justificatory role of truth-preserving deductions for an agent with something else: "*seeing* those truth-preserving deductions" or "*recognizing* those truth-preserving deductions." The same is true of the hatted cat justifying "the cat is in the hat." We don't have to replace the justificatory role of the hatted cat with "*seeing* the cat is in the hat" or "*recognizing* the cat is in the hat." This doesn't mean, of course, that seeing or recognizing aren't pertinent to, or part of, what justifies an agent's thought—but that's insufficient to *require* representational justifications to be experiential.

It might be thought that an always-introducible sensory prefix shows that our actual justificational practices never invoke naked external-world facts, but instead such facts explicitly (or implicitly) within the context of a description of an agent's experience. The hatted cat isn't what justifies an agent's thought that the cat is in the hat, but instead, it's that agent *seeing* that the cat is in the hat that justifies his thought that the cat is in the hat. Against this is that in ordinary practices of justification, experience is only invoked when it's followed by specific content that's actually doing the justificational work. It's not experiences of *that* sort (described intrinsically in terms of the internal properties of that experience—raw sense-data patterns of serrated black and a cylindrical red/white striping, for example) that justifies the agent's thought that the cat is in the hat; it's the experience of *the cat in the hat*. This suggests that the justification, strictly speaking, is the content following the cognitive/sensory route descriptor ("sees," "smells," etc.)—and that the route descriptors are just that, descriptions of agents' routes to the content, and not descriptions of their experiences.

Support for this interpretation of these justificatory uses of sensory prefix + indicative sentences is that, as I indicated in section 1.3, "see" and other sensory descriptions have experience-neutral uses—experience is *not* required of automatons that are correctly described as aware, as noticing, as seeing, and so on.[17] It's *required* of self-driving cars, for example, that they *see* hatted cats on roads (and swerve so that they don't run them over and induce lawsuits); it's as important that self-driving cars don't confuse hatted cats on roads that they see with puddles or shadows. Again, in requiring self-driving cars to see hatted cats *as* hatted cats, it isn't necessary that those cars *experience* hatted cats and recognize that their experience of hatted cats is different from their experiences of puddles or shadows. (That, um, would require car manufacturers to solve the hardest problem there is in the philosophy of mind.)

This is an experience-neutral use of "see" that's not different in meaning from our experience-laden use. Someone can say cogently, sitting in a self-driving car, "both me and the car saw the cat in the hat at the same time." If it were included in the perceived *meaning* of certain seeing attributions that the perceiver must have an experience, this collapse of the two uses of "saw" into one wouldn't be acceptable. (This, recall, is an application of the conjunction-reduction test that I described in the introduction.)

Next, consider this remark by Williams (2001, 97):

> However basic knowledge is understood, it must be capable of standing in logical relations to whatever judgments rest on it. But this means that even basic knowledge must involve propositional content and so cannot consist in a mere relation to a particular.

The response is this. The agent knows that the cat is in the hat. The agent justifies this knowledge claim by saying: "There he is." This second bit of knowledge, "There he is," has propositional content, and stands in logical relations. But the agent is justified in this second bit of knowledge only because the agent *does*

[17] In Metz (2017b, B2), we read: "Researchers like Google's Ian Goodfellow, for example, are exploring ways that hackers could fool A.I. systems into seeing things that aren't there." And later in the article, "Just by changing a few pixels in the photo of [an] elephant, for example, they could fool the neural network into thinking it depicts a car."

stand in a "mere" relation (a sensory/cognitive one) to a particular, namely, the hatted cat that she sees. Unsurprisingly, therefore (or so I claim), a statement like "There he is" or "I see him" in the right sensory/cognitive circumstances is seen as a justificational stopping point by nearly everyone.

So (to summarize), to affirm that representational justification can involve things *other* than the experiential givens of an agent, I've pressed against Sellarsians that (1) without argument, semantic ascent isn't required. The mere use of (without "mentioning") propositions (in inference or for representation) is all that's needed to justify an agent. (2) The Sellarsian assumption that lots of subsidiary knowledge must be presupposed in any knowledge attribution to an agent also introduces a focus on experience—at least in the case of humans. This has been deflected by examples in chapter 1. (I supplement these considerations with further examples and discussion in section 8.6.) Many agents that we attribute specific kinds of knowledge to (or specific instances of knowledge to) may, nevertheless, know little else.

But (3) Sellarsians sometimes motivate the requirement of any knowledge attribution necessarily being accompanied by other knowledge by claiming that the words of our natural languages are semantically interconnected so that learning one of them requires learning *many* of them. Even if language-lacking knowers know very little, language-gifted knowers—by virtue of semantically interconnected words—necessarily know a lot. Aikin observes that semantic-holist views about semantic interconnections between our "phenomenal concepts" and our "more theoretical" concepts have been long assumed by many philosophers of science (e.g., Feyerabend (1962); and Kuhn (1970)). Aikin (2011, 141–142) writes, supportively:

> If the Sellars argument is right that phenomenal concepts (e.g. being appeared to ketchup-bottle-ly or hearing C$^{\#}$) derive their significance from their roles in systems of related concepts for their discriminatory power, the linguistic training in using them is connected to their semantic character. To have such a concept is to have mastered part of an interrelated symbolic system. Surely, this is true with being able to hear C$^{\#}$ as a C$^{\#}$—it requires considerable training to do so, and what gives one a reason to believe she is right in this application of the concept is not an autonomous content, but learned skill at applying that concept reliably. This point generalizes to all recognitional concepts—from C$^{\#}$, to ketchup bottles, faces, colors, and shapes.

The decades after the 1960s have been cruel to semantic-holist views, especially in regard to human "observational" concepts. First, there is the intervening recognition in linguistics (and philosophy) of the absence of definitions for most of our words. This blocks one route to an argument for rich semantic interconnections among our concepts. But there is worse. Recent psychological studies follow suit by showing that although linguistic interconnections between concepts often play *some* role, other psychological factors play more—indeed, those other factors may be what's behind natural languages having certain properties (e.g., particularly with respect to their quantifiers) rather than the reverse.[18] In addition, the neurophysiological (and conceptual) continuities between our observational capacities and those of animals also undercut this view—being language users doesn't change the basic ways we observe (and—sometimes—how we're justified on the basis of observations). Acquiring concepts can be arduous and can require a lot of training; but it doesn't follow that the (long) training is required *because* the acquisition of a concept involves psychologically embedding that concept among its fellows in a system of concepts—as Aikin suggests in what I've just quoted.[19]

What *is* true is that in mathematics and the sciences, practitioners replace our natural-language concepts with *new* concepts that *are* semantically (definitionally) tied together. One indication of this is that these new concepts are inferentially tractable: we can deduce the interconnections between them—something largely impossible in the case of natural-language concepts.[20] These facts complement what I've observed in earlier chapters about natural-language words such as "know(s)," "justification," "see(s)," "aware of," etc. These words *aren't* definitionally tied together, and our usage fully reflects that (as does the continued inability of philosophers to get a grip on these words). Our attributional practices allow these words to be applied (or not) in ways often independent of one another (at least with respect to specific agents, and on the basis of their behavior as well as background knowledge about them).

There is yet another common move to undercut the idea that an agent can have observational knowledge ("that's green") without additional supplementary knowledge either about himself or his relations to the world. This is the thermostat-parrot (calculator-greyhound) charge, which I've cited already. Here is Williams's version of it (2001, 175, italics his):

> To be capable of observational knowledge, it is not enough (as pure reliabilists imagine) simply *to be* a reliable reporter on this and that: a person must *know*

18 See, e.g., Carey (2009, especially chapter 7). I also think that my discussion of the concepts of B.B. and animals, in chapter 5, as well as recent psychological results about human concepts strike down views that ground-level concepts, perceptual ones, for example, are ones that can't be understood without understanding concepts relating to cognitive activities. (Brandon apparently has views like this.) I see no reason to think anything like this is true.

19 One reason for this is that even learning to hear a C# as a C# involves a lot of "know-how" learning, which takes a lot of training, but doesn't seem to include the acquisition of a lot of interrelated concepts.

20 I discuss this in detail in Azzouni (2000a), Azzouni (2013b), and Azzouni (2015).

> *something about* how reliable he is. Again, this sort of reflective epistemic self-knowledge is available only to language-users. Animals and small children do not have it. Accordingly, they are outside the game of giving and asking for reasons.

Notice the sharp dichotomy Williams imposes on his opponent.[21] There are *only* two choices here: either an agent knows something about how reliable he is (and so he's "inside" the game of giving and asking for reasons) or he's not (and so, poor thing, he's like a thermostat, calculator, parrot, or greyhound). *Only* two options: a rich conceptual grasp of one's epistemic practices, or austere rote or mechanical (or "brute") epistemic behavior.

We should reject this sharp dichotomy—it seems, after all, based on a kind of slippery-slope argument coupled with a stipulation. In general, a reasoner, even a quite sophisticated reasoner (with lots of accompanying knowledge) needn't know how reliable he is. He need only *rely on* his reasoning, appropriately and in the right contexts. Doing so is compatible with, as I've just stressed, having lots of connected knowledge without any of it being self-regarding.

A sophisticated animal sees a predator and runs. The animal hides in such-and-such a place (say) that will help him escape (in a crevice between rocks instead of on top of a rock if it's a predator cat he's running from). The animal, that is, exhibits knowledge of the terrain and the implications of that terrain for whether he can escape or not. Furthermore, making mistakes, or the possibility of making mistakes, is always part of having systematic interconnected knowledge, and the animal's capacity to (sometimes) recognize that he's made a mistake is required as well. But this doesn't require any sort of self-regarding knowledge about his reliability or his authority in thinking what he knows. A primitive "oops!" or "what just happened here?" reaction is needed, of course—but that doesn't have to involve semantic ascent.[22] The point, of course, isn't that there are only *three* options: rich semantic ascent knowledge, less rich but very interconnected knowledge, and finally, brute or mechanical knowledge. There is, rather, a gradation of possibilities—that's what our knowledge-attribution practices suggest, anyway.

Supplementing this objection, finally, is the point I made in section 8.2 (against Aikin), that the *iterated knowledge* possessed by an agent gives her justifications no different in kind from our basic two: inference and semantic representation. There is an implicit suggestion running through much of this literature that

[21] Recall the quotation in note 2 from Turri and Klein (2014b), who also ply this sharp dichotomy. These are, of course, two examples among *many*.

[22] A staple of the evidence for child development are the studies of when babies stare longer at scenarios, typically cases where physical items are apparently violating the babies' expectations. (See, e.g., Carey (2009) for many examples.)

somehow self-awareness provides a different kind of knowledge that transforms the agent from something cognitively lowly—something that thinks mechanically like a parrot or thermostat—into a glorious cognizer: a *human*. Why *should* iterative knowledge have such magical properties? Nothing in the preceding chapters on iterated knowledge explains how such a thing could be possible.[23]

Here's one last possible argument that experiences of agents are the only justificational stopping points. Experiences can function justificationally in lieu of *any* corresponding state of affairs. If an animal hallucinates a predator, we may (nevertheless) think the animal is justified in thinking, "That's dangerous," even though there is nothing dangerous there. What's justifying the animal, surely, is the *experience* she's having. But, then, isn't the experience the animal is having, when facing an actual predator that she sees, *also* what justifies her thought?[24]

I'll be brief, since I've done this already. First, as I've noted, experiences *can* be justifiers—that's not the disagreement.[25] The disagreement is over whether *non-experiences* can also be justificational stopping points. Second, if a self-driving car malfunctions and thinks a pedestrian is in the road where one isn't, it isn't the *experience* of the car that justifies its view that there is a pedestrian there. What justifies its view is that *it sees (or thinks it sees) a pedestrian in the road*. If "it sees" or "it thinks it sees," as usage indicates, is (generally) experience-neutral, then these phrases don't imply the car is having an experience. So nothing in the considerations, that animals can have hallucinations that justify their (false) thoughts of this or that, motivates denying that nonpropositional justificational stopping points are possible.

8.5 There *Are* Justificational Stopping Points

We've finally reached the major divide between givenness critics, justification sceptics, and infinitists, on the one hand, and foundationalists, on the other. This is whether justificational stopping points are part of our ordinary justificational practices. Purely pragmatic or politeness stopping points or ones that arise

[23] Nevertheless, metacognition, knowledge or otherwise, definitely provides cognitive advantages. Quickly put: metacognizing allows us to evaluate our methods for knowing things and/or compare them to other methods. That this is a powerful tool can't (and shouldn't) be denied. Nevertheless, we shouldn't overreach in our descriptions of how metacognition advantages agents. Nor should we overlook how it can *disadvantage* agents. A careful discussion of how metacognition causes trouble (indeed, opens agents to threats of scepticism, and worse, "cognitive suicide" or "cognitive catastrophe"), however, I must largely put off to a later book, *Challenging Knowledge*.

[24] Notice the analogy to the argument from hallucination (as described, e.g., by Austin (1962)); notice also that I echo aspects of disjunctivism in my response, although I refuse to echo pretty much anything else that comes along with standard disjunctivist views (as in, e.g., McDowell's work).

[25] I agree with Aikin (2011) about this important point. See, in particular, his chapter 4.

because everyone is tired aren't at stake.[26] What I establish here is that there are genuinely *justificational* stopping points. Agents are often seen (and often see themselves) as justified despite failing to (or refusing to) give justifications, or when they're incapable of giving them. Agents are seen as justified, in particular, even when they don't think of themselves as justified, or when they think they're *not* justified.

As chapter 1 made clear, we often think of epistemic agents as justified when they can't provide justifications, or don't even know what justifications *are*. But, second, even when the agents are successful and competent justification providers, nevertheless there are always (many) statements that they make that they would find completely bizarre to be challenged on. (And this attitude is shared by their peers.)

I thus accompany this far certain epistemic foundationalists. But it seems clear that stopping points don't need to have any specific epistemic qualities or that they need to be permanent (or even stable) features of any agent's knowledge structure.

Here's another way of putting the point I want to establish now: Our notion of justification is sufficiently broad to allow justification regresses to stop because our understanding of when agents are justified doesn't require them to always provide justifications (or to be able to do so)—sometimes (in a phrase) they can point to "the facts" and stop there.[27]

Illuminating, to begin with, are the many cases where we take agents to be justified even though they're incapable of *giving* justifications. Let's start with the many attributions of knowledge to animals discussed in chapter 1. It's simply bizarre, in these cases, to suggest that the animals in question don't have the knowledge being attributed to them because they can't provide any

[26] These are the kinds of reasons Aikin (2011, 170–172) thinks we have when we stop providing justifications, although he also thinks that *we could go on*, and the fact that we don't doesn't establish that we're epistemically justified in not doing so. I also don't think genuine justificational stopping points are what Williams (1996) describes as "methodological necessities," contextually given by the participants engaging in, for example, the study of history. They also aren't the kinds of stopping points that epistemic foundationalists need. I'll indicate illustratively why this is the case in section 8.6. Unfortunately a full discussion of the matter must be postponed beyond the covers of *this* book.

[27] Pryor (2000, 535) argues for something *similar*: "I do not suppose that whenever you have justification for believing p, you will always be able to offer *reasons* or a *justifying argument* in support of your belief. It is important to distinguish between (i) the epistemic *status* of being justified, or having justification for believing something; and (ii) the *activity* of defending or giving a justifying argument for a claim. In my view, the status is epistemologically primary, and does not depend on your being able to engage in the activity. It can be reasonable for you to believe something even if you're not able to show that it's reasonable or explain what makes it reasonable." Aikin (2011, 175) argues against this; I'll discuss some of his arguments later. I will say, however, that there are circumstances where (i) and (ii) can't be cleanly distinguished as Pryor does here. In certain important cases, with certain sophisticated agents, being unable to manage (ii) *does* undercut (i). This isn't generally the case, as I'm showing now.

justifications. Furthermore, as I discussed in section 7.1, it's bizarre to suggest that a monkey that hides from eagles because his conspecific has just made an eagle call isn't justified in thinking there is danger. For that matter, it's bizarre to suggest that a monkey that hides from eagles because a conspecific has (deliberately) made a *deceiving* eagle call isn't equally justified in thinking there's danger. In all the cases in which animals and artifacts have knowledge attributed to them, *providing* justifications just doesn't come into it. That Gettier cases can arise for animals (there's an eagle nearby even though the deceiving conspecific doesn't realize there is) indicates that we take them as capable of being justified in what they think—even though they can't (ever) give justifications as humans *sometimes* can.

It's been suggested that in these cases *someone* can provide the justifications, although not the agent the knowledge is being attributed to; and so the agent (in these cases) is justified in a derivative sense. This won't work if only because, at times, the knowledge attributor is in no better position to provide a justification than the agent is. Nevertheless, both may be justified in what they know and the attributor may be further justified in thinking the agent knows as well.

What *is* important is that these are cases of shared knowledge as well as *shared justifications*, in particular knowledge and justifications that are shared by the agents the knowledge is attributed to and by those attributing the knowledge. This is certainly the case with the knowledge attributions to animals and artifacts I discussed in chapter 1: That there are eagles nearby may be something the knowledge attributor knows for exactly the same reason the monkey does (because the monkey's reliable never-deceiving conspecific has made the call and the human recognizes this). The human can provide the justification (in words); but the animal, nevertheless being justified, doesn't need to be able to do this.

In addition, there are the many common cases of humans who can't provide justifications for what they know, or who can't provide the right justifications; they're taken to be justified (and to know) nevertheless. One of my favorite cases is from Sacks (1990): two severely cognitively impaired twins with no grasp of multiplication or division who could nevertheless detect (large) prime numbers. But this is just the extreme end of a common phenomenon. Humans, even bright ones, often make serious mistakes about how they know what they know. They often sincerely think their reasoning or what they saw took such-and-such a form, when it didn't. ("First I thought this, then I thought . . ."). Our *evaluation* of our ways of establishing what we know can be confused, even when there's nothing wrong with the knowledge methods themselves. This is *common*. The *requirement* that agents always be able to justify what they know obliterates the fact that being justified and being able to appreciate (and explain to oneself or others) that one is justified are different abilities that often come apart. Striking examples of this are mathematicians who know certain results, but are confused or unaware of the proof methods by which they got those results.[28] Included among these cases are the more extreme ones where the person (as a result) doesn't think he knows what he nevertheless does know—the amnesiac who nevertheless remembers where he lives.[29]

The results of earlier chapters illuminate these cases. If iterated knowing comes apart from knowing, as I've argued it does, then of course it will be possible for an epistemic agent to know something but fail to know she knows it precisely because her thinking about how she knows what she knows is wrong.

Lastly, consider a variant of the kind of case that's been much discussed in the literature for, and against, reliabilism.[30] Imagine that

> Samantha has completely reliable clairvoyant powers (ESP). Predictions often pop into her head, ones that are straightforwardly simple—for example, that on next Tuesday the president will be in New York. She often has no reason (apart from the thought popping into her head—along with a weird visceral sensation)—for thinking that her predictions are true. Nevertheless, they always are true (even though, sometimes, as with the location of the president, fake news has been spread so that almost everyone else doesn't know they're true). She doesn't really believe her predictions because she's intelligent and reasonably sensible, and she's read all the massive literature that establishes (to the best that science can establish this) that there is no such thing as ESP. So, she often talks about "all these *amazing coincidences*." (She's a really big fan of *Michael Shermer*, and quotes him to everyone she knows.) On occasion, however, when the prediction is something she can do something about—such as the plane her son is going to take in a few days crashing—she'll surreptitiously maneuver

[28] Ramanujan is a famous case. Hardy (1941) wrote that Ramanujan's results were "arrived at by a process of mingled argument, intuition and induction, of which he was entirely unable to give a coherent account." There are many anecdotes—both in the oral tradition and in print—about different mathematicians coupling substantial new results with seriously invalid proofs. Von Neumann apparently often provided bad proofs for results he was nevertheless taken to know. (The reason for attributing knowledge to mathematicians in these cases is that the results are right and the likelihood of *guessing* them or getting them by accident via an invalid proof is near zero.) Moderate versions of this are common in mathematics. If the proofs mathematicians give are supposed to be the justifications they have for what they know, then mathematicians quite often *can't give* justifications for what they're (nevertheless) clearly justified in believing. It can take years (especially with long proofs) to clean up the flawed justification a mathematician has given (and published) for what he and others nevertheless *know*.

[29] Harman (1970, 844) knows this, but then overreaches. He writes: "People often believe things for good reasons, which give them knowledge, even though they cannot say what those reasons are.... In most cases a person is unable to state his reasons in any sort of detail. At best he can give only the vaguest indication of the reasons that convince him. It is only in rare cases that we can tell a person's reasons from what he can say about them. Indeed, it is doubtful that a person can ever fully identify his reasons." I won't endorse the more extreme claim Harman makes here. (On the other hand, I won't refute it either. Sometimes, sure. Almost always? I wouldn't know; and I doubt Harman does.)

[30] See BonJour (1978).

> him onto another plane by, say, canceling his ticket behind his back and purchasing a new one for a different flight. (She doesn't do this because she believes the original plane will crash—so she says to herself—but because "I couldn't live with myself if I didn't and he died because of another one of those *amazing coincidences*.") As a result, she has saved her son's life numerous times, as well as the lives of a number of her other relatives and friends.

A preliminary question: Does Samantha *believe* her predictions? It's true she thinks she shouldn't believe them. But nevertheless, when she can, she (secretly) maneuvers things to protect the people she cares about. This suggests (recall Williamson's case, discussed in note 26 of chapter 1) that she really does believe them. But perhaps not, since humans can be genuinely ambivalent on matters like this, and their behavior can reflect that ambivalence.

Does she, on the other hand, *know* what her ESP enables her to predict? Compelling is this: Suppose science subsequently discovers that ESP is real.[31] There is no doubt that many people would feel they had been vindicated, that they really did know the things they thought they knew; and it's clear, as well, that this feeling would be widely shared. It wouldn't be thought that only *now*, now that ESP has been scientifically vindicated, Samantha knows what her ESP reveals to her, but she didn't know this *before*. This suggestion is bizarre because, according to it, it isn't that science has *discovered* that people can know the future—that there is ESP. It's, instead, that science has made that kind of knowledge *possible* by whatever it was that it has discovered. But that sounds *silly*...

8.6 Justificational Stopping Points in Conversation

It's time to face the claim (asserted by many) that our justificational practices require justificational regresses. Klein (2003, 40) argues that foundationalism involves an inherent irrationality—that of "asserting a proposition for no reason at all." It's important to avoid argument by sheer wordplay: It can't be true that it's irrational to assert something "without a reason" because (after all) if one doesn't have a reason, then (by definition) one isn't "reasoning," and therefore one is being "irrational." We *do* sometimes criticize people for doing things "without a reason," but that's when people do things where we think those people should either have reasons for what they're doing or otherwise they shouldn't do them at all. It doesn't follow that we think *every case* is like

[31] I want to stress that I *do not believe* ESP is real. This is a *thought experiment*.

this. If, in fact, it is (for us) an acceptable justificational practice to sometimes assert something even if one doesn't have a reason for it, then although that's "asserting a proposition for no reason at all," it doesn't follow that such a thing is "irrational." Klein must have a substantial reason for thinking foundationalism is irrational beyond mere wordplay. And he does. He thinks requiring a justification for a claim is always appropriate; failing to provide one when challenged is *never* appropriate.

Here is Klein's illustration. Fred claims to know *p*. Sally asks why Fred thinks *p* is true. Fred says *q*. Sally asks the same question about *q*. Fred says *r*. (This goes on for a while . . .) Finally, Fred gives a justificational stopping point *b*. (In the language Klein uses, Fred, being a foundationalist, claims *b* has "autonomous warrant.") Sally asks Fred why he should believe *b* because it has autonomous warrant. Now Fred has a dilemma. Klein (2003, 40) writes, "Either Fred will give a reason for thinking that the possession of autonomous warrant is at least somewhat truth-conducive or he won't." If he does, the regress continues (because he's given a justification for believing *b*). But if he hasn't, then he isn't justified in thinking *b* (because he hasn't a reason for thinking it's true). Consider this example: Fred's *b* is "I saw it." Sally's question is "why do you think you saw it?" Fred's response is that "I saw it" has autonomous warrant. Sally's next question, according to Klein, is why should Fred trust that something having autonomous warrant means it's more likely to be true (why is believing items with autonomous warrant a truth-conducive practice)? Fred is required to respond to this question.

Something's wrong.[32] First the small point. As Aikin points out, Fred's response isn't a justification for "I saw it" (the justification for *that* is that he *did* see it); Fred's response is to Sally's challenge that justifying what he thinks this way is *itself* justified. As Aikin (2011, 95) puts it, Fred "has other coordinating beliefs and interpretive skills that can be manifested in further dialogue," that is, Fred has resources to further defend himself against Sally's challenges. That's why Klein's picture of an infinite linear sequence of justifiers is wrong as a picture of how the regress goes (*if* it goes). It's not a matter of J_1 justifying J_2 justifying J_3, . . ., and so on (a *linear* linked chain of justifiers). Instead, if Klein is right about there being a regress, it's because the justifications *branch* (as I described them doing in section 7.4.1): new statements are being challenged, not ones Fred

32 Maybe a third thing is wrong besides the two I go on to give. If every challenge to a claim (tacit or otherwise) is legitimate, then can't Fred challenge Sally with "What justifies you in thinking that's a reasonable question?"? If so . . . what's supposed to happen now? Do they take turns demanding justifications from each other? Does each one demand that the other answer his/her question first? It looks like we face a "dialogue crash"—rational exchange is short-circuited. I'll not pursue this question further. (I owe the suggestion that Fred can challenge Sally's question and that the result leads to a standoff to Elson Hunter, September 2019.)

has offered, but additional ones that support what Fred has said, in one way or another. Nearly enough, Sally's challenge is always a simple "but what justifies *that*?"—where *that* needn't be what Fred has just said. That is, it's a regress of the form J_1 justifies J_2, J_3 justifies *that J_1 justifies J_2*, . . ., J_4 justifies . . . Of course, J_3 does justify J_2 (it justifies "I saw it" to point out that seeing something justifies "I saw it"), but it doesn't do so by itself being tacked onto a justifying chain by its justifying J_2. Seeing justifications as branching trees makes clear what it is that's going on here. Both *seeing something*, together with *seeing something justifies "I see it,"* justifies "I see it." There are two branches here. Sally's challenges (according to Klein) can make Fred focus on *any* branch.

Now the big point: Klein is wrong about it being "irrational" to assert propositions "without reasons." The way to see this is to notice that his little playlet about Fred and Sally doesn't correctly depict how the rational agents react when their justificational stopping points are challenged by their opponents, or when they're challenged on why they should think their justificational stopping points are justificational stopping points. Instead, what occurs is one or another version of total irritated exasperation.

Consider a real-life case. Rachel North in early July 2005 witnessed a bombing in a carriage on the Piccadilly tube line in Finsbury Park, North London. Subsequently, a number of conspiracy theorists became convinced that the bombing event was a hoax.[33] Among them was David Shayler. Jon Ronson (2011, 193–195) subsequently wrote about an interview he had with Shayler. Some of it went like this:

> and then the conversation turned to Rachel North. He was, he said, still convinced that she didn't exist.
>
> "Let me talk about Rachel North being a composite MI5 person," he said. "That's exactly the kind of thing the intelligence services would do."
>
> "But you've met her," I said.
>
> "Yes, I know I've MET her," he said. His voice was rising now, getting faster. "She may exist as a human being but that's not to say there aren't five people behind her posting in her name on the Internet."
>
> "Oh come *on*," I said.
>
> "You should look at the evidence of her copious postings," David said. "You should look at the evidence of how many posts she was doing at one point."
>
> "She was posting a lot," I said. "I have no doubt of that."
>
> "People in the movement have come to the conclusion that there were far too many posts to have come from one person," David said.

[33] This is dismayingly common, e.g., Alex Jones and the Sandy Hook elementary school shooting.

"Oh, you know what bloggers are like," I said. "They write and write and write. I don't know why, because they're not being paid."

"I am also very suspicious of the fact that she refuses to sit down and have a dispassionate briefing about 7/7," David said. "Why won't she allow somebody to patiently talk her through the evidence?"

"She was in the *carriage*!" I said. "She was in the CARRIAGE. You really want her to sit down with someone who was on the *Internet* while she was in the *carriage* and have them explain to her that there *was no bomb*?"[34]

We glared angrily at each other. I had won that round. But then he smiled, as if to say he had something better. It was, his smile said, time to pull out the big guns.

"When Rachel North came to one of our meetings in the upstairs room of a pub," he said, "I thought her behavior showed signs of"—he paused—"mental illness."

"You think Rachel's *mentally ill*?" I said. It was a low blow.

"It was the degree to which she attacked me," David said. "She stood up and came running towards me and shouted at me. There was a *madness* to this—"

"But that's because she thinks it's nonsense—" I interrupted.

"She won't look at the *evidence*," interrupted David. "I'm getting the same sort of vibe off you here, Jon. A viewpoint arrived at without evidence is *prejudice*. To say Muslims carried out 7/7—those three guys from Leeds and one from Aylesbury—to say they did it is RACIST, Jon. It's racist. It's racist. You're being RACIST to Muslims if you think they carried out that attack on the evidence there."

There was a short silence.

"Oh, *fuck off*," I said.

There are epistemic lessons to draw here. First, what makes a conspiracy nut a *nut* isn't the beliefs he has; it's his epistemic practices; it's that he demands justifications where justifications are unneeded! (It's that he's a nut about *evidence*; that he's nutty about what he believes is a strictly *derivative* fact.) This isn't, pace Aikin and other justification-regress plyers, a matter of pragmatics. It's especially important to realize it's not seen this way by most people.[35] Second, philosophers—even ones who believe in justificational stopping points—haven't been sure exactly how one is supposed to respond to a demand for justification

[34] A personal note. I laugh every time I read this bit, I really do. But I'm quite sure that emotional reaction is covering up something else. *Fear*, if I'm not mistaken.

[35] After this interview was aired on BBC Radio 4, Ronson was afraid to check his email. When he did, however (2011, 196), "it was—I discovered to my delight—filled with congratulations from listeners. The consensus was that I had struck a blow for rational thinking. This felt good: it is always good to be commended for thinking rationally."

when it's directed toward a justificational stopping point. Often mentioned is the Ducassean (Ducasse (1944)) suggestion that one simply repeats one's claim. It's not realized, apparently, that this can only be done in real conversations either out of exasperation or irritation or because of the impression that the hearer *couldn't* have heard what was just said. To *nakedly challenge* a justificational stopping point by asking *why* the agent believes it is absurd; and the agent naturally responds to the absurdity in any of the number of ways my extensive quotation from Ronson illustrates. By repeating obvious truisms slowly (or rapidly, if one is very annoyed), by being sarcastic or getting very angry (if, for example, you're covered in debris and the person is asking how you *know* you're covered in debris), by using words like "nonsense" or phrases like "Oh, come *on*," or even obscenities. Third, notice that the justificational stopping points aren't to be straightforwardly described as falling into the traditional categories that philosophers typically reach for: immediate sense experience, a priori truths, and the like. The stopping points are mostly "external-world" truisms—"facts."

Apart from these lessons, a methodological point is worth stressing: Giving clear, straightforward, concrete cases is better than making one's case in the abstract (although, of course, abstract presentations can rhetorically pay off in *spades*). Aikin (2011, 4) writes:

> Being justified requires that you be able to give reasons you justifiably hold are good reasons. It seems a simple truism. Who would say someone knows that p [when], if asked why he believes it, he shrugged his shoulders and uttered an inarticulate "Hmmmm, I dunno." Or alternatively, concedes, "I feel like I know, but I can't explain or show how"?

Put this way, it *does* sound weird. But that's because of Aikin's abstract presentation. When we look at specific cases such as Ronson's response (and North's, for that matter) to Shayler's demand that they look more closely at "the evidence," it's perfectly clear how reasonable rejecting his demand is. What's important is to see how and when demands for justification can and can't be justifiably rejected—why naked challenges aren't acceptable.[36]

[36] There is more to say here, that I can't say in this book. My use of "naked challenge" is meant to echo Brandom and Williams's default and challenge conception, according to which (2001, 150–151) knowledge challengers can't simply demand justifications but must have "specific reasons for questioning either the truth of the target belief or the claimant's entitlement to hold it." The default and challenge conception, however, shares the Sellersian assumption with the infinitist that both knowledge claimants and critics have justificational obligations—a picture I've already undermined in this chapter, in chapter 1, and that I'll undermine (further) in the next section. The upshot: We need another explanation for why rebuffing demands for justification are legitimate—when they are. Again, I must defer details to *Challenging Knowledge*.

I've raised one of Aikin's considerations about what drives the justificational regress; I should also rebut two other objections Aikin raises to the suggestion that sometimes we aren't required to justify knowledge that we're nevertheless justified in having. Aikin (2011, 175) claims that such cases are all *special cases*: children, animals—and incompetent adults. This is wrong; these are *not* special cases, as the real cases of (numerous) mathematicians and that of North and Ronson (all cases of competent adults) show. I don't deny that we need to know what's behind the distinction between legitimate and illegitimate justification demands—but it cannot be denied that there is such a distinction and that prima facie it's not pragmatic (or the like) but purely epistemic. Aikin gives a second argument, in the context of the issue of whether the sceptic (or his knowledge-claiming opponent) has the burden of proof. Aikin (175) writes:

> even if the skeptic's principles are false, it doesn't follow that we are justified, unless we think that the burden of proof is always and only on the skeptic. And that seems to get things utterly backwards—if you're claiming you know, then *you* have the burden of proof.

Wait. Why do *you* have the burden of proof if you claim to know something? Just by the sheer fact that you claim to know something? Surely that needs an argument. It does seem to be common sense to think that your taking yourself to know something *doesn't mean* you have the burden of proof—rather, when you're challenged, *you have to see that the challenge has been sustained* for you to rationally drop your claim to know. This suggests that what Williams calls "naked challenges"—mere demands that you justify that you know what you know, which are the sorts of challenges Klein uses to drive the justification regress—aren't acceptable. But this needs further exploration because, as I've just indicated, we need something more basic that will enable us to understand why naked challenges are ruled out (if and when they are) and exactly what makes a challenge legitimate. In any case, opponents have to stop thinking it's *obvious* that it's either sceptics or it's knowledge claimants who *always* have the burden of proof. Surely there's an argument for when this happens and when it doesn't. And if there is, the result of it probably won't be a general claim that knowledge challengers—or knowledge claimants—*always* have the burden of proof.[37]

[37] Again: I plan to discuss all this in the detail it deserves in *Challenging Knowledge*.

8.7 Metacognitive Motivations for Enriching Justification

There are other thought experiments—about our justification practices—that philosophers have claimed show that the cognitively thin notion of justification I've been arguing for violates the justification practices we routinely engage in; and further, that the distinction between being justified and having a justification that I rely on (and claim is part of our ordinary justification practices) is wrong.[38] Consider a modification of a thought experiment originally due to Mark Kaplan (1991, 135).[39] Imagine a philosopher who (like myself) has a thin notion of justification—one that allows that an agent can be justified without a capacity to articulate reasons. Kaplan imagines that philosopher having the following nightmare (I've modified the example so that it puts more direct pressure on my view):

> Imagine that you are sitting in a doctor's crowded waiting room. The novel you have brought to read while you wait has just become interesting when the man sitting three seats to your left rises, points to you, and declares, in a voice loud enough for all to hear, "This person is a traitor to our country!" Needless to say, you are taken aback. "What, if anything, justifies your belief that I am a traitor?" you ask the man. Your accuser is calm. He explains that, although he recognizes that in accusing you of treason, he has made the sort of claim that may well require justification, he cannot at present produce the justification for you. Nevertheless, he continues, he is confident that he is indeed justified in his belief that you are a traitor and, thus, he is confident that, with enough time and effort (similar to the time and effort that cognitive ethologists expend when studying animals), an appropriate justification for this belief can be elicited from him.

Kaplan (135) thinks that the following response isn't available to the dreamer (I've again modified the response to fit the specific case I'm looking at):

[38] As I noted in note 12, *many* philosophers like this distinction. Leite (2004, 220) resists, writing: "Being justified, I will propose, is ordinarily a matter of being able to justify one's belief—that is, of being able to develop and provide an appropriate and adequate defense of one's belief when asked to do so under appropriate conditions." Unsurprisingly, Leite (2004, 250 n. 34) resists talking about animals "reasoning," writing that, "If we fail to recognize that [this talk] is an extension to the more primitive case of notions which apply in the first instance to the more sophisticated adult case, then we might be tempted to treat the adult case as being merely the more primitive case along with something added (the ability for explicit reflection, deliberation, etc.)." I discuss the usage evidence Leite gives for his claims later in this section.

[39] I'm grateful to Ram Neta for urging me to engage with Kaplan (1991) and Leite (2004).

> It is irresponsible to make a claim—and, more to the point, intellectually dishonest to believe a claim—for which one admits he is not now able to produce appropriate justification. It is the justification one produces that should convince a person of the justifiability of the claim, not the person's conviction in the justifiability of the person's claim that should convince him that there must be a justification that can be produced for it.

It's not available because:

> [On the view of the philosopher in question] there is nothing intellectually dishonest in believing a claim to be true, and believing oneself to be justified in believing that claim to be true, while admitting, at the same time, both that it is the kind of claim that may well require justification and that one cannot at present produce appropriate justification for believing the claim to be true.[40]

There are a number of complexities in Kaplan's case that should immediately make us suspicious. Let's start by considering a seeing-eye dog which has been trained to recognize the presence of black ice. Such a dog, when guiding a blind person, and when faced with black ice, will stop walking. If the person the dog is guiding urges the dog to move, the dog will refuse, sitting down, etc. rather than walk the person over the black ice. The dog, presumably cannot explain how she knows about the black ice; she can't explain how her own perceptual faculties work—that "look, there's black ice in front of us that I can see and you can't." Similarly, if we recognize that an animal knows something (for example, in spring as so many animals do, the way back to where he was born), we can ask ourselves, "how does the animal know this?" and we can try to figure it out; but we won't ask the animal! The same is the case with amnesiacs or other cases of human knowers who have no access to the particulars of their own knowing relations; they don't even know they know what they know, let alone know any facts about that knowing relation. (In such a case, to say to the amnesic: "how did you know how to get home?" is to invite the answer, "I don't know.")

Kaplan's case of the man sitting three seats to your left in the doctor's waiting room is quite different. (Call the man "the accuser"; call you, "the dreamer.") We presume—as in a large number of cases with normal articulate humans—that (as I put it in section 6.4) if the accuser knows that he knows you're a traitor, he must have *some* additional knowledge about himself or about the particulars of his cognitive relation to the fact that you're a traitor.

40 Kaplan's specific charge, at this point, is directed toward Chisholm, although he later generalizes it. I'm only focused on whether the charge can be directed toward my position.

And, indeed, when the dreamer protests, "what, if anything, justifies your belief that I am a traitor?" what's being presumed by the dreamer (reasonably enough) is that the accuser knows why he knows you're a traitor. The challenge, therefore, is clearly a metacognitive one—the dreamer is demanding that the accuser provide some particulars about his knowing relation to the proposition that the dreamer is a traitor. That's what a request for justification amounts to. And this is where things in the dream get weird. Recall again what Kaplan writes:

> It is irresponsible to make a claim—and, more to the point, intellectually dishonest to believe a claim—for which one admits he is not now able to produce appropriate justification. It is the justification one produces that should convince a person of the justifiability of the claim, not the person's conviction in the justifiability of the person's claim that should convince him that there must be a justification that can be produced for it.

A couple of things are being run together here that should be separated. First of all, consider a mathematician like Ramanujan (chapter 6, n. 50), or others, such as von Neumann—where in Ramanujan's case no proofs were usually offered for what he, nevertheless, knew, and in von Neumann's case, the proofs that he gave were often wrong. In both cases, it's precisely the confidence of those particular mathematicians' convictions in the justifiability of their claims that convinces others that they know what they claim to know. In such cases, the mathematician can say, as he's said correctly in the past, "oh I can find a proof if you need one," or even, "I can't find a proof—but *you* can find a proof, I'm sure, if you need one." So it is *not* always "intellectually dishonest" to believe a claim that one can't now give a justification for—sometimes yes, sometimes no. But Kaplan's case is weird because the accuser—a stranger—seems to be expecting the dreamer to accept his confidence *all by itself* as a reason to be convinced that the accuser knows the dreamer is a traitor. Even weirder, the accuser seems to think his expression of sheer confidence should convince someone—a stranger—that he knows what he claims to know. For consider: The accuser is claiming to know something on the grounds of his own sheer confidence that "with enough time and effort an appropriate justification for this belief can be elicited from him," without explaining why the dreamer should believe *that*.[41] But nevertheless, the accuser is expecting the dreamer to accept this—to be convinced by this. Unless we know something special about the knowledge claimant (as the mathematicians

[41] Imagine this alternative to Kaplan's case, the accuser says instead, "Whenever I have a special feeling of confidence like I have now that *p*, it always turns out *p*." In this case the dreamer might be telling the truth although it's clear that, nevertheless, a stranger in a waiting room has no reason to *believe* him.

around Ramanujan or von Neumann did know about them) this isn't compelling. The accuser is offering a metacognitive statement that amounts to this: "I know nothing about my own cognitive relationship to *p* except that I'm confident of *p*.[42] But don't worry; that's enough to be confident I know *p* anyway. And you—the dreamer—should be similarly confident." *No* epistemic view, I would expect (mine included) claims that, when a justification is asked for, it's sufficient to respond—without giving any further considerations—that one doesn't have a justification but (don't worry) it exists somewhere or other. (My thanks to Noelle Ballesteros for the seeing-eye dog example, and for discussion that made it clear I needed to say more about Kaplan's case than I originally did. I replaced two of the original paragraphs on Kaplan's case with these several paragraphs on March 26, 2020.)

The more general point (and warning) is that we should be very careful about taking cases that involve interactions—challenges to knowledge—and treating the metacognitive maneuvers that (must) occur there as automatically yielding results about when and how our notions of knowledge and justification can be attributed to agents or vice versa. (As I've said several times already, this is a topic I take up in the detail it deserves in *Challenging Knowledge*.)

Nevertheless, I want to illustrate this warning again, this time by discussing Leite's subtle and sophisticated arguments against those who take seriously the distinction between being justified and having a justification. He claims that a fundamental error of "the Spectatorial Conception" of justification is that such a view sees being justified as (2004, 222, italics his)

> something which *happens to you*. . . . [T]he justification status of a person's belief is determined by certain facts which obtain prior to and independently of the activity of justifying. The activity itself plays no role in determining justificatory status; it is simply a secondary and optional matter of attempting to determine and report, as far as is conversationally necessary, the prior and independent facts which determine the justificatory status of one's belief. . . . On this conception, one stands in a primarily theoretical or epistemic relation to the justificatory status of one's beliefs: positive justificatory status is something which one finds out about, not something which one brings about.

Leite is arguing for a *very strong* position: Being justified is always a *doing*—in particular, it's always a commitment.[43] Therefore, the opponent position (strictly)

[42] Maybe he doesn't even have this; maybe he's only confident that he knows *p*; he's only indirectly confident about *p* itself.

[43] Neta (2019) share this commitment view. I discuss some of Neta's positive arguments for the position shortly.

is: Justification isn't *always* a doing. This is important precisely because Leite officially targets an opponent position on which being justified is *never* a doing. I'll argue for a position (one I *have*) on which being justified is *sometimes* a doing.[44]

I'll start by noting Leite's objection that there is something epistemically off about the Spectatorial Conception; this is that, on such a view, one is—as it were—inspecting one's own psychology in order to find the reasons one has for one's position. Leite (2004, 226) claims this view "fits poorly with what often goes on when people develop or offer reasons for their beliefs." For consider (italics his):

> You confidently hold a particular belief which you did not arrive at through an explicit process of inference or reasoning. Someone challenges you: "On what do you base that belief? Why do you think it is true?" To answer this question you do not consider facts about yourself or your psychology, such as how you came to hold the belief, but instead what there is to be said in favor of the belief—whether and why you should hold it. So in many cases, deliberating about whether a consideration represents one of your reasons is a matter of *evaluating possible reasons for holding the belief.* It is a matter of looking outward, as it were, considering or reconsidering the issue at hand and taking a stand on particular grounds, not of looking inward and attempting to ferret out prior facts about the explanation of your beliefs.

This description trades on a false dichotomy: That I'm to investigate my reasons for something can't be both an attempt to ferret out prior facts and simultaneously to consider or (especially) reconsider those facts. After all, I can always say (and people often do say), "Actually, I thought *p*, but that's not quite right . . ." Most people assume two things when challenged to offer their reasons. First, that if they have a position for reasons, the best way to figure out what those reasons are is to investigate what reasons one has (or can think up) for a claim. This can, and with thoughtful introspective people often does, lead to a mismatch between what they realize they thought and what they think now (what they think they should have as reasons). Nothing about being justified being a commitment follows from *this*.

But the second thing most people assume about their reasons is that those reasons are visible to them. This is some version of a mental transparency view—but, after all, transparency views about the human mind are rooted in our all-too-common ordinary assumption that what's going on in our minds—*especially*

[44] It might be thought that this will at least lead to there being two ways of being justified; two "kinds" of justification, if you will. But really, as I'll indicate momentarily, tense is tripping us up. Perhaps an agent's being justified always turns on that agent (at some time) having done something. (Perhaps this is even true of animals, even if they're not conscious of what they've done.) It doesn't follow that *being justified* must always *be* a doing.

at the present moment—is easily accessible. This explains a second purported mismatch Leite (2004, 226) attributes to the Spectatorial Conception vis-à-vis "what people say in defense of their beliefs" (again, italics his):

> According to the Spectatorial Conception, to ask for a person's reactions for holding a belief is to ask the person to describe or report certain facts about his belief which obtain independently of and prior to his consideration of them. However, we do not ordinarily proceed as if stating one's reasons were a matter of making this sort of report. Instead, we proceed as if someone who deliberates about or offers reasons in justification of a belief is doing something which fixes what her reasons are: namely, *committing to particular reasons for holding the belief.*

For example, we can ask, "Are you really willing to base your belief in the suspect's innocence upon the testimony of a convicted felon?" Leite (227) writes (italics his):

> Such questions indicate that we generally don't treat what people say in defense of their beliefs as merely *evidence about*, or an *indication of*, the reasons for which they hold their beliefs, but rather as a direct expression of their rational activity.

"Consider," he writes,:

> someone who replied to the question, "Upon what reasons do you base that belief? What are your reasons for holding it?" by saying, "to the best of my knowledge, they are ____. Yes, I am pretty sure they are ____." In many cases we would not reply to such a statement by urging the person to investigate his psychology further. [Leite's n. 24 appears here—see below.] Instead, we would say something along the lines of, "Make up your mind! Are those the reasons for which you believe that, or aren't "they?" What he needs to do is deliberate further about what he is willing to offer as a basis for his claim. His uncertainty about his reasons would be unintelligible in many cases unless we treat it as a consequence of his failure (or unwillingness) to commit to holding his belief upon particular grounds. One cannot always treat one's relation to one's own reasons as if it were merely a topic for investigation and report.

We are again being forced to consider a false dichotomy. And what gives the game away is an observation Leite (2004, 248 n. 24) mentions, due to Fred Schmitt, about the relevance of *tense*. When people try to reconstruct an explicit pattern of inference they once went through to arrive at a belief, it *is* natural to tell the person to investigate his psychology further.

But we can imagine a case where a person is trying not only to reconstruct his previous inference, but simultaneously to evaluate whether he should stand by it. And indeed, this is the sort of thing that goes on *most of the time*. We have to realize that, again, a metacognitive process is complicating the analysis we have to run of these cases.

And that's not all that's complicating the analysis! The first point to mention is that committing oneself isn't a particularly special agential activity. That's why it can't do the work Leite (and Neta, as I'll indicate in a moment) want it to do. I commit myself, under a broad range of circumstances (for example), to whatever it is I'm saying when I assert it.[45] Doing so isn't (so I've argued) to do anything even remotely metacognitive—not necessarily, that is. Committing oneself, therefore, is fairly low-level cognitively speaking. The second point (that can easily trip us up), however, is that committing is always a present-tense activity. If I'm committing myself, I'm doing so at the moment. I can *maintain* a commitment (I've made in the past) and I can do so without explicitly thinking of it; but that isn't to recommit in the present moment. Being justified may be based on a previous commitment; that doesn't make it a current commitment except in the ordinary sense that an agent still has all her old commitments if she doesn't drop them.

Let's see how this plays out with respect to Neta's (2019) argument that a certain kind of (self-referential metacognitive) psychological event is *required* to explain certain intricacies about justification.[46] Neta notices something striking. Suppose an agent for very good reasons thinks *p*. Unfortunately, she's also given at that moment excellent reasons to think that her very good reasons aren't good reasons; and, also unfortunately, the excellent reasons are misleading ones.[47] This is a case where the misleading evidence seems to pressure the agent's justifiably drawing the conclusion *p*. But what's clear (and striking) is that if that agent

[45] Not always, of course, as I showed in chapter 4.

[46] I won't dwell on this, but Neta claims that what's needed is a kind of cognitive action that *simultaneously* is a doing and an awareness of that doing: a phenomenologically self-referential cognitive act. (We might call it "metacognition with a vengeance.") He claims this is necessary to explain both the temporal power of the agent's present-moment evaluation of her own reasons (to be described in a moment) *and* that the agent can't be wrong about her present-tense psychological commitments. What I won't dwell on is that—independently of Neta's arguments that only this kind of self-referential cognitive act can explain the phenomena mentioned in the last sentence (which I'll argue against)—I find the attribution of such a cognitive act to *anyone*, however mentally sophisticated, bizarre and implausible. (And this is despite such an attribution having venerable antecedents in Kantian apperception.)

[47] Neta's (2019, 187–188) example. So-Hyun for a number of good reasons R believes Russian forces have bombed civilian targets in Syria. An expert (a "mind-reading logician and statistician") tells So-Hyun that in fact, although R is completely correct, it doesn't support the hypothesis that Russian forces have bombed civilian targets in Syria. Although So-Hyun continues to "*have* good normative reasons to believe that Russian forces bombed civilian targets in Syria," if she has no reason to discount the expert's testimony, then "her belief concerning Russian forces loses ex post justifiedness." Neta is deliberately cautious about the conclusions he draws. But there are many similar examples, which put pressure, one way or another, on an agent being justified in such circumstances.

learns of the misleading evidence *later*, it doesn't pressure her previously being justified in thinking *p*. Also clear (and striking) is that if a third party who takes that misleading evidence seriously evaluates the agent and knows the agent is unaware of the misleading evidence, he won't find that that evidence plays a role in pressuring the agent's being justified.[48]

How is this to be explained? (How is it to be explained, that is, without having to claim that "justification" is a special present-tense psychological act of commitment the way that Leite and Neta do, and without having to undercut the distinction between being justified and being able to give a justification?) This way. What's relevant to an agent being justified at a moment is whatever it is—at that moment—that the agent is cognizant of. Being justified is something the grounds for which shift over time. At a moment what justifies my belief that I'm face to face with a predator is being face to face with that predator. Later, what justifies my belief that I was face to face with a predator is my memory of being face to face with that predator. I can be justified in believing *p* at one moment and not be a moment later just because what I'm aware of has changed.

Nothing changes with respect to being able to express my justifications (and nothing should, since being able to explain why I'm justified is—in the best circumstances—being able to describe what it is that makes me justified). Here too, things can (and do) change moment to moment. It's no surprise, therefore, that if misleading evidence is brought to my attention later, the fact that it's brought to my attention *later* can have no effect on whether I'm justified or not *earlier*. So too, if a third party has evidence (misleading or otherwise) that I don't have—unless my lacking that evidence bears on whether I'm justified—it has no effect. All of this can be explained without having to hypothesize that agents who are justified are, by virtue of that, doing something that's present-tense special and needs therefore to be analyzed in a way that invokes a special psychological state that's metacognitive, or committing, or in some other way, an *action*.

8.8 Concluding Remarks

I close this chapter by describing two tasks, one which I take on in the rest of this book and the second which I don't. There seem sharp differences between the demands placed on different kinds of knowers, or even on the same knowers in

[48] In terms of the jargon I use later—in chapter 11—"justif(y/ies)" is criterion-immanent, in contrast to "know(s)," which is criterion-transcendent. I'm putting this carefully because our reactions to misleading evidence that an agent faces (at a moment), and in particular, to what ways that agent has or hasn't access to the misleading evidence, are complicated (and not well understood); and so there is controversy about it. See my discussion of this in section 9.3, as well as the material I cite in note 12 of chapter 9.

different situations (or with respect to different items of knowledge). Sometimes, it seems, knowers really do strike us as required to provide correct justifications if they're to know what they claim to know. The considerations that seem to make sceptical arguments so compelling, for example, apparently turn on knowers needing to *provide* adequate justifications (and not merely *having* such justifications). On the other hand, we also seem to let knowers off the hook even when their justifications are obviously inadequate or nonexistent. This isn't just the case with animals and artifacts—creatures that can't provide justifications; it's also the case for competent reasoning humans, as I illustrated in section 8.5.

This difference, I think, isn't to be handled by saying, as Pryor does, that there is a difference between being justified and being able to provide justifications (and that's the end of it) or by saying, as Aikin does, that if you are a competent adult (and not an epistemically limited agent—a child or animal), then, of course, you *have to* provide justifications. Because you're the adult, after all! (Aikin (2011, 175)). Similarly, it's wrong to think that making a knowledge claim means you have the burden of proof. Or, instead, that by the sheer virtue of having a belief, you're entitled to think it's presumptively true.[49] Or that in justifying oneself—deductively or otherwise—one is engaging in a potentially self-conscious mental act with special phenomenological qualities. Usage data is incompatible with all of these positions. The data is also incompatible with a contextualist view of justification—which some will be tempted to solve this challenge by means of.

So here are the two tasks. The first is to explain enough about our concepts of knowledge, knowing, and the like to understand why a single word fits with what this chapter and the preceding ones reveal about the diversity of the agents we routinely attribute knowledge to. The second is to illuminate what's behind the distinction between when we're required to justify ourselves and when we're not. I take up the first task in the rest of this book; I take up the second in a later book (as I keep promising).

[49] Fogelin (1994, 147) writes: "Typically, the negative coherentist does not accept the principle that a belief can be justified only by another belief, but holds, instead, that a belief—just in being a belief—is presumptively true; innocent until proven guilty." This view, as stated, is very similar to the default and challenge conception where, as Williams (2001, 24) says, "entitlement to one's beliefs is the default position; but entitlement is always vulnerable to undermining by evidence that one's epistemic performance is not up to par." These views *cannot* be the right way to put the matter, if only because the sensible agent (the sensible agent who is capable of doing this, I mean) always thinks: "Some of these beliefs of mine *can't* be right. I wonder where the mistakes are?" (Think of someone who has just finished a very big book, one that's full of pronouncements—something, maybe, like *this* big book.) The default in question can't be characterized in terms of single beliefs, as it is in these formulations.

9

Confidence, Belief, and Knowledge; The Vagueness of "Know(s)"

9.1 Introduction

In the course of these last three chapters (9, 10, and 11), all the previous jigsaw pieces about knowledge, "know(s)," "justif(y/ies)," and justification—about the semantics and usage of these and other epistemic words, assertion actions and their relations (or non-relations) to knowledge, iterated and ground-floor cognitions, empirical studies and our ordinary cognition-attribution practices—along with a couple of new pieces, will finally be assembled into a cohesive picture of how these words, and our accompanying concepts, work. One indication that I've succeeded (*if* I succeed) is that a number of long-standing puzzles about epistemic words and phrases are resolved.

The plot for this chapter: In section 9.2, I review and illustrate the "piecemeal landscape" of knowledge: that the knowledge of epistemic agents and the justifications they possess for that knowledge, if any, are fragmentary. This fragmentedness has two dimensions: hierarchical, because knowledge isn't iterated knowledge, and lateral, because knowledge of *p* can be accompanied by ignorance of closely related *q*, *r*, . . ., etc. I show in section 9.3 how being clear about when an agent is engaged in iterated cognition and when not helps us to distinguish among the different cases where an agent knows things without being confident of that knowledge or the truth of those things. Although the confidence of an agent in *p* isn't a necessary condition on that agent knowing *p*, still remaining is a more nuanced position: an agent's confidence in *p* is a necessary condition on that agent knowing *p* only if that confidence is constitutive of or supervenient on how she comes to know *p*.

In section 9.4, I explore an important corollary of the fragmentedness of knowledge. Given that having knowledge requires meeting certain standards (e.g., of reliability), the epistemic standards of agents are inaccessible to those agents—regardless of how sophisticated they are, and (usually) regardless of whether or not they have iterated knowledge. It's like our knowledge of natural languages: speaker-hearers easily distinguish grammatical from ungrammatical sentences; they *know* which strings of words are grammatical and which aren't

Attributing Knowledge. Jody Azzouni, Oxford University Press (2020). © Oxford University Press.
DOI: 10.1093/oso/9780197508817.001.0001.

(apart from issues of performance, like being unable to grasp long sentences). Despite this, they have no idea what rules (if any) psychologically enable grammatical-ungrammatical distinctions. Not only are knowledge standards and other related epistemic standards (e.g., justification standards, belief standards, if any, etc.) inaccessible to epistemic agents, but they're vague insofar as the same agent can shift in the stringency of the standards she's using over time. Different agents—at the same time, even when conversing with one another—can also differ in the stringency of the standards they're (respectively) using.

Understanding the vagueness of "know(s)" requires having the right picture of vagueness itself (the main foil is Williamson's (1994) epistemicism, but many standard approaches to vagueness in semantics are also targets) as well as seeing how vagueness affects knowledge attribution—in particular, the apparent shiftiness in knowledge standards that motivates contextualism, anti-intellectualism, and knowledge relativism.

Vagueness can be visible or invisible. Natural-language words apply via paradigms and foils, and the "resemblances" between candidate referents and these paradigms and foils are vague. These "resemblances," however—as well as the paradigms and foils themselves—can be simple and obvious (e.g., colors) or intricate and not visible. Because the standard for baldness is obvious to speaker-hearers—it's on the surface of how we're taught the word—speaker-hearers don't argue about whether someone is bald or not. It's fairly obvious to everyone that, and why, "bald" is vague (and people don't argue over obvious vagueness unless they're having fun with one another); it's also obvious that there's no real principle about this to be recognized or adjudicated.

The vagueness of many words is like that of "bald"—color words, as mentioned, as well as other expressions for sensory qualities, quantifiers like "most," and, of course, the always-popular "heap." It's important to realize, however, that some words aren't like this, that the vagueness of the epistemic standards for words like "know(s)" and "justif(y/ies)" are quite invisible to speaker-hearers, whether those speaker-hearers are sophisticated or not. This is because the mechanisms by which (for example) we recognize someone to know or not to know something (or to be justified in a claim) aren't obvious *at all*—not even after careful thought. Thus, epistemic agents can—and often do—disagree about whether someone knows something, or is justified. That agents disagree in this way is an important datum: it's one of the keys, in particular, to the solution to a number of philosophical puzzles about knowledge.[1]

[1] Schiffer (1996) doesn't recognize the obvious/unobvious vagueness distinction; he thinks all vagueness is visible. That's why he's pessimistic about a vagueness approach handling the apparent shiftiness of knowledge standards.

Many philosophers interpret the semantics of vague expressions as accountable for vagueness—for example, requiring a word to have by virtue of its meaning a three-way relationship to items in the world: applying, not applying, and, thirdly, neither applying nor not applying.[2] An approach to vagueness is "epistemic" if, instead, it places vagueness within the scope of the epistemic expression of ignorance—if it's *not* handled by the word's (semantically defined) application conditions.[3] There are two versions of *epistemicism*: they don't differ in their descriptions of how we use epistemic expressions of ignorance (both take vague cases as ones where agents "don't know" whether a sentence is true or a predicate applies to something) but rather, in their "metaphysical" assumptions.

Williamson's (1994) "epistemicism" requires our (collective) adherence to bivalence as treating "not knowing *p*" as nevertheless metaphysically committed to *p* being or not being the case "in reality."[4] Given any predicate G and any candidate b that G may apply to, *in fact* G holds of b *or* it doesn't. This is true regardless of whether there is a method—even in principle—by which this supposed metaphysical fact can be determined, and regardless of whether we can tell a metaphysical story (related to the use of our words) about what does, in fact, determine the application (or not) of G to b. My "epistemicism," instead, regards expressions of ignorance ("I don't know whether he's bald or not") as placing no metaphysical constraints on the facts: he may, "in reality," be bald or not bald, or there may be no fact of the matter about whether he's bald.

For that matter, a commitment to classical two-valued logic places no metaphysical constraints on reality either.[5] On the contrary, a literal and straightforward adoption of classical two-valued logic (along with accompanying expressions of ignorance, in cases of vagueness) is *not*, as Quine (1981b, 32) writes, "the hallmark of realism."[6] The disagreement between these epistemicist positions may seem "pure metaphysics," resolvable only by a focus on reality (and an accompanying focus on the "machinery" that semantically

[2] The options are complicated: there's a *big* literature on the semantics of vagueness. For example, if the targeted items are graded, application conditions for words may acknowledge that by failing to draw sharp borders in any number of ways between items words apply to and ones they don't. I've implicitly described semantic approaches as deserting two-valuedness by introducing a third way apart from a word applying or not applying to an item. Although semantic approaches to vagueness are often like this, it's not mandatory. A language could have a logic that isn't two-valued, where apart from its three or more truth values, vagueness is additionally handled semantically.

[3] Epistemicist approaches, formally, couple axioms for a semantic theory of a language with those for a "know(s)" operator: together they handle vagueness while being conservative on the implications of the semantic theory alone. See Azzouni (2017b, section 4.5) for further details.

[4] As I noted in note 2, this description can be generalized beyond the two-valued case.

[5] See Azzouni (2017b, section 4.5).

[6] Quine attributes the catchphrase to Dummett, writing (1981b, 32), "as Dummett argues . . ." But "bivalence is the hallmark of realism"—widely used thereafter by others—isn't in Dummett (1963), and an example that Dummett does give in that paper (155–156) suggests he wouldn't accept it. (For that matter, Quine must know that his catchphrase is misleadingly loose.)

attaches our words to reality). Not so: differences in these views affect the topics of this book—the position I argue for is unavailable to those with Williamson's view on vagueness, as I'll illustrate in this chapter and the next one.

In section 9.5, I consider Williamson's argument against KK. It doesn't work because it presupposes the necessity of confidence for knowledge; this is ironic because seeing that confidence isn't necessary for knowledge requires already realizing that KK and other cognitive iteration theses are false. To undercut KK, we must approach it as I have in this book—directly recognizing that the attitude the word expresses belongs to a family of cognitive (and emotional) attitudes, where no general iterative thesis about any of these is true; and also recognizing that when an iteration of cognitive attitudes *is* true, it itself is a substantial attribution to an agent. This is something I've been laboring to establish in different ways in *many* chapters (5, 6, 7, and 8). In section 9.6, I summarize, and prepare for the next chapter.

9.2 Piecemeal Knowledge and Piecemeal Iterated Knowledge

I start the analysis, as promised, by revisiting fragmentary knowledge. Consider a case of perception accompanied by iterated cognitions. Suppose I know *that there is a lizard on the ground in front of me* because I see it. Suppose, further, I know *that I see that there is a lizard on the ground in front of me.* Still further yet, I know *that I know that there is a lizard on the ground in front of me* because I grasp that this specific knowing relationship between me and the lizard is based on my seeing that lizard. In knowing that I know that there is a lizard on the ground, I nevertheless can (and do) remain ignorant of much else about the nature of perception (as humans have for millennia, and as most humans continue to: only recently do vision scientists know *something* of what's involved in this sensory relationship). Knowing that *p* and knowing that one knows that *p* (for that matter) are always pinprick-bright moments in what's otherwise complete darkness about so much else that's related both to knowing that *p* and to knowing that one knows that *p*. This is true for all *p*.

What's widely called the "holism of the mental" or, less poetically, the *systematicity* of mental phenomena has been stressed repeatedly over the last century by, e.g., Davidson, Dennett, Dretske, Fodor, and many others. But the "holism of the mental" slogan and the accompanying view commonly run an insight together with a mistake. The mistake is assuming that knowledge and beliefs must be rich—hierarchically and laterally. No—as I've been arguing throughout this book. It *is* true that beliefs, knowledge, desires, etc., operate as an inferential package that agents employ to navigate and understand their worlds (and that we, correspondingly, interpret them with). The insight doesn't need the mistake: drones and simple-minded animals embody similar "holisms of the mind"—inferential packages the contents of which (in tandem) they use to handle behavior, desires, beliefs, and knowledge. B.B. of section 6.3 exhibits a holism of the mind similar to ours—despite the meager contents of its thinking. Determining what concepts B.B. has—the project of that section—presupposes the constraints of the holism of B.B.'s mind.

A second point about, specifically, knowledge: An agent's knowledge, we think, is much more than what that agent is occurrently aware of. I'm taken (by myself and others) to know 2 plus 2 is 4 even when I'm not thinking about it (which, happily, I'm usually not); perhaps I know 2 plus 2 is 4 even when I'm asleep—although that's controversial. I'm obviously not aware that *I'm* perceiving a lizard every time I do perceive one. We think, nevertheless, that I know I'm perceiving a lizard whenever I'm perceiving one regardless of whether I'm occurrently thinking about that—and even if I'm incapable (at that moment) of becoming occurrently aware of my knowing relation to the lizard, because, say, I'm too frightened to be aware of anything else *but* that (40-foot) lizard. If my brain is damaged so I no longer can iterate knowledge, then I'll no longer know that I'm perceiving a lizard (whatever its size), and I'll no longer know that I know that there is a lizard in front of me (when I'm watching one). Whether someone knows 2 plus 2 is 4 when she's sleeping is controversial, I think, because knowledge attributions being suitable on the basis of a capacity to bring certain occurrent thoughts to mind doesn't clearly dictate an answer one way or the other in this case. Is S's incapacity to think about 2 plus 2 being 4 when she's asleep like being too frightened to think about it, or is it more like a case of a disabled capacity? I suspect there is no non-stipulative way to decide this.

Recall from chapter 5 how easily we confuse ground-floor knowledge with (one-level) iterated knowledge—this contributes to thinking KK is true. It can be asked: "Do you know a lot of mathematics?" And the answer can be: "Yes, I do." This is iterated knowledge—despite no explicit "know(s)" iteration. The respondent knows that he knows a lot of mathematics (he knows that he knows many mathematical propositions, for example). "Do you know where Nicole is?" could be asked of someone; and the answer might be: "Yes, I remember where she told me she would be this afternoon." This is an exhibition of iterated knowledge as well, despite no explicit "know(s)" iteration.[7] Similarly, I might think: "I know *p* because I remember it" (or "because I saw it")—this is iterated cognition.

So consider an agent who knows that *p* without knowing that she knows that *p*. Does this mean she doesn't know whether she's remembering that *p*, seeing

[7] On the other hand, recall from section 5.2 that this identical question needn't request or yield an exhibition of iterative knowledge.

that *p*, or just guessing? Consider: If she knows that she remembers that *p*, then (because her remembering that *p* implies that she knows that *p*) she knows that she knows that *p*.[8] If she knows she's not guessing that *p* (or if she knows she's not doing something else rather than remembering that *p*), then she knows that she knows that *p* because she knows that she's remembering that *p*. If we think we have sure signs that we're remembering something instead of, say, confabulating apparent memories, this makes KK look trivially true. But memory has been shown as quite unreliable (at least as far as the experience of subjective certainty is concerned). So this iterated knowledge is *not* trivial, if it's had—despite the just-rehearsed reasoning.

This reasoning has additional issues. Recall my suggestion (section 6.7) that an agent can have concepts of perception and memory without having that of knowledge. This is unlikely with humans because the concept of "know(s)," developmentally, emerges early—but it seems possible because that notion is so general. I hazarded, in section 6.7, that chimpanzees don't have the notion of knowledge even if they do have one of perception or perhaps, more narrowly, "gaze." Also recall we can attribute propositional attitudes to agents without attributing to them, or needing to, a grasp of or the mere having of either the concepts in those propositions or the cognitive attitude itself directed toward those propositions. So, despite that an agent's remembering that *p* implies her knowing that *p*, it doesn't follow that because *she* knows that she remembers that *p*, then (because her remembering that *p* implies that she knows that *p*) *she* knows that she knows that *p*. The fallacious move here is to push an implication of knowledge from memory, an inference *outside* the agent's own knowledge, to one *within* that scope. Just because remembering *p* (on a sense of "remember") implies knowing *p*, it doesn't follow that because an agent knows that she remembers that *p*, she therefore knows that she knows that *p*. (We'll see in detail in chapter 10 why this doesn't follow.) The iterative cognitions that can be attributed to agents thus come apart: "S knows that she *remembers* that *p*" doesn't imply "S knows that she *knows* that *p*," even though remembering that *p* implies knowing that *p*.

Suppose we describe Rover (the dog) as perceiving that *p*, and therefore as knowing that *p* ("Rover knows that the cat is in that tree"). Rover is *in* a knowing state (Rover *has* knowledge), but he doesn't know he has knowledge, he doesn't know that he's in a state of knowing, and further, he doesn't have, let alone grasp, the concept of knowing something. Suppose Rover sees that the cat is in the tree; it isn't that Rover is remembering that the cat is in the tree. Further, Rover can tell the difference between seeing that a cat is in a tree and remembering that a cat is in a tree—after all, Rover acts differently when he sees that a cat is in a

[8] I'm relying on the factive use of "remember," not the nonfactive one. This note is for those whose "remember" allows both uses (note 44 of the introduction).

tree as opposed to when he remembers that a cat is in a tree. Recall Sultan from section 5.4: Sultan, one might think, knows the difference between remembering that *p* and seeing that *p*. After all, he too acts differently in each case. No, acting differently doesn't mean Sultan or Rover (i) knows the difference between remembering that something and seeing that something, or (ii) has—let alone grasps—the concepts of remembering and/or perceiving. Being in a state of remembering that something, as opposed to being in a state of perceiving that something, suffices to explain their different behaviors.

Recall the subordinate primate I described in section 6.7. Here, because the primate apparently averts her eyes so the dominant chimp doesn't realize where the banana is, or because she deliberately gazes toward a buried cucumber to entice the dominant chimp to pursue it instead of the more delectable banana buried elsewhere, it's natural to say she knows that the dominant chimp knows that she knows where food is buried. But *S knows that Q knows that S knows that p* implies *S knows that S herself knows that p*. Are we (given the situation is as I've described it) to attribute iterated knowledge to the subordinate chimp? Are we, further, to attribute possession of the concept of knowledge to that chimp?

No, neither of these. First, it's insufficient for knowing *q* to know *p*, and for *p* to imply *q* (pace Lewis (1996)). The agent can simply fail to recognize (or know of) the inference. Second, we must remain aware (from section 5.4) that we can describe S knowing that *p* without being required to attribute to S either the having or the grasping of the concepts occurring in *p*. This generalization includes "know(s)": S knows that S knows that *p* doesn't require S to grasp (or even have) the notion of "know(s)." Compare: "Rover knows that the cat is in the tree" doesn't require Rover to grasp or have the notion of "tree"—not *our* notion of "tree," anyway. Rover, of course, has some *concept or other* of the tree in front of him and the cat as well (concept attribution, as B.B. shows, is lightweight, although the attributed concepts may have to be designed—"engineered," if you like—to fit an agent, not ones we already have). So too, the subordinate chimp has *some* self-regarding concept or other—not knowledge, but perhaps a conceptually narrower notion of *gazing*.

It's easy to hear the legitimate cancellation of the grasping (or the having) of particular concepts in the case of "Rover knows that Olga is playing chess": "Rover knows that Olga is playing chess, although, of course, he doesn't know what chess is." It's harder to hear it in cases of iterated knowledge. "The chimp knows that she knows where the banana is, although, of course, she doesn't have a concept of knowledge." The cancellation can be heard as legitimate with more care—mentioning "seeing" or "gazing" helps—but it may still sound off, and because of this, one wants to avoid the word "know(s)" altogether, instead going straight to engineered concepts more comfortably attributed to chimps, like "gaze(s)."

Perhaps "know(s)" is different from the other lexical items, "chess," "cupboard," etc., because the implications governing it filter across epistemic phrases. More plausible, I think, than this exceptionalist doctrine for "know(s)" is that we rarely attribute *iterated* knowledge to nonhumans—only in theoretical settings. Thus, we're habitualized to expect any epistemic agent to whom we attribute iterated knowledge to also grasp the concept of knowledge. (Intuitions about Gricean cancellations are sensitive to whether or not we articulate those cancellations regularly.)

In any case, it's reasonable to think that humans know a lot about what they know. Further, given we're talking about "ourselves" (our fellow humans), it's even more natural to presume, first, that the concepts *we* use in attributing knowledge or beliefs are ones "we" possess and grasp as well.[9] And, apart from cases where we're confused or wrong, we also know that *we know something because we've seen it*, as opposed to having heard about it, or remembered it. A lot of what we (sophisticated and self-aware humans) know that we know isn't captured by the sterile formulation: S knows that she knows that *p*. If S knows that *p* because S remembers that *p* or because S sees that *p* or because S hears that *p*, and S, the human, *knows* this, that's enough for S to have an iterated knowledge cognition; those additional iterated cognitions, however, are also part of what that agent knows.

9.3 Confidence, Knowledge, and Iterated Knowledge

I not only accept that "know(s)" hasn't a definition, but in earlier chapters, I've undercut several traditional necessary conditions on "know(s)" that (most) philosophers have retained despite rejecting the possibility of a definition for "know(s)"—notably the condition that *if an agent knows p then that agent believes p*, or the condition that *if an agent knows p then that agent is conscious of p* (or *conscious at all)*. I also reject as necessary conditions that if an agent knows *p*, then that agent is confident that *p*, or confident that she knows that *p* (these aren't the same). Further illustrative detail is needed because, as has happened before, when we distinguish iterated cognitions from ground-floor cognitions, the options for cognitive states increase: we must carefully imagine cases on pain of obscuring differences. These revealed distinctions illustrate how an agent's knowledge of her own methods of knowing things can play—or not play—a

[9] We *shouldn't* assume this. Perhaps the targeted humans don't grasp certain concepts (understand them) even though they have them. We can't rule this possibility out, although we seem to—in practice, anyway: doing so is engaging in "conceptual imperialism."

constitutive role in her ground-floor knowledge (given, of course, she *has* knowledge of her own methods of knowing things).

Recall the timid-student (or timid Dorothy) cases from section 1.6 and later. Someone, we think, can know something but lack enough confidence about how she knows this that she doubts that she does know it. Her lack of confidence undercuts her knowing that she knows what she does (in fact) know. An agent's confidence *in* her memory, when she knows her memory is how she knows that *p*, is especially threatening to her thinking (believing) that she knows that something—and therefore, to her knowing that she knows it. It's common (despite these cases being characterized as rare outliers) for agents to doubt they know certain things, because (for example) they doubt they still remember them. And yet, because in many cases they *do* still remember them, they know them as well (and others, apart from the agents themselves, will take them to know these things if those agents' needed memories are demonstrably intact). S knowing that *p* and S knowing that S knows that *p* come apart in these cases because agents recognize (and thus know) something about how they know that *p*: they recognize that remembering that *p* (understood factively) is *sufficient for* knowing that *p*—that allows them to remember something without realizing they remember it, and therefore to *know* something without knowing that they know it.

A philosopher may challenge this:

> Just as someone can know something without believing it, can't he know that he knows it without believing it and without having confidence in it? Perhaps KK is true in the timid-student case: the student not only knows the historical facts about France (that he thinks he doesn't know), but he also knows that he knows them (although he thinks he doesn't). In both cases he lacks belief and confidence.

Response: This too is possible. There are two sorts of timid students: those who know what they know and those who don't. Suppose a student denies he remembers historical facts about France even though (i) he and everyone else witnessing his performance sees how he keeps "guessing" the correct answers, and (ii) he and these witnesses know that he once learned these facts. This case (once the student answers correctly often enough) is an example of "false modesty." Since the student recognizes his memory is intact, not only does he know historical facts about France that he denies knowing, but he also knows that he knows these facts because (i) he as well as the witnesses have access to the (inductive) evidence that his memory of these facts is fully intact, and (ii) he as well as the witnesses know that his memory is the sole cognitive/evidential basis on which he has knowledge of these historical facts. With respect to both knowing the facts and knowing that he knows the facts, however, he lacks belief and confidence although not knowledge.

This case must be distinguished from that of a student who hasn't (yet) seen the inductive evidence that her memory is intact—she's only answered a few questions correctly, so far, and she's therefore appropriately unsure about whether she *does* know these facts. Although she does, she doesn't know that she knows them. And witnesses will react similarly. "Let's see how she does with other questions," they'll say. This means, with additional questions, witnesses can determine whether she *does* know this material; it won't be that after answering these questions, she *now* knows the facts, but didn't before. (That's *silly*—she doesn't *acquire* knowledge of the material by answering correctly, although she does, or should, acquire knowledge of *what she knows* by answering correctly.) That timid-student cases sort out differently with respect to iterative knowing facts is a strength of the analysis I'm offering.

The same is true of deduction: after an intricate deduction, even a superlative logician can reasonably doubt whether it's right. The logician recognizes that a sufficient condition (in this case) of knowing the conclusion q is carrying out the deduction *correctly*: if he has done so, he knows q is true. But his confidence that he has carried out the deduction correctly isn't itself a factor in whether he *has* carried it out correctly. We can, thus, describe this person as knowing that q follows from p, after having deduced q correctly, even though we can also describe him as not knowing that he knows this—because his lack of confidence is due to his knowledge that (in cases like this one) he often makes mistakes. So here, he knows that q follows from p although he isn't confident (yet) that q follows from p, nor does he believe it (yet), nor does he know that he knows this (yet). This is a mundane case: I check over my deductive work three times (say). I *know* that q follows from p *the first time* I carry through the deduction correctly, although I'm neither confident of it, nor do I believe it. Only after the third time do I know that I know q follows from p (because I understand the method by which I come to learn deductions, and only now do I think I've verified that I haven't made a mistake); concomitantly, only after the third time am I confident, and only now do I *believe* that q follows from p. Diagnosis: Confounding iterated knowledge with ground-floor knowledge gives the false impression that confidence is a necessary condition of ground-floor knowledge.[10]

[10] A different case is possible. My *method* of reasoning might not be *simply* deducing; instead, it might be deduction *always* followed by a fixed number of checks on the resulting deduction. In this case, I don't know q follows from p the first time (because I'm not yet finished with the "inference"); I only know it after I've done the checks. (This is plausible if, say, my deduction is a multiplication, and I've memorized "checking.") Characterizations of methods of knowing are open to this kind of variability, depending on the agent. I discuss this further in chapter 10.

As I've said, these are ordinary cases: *many* times neither belief in *p* nor confidence about the truth of *p* is required to know that *p*. Philosophers, typically, suggest (or presume) that confidence (or the subjective impression of certainty) is a necessary condition on knowing something. In some cases—but not all—this is because of an antecedent claim that belief is necessary for knowledge; and, of course, it *does seem* that confidence is necessary for belief.[11] My counter-suggestion: confidence is *only* a necessary condition on knowing something when lack of confidence damages how an agent's knowledge would have otherwise been achieved. What follows are illustrations of how this more restricted necessary condition plays out.

The most obvious case where an agent's confidence is constitutive of her abilities to know (how, but also that) is in sports, where confidence often directly affects performance. But the same is true of cognitive tasks: performance anxiety can hamper successfully carrying out inferences or recollection. Anxiety can similarly—via undercutting iterated knowledge—undercut ground-level knowledge. Suppose I suddenly think I've discovered a fallacy in some reasoning that I've—contrary to my sudden impression—carried out appropriately (as I usually do). I can lose confidence that (and, so, lack the knowledge that) *q* follows from *p*. I may, thus, continue to lack this knowledge that *q*—if my only reason for thinking *q* is that it follows from *p*—if I continue to think I *see* (believe that there is) a fallacy in my reasoning.

Here is how lacking knowledge works in these cases. My loss of confidence undercuts what would have been my knowledge that *q*; that loss of confidence is due to my thinking I see a fallacy in my reasoning. As long as I think I see a fallacy, I won't *accept* what otherwise would have been an impeccable inference. Because I think I see a fallacy, I lack confidence in the reasoning, *and I refuse to acknowledge that I've carried it out successfully or to allow my having carried it out to license the conclusion q for me.*

I hypothesize all cases of lack of confidence (when they prevent knowledge) are like this. One consciously *doubts* one knows *q* in a way that *prevents* knowing

[11] DeRose (2009, 186) writes: "Intellectualism should be construed so that, in addition to truth-relevant factors, what attitude the subject has towards the proposition in question—how confident she is that the proposition is true, how strongly she believes it—can matter to whether the subject knows." DeRose is proposing that subjects (sometimes) have enough confidence to believe something although not enough to know it. Harman (1973), on the other hand, takes knowledge of *p* to have the traditional tripartite necessary conditions of belief, justification, and factivity. Confidence, for him, is thus a requirement for belief. Harman gives examples of "loss of knowledge" of *p*, cases where confidence (and thus belief) in *p* is lost (because of misleading evidence) or would be lost (because of misleading evidence the agent doesn't possess, e.g., Harman (1973, 142), the Tom-the-book-thief case due to Lehrer and Paxson (1969)). This particular chain of necessities, on my view, is undercut because neither belief nor confidence is necessary for knowledge. I'll show in chapter 10 and section 11.4 that the factivity of "know(s)," in any case, rules out purported misleading-evidence loss-of-knowledge cases (also see note 12 and the discussion later in this section).

q: One fails to know that one knows *q*, and then, lacking confidence in *q*, one *deliberately short-circuits how one would come to know q*. Imagine I'm convinced I'm hallucinating a lizard—not seeing a real one, although I am. If I refuse to look at the lizard or use my eyes to guide me (vis-à-vis that lizard), then my lack of confidence undercuts how I'd otherwise know a lizard is in front of me.[12]

Contrast this with Jessica, who is "neurotically" insecure about her *reasoning*: Jessica *always* doubts that she has thought through something correctly even though she (almost always) has.[13] It might even be that others regularly rely on her reasoning even though she refuses to because she's too insecure. Others will say: "Talk to Jessica about it. She always recognizes [or "knows"] the implications of a situation [or "she always gives great advice"] even though she never trusts herself." Some may say that Jessica knows that *p* although she doesn't know that she knows that *p* (or, as it's quite commonly put: "she doesn't realize that she knows that *p*"). Imagine, further, that Jessica always becomes confident of her reasoning only after she has "run it by" several people she trusts. Only then, it may be said, does she come to know that she knows it. (She comes to know, in particular, that her reasoning is impeccable.) She may even say later, with her typically nervous laugh: "I guess I did know it." And a friend may say: "You always do." She may respond: "I guess that's right." But this won't stop her from going through the same process again. In this case, notice, we can also say: "She knows that she knows this; but she's too nervous to stop herself from asking a dozen people nevertheless."

I've suggested two possibilities: Perhaps Jessica knows that *p* but doesn't know that she knows that *p*; perhaps she knows that *p* and knows that she knows that *p*. In both cases, she isn't confident (until later) about *p*; similarly, only later does she believe that *p* (and believe that she knows that *p*). The difference here with respect to iterated "know(s)" is due to differing diagnoses of how Jessica establishes

[12] It's unnatural to speak of knowledge "being lost" except when it's *forgotten*. We often talk about having forgotten how to do something because too much time has passed or (less commonly) because of a head injury. It feels weird to talk about losing knowledge when confidence is undercut because of misleading evidence (see the discussion of this toward the end of this section). Harman (1973, 148–149) writes: "Since I now know that Tom stole the book, I now know that any evidence that appears to indicate something else is misleading. That does not warrant me in simply disregarding any further evidence, since getting that further evidence can change what I know. In particular, after I get such further evidence I may no longer know that it is misleading." It sounds *extremely* odd to describe knowledge being lost *this* way—where the individual's faculties *aren't* damaged by a process (like memory loss). I discuss this further several paragraphs later. Also, see section 10.2, where I discuss Kripke's paradox explicitly: I don't solve it the way Harman tries to here (nor does Kripke (2011b, 49) endorse Harman's solution, although he agrees with Harman that knowledge can be lost this way, and he uses knowledge loss through misleading evidence as part of his solution to the surprise-exam paradox; see the appendix). Williamson (2000, 138) also thinks that knowledge can be lost because of misleading evidence, although he claims knowledge, generally, is "robust" in ways that "believing truly" isn't (62).

[13] Jessica is like certain chronically insecure friends of mine (although no friend of mine is named Jessica; people deserve their privacy). I'm sure you have friends like this too: people who just *never* trust themselves (with certain tasks or with respect to almost *everything*) although they *should*.

her iterated knowledge. Where her friends think of her as not knowing that she knows *p*, the thought is that her insecurities prevent her from relying on her own reasoning prowess to accept it as true that she knows something. She instead always relies on others to determine that she knows things, and so she doesn't know that she knows *p* until she's told (by enough people) that she does. Nevertheless, her reasoning capacities are good, and so she often knows things by reasoning them through even though she doesn't know this. The second case (motivated by her admission, let's say, that "yeah, I guess I always do know these things, but I can't stop myself because I'm so insecure") is that she *does* recognize that she knows things by inference and that her inferences can be trusted; this means that she knows that she knows that *p* once she's deduced it. She just isn't confident that she knows these things. Just as we should expect, the difference between knowing that one knows that *p* and not knowing that one knows that *p*—in this case—turns on one's (cognitive) relationship to one's own knowing relations, one's awareness and attitude toward how one knows things in these cases.

It's not, generally, easy to distinguish what's what with a particular agent; agents needn't even be consistent about this; maybe sometimes (with an insecure agent) one thing is going on and sometimes the other—sometimes he has iterated knowledge along with knowledge, and sometimes he doesn't. The point is that this analysis allows different attributions, and grounds those different attributions in the particular ways agents differ in exactly how they're insecure about what (and how) they know things.

Let's return to the case described several paragraphs back, where lack of confidence (induced doubt) doesn't induce memory failure. Remembering remains intact; but the person distrusts the apparent evidence for *p*. *Provided she's right to do so*, knowing that she knows that *p* is undercut by her lack of confidence, but not her knowing that *p*. If knowing that *p* generally comes apart from knowing that one knows that *p*, then of course there can be cases where lack of confidence undercuts one but not the other. But it's acceptable for lack of confidence to undercut knowledge, in any case, only when the loss of confidence is due to one's recognition that evidence is apparently missing or insufficient. Loss of confidence in *p* can be induced by recognition that the evidence for *p* is insufficient; losing confidence, being a psychological state, can also occur for "evidentially independent" reasons. That's why, in general, confidence isn't a necessary condition on knowledge: evidentially independent lack of confidence isn't accepted (by us) as undercutting knowledge. Confidence that's evidentially induced, however, although it accompanies knowledge, is concomitant on the grasping of the nature of the evidence.

Conclusion: confidence isn't a factor (for an agent's knowledge) independently of that agent's grasp of evidence (either for what she knows or for what she knows that she knows). Confidence does seem to function this way for belief;

that's why (sheer) confidence seems to be a necessary condition on belief. In any case, this disconnect between confidence and knowledge suffices to undercut Williamson's argument against KK—I show this in section 9.5.

Lastly, consider misleading-evidence cases. Kripke and Harman think misleading evidence can undercut knowledge. Kripke (2011b, 36) even describes such cases as "fairly straightforward common sense." *No*—apart from forgetting, cognitive damage, and the like, it's *not* fairly straightforward common sense to think misleading evidence can undercut knowledge. *We* never talk this way. We *never* say: "I knew *p*, but then, because S lied to me (and I believed him), I didn't know it anymore," or "I knew *p* once, but then, because usually trustworthy S misled me, I stopped knowing it."[14] This leads to two questions. First: Why *don't* we speak this way? (I answer this in the next paragraph.) Second: Is this a negotiable characteristic of "know(s)"? Can we, that is, change how the word operates without interfering with what we need the word for so that we can *then* talk this way? I puzzle over this second question in section 11.4. (There is also a third question we can ask: Why is the view that we often lose knowledge because of misleading evidence so widespread among epistemologists studying these topics? See note 14. It can't merely be that this is widely seen as the only way to solve Kripke's dogmatism paradox. For one thing, Lasonen-Aarnio (2014), while subscribing to it, nevertheless denies it can be used to solve Kripke's dogmatism puzzle. I discuss this question in chapter 11.)

One reason talk of losing knowledge in such cases *isn't* straightforward common sense is because of a deep conflict in our knowledge-attribution practices. We *retract* our knowledge claims when faced with evidence that undercuts them; further, official retractions of knowledge are in many cases—not cases of severe insecurity, as we've seen—sufficient for not having knowledge: "I thought I knew *p*, although I didn't."[15] But good although *misleading* evidence

[14] Am *I* open to the charge (Pohlhaus (2015, 11)) of presupposing the "homogeneity of the 'we' who make judgments deemed to be 'obvious' in philosophy"? I don't think so. First of all, my claim *can't* be obvious, since Kripke, Harman, and Williamson disagree. So do Wright and Sudbury (1977) and Jackson (1987). For that matter, so do Ginet (1980), Sorensen (1988a), Conee (2004), Hawthorne (2004), Kelly (2008), Worsnip (2015), and Lasonen-Aarnio (2014). The view that faced with misleading evidence we can "lose" knowledge is the closest thing to a widespread *orthodoxy* in philosophy that I've seen in some time. More importantly, my counterclaim to this particular bit of orthodoxy is based on widespread listening and reading, especially the reading of numerous detective and crime novels, *where misleading evidence is a staple of these genres* and where one would expect common-sense talk of loss of knowledge to come up *often*—if it were common-sense talk at all. Another place where one should expect this way of speaking to be *common* (if it existed at all) is in history books and in contemporary commentary on political events. Attempts to mislead people (importantly, attempts that are successful for a while—like those of many politicians) are common, and yet talk of knowledge lost (and then, sometimes, regained) does *not* occur. In history of science and philosophy of science, finally, one never reads, for example, about the emergence of what was subsequently revealed to be misleading evidence against a correct scientific theory that its proponents knew it for a while and then didn't (and then knew it again). I thank Samia Hesni for alerting me to Pohlhaus (2015).

[15] Recall the discussion of the retraction of knowledge claims in chapter 3.

induces sincere and appropriate first-person retraction too. Where we think the reasons an agent originally had for thinking *p* are sufficient for knowledge, we (from the third-person perspective) attribute knowledge to that person. But if the misleading evidence that the person is (or becomes) aware of is good enough, we then think that the person doesn't know.[16] The agent's confidence, in any case, isn't at issue; rather, the evidential basis the agent is relying on—or that the agent should be relying on, in some possibly extended sense of "should"—has shifted.

If we think about how nonphilosophers react when misleading evidence is exposed, we'll realize that agents often take themselves as having *known all along*. D sees B and C (who are supposedly only distant acquaintances) at a concert. Given how B and C are acting (although not *too* explicitly, let's say), D realizes they're having an affair. But then she's told (by B and C separately) something like: "What an amazing coincidence! We independently bought tickets for seats that were next to each other! He [she] is a really nice person. Who knew?" D believes them and concludes she's wrong about the affair. Later she discovers they *were* having an affair. "I *knew* it," D says (as many of us would).

Perhaps it would be nice to speak in cases of misleading evidence of losing (and regaining) knowledge. (That's to be determined: whether our usage of "know(s)" can be re-engineered in this way.) But we don't. We instead do either of two things, both when speaking about whether we ourselves knew or didn't know something and when speaking about someone else's knowledge. We describe the agent as having known all along, but as having lost confidence in what she (nevertheless) continues to know. Or we describe the agent as having never known the fact in question to begin with.

In many of these cases, especially if the misleading evidence—as evidence—is good, it may be disputed whether the agent knows or not. And some of these disagreements, at least as far as standards for knowledge are concerned, may be genuinely indeterminate, because those standards are vague. I turn to this topic now.

9.4 The Invisibility of Epistemic Standards; the Invisibility of the Vagueness of Epistemic Standards

It should be a truism that our standards for knowledge—whatever they are (and however they change)—are nearly completely invisible to those competent with "know(s)," even those who grasp the notion. This is worth dwelling on,

16 Some of us think this even if the person doesn't know of this misleading evidence; examples designed along the lines of Lehrer and Paxson (1969)—see Harman (1973)—illustrate this, e.g., misleading evidence like letters (or emails) in a person's possession that he hasn't opened yet.

nevertheless, because of the *richness* of our ignorance of those standards. This is an odd way to put it—describing ignorance as "rich"—but the point of the phrase will become clear quickly. I'll add that it's perhaps surprising, given the kind of knowledge some of us have about some of our methods of knowing things—memory, deduction, and the like—that nevertheless those knowledgeable some of us are *still* quite ignorant about our standards of knowledge.

Epistemic contextualists believe there are context-sensitive mechanisms that shift standards for knowledge; their views differ on whether these mechanisms directly manipulate standards or indirectly manipulate something else. These postulated mechanisms range from those that directly narrow or widen bands of relevant possibilities in logical space, to ones sensitive to what's salient to speakers, where such saliences are conversationally induced (or triggered by events), to ones employing calculational estimates of probabilities. What allows this range of options for context-shifting-standards mechanisms is the nature of the available evidence: these mechanisms are completely invisible to the agents embodying them (to all of us).

A comparison to speaker-hearers' knowledge of (native) languages helps. Speaker-hearers have only *individual-item knowledge* of sentences: *q* is grammatical, *p* isn't. They don't grasp nearly enough *any* generalization about sentences or sentential components; these fall entirely on the side of theory: it's *theorists* who determine what mechanisms—rules, or something else—enable speaker-hearers' individual-item judgments. It isn't true, of course, that the data for these mechanisms is similarly restricted to speaker-hearer judgments about individual items. Pertinent, for example (at least in principle), are the varying processing speeds by which speaker-hearers recognize grammaticality or ungrammaticality. Pertinent also are the kinds of mistakes that children make and don't make when acquiring a native language. Speaker-hearers themselves provide no direct access to the rules (or mechanisms) by which they make judgments. They offer nothing directly relevant—for example, an ability to recognize an operative set of rules by which they distinguish grammatical strings from ungrammatical strings. Indeed, any impressions speaker-hearers have about such matters are largely irrelevant. That (most) speaker-hearers don't understand variables, for example, doesn't bear on whether variables are essential to the formulation of grammatical rules; a similar point holds of the theoretical predicates and relations posited by theorists to explain the grammatical abilities of speaker-hearers. There is no requirement on theorizing that speaker-hearers grasp these concepts—or that these items even be on the surface of the apparent grammar of languages. This is a corollary of the almost complete invisibility of the structure of grammatical capacity to those who have it.[17]

[17] Speaker-hearers don't even have (much) access to comparative judgments about how difficult or easy their judgments are. The comparative difficulties in question might only be revealed by timing

The analogy to the epistemic case is tight. Whether standards for knowledge are couched in terms of possible worlds or a probability space or involve some shortcut expediency method is completely invisible to we who, often effortlessly, make judgments about who knows and who doesn't. It follows from this, pretty easily, that how *vagueness* occurs in these standards is also invisible to us. Compare, again, judgments about baldness. Speaker-hearers *know* that someone being bald amounts only to the distribution and number of hairs on her head. And further, they know baldness isn't just distribution of hairs or instead just their numbers—except in extreme cases. This is because they *know* baldness is how hair on heads *appears*. Two individuals can have the same amount of hair on their heads, one bald, the other not, because the hair is distributed evenly but thinly in one case, and in the other, there is no hair on the crown at all.[18] As a result, people often (perhaps usually) recognize the source of vagueness in baldness attributions; for example, they can *see* that particular distributions of hair will be cases where people aren't sure. The standards for baldness *and how they're vague* are visible.

"Know(s)" isn't like this. Characterize, as a first pass, knowledge standards as what determine relationships between the evidence that an agent S possesses (either consciously or unconsciously) and the knowing relations between that agent and the propositions that she knows. Even epistemically sophisticated agents and attributors of knowledge have little understanding of the structure and nature of evidence (that is, exactly *what* evidence is and how it determines when agents have or don't have knowledge); in particular, even sophisticated agents have little understanding of how much evidence suffices for knowledge—or even whether evidence is quantifiable, and if so, on what basis (for example, in terms of probabilities).

tests that show processing differences that are below conscious thresholds. When I say "we" have a good grasp of "grammaticality," I *don't* mean that experimental philosophers can easily operationalize this grasp via survey questions with words like "grammatical." Many think a split infinitive *isn't* grammatical because of what they "learned" in school. (I owe this example to Vann McGee, given during his question at a talk at MIT on November 8, 2018.) Operationalizing speaker-hearers' grasp of grammaticality is *really* hard because of grammatical norms most speaker-hearers have acquired—these are confounders. Chomsky has stressed the misleading impact of education-induced norms for decades.

[18] Well, *that's* not exactly accurate: individuals who are (appear) completely bald usually have lots of fine, nearly invisible hair on the "bald spots" on their heads nevertheless. I should add that in one sense the vagueness of "know(s)" is as visible as the vagueness of "bald": Sorities paradoxes can be easily designed for both words. But that's philosophically sophisticated. The invisibility/visibility contrast between "know(s)" and "bald" that I'm speaking of here is one that prevents people from arguing with one another over whether someone is bald or not, although debates over whether someone knows something or not that are due to the vagueness of the word "know(s)" do occur (and relatively often), as I discuss in section 10.4.

Long-standing Gettier controversies illustrate this. Something is wrong in how evidence relates to judgments in these cases. But speaker-hearers have no insights to contribute here; theory (and thus controversy) is needed. Indeed, the standard approach to solving Gettier puzzles has been to hypothesize generalizations—characterizations of suitable relationships between the evidence an agent has and that agent's judgment being knowledge—and then test the generalizations by additional individual-item judgments in specific cases (thus the typical flavor of the Gettier literature: generalization followed by counterexample followed by patch-repaired generalization followed by counterexample . . .).

Epistemic agents don't appreciate that their standards for evidence (when or if they ever think about them) are *tri-scoped*: Epistemic standards leave significant numbers of items outside both the extension and the anti-extension of what's known by any agent. For each S, and for many *p*, there are cases where epistemic standards—the application conditions for the word "know(s)"—don't determine the truth or falsity of "S knows *p*." Call the application conditions for a word *bi-scoped* if those conditions determine every application of it as either in its extension or in its anti-extension. I suggested in section 9.3 that it may be indeterminate—in many cases—whether an agent, in possession of misleading evidence that $\neg p$, nevertheless knows *p*. But tri-scoped-ness, all by itself, causes disputes when it's invisible.

"Know(s)" and probably all of our ordinary-language words are also *application-indeterminate*, as I just indicated. An application-*determinate* condition for a tri-scoped predicate P determines, for every item o, that P holds of o, that it doesn't hold of o, or that it neither holds nor doesn't hold of o. That's not how our standards for "know(s)" work; they simply *fail to determine*, in a number of cases, that S knows *p*, or that S doesn't know *p*, or that S neither knows nor doesn't know *p*.[19]

Here's an illustration of application indeterminacy. Suppose the standard for cleaning a room is: Remove *most* of the dust. This standard is application-indeterminate because it's unclear for a range of cases, given the standard's characterization, whether "most" of the dust has been removed. "Most" is the culprit. Apart from sheer stipulation, nothing about it or its usage determines any particular quantitative gloss, e.g., 80 percent, 95 percent, 99 percent, 99.999 percent, etc.; nothing about how we use the word in any context determines a quantitative

[19] The semantically adventurous can iterate this condition: at any stage where we have several agential states (which for ease of understanding I separate by curly brackets that I quantify into): {S knows *p*}, {S doesn't know *p*}, {S neither {knows *p*} nor {doesn't know *p*}}, {S neither {knows *p*}, {doesn't know *p*}, nor {{knows *p*} nor {doesn't know *p*}}, . . . {S neither { . . . } . . .}, they can introduce a *new* state: {S neither { . . . } . . . }, where what follow the "neither" and are separated by "nors" are all the previously defined states. I forgo this because it doesn't matter. Our ordinary words seem application-indeterminate (in these generalized senses), regardless of how many additional states we coin the existence of.

gloss either. We can (in certain cases—not all) *stipulate* a quantitative gloss for our use of it, but such stipulations are open to negotiation. The illusion that natural-language quantifiers are restricted to natural-language correspondents of the formal "there is an x . . ." and "for all x . . ." can engender a second illusion that vagueness doesn't infect natural-language quantifiers. Quantifier vagueness in natural language, it should be added, pretty much affects *all* our standards, not just our epistemic ones, as indicated by phrases like "beyond a reasonable doubt," "a sufficiently high number," and similar expressions.

Vagueness is typically handled semantically either by stipulating it away[20] or by introducing devices, such as many-valued logics, fuzzy sets, or supervaluations. These latter strategies replace vagueness with a precisified characterization of it with a resulting desertion of classical logic. A different approach (which I think is the right one) is to match the vagueness in the object language with a corresponding vagueness in the metalanguage, for example, as in the classic Barwise and Cooper (1981, 164), where the ordinary-language phrase "most N" is semantically characterized like so: $||\text{Most N}|| = \{X \subseteq \text{E} | \, X \text{ contains most Ns}\}$. Here, notice that the vagueness of "most" isn't characterized by a mechanism in a precise metalanguage; instead, it's carried up into the metalanguage directly by the use of a phrase that replicates the meaning of the phrase being interpreted.[21] This is how I think the vagueness exhibited by "know(s)" should be understood: a semantics characterizing the word in terms of, for example, a reliable process, or standards, or whatever, should help itself to vague terminology when characterizing, for example, stringency or reliability or suchlike. Indeed, with rare exceptions, I suspect all vagueness in natural language should be handled this way. Notice that this way to approaching vagueness, semantically, doesn't treat it as a phenomenon to be characterized explicitly by semantic tools; rather, it's exhibited by the language of the semantics (of a language) just as it's exhibited by the language the semantics is for. More generally, vagueness arises because the materials out of which our semantics is built (e.g., characterizations in language, or psychological mechanisms by which we apply words to the world, or . . .) are themselves susceptible to vagueness.

This aside, *all* our words, as I said, seem tri-scoped and application-indeterminate, although in some cases we can stipulate application determinacy and/or bi-scoped-ness—if there is any value to doing so (there rarely is). Thus, in practice, there are always cases where we can't tell whether our standards

[20] E.g., often, as in some of the generalized quantifier literature, see Westerståhl (2011, n. 9), where "most" is characterized precisely as "more than half."

[21] This is how the classic Tarski metalanguages approach the semantic interpretation of languages: the object language logical particles, ∃, &, ¬, etc., and their meanings, are replicated by metalanguage ∃, &, ¬, etc., and their meanings (see Tarski (1983)).

determine a truth value or not. This is most obvious with our old standby vague words like "red" or "bald"; but as I mentioned, it's true of "most" as well.[22]

Last point. The difference between Williamson's epistemicism and mine can be put this way: On Williamson's view, application indeterminacy is an illusion; all words are application-determinate and bi-scoped. On my view, application indeterminacy arises from language in the sense that semantic characterizations of words—whatever they are—yield application indeterminacy. This can be for as simple a reason (as I've indicated) as that the semantic characterizations of words themselves contain vague expressions.

9.5 Williamson on KK

Williamson (2000, chapter 4) tries to use application indeterminacy to undercut KK via a more general result—that luminosity fails for all conditions C—where luminosity is: For every case α, if in α C obtains, then in α one is in a position to know that C obtains (Williamson 2000, 95). Williamson uses slippery-slope symptoms of the vagueness of conditions—that anything an agent knows (e.g., that she's cold) is graduated (can slowly shift from cold to warm). But (so Williamson says) an agent's confidence in and her reliability about what she knows require a penumbra around any individual case c of knowing (that she's cold) in which all the neighboring cases are ones in which what she knows in c is true (that she *is* cold). Here's the rub: necessarily included among such penumbral cases (because of graduated scaling) are ones in which she's *not* cold. The falsity of KK is a corollary of this general failure of luminosity.

The assumptive gear on which Williamson's argument turns is that *reliable confidence* is a necessary requirement on knowledge. Imagine (Williamson (2000, 96–97)) the temperature in a room slowly increases—so slowly that "one is not aware of any change in [one's feelings of heat and cold] over one millisecond." Nevertheless, one changes from feeling cold to not feeling cold, and from being in a position to know that one feels cold to not being in that position.[23] And because the condition that one feels cold is "luminous," these changes in one's feelings and in one's being in a position to know that one feels as one does are simultaneous.

[22] A complication I won't dwell on outside this note: True, false, and neither are all semantic states of sentences in natural languages, *apart from vagueness*. It really doesn't make sense to say toads are bald (or not). But this isn't because "bald" is vague—although it is.

[23] Williamson's (2000, 95) "being in a position to know" is a dispositional characterization introduced to handle what I discussed earlier: agents being capable of putting themselves in a position to occurrently know something (by focusing on it, for example), although (as I described it) they know it nevertheless. The difference between Williamson's formulation and mine looks purely terminological.

Imagine also that "throughout the process one thoroughly considers how cold or hot one feels." (Given luminosity, one *can* do this.) One's confidence that one feels cold gradually decreases (and after a period where one just "isn't sure," one's confidence that one doesn't feel cold gradually increases)—and in a way that manifests vagueness. One's initial answers to "Do you feel cold?" are firmly positive, then hesitant, then neutral—e.g., "It's hard to say" or "I don't know"—then one denies feeling cold, hesitantly, and then confidently ("firmly") negative.

So what? Williamson (2000, 97) offers this family of conditionals about the shift in time over milliseconds, about feeling cold and knowing that one feels cold:

(I_i) If in α_i one knows that one feels cold, then in α_{i+1} one feels cold.

Luminosity, however, in addition requires this family of conditionals:

(2_i) If in α_i one feels cold, then in α_i one knows that one feels cold.

Together these yield the conclusion that one is cold at noon (t_n) when, on the contrary, one is hot. (I_i) is to be faulted (if anything is). What is Williamson's (97) argument for it? This:

> Consider a time t_i between t_0 and t_n, and suppose that at t_i one knows that one feels cold. Thus one is at least reasonably confident that one feels cold, for otherwise one would not know. Moreover, this confidence must be reliably based, for otherwise one would still not know that one feels cold. Now at t_{i+1} one is almost equally confident that one feels cold, by the description of the case. So if one does not feel cold at t_{i+1}, then one's confidence at t_i that one feels cold is not reliably based, for one's almost equal confidence on a similar basis a millisecond later that one felt cold is mistaken.

I showed, in section 9.4, that the second sentence is in general false: confidence, let alone reliable confidence, *isn't* required to know. But there is an escape clause: confidence isn't required for knowledge unless confidence is constitutively involved in the mechanisms by which the agent (in those cases) knows—and in those cases, presumably, the confidence that's constitutively involved had better be reliable confidence. So, what about *this* specific case? Is there an argument that when feeling cold, one's confidence that one is cold *is* the (psychological) mechanism by which one recognizes that fact? (If so, then although Williamson's attempt to generalize on his example fails, at least he still gets to keep the example.) I rather doubt it. One becomes confident that one is cold (often) insofar—and only insofar—as one recognizes that one *is* cold ("Oh, man, I *feel* cold" or "I'm *shivering*; I'm really cold"), not the other way around.

Are there reasons, independent of purported linkages between confidence and knowledge, for accepting the conditionals (I_i)? One might try to establish them via a necessary reliability consideration on knowledge, something to the effect of: If an agent "can't tell the difference" between being in condition C_1 and condition C_2, then that agent knows she is in condition C_1 if and only if she knows she is in condition C_2—where "can't tell the difference" is open to philosophical negotiation, e.g., whether it's to be construed purely introspectively or not. Indeed, this *has* been offered as a (an internalist) requirement for knowledge. This *isn't* Williamson's argument, however. I'll take up a discussion of this condition (under the rubric of "parity reasoning"), and which forms of it, if any, it should be taken seriously, when I discuss lottery paradoxes in section 10.4.

9.6 Concluding Remarks

Let's return to the empirically established shiftiness of "know(s)" attributions that was so important to the discussion in chapter 3. Recall that the cases like *Low Stakes, High Stakes*, etc., discussed in section 3.2, seem to directly threaten CI (classical invariantism). Here is a possible version of the view:[24]

> Regardless of the attributor's conversational situation and pragmatic needs, and regardless of the subject's conversational situation and pragmatic needs, one set of epistemic standards (relative to the subject's epistemic capacities) comprise the relevant truth conditions that govern all knowledge-attributing and knowledge-denying claims.

The invisible vagueness of these standards offers a way out. This is that if such standards are vague, they're open to shiftiness. If the standards were visibly vague, the shiftiness they're open to would have to fit their character—e.g., that only shiftiness involving strengthening or weakening purely epistemic standards (truth-conducing ones) would be admissible. The standards being invisible, however, allows impure factors to play a role as well. If, for example, an agent, in a rush, is late for a train, she may (unconsciously) lower the standards for knowing the train's schedule.[25] She'll similarly raise the standards, however, if the penalties for missing the train are severe enough. When imagining cases of other

[24] I've modified DeRose's (2009, 26) formulation.

[25] Relevant are results that show that, depending on how tired we are, we *experience* distances as correspondingly longer or shorter. See, e.g., Zadra and Clore (2011).

agents, or imagining conversations or debates over knowledge, other factors can intrude as well, and agents can attribute their own knowledge to others; also, in debates, the person who speaks first sets the point from which deviations can be negotiated. All the minutia of shifting-knowledge cases, that is, are empirical fodder for details about what kind of factors can infiltrate our (subliminal) grasp of the strength of our standards; they don't bear on the question of whether those standards are invariant. Notice that in this way, the invisible-vagueness classical invariantist view is more empirically robust than its opponents. The opponent views are sensitive to the minutia of the details of shifting-"know(s)" cases because those shifts are, on these views, part of how "know(s)" works; they aren't psychological adjuncts to our failure to recognize the vagueness of our invariant standards. This breaks the logjam I opened section 3.8 with: *Nothing* (canvassed) seems to work.

During debates over whether an agent knows or not, failing to recognize the vagueness of "know(s)" can lead to such debates (between nonphilosophers) being irresolvable—I'll illustrate this in the next chapter. In such cases, the (vague) standards don't determine an answer: Agent S knows or not? They're *understood* by all parties to the debate, however, to determine an answer. That's why such debates, despite being irresolvable, nevertheless occur between rational individuals. "Shifting standards" doesn't have to mean—and I think it doesn't mean—that a specifically calibrated standard shifts up or down. The situation, rather, is like with "most": we can "read the standard" more or less stringently.

In the next chapter, I'll show that the invisible vagueness of "know(s)" is extremely important in another way: it's confusing, both to nonphilosophers and to theorists, especially when that vagueness dovetails with other confusing aspects of the word—both iterated cognition phenomena and (as I'll explain in the next chapter) its factivity. Not only should the exposure of these structures of the semantics and usage of "know(s)" clarify the role of the word, but they should also make clear why that word (and what it refers to) has puzzled philosophers for so long.

10
Usage Challenges to Fallibilism

10.1 Introduction

In describing "know(s)" as vague, as I have in chapter 9, I've presupposed fallibilism—roughly, an agent can know *p* even though it's "possible" for the agent to be wrong about this. I've not really discussed fallibilism earlier (although my discussion all along has similarly presupposed and/or implied it); fallibilism is finally taken up now. Taking epistemic agents to be fallible is the most straightforward way to theoretically conform a characterization of "know(s)" with our widespread practices of attributing knowledge to ourselves and others under what look like evidentially imperfect circumstances.

Nevertheless, epistemology is a mass of puzzle topics in large measure because of usage facts that seem to pressure the interpretation of our ordinary "know(s)" in an infallibilist direction. Moorean remarks, "I know *p*, but I could be wrong"—when we feel their force—look like they refute fallibility (Lewis (1996, 419)); similarly, we have "intuitions," many philosophers claim, that, regardless of how unlikely it is someone will win a lottery (or be hit by lightning numerous times in the same place), we still "don't know" that person won't win that lottery or be hit by lightning numerous times in the same place (Vogel (1990), Hawthorne (2004, chapter 1)). Finally—noted already (in section 3.4) and related to the last-made point—when agents disagree on cases of purported knowledge, or reconsider those cases, they often appear to shift their judgments in "sceptical" directions—upping their standards for "know(s)," with respect to themselves and/or others.[1] This suggests that their carefully-thought-out standards for knowledge—as opposed to their sloppy-on-the-spot standards—are quite high, indeed, infallibilist.

Philosophical resistance to infallibilism arises primarily from the scepticism it seems to entail: If we have invariant infallibilist standards, the result, nearly

[1] Agents, recall, don't consciously turn dials (as it were) on a device in their heads marked "standards for knowledge." They have, pretty much, no access to their knowledge standards, as described in section 9.4; they shift on particular cases in the moment (and they're rarely aware of those shifts). I should add that what's going on isn't just sceptical shifts but "going to extremes." People either shift in sceptical directions or they "dig in their heels" and assert that there's no possibility that they're wrong about something they know. Both shifts apparently support infallibilism.

Attributing Knowledge. Jody Azzouni, Oxford University Press (2020). © Oxford University Press.
DOI: 10.1093/oso/9780197508817.001.0001.

enough, is that no one knows anything (Unger (1975)); that puts pressure on our ordinary widespread attributions of knowledge being *correct*. I won't (in this book) directly address *Cartesian* scepticism[2]—that's for later work—but before taking up lottery scepticism, in sections 10.2 and 10.3, I undercut some of the other considerations mentioned in the last paragraph, and arising from usage, that motivate infallibilism. In section 10.2, I define fallibilism and infallibilism. In section 10.3, I examine the ways factivity, an innocent-looking aspect of "know(s)," makes it seem that infallibility about what one knows is an implication of having that knowledge. Factivity confounds epistemological theorizing almost as much as iterated-cognition phenomena do: many of the usage facts that apparently reveal the machinations of the infallibility of "know(s)" are only due to its factivity. Unfortunately, this isn't true of *everything* about usage that seems to compel infallibility—if so, this book would have been about fifty pages shorter.

In section 10.4, I use usage insights about iterated cognition and factivity to resolve Kripke's dogmatism paradox. In section 10.5, I illustrate how the invisibility of vagueness (described in section 9.4) can generate irresolvable disputes—disagreements about what's known—without the disputants realizing that no resolution is, even in principle, possible. Our disputes over whether we know that someone has a losing lottery ticket (just by virtue of having bought it) are good examples. Nevertheless, our "intuitions" about lotteries can't be resolved by revealing the role of the vagueness of "know(s)" in them: impressions about lotteries challenge fallibility too because the vagueness of "know(s)" is only part of the problem; parity reasoning is also an issue: parity reasoning is inconsistent with fallibility, as I show in section 10.2.

I discuss "going to extremes" in section 10.6, that speaker-hearers, in debates, either shift toward positions of knowledge denial rather than knowledge assertion, or bolster their knowledge claims with denials that it's possible for them to be wrong. This is due, surprisingly, to the vagueness of "know(s)," and to our misunderstanding of that vagueness (our failure—actually—to recognize it exists). The same thing happens, consequently, with other vague words as well and in a way irrelevant to epistemics. This shows that going to extremes doesn't indicate that we (always) favor more stringent knowledge standards over less stringent knowledge standards. In section 10.7, I take up prefaces and return to lottery paradoxes, illustrating the resources we have for handling some preface remarks—for acknowledging our fallibility; but

[2] Scepticism is a three-dimensional challenge to knowledge: Cartesian scepticism, justification scepticism, and lottery scepticism. Vogel (1990) calls lottery scepticism "semi-scepticism" because its challenge to knowledge is substantial but not total. I've taken up justification scepticism in chapters 7 and 8; I take up lottery scepticism here.

I indicate why the threat lottery impressions pose to fallibilism can't be handled this way. Fallibilism implies the denial of straightforward principles of knowledge closure; this is the theme of section 10.8. Failures of straightforward principles of knowledge closure, however, don't show up in *most* obvious inferences (like ones from having hands to not being brains in vats)—on the contrary. So, fallibilist failures of knowledge closure can't be used to protect ordinary knowledge from scepticism. Knowledge closure, however, does fail for lottery inferences; parity reasoning fails there as well. That we experience knowledge closure and parity reasoning as exceptionless arises from a confluence of usage factors and confusions—including the usage factors that make us think knowing agents are infallible; knowledge closure, in addition, arises from how we take obviousness to indicate epistemic security. All this explains why our adherence to knowledge closure and parity reasoning doesn't arise from a folk appreciation of what the word "know(s)" means. I show that parallel arguments (as well as additional considerations) show that various closure principles also fail for belief, rational belief, justification, and the like. Section 10.9 summarizes.

Neither the vagueness and factivity of "know(s)" nor the failure of knowledge closure and parity reasoning illuminate Gettier puzzles; details about the methods we use to know things are additionally needed. Gettier puzzles, that is, aren't caused by the vagueness of "know(s)" or the other aspects of our usage of "know(s)" but instead arise because the *methods* we use to learn the things we *know* can't be characterized so that they yield *only* knowledge: there will always be failures to know that fall under any (non-pleonastic) characterization of any method of acquiring knowledge. Nevertheless, Gettier puzzles aren't why "know(s)" eludes definition, nor is it that "know(s)" is vague: nothing stops vague words, in general, from having definitions as long as those definitions match umbras to umbras and penumbras to penumbras (as Quine (1960, 41) once put it). It's the failure of parity reasoning that does it. This, along with a characterization of the meaning of "know(s)," is the topic of chapter 11.

10.2 Preliminaries: Characterizing Fallibilism, Infallibilism, and Parity Reasoning

A fallible agent S who knows that *p*, we might say, is one who *could have been* wrong about *p*. If S knows that *p*, however, then *p* is *true*. We shouldn't characterize how S could have been wrong about *p* by noting that *p* could have been *false*, contrary to what S thinks. (*We* shouldn't characterize S's fallibility this way—but this has certainly been done.) This bad idea unpleasantly leads to: S can be fallible about whether bees have gone extinct, but S can't be fallible about 11,895,224 plus 89,566,332 being 101,461,556, because 11,895,224 plus 89,566,332 being 101,461,556 is "necessarily" true.[3]

Cognitive qualities of an *agent* (e.g., her methods for knowing) should be in focus when she's described as either fallible or infallible—not the metaphysical status of the propositions she knows. So let's try again (with infallibility this time). Infallibility is: *The method that an agent uses to establish p couldn't have yielded a wrong answer.* This can be similarly misinterpreted. We don't want: The method couldn't have yielded a wrong answer because the answer it yields, *p*, couldn't have been false.

Methods are ways in which agents go about learning things (go about coming to know things). Methods are individuated in terms of the actions of the agent ("actions" can be purely mental), and they're open to being individuated in different ways, as I've indicated in chapter 9. *Circumstances* are the situations in which agents apply methods. Agents sometimes think they're applying one method when they're actually applying a different one; they make computational mistakes, for example. Agents also sometimes think they're in one circumstance rather than another. They think they're watching one kind of rodent when they're watching another. Or they think there's a "5" in the carry slot in an addition computation when it's a "6." Call methods M and M*, circumstances C and C*, "S-indistinguishable" for an agent S if S doesn't (can't) distinguish between them. (So, of course, methods M, and circumstances C, are S-indistinguishable from themselves.) We can entertain stronger and weaker notions of S indistinguishability, as the above parenthetical "can't" indicates. A weak notion is best, but I won't argue for that now because the choice doesn't affect the issues at hand. What's instead important is that by characterizing the fallibility of an agent as "she could be wrong" (or by attempting to capture this with an operator "necessarily," we can confuse ourselves over what should be in the scope of the conditional that's implicitly involved. What's wanted is this:

> *An agent S is infallible with respect to p when using method M in circumstance C iff*: For all M* and C* that are S-indistinguishable, respectively, from M and C, M*, when applied in circumstance C*, yields *p*'s truth value.[4]

[3] The opening remarks of Vogel (2000, 603) can be criticized along these lines. So can "entailment gap" definitions of fallibility, e.g., "To fallibly know that *p* is to know that *p* on the basis of evidence that fails to entail that *p*." See Fantl and McGrath (2009, 7–8), especially their n. 8, where they list the many proponents of versions of this definition. As I show, entailment is irrelevant: even if our evidence does entail *p*, we can still only fallibly know it. I should add that falling for this bad idea is an *old* weakness of philosophers. See Pasnau (2017, especially 194), for discussion, and where Pasnau attributes the right idea to Buridan.

[4] In an earlier version of this characterization of infallibility, I had instead: "Necessarily (M* applied in circumstance C* yields *p*'s truth value)." I did this to illustrate how modal talk induces scope confusions. But really (and in any case), I interpret the dangerously modal-sounding items in these formulations deflationistically—I interpret ordinary-language talk of possibility when epistemically understood, in terms of likelihood assumptions; in this earlier version, I wrote: "at a future time I intend to offer a modality grounded in the actual facts of the methods agents use and how they

Because methods and circumstances can be characterized to different degrees of fineness, we have latitude in descriptions of cases. When S makes a computational mistake, she can be described as using a different method M* she can't distinguish from the one, M, she thought she was using—in this case, we define "methods" quite finely, allowing that failing to carry a numeral is using a different method of adding. Alternatively, we can describe S as using the same method M, but in different circumstances that she can't distinguish between (where the circumstances include the locations of numerals on a page, etc.). Other cases can be similarly differently described, as involving S-indistinguishable methods and/or circumstances, depending on how finely we individuate those methods and/or circumstances.[5]

Considering "S-indistinguishable" circumstances and methods differing from those S actually uses is a virtue. God is infallible, presumably, because C and M are God-indistinguishable from C* and M* iff C = C* and M = M*, for all M, M*, C, and C*. Relativizing infallibility to methods and circumstances seems compatible with infallibility, as classically construed. Descartes's method M_D of seeing something clearly and distinctly is taken (by him) to work in all circumstances, and to be a method that, for any agent S, is S-indistinguishable from any M iff $M = M_D$. Correspondingly, we can easily introduce a notion of infallibility that's not relativized to circumstances, if infallibility needs that.[6]

are open to variations in execution." I also cited Kripke's (2011a) discussion as giving reasons for avoiding modal approaches to "know(s)" and knowledge, and not merely because Kripke's target (Nozick (1981)) fails at this. But these are promises about future work. Corey Dethier (email, May 28, 2019) wondered why I didn't just substitute "all" and "some" in my formulations of fallibility and infallibility. He's right, and so I have.

[5] This "indeterminacy" between how we can describe cases is because the individuation of methods and circumstances turns on the methodological habits of agents, and the strengths (and weaknesses) of their faculties—e.g., perceptual or inferential (see section 10.7). I don't interpret methods "radically internally" as Nozick (1981, 184–185) does—see Kripke (2011a, 165)—nor should the slack between characterizing something as an aspect of an agent's method or her circumstances (e.g., with carrying numerals) be significant. I'll treat these as different cases—different cases of possible agents—where it sometimes may be impossible to determine (from an agent's behavior and our knowledge of her faculties) how that agent should be characterized.

[6] Fantl and McGrath (2009, 9–15) give different characterizations of fallibilism. Their weak epistemic fallibilism is: You can know something even though it is not maximally justified for you. Their strong epistemic fallibilism is: You can know that *p* even though there is a nonzero epistemic chance for you that not-*p*. Their weak notion is motivated by thinking of entailment as the best possible (maximally justified) form of justification. As I've noted, this is way off: so, correspondingly, is any characterization in terms of "maximal justification." We could instead characterize the weak notion directly like so: You can know something even though error is still possible—even though you can still be wrong. This needs further analysis: what does "error is still possible" or "can still be wrong" *mean*? Thus: my analysis in terms of methods, above. Similar remarks apply to their strong epistemic fallibilism; what's a nonzero "epistemic chance"? I think, similarly, a characterization in terms of the epistemic agent's methods is called for. "Classical infallibilism" is characterized by Dutant (2015, 99) as: One knows *p* iff *p* bears a *discernible mark of truth*, where: A property of a belief is a *mark of truth* iff necessarily, only true beliefs have it; and a property of belief is *discernible* iff necessarily, a sufficiently attentive subject believes that a belief of hers has it iff it has it. This is a (purported) method, and so falls under my definition. Notice, though, that metacognition on this view is built into our ability to recognize *truths*.

As we ordinarily speak, we often use epistemic talk of necessity and possibility. Speaking this way allows us to say something like:

> *An agent S is infallible with respect to p when using method M in circumstance C iff*: Necessarily, if M* and C* are S-indistinguishable, respectively, from M and C, M*, when applied in circumstance C*, yields *p*'s truth value.

Apart from introducing interpretation complications with respect to the "Necessarily," this formulation allows a scope confusion: a mistaken interpretation that includes the truth value of *p* in the conditional governed by a necessity operator:

> *An agent S is infallible with respect to p when using method M in circumstance C iff*: If M* and C* are S-indistinguishable, respectively, from M and C, necessarily (*p* is true [false] and (M* applied in circumstance C* yields *p*'s truth value)).

Corresponding to the first (correct) characterization of infallibility, we want a description of fallibility that looks like this:

> *An agent S is fallible with respect to p when using method M in circumstance C iff*: There are M* and C* that are S-indistinguishable, respectively, from M and C, M, applied in circumstance C, yields *p*'s truth value, but M*, applied in circumstance C*, doesn't yield *p*'s truth value.

We needn't require *p* to be necessarily true for infallibility. When we speak in natural language of fallibility, "B could have been wrong about *p*," we naturally (but confusedly) take only the truth value of *p* to fall within the scope of the possibility we're considering—we focus on the "about *p*" and not on the "wrong." (Many philosophers in addition compound the error by interpreting the necessity in question in some metaphysical way.) The factivity of "know(s)" then makes us think that the possibility being described must be one where *p* is false.

It looks like a corollary of the definition of fallibility I've given that it's sometimes (maybe often?) rational to claim to know *p* in circumstances where $\neg p$. This isn't a *strict* corollary; it follows when that definition is coupled with a supplementary characterization of rationality as well as conditions on "claiming to know." I'll skip refining the latter notions (except for some remarks about rational-action principles in sections 10.4 and 10.5), both because they're quite complicated and somewhat controversial (and so require entire books to do right), and because I'm largely after different game in this chapter that refining these notions, one way or the other, won't affect.

Fallibility, so defined, is relative to methods and circumstances. Descartes (notoriously) didn't think *all* epistemic methods were fallible—he thought he had one that wasn't. I believe (but won't pause to try to show here) that Descartes was wrong: all human epistemic methods are fallible. For present purposes, what's needed is only a characterization of what's meant by describing the word "know(s)" as fallibilist. Here's the idea: To claim that our word/concept "know(s)" is fallibilist is to say:

> There is an agent S who's fallible with respect to *p* when using method M in circumstance C, and there is a case where S, after using M in circumstance C, knows *p* is true (or false).

Notice the requirement on our *word* "know(s)" being fallibilist is appropriately very weak. We only need there to be a single case where an agent uses a fallible method to know something successfully. (It could be, compatibly with the meaning of the word, that almost everyone is infallible almost all the time.) How fallible we are—how common and widespread our fallibility is—is an empirical question. As I noted, it strikes me that, without exception, we allow that people know things via methods that are obviously ones those people are quite fallible with respect to. This is especially true of mathematics and logic—which we recognize to be *hard*. In describing our word "know(s)" as compatible with agential fallibility, I'm *not* claiming that the meaning of the word itself *requires* fallibility the way that it apparently requires factivity. On the contrary, it could be (it could have been)—as far as the meaning of the word is concerned—that we only use methods with respect to which we're infallible. Furthermore, it's not incoherent to use the same word "know(s)" to describe both ourselves and God as knowing certain things (e.g., that he exists), even though he's infallible and we're not.

What follows now is a characterization of parity reasoning that's modeled (with some modifications) on Hawthorne's (2004, 16). His and my characterizations are close cousins.

> *Parity Reasoning.* Consider a set of propositions $p_1, \ldots, p_n$, where one has no appreciably stronger reason for thinking that any given member of the set will not obtain than one has for thinking that any other member will not obtain. Insofar as one reckons it absurd to suppose that one knows any one of $p_1, \ldots, p_n$, one reckons it absurd to suppose that one knows any other of $p_1, \ldots, p_n$.

Despite my changes, this is still oddly put: why the word "reckon"? (Hawthorne (2004, 16) uses "reckon" in his formulation of parity reasoning, and I've retained it.) Does an agent so "reckoning" amount to the agent so knowing what she reckons? As parity reasoning is used (and understood) to describe thinking about lotteries (and other epistemic phenomena), I take the answer to be yes.

Fallibilism and parity reasoning, as I've characterized them here, are incompatible. Here's the argument:

> If an agent S is fallible with respect to her methods of knowing $p_1, \ldots, p_n$ in various circumstances, then it is *possible* for her to know one particular item from $p_1, \ldots, p_n$ using a method M_i in circumstance C_i while not knowing another item from $p_1, \ldots, p_n$, using any (respectively S-indistinguishable) methods M_j in circumstances C_j. That is, it's possible for an agent to have no appreciably stronger reason for thinking that any given member of the set will not obtain than she has for thinking that any other member will not obtain, even though she knows one member does obtain but doesn't know that another does. But if this is possible, then it *should be* false that insofar as one reckons it absurd to suppose that one knows any particular item of $p_1, \ldots, p_n$, one reckons it absurd to suppose that one knows any different item of $p_1, \ldots, p_n$.[7]

Some comments about this:

(i) Parity reasoning, as I've characterized it (and as Hawthorne characterizes it) is an iterated "know(s)" claim about agents. "One" *reckons* something absurd to *know* or something not absurd to *know*. The argument that fallibilism implies the denial of parity reasoning, however, is a third-party argument: it's not (self-)iterated knowledge. It functions that way, and undercuts parity reasoning for an agent S when she herself carries through the argument.

[7] Hill and Schechter (2007) reject parity by rejecting multi-premise closure and conjunction introduction. I instead centralize fallibility and use *that* to undercut closure principles, conjunction introduction, and parity. So my strategy is closer to the ones exhibited by Lasonen-Aarnio (2008) and Schechter (2013), although significant differences remain, due (primarily) to my rejection of confidence, consciously grasped justification, and metacognitions (of all sorts) as necessary conditions on knowing via deduction (and, of course, on knowing generally). Nevertheless, the earlier insights of Hume and Locke—see Schechter (2013, 437–438)—about human fallibility are being exploited by all of us. (I'm grateful to Ram Neta for drawing my attention to Schechter (2013).) Similar arguments to the one I've just given show that (given fallibility) Fantl and McGrath's (2007, 558; 2009, 28) "epistemic purism"—a supervenience thesis—is also false. Their purism is: For any two possible subjects S and S′, if S and S′ are alike with respect to the strength of their epistemic position regarding a true proposition *p*, then S and S′ are alike with respect to being in a position to know that *p*. Fantl and McGrath claim their purism characterizes the view that knowledge is purely epistemic. It *doesn't*—the falsity of purism is compatible with pragmatic factors playing no role in knowledge. If knowledge standards are *precise*, then something else—besides such standards—*must* explain purism's failure: the agent's own pragmatic goals are good candidates (although there are other options). But the vagueness of knowledge standards induces a failure of purism all on its own.

(ii) Parity reasoning is "intuitive"; my impression is that when philosophers and nonphilosophers understand a characterization of it, they think it's obviously true and that our epistemic practices are obviously in accord with it. But it's dire for our knowledge-attribution practices. As Vogel (1990) and Hawthorne (2004, chapter 1) show, parity reasoning directly motivates the impression we can never know in fair lotteries—where there must be winners and where we've purchased a ticket—that (before we know which winning tickets have been selected) we'll lose. Worse, fairly straightforward extensions of parity reasoning to a broad range of other kinds of knowledge undercut our ability to know things about the future or even what we take ourselves to know about the present. This is because, in strict analogy with lotteries, we don't know that otherwise low-probability events won't happen or aren't happening. (I turn to this in section 10.4.)[8]

(iii) Speaker-hearer impressions of usage here are typical of speaker-hearer impressions of usage generalizations of most of their words. That it *strikes* most of us (when first presented with a characterization of parity reasoning—which is a generalization) that our epistemic practices are in accord with it doesn't indicate that our epistemic practices *are* in accord with it—it doesn't even show that our epistemic practices are mostly (or even somewhat or once in a while) in accord with it.[9] Indeed, generally, they aren't; this is widely recognized as an implication of our attributions of knowledge to ourselves and others being *evidently* fallibilist.

(iv) The impression that parity reasoning is true supports a second impression about knowledge: "luck" isn't involved. "Luck," here, isn't understood as one's being lucky to know *p* because of accidental circumstances that put one in a position to know *p* (a position to know *p* that one wouldn't otherwise have been in). Rather, it's understood as one knowing *p* or not turning on factors beyond the reach of the methods one has to determine *p* (and beyond the reach of one's capacity to evaluate the suitability of those methods in various circumstances). That knowledge never involves "luck" is, of course, another generalization.

(v) The falsity of parity reasoning undercuts an otherwise apparently natural sufficient condition on knowledge. Call *evidentialism* the view that *necessary* for an agent A to know *p* is that A's overall reasons and evidence

[8] Hawthorne (2004, chapter 4) shows this with respect to his version of parity reasoning, of course; but the results are easily shown to hold of my version too. I omit details.

[9] I'm again relying on the fact that generalizations and systematic insights about word usage aren't grasped by the usual speaker-hearer unfamiliar with the kinds of generalization established in linguistics. This is as true of ordinary words like "house" or "this" as it is of sophisticated philosophically contentious words, like "know(s)." Recall the opening remarks of section 9.4. See Azzouni (2013b), especially its discussions of phenomenological compartmentalization.

for p (call this A's "evidential support for p") must be sufficiently high.[10] We can't turn this into a sufficient condition compatibly with fallibilism. If the latter holds, then parity reasoning is false and, thus, there can be circumstances where despite A's overall reasons and evidence for p being as high as one likes, A nevertheless doesn't know p because p is false. Describing evidentialism as providing only a necessary condition for knowing preserves its compatibility with fallibilism.

(vi) Another (perhaps surprising) point, related to (v), follows from the failure of parity reasoning—more accurately, from those failures being *widespread*. Imagine we define a notion, *kjustification* (the "j" is silent), where an agent is kjustified in believing p iff her reasons and evidence (evidential support) covary with her knowing p. Suppose, though, we're *seriously fallible*: for any method M, and any pair of propositions p_1 and p_2, there is a failure of parity reasoning. Then there are no cases of kjustification.[11] We can define kjustification so that its relationship to knowledge is weaker, and then, even given seriously fallibility, it won't be empty: An agent is kjustified in believing p iff her reasons and evidence (evidential support) E yield p, and if there are cases where E is sufficient for her knowing p. (We'll see this second weaker notion of kjustification later, in section 11.5, where I'll use it against certain social-role epistemology positions.)

(vii) Two popular approaches to "know(s)," placing conditions of safety and/or sensitivity on it, fail if the above characterization—of the failure of parity reasoning being due to our fallibility—is right. The failure of safety is pretty obvious if we characterize safety like so: S knows p only if there is no risk or danger that S believes falsely in a similar case. Next consider sensitivity. Understood modally, it can't be that in appropriately characterized nearby worlds, if S doesn't know p, then S doesn't believe p. Leaving aside the limitations of this characterization because it only applies to cases where knowledge is accompanied by belief, there can be lotteries (see my discussion of lotteries in section 10.5) where S knows and believes she won't win, but in extremely close nearby worlds, S doesn't know this although she still

[10] Conee and Feldman (2004, 1) describe evidentialism as "a supervenience thesis according to which facts about whether or not a person is justified in believing a proposition supervene on facts describing the evidence that the person has." So only with subsidiary theses—e.g., that to know, an agent must be justified—as well as a characterization of what "a person has" means, will this imply the thesis I'm describing as evidentialism.

[11] Are *we* seriously fallible? Philosophers certainly disagree about this. I think we are. Things can be *so* bad vis-à-vis an epistemic agent that he's confused about what he thinks he sees (how things appear to him) or about simple obvious truths. This is the case even with things that such a confused agent stipulates (to himself) to be true. Another way to establish serious fallibility is to agree (as I argue below) that parity reasoning fails for lotteries. If lottery reasoning can be extended to (nearly) everything that we take ourselves to know (as Hawthorne (2004, chapter 1) and Vogel (1990, especially 20–21) argue), then we're seriously fallible.

believes it because she will win. (Imagine a randomized process of selecting winning numbers which involves extremely tiny changes in worlds to shift those numbers.)

(viii) This characterization of parity reasoning is quite broad. It covers, potentially anyway, both errors in deductions and foolings by evil demons.[12]

10.3 When Factivity Misleads

Characterizing fallibility and infallibility has turned out to be surprisingly complicated. Adding to the complexity is that infallibility—even when we understand it—looks like it's implied, or presupposed, by other things we say. I'll illustrate this point about usage by showing that although "know(s)" *is* compatible with a simultaneously explicit expression of the fallibility of the knowing agent, the factivity of "know(s)"—and *only* the factivity of "know(s)"—makes this hard to do straightforwardly.

Let's first reconsider Moorean remarks.[13] In chapter 4, I circumscribed the contexts where such remarks are bizarre: They aren't bizarre when uttered by salespersons, by spokespersons, in advertisements, etc. For current purposes, consider such remarks where they *do* sound bizarre: speakers attempting to straightforwardly convey things that they *know*. Imagine such a speaker also wants to convey her fallibility—that, despite knowing something, she could be wrong about it. Factivity—that S knows *p* implies *p*—*all by itself* impedes this. To say, for example,

I know *p*, but I might be wrong,

sincerely, intending to convey what one knows, is to say something unacceptable. This is because, as just mentioned, "I know *p*" implies *p*, and *that* rules out that *in the circumstances of utterance*, $\neg p$. "I might be wrong (about *p*)," however, denies *in the (same) circumstances of utterance* that $\neg p$ can be ruled out. The (Moorean) awkwardness of "I know *p*, but I might be wrong," that is, is due only to the factivity of "know(s)" and not to anything stronger—like an

[12] That is, failures of parity reasoning can be extended to include challenges to knowledge that are undermined by what Hawthorne (2004, 17) calls "duplicate reasoning."

[13] Worsnip (2015) attempts to defend fallibilism against certain "concessive knowledge attributions," in the family of Moorean remarks that look like usage data for infallibilism. He does so, primarily, by providing a contextualist semantic model (in terms of quantifier-domain restriction) that explains the badness of these usages compatibly with fallibilism. I don't think a contextualist use of quantifier-domain-restriction mechanisms does much to explain this data. (I'm grateful to Ram Neta for drawing my attention to Worsnip (2015).)

infallibility condition. Factivity alone, we can see, is causing the problem with acknowledging fallibility.[14] The following remark, in the same circumstances, is awkward:

I correctly guess that *p*, but I might be wrong.

But

I guess that *p*, but I might be wrong,

isn't similarly awkward. The difference here is only the factivity induced by "correctly."[15]

Is there a way to simultaneously assert knowledge and fallibility in English? Can we, that is, "factor out" factivity from "know(s)" self-attributions? Not *literally*—because a semantically necessary condition on know(s) attributions can't be canceled, factored out, etc.[16] One *can*, however, say this:

I take myself to know *p*, but (of course) I might be wrong.

This doesn't sound similarly awkward. It conveys that one, *as far as one knows*, is in a knowing state, as well as fallible.

"Take myself" needs more discussion. First, it seems similar (synonymous, perhaps, but maybe not) with other expressions that are—in some cases—archaic, precious, or at least rare: "esteem myself," "consider myself," "flatter myself," perhaps even "think myself" or "believe myself." We can say (without awkwardness) any of the following:

[14] Once knowledge-assertion norms and the like are refuted (see chapter 4), the fact that "*p*, but I might be wrong," is equally awkward in the same circumstances proves factivity is the sole culprit. I establish this point, in a moment, independently of my denial of knowledge norms.

[15] This factivity diagnosis works for all Moorean remarks: when we experience them as disconcerting, we do so solely because of factivity—this is true of "I know *p*, but there is some risk that *p* is false" (an example from DeRose (2017, 169)), "*p* is true, but it might not be," "I correctly think that *p*, but maybe *p* is false," "I know *p*, but I don't believe *p*," etc. This also explains "third-person" Moorean remarks, like (Fantl and McGrath (2009, 15)), "She knows *p*, but *p* could be wrong." Here, factivity guarantees that *the speaker* by attributing knowledge to "she" is implying *p*, and then adding "but *p* could be wrong." Thus my first-person analysis applies. Fantl and McGrath (18–19) argue against scope confusions plus factivity explaining what's going on. That's right—there are no scope confusions involved here; factivity suffices.

[16] One can only speak of "knowing" nonfactively by using "know(s)" metaphorically in a way that's open to misinterpretation (and thus retraction) if the listener mistakenly thinks literality is intended. Recall the discussion of Hazlett's views in introduction section vi. As we've also seen—section 10.2, (vi)—we can't coin a word "kjustified" that's otherwise identical to "know(s)," except that it's not factive.

I esteem myself to know *p*, but I might be wrong,
I consider myself to know *p*, but I might be wrong,
I flatter myself to know [as knowing] *p*, but I might be wrong,
I believe myself to know *p*, but I might be wrong.

Second, all of these are iterated cognitions; although (obviously) they aren't iterated *know(s)* cognitions; they instead involve different propositional attitudes toward one's knowledge, *taking, considering, flattering*, and the like. Third, the only aspect of a "know(s)" self-attribution they're circumventing is the factivity of "know(s)" this is revealed by the awkwardness of the following statements (in what immediately follows I'm explicitly relying on a denial of assertion norms for "know(s)" and the like):

p, but I might be wrong,
p is true, but I might be wrong,

although none of the following is similarly awkward:[17]

I think *p*, but I might be wrong,
I think *p* to be true, but I might be wrong,
I believe *p*, but I might be wrong,
I believe *p* to be true, but I might be wrong,
I take *p* to be true, but I might be wrong,
I esteem *p* to be true, but I might be wrong,
I consider *p* to be true, but I might be wrong.

I've claimed "I take myself to know *p*" strips only factivity from "I know *p*," despite that in so asserting the former, I explicitly acknowledge awareness of the cognitive side of my (purported) knowledge state. This is because, as I indicated in section 5.2, "I know *p*" literally states that oneself bears the know(s) relation to *p*. To avoid this, recall, one must desert English by asserting something like "Know: *p*." This isn't so for third-person attributions. To say "S knows *p*" isn't to

[17] These examples, however, do invite an interesting question. Consider "I take *p* to be true," where *p* is a sentence. We can't say "I take *p*." Does "*p* is true" *not mean* the same thing as *p*? No, they're different in meaning—so say I (and so have said I for a while—Azzouni (2006, section 1.1)). A second question, therefore: How does "*p* is true" differ in meaning from *p*? In no substantial way (so say I again), but they are different enough to explain why substituting "*p*" for "*p* is true" fails in "I take—." The difference has been obscured by my (deliberately) slurring over use and mention: some device (Quinean corner quotes, or something else to the same effect) is needed to indicate that the variable "*p*," as it appears in "*p* is true" stands in for noun phrases; it stands in for sentences (or, more generally, sentential expressions) when that variable appears freestanding. *That syntactic difference* is sufficient for a difference in meaning, and it gives enough content to "is true," over and above factivity, for there to be content left when "I take *p* to be true" strips "true" in that context of its factivity.

say that S is aware of the knowing relation she has to *p*—unless S is oneself. To say "S takes herself to know *p*" *is* to say this.

Notice an effect of "I take myself to know *p*" stripping factivity from "know." The truth conditions for "I know *p*" require *knowing p*. The truth conditions for "I take myself to know *p*" don't require knowing *p*—I could merely think I know *p* (or think *p*), but be wrong.

Does, then, "taking myself to know *p*" correspond to a different mental state (or epistemic state) from knowing *p* to be true, or knowing that one knows *p* to be true?[18] Yes—insofar as knowing *p* is a ground-level epistemic state and taking oneself to know *p* isn't. Yes—insofar as taking oneself to know *p* isn't knowing oneself to know *p*. But apart from factivity, the mental state isn't different otherwise, as I've analyzed these locutions here. Stripping away factivity (alone) is explicitly *not* changing any of the relevant truth conditions on the cognitive conditions of the *agent* knowing *p* (whatever those happen to be).

I stress again: None of the foregoing shows (or proves) that ordinary usage (uniformly) treats "know(s)" as fallible.[19] All I've tried to show (so far) is that Moorean remarks, despite appearances, aren't incompatible with fallibilism.

One last point about conveying knowledge *and* conveying fallibility: A tempting approach is via an iterated know(s) attribution, "She knows *p*, but she doesn't *know* that she knows *p*." This doesn't always manage what's needed because if "know(s)" is perceived as requiring infallibility, iterating "know(s)"s won't change this. It's true, however (and I'll put this to use in the next section when analyzing Kripke's dogmatism paradox), that iterated "know(s)" attributions sometimes convey greater confidence and/or supplementary knowledge that puts one in a superior epistemic position. Consider: "He not only knows *p*; he *knows* that he knows it." A freestanding utterance of "he knows that he knows" is hard to make sense of without context: "He not only knows that Ji-hye is at the movies; he *knows* that he knows that." (Huh?) Given a context where how an agent knows what he knows is under scrutiny, the utterance of such an iterated "know(s)" attribution makes sense—as in the case of checking

[18] Eric Dean reminds me that I can "take *p* to be true" without taking myself to know *p*. This is because I can defer to experts who claim *p* without (so I may think) that being sufficient for me to claim that I know *p* on that basis. Matters are subtle because often, as I've indicated earlier, we *do* take ourselves to know *p* on the basis of an expert knowing *p*. I think what's happening in these cases is that the agent is implicitly distinguishing between her own personal knowledge and the public knowledge we otherwise take ourselves to share. Further analysis of this goes beyond this book.

[19] Consider the phrase "take to be true." Seth and Smith (forthcoming) and Smith (elsewhere) regard the use of "take to be true" to indicate an "intermediate standing" short of being true. They write: "The phrase 'take to be true' alone is enough to indicate that the evidence required for a proposition to acquire this intermediate standing is something short of evidence that it is true." I disagree: more is required for "take to be true" to indicate a special evidential status than merely stripping factivity from "true." I discuss their view, and the historical setting they apply their view to (in that book), in more detail in Azzouni (forthcoming c).

one's proof that *q* that I discussed in section 9.3, as well as cases like Dorothy, where her lack of confidence affects what she would otherwise know, precisely because it affects her knowledge of what she knows.

Freestanding iterated "know(s)" assertions are more transparent when the "knowledge" of an agent—a mass term—is under discussion. "Vero not only knows the calculus; she knows that she knows the calculus"—here the "know(s)" iteration transparently does two jobs. It conveys Vero's confidence in what she knows, and it conveys that confidence being due to her recognition of her mastery: her mastery of a *lot* of propositions (and know-how too). That is, it really is conveying that an iterated "know(s)" attribution to Vero is correct: she knows that she knows the calculus.

10.4 The Factivity of "Know(s)" and Kripke's Dogmatism Paradox

I'll now make the same point about Kripke's dogmatism paradox that I've just made about Moorean remarks: The dogmatism paradox (despite appearances) puts no pressure on fallibilism. Instead, confusions about iterated cognition and the factivity of "know(s)" together create an appearance of a "paradox." (Along the way, therefore, I'll "solve" the paradox—but *that's* not so important.[20]) Kripke (2011b, 43) characterizes his paradox this way:

> (*i*) If *A* knows that *p* and *A* knows that *p* entails *q*, and, on the basis of such knowledge, *A* concludes that *q* then *A* knows that *q*.
> (*ii*) *p* entails the following hypothetical: any evidence against *p* is misleading (where misleading is to mean *leads to a false conclusion*).
> (*iii*) The subject *A* knows that *p*, and *A* knows (*ii*).

[20] Sharon and Spectre (2010, 307) write that "The puzzle is widely regarded as having been solved." I was shocked to read this—although I don't dispute their sociological claim—because this presumed solution (Sharon and Spectre (2010, 308)), "a developed version of Harman's own proposal," relies crucially on allowing the loss of knowledge apart from the possibilities of forgetting or cognitive injuries; recall my observations, in section 9.3, about how hostile ordinary talk of "know(s)" is to this suggestion. (Indeed, this aspect of "know(s)," it seems to me, is as entrenched in ordinary usage as its factivity is—see chapter 11.) Sharon and Spectre don't criticize either Harman's original proposal or the developed versions of it the way I do; they instead raise technical objections to the developed version of it and describe the original proposal as fine as far as it goes but as not really getting to the root of the problem: the paradox is (Sharon and Spectre (2010, 320)) "instructive regarding formal features of knowledge, in particular the closure of knowledge under entailment." Although I accept failures of closure of knowledge under known entailment, I won't accept that such failures are at work in cases in which Kripke's paradox arises. (See my discussion of knowledge closure in section 10.7.) Lasonen-Aarnio (2014, 421) echoes Sharon and Spectre's sociological claim. She argues, further, that "the defeat solution" (allowing knowledge to be lost) doesn't handle a residue dogmatist puzzle. This is that what she (419) calls "*Entitlement*" must also be rejected to avoid dogmatism:

(*iv*) *A* knows that any evidence against *p* is misleading.[21]
(*v*) If *A* knows that taking an action of type *T* leads to consequence *C*, and *A* wishes above all else to avoid *C* (i.e. this is the only relevant issue), then *A* should resolve now not to take any action of type *T*.
(*vi*) *A* should resolve not to be influenced by any evidence against *p*.

Kripke (2011b, 49)—in an appendix written perhaps around 2011—notices that sometimes we do ignore evidence (and feel right to do so).[22] The problem isn't that we can sometimes ignore evidence about something we know; the problem is that this argument seems to justify *always* ignoring evidence relevant to *any* known *p*.[23]

What's wrong with (*i*)–(*iv*)? Nothing, actually. *It's our interpretation of the reasoning that's problematic.* Here's how a fallibilist should interpret it. If *p* is true, then any evidence for *p* being false is misleading. Therefore if one knows that *p* is true (and if one carries out the reasoning described here), one also knows that any evidence against *p* is misleading. If, however, one can be wrong that *p*, despite thinking one knows *p*, then one can be wrong that all evidence against *p* is misleading, despite thinking one knows that all evidence against *p* is misleading.

Knowing *p* and knowing *all evidence against p is misleading* are exactly on a par despite "intuitions" that suggest otherwise. There's no problem with this

> *Entitlement*: For any time *t*, subject *s*, a proposition *h*, and piece of evidence E, if at *t s* knows that E is misleading evidence against *h*, then at *t s* is justified in disregarding E as it bears on *h*.

I'll indicate in note 27 why any fallibilist—in any case—should reject *Entitlement*; focusing on it, therefore, doesn't raise fresh issues. I'm grateful to Ram Neta for drawing my attention to Lasonen-Aarnio (2014).

[21] Kripke (2011b, 43) writes, after (*iv*): "This already seems very strange: that just by knowing some common or garden-variety statement, which I am calling *p*, one knows a sweeping thing: that any future evidence against *p* will be misleading." This *isn't* strange. If one knows *p*, one isn't wrong about *p* being true (which isn't to say one "couldn't" have been wrong about this—recall the characterization of fallible/infallible construals of "know(s)" in section 10.2). So, on those grounds alone, any future evidence against *p* is misleading. But further, if one knows that any future evidence against *p* is misleading, then one could have been wrong about that in exactly the same sense that one could have been wrong about *p*. So what's strange? What's written suggests that knowing a common or garden-variety thing leading to one knowing a sweeping thing is "strange" *all by itself*—but why? (If you know *that's* a rock, then you know that it's not *all* these other things that aren't rocks.) What this amounts to is (using sentential quantification) that $p \to (q)((q \to \neg p) \to \neg q)$. Does this, with *p*, enable an inference to something particularly *impressive*? I don't see it.

[22] Recall the discussion of this in section 8.6. Rachel North (or Jon Ronson) could have put the problem with David Shayler's "so-called" evidence just this way. *Of course*, Shayler's "evidence" against the bombing North witnessed is (*patently*) misleading; that's why everyone (sensible) is so impatient with and irritated by Shayler.

[23] Kripke (2011b, 49) writes that "sometimes the dogmatic strategy is a rational one," e.g., toward astrology, necromancy, the supposed murder of Vincent Foster by the Clintons, and Holocaust denials (all accompanied by presumed evidence).

deduction, although the conclusion about all evidence against *p* being misleading doesn't *sound* on a par with knowing that *p*. Knowing that *p* sounds weaker than knowing that all evidence against *p* is misleading. But why? One reason is that the English "all evidence against *p* is misleading" sounds like a "know(s)" iteration.[24] As I noted in section 10.3, "know(s)" iterations often sound like they have content that amounts to having a better grip on what's known than a ground-floor "know(s)" attribution. That would push us toward an infallibilist interpretation of knowing that all evidence against *p* is misleading, even if we don't take that interpretation about knowing that *p*.

But really, what should be scrutinized is principle (*v*)—one that Kripke (2011b, 43) admits is "hard to state in a nice, rigorous way, especially giving it the necessary generality":

> If *A* knows that taking an action of type *T* leads to consequence *C*, and *A* wishes above all else to avoid *C* (i.e. this is the only relevant issue), then *A* should resolve now not to take any action of type *T*.

For example (Kripke's example), suppose an agent knows that if he opens a door, someone on the other side will shoot him. Kripke (2011b, 44) dryly remarks, "It would then be a reasonable thing for him to resolve not to open the door."

I'll first make a point that's shown up in an extensive literature that's emerged on purported knowledge norms for *action*. Focusing on formulations like (*v*), and claiming that they reveal a knowledge norm for action because we criticize people for failing to act on the basis of something they *know*, overlooks that we do the same thing when people have certain nonfactive attitudes toward propositions.[25] Consider (*v**):

> If *A* is *really really sure* that taking an action of type *T* leads to consequence *C*, and *A* wishes above all else to avoid *C* (i.e. this is the only relevant issue), then *A* should resolve now not to take any action of type *T*.

[24] And maybe that's because it *is* a "know(s)" iteration. Kripke writes, after stating (*ii*), "notice that (*ii*) does not say anything about knowledge—any evidence against it is misleading, that is, leads to the false conclusion that not-*p*." Arguably, this is not how we understand "any evidence against *p* is misleading"—we understand it as a "know(s)" iteration because we understand "evidence" as "considerations that indicate *knowledge*." I don't claim "evidence" must or should mean this; I'm explaining a relative-strength impression about the two natural-language locutions, *p* and *all evidence against p is misleading*. More weakly, maybe we understand "evidence for *p*" as a metalanguage remark about *p* (e.g., "evidence for *p*" mentions *p*; it doesn't use *p*; as opposed, say, to the substitutional propositional characterization I gave in note 21). This still *sounds* stronger to the nonphilosophical ear: *p* is true sounds stronger than *p*. (In one sense it *is* stronger: it's "about" more—that's why the two locutions don't mean the same thing. But that's not to be necessarily stronger logically.)

[25] See Hawthorne and Stanley (2008), Gerken (2011), Neta (2009), and others—but especially Brown (2008), who observes the point I'm making here about nonfactive cognitive attitudes.

Here too we can observe (dryly) that if one is really really sure (or even only "pretty sure") that there's a gunman on the other side of the door, "It would then be a reasonable thing for him to resolve not to open the door."

Both principles (actually) sound right, despite whatever rigor they need. So what's gone wrong in the deduction from (*v*) or (*v**) to (*vi*)? Well, again, actually, nothing's gone wrong. The key phrase is Kripke's parenthetical clause "(i.e. this is the only relevant issue)." *Iterated* cognition facts, when they intrude, give teeth to this escape clause. In particular, it's because we fail to so easily recognize iterated cognitions are distinct from ground-floor cognitions that (*v*) and (*v**) seem to apply as widely to rational action as they seem to—that they seem to imply a broadly applicable (*vi*)—as opposed to a quite narrowly applicable (*vi*). And it's *this* that gives the impression that Kripke's reasoning leads to a dogmatism *paradox*.

Consider an ordinary student checking his math homework—I described one version in section 9.3. *Some* of these students, I've argued, know in many cases that *q* follows from *p the first time* they derive it. But they don't yet know that they know this. Given their understanding of how they've established *q* (*if* they've established *q*), they'll know the latter as soon as they check their deductions a few times. It, of course, follows from their knowledge of *q* that any evidence against *q* is misleading. But just as they don't (yet) know they know *q* (until they check over their results), they don't (yet) know that they know that all evidence against *q* is misleading. They know *q*; they know that any evidence against *q* is misleading; they don't know that they know *q*; they don't know that they know that any evidence against *q* is misleading. That's why they need to check their results a few times; that's why it's rational for them to do this.

In these cases, as in many cases, there is more than one issue involved: there is the knowledge, and there are the iterated cognitions regarding that knowledge; and that's what the capacity for iterated knowledge does *to agents that have it*; it raises issues about evidence for those agents. That bears directly on condition (*vi*): my resolution not to be influenced by any evidence against *p* turns on the nature of that evidence, and my cognitive relation *to it*. Thus, for example (section 8.6), North's having been in the carriage where an explosion took place is what makes her drawing conclusion (*vi*) with respect to *p* ("There was an explosion . . .") reasonable. Shayler's quite different relation to quite different evidence for the proposition $\neg p$ is what makes his drawing conclusion (*vi*) with respect to that proposition inappropriate.

It may seem these remarks don't help with the dogmatism paradox. After all, if a student checks his deduction three times, surely that's insufficient for him to conclude that he now knows *that all evidence against q is misleading*—that's just too strong a conclusion to draw. No, checking the proof three times may actually be sufficient for a student to know that all evidence against *q* is misleading. But the fallibilist will stress (again) that "knowing that all evidence against *q*" is misleading isn't to be infallibly interpreted. Furthermore, if we're fallibilists (about our own knowledge), then given *anything* we (take ourselves to) know, and *given the particulars of the new evidence*, it may be reasonable to revisit that purported knowledge, and re-evaluate it. This includes our knowledge that any evidence against what we know is misleading.[26] This interpretation of (*iv*) depends on interpreting it as (implicitly) know(s)-iterative.

Given this, principles (*v*) and (*v**) gain a great deal of (illegitimate) scope from the exceptions to them (that I've described) being hard to characterize in ordinary language in clear terms. (It takes a whole book to clarify them.) Consider again a student who checks her multiplication results three times, a student who knows her result when she first carries out the calculation, and is now checking that she knows this (understand this literally!) because she knows how she comes to know such results. A number of factors, we've seen, impede recognizing and expressing this interpretation of her: (1) we routinely collapse second-level know(s) iterations to first-level ones (thus my warning to take "checking that she knows this" literally, instead of interpreting "knows," above, as redundant); (2) we find it hard to express the fallibility of "know(s)" ("I know *p*, but I might be wrong"), and therefore we find it hard to express how it makes sense (and is possible) to check one's "knowledge" instead of what that knowledge is knowledge of—which is a different case; (3) our grasp of our methods of knowing are sloppy, so it's easy for us to slide from methods of knowing that are subsequently checked to (different) methods that include those checks, and (4) in any case, in near neighborhoods of cases where agents are checking what they already know are cases where (different) agents are instead establishing knowledge (because their methods are different). Together, these are the reasons our widespread *second-order* practices of checking and evaluating what we know are almost universally misdescribed as first-order practices of establishing knowledge.

Let me enforce the lessons I'm drawing here about the relationship of knowledge to action by discussing Fantl and McGrath's (2007; 2009) clever argument for pragmatic encroachment. Crucial to their argument is "KA": If a subject knows that *p*, then she is rational to act as if *p*. No—this principle needs to be hedged before a candidate will emerge that has a chance of being true. If I know *p* but suspect I might not (an iterated thought), I certainly *shouldn't* act as if *p*; that isn't *rational*. Consider, instead, the principle that: If I know *p* and I believe *p too*

[26] That is, there is evidence—in principle, anyway—that if presented to North (or Ronson) would make it appropriate for her or him to revisit their taking themselves to know there had been an explosion. It's just that there isn't any evidence that Shayler (or his fellow trolls) have that makes it rational for North or Ronson to revisit the question. (And, of course, this is generally the case with the "evidence" possessed by conspiracy theorists and their fellow trolls.)

(since knowledge *doesn't* imply belief, this isn't redundant), then I should act as if *p*. Will this do? The problem is that, again, although I know *p* and I believe *p*, I may be aware (because I'm aware of the methods I use to come to know *p*) that I shouldn't be sure that I know this (even if I *do* know it): I need to check those methods carefully.[27]

10.5 The Factivity and Fallibility of "Know(s)"; and Lotteries

For quite a while it's been thought by many epistemologists that given a fair lottery, no matter how long the odds of an agent winning it are, that agent can't (rationally) claim to know that he *won't* win the lottery; similarly, he can't *know* he won't win that lottery. Call this "the sceptical lottery impression." The sceptical lottery impression (which most epistemologists think all of us share)[28] is taken as indicated by slogans like "Hey, you never know," once used by the New York State Lottery in advertisements.[29] On this basis, some philosophers

[27] These considerations fault Fantl and McGrath's (2009, 59–60) principles, *Action, Best Results, Preference*, and *Inquiry*. Only in specialized circumstances do principles like these work; the general fault of those who push such principles is a failure to appreciate that the hierarchical fragmentedness of what we know bears on the holism of what we think it's rational to do, to prefer, to inquire about, and so on. When, for example, saying (Fantl and McGrath (2009, 60)), "Why do I prefer red wine? Because I know we're having steak," not just the knowledge that we're having steak is relevant to the acceptability of this statement, even though what "I" say foregrounds only that. Fantl and McGrath (61–63) consider counterexamples—due to Brown (2008) and Reed (2010)—but argue those counterexamples are compatible with the principles allowing pragmatic factors to influence what one knows. My counterexamples aren't so compatible—unless we so eviscerate "pragmatic factors" that sheer "wanting to know if *p* is true" becomes such a factor. Similar remarks apply to Fantl and McGrath's defense of KJ (2009, 66): "If you know that *p*, then *p* is warranted enough to justify you in φ-ing, for any φ," and other principles. (Modifying KJ by softening the antecedent to: "If you know and believe *p* . . .") isn't right either, as I've indicated. Fantl and McGrath are concerned with counterexamples to KK involving "close calls" (89–93), and they're aware that "radical externalism refutes KJ (105–108—they use BonJour's (1978) original ESP case as an illustration of this; see the Samantha case in section 8.5). But cases of nonhuman knowledge fit radical-externalist models of knowledge (and aren't easily dismissed by a modus tollens supporting KJ), as Fantl and McGrath suggest. Timid-student cases aren't "close-call" cases. In general, there are too many cases of knowledge that violate KJ (and its relatives) to take these principles seriously; this is clear once we recognize what kind of cases of knowledge are possible, given the falsity of KK. Principles connecting knowing *p* to reasons one has for φ-ing (offered by Unger (1974), Hyman (1999) and Hawthorne and Stanley (2008)) are similarly faulty. Finally, notice these considerations can be used to undercut Lasonen-Aarnio's Entitlement as well (see note 20).

[28] McKinnon (2013, 524): "A growing consensus has formed that [Ticket *n* will lose] and propositions like it are neither knowable nor assertable." DeRose (2017, 134 n. 3) quotes McKinnon but demurs on whether he (DeRose) knows this sociological claim one way or the other.

[29] That's already suspicious . . . especially because the tickets themselves (as of November 27, 2018, anyway) contain the printed text: "IF GAMBLING OF ANY KIND IS A PROBLEM FOR YOU OR SOMEONE YOU KNOW, CALL 1-877-HOPENY OR TEXT TO 467369" (capitalization theirs). This implies, notice, that we *know* most people who play repeatedly are going to *lose* every time; this is something most people think is true, by the way: we don't have the sceptical lottery impression

have argued that by consistently extending the lottery impression to all the improbable possibilities that arise in one's ordinary life (being hit by a bus when crossing a low-trafficked street; the ceiling of one's home collapsing on one suddenly; being struck by lightning numerous times; predicting the future correctly whenever one guesses it, for the rest of one's life; quantum tunneling through a wall; seeing what looks like one's friends in one's living room but actually being surrounded by "facades" of real objects . . .); nonphilosophers are convicted by their own attitudes toward lotteries as knowing almost nothing about what they (seem to) think they know (Vogel (1990, especially 20–21)), Hawthorne (2004, chapter 1)).[30] Others have used the sceptical lottery impression to show that neither belief nor knowledge can have probabilistic thresholds (Harman (1973, 118), BonJour (1978, 2, n. 3)), to undercut reliabilism (Hawthorne (2004, 9)) or sensitivity requirements (Hawthorne (2004, 11)), to show that we can't grasp the mental component of knowledge independently of grasping the concept of knowledge itself (Williamson (2000, 58–59)),[31] to show that only knowledge provides proper warrant for assertion (Dudman (1992, 205), Williamson (2000, 246–249)), or to show that justification (no matter how much a substantial notion of this is beefed up) can't be a sufficient condition for knowledge (Lewis (1996, 421)). Sceptical lottery impressions can do a lot of philosophically unexpected work for creative epistemologists.

with respect to *everyone*. But of course—with lotteries like Mega Millions, where *anyone* has a nonzero probability of winning—*everyone* winning has a nonzero probability too. Hawthorne (2004, 20) notes that single lotteries can be easily designed to match, for a given lottery, the probability of winning if one plays once a year for thirty years. (This, of course, is also true for the possibility that everyone wins; in both cases people, I've found, think they know they won't win.) Hawthorne writes that although everyone reckons themselves to know they won't win for thirty years, if they're presented with the redesigned single lottery draw with the same probability, "intuitions would then switch." This has *not* been my experience with nonphilosophers. By this point, usually (so it seems to me), a conversation about lotteries with this kind of detail has gone on too long for most of them; as a result, they embrace dramatic sceptical, "well, you never know anything" positions, or they dig in their heels and continue to assert contradictory positions on what they know or don't know (or they, sometimes politely, exit the conversation). Again, see section 10.6 for a linguistic explanation of this "going to extremes" behavior.

[30] Some philosophers—e.g., Harman (1973)—attempt to escape lottery scepticism by denying that our knowledge of quotidian facts (e.g., what's known by perception or on the basis of inference) relies on probabilities. This won't fly; the issue isn't about what the purported knowledge is based on; rather, this is a challenge to knowledge claims based on parity reasoning. Other philosophers, despite extensive use of the sceptical lottery impression for other philosophical purposes, seem to just ignore the awful "we-know-almost-nothing" implication of the sceptical lottery impression. Hawthorne (2004, 3 n. 7) plaintively writes, "In his otherwise synoptic book it is odd that Williamson does not address this problem." It's especially odd since, as far as I can see, the implications Williamson (and other philosophers) draw from sceptical lottery impressions arise solely from their sceptical implications—although when philosophers so use these impressions, they often avoid straightforward sceptical implications in inadvertently ad hoc ways. I won't dwell on this point any further.

[31] This is *one* of the arguments Williamson tries to use to establish this position.

It's important, therefore, to point out that sceptical lottery impressions *aren't* uniformly experienced by nonphilosophers. Nonphilosophers *often* claim they know that they, or someone else, will lose a lottery in which they have a (very small) chance of winning. Nonphilosophers, that is, often have *nonsceptical* lottery impressions. As commonly, nonphilosophers often claim that someone else who has purchased a ticket has wasted her money—this is especially the case if that someone else has spent a *lot* of money to purchase a *lot* of tickets (or if that someone does so regularly, e.g., "has a gambling problem").[32]

Nonsceptical lottery impressions are, generally, stronger the more money is involved *regardless* of the expected utility of participating in a lottery event—even, that is, if the expected utility is extremely high (because the potential payout is extremely high). This suggests something that there is, anyway, a lot of evidence for: that our ability to determine rational behavior on the basis of utilities is exceedingly poor—to be generous about it.[33] The calculated payout can yield expected utilities as high as we like (as has been happening of late with billion-dollar payouts for Mega Millions), and yet claims that it's *known* that the purchaser of a ticket will lose get stronger and more rigid *relative to the amount of resources the purchaser has*, and *independently* of the expected utility.[34]

Apart from this, many people *describe themselves* as being irrational when purchasing lottery tickets, and they say so—*often while purchasing the ticket*.[35] This is a not-atypical dialogue. "This ticket was a waste of money." "Well, you never know." "Um, I do know . . . this ticket is a waste of money." Williamson (2000, 246) suggests that if someone claims the purchaser of the ticket will lose,

[32] Hawthorne (2004, 18) knows this, writing: "when someone is deliberating about whether to buy a lottery ticket, ordinary people will often say 'You know you are wasting your money.'" Hill and Schechter (2007) notice this too—but they attempt to describe the mechanisms of when people do or don't accept sceptical lottery claims (what they call "lottery propositions") via Gricean mechanisms that make speakers sensitive to the information relevant to a hearer. This doesn't handle all the cases on which two debating speakers differ in whether they accept or reject claims about knowing one will lose a lottery. I hypothesize that several different mechanisms are at work making people accept or reject lottery claims; see what follows.

[33] Amos Tversky and Daniel Kahneman, as well as a number of other researchers, have made careers out of studying these forms of irrationality. See, in particular, Tversky and Kahneman's numerous papers (and books) on the topic.

[34] Imagine a person gambles his entire paycheck (again) . . . his wife and children are holding him back, crying out that he'll lose and they'll have nothing to eat again: "No, I won't!" he says. "Yes, you will, just like you have hundreds of times before!" they respond. The melodrama of the exchange detracts neither from its realism nor from its being a nonsceptical lottery impression that the family (and the acquaintances) of the chronic gambler have—one it's reasonable to claim the gambler has too (but is willfully ignoring because of his gambling *compulsion*). Again, note the warning on lottery tickets I quoted in note 29.

[35] I've *overheard*, "Well, this is dumb, but it *is* only two dollars . . ." It's a good idea, if you see a long line of people waiting to buy lottery tickets at a cash register, to get on that line and *just listen*. Or, if necessary, because no one is already talking, to start "innocent" conversations with the people around you about the expensive vacations you're planning to take. (This was written early in 2019, before the emergence of Covid-19.)

that purchaser (after discovering the claimant has no special inside information about the lottery's outcome) is "entitled" to feel "resentment." During a debate over whether it's known that the purchaser will lose, the purchaser *might* "feel resentment," but it's equally clear his opponent can push back against the legitimacy of that very emotion, by saying, "You're *going to* lose . . . like you have a thousand times already," where the "inside information" isn't anything specific about the lottery but only about the gambler's bad habits.[36] Resentment, if there is any, arises as it often does because two parties are having an argument (a "fight") and not because of any "entitlement" one supposedly has to that particular emotion.[37]

It's especially striking that people often use *probabilistic* considerations to argue for their *knowledge* that someone will lose in a lottery situation, for example, "You're more likely to get struck by lightning several times while picking up your winnings than you are getting any winnings to begin with"—where what's implied is that it's known (and by *you* too) that you're not going to get struck by lightning several times.

DeRose (2017, 156–157) recognizes that there are times when nonphilosophers think they know they or others will lose lotteries, and times when they think they know they won't; he puts this in terms of psychological ambivalence, a matter of "intuitive pulls" in conflicting directions. Framing the issue this way allows him to diagnose the source of these conflicting intuitive pulls as due to a conflict in how we evaluate when agents know. That one would believe one had lost the lottery even if the ticket were a winning one (what's called "insensitivity") pulls us toward the denial that one knows that oneself or others have losing tickets (before the draw). On the other hand, ordinary standards for knowledge typically employed indicate we know we've lost.

The primary manifestation of these "intuitive pulls" aren't divided souls ("I know; I don't know"—said by someone to her mirror, holding her lottery ticket up in front of her), but irresolvable arguments between different nonphilosophers, as I indicated in note 34. DeRose's diagnosis can accommodate this, I suppose, by claiming knowledge deniers have embraced intuitions generated by sensitivity considerations and knowledge claimants' intuitions are generated by our ordinary standards; but there are further subtleties about such debates that any such

[36] Hawthorne (2004, especially 18 and n. 43) is good on this. He writes, "Try raising the possibility of lottery success to people who are planning out their lives. Very often, they will respond with 'You know that's not going to happen' or 'I know full well I'm not going to get that lucky.' And he sensibly advises (18 n. 43), "Observe ordinary practice. Try raising questions about lotteries in ordinary conversation." I've *done* this; interestingly, the response is usually a "that's irrelevant" reaction—like the responses I'd get when (in my youth) I'd bring up evil-demon scenarios to the adults around me who were discussing their taxes.

[37] Both Hawthorne (2004, 18 n. 43) and DeRose (2017, 159–160) push back against this idiosyncratic claim of Williamson's.

diagnosis of "intuitions" must take account of. The mechanisms by which these "intuitions" are manufactured are *very* intricate.

Consider a purchaser who claims the purchase was a waste of money; we can further push the dialogue I gave above, along the lines Hawthorne (2004, 29) suggests:

> "This ticket was a waste of money." (said by the purchaser)
> "Well, you never know." (said by the friend)
> "Um, I do know . . . this is a waste of money."
> "Then throw the ticket away. Or better yet, I'll buy it from you for a penny. At least you'll have a penny."
> "No . . . I don't want to sell it for a penny."

Several points need to be made about the resistance almost anyone will feel about selling their just-purchased ticket for a penny. First of all, if standards for "know(s)" are vague (as I argued they are in chapter 9), then that fact—*all by itself*—will generate irresolvable disagreements over whether one knows one will lose a lottery or not. After all, if the standards are strong enough, one doesn't know one will lose; otherwise one does. If nothing in the standards determines exactly how strong they are, nothing the debaters can say to one another will resolve the debate in anyone's favor.[38] It *does* seem, despite this, that the proponent of stronger standards (the one saying "you never know") has the rhetorical advantage; this suggests that the vagueness of knowledge standards can't be the whole story here: it *looks like* more stringent standards always have higher epistemic privileges. I'll take this up in section 10.6.

Second, some philosophers (e.g., Williamson (2000), Hawthorne (2004)) say that someone who right after purchasing a ticket for a dollar refuses to sell it for a penny reveals herself on that basis alone not to know that she'll lose. After all, if she knows she'll lose, it isn't rational to keep a worthless ticket. (A penny is worth a whole lot more than nothing.) The suggestion is that knowing p connects to rational behavior in a way that being really really sure that p doesn't. No. Suppose someone is *really really* sure that he'll lose. Then (provided his real real surety is high enough to damp out the contrast between the value of a penny and the expected utility of winning), it *is* rational for him to sell his ticket for a penny. But no matter how high the odds against winning the lottery, he still won't want to—this is regardless of how high one's real real surety is (as long as it's not 1)—so

[38] Where vagueness is involved, well-studied anchoring effects influence why debaters are in different places that they resist moving from. See, e.g., LeBoeuf and Shafir (2006). Pragmatic factors (differing goals and concerns of the debaters) can also play a role. Vagueness allows infiltration of non-epistemic factors that, nevertheless, speaker-hearers (when apprised of them) will reject as legitimate.

being really really sure exhibits the same (irrational) resistance to suitable behavior as knowledge does.

More important, any impression that knowledge and real real surety (a nonfactive state) generate different pragmatic implications is due only to the factivity of "know(s)," and not to anything that differs (cognitively) between knowing something and being really really sure of it. After all, here is how the reasoning seems to go: if an agent knows p, then p is true. Thus, the agent *will* lose. If the agent *will* lose, then the agent would be best off selling the ticket for a penny (regardless of whether she realizes this or not). But if knowledge is fallible, then the agent, cognitively, may be no different from someone who's really really sure. Provided her rationality is to be characterized internally, it's no less (or more) rational to refuse to sell the ticket for a penny if one knows it will lose than if one's really really sure it will lose.

I relied on the factivity of "know(s)" to draw a pragmatic implication in the last paragraph. Let's focus on this, because it's one source of the false impression that "know(s)" has a special relation to rational action not possessed by nonfactive states (like being really really sure—where "really really sure" means, say, one of any extremely high "sureties"—short of factive, of course.). We (often) reason like so:

S know(s) p.
Therefore p.
Therefore it's rational for S to r,

where r is something that's rational to do, given that p is true. We *do* often talk this way: "Given that p is true, r is the rational thing to do." We don't usually, that is, explicitly conditionalize S's rational behavior to S's knowledge like so: "Given that p is known (by agent S), r is the rational thing for S to do." And no nonfactive attitude can allow the exhibited inference because nonfactivity disallows the second step. This suggests "know(s)" and other factive states allow rational-action inferences that nonfactive states don't. But there is the reasonable challenge that one *can't* draw any conclusions about what's rational for S to do solely on the basis of what's true (leaving, that is, S's cognitive state entirely out of it); the conclusion from this challenge is that this common inference pattern is mistaken (or, less severely, enthymematic).[39] The conclusion, that is, is that rational-action principles should always involve inferences from items to items all of which

[39] Compare: Is it ever rational to assert a contradiction? One *is* tempted to say no. But *of course* it's sometimes rational because one needn't know (or even suspect) that the something one's saying is contradictory. Is it rational to *knowingly* assert a contradiction? Ah, then, we might think: *of course* not. See, however, the discussion on this at the end of section 10.8.

remain within the scope of some sort of operator such as "It is rational to . . ." or "One should . . ." or the like.

If we accept this (and I think we should), what follows is that rationality-action principles don't have a special relationship to factive states, like "know(s)," but follow from a *number* of different cognitive states—factive and otherwise—that agents can be in, something I've already illustrated during the discussion of Kripke's dogmatism paradox in section 10.4.

It's important evidence for fallibilism that agents who are really really sure of something also resist acting against that something, even if *they know* the expected utility of the outcome makes it rational to act against what they're really really sure of. That is, the psychological resistance people have to selling tickets when they know (because of the odds) that they're losing tickets matches the psychological resistance to selling tickets when they're really really sure they have losing tickets. In particular, the psychological studies that reveal sources of resistance illuminate both kinds of resistance in the same ways (and that supports fallibilist claims that, psychologically speaking, knowing p is on a par with being really really sure of p).

What are these psychological factors? There are "sunk-cost" fallacies—if I *bought* the ticket, I'm resistant to selling it at a loss, regardless of what I subsequently realize about its expected value. Apart from this, there is also that we (to varying degrees) experience outcomes with a prospect of loss as far worse than equivalent prospects without a loss. This, *all by itself*, explains why we resist selling a lottery ticket that we know (or even suspect) is a losing ticket for a penny—even if we found it on the sidewalk and paid nothing for it. Once we pick it up, we possess it; and if it (against the long odds) is a winning ticket, then selling it for a penny incurs a *loss*. In addition, the background resources of agents (what's called "the reference point") also create resistance, as I've mentioned.[40]

Even if an agent can get past her psychological resistance to selling a ticket that she knows or is really really sure is a losing one because of its odds, there is still the problem described at the end of section 10.4, that it's almost impossible for that agent to consistently explain her own behavior when it appears to violate (v), as refusing to sell a low-odds lottery ticket for a penny appears to. (You might

40 See Kahneman and Tversky (1979) and Kahneman and Tversky (1984). Novemsky and Kahneman (2005) is a more recent measurement of loss-aversion ratios for certain cases. Regret and disappointment also affect penny intuitions. A popular overview of what we—as of 2011—know about these psychological factors with nice examples (and some citations) is in Kahneman (2011, chapter 26). The joke I made earlier ("A penny is worth a whole lot more than nothing") turns on implicitly recognizing reference points: a penny doesn't enhance *anyone's* resources.

think this would make agents more likely to sell a ticket; I think it just makes them stubborn. We should *never* underestimate factors like this, what once upon a time used to be called "sheer cussedness.")

The foregoing discussion of sceptical lottery impressions and penny arguments still leaves intact two threats to fallibilism. Still at large, first, are the sceptical shifts—and, more generally, going to extremes—that debates about knowledge exhibit; if these can't be explained away (or shown to be a result of a more general phenomenon that's not epistemic), it suggests that there is something about knowledge that advantages more stringent standards. Going to extremes is an issue for contextualists as much as it is for "moderate invariantists"—or fallibilists—because they seem to privilege certain epistemic stances over others, regardless of context.[41] I take this up in the next section.

The second issue is that parity reasoning seems to be a condition on knowledge, and as I've indicated, that supports infallibilism all by itself. I take this up in section 10.7.

10.6 Going to Extremes

I intimated the strategy I employ to handle going to extremes at the end of the last section: Going to extremes is due to a general aspect of vagueness that isn't specifically epistemic. Consider the following dialogues (both quoted in Fantl and McGrath (2009, 16); the second originally from Hawthorne (2004)):

Dialogue 1.
Attorney: Is there a chance that the man sitting here in the courtroom today is not the man you saw that night?
Witness: I know he's the guy. So, no, there's no chance.

Dialogue 2.
Witness: OK, I admit, there's a chance that the man sitting there isn't the guy I saw that night.
Attorney: Ah, so you don't know this is the man you saw, do you?
Witness: No, I don't.

[41] They show up as a challenge to Lewis's (1996) approach, one he ignores: an asymmetry in how standards shift up and down. We seem able to push standards up by simply raising possibilities in conversation (although there is some opportunity for pushback available as when these possibilities are described as "irrelevant"); on the other hand, we seem only capable of pushing standards down by forgetting the possibilities that have been raised. This asymmetry in how standards seem to rise or fall needs an explanation, one not easily available to contextualists.

I've called this "going to extremes." To handle it, let's start with a philosophically uncontroversial example, "flat," although this example has a long history of being exploited for epistemological purposes.[42] There are two broad ways that the vagueness of "flat" can be conceptualized—they run along the divide between the two epistemicist positions I described in chapter 9. One treats the semantics of vague words as not characterizing their vagueness—although such words are open to sloppy usage—the second treats the semantics of such words as inducing their vagueness.[43] A common impression of speaker-hearers about vagueness is a *normative* one: *the way* a word is used, in many cases, is sloppy, but we can be more precise in our usage if we're careful. On a view like that, the word itself isn't vague; it's only our usage of it that is,[44] and so, only a stringent use of the word is a usage that corresponds to what the word "really" means.

"Flat" (that is, Unger's (1975) understanding of "flat"), exemplifies this viewpoint.[45] "Flat," strictly speaking, applies only to surfaces that have no irregularities *whatsoever*—surfaces, that is, that are such that "nothing could ever possibly be even the least bit flatter" (Unger (1975, 49)). Otherwise, we're using "flat" metaphorically, or sloppily; and, as a result, we're almost never using "flat" correctly—we pretty much *never can* use the word correctly because of the kind of world we live in. Applied to "know(s)," this yields that we also almost never use "know(s)" correctly."[46] These results rule out a moderate "semantic invariantism"—a perspective on which we can correctly use "know(s)" or "flat" with less than perfect standards. The important point is that the view in question isn't one that's especially geared toward "know(s)": any vague word open to precisification suffers the same fate.

The second perspective treats "flat" and "know(s)" as genuinely—semantically—vague. That is, the semantics of these words—their meanings—doesn't determine a specification, precise or otherwise, as the (only) correct applications of these words. "Flat," "certain," "know(s)," "useless," and many other words, as we ordinarily use them, are used *correctly* in a wide range of

[42] See Unger (1975), especially chapter II, and chapter III, section 5. Also see DeRose's (2017, 170–173) revisit of Unger's discussion.

[43] Recall from the end of section 9.4 that it needn't be that the semantics of a vague word explicitly marks it as vague—because "vagueness" is a semantic category, or family of such—but rather that words inherit vagueness from the antecedent vagueness in the semantics itself—more precisely, in the terms in the semantics that characterize the meanings of these words.

[44] Such a view can be formalized by means of a pragmatic "sloppiness" operator that "fuzzifies" the referential targets of words falling within its scope.

[45] Unger (1975, 49) writes (his italics): "English is a language with absolute terms. Among these terms, 'flat' and 'certain' are *basic* ones. Due to these terms' characteristic features, and because the world is not so simple as it might be, we do not speak truly, at least as a rule, when we say of a real object, 'That has a top which is flat,' or when we say of a real person, 'He is certain that it is raining.' "

[46] Unger (1975) gets this result with "know(s)" via a purported necessary condition on knowledge of certainty: "certainty" is the purportedly absolute term he applies this argument to. But it can be run directly on "know(s)" without that assumption.

circumstances, to apply to surfaces that are (somewhat) irregular, people who are (somewhat) certain, those whose knowledge standards are moderate, and the many devices that (to one degree or another) there's no point to.

Which view of vagueness is better supported by usage facts? Here are some facts that oppose the absolutist viewpoint and support the genuinely vague perspective:

First, "flat," "certain," "useless," and other similar words are widely applied to a gigantic class of objects, events, and the like; they're not experienced by speaker-hearers as words that, in reality, have no (or nearly no) applications. In particular, "flat" is applied to all sorts of bumpy surfaces; "know(s)" is applied to agents who vary greatly in fallibility and epistemic competence.

Second (pace Unger (1975, 114)), modifiers such as "absolutely," "completely," and "perfectly" when applied to these words are *not* redundant ("apart from emphasis"—as Unger puts it). Their purpose, rather, is to shift the range of the vague word falling within their scope *toward* a precisification of it. In particular, "perfectly flat" or "really flat" can still refer to surfaces, like that of a billiard table or a football field, which aren't flat when examined up close, even with the naked eye. This is true of all these words, in general. "Perfectly useless" often applies to devices that aren't useless in *every* possible way.[47] "Perfectly knowledgeable" is often applied to agents that—nevertheless—are wrong about some of what they believe.

Third, attempts to correct the application of "flat" or even "perfectly flat" to a football field or a billiard table by a speaker-hearer can provoke push-back. Imagine a proud maintenance worker describing a just-restored football field: "Now, *that's* flat—just the way it's supposed to be." Someone responding, "That's not flat; it can't be because of all the irregular blades of grass," will be greeted by either incomprehension or by an annoyed: "That's what flat means!"

This is the usage evidence for the genuinely vague perspective on these words and against the absolutist view championed by Unger (1975). To draw the conclusion (from this) that involved in going to extremes is nothing intrinsically epistemic—as the use of "know(s)" instead involving a favoritism toward more stringent rather than less stringent standards would be—a second bit that's needed is that these semantic facts about these vague expressions aren't appreciated by nonphilosophers (and by many philosophers too). In point of fact, when nonprofessional speaker-hearers are apprised of the vagueness of a word, they presume (by default) this to be a matter of sloppy usage, not of the meaning of the word.[48] But this leads, in every case where it's possible, to a stringent

[47] After all, nearly anything—nearly anything "perfectly useless"—can be at least used as a paperweight, or as a philosophical example of an "object."

[48] See Azzouni (2013b, 235–239) on the phenomenology of vagueness.

precisification—even in the case of "bald." Again, people can (and do) push back against precisifications: "Oh, come on, get real! You've got so little hair left that of course you're bald." However, because it's so natural for nonphilosophers to understand vagueness as normative (as use-sloppiness), those pushing precisification with this family of words often have the rhetorical advantage.[49]

Together, these points explain both sceptical shifts and digging in one's heels without involving anything special about our attitudes (implicit or explicit) toward epistemic standards. Speaker-hearers, faced with vagueness—especially when they don't recognize this—will treat it as sloppiness. They'll then often reach for a stable precisification that they take the word, when it's not being used "sloppily," to pick out. Invariably, the resulting precisification eradicates nearly all the *normal* uses of the word. In the case of "know(s)," the corollary is scepticism. If they push back, the result—in the case of "know(s)"—is "dogmatism."

The foregoing is a powerful consideration against the idea that "know(s)," *as it's ordinarily used*, requires absolutely severe (agent-infallible) standards. That's because (i) ordinary practice with the word, like ordinary practice with many other vague words, applies it to numerous (agent-fallible) cases, and (ii) our tendency to slide toward an infallibilist precisification—again, like the same tendency with many other vague words—has been diagnosed by speaker-hearer misapprehensions about the nature of vagueness.

Let's turn to our apparent ("intuitive") acceptance of parity reasoning. Recall the point (made in section 10.2) that parity reasoning is an iterated cognition claim. That is, it's a claim about a generalization about *how* justification works. One, therefore, doesn't have an "intuition" that it's right—not one (anyway) that anyone should take seriously. Furthermore, as a generalization about our practices, it's dubious: We don't, in general, attribute knowledge to agents according to its dictates.

There is an important consideration, however, that pushes all of us—philosophers and nonphilosophers alike—toward the acceptance of parity reasoning, and, as a result, toward infallibilist standards for knowledge; and this consideration *can't* be nullified by the diagnosis of going to extremes that I've just given. This is that our grounds for (first-person) assertion of knowledge of *p* can only be, roughly (using the language of *Parity Reasoning*—section 10.2), "reasons for thinking *p*." But this looks problematic in lottery cases, and indeed, in any other case where speaker-hearers are apprised of an "inconsistency" in their knowledge-attribution practices. I claim I know that my ticket is a losing

[49] "Heap" is something of a special case because it's *obvious* that there is no natural—non-arbitrary—precisification of "heap." This is probably why it emerged so early in (ancient) philosophy as a definitive illustration of vagueness. "Table" and other words, Unger (1980) and Geach (1967) show, are similar to "heap" in this respect: eluding precisifications. Lewis (1993), with his typical ingenuity, invents a quite artificial work-around for this problem.

one (because of the extremely long odds). But say I'm playing one of those lotteries where *someone* will win. Then I can assert I know someone will win. But my reasons for thinking that any particular someone will lose are exactly the same as they are for me. So it seems that I should claim of anyone that they will lose, and indeed, I should claim that *every* person (playing) will lose. I'm in the following quandary: I know S will lose for every S, and I know some S will win. (I *don't know* that every S will lose.) This *is* a contradiction; and notice it seems to be a contradiction that's *not* due to the factivity of "know(s)": it looks like the same argument can be run with "really really sure." The only way that nonphilosophers (and most philosophers too) can think of to avoid this quandary is to withdraw the initial knowledge claim. But this pushes everyone toward infallibilist standards because only with those standards is there no problem with lottery knowledge. Things are complicated; so I need to take this up in a new section.

10.7 Prefaces and Lotteries

The *lottery paradox* (called this by Harman (1973, 118) and due originally to Kyburg (1961)): Presume a fair lottery in which $S_1, \ldots, S_m$ are all participating, where one of them *will* win, and where the odds of any individual losing are high enough to meet fallibilist standards for knowledge. The fallibilist—it seems—allows that one can know that S_1 will lose, . . ., can know that S_m will lose; and therefore can know that *each person* will lose. (But each person won't lose!) Belief runs along a similarly awful track: one believes that S_1 will lose . . ., believes that S_m will lose; one therefore believes that each person will lose . . . but one knows (and therefore, in this case, believes) that someone will win. *Contradictions.*

A version of the preface paradox (it has been noticed) has a similar structure. J.A. has finished a very long book, each sentence of which he has worked very hard to *establish.* J.A. writes, "Despite my best efforts, falsehoods remain. I apologize for them." If J.A. claims to know of each sentence in the book that it is true (which is a sensible claim if he's been careful enough to meet—even high—fallibilist standards, and the fallibilist is right that knowledge claims are fallible), and it also looks sensible for him to claim to know that falsehoods occur in the book (because, after all, consider its size) then it's apparently sensible for him—given factivity—to assert a contradiction.[50] Worse, if we know he's met—even high—fallibilist standards for each sentence in his book, then we get to assert a contradiction as well: J.A. knows Si, for every i, yields J.A. knows $(x)Sx$, and we agree.

[50] J.A. may instead say, "I suspect mistakes remain." This isn't a contradiction; it's a Moorean remark. Notice: we may run the argument in a way that avoids dependence on factivity, by focusing purely on "know(s)" assertions.

But in the preface J.A. states that he knows $(\exists x)\neg Sx$, and we agree with that too That gives us, in short order, $(x)Sx \& (\exists x)\neg Sx$, regardless of whether a third party asserts this or J.A. himself does so.

A different version of the paradox instead uses belief, and leads to inconsistent beliefs: J.A. believes each sentence in the book; he also believes he's made mistakes, that there are falsehoods. For each sentence Si, he believes Si; this seems to show that he believes $(x)Sx$; but surely he also thinks $(\exists x)\neg Sx$. So he believes $(x)Sx \& (\exists x)\neg Sx$, which is a contradiction.

To see how we should understand preface-paradox possibilities (because there is more than one), and whether (as a result) there are prefaces J.A. can write that both are consistent with his assertion of knowledge of the contents of the book and indicate fallibility, I'll briefly revisit (yet again) someone checking over a mathematical proof. In each case in which I described the example, I had the epistemic agent check the proof three times. Why *three* times? For no good reason, actually. Mathematicians in practice check more times (or fewer) depending on the length of the proof they're dealing with.[51] Mathematicians are rational to do so. They understand fairly well how they come to know the results they know, and they understand how mistakes can arise. So, in many cases, even though they know that *q* follows from *p when they first construct the valid proof*, they only come to *know that they know this* later.

Recall the two sorts of cases possible. One is where the agent is as above: she knows *q* follows from *p* because her method (one she sometimes checks, but not always) is straight deduction. The second case is one in which the agent doesn't know *q* until he has deduced *q* from *p and* checked his deduction of *q* from *p* a certain number of times, because, in this case, that agent's *method* of knowing that *q* follows from *p* isn't the same as the first agent's. In the first case, that is, the agent knows *q*; what she's verifying is her knowledge that she knows *q*.

This distinction, in the first case, can be applied to the preface paradox as well, and on this way of understanding what J.A.'s claim is based on, there is no paradox—no contradiction—*if J.A. puts the point right*. J.A.'s way of coming to know each sentence S_i determines (or not) whether J.A. knows S_i. And when J.A. asserts on the basis of this, of each sentence Si, that he knows Si, he may be right or wrong—because "know(s)" is fallible. When he asserts in the preface, however, that, "despite my best efforts, falsehoods remain," he's claiming

[51] Not quite "depending on the length of the proof." Mathematical proofs, almost invariably, aren't mechanically checkable; they're, as it's put, "informally rigorous"—heterogeneous combinations of mechanical calculations, shortcuts, meta-proof considerations, and conceptual maneuvers. I'm idealizing to the case, familiar from formal logic, of mechanically checkable proofs. But, more accurately, mathematicians check their proofs more or fewer times depending on the conceptual intricacy of the proof, the nature and scope of the computational aspects of the proof, recognition of their own cognitive strengths and weaknesses, etc. They also confer with their colleagues, depending on the same considerations.

something else: he's claiming that he knows that he doesn't know $(x)Sx$, because $(x)Sx$ is false—because he knows $(\exists x)\neg Sx$. The factivity of "know(s)" then implies he's asserting a contradiction. A contradiction even more quickly arises if he says: "despite my best efforts, I know falsehoods remain." Why do I want to claim that "despite my best efforts, falsehoods remain" involves metacognition? Why isn't the assertion of this phrase merely a denial of $(x)Sx$? (I owe this suggestion to Patrick McKee—April 14, 2020.) Because, "despite my best efforts," isn't idle; it indicates that despite purportedly-impeccable epistemic methods (say) falsehoods nevertheless remain.

But there are other prefatory remarks J.A. could have made, ones which don't imply contradictions. He can say, for example: "I know S*i*, for all *i*; I therefore know $(x)S(x)$, but I don't know that I know this (because I know that the methods I used to establish every S*i* are fallible, and I established enough of them that I have my doubts that the methods I used didn't yield falsehoods)." He can also say: "I take myself to know S*i*, for all *i*, but (of course) I could be wrong." He can even say something stronger via the "take myself to know" locution: "I take myself to know S*i*, for all *i*, but (of course) I'm wrong (about one or another S*i*)."

We're in a position (at this point in the book) to distinguish these remarks from contradictory preface remarks because we can now appreciate that knowing *p* isn't knowing that one knows *p* and because we can appreciate that we must acknowledge fallibility (which is what the preface remark is doing) in an indirect way because of (and only because of) the factivity of "know(s)." Factivity is why we can't say, straight out, I know, of each sentence in the book, that it's true but one of them is wrong" (or "likely to be wrong").

But isn't all this prefatory indirection a bit . . . weird? It *seems* weird because (i) we tend to assimilate knowing that one knows *p* to knowing *p*. Thus, it seems that if I know that *p*, for all *p*, then I know that I know *p*, for all *p*. And that seems to foreclose on saying that I know *p*, for all *p*, but I don't know that I know this. It also seems weird because (ii) we naturally collapse the considerations we use to establish each *p*, and the ones raised in the preface that make us worried about the considerations we used to establish each *p*, into one method for knowing things. That forces the idea that the considerations used to raise doubts about knowledge that we know *p* (for all *p*) are instead considerations that directly undercut knowledge that *p* for each (or some) *p*.

Despite the foregoing, one might argue like so: The preface acknowledges I *know* one of the sentences in the book is *wrong*. It doesn't (or, anyway, doesn't have to) acknowledge that I don't know if I know every sentence is right; it doesn't (or, anyway, doesn't have to) acknowledge that I take every sentence to be right, but of course I might be wrong. I can (so it seems) *know* there's a mistake in a big book I've written.

Response: *Fine.* If *that's* what you want to assert, you can't assert of each sentence of the book knowledge of it *too* because you can't do the impossible (slogan: The impossible is impossible). The preface paradox—if it's a paradox to worry about—is worrying because it seems to force us to a place where we can't acknowledge fallibility *at all.* To show that we can (and do) acknowledge fallibility, and to show why it seems to us we can't, tames the preface paradox. That said, if my reasons for asserting knowledge of each sentence in the book are on a par, then I can't acknowledge knowing *any* of them (if I want to acknowledge in the preface that one of them is false). This is an application of parity reasoning. This maneuver arises in this form with lotteries as it doesn't with a book. The various reasons an author has for thinking the sentences in her book are true are surely not all on a par.

Consider, though, a lottery where I *know* someone will win, and where everyone has the same chance of winning. I *can't* say, I know, of each participant, that she'll lose, but then merely add: I don't know that I know everyone will lose. I *know* someone will win; and this can't be avoided by separating a focus on my methods for knowing something from my knowing that something—so iterated cognition doesn't seem to come into it either.

What needs to go is unrestricted "aggregation" (as Kyburg (1961) urges), both for knowledge and for (rational) belief. Actually, what must go—more generally—is unrestricted epistemic closure, any *universal* principle of known closure under knowledge, as well as any corresponding unrestricted principle for rational belief, and other similar nonfactive mental states—being really really sure, for example. I now indicate (i) why this is so and (ii) why this doesn't entail a "cognitive collapse," one depriving us of the use of logical principles in our everyday and scientific reasoning for purposes of *knowledge* or rational belief, etc.

10.8 Fallibility Implies the Denial of Knowledge Closure

The fallibilist *must* deny knowledge closure; we can see this independently of lottery considerations. Call the "fallibility point" that point that the evidential standards for a proposition p require the evidence of an agent to meet in order for that agent to know p. Vagueness induces there not being, in general, a fallibility *point.* Nevertheless, idealize a point F as the fallibility point for a method M that an agent uses (doing so won't fault the proof that fallibility implies the denial of knowledge closure). Just because an agent's method determines that the agent's knowledge of p and her knowledge that $p \rightarrow q$ are both above F, it never *follows* inevitably that, fully consciously drawing the conclusion q (and doing so on the basis of her recognition of the inference of q from p), that agent's grasp of

q is still above F. There are always cases where this doesn't happen. Thus, knowledge closure fails, although the question remains: how many and what kinds of exceptions are there? (Can anything *relatively systematic* be said about this?)

Take a simple case of carrying out a long chain of inferences. Sheer fatigue can set in as one executes the task (a tedious arithmetic computation is the best kind of example), and the chance of making a mistake increases over time until it can no longer be said that one knows that the conclusion drawn is right. Mere boredom without any diminution of one's abilities will do the same. How is this to be analyzed?

Here's one approach. Treat the method M being used by these agents as one of "carrying out inferences," where the individuation of the method M used by agents is in terms of proof-theoretic validity.[52] Agents can make mistakes, but (up to a point) we can regard them as knowing p_i up to and including every reasoning step they've correctly taken, even if they don't know they know this. Their fallibility is cashed out in terms of the possibility of their failing to implement method M but instead a different method M* that they've (at that moment) failed to distinguish from M.[53] Even though, that is, at a certain stage, an agent knows p_i and knows $p_i \rightarrow p_{i+1}$, she doesn't know p_{i+1} even if she correctly recognizes that p_{i+1} follows from p_i and $p_i \rightarrow p_{i+1}$. This is because her grasp of p_{i+1} (because of boredom, let's say) has now fallen below the fallibility point required for knowledge.

Nothing I've said so far (so I claim) is specific to knowledge as opposed to rational belief or real real surety, since these also have fallibility points (or bands). Just because I'm really really sure of p_1, I'm really really sure that p_1 implies p_2 . . . and I'm really really sure that p_{n-1} implies p_n, it doesn't follow I'm really really sure that p_n; at that very point my grasp of the inference may have fallen below the fallibility point for real real surety. ("Look," I might say, "this has been going on for a while—I'm getting tired; I can't focus anymore; I have no confidence left in what I'm thinking.") And similar considerations seem to hold of rational belief. Given that I'm getting tired (given that my eyes are starting to cross . . .), it seems *rational* to say, "OK, I'm not mentally there anymore—I don't

[52] As I've noted before, we should recognize this is *psychologically unreal*, and use instead a second approach: describe the method M as a hodgepodge of psychologically real processes of imagery, partial rule-following, etc. On this second approach, the method an agent uses to reason will deviate from a method individuated in terms of proof-theoretic validity. In particular, some of the errors an agent makes (errors from the perspective of proof-theoretic validity) will be built into her method of reasoning, rather than arising as described here, because of a mistaken implementation of another method at some stage in the reasoning. I described these inferential methods (in section 7.4.2, note 41) as not "everywhere truth-preserving." That underdescribes things. Rather more accurate is that they're "almost nowhere truth-preserving," although they're pretty good on the inferences we usually carry out. Anyway, the points about fallibility and knowledge closure that I'm making carry through under either approach. (See section 11.3 for further discussion of this.)

[53] Recall that this isn't the only way to categorize their mistakes; it can also be done in terms of circumstances they're not distinguishing.

trust myself."[54] It's also reasonable to say the same about third parties: He doesn't know p_n because the chances of an error (even if he didn't make one!) have risen too far.

There is an unruly family of (hedged) closure principles that do hold. These are specific agent-relative principles that allow knowledge or confidence in reasoning about proofs up to certain sizes, or for certain amounts of time, or involving steps of only such-and-such complexity, as well as involving specific details about what the agent had for lunch, how much sleep she had, whether personal factors (and of what sort) are intruding into her thinking, and so on. These hedged closure principles (dare I call them *principles*?) are agent-relative because agents differ in their abilities (their strengths) in reasoning; sheer human fallibility, of course, puts a ceiling on *everyone*. This way of hedging closure principles doesn't infirm the role of logic in the sciences and ordinary life. On the contrary, it ratifies how we ordinarily reason and check our (and others') reasoning—both individually and collectively. We (we careful and responsible smart ones, anyway) repeatedly check our reasoning, both as individuals and in groups—we do so more diligently the riskier the inferences or the circumstances of the reasoning strike us. To the extent that we recheck our reasoning (and practice reasoning) we get better at reasoning, and become sure of or know results from long and careful reasoning that we couldn't be sure of or know before.[55]

One result of the foregoing is that *fallibilist* knowledge closure failure *can't* be used by those philosophers (e.g., Dretske (1970) and Nozick (1981)) to protect

[54] There is no reason, of course, to think the "fallibility points" or, more accurately, the "fallibility bands" for knowledge, real real surety, or rational belief are the same. Notice: I'm claiming that standard closure principles fail for these notions *independently*. This is, in particular, because (consciously held) justification, rational belief, real real surety, and knowledge have all come apart. So the fallibilist-based argument I've given here must be run independently on all of them although *in parallel*. My approach, in this way—but also in other ways—contrasts with the attacks on closure principles mounted by Lasonen-Aarnio (2008) and Schechter (2013). I'll return to this argument for the cases of belief and rational belief because special issues arise not shared by the case of knowledge; I'll at that point also address Neta's (2015) defense of the consistency of fallibilism with "closure (at least for propositional justification if not [for] doxastic justification or knowledge." (I've borrowed this way of describing Neta's position from his then-anonymous comments on a manuscript incarnation of this book, June 24, 2019). He there also noted that Simon Evnine and Ralph Wedgwood give similar arguments; and he suggested that the considerations raised may not be that different from the considerations—about agent-specific fallibilities—that I give to support hedged closure principles. This is an issue I may have to revisit in the future, since I (at the present time, early October 2019) don't have time to give this the full attention it deserves. I *will* say that I'll momentarily indicate that the agent-relative hedged closure principles I'm thinking of are likely to be horribly specific and exception-ridden—not at all the sort of thing one would normally describe as, for example, a "structural constraint" on an agent's beliefs.

[55] One of the striking historical facts about mathematical proof is that mathematicians—as a professional group—can handle far longer and more complex proofs than at any time previously. Mathematicians have managed this, pretty much, by developing a battery of sociological tools for checking and verifying long proofs. One "tool" is just the sheer number of mathematicians that exist today. What amounts to the practice among mathematicians (nearly enough) of "crowdsourcing," the checking of certain proofs illustrates this.

knowledge from scepticism or from inferences of *those animals* not being mules disguised as zebras from *those animals* being zebras. These *are* (relatively) unchallengeable cases of inferential closure; indeed, *nearly* all the instances of inferential closure we've thought carefully about are to that extent unchallengeable.

This is because, *generally*, fallibilist failures of knowledge closure don't occur when we're being careful, scrutinizing an inference, and carefully considering all the reasons it might be false—something that occurs, say, when you're thoughtfully considering whether it follows from your having hands that you're not a hallucinating bodiless brain in a vat.

Kripke (2011a, 200 n. 60) writes, "the cases where knowledge fails to be closed under known logical implication ought to be rare exceptions." Nope: they're *numerous*, but not ones we're particularly (or, perhaps, ever) aware of. This suffices to explain our "intuitive" resistance to denying knowledge closure. If in all the cases where we *focus on* inferences knowledge *is* closed, then it won't seem to us that there are cases where knowledge *isn't* closed. Focusing on an inference, importantly, is a way of *lowering* the riskiness of that inference; thus, the suggestion that knowledge closure could fail in cases where we're focusing hard on inferences seems especially implausible (as it does with zebra/hand inferences).[56]

What's atypical of lottery cases is that we can focus carefully and repeatedly on certain inferences, know the premises, and knowledge of the conclusion fails anyway. For, in general, if our knowledge of p (S has a losing ticket) has fallibility point i and our knowledge of q (R has a losing ticket) has fallibility point j, our knowledge of p & q, where p and q are independent of each other, has fallibility point ij (i multiplied by j). These conditions are satisfied in (certain) lotteries; and so conjunction-introduction inferences from the knowledge (or belief) that particular individuals will lose to knowledge of groups of such individuals all losing rapidly make the fallibility points of the resulting conjunctions fall below appropriate standards for knowledge (regardless of how low those standards are); our scrutinizing those inferences carefully doesn't change this.

There's no getting past how weird it feels to claim that if one focuses on p (which one knows) and focuses on q (which one knows) and carefully draws the inference p & q, nevertheless knowledge of p & q can fail! This sensation of weirdness arises with *any* inference from p to q that's "obvious." That explains our resistance to denials of knowledge closure (and denials of rational-belief closure). Philosophers, having learned that deductive inferences are truth-preserving, might claim that such inferences are epistemically *risk-free* (epistemically

[56] This explains why multi- and single-premise knowledge closure seems "intuitive." Hill and Schechter (2007, 120) explain this instead via "overgeneralization" from paradigm cases where our confidence of the *premises* of the reasoning is extremely high. I think the mistake is more subtle and (for that matter) more sophisticated than that.

frictionless). The fallibilist denies this: *No* psychological process of inference—deductive or otherwise—can be epistemically risk-free. That's, um, *crazy*—that's to treat a logical property of propositions as yielding an infallibility condition on *agents*.[57] The nonphilosopher's adherence to knowledge closure, however, isn't due to an appreciation of the truth-preserving qualities of deduction (since, generally, nonphilosophers aren't aware of this metalogical nicety); it's due, instead, to an assimilation of epistemic riskiness with the impression of obviousness.[58]

And this is a major factor (if not *the* major factor) giving rise to sceptical lottery impressions. Inferences from *this participant will lose, that participant will lose, this other participant will lose* (and so on to include every participant), to *every participant will lose* look obvious. And inferences that look obvious also look epistemically risk-free; and so, they look like ones fallibilist considerations can't undercut.

The foregoing analysis has characterized the failed inference pattern the revelation of which tames (and explains) the lottery paradox as one of an unacknowledged fallibilist knowledge-closure failure, in particular the one that licenses $Kp \ \& \ Kq \rightarrow K(p \ \& \ q)$, for all p and q. But the factivity of "know(s)" seems to allow a workaround of the necessity of this inference to the lottery paradox. Instead, use $(Kp \rightarrow p) \ \& \ (Kq \rightarrow Kq) \rightarrow (p \ \& \ q)$. From this (by focusing on the inference just carried out), we conclude $K(p \ \& \ q)$. Here too, however, the last inference causes a precipitous rise in one's fallibility so that (regardless of how low one's standards are) one fails to know the conclusion.

The result, so far, is this. Fallibilist failures of knowledge closure are, generally, not ones where inferences are scrutinized carefully; this explains why we're resistant both to the suggestion that a universal knowledge-closure principle is false and to the scrutinized purported examples of failures of knowledge closure (e.g., zebra/hand inferences) being examples of these. But inferences about lotteries, as I've shown, due to the precipitous rise in fallibility, are cases where knowledge closure, of even scrutinized (and obvious) inferences, fails.

Although in lottery cases, the application of parity reasoning enables inferences similar to those invalidated by a denial of knowledge closure, the argument for rejecting parity reasoning runs independently of the rejection of knowledge closure (although both turn on the fallibility of knowing agents). Consider: I know someone will win. Call that person "the-person-who-will-win" (this is a name/label for whoever that is). So I know "the-person-who-will-win will win. But I know I will lose. By parity reasoning I know the-person-who-will-win

[57] And so that's to make a companion error to the one I diagnosed at work in section 10.2: the thought that one can't be wrong about necessary truths.

[58] Degree of obviousness as a perceived indicator of degree of epistemic riskiness is closely related to answer fluency. Recall the discussion of this well-studied psychological phenomenon in section 6.5.

will lose as well. So I know the-person-who-will-win will win and I know the-person-who-will-win will lose. By factivity, the-person-who-will-win will win and the-person-who-will-win will lose.[59] Contradiction. Here (or so it seems to me) there is no fallibility rise in the inferences (or it's negligible).[60] So parity reasoning must be directly targeted independently of knowledge closure. Since fallibility *directly* implies parity reasoning is false, we have what's needed.

Do we have "intuitions" that support parity reasoning independently of the usage factors that impel us to experience "know(s)" as requiring infallibility of the knowing agent? I think not. This is because any such intuitions arise from iterated cognition considerations: the faulty impression of speaker-hearers (or seasoned philosophers) that our justification practices are in accord with parity reasoning.

In addition, although it may seem that we—nearly universally—accept parity reasoning (when we're brought to consider it), this isn't so. Consider a case where I've carried out a simple deduction. It might be said against my knowledge of my result that I could have made a mistake. (And suppose it's true: I *could have* made a mistake.) Nevertheless, I haven't. And I can know this. Agents *often* push back in cases like this—against denials that they know these results—*despite those agents acknowledging the possibility*. One sometimes says confidently, "Yes, it's *possible* I made a mistake, but I didn't." This is to reject parity reasoning.[61] Notice the move: "I" am *accepting* the possibility that I made a mistake, but using the factivity of "know(s)" and my certainty about what I know to deny that possibility is realized.

The tendency most of us have in ordinary circumstances to treat as irrelevant the possibility of being fooled by an evil demon might also look like a rejection of parity reasoning. I think it's not; it's more likely a rejection of the evil-demon possibility altogether. I'm putting off to *Challenging Knowledge* the evaluation of when we do and don't (when we can and can't) reject possibilities that challenge our knowledge.

Denying a generalization—like knowledge closure or the parity principle—is never in itself a big deal; it's the nature of the instances of the principle that are consequently denied that matters.[62] What's important to point out, therefore, is

[59] Notice that we can't get to "The-person-who-will-win will win and The-person-who-will-win will lose" via a generalization of some sort, like: (1) Parity reasoning tells me that, *for each person S*, S will lose. (2) So, consider the person who will win. (3) That person will lose. (1) is ruled out by a precipitous rise in fallibility.

[60] So, risk aggregation can't be used to invalidate the inference, and thus (pace Hill and Schechter (2008, specifically 105)), we can't reject this instance of an application of parity on the basis of a rejection of closure principles.

[61] Similarly (Fantl and McGrath (2009, 21), "Of course there is always some chance that I'm wrong, *anything is possible*, but I know that *p*." This is (somewhat) less appealing to say (for reasons I've explained) than the above, but it's still an illustration of pushback.

[62] We can deny all the implications of Peano arithmetic that no one will ever use; that won't negatively affect our practice of arithmetic. We can deny all but one instance of the law of

that by denying these three principles—parity reasoning, knowledge closure, and rational-belief closure—one isn't rejecting all the instances of these principles. Instances are rejected only on the grounds of what can be called "epistemic threshold effects," and in practice—in most cases we're aware of—we can avoid these effects on knowledge and rational-belief closure principles by paying concerted attention to our reasoning.

Our "intuitions" about parity reasoning involve additional factors not operative with respect to knowledge closure. As I've mentioned, a commitment to parity reasoning (by an individual) is directly a matter of beliefs about the nature of justifications; it's not a simple grasping of what "know(s)" means. In addition, the usage factors impelling the impression of infallibility make parity reasoning plausible. Finally, there is a subtle interplay between cases where we assert knowledge despite possibilities we acknowledge as opposed to when we assert knowledge despite possibilities we reject. This confusing dovetailing of various usage factors (and naive speaker-hearer impressions) has been the theme of this chapter.

10.9 Rational Belief and Concluding Remarks

I'll conclude this chapter by developing the point of the last sentence of the last paragraph of the last section, and then by considering one last loose end regarding beliefs, rational beliefs, and prefaces. I've argued elsewhere that the inconsistency of natural languages isn't a result of such languages harboring a single contradiction somewhere within them—such as, say, an inconsistent generalization governing an inconsistent truth predicate[63]—but rather the syncretic combination of various language resources that may have (historically) developed independently of one another. I focus (in, e.g., Azzouni (2013a)), specifically, on the idea that various logical particles, "and," "or," "not," etc., as well as certain referential principle governing words, could themselves have particular (and innocently

non-contradiction; that won't have much effect even on our use of the law of non-contradiction as a generalization. See Azzouni and Armour-Garb (2005) on this. For that matter, see Azzouni (1992, 341–342) on this.

[63] This is a common perspective fueled in large part by the impression that contradictions—like the notion of set governed by an unrestricted comprehension axiom in set theory—can be blamed on a single concept. In the case of liar-paradox phenomena, what's overlooked in taking this perspective is that other language facts, e.g., what logical principles are operating in natural languages, as well as referential practices, and even syntax, *all* contribute to the contradiction. See Scharp (2013) for an approach to the liar paradox based on this criticized view; see Feferman (1982), especially the opening paragraphs, for the marginalized lesson on liar paradoxes that the subsequent literature hasn't absorbed.

consistent) local logical properties that their unrestricted combinations don't have. Only when these operate *together* is the result contradictory—a "paradox."

I've illustrated a far more confusing (and complex) example of the same thing in this chapter. For consider, (i) our pragmatic redundancy practices of interpreting iterated cognitions as ground-floor cognitions, (ii) the factivity of "know(s)," (iii) the invisibility of the vagueness of "know(s)," in particular how it facilitates going to extremes, (iv) various scope confusions (e.g., in rationality principles and in descriptions of fallibility and infallibility),[64] (v) the tendency to experience obvious inferences as epistemically risk-free, (vi) the general opacity of the nature and kinds of methods used by agents that justify what they know, and, related to this last item, (vii) a certain sloppiness in the individuation of methods and/or the circumstances in which those methods are used. *All of this*, as I've illustrated in this chapter, contributes to the knotty character of our thinking about lotteries, rational action, and "know(s)": only by grasping firmly *all* the elements of our usage practices (and understanding them) is it possible to unravel this mess.

In the next chapter, I give an overview of "know(s)" and related epistemic words and phrases. But first, a major loose end: Belief attribution seems descriptive; beliefs are items agents *do* have, not ones they necessarily *should* have.[65] Furthermore, it's surely true that we (sophisticated) agents have inconsistent beliefs. What should we do when we recognize a group of our beliefs is inconsistent—what's the rational thing to do? It might be thought: suspend belief with respect to the contradictory set of propositions.[66] But that means, given that we've certainly got contradictory beliefs that we can't locate, that we should suspend belief with respect to everything we believe—we shouldn't believe anything. Another option is to accept that we believe p, and that we believe $\neg p$ too—which (though) *isn't* to believe $p \& \neg p$.[67]

[64] Scope confusions, of course, show up *everywhere*, even in mathematics, e.g., Cauchy's confusions about pointwise vs. uniform convergence (which involves a quantifier interchange). Scope confusions are due, of course, to the complex (and still not well-understood) mechanisms in natural languages for indicating anaphora (mechanisms that we're—more or less—psychologically trapped into using by our childhood acquisitions of our native natural languages).

[65] This is controversial, however. Some philosophers claim beliefs need to be justified; others that belief attribution isn't purely descriptive. The examples I've given, especially in chapter 1, of nonhuman animals and drones that have beliefs militate against this second view.

[66] Along the lines of: I realize I've believed all along that Dave is honest, but there's evidence, I've come to realize, that he's not. So now I think: I don't know whether he's honest or not, so I don't believe him to be either honest or not honest. (This is a natural exchange: "Well, do you believe Dave's honest?" "I don't know whether he's honest or not," where the second sentence seems to imply, "I don't believe or not believe Dave is honest.")

[67] Imagine: I believe p; I believe $\neg p$; they can't both be right (because I don't believe $p \& \neg p$, in *any* case); something is wrong, but I can't figure out what. This state of mind isn't *irrational*. There is more to say about this—which I'm doing in a moment.

So, belief closure fails too. More importantly—so I claim—rational belief closure fails too. Let me spell this out. There is no test for contradiction (Church (1936)). That is, in many cases, *no matter what an agent does*, she will remain stuck with contradictory beliefs. Neta (2015, 302 n. 1) notes that Millgram (2000) "argues that, even if coherence is achievable, it is impossible to know whether we've achieved it." Neta writes:

> Even if true, this does not tell against the internalist's appeal to coherence as a source of rational duty, achievable solely by dint of our own effort; whether we are obligated to comply with the requirements of coherence, capable of doing so, and at fault if we fail to do so, need not turn our ability to know whether we've done so.

Let's read Millgram (2000) as alluding to Church's result.[68] If so, Neta's focus on being able to tell if one's beliefs harbor a contradiction isn't to the point. The problem, the fallibilist should stress, is that we have *various* methods for rationally establishing epistemic results. There is, for example, the evidence of my having checked a proof. As many philosophers note, there is also the valuable testimony of experts about the validity of such proofs. Cases can arise thus where, as far as I can tell, I should believe p on the basis of very good methods M_1, and I should believe $\neg p$ on the basis of very good methods M_2; and *I haven't any way to resolve this issue.*

I've just given a case involving checking a proof vs. expert testimony. But consistency conflicts can (and do) arise in lots of ways. We may be faced with two different very intricate proofs both of which look equally valid.[69] There can be powerful visual evidence (optical illusions of various sorts) that evidentially impel contradictory results—not to mention all sorts of background conditions that coupled with what I've just described, or other considerations, impel inconsistent claims. There can be, that is, all sorts of (differing) ways to compel my rational belief in p and in $\neg p$—*without my being able to resolve the issue.* This happens—notably—in the sciences *all the time*: All scientific theories face "anomalies."

Neta (2015, 295) requires consistency of rational belief. He simultaneously describes us as being at fault if our beliefs fail to be consistent. But, I claim, this

[68] Millgram (2000) is concerned with the strictly broader issue of the computational complexity that calculations of coherence face—being incomputable altogether is just the worst case of this. "Coherence," as Neta (2015) understands it, involves logical consistency and probabilism (distributing one's confidences in one's beliefs in accord with Kolmogorov's axioms), as well as matching one's confidences appropriately to one's evidence. I restrict my discussion to logical consistency.

[69] Apart from intricate arguments in natural languages (e.g., in philosophy) which can have this appearance, it can also happen with respect to long, informal, rigorous mathematical proofs.

is to demand far too much of rational belief, and of rationality, for that matter. Instead, if we have good reasons to think our beliefs are inconsistent, but we also have good reasons to think that we can't do anything (at this time) to "clean house," it doesn't mean we're thus ejected from the "space of reasons" and our thinking is irrational. On the contrary. It's rational (sometimes) not to believe the consequences of certain things we believe: because, say, we believe p and we believe $\neg p$. But we surely don't believe $p \;\&\; \neg p$! Thus, fallibilism implies rational belief isn't closed under deduction (and that it shouldn't be). Of course, it *is* rational to believe the consequences (that you recognize) of what you rationally believe if you think what you rationally believe is consistent.

Rational belief involves cognitive "duties," for sure. We should avoid inconsistency, *if* we can. We should test for inconsistency, *when* we can. We should isolate the contradiction (if we can't eliminate it), *if* we can—e.g., we shouldn't infer certain things from inconsistencies (or what we suspect are inconsistencies).[70] The important point: It's not my fault (and I can't be blamed) for what I don't know about and/or can't do anything about. No conditions on rationality (or rational belief) should imply otherwise.

For purposes of prefaces, this allows the following: For every statement in the book, p, it's rational to believe p, and yet to also believe that for some p (who knows which) $\neg p$. Again, as with knowledge closure, denying belief closure, as a generalization, doesn't mean we deny most or many inferences from our beliefs. The same considerations raised in this section about knowledge closure and rational belief closure apply to ordinary belief closure. It also seems that belief—this is a matter of how belief, descriptively, sometimes works—violates parity reasoning. One *can* say, "It's so odd, I believe p, but not q, even though I have no reason to treat them differently." One *may* (sometimes) successfully criticize this as irrational—depending on the p and q in question. And in these cases, the criticism doesn't presuppose an adherence to parity reasoning holding of *rational* belief—it just attacks this particular violation of parity reasoning. Still in place are the fallibilist considerations that undercut instances of parity reasoning with respect to rational believing.

What the foregoing suggests is something we should, anyway, take seriously: belief isn't a necessary condition for knowledge; and rational belief isn't a necessary condition for knowledge either. Our beliefs can be contradictory; our rational beliefs can be contradictory. That's not true of what we know because "know(s)" is factive.

[70] Shouldn't we just avoid inconsistencies altogether? Never infer *anything* from them? No: that wouldn't be rational either! It's often good scientific practice to use flagrantly inconsistent scientific/mathematical theories to infer results we otherwise can't get to. See Azzouni (2014) and the citations given there.

11
The (Complex) Structure of the Meaning of "Know(s)"

11.1 Introduction

The last substantial task (to do in *this* book—apart from the appendix) is to describe the structure of the meaning of "know(s)," as well as its relations to other epistemic words. I'll first review what I've claimed about the various necessary conditions and sufficient conditions that govern this word. I'll then describe its meaning in terms familiar from lexical semantics and explain why the word eludes definition. Relevant to this last bit is the failure of priority reasoning. Next, I compare my approach to understanding our concept of *know(s)* with approaches to this taken by social-role epistemologists, in particular Craig (1990), Lawlor (2013), and Reynolds (2017). At a certain distance, my analysis—especially the considerations I raise in this chapter—bears parallels to what social-role epistemologists do: single out a central social functional role for the concept of knowledge and characterize the properties of "know(s)" in those terms. The material in the introduction, part 2, about the distinction between the function(s) of a word and its semantic/syntactic structure is important for seeing how different my approach actually is.

11.2 Necessary Conditions and Sufficient Conditions for "Know(s)"; the Relation of These Conditions to Criterion Transcendence

The lesson that many have drawn from more than a half century of Gettier cases—that no adequate definition of "know(s)," of knowledge, exists—leaves intact the possibility of a nevertheless quite rich set of necessary conditions and sufficient conditions that govern "know(s)." And, indeed, many philosophers have thought "know(s)" *obviously* obeys significant necessary conditions that can be used as lexical scaffolding to characterize their (various) systematic understandings of epistemology. A lot of this book undertakes undercutting and/or hedging many of these. I've denied that S knows *p* requires: S believes *p*, S rationally believes *p*, S is infallible about *p*, S is certain of *p*, S is sure/confident of *p*, S is conscious of

Attributing Knowledge. Jody Azzouni, Oxford University Press (2020). © Oxford University Press.
DOI: 10.1093/oso/9780197508817.001.0001.

p, S is aware of *p*, S is conscious (at all), S can justify *p* (in the sense of: S is aware of, or grasps, or can grasp, or can articulate, reasons that justify *p*), S knows that S knows *p*, or, indeed, S necessarily bears any metacognitive attitude toward S's knowing *p*. (I've, relatedly, denied purported necessary conditions on an agent seeing that *p*, and the like.) Similarly, for an agent to know *p*, S's knowledge of *p* needn't be sensitive or safe. I've also denied the existence of knowledge norms for assertion, belief, inquiry or action, as well as well-behaved closure conditions for knowledge.

None of this is to say (as I've said before) that there are no situations in which specifications of such conditions hold. I'm *not* claiming that agents never metacognize, that knowledge is never closed under specific deductions an agent undertakes, and so on. I *am* claiming that the same word—and concept—is applied across enough cases where one or more of these conditions don't hold: none of these conditions is *necessary* for the correct application of "know(s)."

Versions of the other implicational conditions philosophers have argued for remain nevertheless. Williamson (2000) urges us to take "know(s)" to be the most general factive mental state. Subsidiary claims accompanying this are, e.g., that if φ is any factive mental state, then, if an agent φs that *p*, the agent knows that *p*; for example, if an agent sees that *p*, then that agent knows that *p*. This is also true for all speakers whose "remember that" is factive. (Recall the discussion of this in note 44 of the introduction.) These subsidiary claims about "know(s)" hold, in general, if *all* the usages of a word or phrase φ are factive: any purported implicational relations between words must be checked on *all* their usages. For example, "see(s)" (recall from the introduction) has two conditions, one on which one sees something that's real and one on which one needn't. Because both these usages are factive, however, the inference from an agent seeing that *p* to that agent knowing that *p* goes through for them.

I've also supported in section 9.3 a hedged version of an agent knowing *p* implying that agent is confident or certain of *p*; that is, confidence is a necessary condition on knowing *p* only when lacking that confidence damages an agent's methods of knowing *p*. I've also argued for augmenting/precisifying our ordinary talk about having/possessing concepts and the relationships of having/possessing concepts to knowledge (in section 5.4). This too weakens or eliminates theses about concept-possession conditions on the appropriate attribution of propositional attitudes to epistemic agents that have been popular among many philosophers—and that have done a lot of work for them—for example, that an agent knowing *p* requires that agent to possess (in a very strong sense of "possess") the concepts used to express *p*.

These qualifications aside, I've argued that "know(s)" is governed by two necessary conditions. The easily stated one, factivity, was the star of chapter 10: If

S know(s) p, then p is true. The second isn't easily stated (so I'll do it in a hedgy vague way): If S know(s) p, then S has come to know p by a process that is, to some extent, reliable. The vagueness, I've argued, is ineliminable: "know(s)" purely and simply is vague; it's vague because the (tacit) standards for knowledge are vague. (This is a vagueness that infects "know(s)", therefore, that's over and above the vagueness "know(s)" inherits from "true.") That this isn't a sufficient condition follows from the failure of the parity condition (section 10.2), and thus (ultimately) from the fallibility of knowing agents. A reliable process that's sufficient for an agent's knowledge that p in some circumstances may not be sufficient for knowledge in those *same* circumstances for an otherwise indistinguishable q—lottery cases being the most salient examples of this.

There is another important property of "know(s)" that needs elucidation. This one undermines Harman-style solutions to Kripke's dogmatism paradox (section 9.3), and it's central to the retraction phenomenon that undercuts contextualist/anti-intellectualist/relativist interpretations of "know(s)" (chapter 3), although in neither case did I explicitly refer to it with the terminology I use now. This is that "know(s)" is criterion-transcendent, as opposed to being criterion-immanent.[1] This property of "know(s)" is also important because a word's being criterion-transcendent, normally, prevents that word from having a publicly accessible definition. In what follows, I explain all this.

I'll start with the contrast notion: *criterion immanence*. Consider the phrase "notarized document." This phrase recognizably comes with application conditions. For a document to be successfully notarized requires that certain events occur, ones involving legally endowed agents (with specific specialized tools, in this case a notary stamp). In addition, should laws change—e.g., the tools that are allowed to be used—the word will continue to apply to previous documents then considered notarized, but won't apply to current ones; e.g., we'll describe older documents as *having been* notarized, but the new ones handled by the outdated methods as not having been notarized. Similarly, previous instances of legal tender, although (possibly) unacceptable as current instances of legal tender, will still be described as *having been* legal tender. I call these *weakly retroactive criterion-immanent* words (Azzouni (2000b, 210)).

Other criterion-immanent words are *nonretroactive*. Consider "cell phone." If a new kind of cell phone is introduced by a company (and it comes to dominate the market), no one thinks that the discontinued models aren't cell phones. "Toy" is similar. When new toys are invented, old toys may be set aside by children who've lost interest in them, but they don't cease being *toys*. The changes in

[1] My most recent discussion of this important distinction between words is in Azzouni (2017b, section 2.2). I claimed that "know(s)" and "true" are criterion-transcendent (although "warrantedly assertable" isn't) in Azzouni (2000b, 208).

the publicly known characterizations of these words—what I call criteria—have no effect on their continued application to items that fit the previously acceptable criteria for these words: those items are still instances. Similarly, we may regard medieval thinkers (or many of them, anyway) as having been *justified* in asserting a spherical geocentric unmoving earth, even though *we're* not so justified. "Justified" is also a nonretroactive criterion-immanent word. Other examples of criterion-immanent words are "debt," "contract," "jury," "warrant," "marriage," "day," "touchdown," "chess," and "fictional character."

Many words, however, are *criterion-transcendent*. A criterion-transcendent word is *strongly retroactive*: After a change in the criteria for such a word, it isn't taken to refer to or to ever have referred to instances that don't fit the new criteria. So too, items that fit the new criteria, but not the old ones, are taken to fall under and to always have fallen under the word. Consider "gold." At one time, let's say, the word had the criterion: metallic, yellow, ductile, and inert. And now suppose the criterion for "gold" changes (under the impact of theory development) so that it comes to be instead: a substance composed (mostly) of atoms with atomic number 79. Materials that don't fit the new criterion are denied the status of gold; they're treated as *never having been gold*. New items that weren't "gold" according to the old de facto definition (e.g., gold gas) are now deemed gold, and to always have been gold (although not realized by us at the time). Other examples of criterion-transcendent words are "atom," "zebra," "bird," "vegetable," "electricity," and "God," as well as more abstract words such as "exist," "object," and "true."

The idea, therefore, is that criterion-transcendent and criterion-immanent words operate differently with respect to the criteria we use to apply them, and by which we understand them, and they operate differently when we change their criteria. The references of criterion-transcendent words—more generally, the understood *identity conditions* for these words and their meanings—can float free of their criteria: they can float free of the descriptions by which we understand these words at a time. To put it another way, we don't understand a change in the criterion of a criterion-transcendent word as a change in the "meaning" of that word. We take "gold" to still "mean the same thing" when we shift on its criteria—we think it has always referred to, and will always refer to, the same things.[2]

Criterion-immanent words have a tighter relationship to (certain) descriptions that we take as conveying their meanings. In some cases, this is because the description is recognized to provide a functional description of a kind of artifact: a refrigerator, say, is a device designed to keep foodstuffs cold. Anything that doesn't have that function—or that wasn't designed to have that

[2] We might deliberately and consciously change what the word "gold" means, of course, we may now use it to refer to things we used to refer to with the word "beef"; that's a different matter.

function—isn't a refrigerator (even if it's used to cool foodstuffs, e.g., a box submerged in cold flowing water by a riverbank). I'm not prepared to say the presence of a functional characterization in the meaning of a word is *necessary* for it to be criterion-immanent, but functionality all by itself takes us pretty far. The functional characterizations of types of artifacts appear, of course, right on the surfaces of our understandings of them: an artifact (a tool, for example) is usually designed *for a purpose*, or *set of purposes*, and in coming to understand what a particular artifact is, we usually come to understand how it's "supposed" to be used. "Justifications" aren't artifacts; nevertheless, the word is criterion-immanent. I've suggested (recall section 7.2) that "justif(y/ies)" also has what we can easily describe as a functional characterization that yields a definition: to provide a reason to think a proposition true over and above what was available for this before.

We saw, in chapter 3, how the criterion transcendence of "know(s)" pressures claims that "know(s)" is contextually variable in its standards; the same property wrecks philosophical attempts to claim it's ordinary common sense to say we lose knowledge in situations where only our perceived (or, sometimes, unperceived) evidential relations change (section 9.3, especially note 12). The criterion transcendence of "know(s)" requires retractions, the same as criterion transcendence does for any word it governs. If, in light of a situation in which we realize evidence is sufficient to deny that someone currently knows *p*, we deny that they ever knew *p* (on the basis of that evidence, anyway).

What's the source of the criterion transcendence of "know(s)"? When it comes to words like "gold," "zebra," etc., the temptation (among some philosophers) has been to hypothesize that these words semantically target metaphysically real "natural kinds." This is now recognized as implausible (pace Kripke, Putnam, and others): "ant," "mouse," "vegetable," and other words that are criterion-transcendent *don't* semantically target natural kinds. That "know(s)" characterizes a natural scientific kind (e.g., Kornblith (2002)) is (I think) is even less plausible. So that's not a source of "know(s)" being criterion-transcendent. Factivity doesn't explain it either: the word could be factive without it being criterion-transcendent. Its criterion transcendence is also independent of its connection to reliable processes—especially because these are at best only necessary for "know(s)"—no such processes are sufficient (because of the failure of priority reasoning). Criterion transcendence, therefore, is another important semantic property of "know(s)," apart from its factivity, its compatibility with fallibility, its vagueness, and the necessity (but not sufficiency) of an agent's knowledge being underwritten by reliable cognitive processes. I'm inclined to explain the presence of a criterion-transcendent word like "know(s)" (which, in addition, is factive, for that matter) by the need for a linguistic item with a certain *inferential* role that we use "know(s)" for. I discuss this in section 11.4.

Although criterion-transcendent words, generally, don't have definitions that are perceived to follow from what they mean, this doesn't rule out empirically driven definitions emerging for such words from a developed theoretical understanding of what they refer to; the recent scientific history of words like "gold," "fire," "true," and others illustrates this. Sometimes, as with "gold," the resulting definition cements the word to what looks like a "natural kind" out there in the world—but other times it doesn't. There are lots of useful scientific terms with extensions that aren't "natural kinds"—mineral science and biology are rich sources of examples (but there are many others). In any case, as I've noted, one way our understanding of our world progresses is by our acquisition of definitions for criterion-transcendent words through empirical means. Indeed, the presence of so many criterion-transcendent words can be taken to be a wise acknowledgment by the "designers" of natural languages that what these words apply to isn't dictated by perceived meanings (but instead by whatever surprising facts are, in time, empirically revealed). But despite "know(s)" being a criterion-transcendent word, it doesn't (it can't) have even an empirically driven definition. I show why in the next section.[3]

11.3 Why "Know(s)" Evades a Definition

I first review (and develop further) some of the points made in part 2 of the introduction about natural-language lexicons. I describe words as, generally, having *regions of sufficiency*, demarcated (partially overlapping) areas of application. "Climb(s)" (Jackendoff (1990, 35–36; 1983)) has two independent conceptual conditions: (i) an individual is traveling upward; (ii) the individual is moving with characteristic effortful grasping motions. "X see(s) Y" has "roughly" the two conditions (i) X's gaze makes contact with Y, and (ii) X has a visual experience of Y. We experience the uses, respectively, of the words "climb(s)" and "see(s)" as paradigmatic (as "robin" uses) when both conditions are satisfied, as acceptable; but not as paradigmatic (as "penguin" uses) when only one of the conditions is

[3] Williamson (2000, 30–31) classifies the failure, in the Gettier literature, to find a definition for "know(s)" under the broader linguistic observation that most words in natural-language lexicons lack definitions—and that nothing requires such lexicons to contain the words that would enable definitions to be possible. Although true, this misses the depth of the problem of defining "know(s)." Despite the relevant epistemological literature occurring self-consciously in the vernacular, most philosophers in the Gettier tradition were *not* against precisifying ordinary language or coining new terminology in terms of which "know(s)" (at least in principle) could be defined—something, I've already noted, common with the natural-language words that science makes progress with respect to. (Williamson's own characterization—attempted definition—of knowledge as the most general factive mental state should be described this way.) The interesting question, if it's true that "know(s)" doesn't have—and can't have—a definition, is why this process, so common with words describing phenomena that science makes progress with, won't (or doesn't) work for "know(s)."

satisfied; and as unacceptable (wrong, metaphorical, or a use of the word with a different meaning altogether) when none of the conditions is satisfied.

Let me briefly return to the issue of the necessary conditions of epistemological terms that was raised in section 11.2. In general, checking for the entailments that underwrite such necessary conditions becomes much more subtle given a picture on which the meanings of words, generally, have multiple regions of sufficiency: entailments may hold between some sufficiency regions of particular words but not others. For example, when someone is conscious, not merely of the proposition she knows but of her knowledge of it, it may be a condition of knowledge in those circumstances that she believes the proposition as well. Certain timid students, who know propositions they don't believe they know, don't know they know these propositions either (see sections 1.6 and 9.3). Similarly, I may say of a cash machine, "It believes I'm someone else," when the cash machine refuses my card or doesn't acknowledge my password; but we balk at saying flat out that the cash machine "believes what it says." The latter use of "believes" requires consciousness, but other uses don't. In general, an "entailment tree" for words so related in natural languages, e.g., "know(s)," "believe(s)," "is aware of," "is justified," etc., is a complex diagram that delineates regions of sufficiency for these words along with necessity and sufficiency lines between those regions, but not (generally) between the words themselves. Relatedly, rational belief comes apart from knowledge even in cases where an agent is *aware* of the p that she knows. This is because it can be rational for her to believe $\neg p$ because she's mistaken about how she knows p.

This aside, philosophers will have noticed (and perhaps bristled at) Jackendoff's stated conditions not being quite satisfactory—something Jackendoff himself notes explicitly with his word "roughly." I'll now put to philosophical use that it's often extremely difficult, if not impossible, to provide impeccable conditions for the meanings of words.

Regions of sufficiency involve applications of words that—perhaps often—*cannot* be characterized by other words in the lexicon. Colors are an easy case. The region of sufficiency for, say, "purple" involves the demarcation of an experiential visual range by purely sensory means—words don't help. In general, a region of sufficiency for a word may be induced by a complex pattern of sensory means and some language conditions—but ones insufficient for a definition purely via words of the lexicon. The same is true of more complex words, like "know(s)," which look, at least in principle, like they're amenable to a definition in words purely of the natural-language lexicon—or, at least, if not by means of these words, then with words that might be subsequently coined in one or another relevant scientific discipline.

To illustrate the point for "know(s)," let's preliminarily (and *very* roughly) characterize sufficiency regions for "know(s)" in terms of the traditional domains of knowledge-gathering methods that have emerged in epistemology: truth-preserving inference, non-truth-preserving inference/inference to the best explanation/induction, perception, memory, testimony/authority. It's no accident that Gettier puzzles emerged around 1962, and not (centuries) before. Part of what was needed for philosophers to recognize them was a general discounting of infallibility—or conditions largely equivalent to it—as required of knowers. This isn't because our methods being infallible necessarily makes Gettier cases impossible—it needn't—but because, in any case, it makes them hard to see. (I explain why this is immediately below.)[4]

If there are (some) infallible methods we have of knowing things, if—to use Zagzebski's (1994, 72) language—"there is no degree of independence at all between truth and justification," then these methods are immune to Gettier cases. For the infallibility of an agent (given a certain method) amounts to: justifying that *p* on the basis of that method implies *p* is true.

Does truth-preserving deduction provide such a method of justification for agents? Is (therefore) truth-preserving deduction immune to Gettier cases? Consider a simplified case. Suppose an agent's method of knowing *p* is: determine whether or not *p* is a tautology. *No* method of determining that a proposition is a tautology, one should think, enables agents to be infallible. After all, given even a small amount of confusion, fatigue, momentary distractedness, etc., an agent may misapply the method—even if the method only involves a quick mental inspection of some sort. This is human (agential) fallibility.

Still, which Gettier cases are possible turns on how we characterize an agent being justified, given this antecedent description of knowledge. We can, for example, characterize an agent as justified if the method M that agent uses is a truth-preserving one. According to this characterization, an agent fails to be

[4] Pasnau (2017) describes (with numerous valuable citations) the complex evolution and emergence (among philosophers) of the professionalized words and concepts "certainty," "evident," "scientia"; legal-practice-derived words like "justif(y/ies)," "justification," "warrant," etc.; their complex relationships to one another, and to the word "know(s)," as used by nonprofessionals (in various vernaculars). Thinkers, during this long period, seemed quite aware that placing a condition of certainty or infallibility or "perfection" on knowledge was to introduce something not reflected in ordinary usage. Pasnau (2017, 145–146) quotes Augustine, Grosseteste, and Gassendi on this. In particular, Gassendi (Pasnau (2017, 186 n. 9)) writes: "we are not one of those who reject the familiar and common manner of speech, by which we are said to know [*scire*] many things." Some of the complexity this (long) history exhibits, I think, is because "know(s)" is a semantic universal, although many of the other words eventually accompanying it (even in the vernacular), like "justif(y/ies)," aren't. A word being a semantic universal doesn't prevent it from being modified diachronically in a language, nor are such words resistant to being refined, splintered, or even having (some of) their semantic entailments denied in the way that "tomato" is reclassified as a "fruit," "point" as a location with no dimensions, and "square" as a figure bounded by one dimension. Pasnau (2017 170–172 n. 1) ridicules the idea that "know(s)" is a semantic universal on what I think are weak grounds, although I can't get further into this now. (I *will* add for the record, that Lexicology and Philology *can* be friends—but only if everyone holds hands and plays nice.) I thank Eric Schliesser for recommending Pasnau's book to me early in 2019.

justified in thinking *p* (whether she realizes this or not) if she fails to execute the inference via M. Call this *a proposition-relative model of justification.* We can also, however, treat the agent as justified if, *as far as he can tell*, he has used M. In this case, he may be justified in thinking *p*, although he used a method M* that he thought was M, where M* isn't truth-preserving. Call this *an agent-relative model of justification.*[5]

Which is the right way to go? The first way of characterizing justified inference is popular among philosophers. Against it is that it looks psychologically unreal. Justification shouldn't be characterized in terms of logically impeccable idealized methods we only *simulate*; it should be characterized in terms of the powers and abilities of actual agents.[6] Thus, what actually justifies agents shouldn't be individuated in terms of (formal/mechanical) methods that can be defined in terms of the truth-preserving relations among propositions; instead, it should be characterized in terms of the physical/cognitive movements that agents actually engage in when they try to execute the mechanical proof methods they've acquired. On this view, an agent can be justified even if she fails to use a truth-preserving method M because (*as far as she can tell*) she did use it.

Someone *tries* to carry out an addition task. "You didn't manage it," we say, "because look at what you did here." This is to individuate the method the person used in terms of what he did. It's not that he succeeded in carrying out the addition task (but with an error)—that's not what "you *didn't manage it*" means. It's that he did something else while *trying to* execute an addition task. That's what "trying to ***" means; if you *try* to ***, you can *fail* to ***.[7]

Several interesting cases show we operate (implicitly) in accord with agent-relative models of justification and not proposition-relative ones. Consider this case (Warfield (2005, 407–408)):[8] Warfield worries he hasn't enough handouts for his talk (he has 100). He counts the people in the audience and gets 53. There are, however, 52 people in the audience (he counted someone twice because she'd changed her seat while he was counting—inattentional blindness). "There are 53

[5] This distinction echoes Kitcher's (1980) distinction between "psychologistic" and "apsychologistic" approaches to knowledge; especially see section VII of his article.

[6] Suppose an agent checks over a tax return several times, but a small calculational blunder remains. We think she's justified in thinking she owes the amount to the IRS that she's calculated she owes—we think this even if the IRS subsequently fines her for an underpayment. (The IRS doesn't care if you've made an honest mistake.) This example is like those Warfield (2005) has introduced into the literature; see what follows.

[7] This said, and given the next few paragraphs, it's clear we shift back and forth in how we individuate what a person is doing in these cases (and in many cases): sometimes we individuate "what the person is doing" in terms of what the person actually does and sometimes in terms of what the person tries to do. This phenomenon—of shifting on the individuation of the methods we attribute to people—contributes to the variation manifested in our judgments about whether a person knows, or is justified in believing, *p*. I illustrate this momentarily.

[8] I thank Monika Greco for drawing my attention to Warfield (2005).

people at my talk; therefore 100 handout copies are sufficient," he tells himself.[9] Not only do we think he knows this (as Warfield (2005, 407–408) points out), but we also think he's *justified* (Warfield doesn't point this out). Why justified? Because he's used a method most of us use (*sloppy* counting), but one that's pretty reliable for rough estimates. That is, we individuate the methods agents use in terms of what agents actually do to execute them instead of in terms of the idealized (logically impeccable) ways those methods can be characterized.

Another example from Warfield (2005, 408):

> CNN breaks in with a live report. The headline is "The President is speaking to supporters in Utah." I reason: "The President is in Utah; therefore he is not attending today's NATO talks in Brussels." I know my conclusion but my premise is false: The President is in Nevada—he is speaking at a "border rally" at the border of these two states and the speaking platform on which he is standing is in Nevada. The crowd listening to the speech is in Utah.

That many will accept Warfield's judgments about these examples—that they're illustrations of *knowledge*—makes sense if the knowledge methods of agents are fallible. This fallibility, in the case of counting, arises from the small numerical missteps that always result in answers *near* the correct answer. So, if the correct conclusion of the agent is sustained by a range of false answers clustered around the correct answer, the method is regarded as yielding knowledge. (People will differ in what the penumbra is of acceptable false answers supporting a correct conclusion: this is the vagueness of the standards for "know(s)" intruding, and it also explains why not everyone will accept *all* of Warfield's examples as cases of knowledge.) Inferential cases—like the Nevada case—may look different because there aren't natural numerical ranges that false results can be clustered in; but something similar is at work: the resulting false interim conclusion ("The President is in Nevada") can't be "too far" from the truth ("The President is in Utah").[10]

These examples (and the reader should be able to construct many, in all sorts of ways—or she can read Warfield's article) also illustrate the lessons of chapter 10.

[9] Many of us, aware of the fallibility of our counting skills, conclude with: "There are *about* 53 people in the room; I have enough handouts." This difference affects how we think about other cases, as I indicate shortly.

[10] Warfield's self-avowed sketchy description of why his cases are ones of knowledge looks compatible with my analysis in terms of our acceptance of the fallibility of the methods used by agents. He invokes the stability of the inferences from premises to conclusions insofar as (Warfield (2005, 414)) "It is no accident that the falsehood 'there are 53 people at my talk' gets me to the truth 'my 100 handout copies are sufficient' nor does it seem that I was epistemically lucky in concluding 'the President is not in Brussels' upon coming to (falsely) believe that he is in Utah based on CNN's accurate report of his 'speaking to supporters in Utah.'"

That, in general, knowledge can be acquired in cases where applications of fallible methods *essentially* involve missteps shows our acceptance of the fallibility of knowers. Accompanying this, therefore, is that knowledge doesn't exclude "luck"—as it mustn't on any fallibilist account. (It does, however, *tame* luck: too much luck is no good; see note 15 on this.) Attempted solutions to Gettier cases (e.g., Harman (1973)) that turn on requiring for knowledge *no* false inferences or missteps (characterized in some more general sense) aren't true to the ordinary notion.[11]

Let's return to the question of whether truth-preserving deduction is immune to Gettier cases. Given the agent-relative model of truth-preserving deductive justification, Gettier cases can be easily constructed for them. Imagine that an agent thinks she's using a truth-preserving method M to deduce a proposition *p*. Because of momentary lapses in memory (or several mechanical errors), she instead executes a procedure M* that she thinks is truth-preserving but isn't. Accidents sometimes happen, however, and M* in this case yields the correct answer. (A lengthy addition computation—in which a couple of carrying errors accidentally cancel each other—is a natural example.) She's justified, *p* is true; but she doesn't know that *p*.[12]

According to the proposition-relative model of justification, she's not justified. But a second kind of case is possible.[13] Imagine that, unknown to agent *A*, a drug has been administered to him that both diminishes his ability to reason and diminishes his ability to monitor the quality of his reasoning capacities.[14] The drug's effects, however, are sometimes sporadic—the mind clears momentarily, and one reasons well. *A* has been cognitively muddled by this drug for the last couple of hours (although he's unaware of his mental impairment); just as he undertakes a new addition calculation, his mind suddenly clears and he carries it out correctly; moments before, or after, he would have blundered, as he has and will continue to with the other calculations he's been making. Those who judge

[11] Warfield cases are also helpful in understanding an aspect of the surprise-exam paradox; see the appendix.

[12] Why don't we judge this case the way we judge Warfield's handout case? One reason: Because conclusions like the one Warfield drew are supported by the sloppy method. Not so when we want a precise conclusion that depends on the designated method being executed exactly. Another reason: Counting missteps generate wrong answers that cluster closely to the right answer. Carrying errors, however, can lead to answers *quite far* from the correct answer.

[13] We might call this forthcoming case a Ginet case, a Goldman case, or perhaps a Ginet-Goldman case—it's like the fake-barn cases that first appeared in print in Goldman (1976). Stine (1976, 252) writes, "Alvin Goldman makes this point nicely with the following example which he attributes to Carl Ginet"; Stine seems to be speaking (260 n. 1) of a presentation of Goldman (1976) that Goldman gave in 1973. See Kripke (2011b, 166) on this, and this article, more generally, for a thorough and illuminating discussion of these cases.

[14] The drug resembles alcohol, which diminishes a person's reflexes and other mental capacities while leaving intact a (false) confidence in her capacities—in contrast to, say, marijuana, which undercuts one's confidence in one's abilities along with a diminution of those abilities.

that in fake-barn cases one doesn't know that one's looking at a real barn despite looking at one (because of all the fake barn facades around it) should similarly judge that *A* doesn't know that *p* even though (according to the first characterization of justification) *A* is justified.[15]

Are these *Gettier* cases? It's been suggested both that they are (by some) and that they're not (by others). It depends, of course, on whether the barn viewer is justified or not in thinking he's seeing a barn. If he is, it's a Gettier case; otherwise not. If we adopt proposition-relative models of justification, then *A is* justified. It follows that, regardless of how truth-preserving justification should be characterized, what amounts to Gettier cases remain possible.[16]

Zagzebski (1994, 73) argues(her italics):

> The notion of knowledge requires success, both in reaching the goal of truth, and in reaching it via the right cognitive path. The notion of justification or warrant is less stringent, requiring only that the right path is one that is *usually* successful at getting the truth. It is this difference between the notion of knowledge and the notion of justification that is responsible for Gettier problems.

[15] Consider the various facade cases. An agent is driving through an area and sees what he thinks is a barn. It *is* a barn. But every "barn" he thought he saw up to then (and from then on) are barn facades, and not real barns. So (most of us think) he didn't know he was looking at a barn. Now introduce differences in how many barn facades there are in the area, how close they are to the real barn the agent sees (whether they're in Sweden or not); how well known the barn facade practice is; etc. Notice that judgments about this will vary along dimensions—roughly—of how lucky the agent is as a result. The luckier the agent is (roughly, e.g., the more barn facades there are in the area, as well as their distribution), the more likely we are to discount the suggestion that the agent knows. There is certainly more to analyze here; let me make a couple of remarks. First, it's important not to over-intellectualize or over-precisify these judgments. Everyone uses quite crude means for individuating methods and deciding how reliable they are. In particular, what should be expected aren't just differences between the individuals making judgments but inconsistencies in any one particular person's judgments across time and cases. Second, these claims are empirical; they can—in principle, anyway—be tested using social-psychological tools, like some of the ones employed by xphilosophers. Third, there are three kinds of cases that philosophers classify differently: Warfield cases, misleading-evidence-that-the-agent-doesn't-possess cases (Lehrer and Paxson (1969), Harman (1973)) and fake-barn cases. In all these cases, judgments vary, and the reasons for judgment shifts aren't transparent. I treat the judgment shifts in these cases as involving the same reasons: differing individuations of methods, as well as differing judgments on how fallible the resulting methods can be to still allow knowledge. I leave the details of this for future work.

[16] A caveat: Suppose I'm right that the fallibility of agents allows Gettier cases with respect to deduction; what about being in severe pain? If we then restrict "knowledge" *and* "justification" to "nowledge"—present-tense cases where mental states *are* transparent this way ("clear and distinct")—don't we get a definition? I think yes, and I think Gettier cases can't be introduced via margins of error (pace Williamson (2013)) for reasons closely related to the rejoinder I gave to his argument against KK in section 9.5. Since classical fallibilists were focused on transparent cases of cognition like severe pain, and since they took the cognition of (some) truths, and possibly short deductions, to be similar, if knowledge is restricted to *these* cases, Gettier cases are impossible. Despite appearances, I *don't think* this indicates that the Gettier-case phenomenon is the culprit preventing a definition of "know(s)," as Zagzebski and others have hypothesized. I show this shortly.

The project of defining knowledge as belief + justification + X[17] is taken, by Zagzebski, to fail because of this: There must always be a gap between the package, belief + justification + X, and truth. This is wrong because even if what Zagzebski says is true about justification, that there must always be a gap between the package, belief + justification, and truth, that doesn't imply that there can't be a characterizable X on which there is no gap between belief + justification + X, and truth. All that follows is that justification plus the X that determines truth can't amount to justification tout court.

Given this, we have, so far: (i) the criterion transcendence of "know(s)" doesn't preclude designing a definition of "know(s)" in terms of justification, belief, and X; (ii) Gettier cases don't per se exclude such a definition;[18] (iii) the vagueness of the word "know(s)" doesn't per se exclude such a definition; and (iv) that "know(s)" is a word with several (but finitely many) regions of sufficiency doesn't exclude the possibility either. This is because such a word is still open to a disjunctive definition if each of those regions can be characterized in definitions. That's the lesson of chapters 7 and 8: two sufficiency domains for justification—inferential and representational—are both open to characterizations. If that exhausts the sufficiency domains for justification, then we have a disjunctive definition (as I think we do).

What, if anything, *does* exclude a definition for "know(s)" and knowledge? Apparently, it's just this: Some of the ways of coming to know things can't be captured by a "method-sized" sufficient condition for "know(s)" because our fallibility undercuts parity reasoning with respect to those methods—for example, those that enable us to know we've lost a lottery. In such cases, therefore, there are *p*s and *q*s, where the agent S knows the *p*s but doesn't know the *q*s, where the method M_p and M_q are S-indistinguishable, and where *p* is true and *q* isn't. Sheer fallibility, thus, precludes defining knowledge in terms of the methods by which agents come to know and on which their expressed justifications must be based.

Serious fallibility (recall from section 10.2) isn't needed for this result. Thus, we see yet another motivation for infallibility construals of knowledge: Exclude the methods which undercut parity reasoning, and perhaps a definition of knowledge is within sight.

[17] I specify the definition project that Gettier cases challenge as one of "belief + justification + X" because Gettier cases don't (directly) threaten other in-principle ways of defining knowledge—e.g., Williamson's (2000) definition of knowledge as "the most general factive mental state," as well as ones that give up on one or more of the presumed necessary conditions Gettier assumed are in place for knowing *p*.

[18] This is ironic. It shows that ad hoc attempts to patch purported definitions of knowledge against specific Gettier counterexamples—a practice exhibited by the epistemic literature for *many* years (and often ridiculed for its futility by philosophers hostile to "analytic" philosophy)—were, pace Zagzebski, Williamson, and these others, the right way to go. *General reasons* for why a definition of "know(s)" can't be patched up against counterexamples still elude us. (I'm hoping to change that in the next few paragraphs.)

It seems, in this and the last few chapters, that factivity and fallibility like to take turns making our epistemic lives miserable (at least making our *philosophical* lives miserable: those lives dedicated to *understanding* what we do when we attribute knowledge, anyway). This makes natural the topic of the next section: conceptually re-engineering "know(s)," either by modifying it or by replacing it. Specifically, why would anyone *want* a vague factive fallible notion of knowledge that, furthermore, is vaguely dependent on reliable but fallible methods, but not in a way that allows it to be definable on the basis of those methods; why is a notion like *that* indispensable to us?

11.4 Conceptually Engineering a Successor Notion to "Know(s)"?

I'll start by listing several aspects of "know(s)" that philosophers often contemplate engineering away: its (apparent) infallibility, its vagueness, its criterion transcendence, and its factivity.[19] Quine (1987, 109) writes, for example, "I think that for scientific or philosophical purposes the best we can do is give up the notion of knowledge as a bad job and make do rather with its separate ingredients. We can still speak of a belief as true, and of one belief as firmer or more certain, to the believer's mind, than another." Here, we find an (implicit) focus on infallibility—thus the explicit option of focusing on firmer or less firm certainty.[20] Lewis (1996, 439–440), after describing a horribly messy contextualist notion of knowledge that he's (pretty much) made up, one involving the ignoring of possibilities and various kinds of contextual shifting, writes:

> What is it all for? . . . I venture the guess that it is one of the messy short-cuts—like satisficing, like having indeterminate degrees of belief—that we resort to because we are not smart enough to live up to really high, perfectly Bayesian, standards of rationality.

Here, although Lewis isn't explicit, factivity, among other things, would be given up (by the appropriately smart people he alludes to). Regardless, both Quine and

[19] Because *so many* philosophers think that misleading evidence can lead to the "loss" of knowledge (recall note 14 in chapter 9), the word's criterion transcendence is ignored or overlooked rather than officially engineered away.

[20] Quine's implicit focus on infallibility as an entailment of "know(s)" becomes explicit elsewhere. He (1981a, 180) writes: "[Regarding the question: how can we know that one theory is true and another false? There] is an obstacle . . . in the verb 'know.' Must it imply certainty, infallibility? Then the answer is that we cannot. But if we ask rather how we are better warranted in believing one theory than another, our question is a substantial one. A full answer would be a full theory of observational evidence and scientific method."

Lewis think the notion of "know(s)," as it normally is, is dispensable (at least in principle): something else (or a bundle of something elses) can do the epistemic work we (think we) need "know(s)" for.[21]

Let's first take up dropping factivity, since it has—anyway—proved to be such a constant and ubiquitous troublemaker. Why should "know(s)" be factive?[22]

Well, one thing the factivity of "know(s)" *isn't* indispensable for is justifying an agent's practical inferences (this was shown in section 10.5); other nonfactive notions, being really really sure, being justified, etc., can do *that* all by themselves. We must, instead, look to a use of "know(s)" that's closely related to the use of "true" in blind truth ascription. "True," that is, is indispensable for utterances like "Everything Einstein said yesterday is true," where although I want to assent to everything Einstein said yesterday, I don't exactly remember what it was he *did* say. *One* thing behind the need for blind truth ascriptions, that is, is our need to rely on others who *can* assert *p* to enable our own assent *to p*.[23]

[21] Quine isn't offering new coinage, as he's so often willing to do elsewhere. Lewis, however, *is* eyeing a more formal replacement that would amount to a regimentation or (in more contemporary language) a re-engineering of the concept in terms of technical mathematical tools that are, relatively speaking, quite recent. The main replacement strategy among contemporary philosophers is the replacement of "know(s)" *p* with "evidence for" *p*, where "evidence" is numericalized along probabilistic lines, and the notion is nonfactive. I should add that the dispensability of "folk notions" like "know(s)" or even "justification" (for, e.g., purposes of "naturalized epistemology") are pretty widespread attitudes—especially by those inclined toward formal Bayesian replacements. I've recently (January 8, 2019) heard these views reiterated yet again by Hartry Field and David Papineau during their talks at the Eastern APA. Worth acknowledging is also Papineau's (2019) popularly written article. "Knowledge" is there described as "crude" and a "stone-age concept" on the mere basis that it's purportedly incompatible with statistical reasoning—and the mere basis for *that* claim is Papineau's widely shared misperception that it's an *implication* of the concept of "know(s)" that no one can know that they will lose a lottery. (Sigh.) I'll add that when a semantic property of a word *is* dispensable, what's commonly seen in an otherwise shared language (either diachronically or synchronically) are differences in the language community with respect to that property: individuals whose words idiolectically exhibit the property and ones whose words don't. "Remember that" is like this, with both factive and nonfactive versions of the word occurring among members of the English-speaking population. "Know(s)" *isn't* like this; this is a symptom that a factive, criterion-transcendent, but otherwise fallibilist "know(s)" is indispensable for *something* we do. The question is what?

[22] This is a diagnostic question: by discovering what indispensable role a particular semantic property of a word is used for, we empirically uncover a function it has that we have good reason to think makes the word—with certain properties—indispensable to us. I illustrated this strategy—in part 2 of the introduction—with respect to "true." Recall that the function so discovered (in the case of "true," its use in blind truth ascription) needn't be directly reflected *anywhere* in the syntax or semantics of the word itself. The word "true," I noted, isn't a *device* of blind truth ascription (for that it would need, among other things, *built-in* singular-term and/or quantificational structure, and it has neither); it's an *ordinary* predicate—both semantically and syntactically—that we *use* (along with other "parts of speech," specifically: names and quantifiers) in speech acts to *assert* truths blindly. In this sense, the role of the word comes apart from its syntactic/semantic properties and can even conflict with them—as I suggest happens with "true." We'll see a similar phenomenon at work with "know(s)." I take this up in my discussion of social-role epistemology in section 11.5.

[23] This isn't the only thing that makes blind truth ascription indispensable. We sometimes want to assent to an infinite set of sentences, ones we can't *assert all at once*, e.g., all the theorems of Peano arithmetics.

Something related to this is at work in requiring a word "know(s)" that's factive and criterion-transcendent. I want to state the need carefully (to prevent that need being confused with various social-role needs for "know(s)" that other philosophers have hypothesized the existence of). Each of us has a lot of knowledge that others don't have: knowledge is specialized. Informally speaking, there's an inferential mechanism by which we pass the propositions so known to one another in such a way as to enable the recipients to also know those propositions. Again, informally speaking, we're part of a community that "shares" knowledge in this way. Here is more detail: Some, but not all, of the members of our community have justifications for some of the things they know; these justifications rely on what they've seen or inferred, say, and these justifications aren't shared with the rest of the community—that is, others haven't seen or inferred these things. Others, however, become knowledgeable about the propositions known by these individuals via a justified trust *in* those members.[24]

What's important is that an agent S can know something *p*; and her justification for *p* is that another epistemic agent Q *knows p*; crucially, however, Q's justification is different from S's. This is key: *In "passing knowledge" to one another, the justifications-for/reasons-for-believing-that knowledge are (usually) not passed along.* S knows *p* because Q knows *p*; but Q's justifications for *p* aren't S's justifications. I now show why this requires "know(s)" to have the semantic/syntactic properties it has; more accurately, I'll show why a word with just the semantic/syntactic contours that "know(s)" has been revealed to have in this book is indispensable to us.

Transferring propositions—so that the recipients know those propositions—occurs among relatively unsophisticated agents. Suppose monkey *A* hears an eagle call from his (reliable) conspecific *B* (section 8.5). Because *B* sees a nearby eagle, *B* knows that an eagle is nearby, and because *A* hears *B*'s eagle call, *A* knows this too.[25] Similarly, I know a great many mathematical results (in particular, Fermat's Last Theorem), because others (in particular, Andrew Wiles) know these results; and I have grounds for trusting them. (I know many mathematical results on my own too, of course, because I've gone through the

[24] "Justified" here isn't understood as requiring agents to be able to express or even to be aware of the relevant justifications. Recall the discussion of this in chapter 8. Very worth saying: justified trust isn't the only way I can know things because of what others know. Justified *mistrust* (in the right circumstances) can do the job *too*: being able to recognize exactly how someone is lying.

[25] This doesn't *imply* that *A* knows *himself* to know that an eagle is nearby (recall section 9.3, regarding iterated knowledge). Kripke (2011b, 34) *says* to an audience, "I know that you know that I know that Nixon is president. After all, I just said so. But knowledge implies truth. So if I know that you know something, I must know it myself. Hence, I know that I know that Nixon is president." This argument or a version of it that we could try to attribute to the monkey *A* fails because this instance of knowledge closure fails for that monkey.

proofs—but not Fermat's Last Theorem, and not a number of other results that I nevertheless know.)

It seems, therefore, the reasoning that supports this knowledge-preserving transfer of a proposition *p* is as follows (in the first-person case):

I know that Agent *A* knows that *p*. (Premise)
Agent *A* knows that p implies *p*. (Factivity)
I know that *p*. (Truth-preserving substitution of *p* for "Agent *A* knows that *p*")

Suppose a nonfactive phrase is used instead; then the reasoning fails:

I'm really really sure/certain that Agent *A* is really really sure/certain that *p*.
. . .
I'm really really sure/certain that *p*.

That is, *really real surety/certainty* doesn't transfer the same way. For consider: I'm really really sure/certain that Donald Trump is really really sure/certain that he's got a really really good brain. It *doesn't* follow that *I'm* really really sure/certain that Donald Trump has a really really good brain.

Let's try a "rationally believes" or "is justified in thinking" propositional-transfer deduction:

I rationally believe/am justified in thinking that Agent *A* rationally believes/is justified in thinking that *p*.
. . .
I rationally believe/am justified in thinking that *p*.

We might (momentarily) think rational belief or justification works here; but neither does (because neither is *criterion-transcendent*). I rationally believe (I'm justified in believing) that some educated medievals rationally believed in—were justified in believing in—a spherical unmoving earth located at the center of the universe. After all, *I've* studied (some of) the history and I've studied the reasons some medieval thinkers had for believing this: They had *good* reasons. Nevertheless, I don't *rationally believe in*—I'm not justified in believing in—a spherical unmoving earth located at the center of the universe.

So (diagnosis), the widespread belief—among philosophers—that an epistemic phrase like "know(s)," which is factive and criterion-transcendent, can be replaced by (or in fact is already) a nonfactive and/or criterion-immanent epistemic word, or even a set of these, turns on the mistaken belief that our proposition-transferring practices will be unaffected if the factive criterion-transcendent "know(s)" is dropped. We need, that is, a descriptive phrase P where an originating agent bears P to a proposition *p*, and the transferring of *p* yields that the recipient agent bears P to *p*. "Know(s)" does the job. These other candidates fail to do the job precisely because central to our proposition-passing practices is that we pass propositions to one another in communities, where the justification-pedigrees-of/reasons-for those propositions are *not* passed along.[26] That is, in the vast majority of these cases, even though *A*'s knowledge of *p* derives from *B*'s knowledge of *p*, the *justification A* has for his knowledge of *p* isn't the justification that *B* has for her knowledge. *A*'s justification is—nearly enough—*A*'s justified trust that *B has* a good justification for what she knows.[27]

I *don't* want to give the impression that this transfer-of-proposition role for "know(s)" is intrinsically interpersonal—intrinsically *social*; it's *not*. I mentioned earlier that I know a lot of mathematical results because I've perused their proofs. But my justifications for knowing they're true, at the time I proved them, aren't my justifications for knowing they're true *right now*. I've forgotten the proofs themselves, but I'm justified (for various reasons) in trusting myself as having cognized the validity of those proofs. Although I've forgotten the details or even the overall contour of certain proofs I haven't forgotten how careful I was (years ago) in going over these proofs—and it's the memory of *this* that justifies my current knowledge of mathematical results that I no longer remember the proofs of. There is a lot of shifting over time in what justifies agents in knowing what they nevertheless continue to know. The factivity and criterion transcendence of "know(s)" are crucial to stabilizing the propositions we know *across* these justification shifts—that is, enabling the known propositions so transferred to remain knowledge of the agent.

It should be noticed how *thin* (although utterly indispensable) the role I've described for "know(s)" is. One way to see this is to observe that most attempts to characterize a function for "know(s)" by philosophers rely on one or more of the necessary and/or sufficient conditions for knowledge that I've undercut in this

[26] This point survives a rejection of "justification" or a replacement of it with something else. The Bayesian grounds for one's beliefs, for example, are no more passed along (with knowledge) than justifications are. "Evidence for *p*" isn't factive—however it's construed. For a fascinating description of the trajectory of "evident" and "evidence" among philosophers (over the centuries), see Pasnau (2017).

[27] I've not *shown* that there isn't some other indispensable role "know(s)" plays that *doesn't* involve the transfer of propositions yielding knowledge of the recipient (without requiring a transfer of justification) although I'm pretty sure there isn't. I say a little more about this momentarily. What's not been shown by this—what's, anyway, false—is that *having* (in some weak or strong sense) the notion of "know(s)" is needed by those who are involved in a proposition-transfer practice. *We* can attribute knowledge to monkeys because of how they transfer propositions among themselves; but that isn't to show they've *got* the concept of "know(s)." *We* have that notion, precisely because of certain kinds of iterative cognitions we're—at least in principle—capable of.

book. For the function of knowledge to be that of justifying assertion or belief, either assertion or belief needs to have knowledge as a necessary condition, or at least as a norm. But they don't. Similarly, Fantl and McGrath (2009, 56) write (italics theirs), "In attributing knowledge to a person we are certifying that her epistemic position is good enough to be a basis for action and belief in *all* the stakes-situations under consideration." This is a function they're attributing to knowledge attribution; but as I showed in section 10.4, straightforward principles connecting knowing *p* to actions, beliefs, or assertions are all false—which isn't to say knowledge is irrelevant to action, belief, or assertion. No more (and no less) are there straightforward principles connecting what we have evidence for, what we're justified about, certain of, rationally believe, etc., to action, belief, or assertion; and similarly, these states aren't irrelevant to action, belief, or assertion either. Knowledge doesn't stand out in relation to these with respect to how we use it; it stands out because of its factivity, its criterion transcendence, and how that enables proposition transfers that preserve knowledge. Other criterion-transcendent words, *when used factively*, words such as "infer," "remember," "see," or "hear," thus specify ways of knowing and so imply knowledge. The role I've described for "know(s)" is thin in another sense: it *underwrites* the other purposes that "know(s)" is put to.

A caveat: I'm claiming that "know(s)" is indispensable to enabling the inference forms I described above. We can try to circumvent this by introducing specific *inference bridges* for other notions—by building in specific conditions on "justification" or "rationally believes" so that specific cases of these inferences—that we need—are licensed. I predict that the result will be a baroque mass of special conditions similar to all the special-case closure conditions that we'd get if we tried to specify exactly when a knowledge-closure condition holds of an agent. (Recall the discussion of this in section 10.8.)

An important role for "know(s)" came up in section 6.7; it's inherited from the proposition-transfer role of "know(s). Generalizations like "If an agent knows that something is a banana, then she'll do such-and-such" are hedged *predictions* about agents. They're hedged because knowledge, pretty much, doesn't dictate any particular sort of behavior by an agent without other, and often substantial, assumptions about him, including (but not restricted to) other things he knows. In calling them predictions, I'm pointedly not saying that they state anything about the epistemic position of the agent being good enough to assert, or believe, or whatever. I *am* saying, however, that what we're licensed by a formulation of this sort to assume is that a number of propositions (that *we* know are true) the *agent* knows too.

Let me describe the importance of the criterion transcendence of "know(s)" in relation to the criterion immanence of notions like "rational," etc., in more detail since, after all, this is denied by all those many philosophers who think we can "lose" knowledge. Let's first consider a case that's directly ruled out by factivity. Think again of the justified beliefs of some medieval thinkers in a spherical unmoving earth located at the center of the universe. Let's (attempt to) regard those beliefs as knowledge that these thinkers *had*. (This is to treat knowledge along the line of notarized documents.) But . . . *A* knew *p* implies *p*. So this is ruled out.

Now recall (from section 3.6) the fairly subtle retraction evidence against knowledge relativism described by Wright (2017, 25–28). I may retract a knowing attribution in one of two ways. I can mildly say, "Because of a possibility I overlooked, I didn't know *p*, although I thought I did." This retraction is mandated by the criterion transcendence of "know(s)": I can't say, "despite the possibility I overlooked, I still knew *p*"—not if I'm unwilling to say I know *p* now. But (and it's this retraction that plays against knowledge relativism) I can also say, more strongly, "I should not have claimed to know *p*. I made a mistake."

This second attribution turns on an interesting interaction between the criterion transcendence of "know(s)" and how standards of justification are instead criterion-immanent—allowed to change over time. The criterion transcendence of "know(s)" (alone) won't determine that this second attribution is correct. In claiming I made a mistake in claiming to know *p*, I'm indicating something about the standards of justification *at the time*: that those standards, in this respect, are the same as current standards, according to which I've made a mistake. (This is making clear something that's not in general required because those standards could have changed.) I'm also stating, furthermore, that the "degree of justification" I had then wasn't sufficient for knowledge, nor would it be now—and this latter point is because "know(s)" is criterion-transcendent.

Let's turn to a different property of "know(s)." After all, that the word is vague is annoying *too*. Should we engineer "know(s)" to require infallibility? The thought would be that doing so would eliminate its vagueness. Nearly enough—this is what I think Descartes did: He restricted knowledge to those cases that he took us to infallibly know.[28] Against this, I've first argued that vagueness isn't a drawback for a word or the concept a word corresponds to. (And anyway, do we really want to undertake the project of engineering away the vagueness present in

[28] Well, maybe he didn't. See Pasnau (2017, 172–174 n. 2) for arguments, textual and otherwise, that Descartes wasn't putting such certainty conditions on *knowledge*, but on something else, an idealized and better form of cognition different from (vulgar) knowledge—*scientia*. (If so, read my suggestion as what the lesson from Descartes was eventually taken to be by philosophers—especially relatively contemporary ones—as opposed to careful scholars of intellectual history.) On the other hand, Dutant (2015, 112–113), while evaluating Pasnau's (2013) arguments for this, notes that "Descartes defines *science* (*scientia*) in terms of clear and distinct perception, which is his account of (basic) knowledge (*cognitio*)." Pasnau (2017, 24–26, 206) pushes back, noting that Descartes allows that vulgar (uncertain) "knowledge" is, nevertheless, *knowledge* had (by, for example, atheists). *I* think Descartes is waffling, stumbling over the ordinary fallible use of "know(s)" and what he should think about it; thus, the debate between Pasnau and Dutant is (textually) irresolvable.

all our words? To what end?[29]) Second, and more important, the resulting word and the concept it corresponds to are useless. I'm *not* saying that words without extensions are useless. ("Hercules" is *not* useless; neither is "flying horse.") But if we need to transfer propositions using "know(s)," then we need its extension to be non-empty: if no one has *any* knowledge or only nontransferable first-person present-tense "nowledge" (recall note 16), there's no point to "know(s)."[30]

Let me press the same observation in another way. Many philosophers are tempted by an enriched notion of knowledge (*scientia*), one with special conditions, e.g., the agent being self-aware in certain ways (as able—in principle—to provide justifications for what she knows, say). Even if I'm right that our actual word "know(s)" doesn't have such conditions, maybe we need a (coined) word that does. We might, that is, coin a word to fit mature adult humans, one that requires them to be aware of their knowledge and as able to justify it (at least in principle), and leave the ordinary one, as Aikin (2011, 22) puts it, as "fine for cats and babies."

Against this is that this enriched or cognitively superior knowledge is an unstable fragment of ordinary knowledge for *all* agents (except for, maybe, someone like God), as we realize if we consider the cases I've described already, timid students, mathematicians who are mistaken about their proofs, children who slowly mature into reassessments of what they know, Samantha, who has ESP (and so *knows* the future), and so on. *All of us* are like such agents in some respects some of the time; some of what we know is like this, some of it isn't, and some of it changes over time from one state to another (and back again). What's needed is a word—like "know(s)"—that includes all these as items of "knowledge" along with those where an agent "know(s)" in this suggested stronger way.

Second, once we clearly separate iterated knowledge from ground-floor knowledge, we can see that all the taxonomic needs that a coined enriched or

[29] That said, I'll repeat that precisifying "know(s)" by imposing a *sharp* probabilistic threshold strictly below 1 is compatible with the ordinary "know(s)." Arguments against this compatibility that turn on denials that we ever know before a drawing that we'll lose a lottery were refuted in chapter 10.

[30] This is ironic. If we deliberately narrow (engineer) "knowledge" to "nowledge," we make the word useless. This—and a lot of what I've shown in this book—nicely illustrates a point Austin (1962, 63) made a long time ago, when he wrote: "Certainly, when we have discovered how a word is in fact used, that may not be the end of the matter; there is certainly no reason why, in general, things should be left exactly as we find them; we may wish to tidy the situation up a bit, revise the map here and there, draw the boundaries and distinctions rather differently. But still, it is advisable always to bear in mind (a) that the distinctions embodied in our vast and, for the most part, relatively ancient stock of ordinary words are neither few nor always very obvious, and almost never just arbitrary; (b) that in any case, before indulging in any tampering on our own account, we need to find out what it is that we have to deal with; and (c) that tampering with words in what we take to be one little corner of the field is always liable to have unforeseen repercussions in the adjoining territory. . . . And we must always be particularly wary of the philosophical habit of dismissing some (if not all) the ordinary uses of a word as 'unimportant,' a habit which makes distortion practically unavoidable." Tight entailment relations among words are one obvious way that changing one item affects others—but as the intricacy of "know(s)" and its relations to other words indicates, this isn't the only way this can happen.

cognitively superior notion of "know(s)" would meet are already met by a more fine-grained analysis of an agent's knowledge, her knowledge of her methods of knowing, and the like. The imagined technical vocabulary has no distinctive new role to play in our "know(s)" attributions—not even in the sciences.

The same point can be made about "know(s)"-fragmentation projects—like that of Greco (2015) and others (recall the second paragraph of note 9 in section 5.1)—introducing *several* know notions. Again, the indispensable role that "know(s)" plays for us in proposition transfers (a role, notably, that in important cases turns on our *forgetting* the justifications for propositions we once had) requires a notion that isn't fragmented.[31]

Lastly, I've argued against the idea that "know(s)" admits of pragmatic-stakes encroachments (of *anyone*—the epistemic agent, assessors of that knowledge, etc.) except insofar as our failure to recognize the vagueness of the word, or of its standards, allows inadvertent shifting due to stakes (and other things—like one's initial position in a debate). But what about engineering the word to explicitly include such stakes? Stake inclusion would infirm the proposition-transfer role of "know(s)" since stakes transfer no more than justifications do.

One conclusion (of this section): Conceptually engineering "know(s)" so that it induces fewer cognitive/linguistic traps isn't possible because this word (the one with just *those* annoying semantic properties) is indispensable to our proposition-transferring practices.

As I mentioned earlier, there have been many suggestions made about the function and role of "know(s)." Recent ones—that I've argued against earlier in the book—are that knowledge serves as a presupposition of one or another norm, e.g., for belief, action, or assertion. It does none of these things indispensably because an agent being in other nonfactive epistemic states (e.g., rationally believing) justifies belief, action, or assertion just as well (pace Hawthorne, Stanley, and others). What has, instead, emerged as the indispensable role for "know(s)" is something quite "deflationary": that we need it for certain inferences that enable (although this is something not particularly deflationary) the transfer of statements from agents (including our earlier selves) that we can take to be true without simultaneously transferring what justified the truth of those propositions for those agents. The factivity of "know(s)" is crucial for this. So too is its criterion transcendence.

There's another point to make about the fact that our notion of "know(s)" is compatible with agential fallibility. Notice that we often allow agents to change up—improve—their methods for doing things without that undercutting that

[31] Fragmentation projects of this sort, generally, are popular with philosophers; "true" is another unfortunate victim of such projects. They fail for "true" for reasons closely related to why such projects fail for "know(s)." See my discussion of this in Azzouni (2010, chapter 4).

what they earlier purportedly knew via the earlier methods was knowledge. For example, if I procure better glasses that very much improve what I know on the basis of what I see—in particular, as good glasses do, lowering the number of "false positives" (cases where, for example, I thought I saw A, but I didn't), we don't take it that I *didn't know* all sorts of things on the basis of my earlier worse glasses (or no glasses). There are conditions on this—the earlier methods can't be too bad (e.g., I can't be nearly blind without my glasses), but there's a quite a bit of leeway otherwise. The earlier discussion on the vagueness of "know(s)" should make none of this surprising.

But as a result, there's a topic to be explored here: *epistemic virtue*. It's clear that if we compare methods and replace one method that has a lower yield of truths with another that has a higher yield of truths, we're (epistemically speaking) doing a "good thing." Furthermore, agents can be compared for differences in their epistemic virtuousness—so understood. However: because of the considerations of the last paragraph, we often can't fault a less virtuous agent by penalizing their claims to know things on the basis of their statistically poorer methods. It's just that their methods provide less knowledge (used as a mass term) than otherwise. Still, this explains the main value of metacognition—and it's a real value: metacognition is *the* tool that we use to compare methods and become, as a result, more epistemically virtuous agents.

I leave further details for later work.[32] But the statistical flavor of epistemic virtue invites a discussion of Berker's (2013) attack on "epistemic consequentialism," and so I'll conclude this section with some brief comments on his attack. In my earlier discussion of justification, I adopted the rather widespread (consequentialist) view that justifications are meant to increase (or preserve) the likelihood of the truth of the propositions we so justify. Cleverly modifying (and extending) an example originally due to Firth (1981), Berker endeavors to undercut this characterization of justification. So, consider (Berker (2013, 369)):

> John Doe is a brilliant set [theorist] who is on the cusp of proving [a major new result in set theory]: all he needs is six more months. But . . . John is suffering from a serious illness that, according to his doctors, will almost certainly kill him in two months' time. John stubbornly clings to a belief that he will recover from his illness, and not only does this belief comfort him, but—let us suppose—it in fact significantly raises the chances that he will live for the six

[32] I'll add, however, unlike some views of "epistemic virtue," this approach to it doesn't compete with or present an alternative to the characterization of "know(s)" that I've given in this book. Epistemic virtue—so described—doesn't affect what agents know; it affects, rather, how much they *can* know.

months that he needs both to complete his proof and derive from it [a large number of additional surprising and important results].

Firth and Berker both think we should recognize that John's belief isn't epistemically justified, although—they claim—on a straightforward view of justifications being likelihood-increasing it is.[33] Indeed, both these claims are argued for by neither of them. Presumably, John's belief isn't epistemically justified because all the evidence John has is from his doctors who don't know this surprising fact about his disease. On the other hand, although John stubbornly clinging to a belief despite all evidence *in this case* truth-enhances his resulting beliefs, this isn't the case *in general*. Indeed, his "method" of stubbornly clinging to his beliefs despite counter-evidence, *in the world we live in*, is a method that almost always leads to resulting beliefs less likely to be true. This is why we regard John's acquisition of the belief that he'll recover from his disease as unjustified.

Imagine, however, that John's stubbornly acquired beliefs almost always lead to beliefs that are more likely to be true—perhaps because when he acquires such beliefs, he's carried out subconscious evaluations he has no conscious access to.[34] Then we have cases of justified agents who can't provide their justifications. Or imagine, instead, agents who live in "placebo worlds," places where stubbornly clinging to beliefs has truth-conducing efficacy for those beliefs. In these cases too, such agents are justified; and indeed, if it becomes generally known among them that they live in placebo worlds, then they will not only be justified in their beliefs, they will—in addition—be able to give appropriate justifications. (Oddly, many people among us believe this about their own beliefs: this is called "magical thinking." If the world were well behaved in the way these people think, their magical thinking would be justified.)[35]

[33] More accurately, Berker means us to recognize that Firth has offered us a "recipe" (378) for constructing counterexamples against a variety of epistemic-consequentialist positions. Berker (377) claims this to enable his diagnosis of the problem: Epistemic consequentialism is "forward looking" when instead it should be "backwards-" or at least "sideways-looking." I get to this in due course.

[34] How would this work? Imagine agents who subconsciously evaluate evidence by subconsciously calculating probabilities for events—calculations that they're much better at than the ones they do consciously. And imagine that after a subconscious calculation is completed, agents feel a stubborn (conscious) commitment to the result of the calculation—although, it (consciously) feels as if the belief has just popped into their heads without an accompanying reason. Such agents have certain justifications for their beliefs that they can't give.

[35] It seems to me that ordinary "intuitions" about epistemic consequentialism and moral consequentialism differ on exactly this point—and so it's here where Firth's and Berker's attempt to analogize epistemology to ethics breaks down. Many of us have strong intuitions that a *single* action is right or wrong, based on its consequences, and independent of the agent's intentions or abilities. Rule utilitarianism, therefore, has to be argued for—it doesn't seem quite right otherwise. But the epistemic version of rule utilitarianism sounds completely right—and corresponds to the fact that we evaluate justifications in relation to the methods they're supported by. Our "intuition," therefore, is that if someone uses a method that's truth-conducively poor but their belief is luckily right, they're *not* justified. Indeed, this is why we react to Gettier cases the way we do.

This explains Emily McWilliams's observation (Berker (2013 n. 27, 385)) that certain epistemic norms seem hard to capture in epistemically consequentialist terms. Berker (2013, 377) mentions (italics his) "Epistemic justification is a matter of *responding to* how things appear to you," "Epistemic rationality is a matter of *respecting* one's evidence," and "Epistemic virtue is a matter of *fitting together* one's cognitive states into a coherent whole." None of these epistemic virtues, of course, is a priori. By saying that, I'm noting that their value—if any—is exquisitely sensitive to the kind of world we apply them in. We could be applying them in a world (or, more locally, to phenomena) where thinking up generalizations that turn out to be true will only work if one—fairly arbitrarily—ignores evidence. (Imagine that too much of the evidence about something is misleading.) Indeed, it was an old observation of Kuhn's that sometimes one makes progress in the sciences only by ignoring some of what everyone regards as evidence. The epistemic consequentialist, therefore, should *not* be able to derive virtues like this from the (purported) truth conduciveness of the methods we currently use to justify ourselves. Nor should we treat these "epistemic norms" as genuine *norms* as opposed to evidential principles that only work in certain empirical contexts.

11.5 Social-Role Epistemology

In this last section of this chapter, I compare the foregoing analysis of the concept of "know(s)"—especially the form it has taken in this last chapter—with attempts to use a purportedly central social role of the word "know(s)" as the key to unlocking the word's complexity. It's worth starting with the following point. Consider any word with a given syntactic/semantic structure. We can ask: What sorts of speech acts can be executed with that word? The useless intractable answer (that's nevertheless true) is: *anything anyone can manage to think up*. My approach to locating a role (social or otherwise) for the words I've studied—"true" and "know(s)," in particular—hasn't been to impressionistically focus on one or another role for these words that I've noticed them being used for. That's dangerously too close to the approach I just described of trying to characterize the speech acts a word occurs in without paying attention to the semantic/syntactic structure of the word.

The right method is to instead first characterize the syntactic/semantic structure of the word being studied, and then use that characterization to guide us when asking the question: What function *is* something with this structure indispensable for? It may turn out, of course, that such a function is a broad social one; but it could easily be that such a function instead is a narrowly linguistic one. That's an empirical matter to be determined.

One can nevertheless (and despite my warnings above) flip the methodology I've described myself as engaged in: pick out one or another social role for "know(s)" *first*, and then try to show that everything philosophically puzzling about the word and—more broadly—all our usage data about the word are handled by this social role. Consider Craig's (1990, 2) description of the following "experiment":

> Instead of beginning with ordinary usage, we begin with an ordinary situation. We take some prima facie plausible hypothesis about what the concept of knowledge does for us, what its role in our life might be, and then ask what a concept having that role would be like, what conditions would govern its application.

It's important that Craig is contrasting his procedure with the one I've officially used in this book. An immediate worry is the one I would base on the distinction between the function(s) of a word and its syntactic/semantic structure. I'd imagine, that is, a biologist first asking what flying does for birds and what its role in their lives would be, and on the basis of that, hypothesizing what wings are like—what *physical* conditions would govern such things.

Perhaps this is unfair to Craig. But I think not: Craig thinks there are *two* methodological options here when there aren't: one can't study the social role of *any* word in a syntactic/semantic vacuum. Trying to do so will result in one's nevertheless importing various syntactic/semantic assumptions into one's analysis without having done the accompanying work needed to show those assumptions are justified. I'll illustrate the danger in what follows.

Start by noticing that different philosophers in this literature have found rather many different social-role functions of knowledge attributions. Apart from Craig's "flagging approved sources of information" and Reynolds's (2017) "encouraging acceptable testimony," we have (I borrow the following list, with citations—and spelling choices—from Kusch (2017)):

—signaling that inquiry is at an end (Kappel [2010], Kelp (2011), Rysiew (2012))
—identifying propositions we can treat as reasons for acting (McGrath (2015))
—providing assurance (Austin (1946), Lawlor (2013))
—distinguishing between blameless and blameworthy behavior (Beebe (2012))
—honouring the subject of knowledge attributions (Kusch (2009))

Perhaps one *shouldn't* fear that one's facing an *eeny-meeny-miny-moe* phenomenon here; after all, the idea isn't to pick out *at random* a role that the word uses; one intends to show that centralizing the chosen role is illuminating. Nevertheless, I think we should worry that there really are too many candidates here and that, in any case, their all being compatible, being roles the word "know(s)" actually has, turns on the semantic/syntactic structure of the word "know(s)"—one we should really look at first. Consider assurance, for example. No doubt we often assure people by describing ourselves as knowers; but just as often (and in some academic fields *more* often), we deliberately disconcert people (to put it mildly) by describing ourselves as knowing things they don't. Really, it often seems that the word's role isn't to assure people but to undermine their self-confidence! "You don't know," as in "You don't know what you're talking about," is *very* common. The negation of an expression can be what is most used when executing the central social role of a word. (The importance of investigating negations of expressions is something Austin (1962, 70) noted the importance of long ago.) Assurance characterizations of the role of "know(s)" are patchable possibly along the lines of the function described by Beebe, "assuring and/or disconcerting," or something like that instead being described as the social role of "know(s)." Still, the worry remains that all these differing candidates have equal claim to being *the* social role "know(s)" should be analyzed in terms of.

What seems to be an even more serious problem facing all of these approaches, however, is what I'll call the kjustification challenge (the "j," recall, is silent). Recall observation (vi) from section 10.2. We can define a notion of kjustification which, from the agential point of view, is as good as knowledge. What I mean is, leaving aside whether in fact *p* is true or not, an agent can be in as good a justificatory position regarding *p* as someone who knows *p*. Being in such a state, surely, is sufficient to satisfy all the social roles for knowledge that I've listed. If someone has kjustification for *p* and I know this, that reassures me; that signals that inquiry is at an end (no one can do any better); that honors the kjustifier (she's done everything humanly possible to guarantee *p*); the kjustifier isn't to be blamed, but someone who doesn't rise to the standards of kjustification *is* to be blamed; and so on. If we just focus on the social role of "know(s)," we can't see why a notion of kjustification doesn't fit the bill. If kjustification seems unappealing, consider being "really really epistemically careful and cautious." Why doesn't this satisfy the social roles posited for "know(s)"?[36]

[36] We must be very careful when describing social-role needs that we don't overstate what's needed in order to get those needs to fit how a word/concept works. Reynolds (2017, 22) writes: "We need to have true beliefs about our surroundings in order to survive and do well." This may sound like it requires a concept we can attribute to testifiers that's factive; but it doesn't, because what we need to survive and do well are methods (including listening to reliable other) that yield beliefs for us that are mostly (or even largely) true. Kjustified testifiers are just as good as knowing testifiers for this purpose. Similarly, Reynolds (22): "since the tribe lacks the concept of knowledge, no one will be able to tell [an enquirer], '. . . ask Fred! He knows whether there is a tiger there.'" What's wrong with "very very likely believes truly"? Again, an implicit assumption that only a factive notion will meet the need is being smuggled into the analysis without any argument that it's needed.

Consider Reynolds's (2017) analysis of the social role for "know(s)." He presents a Hobbesian "state of nature" situation where the individuals of a primitive society lack the concept of "know(s)," and tries to show that requirements on testimony force them to acquire that concept. Although he dedicates an entire chapter (10) to "Plato's problem," *why should we prefer knowledge to true belief*, he never consider the question of why we should prefer knowledge to kjustification (or even the nonfactive "really really likely to be right"). Indeed, nothing in his approach shows why the factivity of "know(s)" is required for the social role he diagnoses "know(s)" to have (indicating an acceptable testifier). Surely a kjustified individual *does* provide acceptable testimony, and just for the reasons that an individual who knows does: a kjustified individual has done *everything possible* to satisfy the requirements needed to provide evidence/reasons/etc. for thinking *p* is true.[37]

[37] I'll add that Reynolds's state-of-nature analysis is further vitiated by his assumption that belief is a necessary condition for knowledge. We're to imagine, therefore, people who not only lack the concept of knowledge; they lack the concept of belief too. It therefore becomes very hard to see how they're supposed to manage to evaluate or consider the testimony of others if they can't even talk about what their cohorts believe. Craig (1990), notably, does *not* do this; he instead tries to show that the social role he attributes to "know(s)" can accommodate the relatively exceptional and remote possibilities of knowers who don't believe what they know—the criticism of Craig's approach, therefore, is that such possibilities *aren't* exceptional or remote. Regardless, the individuals in Reynolds's posited state-of-nature not only lack a notion of "know(s)," they lack a notion of "belief" too. (He even suggests (38 n. 8) that members of such a population can't answer a question with "maybe," because "we usually say 'maybe p' to indicate that we *don't know* that not p" (italics his). (Recall chapters 5 and 6 on confusions about metacognition.) In any case, the result is that it's far easier for Reynolds to show that "know(s)" is indispensable to a population who rely on testimony and need concepts about how other people think and what they think, if they can't have a notion of belief without a notion of knowledge. This illustrates my warning at the beginning of this section: Do not attempt social-role epistemology without analyzing the syntactic/semantic structure of the word "know(s)," and its relation to other words, "belief," etc., *first*. (Compare: let's study the social role of axes in this society without first determining what properties their particular axes *have*—e.g., stone versus metal axes.)

Conclusion

Dutant raises a number of interesting historical questions that he poses for future research while trying to establish his New Story—that Gettier cases became salient to philosophers because of the demise (in the mid-twentieth century) of classical infallibilism. One is (Dutant (2015, 120)) "why Classical Infallibilism did not collapse before the mid-twentieth century." Another is "why was Classical Infallibilism so widely and strongly held?" He says:

> a *folk* hypothesis would be that Classical Infallibilism is somehow rooted in the ways (Western) people ascribe knowledge. Since its recent demise in analytic circles is unlikely to have had any influence on non-philosophers, we should be able to observe these roots now. Hence psychology can be brought to bear on the New Story.

This book—and especially chapter 10—contains an explicit response to Dutant's second question. If we look to psychology *and* to linguistics (in particular, lexical semantics), and more generally, to the details of how we attribute knowledge to ourselves and to one another, we see the *many* elements that push us toward an infallibilist interpretation of our knowledge-attribution practices. This isn't to observe "roots"; this is to describe a vital, robust, and indispensable practice of knowledge attribution (one that remains unscathed even in the sciences). To the extent that the elements I describe are shared by all speaker-hearers in all languages, infallibilism (classical or otherwise) is always a likely position for thoughtful people to come to. The first question is answered by the entire book as well. What's required to get past infallibilist views isn't merely the recognition that ordinary (vulgar) talk of knowledge is fallibilist. This *is* something that *was* recognized, as I noted in note 4 of chapter 11—but, really, how could it *not* have been recognized? What was further required was a dramatic change in attitude that would force philosophers to take the details *and minutia* of ordinary usage seriously—and as relevant to epistemology. For related (but somewhat different) complex historical reasons (involving, of course, the emergence of "ordinary language philosophy" on the part of Moore, Wittgenstein, Austin, and others), Malcolm, Austin, and other later postwar philosophers were exactly in this position. Cartesian thought experiments seem to show that *only* what the agent has infallible grounds for is immune to Cartesian challenges—e.g., being fooled by an evil demon, being a brain in a vat, perhaps even

Attributing Knowledge. Jody Azzouni, Oxford University Press (2020). © Oxford University Press.
DOI: 10.1093/oso/9780197508817.001.0001.

the possibility that one's dreaming. (This may have been Descartes's view.) So we can add to the long list of factors (described in chapter 10) that impel us to infallibilist construals of "know(s)" yet one more: Cartesian thought experiments.

On the other hand, fallibilists may be blasé about these thought experiments. We can know *p*, after all, even if it's possible for us to be wrong. Recall Samantha from section 8.5. She actually has ESP, she has actually saved lives, she often *knows* that people are in danger of dying; but she's rational to think she doesn't; she's certainly not certain of it; she doesn't believe any of these people are really in danger.[1] Why not similarly say the same to someone who's challenged himself about the possibility of being fooled by evil demons? If you're *not* being fooled by an evil demon, you know that's an apple in front of you—whether you realize it or not.

Perhaps higher-order scepticism is still a challenge we should be concerned with; we *may* know a lot—but maybe we can never know *this*.[2] Regardless, the Samantha ploy doesn't seem sufficient. After all, we do use possibilities to challenge knowledge successfully. It can't *always* be suitable to respond to a challenge with: "Oh I'm not worried, knowledge is fallible—so I still know." This is directly related to the vagueness of "know(s)." There has to be, that is, a relatively systematic story about which challenges we take seriously and which we don't. No doubt this story must dovetail in the right way with the vagueness of know(s) attributions; the vagueness can't be widespread enough to allow *anything*.[3]

I do want to offer what I hope is a tantalizing hint about how what's been put in place in this book will help handle analyzing sceptical challenges. Consider the following dialogue:

> You could be wrong about *p*.
> Yes, I could. After all, I'm fallible. But I know I'm not wrong about *p*—if *p* is true.

We've seen how hard it is to say something like this because, in particular, "know(s)" is factive. But we can nevertheless convey this (as this *entire* book shows). And we can also see that this debate can derail irresolvably because of the vagueness of "know(s)." Nevertheless (to repeat myself), some challenges

[1] And the case is subtle with respect to how this knowledge of hers bears on *action*. It strikes me as licensing her to take *certain* actions, e.g., secretly changing the dates of her son's flight travel when it doesn't manifestly compromise him. This doesn't, however, license her—in every way (or broadly speaking)—to act as if what she knows is true. As I argued in section 10.4, the straightforwardly simple principles that philosophers—e.g., Unger (1974), Hyman (1999), Hawthorne and Stanley (2008), Fantl and McGrath (2009)—argue connect knowledge to action and belief fall afoul of how knowledge comes apart from propositional attitudes one may have about that knowledge.

[2] This is just how Williams (1996, 93) puts a version of the sceptical challenge: "We may know things about the world, but we will never know that we know them."

[3] In general, vague words are highly constrained; "know(s)" is no exception.

to knowing are sustained and some aren't. That, anyway, is what our practice of challenging knowledge claims looks like; and this is the topic of a subsequent book, *Challenging Knowledge*.

I claim (but will only show there) that a number of seductive factors—fallacies in logic (modal scope confusions, for example), linguistic and psychological pitfalls similar to the ones studied in this book, as well as subtleties about burdens of proof and the rationality of conceding in the face of counterarguments—conspire to make Cartesian challenges to knowledge seem compelling. Issues about burden of proof are related to justificational stopping points (which were discussed in chapter 8). Further required for this analysis is a more detailed examination of what I've called "methods"—the practices that justify what agents know, whether they grasp that they're using these methods, or not.[4]

Part of the complexity involved here is that the epistemic agents to whom Cartesian challenges can be made are *special*. More than one thing is wrong with that philosopher who kneels down in a park in front of a squirrel and says: "Look, buddy, you don't know *that's* a nut in front of you because you might be dreaming." The Cartesian challenge is, ultimately—just as Descartes presents it—a challenge an agent makes to herself; an agent who does so is thus capable of complex iterated cognitions. Further unraveling the role of iterated cognition in Cartesian challenges to knowledge, and how they affect the individuation of a person's methods of knowing, indeed, is a key to understanding exactly how "internalist" considerations affect the cogency of some knowledge attributions to some agents, although not to others. (Thus, it's a key to clearing up debates between external reliabilists and their internalist opponents.) It's also a key to understanding how Cartesian scepticism operates (and how we—certain agents, anyway—can avoid its dire conclusions without trivializing our, nevertheless, fallible knowledge).

[4] Recall the discussion in sections 1.8, 10.2, and 11.3 of how methods of seeing can be regarded slippily, for example, as including checks on whether the light in a room is standard white light, or instead as not including such checks. Whether a challenge of a certain sort undercuts knowledge or iterated knowledge often turns on how methods of an agent for knowing things are individuated.

Appendix
The Aesthetics of Hangman Knots

I

Looking back over this book, I can see why someone might recommend that it instead be titled *The Book of Epistemic Puzzles and Conundrums (and Some Purported Solutions to Them)*. That's ironic because I *hate* solving puzzles. I've never liked crossword or math puzzles, for example; most board games (which in one way or another involve puzzle solving) also bore me. This is a statement of autobiography—not a condemnation of puzzling. Something is clearly missing from my cognitive makeup that stops me from enjoying what many other humans *love*: sheer puzzle solving. Perhaps it's related to my equally strong loathing for vicarious sports; or maybe it's different (maybe I'm missing *more* than one thing, cognitively speaking). Merely winning a race, I'll add, doesn't motivate me either. And puzzle solving often (usually) is getting something taken care of quickly and first (*Yay!!!*). Childhood was rough for me; among other things, it involved lots of competition against peers to achieve things—like gold stars—that there was no independent point to. So too: there seemed (and seems) to me no point to *merely* winning a contest.

What I *do* like are beautiful landscapes, in particular, beautiful *conceptual* landscapes, made up *or* real—both seeing them *all at once* and traveling through them (seeing them, as it were, *in time*). That drives my interest in both mathematics and philosophy—not the puzzle solving that necessarily accompanies success in these fields, but the visions of structure and intricacy that the solving of (some) puzzles gives rise to. *The aesthetics of knots*: the unraveling of a knot is beautiful—it's more than the sheer satisfaction of solving a problem (whatever *that* is)—if the unraveling also reveals why our thinking knotted up in the first place; and if we've been able to untie the knot because we finally see a rich and intricate (conceptual) landscape behind that knot. (A corollary: You don't know how pretty a knot is until you watch it unravel.)

Kripke's dogmatism paradox is pretty in this way. If I'm right (section 10.4), then *many* linguistic and cognitive factors that structurally condition how we talk and think about knowledge crossroad together to beautifully create an argument with a bizarre conclusion that appears compellingly sound and valid. Unknotting this is informative and illuminating. Or, rather, once we see how a number of linguistic and cognitive factors blend together (once we see how the linguistic/cognitive landscape flows into this particularly disturbing argument), we see our way through the landscape of this "paradox."

This is *not* true of the hangman's paradox, or (more benignly) the surprise-exam or prediction paradox. Despite this "paradox" intriguing a large number of thinkers[1] (and its seeming relevant enough to epistemology that Williamson (2000) dedicates a chapter

[1] See Sorensen (1988a) for an extensive citation/discussion of the history of and approaches to the paradox as of that date. See Williamson (2000, chapter 6), for subsequent citations as of 2000.

of his epistemology book to it, and Kripke (2011b) takes one of his two paradoxes about knowledge to be it), there isn't much going on. If I'm right, it's really to be handled by a narrow set of tools involving tacit and explicit expressions of assumptions as well as being clear-headed about reductio. Broader epistemic lessons intrude (and are relevant) only insofar as they explain aspects of why we experience the puzzle the way we do—or think we can solve it in certain ways. That is, there (ultimately) isn't much going on if I'm right about what *is* going on. Hereafter, I'll call it "the Puzzle."

II

A preliminary: Define an exam as a "surprise exam" for a student if that student doesn't know that exam will occur at any point on the day *before* it does so.

Consider this stripped-down version of the Puzzle ("Stripped-down Surprise").[2] A teacher, having full authority about this, tells her students on Monday that an exam will occur that Thursday or Friday, and that it will be a surprise exam for every student. *All* the students are shocked because the teacher has *evidently* uttered a contradiction. After all (notice how easy this reasoning is), if the exam doesn't take place that Thursday, all the students will know after class (on *Thursday*) that the exam must take place on Friday (if the teacher's remarks are true); but in that case, the Friday exam won't be a surprise (so the teacher's remarks will be false). This means that if the exam is to be a surprise (again, in order for the teacher's remarks to be true), it must take place on the only day left: Thursday. But it won't be a surprise then, either, since the students *have now* (on Monday, two days before Wednesday) deduced that it must take place on Thursday; and they aren't going to forget this by Wednesday. The teacher's remarks can't be true: she's uttered a contradiction. Call this "Contradiction."

The students reason further. Because they know the teacher's remarks are false, that is, it's false that: *An exam will occur this Thursday or Friday, and that exam will be a surprise for every student*, they conclude: Either the exam won't occur on Thursday or Friday, or it won't surprise every student. Call this "Either No Surprise or No Exam."[3]

The number of days doesn't seem relevant to the validity and soundness of the reasoning. If there are three days, or seventeen, versions of the same two results seem to follow: Contradiction, and Either No Surprise or No Exam.[4]

Suppose one of the students argues this way instead: Wait a minute! What we've actually shown is that the teacher's remarks are contradictory. So in reasoning further to Either No Surprise or No Exam, we made a mistake. After all, if the teacher's remarks are contradictory, then *everything* follows from them—not just the conclusion that the exam won't be given or that it won't be a surprise. What *also* follows is that the sun is purple, that

[2] Kripke (2011b, 28–29) gives this version of the puzzle, using cards instead.

[3] Kripke (2011b, 28) has a student conclude, pretty much, this. In Quine (1953) (where a judge, cruelly, has sentenced: the prisoner will hang the following week, and the event will be a surprise for him), the prisoner concludes: the sentence will not be executed.

[4] A weeklong version: the teacher makes the announcement on Friday that the surprise exam will occur on one day the following week. The students can say to one another, after taking the Thursday step: "See? You can keep doing this to exclude all the days." Kripke and Williamson deny this; they claim the number of days affects our impression of the reasoning. See appendix section IV.

there are no such things as exams or teachers, that there *are* many unicorns, *and a whole lot of other stuff.*

Here's an argument the students might therefore run (call it "Knowledge-Basis"):

> First leave aside what the teacher told us. On only the basis of everything else we know, on whatever day an exam occurs, it will be a surprise exam. This includes Thursday or Friday. Now let's include provisionally, in what we know, the teacher's assertions. If we do this, then "what we know" is contradictory; we can't use "what we know" to draw any conclusions about exams (or about anything else). So, we have to go back to before the teacher said anything. In that case the exam will be a surprise, whenever it is given.

I've presented Knowledge-Basis as straightforward reasoning that students could have invented—provided they'd learned that contradictions aren't informative. (I'd heard this much in *high school* about contradictions; so had my friends.) But there's an obvious problem with Knowledge-Basis: contradictions can't be *true.*[5] If the exam takes place on Thursday *or* Friday, it *will be* a surprise. And then, what the teacher has said is true. So we can (so it seems) set aside Knowledge-Basis, diagnosing the error the student has made as this: She's confusing reductio ad absurdum (to show that a statement contradicts a background set of statements) with reasoning (using reductio ad absurdum—or any logical principles, for that matter) from a contradiction. The teacher's remarks contradict background presuppositions about time, knowledge, surprises, and the like; her remarks aren't *in themselves* contradictory. But something's *still* wrong because, after all, when the exam takes place on Thursday or Friday, it's still a surprise. The teacher's remarks don't contradict *the facts* about time, knowledge, surprises, and the like—that's why the teacher's remarks can be true. So there must be a fallacy in Contradiction because of presuppositions about time, knowledge, surprises, and the like, ones that aren't true to the facts about time, knowledge, surprises, and the like.

This analysis invites "solutions" to the Puzzle that make explicit presuppositions about time, knowledge, surprises, and the like, that the students have implicitly used to show the teacher's remarks can't be true, but which are incompatible with the teacher's (true) remarks; and, indeed (because the teacher's remarks *are* true), aren't themselves true, or, relatedly, solutions that reveal fallacious steps in Contradiction.

So (for example), one might argue that "surprise," as defined, involves an ambiguity that generates a false conclusion (but no, "surprise," as defined, *isn't* ambiguous); or that "know(s)" itself is ambiguous relevantly to drawing a false conclusion (see Kripke (2011b) for discussion of this option—which, in any case, I reject). One might also note, as Williamson (2000, chapter 6) and Kripke (2011b) do, the use of KK that arises because the reasoning occurs in stages: Friday is first ruled out, and then *knowing that Friday has been ruled out*, Thursday is next ruled out.[6] One might deny that this use of KK is

[5] I'm not considering adopting a paraconsistent logic as a way out of this. If we can't find a way out of the Puzzle that's compatible with *classical* logic, then the surprise-exam/hangman paradox becomes an argument *for* changing logic—and some have seen it that way.

[6] And so on, the more days are involved. The reasoning the students engage in correspondingly gets more complex, in part because of ever more iterated uses of KK. Kripke (2011b) argues that KK is "nearly true." Williamson (2000, 140) notes that KK isn't essential; various iterations of knowledge work as well. He argues that "the iteration of knowledge operators leads sooner or later to falsity through

legitimate. Whatever force this suggestion has for versions of the Puzzle that involve more than two days (and I'll argue in section IV that it has none), it's implausible as a solution for Stripped-down Surprise. The needed single use of KK or the grasp of an iterated "know(s)" claim to reason through Contradiction is surely within (nearly) everyone's grasp, and *completely legitimated by the fact that the students understand the argument.*

Kripke's solution is two-pronged. When there are more than two days involved in the setup of the puzzle, he claims that knowledge can be lost on the basis of misleading evidence. With respect to cases like Stripped-down Surprise, he notes that nearly everyone will recognize something is wrong; they will recognize (Kripke (2011b, 38)) the Moore-like "paradoxical flavor."[7] But merely invoking Moore's "It's raining, but I don't know this," and noting the Puzzle has the same flavor, doesn't really explain an important puzzle about the Puzzle.

Consider this case. The teacher says to her class: "There will be a test tomorrow; it will be a surprise exam." Given that "surprise exam" means an exam that the students (on the day before the test) don't know will take place, the teacher's remarks amount to: "There will be a test tomorrow, and you will not know until tomorrow that there will be a test tomorrow." This is a statement that, *regardless of whether it's said to the students or not*, will be true if the teacher gives a test tomorrow that the students get no information about apart from what the teacher has said. The teacher could think to herself: *There will be a test tomorrow; it will be a surprise [to all the students]*. If she says nothing to the students about the test, the statement is true. On the other hand, because the students can't give an interpretation of the teacher's statement that makes it true, the test will (again) be a surprise to them. So the remark looks Moorean, as Kripke says.

Here's the puzzle about the Puzzle. The empirical facts make it look right for the students to reject the teacher's statement, "there will be a test tomorrow; it will be a surprise," *altogether*, and then, when the test occurs, being surprised. But what makes *this rejection* "legal"? Is it part of the definition of "Moorean remarks" that one *shouldn't* negate them, after reasoning to the result that they're false (and thus, that their negations are true) but instead ignore them? It's hard to see how to justify this maneuver. What makes the statement Moorean is that the utterance of it looks contradictory. But that, after all, is the problem. If the teacher's remarks *are* contradictory, we should be able to negate them, and the result of negating them should be true. But the negation of the teacher's statement yields "There won't be a test tomorrow or it won't be a surprise." And this statement is false.

a process of erosion resulting from the need for margins for error." (I'll say more about this shortly; KK is false and iterated knowledge can fail for an agent—but not in cases where students understand the Puzzle.) Keeping the reasoning in mind each day until the last day the exam can take place (and the teacher's remarks still be true) also allows the possibility of the students losing their knowledge through misleading evidence. Kripke adopts this solution for many-days version of the paradox; so do Wright and Sudbury (1977) and Jackson (1987). Williamson (2000, 138) writes of this approach: "There is clearly something to it." I've ruled this option out in section 9.3, especially in note 12.

[7] Williamson's solution is similarly two-pronged. He (2000, 142) writes: "Most people are simply confused by the one-day version of the paradox, 'There will be an examination today and you do not know it.' The more days are involved, the clearer it is that the pupils can know the truth of the teacher's announcement." Both sentences misdescribe the data. Relevant now is what's wrong with his first sentence: most people are "simply confused" by the one-day version of the paradox *because they see it can't be true.* (So what they're "confused about" is why the teacher would say it.) I discuss his second sentence in section IV.

We need to legitimate the students' *ignoring* the teacher's (true) remarks rather than negating them (as the process of recognizing the statement to be contradictory apparently licenses them to do). All the versions of the Puzzle generated from the Stripped-down Surprise setup, regardless of the number of days involved, look the same in this respect: *all of them* yield a statement that the students can apply Contradiction to, and then draw a version of Either No Surprise or No Exam. And, unfortunately, these statements shouldn't be negated—because their negations can be falsified (by the test occurring on an appropriate day). This is why Kripke's (and Williamson's) remarks about the Moorean nature of this case are inadequate. To describe the teacher's remarks as Moorean isn't to explain why negating them is ruled out.

Here's how to solve the puzzle about the Puzzle, and so solve the Puzzle too. Some contradictions are fully explicit and some aren't. When contradictions aren't fully explicit, we blunder if we negate (and only negate) the explicit part of the contradiction. (If the explicit part of the contradiction is, for example, (p and q), but the whole contradiction is (p and q and r), then if we conclude ($\neg p$ or $\neg q$), we've blundered: we're only licensed to conclude the weaker ($\neg p$ or $\neg q$ or $\neg r$). The teacher's statements, regardless of the days involved in the cases I've described, are an explicit *part of* a larger implicit contradiction. The students who give the contradiction argument don't negate the full implicit contradiction; they negate only what's been stated explicitly—just the teacher's remarks. That's why they get in trouble. I now try to establish this.

III

Here's an alternative statement the teacher could have uttered ("Alternative"):

> The next two sentences I say are true; you know they're true as a result of my saying them. The exam will occur on Thursday or Friday. It will be a surprise exam.

When the exam surprisingly occurs on Thursday or Friday, the only false clause is "you know they're true as a result of my saying them." This is because students *can't know* these two propositions are true by the teacher saying so. Let's spell this out. The negation of alternative is ("Negation of Alternative"):

> Not (the next two sentences I say are true) *or* Not (You know they're true as a result of my saying so) *or* Not (The exam will occur on Thursday or Friday) *or* Not (The exam will be a surprise).

If the exam occurs on some day other than Thursday or Friday, then the third clause is true. If the exam occurs on either Thursday or Friday, then the second clause is true because the students know the sentence, "The exam will occur on Thursday or Friday," and "The exam is a surprise" but *not* on the basis of the teacher's words.

Similarly, suppose the teacher says this ("Alternative 2"):

> The following two propositions can be included by you as part of what you know, and they can be used in inferences about the day of the exam and whether the exam on that day is a surprise exam or not: The exam will occur on Friday or Thursday. It will be a surprise exam.

We can see that Alternative 2 is contradictory using similar reasoning on its negation.

Kripke (2011b, 33) writes:

> Quine says the fallacy derives from the fact that the prisoner does not *know* that the judge is telling the truth, or that the student does not *know* that there will be an exam given at all. But often, I think, you do *know* something simply because a good teacher has told you so. If a teacher were to announce a surprise exam to be given within a month, a student who did badly could not excuse herself by saying that she did not *know* that there was going to be an exam. If there is only one day, we have the anomalous situation I have just mentioned [the hearer will not know what to believe, given the strangeness of the performance, and therefore will not have knowledge on the basis of what the teacher says]. But if there are many days, then it is natural to give the students knowledge on the basis of what the teacher tells them.

Consider now a modification of Knowledge-Basis (call this "Modified Knowledge-Basis"):

> Let's first assume that what the teacher told us *isn't* something we *know*. Then, on the basis of everything we *do* know in this case, on whatever day an exam occurs, it will be a surprise exam. This includes, of course, Thursday or Friday. Next, let's assume that we know what the teacher has told us. If we do this, then we derive a contradiction (along the lines of Contradiction). So we *don't know* what the teacher has told us in this case either; and so the exam, whenever it takes place, will be a surprise in this case too. Conclusion: The exam will be a surprise exam, whenever it is given.

The reasoning is good; it's of the form: If (p or $\neg p$) implies q, then q. The reasoning in Contradiction is good *too*. If what the teacher told the students *does* give them knowledge, then it *does* follow that either the exam won't be a surprise or it won't occur on Thursday or Friday. But what the teacher told the students doesn't give them knowledge; the students made a mistake in assuming it does. Quine's prisoner similarly, by assuming what the judge said gave him knowledge, also made a mistake. So, according to this solution, there isn't a fallacy in *reasoning*; the *soundness* of the reasoning is at fault; a falsity was (tacitly) assumed.

Am I offering Quine's solution to the Puzzle? No. Quine is criticized by Kripke for denying that prisoners can know things on the basis of what judges say. Similarly, Sorensen (1988, 296, 310) writes:

> The hidden cost [of Quine's solution is] epistemological . . .: scepticism about either authority or the future [because] Quine maintains that . . . the judge's declaration is insufficient evidence for [the prisoner] to know that he will be hung on an unforeseen day.

Is Quine's (1953) solution a sceptical one about authority or the future? Are these the correct interpretations of what he writes? Yes, for a slightly subtle textual reason. He describes the prisoner as committing a "fallacy" in his reasoning (e.g., Quine (1953, 21)). That implies the prisoner has adopted a fallacious principle about knowledge. Kripke's criticism of Quine's solution, quoted here, is used to conclude (Kripke (2011b, 33)): "In the cases where there are many days, it is natural to give the students knowledge on the basis of what the teacher tells them."[8]

[8] Williamson (2000, 139) similarly assumes (in many-days cases) that "any adequate diagnosis of the Surprise Examination should allow the pupils to know that there will be a surprise examination." Wright and Sudbury (1977, 42) think the same. I'm disputing this, with a caveat; or rather, I agree, but not in the way Kripke, Williamson, and Wright and Sudbury, mean. See note 10.

What Quine should have said instead is that the prisoner didn't commit a fallacy; he just tacitly assumed a false premise (something easy to do with unstated assumptions). The false premise is that teacher's/judge's statement provides knowledge. It's not true that *all* statements by teachers and judges *don't* provide knowledge; but *some* really don't. Were the judge to have uttered a simple contradiction, "You will be hung and you will not be hung," the remark wouldn't have provided knowledge. If he had said tautologously, "You will be hung or you will not be hung," he wouldn't have provided knowledge either. Often the assumption that what the person has provided is knowledge (or isn't knowledge) is an idle wheel for the inferences we make on the basis of what's said. But not always, as the Puzzle makes clear.

All of us who find the Puzzle compelling make the same mistake: We treat the words of the teacher/judge as freestanding, and when we deduce a contradiction, we think the explicit words uttered are *where the contradiction is located.* But that the teacher's/judge's words are true proves this isn't where the contradiction is located.[9] The way to locate the contradiction is to include with the teacher's words the additional background assumption, and see that the resulting statement *is* contradictory; this is what I've done in Alternative.

Kripke writes about the cases where there are many days that "it is natural to give the students knowledge on the basis of what the teacher tells them," as I quoted him. Nope—no more than it's natural in Stripped-down Surprise. Whether what's told to students by a teacher conveys knowledge to those students *solely on the basis of what the teacher has said* turns not only on circumstances but on what's said, and whether what's said *can* convey knowledge. If an unwitting teacher says an exam will be given within a month, and that it will be a surprise, because this remark (along with the background assumption that it conveys knowledge) results in a contradiction, the remark *isn't* informative; *it* can't be knowledge.

The wily student who realizes this (when she hears what the unwitting teacher has said) will also realize, however, that there *will be* an exam within a month. She realizes this because: (1) she realizes the unwitting teacher didn't recognize that he said something that can't be knowledge for the students who heard him; (2) she realizes that the unwitting teacher, nevertheless, intended to convey knowledge; (3) given other background information (e.g., about the psychology of the unwitting teacher), she realizes that the only thing the unwitting teacher could have intended to convey was that there would be a surprise exam within the month; (4) given other background information (e.g., that the unwitting teacher is in full control of when the exam will be given; the unwitting teacher is normally straightforward; he wouldn't want to mislead; etc.), the student can infer there will be a surprise exam within the month. This is *not* to take what the unwitting teacher said as true or as knowledge. The student's justification that there will be an exam within a month isn't that the unwitting teacher said p and p implies "there will be a surprise exam within a month"; her justification is that, given what she knows about the unwitting teacher, this is what he must have meant to convey by uttering p; and what he meant to convey is what he will do.

The wily student also knows that if she tries to get out of having to take the exam on the grounds that the unwitting teacher uttered something that couldn't have conveyed to

[9] Church's (1936) result that there is no decision procedure for logical contradictions is relevant; from this it follows there is no syntactically describable form that contradictions take—many, most (in an acceptable form of "most"), *aren't* of the form: $p \,\&\, \neg p$. This makes contradictions (in general) hard to see; they're even harder to see when some of their relevant content is tacit.

the students that there will be a surprise exam, either no one will understand what's she claimed (and she'll be punished anyway), or, worse, a really smart principal will point out the reasoning (1)–(4) that shows that the student had to have realized that there *would be* an exam. Furthermore, suppose the wily student has a different (witty) teacher, who uttered the remark, knowing it couldn't be used by the students to know that there will be a surprise exam during that month. If the wily student figures this out, she *will be* justified in saying that she didn't know there would be an exam. (And the witty teacher, if honest, would have to admit she's right.)

But back to the unwitting-teacher case: what about the rest of the students, who, like the unwitting teacher, don't recognize that the statement the unwitting teacher has uttered doesn't convey knowledge to them about a surprise exam? When these students conclude there will be a surprise exam within the month, do they *not* know this? No—they do know it because this is a Warfield case (section 11.3). The students know (despite a false assumption) that there will be a surprise exam.[10]

IV

Left are final remarks about the phenomenology of the Puzzle: what in our experience of the Puzzle makes it *feel* like a puzzle. I'll also mention a point about certain variations on the Puzzle.

When someone asserts something to me, their assertion may or may not provide me with knowledge. If it doesn't, in some of those cases the assumption—that what has been said provides me with knowledge—contradicts what the person has said. This is explicit and unsurprising in cases where someone says, for example, "It's snowing, and you don't know this on the basis of what I've just said." This would have the form of some kind of liar paradox, if it were built into the uttered sentence somehow, that the listener knows what the speaker is saying.[11] But it's not built into this sentence; instead, sometimes we

[10] This is cool. The unwitting teacher thinks he's conveyed knowledge by his utterance; he has, but not in the way he thinks. And life, I've noticed (and you have too), is really like this. In note 8, I quoted Williamson: "Any adequate diagnosis of the Surprise Examination should allow the pupils to know that there will be a surprise examination." Also, Wright and Sudbury (1977, 42) write, "The account should make it possible for the pupils to be *informed* by the announcement: we want the reaction of someone who notices no peculiarity but just gets on with his revision to be logically unobjectionable." I don't accept this constraint in quite the form they give it—this is why I describe unwily students learning about the surprise exam as a Warfield case. (I'll note parenthetically that my solution meets the other five conditions Wright and Sudbury give for an adequate solution of the puzzle.) If the teacher is unwitting then all his students, wily and otherwise, learn *via* his utterance about the surprise exam within a month. Of course, if the teacher is wittingly saying what he says, then the unwily students learn there will be a surprise exam within a month—if there is one—and the wily students (with the appropriate background knowledge) learn this too.

[11] For example, if it was a presupposition of utterance that what's conveyed is supposed to be knowledge. That it's not such a presupposition (or norm) is argued in chapter 4. Many of the articles in the hangman/surprise-exam/prediction literature attempt to show these puzzles involve paradoxical utterances; although there are versions of the Puzzle in the literature where what's uttered by the teacher/judge are paradoxes, the ones I've discussed aren't. (See Sorensen (1988a) for overview, criticism, and citations as of 1988.) One of the most misleading aspects of the Puzzle is that it lives so close to paradoxical formulations that it looks like it should be one. It's natural, therefore, to spend *days* trying to massage it into a formulation that's really paradoxical *while retaining what is actually said.* (I couldn't do it.)

assume what we're hearing will yield knowledge and sometimes we don't. The problem is that when we assume that something someone has told us gives us knowledge, we don't recognize that we're assuming this; we just assume it. And similarly (more surprisingly, perhaps), when we assume that someone has told us something that doesn't give us knowledge, we also just assume it; we needn't realize we're doing so. (To realize what we're assuming or not assuming, in either case, is an iterated cognition—which we needn't have; recall the discussion of this in chapters 5 and 6.) We say, usually, "You're lying" or "That's false," but we don't usually say: "Therefore what you've told me isn't knowledge," even though this follows. This is why we (we "theorists" trying to solve the Puzzle) tend *ourselves* to reason as the students do in Contradiction and not as the students do in Modified Knowledge-Basis.

The second point is this. Kripke (2011b) and Williamson (2000, chapter 6) both include in the phenomenology of these arguments that the number of days affects the impression of the *plausibility* of the Contradiction argument—they both claim that the reasoning in the Contradiction argument seems progressively less plausible, the larger the number of days on which the test may occur. Both of them explain this with something true, that the proof takes place in stages, starting with the last day on which the test can take place, and, with progressively more days, the principles needed to justify the inferences ruling out days increase in complexity, the steps gone through increase in number, and finally, the students must retain the knowledge for a longer number of days. Pressure is put on knowledge closure, iterated knowledge cognition and/or KK, as well as the retention of the knowledge on the successive days that the students live through up to the last day that the test can take place (and the teacher's remarks be true). Williamson and Kripke both argue that their solutions are supported by the experience of the person considering the Puzzle to find the reasoning progressively less plausible as the number of days in the setup of the puzzle is increased,

But our experience of the reasoning *isn't* sensitive to the number of days in the Puzzle case. It *is* true that when going through the steps of Contradiction (stating exactly each premise that's used), one easily loses the details, and the argument looks shaky. But this is an experience typical of many mathematical proofs. The more details we supply, the less sure we are that the proofs are right. Leaving details out often (usually, actually) makes it transparent that the proof is good. This is why typical remarks in many proofs are: *the other cases are the same*, or *do the same in the other cases*. There are things to explain here, but they're about the epistemology of proof, in particular the epistemic relation between ordinary proofs and precise formal derivations;[12] there's nothing special going on here with respect to the Puzzle.

I've found nonphilosophers always find the Puzzle pretty clear when presented this way:

> The surprise exam must take place in the next week, Monday through Friday. It *can't* occur on Friday and be a surprise because on Thursday night there's only one day left; so we know the surprise exam won't happen on Friday. But then, on Wednesday night, we know it won't be a surprise on Thursday either. This is because if it's to be a surprise, we already know it can't be on Friday; we already know this on Wednesday night. So if it's going to be a surprise (so we think on Wednesday night), then it has to happen Thursday, tomorrow; but since we just showed this, it won't be a surprise

[12] See, e.g., Azzouni (2017a), and the other articles cited there.

on Thursday either. *Now notice that we can keep on doing this* as long as needed to exclude *all* the days.

I've found that everyone gets it.[13] So the purported phenomenological datum that the reasoning looks increasingly shaky is wrong. What's true is that it's obvious, when there are many days the teacher has to choose from, that a surprise exam can be easily given. But this isn't an experience of the *reasoning* becoming shaky as the number of days involved increases. This is only that it becomes blatantly obvious *something* is wrong with the reasoning because the conclusion is so clearly contradicted by the facts.

I've analyzed a particular setup, where the teacher authorizes the date of the exam. If we change the example by introducing, for example, a school rule that dictates what week the exam must take place in, the solution to the Puzzle is unaffected. What changes is what days the exam will be a surprise on, when leaving aside what the teacher has said. If the school rules state that the exam must occur on any day in the last full week of April, for example, then the exam occurring on the Friday of that week won't be a surprise in any case. Other changes (e.g., as in Williamson (2000, 136), where someone else relays the facts) similarly affect what background knowledge students have before the teacher's remarks are conveyed or spoken.

[13] Everyone gets it, that is, who gets it *at all*. If I can get someone to see Friday and Thursday are ruled out, I can always get that person to see this is true of the rest of the week—*and I can do it in one shot*. (This also works if the Puzzle is about a surprise exam in the next month—or *year*.) On the other hand, if I borrow Kripke's notation (2011b), or that of Wright and Sudbury, or Williamson's, or the notation of any number of other presentations of the Puzzle, if I explain that notation *really really* simply and clearly, and I spell out the argument explicitly in that notation, *I'll lose almost everyone*—and this is true even if I'm as liberal with ellipses as I can possibly be. Notice what's going on: someone can see the validity of a proof without having to *go through* the proof; indeed, this is fairly typical when grasping mathematical proofs. Recall my discussion of *reasoning through* and *reasoning about* in section 7.4.3.

Bibliography

Abramson, José Z., Victoria Hernández-Lloreda, Josep Call, and Fernando Colmenares. 2012. Experimental evidence for action imitation in killer whales (Orcinus orca). *Animal Cognition* 16, no. 1: 11–22.

Adler, Jonathan E. 1981. Skepticism and universalizability. *Journal of Philosophy* 77: 143–156.

Aikin, Scott F. 2011. *Epistemology and the regress problem*. New York: Routledge.

Aikin, Scott F. 2014. Knowing better, cognitive command, and epistemic infinitism. In (John Turri and Peter D. Klein, ed.) *Ad infinitum: New essays on epistemological infinitism*, 18–36. Oxford: Oxford University Press.

Alston, William P. 1971. How does one tell whether a word has one, several or many senses? In (Danny D. Steinberg and Leon A. Jakobovits, ed.) *Semantics: An interdisciplinary reader in philosophy, linguistics and psychology*, 35–47. Cambridge: Cambridge University Press.

Alston, William P. 1980. Level-confusions in epistemology. In (William P. Alston) *Epistemic justification* (1989), 153–182. Ithaca: Cornell University Press.

Alston, William P. 2000. *Illocutionary acts and sentence meaning*. Ithaca: Cornell University Press.

Antony, Louise. 2004. A naturalized approach to the a priori. *Philosophical Issues* 14, no. 1: 1–17.

Armstrong, David M. 1973. *Belief, truth and knowledge*. Cambridge: Cambridge University Press.

Atkinson, David, and Jeanne Peijnenburg. 2017. *Fading foundations: Probability and the regress problem*. Cham, Switzerland: Springer Open.

Austin, J. L. 1946. Other minds. In (J. L. Austin, 1979) *Philosophical papers*, 3rd ed., 76–116. Oxford: Oxford University Press.

Austin, J. L. 1962. *Sense and sensibilia*. Oxford: Oxford University Press.

Ayer, A. J. 1940. *The foundations of empirical knowledge*. London: Macmillan.

Azzouni, Jody. 1992. A priori truth. *Erkenntnis* 37: 327–346.

Azzouni, Jody. 2000a. Applying mathematics: An attempt to design a philosophical problem. *Monist* 83, no. 2: 209–227.

Azzouni, Jody. 2000b. *Knowledge and reference in empirical science*. London: Routledge.

Azzouni, Jody. 2001. Truth via anaphorically unrestricted quantifiers. *Journal of Philosophical Logic* 30: 329–354.

Azzouni, Jody. 2004. Tarski, Quine, and the transcendence of the vernacular "true." *Synthese* 142: 273–288.

Azzouni, Jody. 2006. *Tracking reason: Proof, consequence, and truth*. Oxford: Oxford University Press.

Azzouni, Jody. 2007. The inconsistency of natural languages: How we live with it. *Inquiry* 50, no. 6: 590–605.

Azzouni, Jody. 2009. Why do informal proofs conform to formal norms? *Foundations of Science* 14: 9–26.

Azzouni, Jody. 2010. *Talking about nothing: Numbers, hallucinations, and fictions*. Oxford: Oxford University Press.

Azzouni, Jody. 2013a. Inconsistency in natural languages. *Synthese* 190: 3175–3184.

Azzouni, Jody. 2013b. *Semantic perception: How the illusion of a public language arises and persists*. Oxford: Oxford University Press.

Azzouni, Jody. 2014. A new characterization of scientific theories. *Synthese* 19: 2993–3008. doi: 10.1007/s11229-014-0469-3.

Azzouni, Jody. 2015. Mathematical fictions. In (Ananta Ch. Suka, ed.) *Fiction and art: Explorations in contemporary theory*, 63–77. London: Bloomsbury.

Azzouni, Jody. 2017a. Does reason evolve? (Does the reasoning in mathematics evolve?) In (Bharath Sriraman, ed.) *Humanizing mathematics and its philosophy: Essays celebrating the 90th birthday of Reuben Hersh*, 253–289. Birkhäuser: Springer.

Azzouni, Jody. 2017b. *Ontology without borders*. Oxford: Oxford University Press.

Azzouni, Jody. 2017c. *The rule-following paradox and its implications for metaphysics*. Cham, Switzerland: Springer.

Azzouni, Jody. 2018. Deflationist truth. In (Michael Glanzberg, ed.) *The Oxford handbook of truth*, 477–502. Oxford: Oxford University Press.

Azzouni, Jody. 2020. Defending the importance of ordinary existence questions and debates. In (Ricki Leigh Bliss and James Miller, ed.) *Routledge handbook of metametaphysics*, 171–183. London: Routledge.

Azzouni, Jody. Forthcoming b. The implicature view of ontological commitments and denials.

Azzouni, Jody. Forthcoming c. Smith, Seth and Smith, and Newton on "taking to be true." In (Eric Schliesser, Chris Smeenk, and Marius Stan, ed.) *Theory, evidence, data: The philosophical legacy of George E. Smith*.

Azzouni, Jody. Forthcoming d. Telling tales. In (Alexandra King and Christy Mag Uidhir, ed.) *Philosophy and art: New essays at the intersection*, XXX–XXX. Oxford: Oxford University Press.

Azzouni, Jody, and Bradley Armour-Garb. 2005. Standing on common ground. *Journal of Philosophy* 102, no. 10: 532–544.

Bach, Kent. 2001. Speaking loosely: Sentence nonliterality. In (Peter French and Howard Wettstein, ed.) *Midwest studies in philosophy*, vol. 25, 51–89. Malden, MA: Blackwell.

Bach, Kent. 2005. The emperor's new "knows." In (Gerhard Preyer and Georg Peter, ed.) *Contextualism in philosophy: Knowledge, meaning, and truth*, 51–89. Oxford: Oxford University Press.

Baddeley, Bart, Paul Graham, Philip Husbands, and Andrew Philippides. 2012. A model of ant route navigation driven by scene familiarity. *PLOS Computational Biology* 8, no. 1: 1–16.

Barwise, Jon, and Robin Cooper. 1981. Generalized quantifiers and natural language. *Linguistics and Philosophy* 4: 159–219.

Basile, Benjamin M., Gabriel R. Schroeder, Emily Kathryn Brown, Victoria L. Templer, and Robert R. Hampton. 2014. Evaluation of seven hypotheses for metamemory performance in Rhesus monkeys. *Journal of Experimental Psychology: General* 144: 85–102.

Baz, Avner. 2012. *When words are called for: A defense of ordinary language philosophy*. Cambridge, MA: Harvard University Press.

Bearzi, M., and C. B. Stanford. 2008. *Beautiful minds: The parallel lives of great apes and dolphins*. Cambridge, MA: Harvard University Press.

Beebe, J. R. 2012. Social functions of knowledge attributions. In (M. Gerken and J. Brown, ed.) *Knowledge ascriptions*, 220–242. Oxford: Oxford University Press.

Benjamin, A. S., R. A. Bjork, and B. L. Schwartz. 1998. The mismeasure of memory: When retrieval fluency is misleading as a metamnemonic index. *Journal of Experimental Psychology: General* 127: 55–68.

Bentall, R.P. 1990. The illusion of reality: A review and integration of psychological research on hallucinations. *Psychological Bulletin* 107: 82–95.

Beran, Michael J., Johannes L. Brandl, Josef Perner, and Joëlle Proust. 2012. On the nature, evolution, development, and epistemology of metacognition: Introductory thoughts. In (Michael J. Beran, Johannes L. Brandl, Josef Perner, Joëlle Proust, ed.) *Foundations of metacognition*, 1–18. Oxford: Oxford University Press.

Beran, Michael J., and J. David Smith. 2011. Information seeking by rhesus monkeys (*Macaca mulatta*) and capuchin monkeys (*Cebus paella*). *Cognition* 120: 90–105.

Berker, Selim. 2013. The rejection of epistemic consequentialism. *Philosophical Issues* 23, no. 1: 363–387.

Beynon-Davies, Paul. 2011. In-formation on the prairie: Signs, patterns, systems and prairie dogs. *International Journal of Information Management* 31, no. 4: 307–316.

Bilger, Burkhard. 2013. Has the self-driving car at last arrived? *New Yorker*, November 25.

Black, Oliver. 1988. Infinite regresses of justification. *International Philosophical Quarterly* 28, no. 4: 421–437.

Blanshard, Brand. 1939. *The nature of thought*, 2 vols. New York: Macmillan.

Bloom, P. 2004. Can a dog learn a word? *Science* 304: 1605–1606.

BonJour, Laurence. 1978. Can empirical knowledge have a foundation? *American Philosophical Quarterly* 15, no. 1: 1–13.

BonJour, Laurence. 1985. *The structure of empirical knowledge*. Cambridge, MA: Harvard University Press.

Borg, Emma. 2012. *Pursuing meaning*. Oxford: Oxford University Press.

Boudette, Neal E. 2016a. Elon Musk says pending Tesla updates could have prevented fatal crash. *New York Times*, September 11, B1.

Boudette, Neal E. 2016b. 5 things that give self-driving cars headaches. *New York Times*, June 6.

Box, Hilary O. 2003. Characteristics and propensities of marmosets and tamarins: Implications for studies of innovation. In (Simon M. Reader and Kevin N. Laland, ed.) *Animal innovation*, 197–219. Oxford: Oxford University Press.

Brandl, Johannes L. 2012. Pretend play in early childhood: The road between mentalism and behaviourism. In (Michael J. Beran et al., ed.) *Foundations of metacognition*, 1–18. Oxford: Oxford University Press.

Brandom, Robert. 1994. *Making it explicit: Reasoning, representing, and discursive commitment*. Cambridge, MA: Harvard University Press.

Brandom, Robert. 1995. Knowledge and the social articulation of the space of reasons. *Philosophy and Phenomenological Research* 55: 895–908.

Brown, Jessica. 2006. Contextualism and warranted assertibility manoeuvres. *Philosophical Studies* 130: 407–435.

Brown, Jessica. 2008. Subject-sensitive invariantism and the knowledge norm for practical reasoning. *Noûs* 42, no. 2: 167–189.

Brown, Jessica, and Herman Cappelen. 2011. Assertion: An introduction and overview. In (Jessica Brown and Herman Cappelen, ed.) *Assertion: New philosophical essays*, 1–17. Oxford: Oxford University Press.

Brown, Jessica, and Mikkel Gerken (ed.). 2012. *Knowledge ascriptions*. Oxford: Oxford University Press.

Brunk, J. N. 2013. Decades-long social memory in bottlenose dolphins. *Proceedings of the Royal Society B* 280, no. 1768: 1726.

Bueno, Otávio, and Jody Azzouni. 2005. Review of Donald MacKenzie, Mechanizing proof: Computing, risk, and trust. *Philosophia Mathematica* 13, no. 3: 319–325.

Burge, Tyler. 1993. Content preservation. Reprinted 2013 in (Tyler Burge) *Philosophical essays*, Vol. 3: *Cognition through Understanding: Self-knowledge, interlocution, reasoning*, 229–253. Oxford: Oxford University Press.

Byrne, Richard W. 2016. *Evolving insight*. Oxford: Oxford University Press.

Call, Josep, and M. Carpenter. 2001. Do apes and children know what they have seen? *Animal Cognition* 4: 207–220.

Call, Josep, and Michael Tomasello. 2008. Does the chimpanzee have a theory of mind? 30 years later. *Trends in Cognitive Science* 12, no. 5: 187–192.

Cappelen, Herman. 2011. Against assertion. In (Jessica Brown and Herman Cappelen, ed.) *Assertion: New philosophical essays*, 21–47. Oxford: Oxford University Press.

Cappelen, Herman. 2012. *Philosophy without intuitions*. Oxford: Oxford University Press.

Carey, Susan. 2009. *The origin of concepts*. Oxford: Oxford University Press.

Carruthers, Peter. 2008. Meta-cognition in animals: A skeptical look. *Mind & Language* 23, no. 1: 58–89.

Carruthers, Peter, and J. Brendan Ritchie. 2012. The emergence of metacognition: Affect and uncertainty in animals. In (Michael J. Beran et al., ed.) *Foundations of metacognition*, 76–93. Oxford: Oxford University Press.

Carston, Robyn. 1996. Metalinguistic negation and echoic use. *Journal of Pragmatics* 25: 309–330.

Chisholm, Roderick M. 1964. Theory of knowledge. In (Roderick M. Chisholm, Herbert Feigl, William K. Frankena, John Passmore, and Manley Thompson) *Philosophy*, 233–344. Englewood Cliffs: Prentice-Hall.

Chomsky, Noam. 1980. *Rules and representations*. New York: Columbia University Press.

Chomsky, Noam. 2000. *New horizons in the study of language and mind*. Cambridge: Cambridge University Press.

Church, Alonzo. 1936. A note on the Entscheidungsproblem. *Journal of Symbolic Logic* 1, nos. 40–41: 101–102.

Cohen, Stewart. 1998. Contextualist solutions to epistemological problems: Scepticism, Gettier, and the lottery. *Australasian Journal of Philosophy* 76, no. 2: 289–306.

Cohen, Stewart. 1999. Contextualism, skepticism, and the structure of reasons. *Philosophical Perspectives* 13: 57–89.

Cohen, Stewart. 2016. Theorizing about the epistemic. *Inquiry* 59, nos. 7–8: 839–857.

Collett, Thomas S., and Matthew Collett. 2002. Memory use in insect visual navigation. *Nature Reviews Neuroscience* 3, no. 7: 542–552.

Collins, John. 2017. The copredication argument. *Inquiry* 60, no. 7: 675–702.

Conee, Earl. 2004. Evidentialism. In (Earl Conee and Richard Feldman, ed.) *Evidentialism: Essays in epistemology*, 83–107. Oxford: Oxford University Press.

Conee, Earl, and Richard Feldman. 2004. Introduction. In (Earl Conee and Richard Feldman, ed.) *Evidentialism: Essays in epistemology*, 1–7. Oxford: Oxford University Press.

Cooper, J. J., C. Ashton, S. Bishop, R. West, D. S. Mills, and R. J. Young. 2003. Clever hounds: Social cognition in the domestic dog (*Canis familiaris*). *Applied Animal Behavior Sciences* 81: 229–244.

Craig, Edward. 1990. *Knowledge and the state of nature*. Oxford: Oxford University Press.

Cullen, S. 2010. Survey-driven romanticism. *Review of Philosophy and Psychology* 1: 275–296.

Davidson, Donald. 1982. Rational animals. In (Donald Davidson) *Subjective, intersubjective, objective* (2001), 95–105. Oxford: Oxford University Press.

Davidson, Donald. 1986. A coherence theory of knowledge and truth. In (Ernest LePore, ed.) *Truth and interpretation*, 307–319. Oxford: Blackwell.

Dennett, Daniel C. 1987. True believers. In (Damiel C. Dennett) *The intentional stance*, 13–35. Cambridge, MA: MIT Press.

DeRose, Keith. 1995. Solving the skeptical problem. *Philosophical Review* 104, no. 1: 1–52.

DeRose, Keith. 2009. *The case for contextualism: Knowledge, skepticism, and context, Volume 1*. Oxford: Oxford University Press.

DeRose, Keith. 2017. *The appearance of ignorance: Knowledge, skepticism, and context, Volume 2*. Oxford: Oxford University Press.

Deutsch, Max. 2015. *The myth of the intuitive: Experimental philosophy and philosophical method*. Cambridge, MA: MIT Press.

De Waal, Frans. 2016. *Are we smart enough to know how smart animals are?* New York: W. W. Norton.

Dienes, Zoltan, and Josef Perner. 2001. The metacognitive implications of the implicit-explicit distinction. In (P. Chambres, M. Izaute, and P.-J. Marescaux, ed.) *Metacognition, process, function, and use*, 171–189. Dordrecht: Kluwer Academic.

Dokic, Jérôme, and Paul Égré. 2009. Margin for error and the transparency of knowledge. *Synthese* 166: 1–20.

Dominus, Susan. 2017. When the revolution came for Amy Cuddy. *New York Times Magazine*, October 22, 28–33, 50, 52–53, 55.

Dretske, Fred. 1970. Epistemic operators. *Journal of Philosophy* 67, no. 24: 1007–1023.

Dretske, Fred. 1993. Conscious experience. *Mind* 102, no. 406: 263–283.

Dretske, Fred. 1999. The mind's awareness of itself. *Philosophical Studies* 95, nos. 1–2: 103–124.

Ducasse, C. J. 1944. Propositions, truth, and the ultimate criterion of truth. *Philosophy and Phenomenological Research* 4: 317–340.

Dudman, V. H. 1992. Probability and assertion. *Analysis* 52, no. 4: 204–211.

Dummett, Michael. 1963. Realism. In (Michael Dummett) *Truth and other enigmas* (1978) 145–165. Cambridge, MA: Harvard University Press.

Dunlosky, J., and R. A. Bjork (ed.). 2008. *Handbook of metamemory and memory*. New York: Psychology Press.

Dunn, J. Michael, and Nuel D. Belnap, Jr. 1968. The substitution interpretation of the quantifiers. *Noûs* 2, no. 2: 177–185.

Dunning, D., K. Johnson, J. Ehrlinger, and J. Kruger. 2003. Why people fail to recognize their own incompetence. *Current Directions in Psychological Science* 12: 83–87.

Dutant, Julien. 2015. The legend of the justified true belief analysis. *Philosophical Perspectives* 29: 95–145.

Esken, Frank. 2012. Early forms of metacognition in human children. In (Michael J. Beran et al., ed.) *Foundations of metacognition*, 134–145. Oxford: Oxford University Press.

Evans, J. St. B. T. 2006. The heuristic-analytic theory of reasoning: Extension and evaluation. *Psychonomic Bulletin and Review* 13: 378–395.

Evans, J. St. B. T., and K. Frankish. 2009. *In two minds: Dual processes and beyond.* Oxford: Oxford University Press.

Evans, Garath. 1982. *The varieties of reference*. Oxford: Oxford University Press.

Fantl, Jeremy, and Matthew McGrath. 2002. Evidence, pragmatics, and justification. *Philosophical Review* 111, no. 1: 67–94.

Fantl, Jeremy, and Matthew McGrath. 2007. On pragmatic encroachment in epistemology. *Philosophy and Phenomenological Research* 75, no. 3: 558–589.

Fantl, Jeremy, and Matthew McGrath. 2009. *Knowledge in an uncertain world.* Oxford: Oxford University Press.

Feferman, S. 1982. Towards useful type-free theories, I. *Journal of Symbolic Logic* 49, no. 1: 75–111.

Feyerabend, Paul. 1962. Explanation, reduction, and empiricism. *Minnesota Studies in the Philosophy of Science* 3: 337–69.

Figdor, Carrie. 2018. *Pieces of mind: The proper domain of psychological predicates.* Oxford: Oxford University Press.

Fillmore, C. 1982. Towards a descriptive framework for deixis. In (R. Jarvella and W. Klein, ed.) *Speech, place, and action*, 31–52. New York: Holt, Rinehart and Winston.

Firth, Roderick. 1981. Epistemic merit, intrinsic and instrumental. *Proceedings and Addresses of the American Philosophical Association* 55: 5–23. (Presidential address delivered at the Annual Eastern Meeting of the American Philosophical Association in December 1980.)

Flavell, J. H. 1979. Metacognition and cognitive reasoning: A new area of cognitive-developmental inquiry. *American Psychologist* 34: 906–911.

Fodor, J. A., M. Garrett, E. Walker, and C. Parkes. 1980. *Against definitions. Cognition* 8: 263–367.

Fodor, Jerry A. 1983. *The modularity of mind: An essay on faculty psychology*. Cambridge, MA.: MIT Press.

Fodor, Jerry A. 1998. *Concepts: Where cognitive science went wrong*. Oxford: Oxford University Press.

Fogelin, Robert J. 1994. *Pyrrhonian reflections on knowledge and justification*. Oxford: Oxford University Press.

Foly, Richard. 1978. Inferential justification and the infinite regress. *American Philosophical Quarterly* 15: 311–316.

Foote, A. D., R. M. Griffin, D. Howitt, L. Larsson, P. J. O. Miller, and A. Rus Hoelzel. 2006. Killer whales are capable of vocal learning. *Biology Letters* 2, no. 4: 509–512.

Franks, N. R., S.C. Pratt, E. B. Mallon, N. F. Britton, and D. J. T. Sumpter. 2002. Information flow, opinion polling and collective intelligence in house-hunting social insects. *Philosophical Transactions of the Royal Society B: Biological Sciences* 357, no. 1427: 1567–1583.

Fricker, Elizabeth. 2006. Martians and meetings: Against Burge's neo-Kantian apriorism about testimony. *Philosophia* 78: 69–84.

Fujita, Kazuo, Noriyuki Nakamura, Sumie Iwasaki, and Sota Watanabe. 2012. Are birds metacognitive? In (Michael J. Beran et al., ed.) *Foundations of metacognition*, 50–61. Oxford: Oxford University Press.

Fumerton, Richard. 1995. *Metaepistemology and skepticism*. Lanham, Maryland: Rowman & Littlefield Publishers, Inc.

Gao, Jie, Mikkel Gerken, and Stephen B. Ryan. 2017. Does contextualism hinge on a methodological dispute? In (Jonathan Jenkins Ichikawa, ed.) *The Routledge handbook of epistemic contextualism*, 81–93. London: Routledge.

Geach, Peter T. 1967. Identity. *Review of Metaphysics* 21: 3–12.

Gerken, Mikkel. 2011. Warrant and action. *Synthese* 178, no. 3: 529–547.

Gettier, Edmund. 1963. Is justified true belief knowledge? *Analysis* 23: 121–123.

Gillett, Carl. 2003. Infinitism redux? A response to Klein. *Philosophy and Phenomenological Research* 66, no. 3: 699–717.

Ginet, Carl. 1980. Knowing less by knowing more. *Midwest Studies in Philosophy* 51, no. 1: 151–162.

Goldberg, Sanford C. 2013. Anonymous assertions. *Episteme* 10: 135–151.

Goldman, Alvin. 1976. Discrimination and perceptual knowledge. *Journal of Philosophy* 73, no. 20: 771–791.

Goldman, Alvin, and Bob Beddor. 2016. Reliabilist epistemology. In (Edward N. Zalta, ed.) *The Stanford encyclopedia of philosophy* (Winter), https://plato.stanford.edu/archives/win2016/entries/reliabilism.

Gräfenhain, M., T. Behne, M. Carpenter, and M. Tomasello. 2009. One-year-olds' understanding of nonverbally expressed communicative intentions directed to a third person. *Cognitive Development* 24: 23–33.

Grandin, Temple, and Catherine Johnson. 2005. *Animals in translation: Using the mysteries of autism to decode animal behavior*. New York: Simon & Schuster.

Greco, Daniel. 2014. Could KK be OK? *Journal of Philosophy* 111, no. 4: 169–197.

Greco, Daniel. 2015. Iteration and fragmentation. *Philosophy and Phenomenological Research* 91, no. 3: 656–673.

Green, Mitchell. 2015. Speech acts. In (Edward N. Zalta, ed.) *Stanford encyclopedia of philosophy* (Summer 2015), https://plato.stanford.edu/archives/sum2015/entries/speech-acts.

Gunther, York H. (ed.). 2003. *Essays on nonconceptual content*. Cambridge, MA: MIT Press.

Hall, Katie, Mike W. Oram, Matthew Campbell, Timothy M. Eppley, Richard W. Byrne, and Frans B. M. de Waal. 2016. Chimpanzee uses manipulative gaze cues to conceal and reveal information to foraging competitor. *American Journal of Primatology* 9999: 1–11.

Halliday, Daniel. 2007. Contextualism, comparatives, and gradability. *Philosophical Studies* 132: 381–393.

Hampton, R. 2001. Rhesus monkeys know when they remember. *Proceedings of the National Academy of Sciences* 98: 5359–5362.

Hampton, R. 2009. Multiple demonstrations of metacognition in nonhumans: Converging evidence or multiple mechanisms. *Comparative Cognition & Behavior Reviews* 4: 17–28.

Hampton, R., A, Zivin, and E. Murray. 2004. Rhesus monkeys (*Macaca mulatta*) discriminate between knowing and not knowing and collect information as needed before acting. *Animal Cognition* 7: 239–246.

Hardy, G. H. 1941. *The Indian mathematician Ramanujan: Twelve lectures on subjects suggested by his life and work. Mathematical Proceedings of the Cambridge Philosophical Society* 37, no. 3, rept. 1999, no. 136. Chelsea, NY: AMS Chelsea.

Hare, Brian, and Michael Tomasello. 2005. Human-like social skills in dogs? *Trends in Cognitive Science* 9, no. 9: 439–444.

Harman, Gilbert. 1970. Knowledge, reasons, and causes. *Journal of Philosophy* 67: 841–855.

Harman, Gilbert. 1973. *Thought*. Princeton: Princeton University Press.

Hawthorne, John. 2004. *Knowledge and lotteries*. Oxford: Oxford University Press.

Hawthorne, John, and Jason Stanley. 2008. Knowledge and action. *Journal of Philosophy* 105, no. 10: 571–590.

Hazlett, Alan. 2010. The myth of factive verbs. *Philosophy and Phenomenological Research* 80, no. 3: 497–522.

Hill, Christopher S., and Joshua Schechter. 2007. Hawthorne's lottery puzzle and the nature of belief. *Philosophical Issues* 17: 102–122.

Hintikka, J. 1962. *Knowledge and belief*. Ithaca: Cornell University Press.

Hofweber, Thomas. 2016. *Ontology and the ambitions of metaphysics*. Oxford: Oxford University Press.

Holekamp, Kay E., Sharleen T. Sakai, and Barbara L. Lundrigan. 2007. Social intelligence in the spotted hyena (*Crocuta crocuta*). *Philosophical Transactions of the Royal Society B—Biological Sciences* 362, no. 1480: 523–538.

Hookway, Christopher. 1990. *Scepticism*. London: Routledge.

Huber, Ludwig. 2016. How dogs perceive and understand us. *Current Directions in Psychological Science* 25, no. 5: 399–344.

Hume, David. 1977. *An enquiry concerning human understanding/A letter from a gentleman to his friend in Edinburgh*. Indianapolis: Hackett.

Hylton, Peter. 2014. Quine's naturalism revisited. In (Gilbert Harman and Ernie Lepore, ed.) *A companion to W. V. O. Quine*, 148–162. Chichester: Blackwell.

Hyman, John. 1999. How knowledge works. *Philosophical Quarterly* 49: 433–451.

Ichikawa, Jonathan. 2017. *Contextualizing knowledge: Epistemology and semantics*. Oxford: Oxford University Press.

Ichikawa, Jonathan, and Benjamin Jarvis. 2009. Thought-experiment intuitions and truth in fiction. *Philosophical Studies* 142: 221–246.

Jabr, Ferris. 2017. Can prairie dogs talk? *New York Times Magazine*, May 12.

Jackendoff, Ray. 1983. *Semantics and cognition*. Cambridge, MA: MIT Press.

Jackendoff, Ray. 1990. *Semantic structures*. Cambridge, MA: MIT Press.

Jackson, Frank. 1987. *Conditionals*. Oxford: Blackwell.

Jacoby, L. L., C. M. Kelley, and J. Dywan. 1989. Memory attributions. In (J. L. Roediger III and F. I. M. Craik, ed.) *Varieties of memory and consciousness: Essays in honour of Endel Tulving*, 391–422. Hillsdale, NJ.: Erlbaum.

Johnson, Casey Rebecca. 2018. What norm of assertion? *Acta Analytica* 33: 51–67.

Kahneman, Daniel. 2003. A perspective on judgment and choice: Mapping bounded rationality. *American Psychologist* 58: 697–720.

Kahneman, Daniel. 2011. *Thinking, fast and slow*. New York: Farrar, Straus and Giroux.

Kahneman, Daniel, and Amos Tversky. 1979. Prospect theory: An analysis of decision under risk. *Econometrica* 47, no. 2: 263–292.

Kahneman, Daniel, and Amos Tversky. 1984. Choices, values, and frames. *American Psychologist* 39, no. 4: 341–350.

Kaminski, J., J. Call, and J. Fischer. 2004. Word learning in a domestic dog: Evidence for "fast mapping." *Science* 304: 1682–1683.

Kaminski, Juliane, Linda Schultz, and Michael Tomasello. 2011. How dogs know when communication is intended for them. *Developmental Science* 15, no. 2: 222–232.

Kant, Immanuel. 1929. *Critique of pure reason* (trans. Norman Kemp Smith). London: Macmillan.

Kant, Immanuel. 1934. *Religion within the limits of reason alone*. La Salle, IL: Open Court.

Kaplan, Mark. 1991. Epistemology on holiday. *Journal of Philosophy* 88, no. 3: 132–154.

Kappel, K. 2010. On saying that someone knows: Themes from Craig. In (A. Haddock, A. Millar, and D. Pritchard, ed.) *Social epistemology*, 69–88. Oxford: Oxford University Press.

Kelly, Thomas. 2008. Disagreement, dogmatism, and belief polarization. *Journal of Philosophy* 105, no. 10: 611–633.

Kelp, Christoph. 2011. What's the Point of "Knowledge" Anyway? *Episteme* 8: 53–66.

Kitcher, Philip. 1980. A priori knowledge. *Philosophical Review* 86: 3–23.

Kleene, Stephen C. 1971. *Introduction to metamathematics*. Amsterdam: North-Holland.

Klein, Peter. 2003. How a Pyrrhonian skeptic might respond to academic skepticism. In (Steven Loper, ed.) *The skeptics: Contemporary essays*, 75–94. Aldershot: Ashgate.

Klein, Peter. 2007. Human knowledge and the infinite progress of reason. *Philosophical Studies* 134: 1–17.

Kloo, Daniel, and Michael Rohwer. 2012. The development of earlier and later forms of metacognitive abilities: Reflections on agency and ignorance. In (Michael J. Beran et al., ed.) *Foundations of metacognition*, 167–180. Oxford: Oxford University Press.

Knobe, Joshua, and Shaun Nichols (ed.). 2008. *Experimental philosophy*. Oxford: Oxford University Press.

Knobe, Joshua, and Shaun Nichols (ed.). 2014. *Experimental philosophy*, Vol. 2. Oxford: Oxford University Press.

Kölbel, Max. 2011. Conversational score, assertion, and testimony. In (Jessica Brown and Herman Cappelen, ed.) *Assertion: New philosophical essays*, 49–77. Oxford: Oxford University Press.

Kompa, Nikola. 2002. The context sensitivity of knowledge ascriptions. *Grazer Philosophische Studien* 64: 1–18.

Koriat, A. 2000. The feeling of knowing: Some meta-theoretical implications for consciousness and control. *Consciousness and Cognition* 9: 149–171.

Koriat, A. 2007. Metacognition and consciousness. In (P. D. Zelazo, M. Moscovitch, and E. Thompson, ed.) *The Cambridge handbook of consciousness*, 289-326. Cambridge: Cambridge University Press.

Koriat, A., and H. Ma'ayan. 2005. The effects of encoding fluency and retrieval fluency on judgments of learning. *Journal of Memory and Language* 52: 478–492.

Koriat, A., H. Ma'ayan, and R. Nussinson. 2006. The intricate relationships between monitoring and control in metacognition: Lessons for the cause-and-effect relation between subjective experience and behavior. *Journal of Experimental Psychology: General* 135: 36–69.

Kornblith, Hilary. 2002. *Knowledge and its place in nature*. Oxford: Oxford University Press.

Kornell, N., L. Son, and H. Terrace. 2007. Transfer of metacognitive skills and hint seeking in monkeys. *Psychological Science* 18: 64–71.

Kripke, Saul. 1975. Outline of a theory of truth. *Journal of Philosophy* 72: 690–716.

Kripke, Saul. 2011a. Nozick on knowledge. In (Saul Kripke) *Philosophical troubles: Collected papers*, vol. 1, 162–224. Oxford: Oxford University Press.

Kripke, Saul. 2011b. On two paradoxes of knowledge. In (Saul Kripke) *Philosophical troubles: Collected papers*, vol. 1, 27–51. Oxford: Oxford University Press.

Kuhn, Thomas S. 1970. *The structure of scientific revolutions*. Chicago: University of Chicago Press.

Kummer, Hans, and Jane Goodall. 2003. Innovative behavior in primates. In (Simon M. Reader and Kevin N. Laland, ed.) *Animal Innovation*, 223–235. Oxford: Oxford University Press.

Kusch, Martin. 2009. Testimony and the value of knowledge. In (A. Haddock, A. Millar, and D. Pritchard, ed.) *Epistemic value*, 60–94. Oxford: Oxford University Press.

Kusch, Martin. 2017. Review of "Knowledge as acceptable testimony." *Notre Dame Reviews*, November 17, https://ndpr.nd.edu/news/knowledge-as-acceptable-testimony/.

Kvanvig, J. 2009. Assertion, knowledge, and lotteries. In (Patrick Greenough and Duncan Pritchard, ed.) *Williamson on knowledge*, 140–160. Oxford: Oxford University Press.

Kyburg, Henry. 1961. *Probability and the logic of rational belief*. Middletown: Wesleyan University Press.

Lackey, Jennifer. 2007. Norms of assertion. *Noûs* 41: 594–626.

Lasonen-Aarnio, Maria. 2008. Single premise deduction and risk. *Philosophical Studies* 141: 157–173.

Lasonen-Aarnio, Maria. 2014. The dogmatism paradox. *Australasian Journal of Philosophy* 92, no. 3: 417–432.

Lauer, Martin, Roland Hafner, Sascha Lange, and Martin Riedmiller. 2010. Cognitive concepts in autonomous soccer playing robots. *Cognitive Systems Research* 11, no. 3: 287–309.

Lawlor, Krista. 2013. *Assurance: An Austinian view of knowledge and knowledge claims*. Oxford: Oxford University Press.

LeBoeuf, Robyn, and Eldar Shafir. 2006. The long and short of it: Physical anchoring effects. *Journal of Behavioral Decision Making* 19: 393–406.

Lehrer, Keith, and Thomas Paxson, Jr. 1969. Knowledge: Undefeated justified true belief. *Journal of Philosophy* 66, no. 8: 225–237.

Leite, Adam. 2004. On justifying and being justified. *Philosophical Issues* 14: 219–253.

Lewis, David. 1969. *Convention*. Cambridge, MA: Harvard University Press.

Lewis, David. 1993. Many, but almost one. In (David Lewis) *Papers in metaphysics and epistemology* (1999), 164–182. Cambridge: Cambridge University Press.

Lewis, David. 1996. Elusive knowledge. In (David Lewis) *Papers in metaphysics and epistemology* (1999), 418–445. Cambridge: Cambridge University Press.

Ludlow, Peter. 2005. Contextualism and the new linguistic turn in epistemology. In (Gerhard Preyer and Georg Peter, ed.) *Contextualism in philosophy: Knowledge, meaning, and truth*, 11–50. Oxford: Oxford University Press.

MacFarlane, John. 2005. The assessment sensitivity of knowledge attributions. In (Tamar Szabó Gendler and John Hawthorne, ed.) *Oxford studies in epistemology*, vol. 1, 197–233. New York: Oxford University Press.

MacFarlane, John. 2014. *Assessment sensitivity: Relative truth and its applications*. Oxford: Oxford University Press.

Malcolm, Norman. 1952. Knowledge and belief. *Mind* 61, no. 242: 178–189.

Malcolm, Norman. 1972–1973. Thoughtless brutes. *Proceedings and Addresses of the American Philosophical Association* 46: 5–20.

Malmgren, Anna-Sara. 2011. Rationalism and the content of intuitive judgements. *Mind* 120 (478): 263–327.

Maney, Kevin. 2016. Once drones get artificial intelligence, they'll rule the world. *Newsweek*, September 4,https://www.newsweek.com/once-drones-get-artificial-intelligence-theyll-rule-world-495417.

Mcbride, Neil. 2016. The ethics of driverless cars. *ACM SIGAS Computers and Society* 45, no. 3: 179–184.

McDowell, John. 1996. *Mind and world*. Cambridge, MA: Harvard University Press.

McGrath, M. 2015. *Assessment sensitivity: Relative truth and its applications*. Oxford: Oxford University Press.

McHugh, Conor. 2010. Self-knowledge and the KK principle. *Synthese* 173, no. 3: 231–257.

McKinnon, R. 2012. What I learned in the lunch room about assertion and practical reasoning. *Logos and Episteme* 3, no. 4: 565–569.

McKinnon, Rachel. 2013. Lotteries, knowledge, and irrelevant alternatives. *Dialogue* 52: 523–549.

Mech, David L. 2009. Possible use of foresight, understanding, and planning by wolves hunting muskoxen. *Arctic* 60, no. 2: 144–149.

Melia, Joseph. 2000. Weaseling away the indispensability argument. *Mind* 109, no. 435: 455–479.

Metz, Cade. 2017a. In Toronto, developing a new way for machines to see. *New York Times*, December 1, B3.

Metz, Cade. 2017b. When robots have minds of their own. *New York Times*, August 14, B1–B2.

Miller, G., and P. Johnson-Laird. 1976. *Language and perception*. Cambridge, MA: Harvard University Press.

Millgram, Elijah. 2000. Coherence: The price of the ticket. *Journal of Philosophy* 97, no. 2: 82–93.

Minsky, Marvin. 1967. *Computation: Finite and infinite machines*. Englewood Cliffs: Prentice-Hall.

Molnar, Barbara, Julien Fattebert, Rupert Palme, Paolo Ciucci, Bruno Betschart, Douglas W. Smith, and Peter Allan Diehl. 2015. Environmental and intrinsic correlates of stress in free-ranging wolves. PLOS One 10, no. 9: 1–25. doi: 10.1371/journal.pone.0137378.

Moore, G. E. 1959. Four forms of skepticism. In (G. E. Moore) *Philosophical Papers*, 193–222. New York: Collier Books (1962).

Moran, Richard. 2005. Getting told and being believed. *Philosophers' Imprint* 5, no. 5, 1–29, https://quod.lib.umich.edu/p/phimp/3521354.0005.005/1.

Muller, M., and R. Wehner. 2010. Path integration provides a scaffold for landmark learning in desert ants. *Current Biology* 20: 1368–1371.

Muser, B., S. Sommer, H. Wolf, and R. Wehner. 2005. Foraging ecology of the thermophilic Australian desert ant, *Melophorus bagoti*. *Australian Journal of Zoology* 53: 301–311.

Nagel, Jennifer. 2010. Knowledge ascriptions and the psychological consequences of thinking about error. *Philosophical Quarterly* 60, no. 239: 286–309.

Nelson, T. O. 1996. Consciousness and metacognition. *American Psychologist* 51(2): 102–116, February.

Neta, Ram. 2003. Contextualism and the problem of the external world. *Philosophy and Phenomenological Research* 66, no. 1: 1–31.

Neta, Ram. 2007. Anti-intellectualism and the knowledge-action principle. *Philosophy and Phenomenological Research* 75: 180–187.

Neta, Ram. 2009. Treating something as a reason for action. *Noûs* 43, no. 4: 684–699.

Neta, Ram. 2012. Knowing from the armchair that our intuitions are reliable. *Monist* 95, no. 2: 329–351.

Neta, Ram. 2014. Klein's case for infinitism. In (John Turri and Peter D. Klein, ed.) *Ad infinitum*, 143–161. Oxford: Oxford University Press.

Neta, Ram. 2015. Coherence and deontology. *Philosophical Perspectives* 29: 284–304.

Neta, Ram. 2019. The basing relation. *Philosophical Review* 129, no. 9: 179–217.

Novemsky, Nathan, and Daniel Kahneman. 2005. The boundaries of loss aversion. *Journal of Marketing Research* 92: 119–128.

Nozick, Robert. 1981. *Philosophical explanations*. Cambridge, MA: Harvard University Press.

Owens, David. 2000. *Reason without freedom: The problem of epistemic normativity*. London: Routledge.

Pagin, Peter. 2011. Information and assertoric force. In (Jessica Brown and Herman Cappelen, ed.) *Assertion: New philosophical essays*, 97–135. Oxford: Oxford University Press.

Pagin, Peter. 2016. Assertion. In (Edward N. Zalta, ed.) *The Stanford encyclopedia of philosophy* (Winter), https://plato.stanford.edu/archives/win2016/entries/assertion.

Palagi, Elizabetta, and Giada Cordoni. 2009. Postconflict third-party affiliation in *Canis lupus*: Do wolves share similarities with the great apes? *Animal Behaviour* 78: 979–986.

Palladino, Valentina. 2015. IRobot's Roomba 980 maps your home while making your floors sparkle. *Ars Technica*, September 17, https://arstechnica.com/gadgets/2015/09/irobots-roomba-980-maps-your-home-while-making-your-floors-sparkle.

Papineau, David. 2019. Knowledge is crude. *Aeon Essays*, June, https://aeon.co/essays/knowledge-is-a-stone-age-concept-were-better-off-without-it.

Pasnau, Robert. 2013. Epistemology idealized. *Mind* 122: 988–1021.

Pasnau, Robert. 2017. *After certainty: A history of our epistemic ideas and illusions*. Oxford: Oxford University Press.

Perner, Josef. 2012. MiniMeta: In search of minimal criteria for metacognition. In (Michael J. Beran et al., ed.) *Foundations of metacognition*, 94–116. Oxford: Oxford University Press.

Pinillos, Ángel. 2012. Knowledge, experiments, and practical interests. In (Jessica Brown and Mikkel Gerken, ed.) *Knowledge ascriptions*, 192–219. Oxford: Oxford University Press.

Pinillos, Ángel, and Simpson, Shawn. 2014. Experimental evidence supporting anti-intellectualism about knowledge. In (James R. Beebe, ed.) *Advances in experimental philosophy*, 9–43. London: Bloomsbury.

Podlaskowski, Adam C., and Joshua A. Smith. 2014. Probabilistic regresses and the availability problem for infinitism. *Metaphilosophy* 45, no. 2: 211–220.

Pohlhaus, Gaile. 2015. Different voices, perfect storms, and asking Grandma what she thinks: Situating experimental philosophy in relation to feminist philosophy. *Feminist Philosophy Quarterly* 1, no. 1: 1–23.

Post, John. 1980. Infinite regresses of justification and explanation. *Philosophical Studies* 34: 31–52.

Proust, Joëlle. 2006. Rationality and metacognition in non-human animals. In (S. Hurley and M. Nudds, ed.) *Rational animals?* 247–274. Oxford: Oxford University Press.

Proust, Joëlle. 2007. Metacognition and metarepresentation: Is a self-directed theory of mind a precondition for metacognition? *Synthese* 2: 271–295.

Proust, Joëlle. 2012. Metacognition and mind reading: One or two functions. In (Michael, J. Beran, Johannes L. Brandl, Josef Perner, and Joëlle Proust, ed.) *Foundations of metacognition*, 234–251. Oxford: Oxford University Press.

Prowse Turner, J. A., and V. A. Thompson. 2009. The role of training, alternative models, and logical necessity in determining confidence in syllogistic reasoning. *Thinking & Reasoning* 15: 69–100.

Pryor, James. 2000. The skeptic and the dogmatist. *Noûs* 34, no. 4: 517–549.

Pullen, John Patrick. 2015. This is how drones work. *Time*, https://time.com/3769831/this-is-how-drones-work/.

Pust, Joel. 2000. *Intuitions as evidence*. London: Taylor & Francis.

Pynn, Geoff. 2017. The intuitive basis for contextualism. In (Jonathan Jenkins Ichikawa, ed.) *The Routledge handbook of epistemic contextualism*, 32–43. London: Routledge.

Quain, John R. 2019. Wheels. *New York Times*, September 27, B8.

Quine, W. V. 1953. On a supposed antinomy. Reprinted in (W. V. Quine) *The ways of paradox and other essays*, rev. ed., 19–20. Cambridge, MA: Harvard University Press (1977).

Quine, W. V. 1960. *Word and object*. Cambridge, MA: Harvard University Press.

Quine, W. V. 1969. Epistemology naturalized. In (W. V. Quine) *Ontological relativity and other essays*, 69–90. New York: Columbia University Press.

Quine, W. V. 1970. *Philosophy of logic*. Englewood Cliffs: Prentice-Hall.

Quine, W. V. 1981a. Responses. In (W. V. Quine) *Theories and things*, 173–186. Cambridge, MA: Harvard University Press.

Quine, W. V. 1981b. What price bivalence? In *Theories and things*, 31–37. Cambridge, MA: Harvard University Press.

Quine, W. V. 1987. *Quiddities*. Cambridge, MA: Harvard University Press.

Radford, Colin. 1966. Knowledge—by examples. *Analysis* 27: 1–11.

Rapaport, L. G. 1999. Provisioning of young in golden lion tamarins (Callitrichidea, *Leontopithecus rosalia*): A test of the information hypothesis. *Ethology* 105: 619–636.

Rav, Yehuda. 2007. A critique of a formalist-mechanist version of the justification of arguments in mathematicians' proof practices. *Philosophia Mathematica* 15, no. 3: 291–320.

Reed, Baron. 2010. A defense of stable invariantism. *Noûs* 44, no. 2: 224–244.

Reynolds, Steven L. 2017. *Knowledge as acceptable testimony*. Cambridge: Cambridge University Press.

Richard, Mark. 2004. Contextualism and relativism. *Philosophical Studies* 119, nos. 1–2: 215–241.

Roberts, Andrew. 2015. *Napoleon: A life*, rpt. ed. New York: Penguin.

Ronson, Jon. 2011. *The psychopath test: A journey through the madness industry*. New York: Penguin.

Rosch, E. 1978. Principles of categorization. In (E. Rosch and B. Lloyd, ed.) *Cognition and categorization*, 27–48. Hillsdale, NJ: Erlbaum.

Rosch, E., and C. Mervis. 1975. Family resemblances: Studies in the internal structure of categories. *Cognitive Psychology* 7: 573–605.

Rosenberg, Matthew, and John Markoff. 2016. The Pentagon's "Terminator Conundrum": Robots that could kill on their own. *New York Times*, October 25, https://www.nytimes.com/2016/10/26/us/pentagon-artificial-intelligence-terminator.html.

Rothman, Joshua. 2018. As real as it gets. *New Yorker*, April 2, 30–36.

Rowlands, Mark. 2019. Fellow passengers. *Hedgehog Review* (Spring): 16–30.

Russell, Bertrand. 1948. *Human knowledge: Its scope and limits*. London: Routledge (reprint 1992).

Rysiew, Patrick. 2001. The context-sensitivity of knowledge attributions. *Noûs* 35, no. 4: 477–514.

Rysiew, Patrick. 2005. Contesting contextualism. *Grazer Philosophische Studien* 69: 51–70.

Rysiew, Patrick. 2007. Speaking of knowing. *Noûs* 41, no. 4: 627–662.

Rysiew, Patrick. 2012. Epistemic scorekeeping. In (J. Brown and M. Gerken, ed.) *Knowledge ascriptions*, 270–294. Oxford: Oxford University Press.

Rysiew, Patrick. 2017. "Knowledge" and pragmatics. In (Jonathan Jenkins Ichikawa, ed.) *The Routledge handbook of epistemic contextualism*, 205–217. London: Routledge.

Sacks, Oliver. 1990. The twins. In (Oliver Sacks) *The man who mistook his wife for a hat and other clinical tales*, 195–213. New York: HarperCollins.

Sacks, Oliver. 2014. The mental life of plants and worms, among others. *New York Review of Books* 61, no. 7.

Safina, Carl. 2015. *Beyond words: What animals think and feel*. New York: Picador.

Sanford, David H. 1972. Begging the question. *Analysis* 32, no. 6: 197–199.

Schaffer, Jonathan. 2004. Skepticism, contextualism, and discrimination. *Philosophy and Phenomenological Research* 69, no. 1: 138–155.

Schaffer, Jonathan. 2005. Contrastive knowledge. In (Tamar Szabó Gendler and John Hawthorne, ed.) *Oxford studies in epistemology*, vol. 1, 235–271. Oxford: Oxford University Press.

Schaffer, Jonathan, and Zoltán Gendler Szabó. 2014. Epistemic comparativism: A contextual semantics for knowledge ascriptions. *Philosophical Studies* 168: 491–543.

Scharp, Kevin. 2013. *Replacing truth*. Oxford: Oxford University Press.

Schechter, Joshua. 2013. Rational self-doubt and the failure of closure. *Philosophical Studies* 163: 429–452.

Schiffer, Stephen. 1972. *Meaning*. Oxford: Oxford University Press.

Schiffer, Stephen. 1996. Contextualist solutions to scepticism. *Proceedings of the Aristotelian Society* 96: 317–333.

Searle, J., and D. Vanderveken. 1985. *Foundations of illocutionary logic*. Cambridge: Cambridge University Press.

Sellars, Wilfrid. 1956. Empiricism and the philosophy of mind. In (Wilfrid Sellars) *Science, perception, and reality* (1963), 127–196. Atascadero, CA: Ridgeview.

Sennet, Adam. 2016. Ambiguity. In (Edward N. Zalta, ed.) *The Stanford Encyclopedia of Philosophy* (Spring), https://plato.stanford.edu/archives/spr2016/entries/ambiguity.

Seth, Raghav, and George Smith. 2020. *Brownian motion and molecular reality: A study in theory-mediated measurement*. Oxford: Oxford University Press.

Sextus Empiricus. 1994. Outlines of scepticism, trans. Julia Annas and Jonathan Barnes. Cambridge: Cambridge University Press.

Shane, Scott, and Mark Mazzetti. 2018. The plot to subvert an election: Unraveling the Russia story so far. *New York Times*, September 20, F1–F11.

Sharon, Assaf, and Levi Spectre. 2010. Dogmatism repuzzled. *Philosophical Studies* 148: 307–321.

Shatz, M., H. M. Wellman, and S. Silber. 1983. The acquisition of mental verbs: A systemic investigation of the child's first reference to mental states. *Cognition* 14: 301–321.

Shields, W., J. Smith, and D. Washburn. 1997. Uncertain responses by huans and rhesus monkeys (*Macaca mulatta*) in a psychological same-different task. *Journal of Experimental Psychology: General* 126: 147–164.

Shope, R. K. 1983. *The analysis of knowing: A decade of research*. Princeton: Princeton University Press.

Siegel, Susanna. 2017. *The rationality of perception*. Oxford: Oxford University Press.

Sloman, S.A. 2002. Two systems of reasoning. In (G.D. Griffin and D. Kahneman, ed.) *Heuristics and biases: The psychology of intuitive judgment*, 379–396. Cambridge: Cambridge University Press.

Slote, Michael A. 1979. Assertion and belief. In (Jonathan Dancy, ed.) *Papers on language and logic*, 177–190. Keele: Keele University Library.

Smith, Carolynn L., and Christopher S. Evans. 2014. Referential signals: A window into animal minds. In (Ken Yasukawa, ed.) *Animal behavior: How and why animals do the things they do*, Vol. 3: *Integration and application with case studies*, 175–208. Santa Barbara: Praeger.

Smith, J. 2005. Studies of uncertainty monitoring and meta-cognition in animals and humans. In (H. Terrace and J. Metcalfe, ed.) *The missing link in cognition: Origins of self-reflective consciousness*, 242–271. Oxford: Oxford University Press.

Smith, J., J. Schull, J. Strote, K. McGree, R. Egnor, and L. Erb. 1995. The uncertain response in the bottlenosed dolphin (*Tursiops truncates*). *Journal of Experimental Psychology: General* 124: 391–408.

Smith, J., W. Shields, J. Schull, and D. Washburn. 1997. The uncertain response in humans and animals. *Cognition* 62: 75–97.

Snowdon, Charles T. 2014. Cotton-top tamarins: Research for conservation and understanding human behavior. In (Ken Yasukawa, ed.) *Animal behavior: How and why animals do the things they do*, Vol. 3: *Integration and application with case studies*, 209–247. Santa Barbara: Praeger.

Son, L., and N. Kornell. 2005. Meta-confidence judgments in rhesus macaques: Explicit versus implicit mechanism. In (H. Terrace and J. Metcalfe, ed.) *The missing link in cognition: Origins of self-reflective consciousness*, 296–320. Oxford: Oxford University Press.

Sorensen, Roy A. 1988a. *Blindspots*. Oxford: Oxford University Press.

Sorensen, Roy A. 1988b. Dogmatism, junk knowledge, and conditionals. *The Philosophical Quarterly* 38:153, 433–54.

Sosa, Ernest. 1980. The raft and the pyramid. *Midwest Studies in Philosophy* 5, no. 1: 3–26.

Sosa, Ernest. 1991. Knowledge and intellectual virtue. In (Ernest Sosa) *Knowledge in perspective: Selected essays in epistemology*, 225–244. Cambridge University Press, 225–244.

Sosa, Ernest. 2000. Skepticism and contextualism. In (Ernest Sosa and Enrique Villanueva, ed.) *Philosophical issues*, vol. 10, 1–18.

Spar, Jessica. 2015. 20 foods (and drinks) that aren't what they seem: Everything you thought about these foods has been wrong. Accessed online December 27.

Spiegel, Alison. 2014. These everyday foods aren't what you think they are. *Huffington Post*, April 9.

Stalnaker, Robert C. 1974. Pragmatic presuppositions. In (Robert C. Stalnaker) *Context and content* (1999), 47–62. Oxford: Oxford University Press.

Stalnaker, Robert C. 1978. Assertion. In (Robert C. Stalnaker) *Context and content* (1999), 78–95. Oxford: Oxford University Press.

Stalnaker, Robert C. 2002. Common ground. *Linguistics and Philosophy* 25: 701–721.

Stanley, Jason. 2004. On the linguistic basis for contextualism. *Philosophical Studies* 119: 19–146.

Stanley, Jason. 2005. *Knowledge and practical interests*. Oxford: Oxford University Press.

Stanovich, K. E. 2004. *The robot's rebellion: Finding meaning in the age of Darwin*. Chicago, IL: University of Chicago Press.

Starmans, C., and O. Friedman. 2012. The folk conception of knowledge. *Cognition* 124: 272–283.

Stine, Gail C. 1976. Skepticism, relevant alternatives and deductive closure. *Philosophical Studies* 29: 249–261.

Stroud, Barry. 1984. *The significance of philosophical scepticism*. Oxford: Oxford University Press.

Swain, S., J. Alexander, and J. M. Weinberg. 2008. The instability of philosophical intuitions: Running hot and cold on Truetemp. *Philosophy and Phenomenological Research* 76: 138–155.

Tanswell, Fenner. 2015. A problem with the dependence of informal proofs on formal proofs. *Philosophia Mathematica* 23, no. 3: 295–310.

Tarski, Alfred. 1969. Truth and proof. *Scientific American* 220: 63–77.

Tarski, Alfred. 1983. The concept of truth in formalized languages. In (J. H. Wooder and John Corcoran, ed.) *Logic, semantics, metamathematics*, 24–37. Indianapolis: Hackett.

Thompson, Valerie A., Jamie A. Prowse Turner, and Gordon Pennycook. 2011. Intuition, reason, and metacognition. *Cognitive Psychology* 63: 107–140.

Topál, József, Ádám Miklósi, Márta Gácsi, Antal Dóka, Péter Pongrácz, Enikő Kubinyi, Zsófia Virányi, and Vilmos Csányi. 2009. The dog as a model for understanding human social behavior. *Advances in the Study of Behavior* 39: 71–116.

Turri, John. 2011. Mythology of the factive. *Logos & Episteme* 2, no. 1: 141–150.

Turri, John. 2015. Skeptical appeal: The source-content bias. *Cognitive Science* 39: 307–324.

Turri, John, and Peter D. Klein, ed. 2014a. *Ad infinitum: New essays on epistemological infinitism*. Oxford: Oxford University Press.

Turri, John, and Peter D. Klein. 2014b. Introduction. In (John Turri and Peter D. Klein, ed.) *Ad infinitum: New essays on epistemological Infinitism*, 1–17. Oxford: Oxford University Press.

Tversky, Amos, and Daniel Kahneman. 1974. Judgment under uncertainty: Heuristics and biases. In (Daniel Kahneman, Paul Slovic, and Amos Tversky, ed.) *Judgment under uncertainty: Heuristics and biases* (1982), 3–20. Cambridge: Cambridge University Press.

Uetz, George, and David Clark. 2014. A tale of two spiders: Investigating communication in two unique model species using video digitization and playback. In (Ken Yasukawa, ed.) *Animal behavior: How and why animals do the things they do*, Vol. 3: *Integration and application with case studies*, 63–98. Santa Barbara: Praeger.

Unger, Peter. 1974. Two types of skepticism. *Philosophical Studies* 25: 77–96.

Unger, Peter. 1975. *Ignorance: A case for scepticism*. Oxford: Oxford University Press.

Unger, Peter. 1980. The problem of the many. *Midwest Studies in Philosophy* 5: 411–467.

Unger, Peter. 1984. *Philosophical relativity*. Minneapolis: University of Minnesota Press.

Verhaegh, Sander. 2017. Boarding Neurath's boat: The early development of Quine's naturalism. *Journal of the History of Philosophy* 55, no. 2: 317–342.

Vogel, Jonathan. 1990. Are there counterexamples to the closure principle? In (Michael D. Roth and Glenn Ross, ed.), *Doubting: Contemporary perspectives on* skepticism, 13–27. Dordrecht: Kluwer.

Vogel, Jonathan. 2000. Reliabilism leveled. *Journal of Philosophy* 97, no. 11: 602–623.

Warfield, Ted A. 2005. Knowledge from falsehoods. *Philosophical Perspectives* 19: 405–416.

Wehner, R. 1990. Do insects have cognitive maps? *Annual Review of Neuroscience* 13, no. 1: 403–414.

Wehner, R., C. Meier, and C. Zollikofer. 2004. The ontogeny of foraging behaviour in desert ants, *Cataglyphis bicolor. Ecol Entomol* 29: 240–250.

Weinberg, J. M., S. Nichols, and S. Stich. 2001. Normativity and epistemic intuitions. *Philosophical Topics* 29: 429–60.

Westerståhl, D. 2011. Generalized quantifiers. In (Edward N. Zalta, ed.) *The Stanford encyclopedia of philosophy* (Winter), http://plato.stanford.edu/archives/win2016/entries/generalized-quantifiers.

Whittlesea, B., and J. P. Leboe. 2003. Two fluency heuristics (and how to tell them apart). *Journal of Memory and Language* 49: 62–79.

Wierzbicka, Anna. 1996. *Semantics: Primes and universals.* Oxford: Oxford University Press.

Williams, Michael. 1996. *Unnatural doubts: Epistemological realism and the basis of scepticism.* Princeton: Princeton University Press.

Williams, Michael. 1999. *Groundless belief: An essay on the possibility of epistemology*, 2nd ed. (1st ed. 1977). Princeton: Princeton University Press.

Williams, Michael. 2001. *Problems of knowledge: A critical introduction to epistemology.* Oxford: Oxford University Press.

Williamson, Timothy. 1994. *Vagueness.* London: Routledge.

Williamson, Timothy. 2000. *Knowledge and its limits.* Oxford: Oxford University Press.

Williamson, Timothy. 2007. *The philosophy of philosophy.* London: Blackwell.

Williamson, Timothy. 2013. Gettier cases in epistemic logic. *Inquiry* 56, no. 1: 1–14.

Wittgenstein, L. 1963. *Philosophical investigations*, trans. G. E. M. Anscombe. Oxford: Basil Blackwell.

Wittgenstein, L. 1969. *On certainty*, ed. G. E. M. Anscombe and G. H. von Wright, trans. Denis Paul and G. E. M. Anscombe. NewYork: Harper & Row.

Worsnip. Alex. 2015. Possibly false knowledge. *Journal of Philosophy* 112, no. 5: 225–246.

Wright, Crispin. 2017. The variability of "knows": An opinionated overview. In (Jonathan Jenkins Ichikawa, ed.) *The Routledge handbook of epistemic contextualism*, 13–31. London: Routledge.

Wright, Crispin, and A. Sudbury. 1977. The paradox of the unexpected examination. *Australasian Journal of Philosophy* 55: 41–58.

Yablo, Stephen. 1998. Does ontology rest on a mistake? *Aristotelian Society Supplementary Volume* 72: 229–261.

Yourgrau, Palle. 1983. Knowledge and relevant alternatives. *Synthese* 55: 175–190.

Zadra, Jonathan R., and Gerald L. Clore. 2011. Emotion and perception: The role of affective information. *Wiley Interdisciplinary Reviews: Cognitive Science* 2(6): 676–685.

Zagzebski, Linda. 1994. The inescapability of Gettier problems. *Philosophical Quarterly* 44, no. 174: 65–73.

Zwicky, Arnold, and Jerrold Sadock. 1975. Ambiguity tests and how to fail them. In (John P. Kimball, ed.) *Syntax and semantics*, vol. 4, 1–36. New York: Academic Press.

Index